EXPERIENCE and EXPRESSION

EXPERIENCE and EXPRESSION

Reading and Responding to Short Fiction

John L. Kimmey
University of South Carolina

Scott, Foresman and Company Glenview, Illinois
Dallas, Tex. Oakland, N.J. Palo Alto, Cal. Tucker, Ga. Brighton, England

Library of Congress Cataloging in Publication Data

Kimmey, John Lansing, 1922–
Experience and expression.

Includes index.
1. Fiction—Collections. 2. Fiction—Technique.
3. College readers. I. Title.
PZ1.K55Ex [PN6014] 808'.04275 75-37901
ISBN 0-673-15016-X

1 2 3 4 5 6 7 8 9 10 -GBC- 80 79 78 77 76 75

ACKNOWLEDGMENTS

COVER: Untitled photograph by Geoffrey R. Gove, used with his permission.

KURT VONNEGUT, JR. "Next Door" Copyright © 1955 by Kurt Vonnegut, Jr. Originally appeared in the COSMOPOLITAN. Reprinted from the book, WELCOME TO THE MONKEY HOUSE, by Kurt Vonnegut, Jr. with permission of DELACORTE PRESS/ SEYMOUR LAWRENCE.
ANTON CHEKHOV. "Enemies" from THE SHORT STORIES OF ANTON CHEKHOV, edited by Robert Linscott, published by Random House, Inc.
WILLIAM FAULKNER. Copyright 1931 and renewed 1959 by William Faulkner. Reprinted by permission of Random House, Inc. An expanded version of this story appears as part of THE HAMLET, byWilliam Faulkner.
PHILIP ROTH. Copyright © 1966 by Philip Roth. Reprinted from WHEN SHE WAS GOOD by Philip Roth, by permission of Random House, Inc.
HENRY JAMES. "Owen Wingrave" by Henry James from THE NOVELS AND TALES OF HENRY JAMES, New York Edition, Volume XVII is reprinted by permission of Charles Scribner's Sons. Copyright 1909 Charles Scribner's Sons.
ALEXANDER SOLZHENITSYN. "Matryona's House" by Alexander Solzhenitsyn from HALF-WAY TO THE MOON edited by Patricia Blake and Max Hayward. Copyright © 1963 by Encounter Ltd. Reprinted by permission of Holt, Rinehart and Winston, Publishers and Weidenfeld & Nicolson Limited.
ERNEST HEMINGWAY. "Indian Camp" (Copyright 1925 Charles Scribner's Sons) is reprinted by permission of Charles Scribner's Sons from IN OUR TIME by Ernest Hemingway.
ISAAC BABEL. "The Sin of Jesus" From LYUBKA THE COSSACK AND OTHER STORIES by Isaac Babel, translated by Andrew R. MacAndrew. Copyright © 1963 by Andrew R. MacAndrew. Reprinted by arrangement with The New American Library, Inc., New York, N.Y.

JAMES BALDWIN. "This Morning, This Evening, So Soon" excerpted from GOING TO MEET THE MAN by James Baldwin. Copyright © 1960 by James Baldwin. Reprinted by permission of the publisher, The Dial Press.
NATHANIEL HAWTHORNE. "Wakefield" by Nathaniel Hawthorne from THE COMPLETE WORKS OF NATHANIEL HAWTHORNE, published by Houghton Mifflin Company, 1883.
HEINRICH BÖLL. "Murke's Collected Silences" from 18 STORIES by Heinrich Böll. Translated by Leila Vennewitz. Copyright © 1966 by Heinrich Böll. Used with permission of McGraw-Hill Book Company.
VLADIMIR NABOKOV. "The Potato Elf" from A RUSSIAN BEAUTY AND OTHER STORIES by Vladimir Nabokov, Copyright © 1973 by McGraw-Hill International, Inc., is reprinted by permission of McGraw-Hill Book Company.
FRANZ KAFKA. "The Metamorphosis" from THE PENAL COLONY by Franz Kafka, translated by Willa and Edwin Muir. Copyright 1948 by Schocken Books Inc. Reprinted by permission of Schocken Books Inc.
JOYCE CAROL OATES. "The Metamorphosis" reprinted from MARRIAGES AND INFIDELITIES by Joyce Carol Oates by permission of the publisher, Vanguard Press, Inc. Copyright © 1968, 1969, 1970, 1971, 1972 by Joyce Carol Oates.
DONALD BARTHELME. "City Life" reprinted with the permission of Farrar, Straus & Giroux, Inc. from CITY LIFE by Donald Barthelme, Copyright © 1969 by Donald Barthelme; "City Life" originally appeared in THE NEW YORKER.
JOHN BARTH. "Lost in the Funhouse," copyright © 1967 by The Atlantic Monthly Company from the book LOST IN THE FUNHOUSE by John Barth. Reprinted by permission from Doubleday & Company, Inc. (Song excerpt from "They're Either Too Young or Too Old" by Schwartz-Loesser. © 1943 M. Witmark & Sons. Copyright Renewed. All Rights Reserved. Used by permission of Warner Bros. Music.)

Preface

The aim of *Experience and Expression* is twofold: (1) to introduce students to a variety of enjoyable works of short fiction in the hope that they will become more perceptive readers; and (2) to guide them in analyzing and writing about short fiction so they can become more skillful in expressing their responses in tightly organized and coherent essays. Admittedly this is an ambitious goal for a single text. To accomplish it, I have chosen thirty-one short stories and four short novels (*Matryona's House, The Secret Sharer, This Morning, This Evening, So Soon,* and Kafka's *The Metamorphosis*). Readers with varying interests and literary backgrounds should respond to these selections with ease and should learn from them with pleasure. They are written by a broad range of nineteenth-century, modern, and contemporary authors of different nationalities and offer a variety of subjects, themes, and techniques. Some are fairly simple to read and interpret; others are more complex. All are by recognized masters of the craft of fiction who have something to say and who say it with power and imagination.

Experience and Expression can be used in a number of ways. As its title suggests, it can serve as a text to help students read and enjoy—*experience*—short fiction on any level. The brief introductions on the basic components of fiction can guide students, in courses from freshman composition to advanced literature, in their analysis and evaluation of the stories. The suggestions on how to write about short fiction—*expression*—should help students who are required to write essays in a composition course. For those who want to write fiction the text offers a variety of models to study. No doubt instructors will adapt the contents and the commentary to their own tastes and requirements.

The text has two parts. The first, consisting of six sections, presents the main elements of fiction—plot, character, point of view, setting, theme, and style. Each section contains an introduction; an explanation of how to write on a particular element, accompanied by a model essay based on the first story in the section; and two stories, each of which is followed by questions for discussion and suggestions for writing. The model essay, brief and to the point, shows students how to analyze a story as well as how to write about it from a particular angle. Taken as a whole, the sections provide material on understanding the art of fiction, but they do not include everything about this art. The aim of the text is to be specific yet general enough to cover many different kinds of stories.

The elements of fiction need not be taken up in the order given here. While each section is self-sufficient, there are numerous references to stories and terms in other sections. The text begins with the simplest element, plot, and ends with the most difficult, style. The questions and topics in each section suggest approaches for analysis and writing, but instructors will certainly want to supply additional questions and topics of their own.

One further point about the stories in the first part: although I have grouped them to illustrate different elements of fiction, they are not exclusively "plot" or "character" or "setting" stories. "Spotted Horses" could just as well be discussed under "character" as under "plot," and "María Concepcíon" might well be considered under "style." In fact, it is to some extent artificial to analyze only one fictional element when all contribute to creating a story more complex and elusive than the sum of its individual parts. Still I believe focusing on one element at a time can help students understand it, and consequently the entire story, more profitably. Certainly when students and instructors consider the stories in the second part of the book, they will discuss them in terms of all the elements, not in terms of only one.

The second part, "Stories for Further Study," includes works of short fiction arranged in order of increasing complexity, without comments or questions. Here students can use what they have learned from analyzing and writing on stories in the first half. In general, the more traditional plot stories appear first and the experimental or avant-garde stories toward the end. The stories are also grouped by technique and theme. Several stories in the beginning, such as those by Bierce and Greene, depend on ironic twists. Several at the end, such as those by Kafka and Oates, employ common approaches to experience. To aid in approaching the stories in this part, an *Instructor's Manual* is available which offers interpretations of the stories, shows the relationships among them in terms of complexity, theme, and structure, and comments on the various elements of fiction they contain. Questions for study and topics for discussion and writing on each story are also included.

Not only must an anthology meet different needs and appeal to all sorts of students, but it must also contain stories that are provocative and exciting. I believe the fiction here has the power to move students and to stimulate them to respond with understanding and pleasure. (One aim of the "Biographical Sketches" at the end of the text is to help students who are particularly struck by a story to learn a little about its author and his or her other works.) Ultimately, of course, the degree of involvement is up to the individual reader. An author writes a story and an editor presents it for study, but only a reader can give it true life and significance.

No book is a solo flight. It takes a dedicated and experienced crew to get it off the ground. Dick Welna, Stan Stoga, and Diane Culhane of Scott, Foresman have worked hard on this text, and I owe them my gratitude.

John L. Kimmey

Contents

I. PLOT: THE PATTERN OF ACTION 1

Kurt Vonnegut, Jr. Next Door 5
WRITING ABOUT PLOT 11
"COMIC COINCIDENCE IN 'NEXT DOOR'" 12
Anton Chekhov Enemies 14
William Faulkner Spotted Horses 23

II. CHARACTER: PEOPLE IN ACTION 37

Philip Roth In Trouble 40
WRITING ABOUT CHARACTER 53
"LUCY IN TROUBLE" 55
Henry James Owen Wingrave 56
Alexander Solzhenitsyn Matryona's House 80

III. POINT OF VIEW: THE ANGLE OF NARRATION 107

Ernest Hemingway Indian Camp 110
WRITING ABOUT POINT OF VIEW 113
"NICK'S INITIATION" 115
Isaac Babel The Sin of Jesus 116
Caroline Gordon The Captive 120

IV. SETTING: WHERE AND WHEN 147

John Cheever The Swimmer 149
WRITING ABOUT SETTING 158
"THE LONELINESS OF THE LONG DISTANCE SWIMMER" 159
Doris Lessing A Sunrise on the Veld 161
Katherine Anne Porter María Concepcíon 167

V. THEME: IDEAS IN ACTION 182

D. H. Lawrence Things 186
WRITING ABOUT THEME 193
"PHONY IDEALISM IN 'THINGS'" 194
Jorge Luis Borges The Gospel According to Mark 196
Stephen Crane The Blue Hotel 200

VI. STYLE: LANGUAGE IN ACTION 221

Eudora Welty Death of a Travelling Salesman 224
WRITING ABOUT STYLE 233
"BOWMAN'S VOICE" 235
John Updike Museums and Women 236
Joseph Conrad The Secret Sharer 245

STORIES FOR FURTHER STUDY

Jack London To Build a Fire 276
Ambrose Bierce A Horseman in the Sky 287
Graham Greene The Blue Film 291
Flannery O'Connor Enoch and the Gorilla 294
James Alan McPherson Gold Coast 300
James Joyce An Encounter 316
Isaac Bashevis Singer Powers 321
Bernard Malamud The Silver Crown 331
Ralph Ellison Battle Royal 344
James Baldwin This Morning, This Evening, So Soon 355
Nathaniel Hawthorne Wakefield 384
Heinrich Böll Murke's Collected Silences 390
Vladimir Nabokov The Potato Elf 405
Franz Kafka The Metamorphosis 420
Joyce Carol Oates The Metamorphosis 453
Donald Barthelme City Life 464
John Barth Lost in the Funhouse 475

BIOGRAPHICAL SKETCHES 491

INDEX OF LITERARY TERMS 503

INDEX OF AUTHORS AND TITLES 505

PLOT: THE PATTERN OF ACTION

Plot is what happens in a story. It is the relationship of the incidents to one another in a meaningful pattern of action. Sometimes it involves violence, suspense, and surprise, but such elements are not necessary or always appropriate. In a successful story like "Next Door" (p. 5), in which a child overhears the shooting of a married man by his mistress, they tend to dominate, but not overwhelm. Too often plot is thought of solely in these terms, however, and we speak of spy stories, mysteries, tales of horror, and melodramas as having strong plots because of their emphasis on conflict and tension. Yet in most successful stories, such as "Enemies" (p. 14) and "Spotted Horses" (p. 23), action is subordinate to or mixed equally with character, setting, and theme so that it is impossible to say that this is entirely a plot story and the only interesting thing to ask about it is what happens, not where, why, or to whom it happens. All of these questions are important in examining successful stories in which plot plays a fundamental, though not exclusive, role.

Two specific aspects of plot should be kept in mind when you read short fiction. First, you should determine the **believability** of the incidents selected. To be believable, a story does not have to avoid presenting fantastic actions that have never actually happened outside of fiction. Certainly "Spotted Horses" has a number of extraordinary scenes that appear unrealistic: the auction, the horses' romp through the countryside, Flem's outwitting of Mrs. Armstid. Believability merely means that these actions must be so convincing the reader accepts the possibility of their occurring. There must be a logic to them, a plausibility. "Spotted Horses" succeeds because everything that happens, no matter how exaggerated, is consistent with the characters and their rural society. Faulkner creates a world you immediately believe in despite its remoteness from you. And you believe in it because everything seems so vivid and so real.

This leads to the second key aspect of plot, the **inevitability** of the sequence of events. You should determine whether, from the first action to the last, each one is closely connected and carefully integrated. The decision of Paul's parents in "Next Door" not to take him to the movies results in a series of unusual but related scenes, one dependent on the other. In order to link these scenes together, coincidence must obviously play a part. No story could start or continue very long without some chance happening—that is, a happening which has no given cause, such as the Leonards in "Next Door" moving into the other side of the old house in which the Hargers live. However, the continued use of coincidence after the initial one must never seem so arbitrary as to invite disbelief. It must be appropriate to the situation and the characters, not imposed on them from without by the heavy hand of the author, especially at the conclusion. The action should evolve in a natural manner, without any last-minute pulling of strings. If there is a surprise ending, it should be tied to what has gone before. The discovery of the *Tabu* scent in Paul's pocket by Mrs. Leonard at the conclusion of "Next Door" may be a surprise to the reader, but not a shock. It is the result of Paul's meeting Mr. Harger's mistress in the hall and her efforts to bribe him.

There are many different ways in which fiction writers develop plots. In some stories the incidents occur in strict chronological order. They follow one another according to a time sequence, moving from the beginning of the action to the end. In others the time sequence may be rearranged. The author may present the conclusion first and then work toward an explanation of it. F. Scott Fitzgerald's novel *The Great Gatsby* is an example. Or the author may move back and forth in time, weaving past and present together in a complicated web. Conrad's novel *Lord Jim* and Faulkner's short story "A Rose for Emily" proceed in this fashion. Once in a while you will find a story which, though it follows a loose chronological order, is composed of seemingly unrelated fragments. Your task is to put all the pieces together. The stories by Barth and Barthelme, for example, in "Stories for Further Study" offer this challenge.

One common and conventional method of development is the arrangement of incidents into three distinct movements: an **exposition,** or introduction of the main situation, scene, and character; a **climax,** or turning point at which the action reaches its peak and moves toward a solution; and the **denouement,** or resolution. In "Next Door" the scene is set, the characters and the circumstances are introduced, and the suspense is created by the time Paul's parents leave for the movie. The climax occurs the moment the woman next door cries "So" after All-Night Sam makes his pitch for reconciliation with the song *Somebody Bad Stole De Wedding Bell.* The denouement comes with the return of Mrs. Harger and Paul's parents. Sometimes it is possible to break the three movements into five and distinguish the **rising action,** or complication after the exposition, and the **falling action,** or unraveling after the climax. The rising action in "Next Door" corresponds to Paul's listening to the fight on the other side of the wall and calling the disc jockey. The falling action corresponds to the shooting and the arrival of the policeman. In many stories the climax is replaced by what is called an **epiphany**. The main character experiences a moment of insight or illumination when he or she comes to a full realization of his or her plight. In "Enemies" Kirilov finally understands what is taking place when Aboguin shows him the photograph of his wife, who he thought was dying but who has actually deserted him. The doctor recognizes he has been played with, treated as a servant, turned into a piece of property by a wealthy gentleman who does not realize what true suffering is.

Every good story, no matter how disorganized it appears or how much it lacks a climax or resolution, has a structure and follows some plan. It hangs together for a purpose. It has a connecting thread. The incidents are chosen for a reason. Before you can discover the author's meaning or begin to analyze the characters, you have to perceive this structure or plan. If nothing else it tells you what is going on, and many times that is the clue to the significance of what is happening. "Spotted Horses" might seem confusing at first because of its mingling of past and present and the tendency of the narrator to wander from the story line. But if you study the plot carefully you will find that, after an introduction to the world of Flem Snopes, it follows a clear pattern of action involving the auctioning off of the wild horses and their effect on the people of the region.

An important device used to enrich plot, to make it more lifelike, more dramatic, more complex, is **irony**—the contrast between what appears to be true and what is true. Often twists and turns of action and comments by characters have ironic implications that you should be aware of if you are to understand the intentions of the author and interpret the story intelligently.

There are three principal kinds of irony in fiction: **irony of situation, dramatic irony,** and **verbal irony**. Irony of situation arises from the difference between how a set of circumstances looks on the surface and what it is in reality, between what literally appears to be the case and what actually is the case. When the son in "Next Door" calls a disc jockey, he thinks he is reconciling a quarreling married couple. To him the situation is a simple fight between husband and wife. Little does he know that the woman is Mr. Harger's mistress. Instead of bringing peace to a troubled household he causes a near murder.

Dramatic irony involves the difference between what characters say or believe about the events surrounding them and what the reader knows about these events. The characters speak without realizing fully what they are saying, without having the reader's grasp of the complete significance of their words. At the end of Vonnegut's story the mother's remarks about her son being a "little adventurer" and about "how dreadfully short childhood is" are made in ignorance of the terrifying experience the boy has just faced. Even the child does not grasp them. Only the reader can see their whole meaning.

Finally, verbal irony is the contrast between what one says and what one means. When the father in "Next Door" notes that the movie he is going to would not "kill" his son and his wife describes it as about "a girl who chooses her friends unwisely," they are both saying one thing and suggesting another. The father is implying the risqué movie would not harm Paul's morals, and his wife is talking about promiscuous women. Their statements contain other than literal significance not only for themselves, but also for the reader, who soon learns the son is party to a shooting that involves an adulterous love affair. Most surprises of this kind are ironic. They are particularly effective at the climax and the denouement. In fact, it is difficult to find a plot that does not employ verbal irony to achieve complexity and verisimilitude, the semblance of truth.

In addition to the devices already mentioned for achieving unity of plot and integration of all the incidents, there are several others. A common one is the **flashback**, which introduces information about the past relevant to the present without interrupting the narrative for too long a time. Some authors are so adept at employing it that the shift in time never disrupts the narrative. After the wild horses running loose throughout the land have been described, the sewing machine salesman in "Spotted Horses" explains how they came to the region and who was responsible for them. Another method of establishing unity is through **foreshadowing**, hinting what is to come through an incident, symbolic detail, or dialogue. The mention in the first sentence of "Spotted Horses" of the sound of thunder the horses make as they race across the wooden bridges creates a sense of the ominous events about to unfold. Still another device is **contrast**, particularly the contrast of two scenes such as the first and last ones in "Next Door." All these techniques help create that unity of impression which is the goal of all short fiction.

One further aspect of plot should be examined, the alternation of dialogue and dramatic scenes with summaries and descriptions. Most writers of fiction engage in this practice. One advantage is variety of pace. Dialogue moves faster than analysis, but does not go so deep. Description, on the other hand, while proceeding more slowly than conversation, enables the reader to participate visually in what is happening. Another advantage of this alternation is that summaries allow a great deal of background material to be introduced in brief, while dialogue and dramatic scenes can make them come alive. And, lastly, the combination permits both the author and the characters to have their say. Just as there is something ponderous about stories without dialogue or dramatic scenes of any kind, so there is something monotonous about those with only conversations. Ultimately the proportion of scene and picture depends on the story and its material.

It is common today to disparage plot as a skeleton, a blueprint. We tend to be more interested in character than action, ideas than incidents. As one critic has remarked, "Serious works get the characters, adventure stories get the plot." But if you look at plot in the broader sense of the term, as something interwoven with character and theme, you realize it has its uses, its own importance. Contemporary fiction writers, despite their avoidance of adventure plots, must still create situations for their characters. Those characters cannot exist in a vacuum. They must do and say things that form a pattern for the reader to follow. Plot may not be the heart of a good story, but without the skeleton there would be no heart.

KURT VONNEGUT, JR.

Next Door

The old house was divided into two dwellings by a thin wall that passed on, with high fidelity, sounds on either side. On the north side were the Leonards. On the south side were the Hargers.

The Leonards—husband, wife, and eight-year-old son—had just moved in. And, aware of the wall, they kept their voices down as they argued in a friendly way as to whether or not the boy, Paul, was old enough to be left alone for the evening.

"Shhhhh!" said Paul's father.

"Was I shouting?" said his mother. "I was talking in a perfectly normal tone."

"If I could hear Harger pulling a cork, he can certainly hear you," said his father.

"I didn't say anything I'd be ashamed to have anybody hear," said Mrs. Leonard.

"You called Paul a baby," said Mr. Leonard. "That certainly embarrasses Paul—and it embarrasses me."

"It's just a way of talking," she said.

"It's a way we've got to stop," he said. "And we can stop treating him like a baby, too—*tonight*. We simply shake his hand, walk out, and go to the movie." He turned to Paul. "You're not afraid—are you, boy?"

"I'll be all right," said Paul. He was very tall for his age, and thin, and had a soft, sleepy, radiant sweetness engendered by his mother. "I'm fine."

"Damn right!" said his father, clouting him on the back. "It'll be an adventure."

"I'd feel better about this adventure, if we could get a sitter," said his mother.

"If it's going to spoil the picture for you," said the father, "let's take him with us."

Mrs. Leonard was shocked. "Oh—it isn't for children."

"I don't care," said Paul amiably. The why of their not wanting him to see certain movies, certain magazines, certain books, certain television shows was a mystery he respected—even relished a little.

"It wouldn't kill him to see it," said father.

"You *know* what it's about," she said.

"What *is* it about?" said Paul innocently.

Mrs. Leonard looked to her husband for help, and got none. "It's about a girl who chooses her friends unwisely," she said.

"Oh," said Paul. "That doesn't sound very interesting."

"Are we going, or aren't we?" said Mr. Leonard impatiently. "The show starts in ten minutes."

Mrs. Leonard bit her lip. "All right!" she said bravely. "You lock the windows and the back door, and I'll write down the telephone numbers for the police and the fire department and the theater and Dr. Failey." She turned to Paul. "You *can* dial, can't you, dear?"

"He's been dialing for years!" cried Mr. Leonard.

"Ssssssh!" said Mrs. Leonard.

"Sorry," Mr. Leonard bowed to the wall. "My apologies."

"Paul, dear," said Mrs. Leonard, "what are you going to do while we're gone?"

"Oh—look through my microscope, I guess," said Paul.

"You're not going to be looking at germs, are you?" she said.

"Nope—just hair, sugar, pepper, stuff like that," said Paul.

His mother frowned judiciously. "I think that would be all right, don't you?" she said to Mr. Leonard.

"Fine!" said Mr. Leonard. "Just as long as the pepper doesn't make him sneeze!"

"I'll be careful," said Paul.

Mr. Leonard winced. "Shhhhh!" he said.

Soon after Paul's parents left, the radio in the Harger apartment went on. It was on softly at first—so softly that Paul, looking through his microscope on the living room coffee table, couldn't make out the announcer's words. The music was frail and dissonant—unidentifiable.

Gamely, Paul tried to listen to the music rather than to the man and woman who were fighting.

Paul squinted through the eyepiece of his microscope at a bit of his hair far below, and he turned a knob to bring the hair into focus. It looked like a glistening brown eel, flecked here and there with tiny spectra where the light struck the hair just so.

There—the voices of the man and woman were getting louder again, drowning out the radio. Paul twisted the microscope knob nervously, and the objective lens ground into the glass slide on which the hair rested.

The woman was shouting now.

Paul unscrewed the lens, and examined it for damage.

Now the man shouted back—shouted something awful, unbelievable.

Paul got a sheet of lens tissue from his bedroom, and dusted at the frosted dot on the lens, where the lens had bitten into the slide. He screwed the lens back in place.

All was quiet again next door—except for the radio.

Paul looked down into the microscope, down into the milky mist of the damaged lens.

Now the fight was beginning again—louder and louder, cruel and crazy.

Trembling, Paul sprinkled grains of salt on a fresh slide, and put it under the microscope.

The woman shouted again, a high, ragged, poisonous shout.

Paul turned the knob too hard, and the fresh slide cracked and fell in triangles to the floor. Paul stood, shaking, wanting to shout, too—to shout in terror and bewilderment. It had to stop. Whatever it was, it *had* to stop!

"If you're going to yell, turn up the radio!" the man cried.

Paul heard the clicking of the woman's heels across the floor. The radio volume swelled until the boom of the bass made Paul feel like he was trapped in a drum.

"And now!" bellowed the radio, "for Katy from Fred! For Nancy from Bob, who thinks she's swell! For Arthur, from one who's worshipped him from afar for six weeks! Here's *Stardust!* Remember! If you have a dedication, call Milton nine-three-thousand! Ask for All-Night Sam, the record man!"

The music picked up the house and shook it.

A door slammed next door. Now someone hammered on a door.

Paul looked down into his microscope once more, looked at nothing—while a prickling sensation spread over his skin. He faced the truth: The man and woman would kill each other, if he didn't stop them.

He beat on the wall with his fist. "Mr. Harger! Stop it!" he cried. "Mrs. Harger! Stop it!"

"For Ollie from Lavinia!" All-Night Sam cried back at him. "For Ruth from Carl, who'll never forget last Tuesday! For Wilber from Mary, who's lonesome tonight! Here's the Sauter-Finnegan Band asking, *Love, What Are You Doing to My Heart?*"

Next door, crockery smashed, filling a split second of radio silence. And then the tidal wave of music drowned everything again.

Paul stood by the wall, trembling in his helplessness. "Mr. Harger! Mrs. Harger! Please."

"Remember the number!" said All-Night Sam. "Milton nine-three-thousand!"

Dazed, Paul went to the phone and dialed the number.

"WJCD," said the switchboard operator.

"Would you kindly connect me with All-Night Sam?" said Paul.

"Hello!" said All-Night Sam. He was eating, talking with a full mouth. In the background, Paul could hear sweet, bleating music, the original of what was rending the radio next door.

"I wonder if I might make a dedication," said Paul.

"Dunno why not," said Sam. "Ever belong to any organization listed as subversive by the Attorney General's office?"

Paul thought a moment. "Nossir—I don't think so, sir," he said.

"Shoot," said Sam.

"From Mr. Lemuel K. Harger to Mrs. Harger," said Paul.

"What's the message?" said Sam.

"I love you," said Paul. "Let's make up and start all over again."

The woman's voice was so shrill with passion that it cut through the din of the radio, and even Sam heard it.

"Kid—are you in trouble?" said Sam. "Your folks fighting?"

Paul was afraid that Sam would hang up on him if he found out that Paul wasn't a blood relative of the Hargers. "Yessir," he said.

"And you're trying to pull 'em back together again with this dedication?" said Sam.

"Yessir," said Paul.

Sam became very emotional. "O.K., kid," he said hoarsely, "I'll give it everything I've got. Maybe it'll work. I once saved a guy from shooting himself the same way."

"How did you do that?" said Paul, fascinated.

"He called up and said he was gonna blow his brains out," said Sam, "and I played *The Bluebird of Happiness.*" He hung up.

Paul dropped the telephone into its cradle. The music stopped, and Paul's hair stood on end. For the first time, the fantastic speed of modern communications was real to him, and he was appalled.

"Folks!" said Sam. "I guess everybody stops and wonders sometimes what the heck he thinks he's doin' with the life the good Lord gave him! It may seem funny to you folks, because I always keep a cheerful front, no matter how I feel inside, that I wonder sometimes, too! And then, just like some angel was trying to tell me, 'Keep going, Sam, keep going,' something like this comes along."

"Folks!" said Sam, "I've been asked to bring a man and his wife back together again through the miracle of radio! I guess there's no sense in kidding ourselves about marriage! It isn't any bowl of cherries! There's ups and downs, and sometimes folks don't see how they can go on!"

Paul was impressed with the wisdom and authority of Sam. Having the radio turned up high made sense now, for Sam was speaking like the right-hand man of God.

When Sam paused for effect, all was still next door. Already the miracle was working.

"Now," said Sam, "a guy in my business has to be half musician, half philosopher, half psychiatrist, and half electrical engineer! And! If I've learned one thing from working with all you wonderful people out there, it's this: if folks would swallow their self-respect and pride, there wouldn't be any more divorces!"

There were affectionate cooings from next door. A lump grew in Paul's throat as he thought about the beautiful thing he and Sam were bringing to pass.

"Folks!" said Sam, "that's all I'm gonna say about love and marriage! That's all anybody needs to know! And now, for Mrs. Lemuel K. Harger, from Mr. Harger—I love you! Let's make up and start all over again!" Sam choked up. "Here's Eartha Kitt, and *Somebody Bad Stole De Wedding Bell!*"

The radio next door went off.

The world lay still.

A purple emotion flooded Paul's being. Childhood dropped away, and he hung, dizzy, on the brink of life, rich, violent, rewarding.

There was movement next door—slow, foot-dragging movement.

"So," said the woman.

"Charlotte—" said the man uneasily. "Honey—I swear."

" 'I love you,' " she said bitterly. " 'Let's make up and start all over again.' "

"Baby," said the man desperately, "it's another Lemuel K. Harger. It's got to be!"

"You want your wife back?" she said. "All right—I won't get in her way. She can have you, Lemuel—you jewel beyond price, you."

"*She* must have called the station," said the man.

"She can have you, you philandering, two-timing, two-bit Lochinvar," she said. "But you won't be in very good condition."

"Charlotte—put down that gun," said the man. "Don't do anything you'll be sorry for."

"That's all behind me, you worm," she said.

There were three shots.

Paul ran out into the hall, and bumped into the woman as she burst from the Harger apartment. She was a big, blonde woman, all soft and awry, like an unmade bed.

She and Paul screamed at the same time, and then she grabbed him as he started to run.

"You want candy?" she said wildly. "Bicycle?"

"No, thank you," said Paul shrilly. "Not at this time."

"You haven't seen or heard a thing!" she said. "You know what happens to squealers?"

"Yes!" cried Paul.

She dug into her purse, and brought out a perfumed mulch of face tissues, bobbypins and cash. "Here!" she panted. "It's yours! And there's more where that came from, if you keep your mouth shut." She stuffed it into his trousers pocket.

She looked at him fiercely, then fled into the street.

Paul ran back into his apartment, jumped into bed, and pulled the covers up over his head. In the hot, dark cave of the bed, he cried because he and All-Night Sam had helped to kill a man.

A policeman came clumping into the house very soon, and he knocked on both apartment doors with his billyclub.

Numb, Paul crept out of the hot, dark cave, and answered the door. Just as he did, the door across the hall opened, and there stood Mr. Harger, haggard but whole.

"Yes, sir?" said Harger. He was a small, balding man, with a hairline mustache. "Can I help you?"

"The neighbors heard some shots," said the policeman.

"Really?" said Harger urbanely. He dampened his mustache with the tip of his little finger. "How bizarre. I heard nothing." He looked at Paul sharply. "Have you been playing with your father's guns again, young man?"

"Oh, nossir!" said Paul, horrified.

"Where are your folks?" said the policeman to Paul.

"At the movies," said Paul.

"You're all alone?" said the policeman.

"Yessir," said Paul. "It's an adventure."

"I'm sorry I said that about the guns," said Harger. "I certainly would have heard any shots in this house. The walls are thin as paper, and I heard nothing."

Paul looked at him gratefully.

"And you didn't hear any shots, either, kid?" said the policeman.

Before Paul could find an answer, there was a disturbance out on the street. A big, motherly woman was getting out of a taxicab and wailing at the top of her lungs. "Lem! Lem, baby."

She barged into the foyer, a suitcase bumping against her leg and tearing her stocking to shreds. She dropped the suitcase, and ran to Harger, throwing her arms around him.

"I got your message, darling," she said, "and I did just what All-Night Sam told me to do. I swallowed my self-respect, and here I am!"

"Rose, Rose, Rose—my little Rose," said Harger. "Don't ever leave me again." They grappled with each other affectionately, and staggered into their apartment.

"Just look at this apartment!" said Mrs. Harger. "Men are just lost without women!" As she closed the door, Paul could see that she was awfully pleased with the mess.

"You *sure* you didn't hear any shots?" said the policeman to Paul.

The ball of money in Paul's pocket seemed to swell to the size of a watermelon. "Yessir," he croaked.

The policeman left.

Paul shut his apartment door, shuffled into his bedroom, and collapsed on the bed.

The next voices Paul heard came from his own side of the wall. The voices were sunny—the voices of his mother and father. His mother was singing a nursery rhyme and his father was undressing him.

"Diddle-diddle-dumpling, my son John," piped his mother, "Went to bed with his stockings on. One shoe off, and one shoe on—diddle-diddle-dumpling, my son John."

Paul opened his eyes.

"Hi, big boy," said his father, "you went to sleep with all your clothes on."

"How's my little adventurer?" said his mother.

"O.K.," said Paul sleepily. "How was the show?"

"It wasn't for children, honey," said his mother. "You would have liked the short subject, though. It was all about bears—cunning little cubs."

Paul's father handed her Paul's trousers, and she shook them out, and hung them neatly on the back of a chair by the bed. She patted them smooth, and felt the ball of money in the pocket. "Little boys' pockets!" she said, delighted. "Full of childhood's mysteries. An enchanted frog? A magic pocketknife from a fairy princess?" She caressed the lump.

"He's not a little boy—he's a big boy," said Paul's father. "And he's too old to be thinking about fairy princesses."

Paul's mother held up her hands. "Don't rush it, don't rush it. When I saw him asleep there, I realized all over again how dreadfully short childhood is." She reached into the pocket and sighed wistfully. "Little boys are so hard on clothes—especially pockets."

She brought out the ball and held it under Paul's nose. "Now, would you mind telling Mommy what we have here?" she said gaily.

The ball bloomed like a frowzy chrysanthemum, with ones, fives, tens, twenties, and lipstick-stained Kleenex for petals. And rising from it, befuddling

Paul's young mind, was the pungent musk of perfume.

Paul's father sniffed the air. "What's that smell?" he said.

Paul's mother rolled her eyes. "*Tabu*," she said.

Writing About Plot

Writing about fiction is not so very different from writing about anything else. In some ways it is much easier since you have your material right in front of you at all times. It is interpreting this material that causes most of the problems. But essentially you approach your subject in the same manner you would any other. First and most important, you want to select a story you like, you understand, and you believe you can write about in an interesting manner. Next you need to decide what element of fiction to treat and what aspect of that element. Your topic must be small and uncomplicated enough to cover in a few pages, yet large and meaningful enough to be of some significance. Another dilemma is deciding on the development and organization. The suggestions offered in each of the sections in this book should help you. They will not solve all your problems, for every story presents new difficulties. But if you follow the guidelines you should get a clear idea of how to write about a story. Example is a greater teacher than a set of instructions when it comes to learning how to write. That is why the model essays may help you more than the discussion of how to write on each element of fiction. Study them to learn as much as possible about how to develop your own topic in your own way.

When you write about plot, the first thing to remember is not to retell the story. To make sure you avoid this danger, choose a topic that keeps you away from plot summaries yet permits you to use incidents to illustrate your points. One such topic is the relationship of the ending to the rest of the story. Another is an analysis of the first scene or even the first paragraph to show how it prepares for or mirrors the whole story. A paper on foreshadowing and how it creates suspense and prepares for the ending is another possibility. You could pick some unifying device peculiar to the story, such as the chaos the wild horses in "Spotted Horses" produce, and indicate how it develops a basic **motif**, that is, a dominant idea, and at the same time how it links the various segments of the action to form a tightly unified plot.

Your first concern, then, is the selection of a topic appropriate to the plot of your story. It must be one you are interested in and understand. The next step is narrowing the topic so you can deal with it adequately in a short essay. Although the length is not so important as the clear and full treatment of your subject, you should try to have at least four or five paragraphs, including an introduction in which you state your main idea, several paragraphs that develop this idea in terms of the story, and a conclusion. Suppose you choose one of the essential features of the plot of "Next Door," coincidence. The topic automatically limits itself. You are not going to focus on suspense, flashbacks, or foreshadowing, only on the part chance happenings play in developing the action.

Your next task is to find a thesis sentence and organize your essay around it. Ask yourself what the role of coincidence is in the story. Three points should come to mind. Coincidence links the various parts of the story together in a plausible and inevitable manner. It creates ironic and humorous situations. It makes possible the surprise comic ending that is a logical outgrowth of the action. With these points in mind you can proceed to the thesis sentence. An appropriate one might be: Comic coincidence is an essential part of "Next Door" with respect to the incidents, the irony, and the unexpected conclusion.

Such a sentence sets up your organization. What you have to do now is choose details to support your generalizations. To do this go through the story looking for examples of coincidence that illustrate the three points mentioned above. They should be fairly obvious and are not too numerous. They include such incidents as Paul's attempt to stop the quarreling, the disc jockey's intervention, and the shooting caused by a misunderstanding. Ironic coincidence concerns Paul's finding women in movies dull and his silence about the whole situation upon his parents' return. The conclusion has two coincidences, the arrival of Mrs. Harger and the discovery of the *Tabu* scent in Paul's pocket. However, you should remember that you are analyzing a technique of fiction, not summarizing the plot. You are using illustrations and examples to support the point you make. Your last paragraph should offer a critical evaluation of how well you think the author handles coincidence. This does not mean you should give a vague impressionistic judgment such as "I liked the way Vonnegut used coincidence." You should offer specific observations about why coincidence works so well in establishing an integrated plot.

Comic Coincidence in "Next Door"

Without coincidence most stories could not exist. The trick is for the author to use it in such a natural way the reader is unaware of its presence. The reader must accept the various actions and not stop to question if they are appropriate and credible. Kurt Vonnegut succeeds admirably in this respect in "Next Door." His coincidences make believable a rather bizarre situation. They create ironic humor on which the whole story depends for its effect. And they lead to an ending that is a natural and inevitable outgrowth of the previous actions.

The initial coincidences are those the reader must take on faith, namely, that two different kinds of families live side by side in an old house, that the Leonards, the new tenants, decide to go to a movie without their son, and that the old tenant, Mr. Harger, is living with his mistress and not his wife. While admittedly the situation is contrived, the reader accepts it because what follows flows so smoothly and appears so reasonable. Paul, frightened by the fighting he hears, wants to stop the noise and concentrate on his microscope. The best way to do this, he thinks, is to call the disc jockey on the radio next door. All-Night Sam prides himself on helping people in trouble. The mistress quite logically thinks her lover sent the radio message to get back his wife. Thus the shooting that results comes as a believable climax to a series of unusual but plausible events that are connected and that, once begun, all fall in place.

The series of events would not be completely successful, however, without irony, which allows the reader to accept the strange situation partly because of the comic implications. This irony involves all the characters, none of whom understands what is actually going on except Paul, and he is a naive eight-year-old boy. One of the humorous touches of irony is his refusal to go to the adult movie because he finds movie girls who choose their friends "unwisely" dull. Another is his silence upon his parents' return, never commenting when his mother remarks, "It wasn't for children." Almost everything in the story has an ironic twist, from the song titles and the sermon Sam delivers to the appearance of Mrs. Harger, "my little Rose," and the Tabu scent found in Paul's pocket. They unify the story as well as entertain the reader.

The appearance of Rose at the end, though a surprise, is not arbitrary. It is quite possible that she could have heard the radio message mentioning her and was touched by the sentiment. In addition, her arrival heightens the irony of the adulterous husband who has been attacked by his mistress for being in love with his wife. His plea to her about never leaving him again is doubly humorous to the reader who has witnessed his hypocrisy with both women. The finding of the strange objects in Paul's pocket is another integral part of the action. Moreover, it adds a final ironic touch. The child who was too young to see an adult movie witnesses an "adventure" that could have killed him.

Coincidence is effective in the story for two reasons. First, it enables the comedy of the situation to unfold in a manner that amuses and does not seem wildly improbable. Second, it permits Vonnegut to spring one irony after another on the reader, all of them appropriate to the incidents and the characters. Unity is achieved. The various actions are carefully integrated, and the humor based on the contrast between what is and what appears to be is consistently maintained. One comes away from the story both believing it could have happened and at the same time laughing at the way it did happen. Coincidence reveals the strange but true behavior of people, and this is as much as we can ask of any device of fiction.

ANTON CHEKHOV

Enemies

About ten o'clock of a dark September evening the Zemstvo doctor Kirilov's only son, six-year-old Andrey, died of diphtheria. As the doctor's wife dropped on to her knees before the dead child's cot and the first paroxysm of despair took hold of her, the bell rang sharply in the hall.

When the diphtheria came all the servants were sent away from the house, that very morning. Kirilov himself went to the door, just as he was, in his shirt-sleeves with his waistcoat unbuttoned, without wiping his wet face or hands, which had been burnt with carbolic acid. It was dark in the hall, and of the person who entered could be distinguished only his middle height, a white scarf and a big, extraordinarily pale face, so pale that it seemed as though its appearance made the hall brighter . . . .

"Is the doctor in?" the visitor asked abruptly.

"I'm at home," answered Kirilov. "What do you want?"

"Oh, you're the doctor? I'm so glad!" The visitor was overjoyed and began to seek for the doctor's hand in the darkness. He found it and squeezed it hard in his own. "I'm very . . . very glad! We were introduced. . . . I am Aboguin . . . had the pleasure of meeting you this summer at Mr. Gnouchev's. I am very glad to have found you at home. . . . For God's sake, don't say you won't come with me immediately. . . . My wife has been taken dangerously ill . . . I have the carriage with me. . . ."

From the visitor's voice and movements it was evident that he had been in a state of violent agitation. Exactly as though he had been frightened by a fire or a mad dog, he could hardly restrain his hurried breathing, and he spoke quickly in a trembling voice. In his speech there sounded a note of real sincerity, of childish fright. Like all men who are frightened and dazed, he spoke in short, abrupt phrases and uttered many superfluous, quite unnecessary, words.

"I was afraid I shouldn't find you at home," he continued. "While I was coming to you I suffered terribly. . . . Dress yourself and let us go, for God's sake. . . . It happened like this, Papchinsky came to me—Alexander Siemionovich, you know him. . . . We were chatting. . . . Then we sat down to tea. Suddenly my wife cries out, presses her hands to her heart, and falls back in her chair. We carried her off to her bed and . . . and I rubbed her forehead with salvolatile, and splashed her with water. . . . She lies like a corpse. . . . I'm afraid that her heart's failed. . . . Let us go. . . . Her father too died of heart-failure."

Kirilov listened in silence as though he did not understand the Russian language.

When Aboguin once more mentioned Papchinsky and his wife's father, and once more began to seek for the doctor's hand in the darkness, the doctor shook his head and said, drawling each word listlessly:

"Excuse me, but I can't go. . . . Five minutes ago my . . . son died."

"Is that true?" Aboguin whispered, stepping back. "My God, what an awful moment to come! It's a terribly fated day . . . terribly! What a coincidence . . . and it might have been on purpose!"

Aboguin took hold of the door handle and dropped his head in meditation. Evidently he was hesitating, not knowing whether to go away, or to ask the doctor once more.

"Listen," he said eagerly, seizing Kirilov by the sleeve. "I fully understand your state! God knows I'm ashamed to try to hold your attention at such a moment, but what can I do? Think yourself—who can I go to? There isn't another doctor here besides you. For heaven's sake come. I'm not asking for myself. It's not I that's ill!"

Silence began. Kirilov turned his back to Aboguin, stood still for a while and slowly went out of the hall into the drawing-room. To judge by his uncertain, machine-like movement, and by the attentiveness with which he arranged the hanging shade on the unlighted lamp in the drawing-room and consulted a thick book which lay on the table—at such a moment he had neither purpose nor desire, nor did he think of anything, and probably had already forgotten that there was a stranger standing in his hall. The gloom and the quiet of the drawing-room apparently increased his insanity. As he went from the drawing-room to his study he raised his right foot higher than he need, felt with his hands for the door-posts, and then one felt a certain perplexity in his whole figure, as though he had entered a strange house by chance, or for the first time in his life had got drunk, and now was giving himself up in bewilderment to the new sensation. A wide line of light stretched across the bookshelves on one wall of the study; this light, together with the heavy stifling smell of carbolic acid and ether, came from the door ajar that led the study into the bedroom. . . . The doctor sank into a chair before the table; for a while he looked drowsily at the shining books, then rose, and went into the bedroom.

Here, in the bedroom dead quiet reigned. Everything, down to the last trifle, spoke eloquently of the tempest undergone, of weariness, and everything rested. The candle which stood among a closed crowd of phials, boxes and jars on the stool and the big lamp on the chest of drawers brightly lit the room. On the bed, by the window, the boy lay open-eyed, with a look of wonder on his face. He did not move, but it seemed that his open eyes became darker and darker every second and sank into his skull. Having laid her hands on his body and hid her face in the folds of the bedclothes, the mother now was on her knees before the bed. Like the boy she did not move, but how much living movement was felt in the coil of her body and in her hands! She was pressing close to the bed with her whole being, with eager vehemence, as though she were afraid to violate the quiet and comfortable pose which she had found at last for her weary body. Blankets, cloths, basins, splashes on the floor, brushes and spoons scattered everywhere, a white bottle of limewater, the stifling heavy air itself—everything died away, and as it were plunged into quietude.

The doctor stopped by his wife, thrust his hands into his trouser pockets and bending his head on one side looked fixedly at his son. His face showed indifference; only the drops which glistened on his beard revealed that he had been lately weeping.

The repulsive terror of which we think when we speak of death was absent from the bedroom. In the pervading dumbness, in the mother's pose, in the indifference of the doctor's face was something attractive that touched the heart, the subtle and elusive beauty of human grief, which it will take men long to understand and describe, and only music, it seems, is able to express. Beauty too was felt in the stern stillness. Kirilov and his wife were silent and did not weep, as though they confessed all the poetry of their condition. As once the season of their youth passed away, so now in this boy their right to bear children had passed away, alas! for ever to eternity. The doctor is forty-four years old, already grey and looks like an old man; his faded sick wife is thirty-five. Andrey was not merely the only son but the last.

In contrast to his wife the doctor's nature belonged to those which feel the necessity of movement when their soul is in pain. After standing by his wife for about five minutes, he passed from the bedroom lifting his right foot too high, into a little room half filled with a big broad divan. From there he went to the kitchen. After wandering about the fireplace and the cook's bed, he stooped through a little door and came into the hall.

Here he saw the white scarf and the pale face again.

"At last," sighed Aboguin, seizing the door handle. "Let us go, please."

The doctor shuddered, glanced at him and remembered.

"Listen. I've told you already that I can't go," he said, livening. "What a strange idea!"

"Doctor, I'm made of flesh and blood, too. I fully understand your condition. I sympathise with you," Aboguin said in an imploring voice, putting his hand to his scarf. "But I am not asking for myself. My wife is dying. If you had heard her cry, if you'd seen her face, you would understand my insistence! My God—and I thought that you'd gone to dress yourself. The time is precious, Doctor! Let us go, I beg of you."

"I can't come," Kirilov said after a pause, and stepped into his drawing-room.

Aboguin followed him and seized him by the sleeve.

"You're in sorrow. I understand. But I'm not asking you to cure a toothache, or to give expert evidence—but to save a human life." He went on imploring like a beggar. "This life is more than any personal grief. I ask you for courage, for a brave deed—in the name of humanity."

"Humanity cuts both ways," Kirilov said irritably. "In the name of the same humanity I ask you not to take me away. My God, what a strange idea! I can hardly stand on my feet and you frighten me with humanity. I'm not fit for anything now. I won't go for anything. With whom shall I leave my wife? No, no. . . ."

Kirilov flung out his open hands and drew back.

"And . . . and don't ask me," he continued, disturbed. "I'm sorry. . . . Under the Laws, Volume XIII., I'm obliged to go and you have the right to drag me by the neck. . . . Well, drag me, but . . . I'm not fit. . . . I'm not even able to speak. Excuse me."

"It's quite unfair to speak to me in that tone, Doctor," said Aboguin, again taking the doctor by the sleeve. "The thirteenth volume be damned! I have no right to do violence to your will. If you want to, come; if you don't, then God be with you; but it's not to your will that I apply, but to your feelings. A young woman is dying! You say your son died just now. Who could understand my terror better than you?"

Aboguin's voice trembled with agitation. His tremor and his tone were much more convincing than his words. Aboguin was sincere, but it is remarkable that every phrase he used came out stilted, soulless, inopportunely florid, and as it were insulted the atmosphere of the doctor's house and the woman who was dying. He felt it himself, and in his fear of being misunderstood he exerted himself to the utmost to make his voice soft and tender so as to convince by the sincerity of his tone at least, if not by his words. As a rule, however deep and beautiful the words they affect only the unconcerned. They cannot always satisfy those who are happy or distressed because the highest expression of happiness or distress is most often silence. Lovers understand each other best when they are silent, and a fervent passionate speech at the graveside affects only outsiders. To the widow and children it seems cold and trivial.

Kirilov stood still and was silent. When Aboguin uttered some more words on the higher vocation of a doctor, and self-sacrifice, the doctor sternly asked:

"Is is far?"

"Thirteen or fourteen versts. I've got good horses, Doctor. I give you my word of honour that I'll take you there and back in an hour. Only an hour."

The last words impressed the doctor more strongly than the references to humanity or the doctor's vocation. He thought for a while and said with a sigh:

"Well, let us go!"

He went off quickly, with a step that was not sure, to his study and soon after returned in a long coat. Aboguin, delighted, danced impatiently round him, helped him on with his overcoat, and accompanied him out of the house.

Outside it was dark, but brighter than in the hall. Now in the darkness the tall stooping figure of the doctor was clearly visible with the long, narrow beard and the aquiline nose. Beside his pale face Aboguin's big face could now be seen and a little student cap which hardly covered the crown of his head. The scarf showed white only in front, but behind it was hid under his long hair.

"Believe me, I'm able to appreciate your magnanimity," murmured Aboguin, as he helped the doctor to a seat in the carriage. "We'll whirl away. Luke, dear man, drive as fast as you can, do!"

The coachman drove quickly. First appeared a row of bare buildings, which stood along the hospital yard. It was dark everywhere, save that at the end of the yard a bright light from someone's window broke through the garden fence, and three windows in the upper story of the separate house seemed to be paler than the air. Then the carriage drove into dense obscurity where you could smell mushroom damp, and hear the whisper of the trees.

The noise of the wheels awoke the rooks who began to stir in the leaves and raised a doleful, bewildered cry as if they knew that the doctor's son was dead and Aboguin's wife ill. Then began to appear separate trees, a shrub. Sternly gleamed the pond, where big black shadows slept. The carriage rolled along over an even plain. Now the cry of the rooks was but faintly heard far away behind. Soon it became completely still.

Almost all the way Kirilov and Aboguin were silent; save that once Aboguin sighed profoundly and mumured:

"It's terrible pain. One never loves his nearest so much as when there is the risk of losing them."

And when the carriage was quietly passing through the river, Kirilov gave a sudden start, as though the dashing of the water frightened him, and he began to move impatiently.

"Let me go," he said in anguish. "I'll come to you later. I only want to send the attendant to my wife. She is all alone."

Aboguin was silent. The carriage, swaying and rattling against the stones, drove over the sandy bank and went on. Kirilov began to toss about in anguish, and glanced around. Behind the road was visible in the scant light of the stars and the willows that fringed the bank disappearing into the darkness. To the right the plain stretched smooth and boundless as heaven. On it in the distance here and there dim lights were burning, probably on the turfpits. To the left, parallel with the road stretched a little hill, tufted with tiny shrubs, and on the hill a big half-moon stood motionless, red, slightly veiled with a mist, and surrounded with fine clouds which seemed to be gazing upon it from every side, and guarding it, lest it should disappear.

In all nature one felt something hopeless and sick. Like a fallen woman who sits alone in a dark room trying not to think of her past, the earth languished with reminiscence of spring and summer and waited in apathy for ineluctable winter. Wherever one's glance turned nature showed everywhere like a dark, cold, bottomless pit, whence neither Kirilov nor Aboguin nor the red half-moon could escape. . . .

The nearer the carriage approached the destination the more impatient did Aboguin become. He moved about, jumped up and stared over the driver's shoulder in front of him. And when at last the carriage drew up at the foot of the grand staircase, nicely covered with a striped linen awning, and he looked up at the lighted windows of the first floor one could hear his breath trembling.

"If anything happens . . . I shan't survive it," he said, entering the hall with the doctor and slowly rubbing his hands in his agitation. "But I can't hear any noise. That means it's all right so far," he added, listening to the stillness.

No voices or steps were heard in the hall. For all the bright illumination the whole house seemed asleep. Now the doctor and Aboguin who had been in darkness up till now could examine each other. The doctor was tall, with a stoop, slovenly dressed, and his face was plain. There was something unpleasantly sharp, ungracious, and severe in his thick negro lips, his aquiline nose and his faded, indifferent look. His tangled hair, his sunken temples, the early grey in his long thin beard, that showed his shining chin, his pale grey complexion and the slipshod awkwardness of his manners—the hardness of it all suggested to the mind bad times undergone, an unjust lot and weariness of life and men. To look at the hard figure of the man, you could not believe that he had a wife and could weep over his child. Aboguin revealed something different. He was robust, solid and fair-haired, with a big head and large, yet soft, features, exquisitely dressed in the latest fashion. In his carriage, his tight-buttoned coat and his mane of hair you felt something noble and leonine. He walked with his head straight and his chest prominent, he spoke in a pleasant baritone, and in his manner of removing his scarf or arranging his hair there appeared a subtle, almost feminine, elegance. Even his pallor and childish fear as he glanced upwards to the staircase while taking off his coat, did not disturb his carriage or take from the satisfaction, the health and aplomb which his figure breathed.

"There's no one about, nothing I can hear," he said, walking upstairs. "No commotion. May God be good!"

He accompanied the doctor through the hall to a large salon, where a big piano showed dark and a lustre hung in a white cover. Thence they both passed into a small and beautiful drawing-room, very cosy, filled with a pleasant, rosy half-darkness.

"Please sit here a moment, Doctor," said Aboguin, "I . . . I won't be a second. I'll just have a look and tell them."

Kirilov was left alone. The luxury of the drawing-room, the pleasant half-darkness, even his presence in a stranger's unfamiliar house evidently did not move him. He sat in a chair looking at his hands burnt with carbolic acid. He had no more than a glimpse of the bright red lampshade, the 'cello case, and when he looked sideways across the room to where the clock was ticking, he noticed a stuffed wolf, as solid and satisfied as Aboguin himself.

It was still. . . . Somewhere far away in the other rooms someone uttered a loud "Ah!" A glass door, probably a cupboard door, rang, and again everything was still. After five minutes had passed, Kirilov did not look at his hands any more. He raised his eyes to the door through which Aboguin had disappeared.

Aboguin was standing on the threshold, but not the same man as went out. The expression of satisfaction and subtle elegance had disappeared from him. His face and hands, the attitude of his body were distorted with a disgusting expression either of horror or of tormenting physical pain. His nose, lips, moustache, all his features were moving and as it were trying to tear themselves away from his face, but the eyes were as though laughing from pain.

Aboguin took a long heavy step into the middle of the room, stooped, moaned, and shook his fists.

"Deceived!" he cried, emphasising the syllable *cei*. "She deceived me! She's gone! She fell ill and sent me for the doctor only to run away with this fool Papchinsky. My God!"

Aboguin stepped heavily towards the doctor, thrust his white soft fists before his face, and went on wailing, shaking his fists the while.

"She's gone off! She's deceived me! But why this lie? My God, my God! Why this dirty, foul trick, this devilish, serpent's game? What have I done to her? She's gone off."

Tears gushed from his eyes. He turned on his heel and began to pace the drawing-room. Now in his short jacket and his fashionable narrow trousers in which his legs seemed too thin for his body, he was extraordinarily like a lion. Curiosity kindled in the doctor's impassive face. He rose and eyed Aboguin.

"Well, where's the patient?"

"The patient, the patient," cried Aboguin, laughing, weeping, and still shaking his fists. "She's not ill, but accursed. Vile—dastardly. The Devil himself couldn't have planned a fouler trick. She sent me so that she could run away with a fool, an utter clown, an Alphonse! My God, far better she should have died. I'll not bear it. I shall not bear it."

The doctor stood up straight. His eyes began to blink, filled with tears; his thin beard began to move with his jaw right and left.

"What's this?" he asked, looking curiously about. "My child's dead. My wife in anguish, alone in all the house. . . . I can hardly stand on my feet, I haven't slept for three nights . . . and I'm made to play in a vulgar comedy, to play the part of a stage property! I don't . . . I don't understand it!"

Aboguin opened one fist, flung a crumpled note on the floor and trod on it, as upon an insect he wished to crush.

"And I didn't see . . . didn't understand," he said through his set teeth, brandishing one fist round his head, with an expression as though someone had trod on a corn. "I didn't notice how he came to see us every day. I didn't notice that he came in a carriage to-day! What was the carriage for? And I didn't see! Innocent!"

"I don't . . . I don't understand," the doctor murmured. "What's it all mean? It's jeering at a man, laughing at a man's suffering! That's impossible. . . . I've never seen it in my life before!"

With the dull bewilderment of a man who has just begun to understand that someone has bitterly offended him, the doctor shrugged his shoulders, waved his hands and not knowing what to say or do, dropped exhausted into a chair.

"Well, she didn't love me any more. She loved another man. Very well. But why the deceit, why this foul treachery?" Aboguin spoke with tears in his voice. "Why, why? What have I done to you? Listen, Doctor," he said passionately approaching Kirilov. "You were the unwilling witness of my misfortune, and I am not going to hide the truth from you. I swear I loved this woman. I loved her with devotion, like a slave. I sacrificed everything for her. I broke with my family, I gave up the service and my music. I forgave her things I could not have forgiven my mother and sister . . . I never once gave her an angry look . . . I never gave her any cause. Why this lie, then? I do not demand love, but why this abominable deceit? If you don't love any more then speak out honestly, above all when you know what I feel about this matter. . . ."

With tears in his eyes and trembling in all his bones, Aboguin was pouring out his soul to the doctor. He spoke passionately, pressing both hands to his heart. He revealed all the family secrets without hesitation, as though he were glad that these secrets were being torn from his heart. Had he spoken thus for an hour or two and poured out all his soul, he would surely have been easier.

Who can say whether, had the doctor listened and given him friendly sympathy, he would not, as so often happens, have been reconciled to his grief unprotesting, without turning to unprofitable follies? But it happened otherwise. While Aboguin was speaking the offended doctor changed countenance visibly. The indifference and amazement in his face gradually gave way to an expression of bitter outrage, indignation, and anger. His features became still sharper, harder, and more forbidding. When Aboguin put before his eyes the photograph of his young wife, with a pretty, but dry, inexpressive face like a nun's, and asked if it were possible to look at that face and grant that it could express a lie, the doctor suddenly started away, with flashing eyes, and said, coarsely forging out each several word:

"Why do you tell me all this? I do not want to hear! I don't want to," he cried and banged his fist upon the table. "I don't want your trivial vulgar secrets—to Hell with them. You dare not tell me such trivialities. Or do you think I have not yet been insulted enough! That I'm a lackey to whom you can give the last insult? Yes?"

Aboguin drew back from Kirilov and stared at him in surprise.

"Why did you bring me here?" the doctor went on, shaking his beard. "You marry out of high spirits, get angry out of high spirits, and make a melodrama—but where do I come in? What have I got to do with your romances? Leave me alone! Get on with your noble grabbing, parade your humane ideas, play"—the doctor gave a side-glance at the 'cello-case—"the double-bass and the trombone, stuff yourselves like capons, but don't dare to jeer at a real man! If you can't respect him, then you can at least spare him your attentions."

"What does all this mean?" Aboguin asked, blushing.

"It means that it's vile and foul to play with a man! I'm a doctor. You consider doctors and all men who work and don't reek of scent and harlotry, your footmen, your *mauvais tons.* Very well, but no one gave you the right to turn a man who suffers into a property."

"How dare you say that?" Aboguin asked quietly. Again his face began to twist about, this time in visible anger.

"How dare *you* bring me here to listen to trivial rubbish, when you know that I'm in sorrow?" the doctor cried and banged his fists on the table once more. "Who gave you the right to jeer at another's grief?"

"You're mad," cried Aboguin. "You're ungenerous. I too am deeply unhappy and . . . and . . ."

"Unhappy"—the doctor gave a sneering laugh—"don't touch the word, it's got nothing to do with you. Wasters who can't get money on a bill call themselves unhappy too. A capon's unhappy, oppressed with all its superfluous fat. You worthless lot!"

"Sir, you're forgetting yourself," Aboguin gave a piercing scream. "For words like those, people are beaten. Do you understand?"

Aboguin thrust his hand into his side pocket, took out a pocket-book, found two notes and flung them on the table.

"There's your fee," he said, and his nostrils trembled. "You're paid."

"You dare not offer me money," said the doctor, and brushed the notes from the table to the floor. "You don't settle an insult with money."

Aboguin and the doctor stood face to face, heaping each other with undeserved insults. Never in their lives, even in a frenzy, had they said so much that was unjust and cruel and absurd. In both the selfishness of the unhappy is violently manifest. Unhappy men are selfish, wicked, unjust, and less able to understand each other than fools. Unhappiness does not unite people, but separates them; and just where one would imagine that people should be united by the community of grief, there is more injustice and cruelty done than among the comparatively contented.

"Send me home, please," the doctor cried, out of breath.

Aboguin rang the bell violently. Nobody came. He rang once more; then flung the bell angrily to the floor. It struck dully on the carpet and gave out a mournful sound like a death-moan. The footman appeared.

"Where have you been hiding, damn you?" The master sprang upon him with clenched fists. "Where have you been just now? Go away and tell them to send the carriage round for this gentleman, and get the brougham ready for me. Wait," he called out as the footman turned to go. "Not a single traitor remains to-morrow. Pack off all of you. I will engage new ones. . . . Rabble!"

While they waited Aboguin and the doctor were silent. Already the expression of satisfaction and the subtle elegance had returned to the former. He paced the drawing-room, shook his head elegantly and evidently was planning something. His anger was not yet cool, but he tried to make as if he did not notice his enemy. . . . The doctor stood with one hand on the edge of the table, looking at Aboguin with that deep, rather cynical, ugly contempt with which only grief and an unjust lot can look, when they see satiety and elegance before them.

A little later, when the doctor took his seat in the carriage and drove away, his eyes still glanced contemptuously. It was dark, much darker than an hour ago. The red half-moon had now disappeared behind the little hill, and the clouds which watched it lay in dark spots round the stars. The brougham with the red lamps began to rattle on the road and passed the doctor. It was Aboguin on his way to protest, to commit all manner of folly.

All the way the doctor thought not of his wife or Andrey, but only of Aboguin and those who lived in the house he just left. His thoughts were unjust, inhuman, and cruel. He passed sentence on Aboguin, his wife, Papchinsky, and all those who live in rosy semi-darkness and smell of scent. All the way he hated them, and his heart ached with his contempt for them. The conviction he formed about them would last his life long.

Time will pass and Kirilov's sorrow, but this conviction, unjust and unworthy of the human heart, will not pass, but will remain in the doctor's mind until the grave.

Questions for Study

1. Where is the climax of the story? Give reasons for your answer.

2. How do the two houses reflect the differences between Kirilov and Aboguin?

3. What makes Kirilov decide to go with Aboguin?
4. What is the purpose of the scene in the carriage during the drive to Aboguin's house?
5. What is ironic about Aboguin's statement at the beginning of the story "While I was coming to you I suffered terribly"? What kind of irony is this?
6. How appropriate is the ending of the story? Has it been prepared for? What does it tell us about Kirilov?
7. What are the ways in which Chekhov maintains suspense?

Topics for Discussion and Writing

1. Explain the part coincidence plays in the story and evaluate its effectiveness.
2. Analyze the scene in the dead boy's bedroom and explain its function in the story.
3. One of the main ironies of the story is that, although the two men are enemies, they have much in common. Write an essay showing their similarities and differences.
4. One of the basic ideas of the story is that a common unhappiness does not unite people, but separates them. Show how the story illustrates this point in an ironic way.

WILLIAM FAULKNER

Spotted Horses

I

Yes sir. Flem Snopes has filled that whole country full of spotted horses. You can hear folks running them all day and all night, whooping and hollering, and the horses running back and forth across them little wooden bridges ever now and then kind of like thunder. Here I was this morning pretty near halfway to town, with the team ambling along and me setting in the buckboard about half asleep, when all of a sudden something come swurging up outen the bushes and jumped the road clean, without touching hoof to it. It flew right over my team big as a billboard and flying through the air like a hawk. It taken me thirty minutes to stop my team and untangle the harness and the buckboard and hitch them up again.

That Flem Snopes. I be dog if he ain't a case, now. One morning about ten years ago the boys was just getting settled down on Varner's porch for a little talk and tobacco, when here come Flem out from behind the counter, with his coat off and his hair all parted, like he might have been clerking for Varner for ten years already. Folks all knowed him; it was a big family of them about five miles down the bottom. That year, at least. Share-cropping. They never stayed on any place over a year. Then they would move on to another place, with the chap or maybe the twins of that year's litter. It was a regular nest of them. But Flem. The rest of them stayed tenant farmers, moving ever year, but here come Flem one day, walking out from behind Jody Varner's counter like he owned it. And he wasn't there but a year or two before folks knowed that if him and Jody was both still in that store in ten years more it would be Jody clerking for Flem Snopes. Why, that fellow could make a nickel where it wasn't but four cents to begin with. He skun me in two trades myself, and the fellow that can do that, I just hope he'll get rich before I do; that's all.

All right. So here Flem was, clerking at Varner's, making a nickel here and there and not telling nobody about it. No, sir. Folks never knowed when Flem got the better of somebody lessen the fellow he beat told it. He'd just set there in the store-chair, chewing his tobacco and keeping his own business to hisself, until about a week later we'd find out it was somebody else's business he was keeping to hisself—provided the fellow he trimmed was mad enough to tell it. That's Flem.

We give him ten years to own ever thing Jody Varner had. But he never waited no ten years. I reckon you-all know that gal of Uncle Billy Varner's, the youngest one, Eula. Jody's sister. Ever Sunday ever yellow-wheeled buggy and curried riding horse in that country would be hitched to Bill Varner's fence, and the young bucks setting on the porch, swarming around Eula like bees around a honey pot. One of these here kind of big, soft-looking gals that could giggle richer than plowed new-ground. Wouldn't none of them leave before the others, and so they would set there on the porch until time to go home, with some of them with nine and ten miles to ride and then get up tomorrow and go back to the field. So they would all leave together and they would ride in a clump down to the creek ford and hitch them curried horses and yellow-wheeled buggies and get out and fight one another. Then they would get in the buggies again and go on home.

Well, one day about a year ago, one of them yellow-wheeled buggies and one of them curried saddle-horses quit this country. We heard they was heading for Texas. The next day Uncle Billy and Eula and Flem come in to town in Uncle Bill's surrey, and when they come back, Flem and Eula was married. And on the next day we heard that two more of them yellow-wheeled buggies had left the country. They mought have gone to Texas, too. It's a big place.

Anyway, about a month after the wedding, Flem and Eula went to Texas, too. They was gone pretty near a year. Then one day last month, Eula come back, with a baby. We figured up, and we decided that it was as well-growed a three-months-old baby as we ever see. It can already pull up on a chair. I reckon Texas makes big men quick, being a big place. Anyway, if it keeps on like it started, it'll be chewing tobacco and voting time it's eight years old.

And so last Friday here come Flem himself. He was on a wagon with another fellow. The other fellow had one of these two-gallon hats and a ivory-handled pistol and a box of gingersnaps sticking out of his pocket, and tied to the tail-gate of the wagon was about two dozen of them Texas ponies, hitched to one another with barbed wire. They was colored like parrots and they was quiet as doves, and ere a one of them would kill you quick as a rattlesnake. Nere a one of them had two eyes the same color, and nere a one of them had ever see a bridle, I reckon; and when that Texas man got down offen the wagon and walked up to them to show how gentle they was, one of them cut his vest clean offen him, same as with a razor.

Flem had done already disappeared; he had went on to see his wife, I reckon, and to see if that ere baby had done gone on to the field to help Uncle Billy plow, maybe. It was the Texas man that taken the horses on to Mrs. Littlejohn's lot. He had a little trouble at first, when they come to the gate, because they hadn't never see a fence before, and when he finally got them in and taken a pair of wire cutters and unhitched them and got them into the barn and poured some shell corn into the trough, they durn nigh tore down the barn. I reckon they thought that shell corn was bugs, maybe. So he left them in the lot and he announced that the auction would begin at sunup tomorrow.

That night we was setting on Mrs. Littlejohn's porch. You-all mind the moon was nigh full that night, and we could watch them spotted varmints swirling along the fence and back and forth across the lot same as minnows in a pond. And then now and then they would all kind of huddle up against the barn and rest themselves by biting and kicking one another. We would hear a squeal, and then a set of hoofs would go Bam! against the barn, like a pistol. It sounded just like a fellow with a pistol, in a nest of cattymounts, taking his time.

II

It wasn't ere a man knowed yet if Flem owned them things or not. They just knowed one thing: that they wasn't never going to know for sho if Flem did or not, or if maybe he didn't just get on that wagon at the edge of town, for the ride or not. Even Eck Snopes didn't know, Flem's own cousin. But wasn't nobody surprised at that. We knowed that Flem would skin Eck quick as he would ere a one of us.

They was there by sunup next morning, some of them come twelve and sixteen miles, with seed-money tied up in tobacco sacks in their overalls, standing along the fence, when the Texas man come out of Mrs. Littlejohn's after breakfast and clumb onto the gate post with that ere white pistol butt sticking outen his hind pocket. He taken a new box of gingersnaps outen his pocket and bit the end offen it like a cigar and spit out the paper, and said the auction was open. And still they was coming up in wagons and a horse- and mule-back and hitching the teams across the road and coming to the fence. Flem wasn't nowhere in sight.

But he couldn't get them started. He begun to work on Eck, because Eck holp him last night to get them into the barn and feed them that shell corn. Eck got out just in time. He come outen that barn like a chip on the crest of a busted dam of water, and clumb into the wagon just in time.

He was working on Eck when Henry Armstid come up in his wagon. Eck was saying he was skeered to bid on one of them, because he might get it, and the Texas man says, "Them ponies? Them little horses?" He clumb down offen the gate post and went toward the horses. They broke and run, and him following them, kind of chirping to them, with his hand out like he was fixing to catch a fly, until he got three or four of them cornered. Then he jumped into them, and then we couldn't see nothing for a while because of the dust. It was a big cloud of it, and them blare-eyed, spotted things swoaring outen it twenty foot to a jump, in forty directions without counting up. Then the dust settled and there they was, that Texas man and the horse. He had its head twisted clean around like a owl's head. Its legs was braced and it was trembling like a new bride and groaning like a sawmill, and him holding its head wrung clean around on its neck so it was snuffing sky. "Look it over," he says, with his heels dug too and that white pistol sticking outen his pocket and his neck swole up like a spreading adder's until you could just tell what he was saying, cussing the horse and talking to us all at once: "Look him over, the fiddle-headed son of fourteen fathers. Try him, buy him; you will get the best—" Then it was all dust again, and we couldn't see nothing but spotted hide and mane, and that ere Texas man's boot-heels like a couple of walnuts on two strings, and after a while that two-gallon hat come sailing out like a fat old hen crossing a fence.

When the dust settled again, he was just getting outen the far fence corner, brushing himself off. He come and got his hat and brushed it off and come and clumb onto the gate post again. He was breathing hard. The hammer-head horse was still running round and round the lot like a merry-go-round at a fair. That was when Henry Armstid come shoving up to the gate in them patched overalls and one of them dangle-armed shirts of hisn. Hadn't nobody noticed him until then. We was all watching the Texas man and the horses. Even Mrs. Littlejohn; she had done come out and built a fire under the wash-pot in her back yard, and she would stand at the fence a while and then go back into the house and come out again with a arm full of wash and stand at the fence again. Well, here come Henry shoving up, and then we see Mrs. Armstid right behind him, in that ere faded wrapper and sunbonnet and them tennis shoes. "Git on back to that wagon," Henry says.

"Henry," she says.

"Here, boys," the Texas man says; "make room for missus to git up and see. Come on Henry," he says; "here's your chance to buy that saddle-horse missus has been wanting. What about ten dollars, Henry?"

"Henry," Mrs. Armstid says. She put her hand on Henry's arm. Henry knocked her hand down.

"Git on back to that wagon, like I told you," he says.

Mrs. Armstid never moved. She stood behind Henry, with her hands rolled into her dress, not looking at nothing. "He hain't no more despair than to buy one of them things," she says. "And us not five dollars ahead of the pore house, he hain't no more despair." It was the truth, too. They ain't never made more than a bare living offen that place of theirs, and them with four chaps and the very clothes they wears she earns by weaving by the firelight at night while Henry's asleep.

"Shut your mouth and git on back to that wagon," Henry says. "Do you want I taken a wagon stake to you here in the big road?"

Well, that Texas man taken one look at her. Then he begun on Eck again, like Henry wasn't even there. But Eck was skeered. "I can git me a snapping turtle or a water moccasin for nothing. I ain't going to buy none."

So the Texas man said he would give Eck a horse. "To start the auction, and because you holp me last night. If you'll start the bidding on the next horse," he says, "I'll give you that fiddle-head horse."

I wish you could have seen them, standing there with their seed-money in their pockets, watching that Texas man give Eck Snopes a live horse, all fixed to call him a fool if he taken it or not. Finally Eck says he'll take it. "Only I just starts the bidding," he says. "I don't have to buy the next one lessen I ain't overtopped." The Texas man said all right, and Eck bid a dollar on the next one, with Henry Armstid standing there with his mouth already open, watching Eck and the Texas man like a mad-dog or something. "A dollar," Eck says.

The Texas man looked at Eck. His mouth was already open too, like he had started to say something and what he was going to say had up and died on him. "A dollar? You mean, *one* dollar, Eck?"

"Durn it," Eck says; "two dollars, then."

Well, sir, I wish you could a seen that Texas man. He taken out that gingersnap box and held it up and looked into it, careful, like it might have been a diamond ring in it, or a spider. Then he throwed it away and wiped his face with a bandanna. "Well," he says. "Well. Two dollars. Two dollars. Is your pulse all right, Eck?" he says. "Do you have ager-sweats at night, maybe?" he says. "Well," he says, "I got to take it. But are you boys going to stand there and see Eck get two horses at a dollar a head?"

That done it. I be dog if he wasn't nigh as smart as Flem Snopes. He hadn't no more than got the words outen his mouth before here was Henry Armstid, waving his hand. "Three dollars," Henry says. Mrs. Armstid tried to hold him again. He knocked her hand off, shoving up to the gate post.

"Mister," Mrs. Armstid says, "we got chaps in the house and not corn to feed the stock. We got five dollars I earned my chaps a-weaving after dark, and him snoring in the bed. And he hain't no more despair."

"Henry bid three dollars," the Texas man says. "Raise him a dollar, Eck, and the horse is yours."

"Henry," Mrs. Armstid says.

"Raise him, Eck," the Texas man says.

"Four dollars," Eck says.

"Five dollars," Henry says, shaking his fist. He shoved up right under the gate post. Mrs. Armstid was looking at the Texas man too.

"Mister," she says, "if you take that five dollars I earned my chaps a-weaving for one of them things, it'll be a curse onto you and yourn during all the time of man."

But it wasn't no stopping Henry. He had shoved up, waving his fist at the Texas man. He opened it; the money was in nickels and quarters, and one dollar bill that looked like a cow's cud. "Five dollars," he says. "And the man that raises it'll have to beat my head off, or I'll beat hisn."

"All right," the Texas man says. "Five dollars is bid. But don't you shake your hand at me."

III

It taken till nigh sundown before the last one was sold. He got them hotted up once and the bidding got up to seven dollars and a quarter, but most of them went around three or four dollars, him setting on the gate post and picking the horses out one at a time by mouth-word, and Mrs. Littlejohn pumping up and down at the tub and stopping and coming to the fence for a while and going back to the tub again. She had done got done too, and the wash was hung on the line in the back yard, and we could smell supper cooking. Finally they was all sold; he swapped the last two and the wagon for a buckboard.

We was all kind of tired, but Henry Armstid looked more like a mad-dog than ever. When he bought, Mrs. Armstid had went back to the wagon, setting in it behind them two rabbit-sized, bone-pore mules, and the wagon itself looking like it would fall all to pieces soon as the mules moved. Henry hadn't even waited to pull it outen the road; it was still in the middle of the road and her setting in it, not looking at nothing, ever since this morning.

Henry was right up against the gate. He went up to the Texas man. "I bought a horse and I paid cash," Henry says. "And yet you expect me to stand around here until they are all sold before I can get my horse. I'm going to take my horse outen that lot."

The Texas man looked at Henry. He talked like he might have been asking for a cup of coffee at the table. "Take your horse," he says.

Then Henry quit looking at the Texas man. He begun to swallow, holding onto the gate. "Ain't you going to help me?" he says.

"It ain't my horse," the Texas man says.

Henry never looked at the Texas man again, he never looked at nobody. "Who'll help me catch my horse?" he says. Never nobody said nothing. "Bring the plowline," Henry says. Mrs. Armstid got outen the wagon and brought the plowline. The Texas man got down offen the post. The woman made to pass him, carrying the rope.

"Don't you go in there, missus," the Texas man says.

Henry opened the gate. He didn't look back. "Come on here," he says.

"Don't you go in there, missus," the Texas man says.

Mrs. Armstid wasn't looking at nobody, neither, with her hands across her middle, holding the rope. "I reckon I better," she says. Her and Henry went into the lot. The horses broke and run. Henry and Mrs. Armstid followed.

"Get him into the corner," Henry says. They got Henry's horse cornered finally, and Henry taken the rope, but Mrs. Armstid let the horse get out. They hemmed it up again, but Mrs. Armstid let it get out again, and Henry turned and hit her with the rope. "Why didn't you head him back?" Henry says. He hit her again. "Why didn't you?" It was about that time I looked around and see Flem Snopes standing there.

It was the Texas man that done something. He moved fast for a big man. He caught the rope before Henry could hit the third time, and Henry whirled and made like he would jump at the Texas man. But he never jumped. The Texas man went and taken Henry's arm and led him outen the lot. Mrs. Armstid come behind them and the Texas man taken some money outen his pocket and he give it into Mrs. Armstid's hand. "Get him into the wagon and take him on home," the Texas man says, like he might have been telling them he enjoyed his supper.

Then here come Flem. "What's that for, Buck?" Flem says.

"Thinks he bought one of them ponies," the Texas man says. "Get him on away, missus."

But Henry wouldn't go. "Give him back that money," he says. "I bought that horse and I aim to have him if I have to shoot him."

And there was Flem, standing there with his hands in his pockets, chewing, like he had just happened to be passing.

"You take your money and I take my horse," Henry says. "Give it back to him," he says to Mrs. Armstid.

"You don't own no horse of mine," the Texas man says. "Get him on home, missus."

Then Henry seen Flem. "You got something to do with these horses," he says. "I bought one. Here's the money for it." He taken the bill outen Mrs. Armstid's hand. He offered it to Flem. "I bought one. Ask him. Here. Here's the money," he says, giving the bill to Flem.

When Flem taken the money, the Texas man dropped the rope he had snatched outen Henry's hand. He had done sent Eck Snopes's boy up to the store for another box of gingersnaps, and he taken the box outen his pocket and looked into it. It was empty and he dropped it on the ground. "Mr. Snopes will have your money for you tomorrow," he says to Mrs. Armstid. "You can get it from him tomorrow. He don't own no horse. You get him into the wagon and get him on home." Mrs. Armstid went back to the wagon and got in. "Where's that ere buckboard I bought?" the Texas man says. It was after sundown then. And then Mrs. Littlejohn come out on the porch and rung the supper bell.

IV

I come on in and et supper. Mrs. Littlejohn would bring in a pan of bread or something, then she would go out to the porch a minute and come back and tell us. The Texas man had hitched his team to the buckboard he had swapped them last two horses for, and him and Flem had gone, and then she told that the rest of them that never had ropes had went back to the store with I. O. Snopes to get some ropes, and wasn't nobody at the gate but Henry Armstid, and Mrs. Armstid setting in the wagon in the road, and Eck Snopes and that boy of hisn. "I don't care how many of them fool men gets killed by them things," Mrs. Littlejohn says, "but I ain't going to let Eck Snopes take that boy into that lot again." So she went down to the gate, but she come back without the boy or Eck neither.

"It ain't no need to worry about that boy," I says. "He's charmed." He was right behind Eck last night when Eck went to help feed them. The whole drove of them jumped clean over that boy's head and never touched him. It was Eck that touched him. Eck snatched him into the wagon and taken a rope and frailed the tar outen him.

So I had done et and went to my room and was undressing, long as I had a long trip to make the next day; I was trying to sell a machine to Mrs. Bundren up past Whiteleaf; when Henry Armstid opened that gate and went in by hisself. They couldn't make him wait for the balance of them to get back with their ropes. Eck Snopes said he tried to make Henry wait, but Henry wouldn't do it. Eck said Henry walked right up to them and that when they broke, they run clean over Henry like a haymow breaking down. Eck said he snatched that boy of hisn out of the way just in time and that them things went through that gate like a creek flood and into the wagons and teams hitched side the road, busting wagon tongues and snapping harness like it was fishing-line, with Mrs. Armstid still setting in their wagon in the middle of it like something carved outen wood. Then they scattered, wild horses and tame mules with pieces of harness and singletrees dangling offen them, both ways up and down the road.

"There goes ourn, paw!" Eck said his boy said. "There it goes, into Mrs. Littlejohn's house." Eck says it run right up the steps and into the house like a boarder late for supper. I reckon so. Anyway, I was in my room, in my underclothes, with one sock on and one sock in my hand, leaning out the window when the commotion busted out, when I heard something run into the melodeon in the hall; it sounded like a railroad engine. Then the door to my room come sailing in like when you throw a tin bucket top into the wind and I looked over my shoulder and see something that looked like a fourteen-foot pinwheel a-blaring its eyes at me. It had to blare them fast, because I was already done jumped out the window.

I reckon it was anxious, too. I reckon it hadn't never seen barbed wire or shell corn before, but I know it hadn't never seen underclothes before, or maybe it was a sewing-machine agent it hadn't never seen. Anyway, it whirled and turned to run back up the hall and outen the house, when it met Eck Snopes and that boy just coming in, carrying a rope. It swirled again and run down the hall and out the back door just in time to meet Mrs. Littlejohn. She had just gathered up the clothes she had washed, and she was coming onto the back porch with a armful of washing in one hand and a scrubbing-board in the other, when the horse skidded up to her, trying to stop and swirl again. It never taken Mrs. Littlejohn no time a-tall.

"Git outen here, you son," she says. She hit it across the face with the scrubbing-board; that ere scrubbing-board split as neat as ere a axe could have done it, and when the horse swirled to run back up the hall, she hit it again with what was left of the scrubbing-board, not on the head this time. "And stay out," she says.

Eck and that boy was halfway down the hall by this time. I reckon that horse looked like a pinwheel to Eck too. "Git to hell outen here, Ad!" Eck says. Only there wasn't time. Eck dropped flat on his face, but the boy never moved. The boy was about a yard tall maybe, in overalls just like Eck's; that horse swoared over his head without touching a hair. I saw that, because I was just coming back up the front steps, still carrying that ere sock and still in my underclothes, when the horse come onto the porch again. It taken one look at me and swirled again and run to the end of the porch and jumped the banisters and the lot fence like a hen-hawk and lit in the lot running and went out the gate again and jumped eight or ten upside-down wagons and went on down the road. It was a full moon then. Mrs. Armstid was still setting in the wagon like she had done been carved outen wood and left there and forgot.

That horse. It ain't never missed a lick. It was going about forty miles an hour when it come to the bridge over the creek. It would have had a clear road, but it so happened that Vernon Tull was already using the bridge when it got there. He was coming back from town; he hadn't heard about the auction; him and his wife and three daughters and Mrs. Tull's aunt, all setting in chairs in the wagon bed, and all asleep, including the mules. They waked up when the horse hit the bridge one time, but Tull said the first he knew was when the mules tried to turn the wagon around in the middle of the bridge and he seen that spotted varmint run right twixt the mules and run up the wagon tongue like a squirrel. He said he just had time to hit it across the face with his whip-stock, because about that time the mules turned the wagon around on that ere one-way bridge and that horse clumb across onto the bridge again and went on, with Vernon standing up in the wagon and kicking at it.

Tull said the mules turned in the harness and clumb back into the wagon too, with Tull trying to beat them out again, with the reins wrapped around his wrist. After that he says all he seen was overturned chairs and women-folk's legs and white drawers shining in the moonlight, and his mules and that spotted horse going on up the road like a ghost.

The mules jerked Tull outen the wagon and drug him a spell on the bridge before the reins broke. They thought at first that he was dead, and while they was kneeling around him, picking the bridge splinters outen him, here come Eck and that boy, still carrying the rope. They was running and breathing a little hard. "Where'd he go?" Eck said.

V

I went back and got my pants and shirt and shoes on just in time to go and help get Henry Armstid outen the trash in the lot. I be dog if he didn't look like he was dead, with his head hanging back and his teeth showing in the moonlight, and a little rim of white under his eye-lids. We could still hear them horses, here and there; hadn't none of them got more than four-five miles away yet, not knowing the country, I reckon. So we could hear them and folks yelling now and then: "Whooey. Head him!"

We toted Henry into Mrs. Littlejohn's. She was in the hall; she hadn't put down the armful of clothes. She taken one look at us, and she laid down the busted scrubbing-board and taken up the lamp and opened a empty door. "Bring him in here," she says.

We toted him in and laid him on the bed. Mrs. Littlejohn set the lamp on the dresser, still carrying the clothes. "I'll declare, you men," she says. Our shadows was way up the wall, tiptoeing too; we could hear ourselves breathing. "Better get his wife," Mrs. Littlejohn says. She went out, carrying the clothes.

"I reckon we had," Quick says. "Go get her, somebody."

"Whyn't you go?" Winterbottom says.

"Let Ernest git her," Durley says. "He lives neighbors with them."

Ernest went to fetch her. I be dog if Henry didn't look like he was dead. Mrs. Littlejohn come back, with a kettle and some towels. She went to work on Henry, and then Mrs. Armstid and Ernest come in. Mrs. Armstid come to the foot of the bed and stood there, with her hands rolled into her apron, watching what Mrs. Littlejohn was doing, I reckon.

"You men get outen the way," Mrs. Littlejohn says. "Git outside," she says. "See if you can't find something else to play with that will kill some more of you."

"Is he dead?" Winterbottom says.

"It ain't your fault if he ain't," Mrs. Littlejohn says. "Go tell Will Varner to come up here. I reckon a man ain't so different from a mule, come long come short. Except maybe a mule's got more sense."

We went to get Uncle Billy. It was a full moon. We could hear them, now and then, four miles away: "Whooey. Head him." The country was full of them, one on ever wooden bridge in the land, running across it like thunder: "Whooey. There he goes. Head him."

We hadn't got far before Henry begun to scream. I reckon Mrs. Littlejohn's water had brung him to; anyway, he wasn't dead. We went on to Uncle Billy's. The house was dark. We called to him, and after a while the window opened and Uncle Billy put his head out, peart as a peckerwood, listening. "Are they still trying to catch them durn rabbits?" he says.

He come down, with his britches on over his night-shirt and his suspenders dangling, carrying his horse-doctoring grip. "Yes, sir," he says, cocking his head like a woodpecker; "they're still a-trying."

We could hear Henry before we reached Mrs. Littlejohn's. He was going Ah-Ah-Ah. We stopped in the yard. Uncle Billy went on in. We could hear Henry. We stood in the yard, hearing them on the bridges, this-a-way and that: "Whooey. Whooey."

"Eck Snopes ought to caught hisn," Ernest says.

"Looks like he ought," Winterbottom said.

Henry was going Ah-Ah-Ah steady in the house; then he begun to scream. "Uncle Billy's started," Quick says. We looked into the hall. We could see the light where the door was. Then Mrs. Littlejohn come out.

"Will needs some help," she says. "You, Ernest. You'll do." Ernest went into the house.

"Hear them?" Quick said. "That one was on Four Mile bridge." We could hear them; it sounded like thunder a long way off; it didn't last long: "Whooey."

We could hear Henry: "Ah-Ah-Ah-Ah-Ah."

"They are both started now," Winterbottom says. "Ernest too."

That was early in the night. Which was a good thing, because it taken a long night for folks to chase them things right and for Henry to lay there and holler, being as Uncle Billy never had none of this here chloryfoam to set Henry's leg with. So it was considerate in Flem to get them started early. And what do you reckon Flem's com-ment was?

That's right. Nothing. Because he wasn't there. Hadn't nobody see him since that Texas man left.

VI

That was Saturday night. I reckon Mrs. Armstid got home about daylight, to see about the chaps. I don't know where they thought her and Henry was. But lucky the oldest one was a gal, about twelve, big enough to take care of the little ones. Which she did for the next two days. Mrs. Armstid would nurse Henry all night and work in the kitchen for hern and Henry's keep, and in the afternoon she would drive home (it was about four miles) to see the chaps. She would cook up a pot of victuals and leave it on the stove, and the gal would bar the house and keep the little ones quiet. I would hear Mrs. Littlejohn and Mrs. Armstid talking in the kitchen. "How are the chaps making out?" Mrs. Littlejohn says.

"All right," Mrs. Armstid says.

"Don't they git skeered at night?" Mrs. Littlejohn says.

"Ina May bars the door when I leave," Mrs. Armstid says. "She's got the axe in bed with her. I reckon she can make out."

I reckon they did. And I reckon Mrs. Armstid was waiting for Flem to come back to town; hadn't nobody seen him until this morning; to get her money the Texas man said Flem was keeping for her. Sho. I reckon she was.

Anyway, I heard Mrs. Armstid and Mrs. Littlejohn talking in the kitchen this morning while I was eating breakfast. Mrs. Littlejohn had just told Mrs. Armstid that Flem was in town. "You can ask him for that five dollars," Mrs. Littlejohn says.

"You reckon he'll give it to me?" Mrs. Armstid says.

Mrs. Littlejohn was washing dishes, washing them like a man, like they was made out of iron. "No," she says. "But asking him won't do no hurt. It might shame him. I don't reckon it will, but it might."

"If he wouldn't give it back, it ain't no use to ask," Mrs. Armstid says.

"Suit yourself," Mrs. Littlejohn says. "It's your money."

I could hear the dishes.

"Do you reckon he might give it back to me?" Mrs. Armstid says. "That Texas man said he would. He said I could get it from Mr. Snopes later."

"Then go and ask him for it," Mrs. Littlejohn says.

I could hear the dishes.

"He won't give it back to me," Mrs. Armstid says.

"All right," Mrs. Littlejohn says. "Don't ask him for it, then."

I could hear the dishes; Mrs. Armstid was helping. "You don't reckon he would, do you?" she says. Mrs. Littlejohn never said nothing. It sounded like she was throwing the dishes at one another. "Maybe I better go and talk to Henry about it," Mrs. Armstid says.

"I would," Mrs. Littlejohn says. I be dog if it didn't sound like she had two plates in her hands, beating them together. "Then Henry can buy another five-dollar horse with it. Maybe he'll buy one next time that will out and out kill him. If I thought that, I'd give you back the money, myself."

"I reckon I better talk to him first," Mrs. Armstid said. Then it sounded like Mrs. Littlejohn taken up all the dishes and throwed them at the cook-stove, and I come away.

That was this morning. I had been up to Bundren's and back, and I thought that things would have kind of settled down. So after breakfast, I went up to the store. And there was Flem, setting in the store chair and whittling, like he might not have ever moved since he come to clerk for Jody Varner. I. O. was leaning in the door, in his shirt sleeves and with his hair parted too, same as Flem was before he turned the clerking job over to I. O. It's a funny thing about them Snopes: they all looks alike, yet there ain't ere a two of them that claims brothers. They're always just cousins, like Flem and Eck and Flem and I. O. Eck was there too, squatting against the wall, him and that boy, eating cheese and crackers outen a sack; they told me that Eck hadn't been home a-tall. And that Lon Quick hadn't got back to town, even. He followed his horse clean down to Samson's Bridge, with a wagon and a camp outfit. Eck finally caught one of hisn. It run into a blind lane at Freeman's and Eck and the boy taken and tied their rope across the end of the lane, about three foot high. The horse come to the end of the lane and whirled and run back without ever stopping. Eck says it never seen the rope a-tall. He says it looked just like one of these here Christmas pinwheels. "Didn't it try to run again?" I says.

"No," Eck says, eating a bite of cheese offen his knife blade. "Just kicked some."

"Kicked some?" I says.

"It broke its neck," Eck says.

Well, they was squatting there, about six of them, talking, talking at Flem; never nobody knowed yet if Flem had ere a interest in them horses or not. So finally I come right out and asked him. "Flem's done skun all of us so much," I says, "that we're proud of him. Come on, Flem," I says, "how much did you and that Texas man make offen them horses? You can tell us. Ain't nobody here but Eck that bought one of them; the others ain't got back to town yet, and Eck's your own cousin; he'll be proud to hear, too. How much did you-all make?"

They was all whittling, not looking at Flem, making like they was studying. But you could a heard a pin drop. And I. O. He had been rubbing his back up and down on the door, but he stopped now, watching Flem like a pointing dog. Flem finished cutting the sliver offen his stick. He spit across the porch, into the road. "Twarn't none of my horses," he said.

I. O. cackled, like a hen, slapping his legs with both hands. "You boys might just as well quit trying to get ahead of Flem," he said.

Well, about that time I see Mrs. Armstid come outen Mrs. Littlejohn's gate, coming up the road. I never said nothing. I says, "Well, if a man can't take care of himself in a trade, he can't blame the man that trims him."

Flem never said nothing, trimming at the stick. He hadn't seen Mrs. Armstid. "Yes, sir," I says. "A fellow like Henry Armstid ain't got nobody but hisself to blame."

"Course he ain't," I. O. says. He ain't seen her, either. "Henry Armstid's a born fool. Always is been. If Flem hadn't a got his money, somebody else would."

We looked at Flem. He never moved. Mrs. Armstid come on up the road.

"That's right," I says. "But come to think of it, Henry never bought no horse." We looked at Flem; you could a heard a match drop. "That Texas man told her to get that five dollars back from Flem next day. I reckon Flem's already taken that money to Mrs. Littlejohn's and give it to Mrs. Armstid."

We watched Flem. I. O. quit rubbing his back against the door again. After a while Flem raised his head and spit across the porch, into the dust. I. O. cackled, just like a hen. "Ain't he a beating fellow, now?" I. O. says.

Mrs. Armstid was getting closer, so I kept on talking, watching to see if Flem would look up and see her. But he never looked up. I went on talking about Tull, about how he was going to sue Flem, and Flem setting there, whittling his stick, not saying nothing else after he said they wasn't none of his horses.

Then I. O. happened to look around. He seen Mrs. Armstid. "Psssst!" he says. Flem looked up. "Here she comes!" I. O. says. "Go out the back. I'll tell her you done went in to town today."

But Flem never moved. He just set there, whittling, and we watched Mrs. Armstid come up onto the porch, in that ere faded sunbonnet and wrapper and them tennis shoes that make a kind of hissing noise on the porch. She come onto the porch and stopped, her hands rolled into her dress in front, not looking at nothing.

"He said Saturday," she says, "that he wouldn't sell Henry no horse. He said I could get the money from you."

Flem looked up. The knife never stopped. It went on trimming off a sliver same as if he was watching it. "He taken that money off with him when he left," Flem says.

Mrs. Armstid never looked at nothing. We never looked at her, neither, except that boy of Eck's. He had a half-et cracker in his hand, watching her, chewing.

"He said Henry hadn't bought no horse," Mrs. Armstid says. "He said for me to get the money from you today."

"I reckon he forgot about it," Flem said. "He taken that money off with him Saturday." He whittled again. I. O. kept on rubbing his back, slow. He licked his lips. After a while the woman looked up the road, where it went on up the hill, toward the graveyard. She looked up that way for a while, with that boy of Eck's watching her and I. O. rubbing his back slow against the door. Then she turned back toward the steps.

"I reckon it's time to get dinner started," she says.

"How's Henry this morning, Mrs. Armstid?" Winterbottom says.

She looked at Winterbottom; she almost stopped. "He's resting, I thank you kindly," she says.

Flem got up, outen the chair, putting his knife away. He spit across the porch. "Wait a minute, Mrs. Armstid," he says. She stopped again. She didn't look at him. Flem went on into the store, with I. O. done quit rubbing his back now, with his head craned after Flem, and Mrs. Armstid standing there with her hands rolled into her dress, not looking at nothing. A wagon come up the road and passed; it was Freeman, on the way to town. Then Flem come out again, with I. O. still watching him. Flem had one of these little striped sacks of Jody Varner's candy; I bet he still owes Jody that nickel, too. He put the sack into Mrs. Armstid's hand, like he would have put it into a hollow stump. He spit again across the porch. "A little sweetening for the chaps," he says.

"You're right kind," Mrs. Armstid says. She held the sack of candy in her hand, not looking at nothing. Eck's boy was watching the sack, the half-et cracker in his hand; he wasn't chewing now. He watched Mrs. Armstid roll the sack into her apron. "I reckon I better get on back and help with dinner," she says. She turned and went back across the porch. Flem set down in the chair again and opened his knife. He spit across the porch again, past Mrs. Armstid where she hadn't went down the steps yet. Then she went on, in that ere sunbonnet and wrapper all the same color, back down the road toward Mrs. Littlejohn's. You couldn't see her dress move, like a natural woman walking. She looked like a old snag still standing up and moving along on a high water. We watched her turn in at Mrs. Littlejohn's and go outen sight. Flem was whittling. I. O. begun to rub his back on the door. Then he begun to cackle, just like a durn hen.

"You boys might just as well quit trying," I. O. says. "You can't git ahead of Flem. You can't touch him. Ain't he a sight, now?"

I be dog if he ain't. If I had brung a herd of wild cattymounts into town and sold them to my neighbors and kinfolks, they would have lynched me. Yes, sir.

Questions for Study

1. Indicate where the exposition, climax, and resolution of the story are.
2. How is the ending prepared for?
3. What is the purpose of detailing Flem Snope's past actions at the beginning of the story?
4. How does the author maintain suspense?
5. How are the actions of Mr. and Mrs. Armstid made credible?
6. What aspects of the story are deliberately exaggerated? What is the purpose of this exaggeration?
7. Explain the irony of Mrs. Littlejohn's comment "See if you can't find something else to play with that will kill some more of you."
8. What is ironic about Flem's giving a bag of candy to Mrs. Armstid?

Topics for Discussion and Writing

1. Discuss the way in which Flem Snopes, though not a major character, dominates the story.
2. Contrast the narrator's view of the events of the story with Mrs. Littlejohn's.
3. Discuss the story in terms of the irony of situation, showing the contrast between how the actions of Flem and the Texan appear to the narrator and how they appear to the reader.
4. Analyze the last scene between Flem and Mrs. Armstid, indicating how it is prepared for and how it resolves the situation.

CHARACTER: PEOPLE IN ACTION

The most memorable feature of a story for many readers is the **characters** in it, the people the author creates to act, to speak, and to represent the significance of what is narrated. More than any other aspect of fiction, such figures arouse curiosity and invite analysis, create empathy and establish credibility. Plot in particular is dependent upon them. Henry James sums up this dependency when he notes, "What is character but the determination of incident? What is incident but the illustration of character?" In James's "Owen Wingrave" (p. 56) the title character acts in accordance with his conscience to defy the family's military tradition and, as a result, what he does reflects who he is. Nothing happens to him by chance. His death is the consequence of his opposition or, as the Greeks would express it, his character is his fate. On the other hand, when the hero or heroine merely serves as an instrument of the plot and the focus is on action rather than motivation or morality, you have an adventure story and what happens takes precedence over why it happens. There are many famous and entertaining stories of this kind, but few are as intriguing or rewarding to read as those in which the individual dominates and reveals something new about human behavior.

In order to understand the nature of a fictional character, there are several things you should consider. First, you need to recognize the different types of characters found in stories. Second, you need to know something about characterization, the way in which the author presents the people that make up his or her world.

Although characters vary tremendously from one story to another, it is possible to divide them into two general groups: the **round** or **dynamic** and the **flat** or **static**. The first type are many-sided, complex, and constantly changing. Often there is an inevitability about their final state of mind or condition, as witness Owen Wingrave. Lucy Nelson in Philip Roth's "In Trouble" (p. 40) changes from a scared and confused girl to a person certain of her course of action. At the same time she acts consistently, and you can detect in her early behavior her later attitude. Since she is the **protagonist,** the central figure in the story, you learn much more about her than you do about anybody else. Many stories employ an **antagonist,** a character whose opposition to the main figure establishes the central conflict. An example is Lucy's father, who, in Lucy's eyes, consistently opposes her attempts to become an individual. Rarely does short fiction feature more than a single important character. Hence one of your first tasks is to locate this individual on whom so much of the action and meaning depend and come to grips with his or her significance and multi-faceted personality.

In contrast, the minor characters are usually **flat characters** or **stock figures,** one-dimensional and unchanging. Like Lucy's mother, they are the same at the end of the story as at the beginning. They possess one or two traits that are immediately apparent and that can be identified through their appearance, mannerisms, or speech. Their function is to bring out various aspects of the main character's personality or to serve as a **foil**—that is, to serve as a vivid contrast to the protagonist—as does Mrs. Nelson to her daughter. Occasionally the principal character is also a stock figure, especially in fiction in which people stand for ideas. Matryona in Solzhenitsyn's "Matryona's House" (p. 80) is fundamentally a representative Russian peasant, despite all the details that individualize her. She stands for heroic endurance in the face of incredible adversity. Yet she transcends the stereotype. The author takes great pains to make her local and unique so that the abstraction is rooted in the real. She is a person before she becomes an idea.

There are several ways an author can present the personalities of his or her characters and what they stand for: by name, by summaries and descriptions, and by dialogue and action. Frequently names denote not only who the characters are, but also what they represent. They give a clue to characters' personalities and social status. "Wingrave" signifies both Owen's serious nature and the fact that, while he wins his battle over his family and rejects the army as a career, he loses his life in the process. His name also has an aristocratic ring to it.

Summaries and descriptions introduce characters through the **reportorial** or **pictorial** method. The author tells you who the characters are, where they come from, and in some instances what might happen to them. The author describes their physical features and their environment in precise detail. The objects that surround them help characterize them. For example, Matryona's house reflects her loneliness and her endurance. The room Wingrave dies in suggests a battlefield on which he loses his life fighting for his cause.

The third method is the **scenic** or **dramatic** approach used in "In Trouble." Roth shows his central character acting and speaking in a particular episode. You learn about Lucy through what she thinks and says and does and through what others say to her. When protagonists tell their own stories, of course, you discover everything through their words. You even do this sometimes when authors present them in the third person. The narrator interrupts the story and allows the protagonist to reveal himself or herself either in an **interior monologue** or in a **stream of consciousness.** In the first the character's thoughts come forth in an orderly fashion. The purpose is to show you what the character is thinking. Roth uses this device in "In Trouble" in the fourth paragraph, when Lucy talks to herself about Roy. In the stream of consciousness the protagonist's thoughts come forth as in a daydream with no logical order. The purpose is to show you how as well as what the character is thinking. James Joyce uses this technique in his novel *Ulysses.*

Authors also develop the personalities of their characters through conflict. No matter what their problems, all characters engage in some sort of conflict, physical, psychological, or moral. If there is no conflict, there can be no full development of a character—in fact, it is doubtful if there can be any meaningful characterization at all. These conflicts usually involve the protagonist in one of three situations or in a combination of them: individual against environment, individual against other individual(s), and individual against himself or herself. "Matryona's House" illustrates the first kind, "In Trouble" the second, and "Owen Wingrave" the third. Matryona is alone against the world. Lucy is fighting her father. Owen is struggling with his conscience. A realization of protagonists' dilemmas and an understanding of how they resolve them can help you determine the kind of people you are reading about, their motivation and significance.

There are certain questions you should ask yourself when confronted with the problem of dealing with character analysis. The first and most vital one is, whose story is it? Next, what is the protagonist's relationship with the minor characters? How similar to and different from the other characters is the protagonist? Is the protagonist comprehensible, consistently developed? Does he or she evoke your sympathy? Do the protagonist's actions and motivations for those actions make sense? What do you think is the attitude of the author toward the protagonist? Usually you can determine the answer to this last question by noting how the narrator describes the protagonist and what happens to the protagonist in the end. The attitude is often an ironic one, concerned but detached.

One final point with respect to characters in fiction. Although they must be lifelike and convincing, recalling people you know or have heard about, they are not real. They are imaginary. As such they are definable, consistent, and recognizable in a way flesh-and-blood individuals are not. You know all about them in terms of the fictional world they inhabit. In many instances you probably become better acquainted with them than with your own friends. This is not to say they can be easily labeled and quickly analyzed. Like living people, they have their contradictions and their mysteries, their unresolved problems and their crises. They remain in the end elusive and haunting. That is, the most fully developed of them do. If they did not, we would scarcely bother reading about them and interpretation would be done by computers instead of by readers.

PHILIP ROTH

In Trouble

That morning when the alarm rang at six thirty, she went off to the bathroom to stick a finger down her throat before the other girls started coming in to brush their teeth. This made her feel herself again, provided she skipped breakfast afterward, and avoided the corridor back of the dining hall, and forced soda crackers down her throat from time to time during the morning. Then she could get through the day's classes pretending that she was the same girl in the same body, and in the same way too—alone.

But what about last night? What about Roy saying he was willing to do his duty by her? The fainting spells had ended two weeks back, and the nausea she could starve to death every morning, but now that Roy's body seemed to be inhabited by some new person—by a man, a responsible, upright, decent man, what she had been pleading with that coward to be for weeks!—the truth came in upon her as it never had before. *A new person was inhabiting hers as well.*

She was stunned. Her predicament was real. It was no plot she had invented to bring them all to their senses. It was no scheme to force them to treat her like flesh and blood, like a human being, like a girl! And it was not going to disappear either, just because somebody besides herself was at long last taking it seriously. It was real! Something was happening which she was helpless to stop! Something was growing inside her body, and without her permission!

And I don't want to marry him! He only said yes because he's afraid—of his family, of me, of everything! He's a weak, frightened, hopeless, childish idiot who if he lives to be a hundred will never be a proper husband or a proper father or even half of a whole human being!

The sun wasn't even above the trees as she ran across Pendleton Park to downtown Fort Kean.

She had to wait an hour in the station for the first bus to the north. Her books were in her lap; she had some idea that she could study on the way up and be back for her two thirty, but then she had not yet a clear idea of why she was suddenly rushing home to Liberty Center, or what would happen there. On the bench in the empty station she tried to calm herself by reading the English assignment she had planned to do in her free hour before lunch; and during lunch, which she didn't eat anyway. "Here you will have a chance to examine, and then practice, several skills used in writing effective sentences. The skills presented are those—"

She didn't want to marry him! He was the last person in the world she would ever want to marry!

She began gagging only a little way beyond Fort Kean. When he heard her, the driver pulled to the side of the road. She dropped out the back door and threw her soiled handkerchief into a puddle. Aboard again, she sat in the rear corner praying that she would not be ill, or faint, or begin to sob. She must not think of food; she must not even think of the crackers she had forgotten in her flight from the dorm; she must not think of what she was going to say, or to whom.

What *was* she going to say?

"Here you will have a chance to examine, and then practice, several skills used in writing effective sentences. The skills presented are those used by writers of the models in the Description Section—" Years ago there was a farm girl at L. C. High who took so large a dose of castor oil to try to make the baby come out that she blew a hole in her stomach. She contracted a terrible case of peritonitis, and lost the baby, but afterward, because she had come so close to dying, everyone forgave her, and kids who hadn't even noticed her before— "Here you will have a chance to examine, and then practice, several skills used in writing—" Curt Bonham, the basketball star . . . He had been a year ahead of her. In March of his last term he and a friend had tried to walk home across the river one night while the ice was breaking up, and Curt had drowned. His whole class voted unanimously to dedicate the yearbook to him, and his graduation photograph appeared all by itself on the opening page of "The Liberty Bell." And beneath the black-bordered picture was written:

Smart lad, to slip betimes away
From fields where glory does not stay . . .
ELLIOT CURTIS BONHAM
1930–1947

"What is it?" her mother asked when she came through the front door. "Lucy, what are you doing here? What's the matter?"

"I got here by bus, Mother. That's how people get from Fort Kean to Liberty Center. Bus."

"But what is it? Lucy, you're so pale."

"Is anyone else home?" she asked. "Where is everyone?"

"Daddy Will took Grandma over to the market in Winnisaw."

"And he went to work? Your husband?"

"Lucy, what is it? Why aren't you in school?"

"I'm getting married Christmas Day," she said, moving into the parlor.

Sadly her mother spoke. "We heard. We know."

"How did you hear?"

"Lucy, weren't you going to tell us?"

"We only decided last night. How did you hear, Mother?"

"Roy's father spoke to Daddy."

"Daddy Will?"

"To your father."

"Oh? And what came of that, may I ask?"

"Well, he took your side. Well, that's what came of it. Lucy, I'm answering your question. He took your side, and without a moment's hesitation. Despite our not having been properly told by our own daughter the day of her own wedding—"

"What did he say, Mother? Exactly."

"He told Mr. Bassart he couldn't speak for Roy, of course— He told Mr. Bassart we feel you are mature enough to know your own mind—"

"Well, maybe I'm not!"

"Lucy, you can't think everything he does is wrong just because he does it: He *believes* in you."

"Tell him not to then!"

"Dear—"

"I'm going to have a baby, Mother. So please tell him not to!"

"Lucy—you are?"

"Yes! Of course I am! Why else would I marry that idiot! I hate him, Mother! I can't stand his guts!"

She ran off to the kitchen just in time to be sick in the sink.

She was put to bed in her room. "Here you will have a chance—" The book slid off the bed onto the floor. What was there to do now but wait?

The mail fell through the slot in the hallway and onto the welcome mat. The vacuum cleaner started up. The car pulled into the driveway. She heard her grandmother's voice down on the front porch. She slept.

Her mother brought her tea and toast. "I told Grandma it was the grippe," she whispered to her daughter. "Is that all right?"

Would her grandmother believe that she had come home because of the grippe? Where was Daddy Will? What had she told *him?*

"He didn't even come inside, Lucy. He'll be back this afternoon."

"Does he know I'm home?"

"Not yet."

Home. But why not? For years they had complained that she acted contemptuous of everything they said or did; for years they complained that she refused to let them give her a single word of advice; she lived among them like a stranger, like an enemy even, unfriendly, uncommunicative, nearly unapproachable. Well, could they say she was behaving like their enemy today? She had come home. So what were they going to do?

She drank some of the tea. She sank back into the pillow her mother had fluffed up for her and drew one finger lightly round and round her lips. Lemon. It smelled so nice. Forget everything else. Just wait. Time will pass. Eventually something will have to be done.

She fell asleep with her face on her fingers.

Her grandmother came up the stairs carrying a wet mustard plaster. The patient let her nightgown be unbuttoned. "That'll loosen it up," said Grandma Berta, pressing it down. "The two important things, rest and heat. Plenty of heat. Much as you can possibly stand," and she piled two blankets more onto the patient.

Lucy closed her eyes. Why hadn't she done this at the start instead of suffering all these weeks while Roy Bassart made up his mind whether or not to do his duty and be a man? Why hadn't she just gotten into bed and left it all to them? Wasn't that what they were always wanting to be, her family?

She was awakened by the piano. Her mother's students had begun to arrive for their lessons. She thought, "*But I don't have the grippe.*" But then she drove the thought, and the panic that accompanied it, right from her mind.

It must have begun snowing while she was asleep. She pulled a blanket off the bed, wrapped it around her, and at the window put her mouth on the cold glass and watched the cars sliding down the street. The window began to grow warm where her mouth was pressed against it. Breathing in and out, she could make the circle of steam on the glass expand and contract. What would happen when her grandmother found out what really was wrong with her? And her grandfather, when he got home? And her father!

She had forgotten to tell her mother not to tell him. Maybe she wouldn't anyway. But then would anything happen?

She scuffed with her slippers across the old worn rug and got back into her bed. She thought to pick her English book up from the floor and work a little on those sentences; instead she got way down under the blankets, and with her faintly lemony fingers under her nose, slept for the sixth or seventh time.

Beyond the window it was dark, though from where she sat propped up in bed the snow could be seen floating through the light of the streetlamp across the street. Her father knocked on her door and asked if he could come in.

"It's not locked," was her response.

"Well," he said, stepping into the room, "so this is how the rich spend their days. Not bad."

She could tell that his words had been prepared. She did not look up from the blanket, but began to smooth it out with her hand. "I have the grippe."

"Smells to me," he said, "like you've been eating hot dogs."

She did not smile or speak.

"I tell you what it smells like. Smells like Comiskey Park, down in Chicago."

"Mustard plaster," she finally said.

"Well," he said, giving the door a push so that it closed, "that's one of your grandmother's real pleasures in life. That's one," he said, lowering his voice, "and the other is—no, I think that about covers it."

She only shrugged, as though she had no opinions on people's habits one way or the other. Was he clowning because he knew, or because he didn't know? She saw from the corner of her eyes that the pale hairs on the back of his hands were wet; he had washed up before coming into her room.

The smell of dinner cooking below caused her to begin to feel ill.

"Mind if I sit at the foot here?" he said.

"If you want to."

She mustn't be sick, not again. She mustn't arouse in him a single suspicion. Oh, she did not want him to know, ever!

"Let's see," he was saying. "Do I want to or don't I want to? I want to."

She yawned; he sat.

"Well," he said, "nice and cozy up here."

She stared straight ahead into the snowy evening.

"Winter's coming in with a rush this time," he said.

He was so close to her, how could she not? She glanced quickly over at him. "I suppose." She turned back to the window instantly and was able to collect herself in that way. She could not remember the last time she had looked directly into his eyes.

"Did I ever tell you," he said, "about the time I sprained my ankle when I was working at McConnell's? It swelled way up, and I came home, and your grandmother just lit up all over. Hot compresses, she said. So I sat down in the kitchen and rolled up my trouser leg. You should have seen her boiling up the water on the stove. Somehow it reminded me of all those cannibals over in Africa. She can't see how it can be good for you, unless it hurts or smells bad."

Suppose she just blurted out the truth to him?

"A lot of people like that," he said. "So," and gave her foot a squeeze where it stuck up at the end of the bed, "how's school going, Goosie?"

"All right."

"I hear you're learning French. *Parlez-vous?*"

"French is one of my subjects, yes."

"And let's see—what else? You and me haven't had a good conversation in a long time now, have we?"

She did not answer.

"Oh, and how's Roy doing?"

Instantly she said, "Fine."

Her father took his hand off her foot at last. "Well," he said, "we heard, you know, about the wedding."

"Where's Daddy Will?"

"I'm talking to you right now, Lucy. What do you want him for while I'm talking to you?"

"I didn't say I wanted him. I only asked where he was."

"Out," her father said. "Your grandfather is out!"

"Isn't he even going to have dinner?"

"He went out!" He rose from the bed. "I don't ask where he goes, or when he eats. How do I know where he is? He's out!" And he left the room.

In a matter of seconds, her mother appeared.

"What happened now?"

"I asked where Daddy Will is, that's all," Lucy answered. "What's wrong with that?"

"But is Daddy Will your father or is your father your father?"

"*But you told him,*" she burst out.

"Lucy," said her mother, shutting the door, "lower your voice."

"But you did. You told him! And I didn't say you should!"

"Lucy, you came home; dear, you said—"

"I don't want him to know! It's not his business!"

"Now you must stop, unless you want others to know too."

"But I don't care who knows! I'm not ashamed! And don't start crying, Mother!"

"Then let him talk to you, *please*. He wants to."

"Oh, does he?"

"Lucy, you have to listen to him. You have to give him a chance."

She turned and hid her face in the pillow. "I didn't want him to *know*, Mother."

Her mother sat on the bed and put her hand on the girl's hair.

"And," said Lucy, moving back, "what was he going to say, anyway? Why didn't he just say it out, if he had anything to say?"

"Because," her mother pleaded, "you didn't give him the chance."

"Well, I'm giving *you* a chance, Mother."

There was a silence.

"Tell me!"

"Lucy—dear, what would you think—what would you say—what would you think, I mean—of going for a visit—"

"Oh, no."

"*Please* let me finish. Of going to visit your father's cousin Vera. In Florida."

"And is that his idea of what to do with me?"

"Lucy, till this is over. For a little while."

"Nine months is no little while, Mother—"

"But it would be warm there, and pleasant—"

"Oh," she said, beginning to cry into the pillow, "very pleasant. Why doesn't he ship me off to a home for wayward girls; wouldn't that be even easier?"

"Don't say that. He doesn't want to send you anywhere, you know that."

"He wishes I'd never been born, Mother. He thinks I'm why everything is so wrong with *him*."

"That's not *so*."

"Then," she said sobbing, "he'd have one less responsibility to feel guilty about. If he even felt guilty to begin with."

"But he does, terribly."

"Well, he should!" she said. "He is!"

Some twenty minutes after her mother had run from the room, her grandfather knocked. Daddy Will was wearing his lumber jacket and held his cap in his hands. The brim was dark where the snow had dampened it.

"Hey, I hear somebody's been asking for me."

"Hullo."

"You sound like death-warmed-over, my friend. You ought to be outside and feel the wind. Then you'd really appreciate being sick in bed."

She did not answer.

"Stomach settle down?" he asked.

"Yes."

He pulled a chair over to the side of the bed. "How's about another mustard plaster? Berta called me at the Erwins, and on the way home I stopped and bought a whole fresh packet. So just say when."

She turned and looked at the wall.

"What is it, Lucy? Maybe you want Dr. Eglund. That's what I told Myra—"

He pulled the chair right up close. "Lucy, I never saw anything like the change in your father this time," he said softly. "Not a drop—not a single solitary drop, Lucy. He is taking this whole decision of yours right in his stride. You set a date, and it was just fine with him. Fine with all of us, Lucy—whatever you think is going to make you and Roy happy."

"I want my mother."

"Don't you feel good again? Maybe the doctor—"

"I want my mother! My mother, and not him!"

She was still looking at the wall when her door opened.

"Myra," her father said, "sit over there. Sit, I said."

"Yes."

"All right, Lucy. Turn over." He was standing by the side of the bed. "Roll over, I said."

"Lucy," her mother begged, "look at us, please."

"I don't have to see that his shoes are shined and his jaw is set and what a new man he is. I don't have to see his necktie, or him either!"

"Lucy—"

"Myra, be quiet. If she wants to act like a two-year-old at a time like this, let her."

She whispered, "Look who's talking about two-year-olds."

"Listen, young lady. Your back talk doesn't faze me one way or the other. There have always been smart-aleck teen-agers, and there always will be, especially this generation. You just listen to me, that's all, and if you're too ashamed to look me in the eye—"

"Ashamed!" she cried, but she did not move.

"Are you or are you not going to visit Cousin Vera?"

"I don't even *know* Cousin Vera."

"That isn't what I'm asking."

"I can't go off alone to someone I don't even know—and what? Make up filthy lies for the neighbors—?"

"But they wouldn't be lies," said her mother.

"What would they be, Mother. The truth?"

"They would be *stories*," her father said. "That you have a husband overseas—in the Army."

"Oh, you know all about stories, I'm sure; but I tell the truth!"

"Then," he said, "just what do you intend to do about getting into trouble with somebody you say you can't even stand?"

She turned violently from the wall as though she intended to hurl herself at him. "Don't you take such a tone with me! Don't you dare!"

"I am not taking any tone!"

"Because I am not ashamed—not in front of you I'm not!"

"Now watch it, you, just watch it. Because I can still give you a licking, smart as you think you are."

"Oh," she said bitterly, "can you?"

"Yes!"

"Go ahead then."

"Oh, wonderful," he said, and walked to the window, where he stood as though looking outside. "Just wonderful."

"Lucy," said her mother, "if you don't want to go to Cousin Vera's, then what do you want to do? Just tell us."

"You're the parents. You were always *dying* to be the parents."

"Now look," said her father, turning to face her once again. "First, Myra, you sit down. And stay down. And you," he said, waving a finger at his daughter, "you give me your attention, do you hear? Now there is a crisis here, you understand that? There is a crisis here involving my daughter, and I am going to deal with it, and it's going to be dealt with."

"Fine," said Lucy. "Deal."

"Then be *still*," her mother pleaded, "and let him talk." But when she made a move to the bed her husband looked at her and she retreated.

"Now either I'm going to do it," he said, speaking between his teeth to his wife, "or I'm not. Now which is it?"

She lowered her eyes.

"Unless, of course, you want to call your daddy in," he said.

"I'm sorry."

"Now," said her father, "if you wanted to marry that Roy Bassart—such as we understood you did, Lucy—that would be one thing. But this is something else entirely. Who he is I see pretty clear now, and the less said about him the better. I understand the whole picture, so there is just no need for raising voices. He was older, back from the service, and just thought to himself he could come back here last year and take advantage of a young seventeen-year-old high school girl. And that's what he did. But he is his father's business, Lucy, and we will have to leave it to his high and mighty father, the big schoolteacher, to teach something into that boy's hide. Oh, his father thinks he is very superior and all in his ways, but I guess he is going to have another guess coming now. But my concern is with you, Lucy, and what is uppermost to you. Do you understand that? My concern is your going to college, which has always been your dream, right? Now, the question is this, do you still want your dream, or don't you?"

She did not favor him with a reply.

"OK," he said, "I am going to go ahead on my assumption that you do, just as you always did. Now, next—to give you your dream I am going to do anything I can— Are you listening to me? Anything that is going to give it to you, do you follow me? Because what that so-called ex-G.I. has done to you, which I would like to put my hands around his throat for, well, that is not going to just take away your dream, lock, stock, and barrel . . . Now, anything," he went on, "even something that isn't usual and ordinary, and that might to some folks seem very—out of the question." He came close to the bed so that he could speak without being heard outside the room. "Now, do you know what *anything* means, before I go to the next step?"

"Giving up whiskey?"

"I want you to go to college, it means! I have given up whiskey, for your information!"

"Really?" she asked. "Again?"

"Lucy, since Thanksgiving," her mother began.

"Myra, you be still."

"I was only telling her—"

"But *I* will tell her," he said. "*I* will do the telling!"

"Yes," his wife said softly.

"Now," he said, turning back to Lucy, "drink is neither here nor there. Drink is not the issue."

"Oh, no?"

"No! A baby is!"

And that made her look away.

"An illegitimate baby is," he said again. "And if you don't *want* that illegitimate baby," his voice had fallen almost to a whisper now, "then maybe we will have to arrange that you don't have it. If Cousin Vera's is still something you are going to consider out of the question."

"It absolutely is! I will not spend nine months lying! I will not get big and pregnant and lie!"

"Shhh!"

"Well, I won't," she muttered.

"OK." He wiped his mouth with his hand. "Then let's do this in order. And without voice-raising, as there are other people who live in this house."

"We're the other people who live here."

"Be still!" he said. "Everybody knows that without your back talk!"

"Then just what are you proposing to me? Say it!"

Her mother rushed to the bed at last. "Lucy," she said, taking hold of her hand, "Lucy, it's only to help *you*—"

And then her father took hold of the other hand, and it was as though some current were about to pass through the three of them. She closed her eyes, waited—and her father spoke. And she let him. And she saw the future. She saw herself seated between her two parents as her father drove them across the bridge to Winnisaw. It would be early morning. The doctor would only just have finished with his breakfast. He would come to the door to greet them, and her father would shake his hand. In his office the doctor would seat himself behind a big dark desk, and she would sit in a chair, and her parents would be together on a sofa, while the doctor explained to them exactly what he was going to do. He would have all his medical degrees right up on the wall, in frames. When she went off with him into the little white operating room, her mother and father would smile at her from the sofa. And they would wait there until it was time to bundle her up and take her home.

When her father had finished, she said, "But it must cost a fortune."

"The object isn't the money, honey," he said.

"The object is you," said her mother.

How nice that sounded. Like a poem. She was just beginning to study poetry, too. Her last English composition had been an interpretation of "Ozymandias." She had only received the paper back on Monday morning, a B plus for the very first interpretation she had ever written of a poem in college. Only on Monday she had thought it was going to be her last. Before Roy had finally returned to Fort Kean with his big brave decision made, her recurring thought had been to run away. And now she didn't have to; and she didn't have to marry him either. Now she could concentrate on one thing and one thing only, on school, on French, history, poetry . . .

The object isn't money,
The object is you.

"But where," she asked softly, "will you get it all?"

"Let me worry about that," her father said. "OK?"

"Will you work?"

"Wow," he said to Myra. "She sure don't pull her punches, your daughter here." The red that had risen into his cheeks remained, even as he tried to maintain a soft joking tone. "Come on, Goosie, what do you say? Give me a break, huh? Where do you think I've been all day today, anyway? Taking a stroll on the boulevard? Playing a tennis game? What do you think I've been doing all my life since I was eighteen years old, and part-time before that? Work, Lucy, just plain old work, day in and day out."

"Not at one job," she said.

"Well, so I moved around—that's true—"

She was going to cry; they were talking!

"Look," he said, "why don't you think of it this way. You have a daddy who is a jack of all trades. You should be proud. Come on, Goosie-pie, how about a smile like I used to get back in prehistoric times?"

She felt her mother squeeze her hand.

"Look," he said, "why do you think people always hire Duane Nelson no matter what? Because he sits around twiddling his thumbs, or because he knows every kind of machine there is, inside out? Now which? That's not a hard question, is it, for a smart college girl?"

Afterward she would read in bed. She would have her assignments mailed up to her while she recuperated in her bed. Yes, a college girl. And without Roy. He wasn't so bad, he just wasn't for her, that was all. He would just disappear, and she could begin to make friends at school, friends to bring home with her when she came to visit on the weekend. For things would have changed.

Could that be? At long last those terrible days of hatred and solitude, over? To think—she could begin again to talk to her family, to tell them about all the things she was studying, to show them her papers. Stuck into her English book right there on the floor was the essay she had written on "Ozymandias." B plus, and across the front the professor had written, "Excellent paragraph development; good understanding of meaning; good use of quotation; but please don't stuff your sentences so." And maybe she *had* overdone the main topic sentence somewhat, but her intention had been to state at the outset all those ideas that she would later take up in the body of the essay. "Even a great king," her paper began, "such as Ozymandias apparently had been, could not predict or control what the future, or Fate, held in store for him and his kingdom; that, I think, is the message that Percy Bysshe Shelley, the poet, means for us to come away with from his romantic poem 'Ozymandias,' which not only reveals the theme of the vanity of human wishes—even a king's—but deals also with the concept of the immensity of 'boundless and bare' life and the inevitability of the 'colossal wreck' of everything, as compared to the 'sneer of cold command,' which is all many mere mortals have at their command, unfortunately."

"But is he clean?" she asked.

"A hundred percent," her father said. "Spotless, Lucy. Like a hospital."

"And how old is he?" she asked.

"Oh," her father said, "middle-aged, I'd say."

A moment passed. Then: "That's the catch, isn't it?"

"What kind of catch?"

"He's too old."

"Now what do you mean 'too old'? If anything, he's real experienced."

"But is this all he does?"

"Lucy, he's a regular doctor who does this as a special favor, that's all."

"But he charges, you said."

"Well, sure, he charges."

"Then it's not a special favor. He does it for money."

"Well, everybody has got bills to meet. Everybody has got to be paid for what they do."

But she saw herself dead. The doctor would be no good, and she would die.

"How do you know about him?"

"Because," and here he stood and hitched up his trousers. "Through a friend," he finally said.

"Who?"

"Lucy, I'm afraid maybe that's got to be a secret."

"But where did you hear about him?" Where *would* he hear about such a doctor? "At Earl's famous Dugout of Buddies? At a *saloon?*"

"Lucy, that's not necessary," said her mother.

Her father walked to the window again. He cleared a pane with the palm of his hand. "Well," he said, "it's stopped snowing. It's stopped snowing, if anybody cares."

"All I meant—" Lucy began.

"*Is what?*" He had turned back to her.

"Is—do you know anybody who he's ever done it to, that's all?"

"Yes, I happen to, for your information!"

"And they're alive?"

"For your information, yes!"

"Well, it's my life. I have a right to know."

"Why don't you just trust me! I'm not going to kill you!"

"Oh, Duane," her mother said, "she *does!*"

"Don't speak for me, Mother!"

"Hear that?" he cried to his wife.

"Well, he might just be some quack drinking friend, who says he's a doctor or something. Well, how do I know, Mother? Maybe it's even Earl himself in his red suspenders!"

"Yeah, that's who it is," her father shouted. "Earl Duval! Sure! What's the matter with you? You think I don't mean it when I say I want you to finish college?"

"Dear, he does. You're his daughter."

"That doesn't mean he knows whether a doctor is good or not, Mother. Suppose I die!"

"But I just told you," he cried, shaking a fist at her, "you won't!"

"But how do you know?"

"Because she didn't, did she!"

"Who?"

No one had to speak for her to understand.

"Oh, no." She dropped slowly back against the headboard.

Her mother covered her face with her hands.

"When?" said Lucy.

"But she's alive, isn't she?" He was pulling at his shirt with his hands. "Answer the point I'm making! I am speaking! She did not die! She did not get hurt in any way at all!"

"Mother," she said, turning to her, "when?"

But her mother only shook her head. Lucy got up out of the bed. "Mother, when did he make you do that?"

"He didn't make me."

"Oh, Mother," she said, standing before her. "You're my *mother.*"

"Lucy, you were a little girl. It was in the Depression times. It was long ago. Oh, it's all forgotten. Daddy Will, Grandma, they don't know," she whispered, "don't have to—"

"But the Depression was over when I was three, when I was four."

"What?" her father cried. "Are you kidding?" To his wife he said, "Is she kidding?"

"Lucy," her mother said, "we did it for you."

"Oh, yes," she said, moving backward onto her bed, "for me, everything was for me."

"Lucy, we couldn't have another baby. Not when we were so far behind and trying so to fight back—"

"But if only he did his job! If he only stopped being a coward!"

"Look," he said, coming angrily at her, "you don't even know when the Depression was, or what it was, either—*so watch what you say!*"

"I do too know!"

"The whole country was behind the eight ball, not just me! If you want to call names, you call the whole United States of America names!"

"Oh, sure, the whole *world.*"

"Don't you know history?" he cried. "Don't you know anything?" he demanded.

"I know what you made her do, you!"

"But," her mother cried, "I *wanted* to."

"Did you hear that?" he shouted. "Did you hear what your mother just said to you?"

"But you're the man!"

"I am also a human being!"

"That's no excuse!"

"Oh, what am I arguing with you for? You don't know *a* from *z* as far as life is concerned, and you never will! You wouldn't know a man's job if I did it!"

Silence.

"Hear, Mother? Hear your husband?" said Lucy. "Did you hear what he just said, right out in the open?"

"Hear what I *mean,*" he cried.

"But what you *said*—"

"I don't care! Stop trapping me! I came in here to solve a crisis, but how can I do it when nobody lets me even begin? Or end! You'd rather trap me—throw me in jail like you did already! That's what you'd rather do! You'd rather humiliate me in this whole town, and make me looked down on as the town joke!"

"Town *drunk!*"

"Drunk?" he said. "Town drunk? You ought to see the town drunk. You think I'm the town drunk? Well, you ought to just see a town drunk, and then think what you're saying twice before you say it. You don't know what a town drunk is. You don't know what anything is! You—you just want me behind bars—that's your big wish in life, and always has been!"

"It's not."

"It is."

"But that's *over,*" cried Myra.

"Sure it's over," said her father. "Sure, people just forget how a daughter threw her own father in jail. Called up the police at the age of fifteen because her own father had one lousy beer too many! Sure, people don't talk about that behind your back. People don't like to tell stories on a person, oh, no. People are always giving other people a chance to change and get their strength back. Sure, that's what this little scene is all about too. You bet it is. Oh, she's got me fixed, boy—and that's the way it's going to be. That's how brilliant she is, your so-called college girl scholarship daughter. Well, go ahead, so-called daughter who knows all the answers, solve your own life. Because I'm not good enough for a person like you, and never have been. What am I anyway? The town drunk to you."

He pulled open the door and went loudly down the stairs. They could hear him in the parlor, bellowing at Daddy Will. "Go ahead, Mr. Carroll. You're the only one can solve things around here. Go ahead, it's Daddy Will everyone wants around here anyway. I'm just extra anyway. I'm just along for the ride, we all know that."

"Shouting won't help anything, Duane—"

"Right, right you are, Berta. Nothing will help anything around here."

"Willard," said Berta, "tell this person—"

"What's the trouble, Duane? What's the fuss?"

"Oh, nothing you can't fix, Willard. Because you're the big daddy, and me, I'm just along for the ride."

"Willard, where is he going? Dinner is all ready."

"Duane, where are you going?"

"I don't know. Maybe I'll go down and see old Tom Whipper."

"Who's he?"

"The town drunk, Willard! That's who the town drunk is, damn it—Tom Whipper!"

The door slammed, and then the house was silent except for the whispering that began downstairs.

Lucy lay without moving on the bed.

Her mother was crying.

"Mother, why, *why* did you let him make you do that?"

"I did what I had to," said her mother mournfully.

"You didn't! You let him trample on your dignity, Mother! You were his doormat! His slave!"

"Lucy, I did what was necessary," she said, sobbing.

"That's not always right, though! You have to do what's *right!*"

"It was." She spoke as in a trance. "It was. It was."

"It wasn't! Not for you! He degrades you, Mother, and you let him! Always! All our lives!"

"Oh, Lucy, whatever we say, our suggestions, you refuse."

"I refuse—I refuse to live your life again, Mother, that's what I refuse!" And so she was married to Roy Bassart on Christmas Day.

Writing About Character

There are three types of themes you can write about character. The easiest and most obvious, and thus the least rewarding and interesting, is the **sketch.** In it you merely detail the characteristics of the protagonist in the story, careful to arrange these characteristics according to a plan. You describe, in order, the protagonist's physical features and behavior, background, and attitude toward others and their attitude toward him or her. You conclude with comments on how well you think the protagonist has been portrayed and what he or she stands for in terms of the story's meaning. Naturally you can work variations on this topic. What you must be wary of is describing the protagonist in a mechanical way, cataloguing instead of interpreting. How the protagonist looks and what he or she says and does are important, but they must serve some central concept you have about the kind of person the protagonist is and what he or she represents. For instance, you would not simply describe Lucy Nelson's appearance, give her background, and tell what she thinks of her family and what they think of her. These details would have to serve some larger aim. Instead you could represent her as an independent-minded girl who defies her family and rejects their way of life. In the struggle she wins a victory, but possibly at the cost of marrying a man she does not love.

The second type of essay is the **character analysis.** Here you dissect a character's motives and conflicts, examine closely that character's actions to see how he or she embodies the basic ideas of the story, trace his or her development from beginning to end. The danger is that, rather than stick to analyzing, you will resort to describing and your paper will consist of lists. To avoid such an approach, concentrate on motivation and conflict. For instance, ask yourself what causes Lucy Nelson to decide to marry Roy and reject her father's advice. What are the forces opposing her decision? What is she seeking? How is she responsible for her own fate? The answers to these questions would lead to an essay on character analysis.

Last there is the theme involving a **contrast** of the protagonist either with the antagonist or with the protagonist in another story. Such a topic is easy to organize and limited enough to cover in a short paper. Most important, it prevents you from retelling the story. In "In Trouble" an obvious contrast is between Lucy and her mother. One is defiant, the other submissive. One is reflective, increasingly disturbed, and isolated, while the other is unthinking, satisfied, and sociable. To develop an essay on the subject you need to organize specific points for comparison. Three possible areas for comparison include: (1) Lucy's superior mind versus her mother's mediocre mind, (2) Lucy's growing estrangement from everyone versus her mother's easy social adjustment to everyone, and (3) Lucy's troubled commitment to her conscience versus her mother's submission to an abortion she may not really have wanted. After an introduction outlining the central idea you should announce in general terms the structure of your essay. The interior paragraphs develop each point in order. The conclusion considers the effectiveness of the comparison of the two women and its larger meaning.

To be more specific with respect to a topic, its organization and development, let us look at "In Trouble" in detail. It is above all concerned with conflict. Such a subject, however, needs narrowing. The way to do this is to focus on the conflicts of the main character, Lucy Nelson, and then to ask yourself what these are. They consist of three basic elements: conflict with her boyfriend Roy Bassart and the problem of their unborn child, conflict with her father and the problem of abortion, and conflict with herself over her decision to get married. A good title to cover these conflicts might simply be "Lucy in Trouble."

Now that the topic is manageable, the next thing to consider is the thesis sentence. If you look closely at the story, you will discover the one thing that links all the conflicts is Lucy's determination to be treated "like flesh and blood" by her family, her determination to find herself and become a person in her own right. A clear thesis sentence based on this idea might be as follows: Lucy Nelson's conflict with her boyfriend, her father, and herself represents her struggle to discover who she is and what her place is in the world. Although the point seems general, it is specifically related to the situation of Lucy as an unmarried mother-to-be. Once looked at closely it should enable you to develop a satisfactory essay.

The organization of the paper follows from the thesis sentence. First you would discuss Lucy's relations with Roy, next with her father, and finally with herself. As in the essay on plot, you would conclude with an evaluation of how successful you think Roth is in presenting Lucy and her dilemma, how convincing, how truthful. As for gathering supporting evidence, this should pose no problem since you are dealing with definite individuals and scenes. All you have to do is to select those details which best support the points you wish to make. The main thing to avoid is repeating what is in the story merely for the sake of establishing your central idea. Each paragraph must start with a basic generalization and in turn be supported by material you glean from the story. Of course, your interpretation of a character is not going to be the same as someone else's. But you must recognize this fact and not be afraid to express your opinions as long as you can back them up with details from the story.

Lucy in Trouble

Although the three principal characters in "In Trouble" are all in difficulty, it is Lucy, the protagonist, who faces the greatest dilemma as an unmarried teenage mother-to-be confronting the prospect of a forced marriage. Her basic problem is threefold. How can she marry a man whom she does not love but whose baby she is carrying? How can she respect a father whose conduct she detests but whose presence continues to haunt her? How can she assert herself before parents who refuse to accept her as an individual?

Her conflict with Roy Bassart is the simplest of the three she experiences. She does not want to marry him because, first, at eighteen she is not ready for such a commitment. Her affair with him represents merely her youthful rebellion against her family. Second, he is weak and irresponsible and, even though she does not realize it, very much like her father. Despite his determination to do his duty by her, he is still immature. Roth suggests that her decision to accept him as a husband shows that she still has not completely found herself. She is acting out of spite rather than love. Her life with Roy promises to continue the struggle with her father.

It is this struggle which is her principal external conflict. In fact, it might be said her problem with Roy is really the continuation of her problem with her father, whom she calls disrespectfully to her mother "your husband." Her disillusionment in him surfaces in her composition on "Ozymandias." He is obviously the king who "could not predict or control what the future, or Fate, held in store for him and his kingdom" and who made inevitable the " 'colossal wreck' of everything." More dramatic expression of her hostility occurs when he confesses her mother had an abortion because of his difficult financial position. After hearing this revelation, Lucy is determined to marry Roy rather than have her father degrade her as he has degraded her mother.

Her mixed feelings toward Roy and her father, her longing to accept them and her realization she cannot, stem from her own uncertainty. Despite the brave show of superiority as a result of her brief college career, she does not know all the answers. She cannot solve the problems of her own life. Although she condemns her mother for allowing her husband to mistreat her and insists she will not repeat her mother's life, she does marry Roy and appears headed toward the same fate. Her flight home, her guilty feelings toward her father, expressed in anger and disappointment, and her fear of dying all show her insecurity. While she is on the verge of marriage and motherhood, she is still a girl trying to write effective sentences in freshman English.

Roth is successful in presenting Lucy's conflict because he does not take sides. He dramatizes her predicament in a realistic manner, showing her bewildered as well as presumptuous, pathetic as well as self-righteous. That she will not live a different life, once married, is evident. Her character is her fate. This honest view of a girl and her sexual and family problems convinces the reader of the accuracy of the author's treatment of Lucy. She is credible, consistent, and clearly motivated. It is easy to see that what began in trouble for her could end in tragedy.

HENRY JAMES

Owen Wingrave

I

"Upon my honour you must be off your head!" cried Spencer Coyle as the young man, with a white face, stood there panting a little and repeating "Really I've quite decided," and "I assure you I've thought it all out." They were both pale, but Owen Wingrave smiled in a manner exasperating to his supervisor, who however still discriminated sufficiently to feel his grimace—it was like an irrelevant leer—the result of extreme and conceivable nervousness.

"It was certainly a mistake to have gone so far; but that's exactly why it strikes me I mustn't go further," poor Owen said, waiting mechanically, almost humbly—he wished not to swagger, and indeed had nothing to swagger about—and carrying through the window to the stupid opposite houses the dry glitter of his eyes.

"I'm unspeakably disgusted. You've made me dreadfully ill"—and Mr. Coyle looked in truth thoroughly upset.

"I'm very sorry. It was the fear of the effect on you that kept me from speaking sooner."

"You should have spoken three months ago. Don't you know your mind from one day to the other?" the elder of the pair demanded.

The young man for a moment held himself: then he quavered his plea. "You're very angry with me and I expected it. I'm awfully obliged to you for all you've done for me. I'll do anything else for you in return, but I can't do that. Every one else will let me have it of course. I'm prepared for that—I'm prepared for everything. It's what has taken the time: to be sure I was prepared. I think it's your displeasure I feel most and regret most. But little by little you'll get over it," Owen wound up.

"*You'll* get over it rather faster, I suppose!" the other satirically exclaimed. He was quite as agitated as his young friend, and they were evidently in no condition to prolong an encounter in which each drew blood. Mr. Coyle was a professional "coach"; he prepared aspirants for the army, taking only three or four at a time, to whom he applied the irresistible stimulus the possession of which was both his secret and his fortune. He hadn't a great establishment; he would have said himself that it was not a wholesale business. Neither his system, his health nor his temper could have concorded with numbers; so he weighed and measured his pupils and turned away more applicants than he passed. He was an artist in his line, caring only for picked subjects and capable of sacrifices almost passionate for the individual. He liked ardent young men—there were types of facility and kinds of capacity to which he was indifferent—and he had taken a particular fancy to Owen Wingrave. This young man's particular shade of ability, to say nothing of his whole personality, almost cast a spell and at any rate worked a charm. Mr. Coyle's candidates usually did wonders, and he might have sent up a multitude. He was a person exactly of the stature of the great Napoleon, with a certain flicker of genius in his light blue eye: it had been said of him that he looked like a concert-giving pianist. The tone of his favourite pupil now expressed, without intention indeed, a superior wisdom that irritated him. He hadn't at all suffered before from Wingrave's high opinion of himself, which had seemed justified by remarkable parts; but to-day, of a sudden, it struck him as intolerable. He cut short the discussion, declining absolutely to regard their relations as terminated, and remarked to his pupil that he had better go off somewhere—down to Eastbourne, say: the sea would bring him round—and take a few days to find his feet and come to his senses. He could afford the time, he was so well up: when Spencer Coyle remembered how well up he was he could have boxed his ears. The tall athletic young man wasn't physically a subject for simplified reasoning; but a troubled gentleness in his handsome face, the index of compunction mixed with resolution, virtually signified that if it could have done any good he would have turned both cheeks. He evidently didn't pretend that his wisdom was superior; he only presented it as his own. It was his own career after all that was in question. He couldn't refuse to go through the form of trying Eastbourne or at least of holding his tongue, though there was that in his manner which implied that if he should do so it would be really to give Mr. Coyle a chance to recuperate. He didn't feel a bit overworked, but there was nothing more natural than that, with their tremendous pressure, Mr. Coyle should be. Mr. Coyle's own intellect would derive an advantage from his pupil's holiday. Mr. Coyle saw what he meant, but controlled himself; he only demanded, as his right, a truce of three days. Owen granted it, though as fostering sad illusions this went visibly against his conscience; but before they separated the famous crammer remarked: "All the same I feel I ought to see some one. I think you mentioned to me that your aunt had come to town?"

"Oh yes—she's in Baker Street. Do go and see her," the boy said for comfort.

His tutor sharply eyed him. "Have you broached this folly to her?"

"Not yet—to no one. I thought it right to speak to you first."

"Oh what you 'think right'!" cried Spencer Coyle, outraged by his young friend's standards. He added that he would probably call on Miss Wingrave; after which the recreant youth got out of the house.

The latter didn't, none the less, start at once for Eastbourne; he only directed his steps to Kensington Gardens, from which Mr. Coyle's desirable residence—he was terribly expensive and had a big house—was not far removed. The famous coach "put up" his pupils, and Owen had mentioned to the butler that he would be back to dinner. The spring day was warm to his young blood, and he had a book in his pocket which, when he had passed into the Gardens and, after a short stroll, dropped into a chair, he took out with the slow soft sigh that finally ushers in a pleasure postponed. He stretched his long legs and began to read it; it was a volume of Goethe's poems. He had been for days in a state of the highest tension, and now that the cord had snapped the relief was proportionate; only it was characteristic of him that this deliverance should take the form of an intellectual pleasure. If he had thrown up the probability of a magnificent career it wasn't to dawdle along Bond

Street nor parade his indifference in the window of a club. At any rate he had in a few moments forgotten everything—the tremendous pressure, Mr. Coyle's disappointment and even his formidable aunt in Baker Street. If these watchers had overtaken him there would surely have been some excuse for their exasperation. There was no doubt he was perverse, for his very choice of a pastime only showed how he had got up his German.

"What the devil's the matter with him, do *you* know?" Spencer Coyle asked that afternoon of young Lechmere, who had never before observed the head of the establishment to set a fellow such an example of bad language. Young Lechmere was not only Wingrave's fellow pupil, he was supposed to be his intimate, indeed quite his best friend, and had unconsciously performed for Mr. Coyle the office of making the promise of his great gifts more vivid by contrast. He was short and sturdy and as a general thing uninspired, and Mr. Coyle, who found no amusement in believing in him, had never thought him less exciting than as he stared now out of a face from which you could no more guess whether he had caught an idea than you could judge of your dinner by looking at a dish-cover. Young Lechmere concealed such achievements as if they had been youthful indiscretions. At any rate he could evidently conceive no reason why it should be thought there was anything more than usual the matter with the companion of his studies; so Mr. Coyle had to continue: "He declines to go up. He chucks the whole shop!"

The first thing that struck young Lechmere in the case was the freshness, as of a forgotten vernacular, it had imparted to the governor's vocabulary. "He doesn't want to go to Sandhurst?"

"He doesn't want to go anywhere. He gives up the army altogether. He objects," said Mr. Coyle in a tone that made young Lechmere almost hold his breath, "to the military profession."

"Why it has been the profession of all his family!"

"Their profession? It has been their religion! Do you know Miss Wingrave?"

"Oh yes. Isn't she awful?" young Lechmere candidly ejaculated.

His instructor demurred. "She's formidable, if you mean that, and it's right she should be; because somehow in her very person, good maiden lady as she is, she represents the might, she represents the traditions and the exploits, of the British army. She represents the expansive property of the English name. I think his family can be trusted to come down on him, but every influence should be set in motion. I want to know what yours is. Can *you* do anything in the matter?"

"I can try a couple of rounds with him," said young Lechmere reflectively. "But he knows a fearful lot. He has the most extraordinary ideas."

"Then he has told you some of them—he has taken you into his confidence?"

"I've heard him jaw by the yard," smiled the honest youth. "He has told me he despises it."

"What *is* it he despises? I can't make out."

The most consecutive of Mr. Coyle's nurslings considered a moment, as if he were conscious of a responsibility. "Why I think just soldiering, don't you know? He says we take the wrong view of it."

"He oughtn't to talk to *you* that way. It's corrupting the youth of Athens. It's sowing sedition."

"Oh I'm all right!" said young Lechmere. "And he never told me he meant to chuck it. I always thought he meant to see it through, simply because he had to. He'll argue on any side you like. He can talk your head off—I will say *that* for him. But it's a tremendous pity—I'm sure he'd have a big career."

"Tell him so then; plead with him; struggle with him—for God's sake."

"I'll do what I can—I'll tell him it's a regular shame."

"Yes, strike *that* note—insist on the disgrace of it."

The young man gave Mr. Coyle a queer look. "I'm sure he wouldn't do anything dishonourable."

"Well—it won't look right. He must be made to feel *that*—work it up. Give him a comrade's point of view—that of a brother-in-arms."

"That's what I thought we were going to be!" young Lechmere mused romantically, much uplifted by the nature of the mission imposed on him. "He's an awfully good sort."

"No one will think so if he backs out!" said Spencer Coyle.

"Well, they mustn't say it to *me!*" his pupil rejoined with a flush.

Mr. Coyle debated, noting his tone and aware that in the perversity of things, though this young man was born a soldier, no excitement would ever attach to *his* alternatives save perhaps on the part of the nice girl to whom at an early day he was sure to be placidly united. "Do you like him very much—do you believe in him?"

Young Lechmere's life in these days was spent in answering terrible questions, but he had never been put through so straight a lot as these. "Believe in him? Rather!"

"Then *save* him!"

The poor boy was puzzled, as if it were forced upon him by this intensity that there was more in such an appeal than could appear on the surface; and he doubtless felt that he was but apprehending a complex situation when after another moment, with his hands in his pockets, he replied hopefully but not pompously: "I dare say I can bring him round!"

II

Before seeing young Lechmere Mr. Coyle had determined to telegraph an enquiry to Miss Wingrave. He had prepaid the answer, which, being promptly put into his hand, brought the interview we have just related to a close. He immediately drove off to Baker Street, where the lady had said she awaited him, and five minutes after he got there, as he sat with Owen Wingrave's remarkable aunt, he repeated several times over, in his angry sadness and with the infallibility of his experience: "He's so intelligent—he's so intelligent!" He had declared it had been a luxury to put such a fellow through.

"Of course he's intelligent; what else could he be? We've never, that I know of, had but *one* idiot in the family!" said Jane Wingrave. This was an allusion that Mr. Coyle could understand, and it brought home to him another of the reasons for the disappointment, the humiliation as it were, of the good people at Paramore, at the same time that it gave an example of the conscientious coarseness he had on former occasions observed in his hostess. Poor Philip Wingrave, her late brother's eldest son, was literally imbecile and banished from view; deformed, unsocial, irretrievable, he had been relegated to a private asylum and had become among the friends of the family only a little hushed lugubrious legend. All the hopes of the house, picturesque Paramore, now unintermittently old Sir Philip's rather melancholy home—his infirmities would keep him there to the last—were therefore gathered on the second boy's head, which nature, as if in compunction for her previous botch, had, in addition to making it strikingly handsome, filled with a marked and general readiness. These two had been the only children of the old man's only son, who, like so many of his ancestors, had given up a gallant young life to the service of his country. Owen Wingrave the elder had received his death-cut, in close quarters, from an Afghan sabre; the blow had come crashing across his skull. His wife, at that time in India, was about to give birth to her third child; and when the event took place, in darkness and anguish, the baby came lifeless into the world and the mother sank under the multiplication of her woes. The second of the little boys in England, who was at Paramore with his grandfather, became the peculiar charge of his aunt, the only unmarried one, and during the interesting Sunday that, by urgent invitation, Spencer Coyle, busy as he was, had, after consenting to put Owen through, spent under that roof, the celebrated crammer received a vivid impression of the influence exerted at least in intention by Miss Wingrave. Indeed the picture of this short visit remained with the observant little man a curious one—the vision of an impoverished Jacobean house, shabby and remarkably "creepy," but full of character still and full of felicity as a setting for the distinguished figure of the peaceful old soldier. Sir Philip Wingrave, a relic rather than a celebrity, was a small brown erect octogenarian, with smouldering eyes and a studied courtesy. He liked to do the diminished honours of his house, but even when with a shaky hand he lighted a bedroom candle for a deprecating guest it was impossible not to feel him, beneath the surface, a merciless old man of blood. The eye of the imagination could glance back into his crowded Eastern past—back at episodes in which his scrupulous forms would only have made him more terrible. He had his legend—and oh there were stories about him!

Mr. Coyle remembered also two other figures—a faded inoffensive Mrs. Julian, domesticated there by a system of frequent visits as the widow of an officer and a particular friend of Miss Wingrave, and a remarkably clever little girl of eighteen, who was this lady's daughter and who struck the speculative visitor as already formed for other relations. She was very impertinent to Owen, and in the course of a long walk that he had taken with the young man and the effect of which, in much talk, had been to clinch his high opinion of him, he had learned—for Owen chattered confidentially—that Mrs. Julian was the sister of a very gallant gentleman, Captain Hume-Walker of the Artillery, who had fallen in the Indian Mutiny and between whom and Miss Wingrave (it had been that lady's one known concession) a passage of some delicacy, taking a tragic turn, was believed to have been enacted. They had been engaged to be married, but she had given way to the jealousy of her nature—had broken with him and sent him off to his fate, which had been horrible. A passionate sense of having wronged him, a hard eternal remorse had thereupon taken possession of her, and when his poor sister, linked also to a soldier, had by a still heavier blow been left almost without resources, she had devoted herself grimly to a long expiation. She had sought comfort in taking Mrs. Julian to live much of the time at Paramore, where she became an unremunerated though not uncriticised housekeeper, and Spencer Coyle rather fancied it a part of this comfort that she could at leisure trample on her. The impression of Jane Wingrave was not the faintest he had gathered on that intensifying Sunday—an occasion singularly tinged for him with the sense of bereavement and mourning and memory, of names never mentioned, of the far-away plaint of widows and the echoes of battles and bad news. It was all military indeed, and Mr. Coyle was made to shudder a little at the profession of which he helped to open the door to otherwise harmless young men. Miss Wingrave might moreover have made such a bad conscience worse—so cold and clear a good one looked at him out of her hard fine eyes and trumpeted in her sonorous voice.

She was a high distinguished person, angular but not awkward, with a large forehead and abundant black hair arranged like that of a woman conceiving perhaps excusably of her head as "noble," and to-day irregularly streaked with white. If however she represented for our troubled friend the genius of a military race it was not that she had the step of a grenadier or the vocabulary of a camp-follower; it was only that such sympathies were vividly implied in the general fact to which her very presence and each of her actions and glances and tones were a constant and direct allusion—the paramount valour of her family. If she was military it was because she sprang from a military house and because she wouldn't for the world have been anything but what the Wingraves had been. She was almost vulgar about her ancestors, and if one had been tempted to quarrel with her one would have found a fair pretext in her defective sense of proportion. This temptation however said nothing to Spencer Coyle, for whom, as a strong character revealing itself in colour and sound, she was almost a "treat" and who was glad to regard her as a force exerted on his own side. He wished her nephew had more of her narrowness instead of being almost cursed with the tendency to look at things in their relations. He wondered why when she came up to town she always resorted to Baker Street for lodgings. He had never known nor heard of Baker Street as a residence—he associated it only with bazaars and photographers. He divined in her a rigid indifference to everything that was not the passion of her life. Nothing really mattered to her but that, and she would have occupied apartments in Whitechapel if they had been an item in her tactics. She had received her visitor in a large cold faded room, furnished with slippery seats and decorated with alabaster vases and wax-flowers. The only little personal comfort for which she appeared to have looked out was a fat catalogue of the Army and Navy Stores, which reposed on a vast desolate table-cover of false blue. Her clear forehead—it was like a porcelain slate, a receptacle for addresses and sums—had flushed when her nephew's crammer told her the extraordinary news; but he saw she was fortunately more angry than frightened. She had essentially, she would always have, too little imagination for fear, and the healthy habit moreover of facing everything had taught her that the occasion usually found her a quantity to reckon with. He saw that her only present fear could have been that of the failure to prevent her nephew's showing publicly for an ass, or for worse, and that to such an apprehension as this she was in fact inaccessible. Practically too she was not troubled by surprise; she recognized none of the futile, none of the subtle sentiments. If Owen had for an hour made a fool of himself she was angry; disconcerted as she would have been on learning that he had confessed to debts or fallen in love with a low girl. But there remained in any annoyance the saving fact that no one could make a fool of *her*.

"I don't know when I've taken such an interest in a young man—I think I've never done it since I began to handle them," Mr. Coyle said. "I like him, I believe in him. It's been a delight to see how he was going."

"Oh I know how they go!" Miss Wingrave threw back her head with an air as acquainted as if a headlong array of the generations had flashed before her with a rattle of their scabbards and spurs. Spencer Coyle recognised the intimation that she had nothing to learn from anybody about the natural carriage of a Wingrave, and he even felt convicted by her next words of being, in her eyes, with the troubled story of his check, his weak complaint of his pupil, rather a poor creature. "If you like him," she exclaimed, "for mercy's sake keep him quiet!"

Mr. Coyle began to explain to her that this was less easy than she appeared to imagine; but it came home to him that she really grasped little of what he said. The more he insisted that the boy had a kind of intellectual independence, the more this struck her as a conclusive proof that her nephew was a Wingrave and a soldier. It was not till he mentioned to her that Owen had spoken of the profession of arms as of something that would be "beneath" him, it was not till her attention was arrested by this intenser light on the complexity of the problem, that she broke out after a moment's stupified reflexion: "Send him to see me at once!"

"That's exactly what I wanted to ask your leave to do. But I've wanted also to prepare you for the worst, to make you understand that he strikes me as really obstinate, and to suggest to you that the most powerful arguments at your command—especially if you should be able to put your hand on some intensely practical one—will be none too effective."

"I think I've got a powerful argument"—and Miss Wingrave looked hard at her visitor. He didn't know in the least what this engine might be, but he begged her to drag it without delay into the field. He promised their young man should come to Baker Street that evening, mentioning however that he had already urged him to spend a couple of the very next days at Eastbourne. This led Jane Wingrave to enquire with surprise what virtue there might be in *that* expensive remedy, and to reply with decision when he had said "The virtue of a little rest, a little change, a little relief to overwrought nerves." "Ah don't coddle him—he's costing us a great deal of money! I'll talk to him and I'll take him down to Paramore; he'll be dealt with there, and I'll send him back to you straightened out."

Spencer Coyle hailed this pledge superficially with satisfaction, but before he quitted the strenuous lady he knew he had really taken on a new anxiety—a restlessness that made him say to himself, groaning inwardly: "Oh she *is* a grenadier at bottom, and she'll have no tact. I don't know what her powerful argument is; I'm only afraid she'll be stupid and make him worse. The old man's better—*he's* capable of tact, though he's not quite an extinct volcano. Owen will probably put him in a rage. In short it's a difficulty that the boy's the best of them."

He felt afresh that evening at dinner that the boy was the best of them. Young Wingrave—who, he was pleased to observe, had not yet proceeded to the seaside—appeared at the repast as usual, looking inevitably a little self-conscious, but not too original for Bayswater. He talked very naturally to Mrs. Coyle, who had thought him from the first the most beautiful young man they had ever received; so that the person most ill at ease was poor Lechmere, who took great trouble, as if from the deepest delicacy, not to meet the eye of his misguided mate. Spencer Coyle however paid the price of his own profundity in feeling more and more worried; he could so easily see that there were all sorts of things in his young friend that the people of Paramore wouldn't understand. He began even already to react against the notion of his being harassed—to reflect that after all he had a right to his ideas—to remember that he was of a substance too fine to be handled with blunt fingers. It was in this way that the ardent little crammer, with his whimsical perceptions and complicated sympathies, was generally condemned not to settle down comfortably either to his displeasures or to his enthusiasms. His love of the real truth never gave him a chance to enjoy them. He mentioned to Wingrave after dinner the propriety of an immediate visit to Baker Street, and the young man, looking "queer," as he thought—that is smiling again with the perverse high spirit in a wrong cause that he had shown in their recent interview—went off to face the ordeal. Spencer Coyle was sure he was scared—he was afraid of his aunt; but somehow this didn't strike him as a sign of pusillanimity. *He* should have been scared, he was aware, in the poor boy's place, and the sight of his pupil marching up to the battery in spite of his terrors was a positive suggestion of the temperament of the soldier. Many a plucky youth would have funked this special exposure.

"He *has* got ideas!" young Lechmere broke out to his instructor after his comrade had quitted the house. He was bewildered and rather rueful—he had an emotion to work off. He had before dinner gone straight at his friend, as Mr. Coyle had requested, and had elicited from him that his scruples were founded on an overwhelming conviction of the stupidity—the "crass barbarism" he called it—of war. His great complaint was that people hadn't invented anything cleverer, and he was determined to show, the only way he could, that *he* wasn't so dull a brute.

"And he thinks all the great generals ought to have been shot, and that Napoleon Bonaparte in particular, the greatest, was a scoundrel, a criminal, a monster for whom language has no adequate name!" Mr. Coyle rejoined, completing young Lechmere's picture. "He favoured you, I see, with exactly the same pearls of wisdom that he produced for me. But I want to know what *you* said."

"I said they were awful rot!" Young Lechmere spoke with emphasis and was slightly surprised to hear Mr. Coyle laugh, out of tune, at this just declaration, and then after a moment continue:

"It's all very curious—I dare say there's something in it. But it's a pity!"

"He told me when it was that the question began to strike him in that light. Four or five years ago, when he did a lot of reading about all the great swells and their campaigns—Hannibal and Julius Caesar, Marlborough and Frederick and Bonaparte. He *has* done a lot of reading, and he says it opened his eyes. He says that a wave of disgust rolled over him. He talked about the 'immeasurable misery' of wars, and asked me why nations don't tear to pieces the governments, the rulers that go in for them. He hates poor old Bonaparte worst of all."

"Well, poor old Bonaparte *was* a scoundrel. He was a frightful ruffian," Mr. Coyle unexpectedly declared. "But I suppose you didn't admit that."

"Oh I dare say he was objectionable, and I'm glad we laid him on his back. But the point I made to Wingrave was that his own behaviour would excite no end of remark." And young Lechmere hung back but an instant before adding: "I told him he must be prepared for the worst."

"Of course he asked you what you meant by the 'worst,' " said Spencer Coyle.

"Yes, he asked me that, and do you know what I said? I said people would call his conscientious scruples and his wave of disgust a mere pretext. Then he asked 'A pretext for what?' "

"Ah he rather had you there!" Mr. Coyle returned with a small laugh that was mystifying to his pupil.

"Not a bit—for I told him."

"What did you tell him?"

Once more, for a few seconds, with his conscious eyes in his instructor's, the young man delayed. "Why what we spoke of a few hours ago. The appearance he'd present of not having—" The honest youth faltered afresh, but brought it out: "The military temperament, don't you know? But do you know how he cheeked us on that?" young Lechmere went on.

"Damn the military temperament!" the crammer promptly replied.

Young Lechmere stared. Mr. Coyle's tone left him uncertain if he were attributing the phrase to Wingrave or uttering his own opinion, but he exclaimed: "Those were exactly his words!"

"He doesn't care," said Mr. Coyle.

"Perhaps not. But it isn't fair for him to abuse *us* fellows. I told him it's the finest temperament in the world, and that there's nothing so splendid as pluck and heroism."

"Ah there you had *him!*"

"I told him it was unworthy of him to abuse a gallant, a magnificent profession. I told him there's no type so fine as that of the soldier doing his duty."

"That's essentially *your* type, my dear boy." Young Lechmere blushed; he couldn't make out—and the danger was naturally unexpected to him—whether at that moment he didn't exist mainly for the recreation of his friend. But he was partly reassured by the genial way his friend continued, laying a hand on his shoulder: "Keep *at* him that way! We may do something. I'm in any case extremely obliged to you."

Another doubt however remained unassuaged—a doubt which led him to overflow yet again before they dropped the painful subject: "He *doesn't* care! But it's awfully odd he shouldn't!"

"So it is, but remember what you said this afternoon—I mean about your not advising people to make insinuations to *you*."

"I believe I should knock the beggar down!" said young Lechmere. Mr. Coyle had got up; the conversation had taken place while they sat together after Mrs. Coyle's withdrawal from the dinner-table, and the head of the establishment administered to his candid charge, on principles that were a part of his thoroughness, a glass of excellent claret. The disciple in question, also on his feet, lingered an instant, not for another "go," as he would have called it, at the decanter, but to wipe his microscopic moustache with prolonged and unusual care. His companion saw he had something to bring out which required a final effort, and waited for him an instant with a hand on the knob of the door. Then as young Lechmere drew nearer Spencer Coyle grew conscious of an unwonted intensity in the round and ingenuous face. The boy was nervous, but tried to behave like a man of the world. "Of course it's between ourselves," he stammered, "and I wouldn't breathe such a word to any one who wasn't interested in poor Wingrave as you are. But do you think he funks it?"

Mr. Coyle looked at him so hard an instant that he was visibly frightened at what he had said. "Funks it! Funks what?"

"Why what we're talking about—the service." Young Lechmere gave a little gulp and added with a want of active wit almost pathetic to Spencer Coyle: "The dangers, you know!"

"Do you mean he's thinking of his skin?"

Young Lechmere's eyes expanded appealingly, and what his instructor saw in his pink face—even thinking he saw a tear—was the dread of a disappointment shocking in the degree in which the loyalty of admiration had been great.

"Is he—is he beastly *afraid?*" repeated the honest lad with a quaver of suspense.

"Dear no!" said Spencer Coyle, turning his back.

On which young Lechmere felt a little snubbed and even a little ashamed. But still more he felt relieved.

III

Less than a week after this the elder man received a note from Miss Wingrave, who had immediately quitted London with her nephew. She proposed he should come down to Paramore for the following Sunday—Owen was really so tiresome. On the spot, in that house of examples and memories and in combination with her poor dear father, who was "dreadfully annoyed," it might be worth their while to make a last stand. Mr. Coyle read between the lines of this letter that the party at Paramore had got over a good deal of ground since Miss Wingrave, in Baker Street, had treated his despair as superficial. She wasn't an insinuating woman, but she went so far as to put the question on the ground of his conferring a particular favour on an afflicted family; and she expressed the pleasure it would give them should he be accompanied by Mrs. Coyle, for whom she enclosed a separate invitation.

She mentioned that she was also writing, subject to Mr. Coyle's approval, to young Lechmere. She thought such a nice manly boy might do her wretched nephew some good. The celebrated crammer decided to embrace this occasion; and now it was the case not so much that he was angry as that he was anxious. As he directed his answer to Miss Wingrave's letter he caught himself smiling at the thought that at bottom he was going to defend his ex-pupil rather than to give him away. He said to his wife, who was a fair fresh slow woman—a person of much more presence than himself—that she had better take Miss Wingrave at her word: it was such an extraordinary, such a fascinating specimen of an old English home. This last allusion was softly sarcastic—he had accused the good lady more than once of being in love with Owen Wingrave. She admitted that she was, she even gloried in her passion; which shows that the subject, between them, was treated in a liberal spirit. She carried out the joke by accepting the invitation with eagerness. Young Lechmere was delighted to do the same; his instructor had good-naturedly taken the view that the little break would freshen him up for his last spurt.

It was the fact that the occupants of Paramore did indeed take their trouble hard that struck our friend after he had been an hour or two in that fine old house. This very short second visit, beginning on the Saturday evening, was to constitute the strangest episode of his life. As soon as he found himself in private with his wife—they had retired to dress for dinner—they called each other's attention with effusion and almost with alarm to the sinister gloom diffused through the place. The house was admirable from its old grey front, which came forward in wings so as to form three sides of a square, but Mrs. Coyle made no scruple to declare that if she had known in advance the sort of impression she was going to receive she would never have put her foot in it. She characterised it as "uncanny" and as looking wicked and weird, and she accused her husband of not having warned her properly. He had named to her in advance some of the appearances she was to expect, but while she almost feverishly dressed she had innumerable questions to ask. He hadn't told her about the girl, the extraordinary girl, Miss Julian—that is, he hadn't told her that this young lady, who in plain terms was a mere dependent, would be in effect, and as a consequence of the way she carried herself, the most important person in the house. Mrs. Coyle was already prepared to announce that she hated Miss Julian's affectations. Her husband above all hadn't told her that they should find their young charge looking five years older.

"I couldn't imagine that," Spencer said, "nor that the character of the crisis here would be quite so perceptible. But I suggested to Miss Wingrave the other day that they should press her nephew in real earnest, and she has taken me at my word. They've cut off his supplies—they're trying to starve him out. That's not what I meant—but indeed I don't quite *know* to-day what I meant. Owen feels the pressure, but he won't yield." The strange thing was that, now he was there, the brooding little coach knew still better, even while half-closing his eyes to it, that his own spirit had been caught up by a wave of reaction. If he was there it was because he was on poor Owen's side. His whole impression, his whole apprehension, had on the spot become much deeper. There was something in the young fanatic's very resistance that began to charm him. When his wife, in the intimacy of the conference I have mentioned, threw off the mask and commended even with extravagance the stand his pupil had taken (he was too good to be a horrid soldier and it was noble of him to suffer for his convictions—wasn't he as upright as a young hero, even though as pale as a Christian martyr?) the good lady only expressed the sympathy which, under cover of regarding his late inmate as a rare exception, he had already recognised in his own soul.

For, half an hour ago, after they had had superficial tea in the brown old hall of the house, that searcher into the reasons of things had proposed to him, before going to dress, a short turn outside, and had even, on the terrace, as they walked together to one of the far ends, passed his hand entreatingly into his companion's arm, permitting himself thus a familiarity unusual between pupil and master and calculated to show he had guessed whom he could most depend on to be kind to him. Spencer Coyle had on his own side guessed something, so that he wasn't surprised at the boy's having a particular confidence to make. He had felt on arriving that each member of the party would want to get hold of him first, and he knew that at that moment Jane Wingrave was peering through the ancient blur of one of the windows—the house had been modernised so little that the thick dim panes were three centuries old—to see whether her nephew looked as if he were poisoning the visitor's mind. Mr. Coyle lost no time therefore in reminding the youth—though careful to turn it to a laugh as he did so—that he hadn't come down to Paramore to be corrupted. He had come down to make, face to face, a last appeal, which he hoped wouldn't be utterly vain. Owen smiled sadly as they went, asking him if he thought he had the general air of a fellow who was going to knock under.

"I think you look odd—I think you look ill," Spencer Coyle said very honestly. They had paused at the end of the terrace.

"I've had to exercise a great power of resistance, and it rather takes it out of one."

"Ah my dear boy, I wish your great power—for you evidently possess it—were exerted in a better cause!"

Owen Wingrave smiled down at his small but erect instructor. "I don't believe that!" Then he added, to explain why: "Isn't what you want (if you're so good as to think well of my character) to see me exert *most* power, in whatever direction? Well, this is the way I exert most." He allowed he had had some terrible hours with his grandfather, who had denounced him in a way to make his hair stand up on his head. He had expected them not to like it, not a bit, but had had no idea they would make such a row. His aunt was different, but she was equally insulting. Oh they had made him feel they were ashamed of him; they accused him of putting a public dishonour on their name. He was the only one who had ever backed out—he was the first for three hundred years. Every one had known he was to go up, and now every one would know him for a young hypocrite who suddenly pretended to have scruples. They talked of his scruples as you wouldn't talk of a cannibal's god. His grandfather had called him outrageous names. "He called me—he called me—" Here Owen faltered and his voice failed him. He looked as haggard as was possible to a young man in such splendid health.

"I probably know!" said Spencer Coyle with a nervous laugh.

His companion's clouded eyes, as if following the last strange consequences of things, rested for an instant on a distant object. Then they met his own and for another moment sounded them deeply. "It isn't true. No, it isn't. It's not *that!*"

"I don't suppose it is! But what *do* you propose instead of it?"

"Instead of what?"

"Instead of the stupid solution of war. If you take that away you should suggest at least a substitute."

"That's for the people in charge, for governments and cabinets," said Owen. "*They'll* arrive soon enough at a substitute, in the particular case, if they're made to understand that they'll be hanged—and also drawn and quartered—if they don't find one. Make it a capital crime; *that* will quicken the wits of ministers!" His eyes brightened as he spoke, and he looked assured and exalted. Mr. Coyle gave a sigh of sad surrender—it was really a stiff obsession. He saw the moment after this when Owen was on the point of asking if he too thought him a coward; but he was relieved to be able to judge that he either didn't suspect him of it or shrank uncomfortably from putting the question to the test. Spencer Coyle wished to show confidence, but somehow a direct assurance that he didn't doubt of his courage was too gross a compliment—it would be like saying he didn't doubt of his honesty. The difficulty was presently averted by Owen's continuing: "My grandfather can't break the entail, but I shall have nothing but this place, which, as you know, is small and, with the way rents are going, has quite ceased to yield an income. He has some money—not much, but such as it is he cuts me off. My aunt does the same—she has let me know her intentions. She was to have left me her six hundred a year. It was all settled, but now what's definite is that I don't get a penny of it if I give up the army. I must add in fairness that I have from my mother three hundred a year of my own. And I tell you the simple truth when I say I don't care a rap for the loss of the money." The young man drew the long slow breath of a creature in pain; then he added: "*That's* not what worries me!"

"What are you going to do instead then?" his friend asked without other comment.

"I don't know—perhaps nothing. Nothing great at all events. Only something peaceful!"

Owen gave a weary smile, as if, worried as he was, he could yet appreciate the humorous effect of such a declaration from a Wingrave; but what it suggested to his guest, who looked up at him with a sense that he was after all not a Wingrave for nothing and had a military steadiness under fire, was the exasperation that such a profession, made in such a way and striking them as the last word of the inglorious, might well have produced on the part of his grandfather and his aunt. "Perhaps nothing"—when he might carry on the great tradition! Yes, he wasn't weak, and he was interesting; but there was clearly a point of view from which he was provoking. "What *is* it then that worries you?" Mr. Coyle demanded.

"Oh the house—the very air and feeling of it. There are strange voices in it that seem to mutter at me—to say dreadful things as I pass. I mean the general consciousness and responsibility of what I'm doing. Of course it hasn't been easy for me—anything rather! I assure you I don't enjoy it." With a light in them that was like a longing for justice Owen again bent his eyes on those of the little coach; then he pursued: "I've started up all the old ghosts. The very portraits glower at me on the walls. There's one of my great-great-grandfather (the one the extraordinary story you know is about—the old fellow who hangs on the second landing of the big staircase) that fairly stirs on the canvas, just heaves a little, when I come near it. I have to go up and down stairs—it's rather awkward! It's what my aunt calls the family-circle, and they sit, ever so grimly, in judgement. The circle's all constituted here, it's a kind of awful encompassing presence, it stretches away into the past, and when I came back with her the other day Miss Wingrave told me I wouldn't have the impudence to stand in the midst of it and say such things. I *had* to say them to my grandfather; but now that I've said them it seems to me the question's ended. I want to go away—I don't care if I never come back again."

"Oh you *are* a soldier; you must fight it out!" Mr. Coyle laughed.

The young man seemed discouraged at his levity, but as they turned round, strolling back in the direction from which they had come, he himself smiled faintly after an instant and replied: "Ah we're tainted all!"

They walked in silence part of the way to the old portico; then the elder of the pair, stopping short after having assured himself he was at a sufficient distance from the house not to be heard, suddenly put the question: "What does Miss Julian say?"

"Miss Julian?" Owen had perceptibly coloured.

"I'm sure *she* hasn't concealed her opinion."

"Oh it's the opinion of the family-circle, for she's a member of it of course. And then she has her own as well."

"Her own opinion?"

"Her own family-circle."

"Do you mean her mother—that patient lady?"

"I mean more particularly her father, who fell in battle. And her grandfather, and *his* father, and her uncles and great-uncles—they all fell in battle."

Mr. Coyle, his face now rather oddly set, took it in. "Hasn't the sacrifice of so many lives been sufficient? Why should she sacrifice *you?*"

"Oh she *hates* me!" Owen declared as they resumed their walk.

"Ah the hatred of pretty girls for fine young men!" cried Spencer Coyle.

He didn't believe in it, but his wife did, it appeared perfectly, when he mentioned this conversation while, in the fashion that has been described, the visitors dressed for dinner. Mrs. Coyle had already discovered that nothing could have been nastier than Miss Julian's manner to the disgraced youth during the half-hour the party had spent in the hall; and it was this lady's judgement that one must have had no eyes in one's head not to see that she was already trying outrageously to flirt with young Lechmere. It was a pity they had brought that silly boy: he was down in the hall with the creature at that moment. Spencer Coyle's version was different—he believed finer elements involved. The girl's footing in the house was inexplicable on any ground save that of her being predestined to Miss Wingrave's nephew. As the niece of Miss Wingrave's own unhappy intended she had been devoted early by this lady to the office of healing by a union with the hope of the race the tragic breach that had separated their elders; and if in reply to this it was to be said that a girl of spirit couldn't enjoy in such a matter having her duty cut out for her, Owen's enlightened friend was ready with the argument that a young person in Miss Julian's position would never be such a fool as really to quarrel with a capital chance. She was familiar at Paramore and she felt safe; therefore she might treat herself to the amusement of pretending she had her option. It was all innocent tricks and airs. She had a curious charm, and it was vain to pretend that the heir of that house wouldn't seem good enough to a girl, clever as she might be, of eighteen. Mrs. Coyle reminded her husband that their late charge was precisely now *not* of that house: this question was among the articles that exercised their wits after the two men had taken the turn on the terrace. Spencer then mentioned to his wife that Owen was afraid of the portrait of his great-great-grandfather. He would show it to her, since she hadn't noticed it, on their way downstairs.

"Why of his great-great-grandfather more than of any of the others?"

"Oh because he's the most formidable. He's the one who's sometimes seen."

"Seen where?" Mrs. Coyle had turned round with a jerk.

"In the room he was found dead in—the White Room they've always called it."

"Do you mean to say the house has a proved *ghost*?" Mrs. Coyle almost shrieked. "You brought me here without telling me?"

"Didn't I mention it after my other visit?"

"Not a word. You only talked about Miss Wingrave."

"Oh I was full of the story—you've simply forgotten."

"Then you should have reminded me!"

"If I had thought of it I'd have held my peace—for you wouldn't have come."

"I wish indeed I hadn't!" cried Mrs. Coyle. "But what," she immediately asked, "*is* the story?"

"Oh a deed of violence that took place here ages ago. I think it was in George the Second's time that Colonel Wingrave, one of their ancestors, struck in a fit of passion one of his children, a lad just growing up, a blow on the head of which the unhappy child died. The matter was hushed up for the hour and some other explanation put about. The poor boy was laid out in one of those rooms on the other side of the house, and amid strange smothered rumours the funeral was hurried on. The next morning, when the household assembled, Colonel Wingrave was missing; he was looked for vainly, and at last it occurred to some one that he might perhaps be in the room from which his child had been carried to burial. The seeker knocked without an answer—then opened the door. The poor man lay dead on the floor, in his clothes, as if he had reeled and fallen back, without a wound, without a mark, without anything in his appearance to indicate that he had either struggled or suffered. He was a strong sound man—there was nothing to account for such a stroke. He's supposed to have gone to the room during the night, just before going to bed, in some fit of compunction or some fascination of dread. It was only after this that the truth about the boy came out. But no one ever sleeps in the room."

Mrs. Coyle had fairly turned pale. "I hope not indeed! Thank heaven they haven't put *us* there!"

"We're at a comfortable distance—I know the scene of the event."

"Do you mean you've been *in*—?"

"For a few moments. They're rather proud of the place and my young friend showed it me when I was here before."

Mrs. Coyle stared. "And what is it like?"

"Simply an empty dull old-fashioned bedroom, rather big and furnished with the things of the 'period.' It's panelled from floor to ceiling, and the panels evidently, years and years ago, were painted white. But the paint has darkened with time and there are three or four quaint little ancient 'samplers,' framed and glazed, hung on the walls."

Mrs. Coyle looked round with a shudder. "I'm glad there are no samplers here! I never heard anything so jumpy! Come down to dinner."

On the staircase as they went her husband showed her the portrait of Colonel Wingrave—a representation, with some force and style, for the place and period, of a gentleman with a hard handsome face, in a red coat and a peruke. Mrs. Coyle pronounced his descendant old Sir Philip wonderfully like him; and her husband could fancy, though he kept it to himself, that if one should have the courage to walk the old corridors of Paramore at night one might meet a figure that resembled him roaming, with the restlessness of a ghost, hand in hand with the figure of a tall boy. As he proceeded to the drawing-room with his wife he found himself suddenly wishing he had made more of a point of his pupil's going to Eastbourne. The evening however seemed to have taken upon itself to dissipate any such whimsical forebodings, for the grimness of the family-circle, as he had preconceived its composition, was mitigated by an infusion of the "neighbourhood." The company at dinner was recruited by two cheerful couples, one of them the vicar and his wife, and by a silent young man who had come down to fish. This was a relief to Mr. Coyle, who had begun to wonder what was after all expected of him and why he had been such a fool as to come, and who now felt that for the first hours at least the situation wouldn't have directly to be dealt with. Indeed he found, as he had found before, sufficient occupation for his ingenuity in reading the various symptoms of which the social scene that spread about him was an expression. He should probably have a trying day on the morrow: he foresaw the difficulty of the long decorous Sunday and how dry Jane Wingrave's ideas, elicited in strenuous conference, would taste. She and her father would make him feel they depended upon him for the impossible, and if they should try to associate him with too tactless a policy he might end by telling them what he thought of it—an accident not required to make his visit a depressed mistake. The old man's actual design was evidently to let their friends see in it a positive mark of their being all right. The presence of the great London coach was tantamount to a profession of faith in the results of the impending examination. It had clearly been obtained from Owen, rather to the principal visitor's surprise, that he would do nothing to interfere with the apparent concord. He let the allusions to his hard work pass and, holding his tongue about his affairs, talked to the ladies as amicably as if he hadn't been "cut off." When Mr. Coyle looked at him once or twice across the table, catching his eye, which showed an indefinable passion, he found a puzzling pathos in his laughing face: one couldn't resist a pang for a young lamb so visibly marked for sacrifice. "Hang him, what a pity he's such a fighter!" he privately sighed—and with a want of logic that was only superficial.

This idea however would have absorbed him more if so much of his attention hadn't been for Kate Julian, who now that he had her well before him struck him as a remarkable and even as a possibly interesting young woman. The interest resided not in any extraordinary prettiness, for if she was handsome, with her long Eastern eyes, her magnificent hair and her general unabashed originality, he had seen complexions rosier and features that pleased him more: it dwelt in a strange impression that she gave of being exactly the sort of person whom, in her position, common considerations, those of prudence and perhaps even a little those of decorum, would have enjoined on her not to be. She was what was vulgarly termed a dependent—penniless patronised tolerated; but something in all her air conveyed that if her situation was inferior her spirit, to make up for it, was above precautions or submissions. It wasn't in the least that she was aggressive—she was too indifferent for that; it was only as if, having nothing either to gain or to lose, she could afford to do as she liked. It occurred to Spencer Coyle that she might really have had more at stake than her imagination appeared to take account of; whatever this quantity might be, at any rate, he had never seen a young woman at less pains to keep the safe side. He wondered inevitably what terms prevailed between Jane Wingrave and such an inmate as this; but those questions of course were unfathomable deeps. Perhaps keen Kate lorded it even over her protectress. The other time he was at Paramore he had received an impression that, with Sir Philip beside her, the girl could fight with her back to the wall. She amused Sir Philip, she charmed him, and he liked people who weren't afraid; between him and his daughter moreover there was no doubt which was the higher in command. Miss Wingrave took many things for granted, and most of all the rigour of discipline and the fate of the vanquished and the captive.

But between their clever boy and so original a companion of his childhood what odd relation would have grown up? It couldn't be indifference, and yet on the part of happy handsome youthful creatures it was still less likely to be aversion. They weren't Paul and Virginia, but they must have had their common summer and their idyll: no nice girl could have disliked such a nice fellow for anything but not liking *her*, and no nice fellow could have resisted such propinquity. Mr. Coyle remembered indeed that Mrs. Julian had spoken to him as if the propinquity had been by no means constant, owing to her daughter's absences at school, to say nothing of Owen's; her visits to a few friends who were so kind as to "take" her from time to time; her sojourns in London—so difficult to manage, but still managed by God's help—for "advantages," for drawing and singing, especially drawing, or rather painting in oils, for which she had gained high credit. But the good lady had also mentioned that the young people were quite brother and sister, which *was* a little, after all, like Paul and Virginia. Mrs. Coyle had been right, and it was apparent that Virginia was doing her best to make the time pass agreeably for young Lechmere. There was no such whirl of conversation as to render it an effort for our critic to reflect on these things: the tone of the occasion, thanks principally to the other guests, was not disposed to stray—it tended to the repetition of anecdote and the discussion of rents, topics that huddled together like uneasy animals. He could judge how intensely his hosts wished the evening to pass off as if nothing had happened; and this gave him the measure of their private resentment. Before dinner was over he found himself fidgety about his second pupil. Young Lechmere, since he began to cram, had done all that might have been expected of him; but this couldn't blind his instructor to a present perception of his being in moments of relaxation as innocent as a babe. Mr. Coyle had considered that the amusements of Paramore would probably give him a fillip, and the poor youth's manner testified to the soundness of the forecast. The fillip had been unmistakeably administered; it had come in the form of a revelation. The light on young Lechmere's brow announced with a candour that was almost an appeal for compassion, or at least a deprecation of ridicule, that he had never seen anything like Miss Julian.

IV

In the drawing-room after dinner the girl found a chance to approach Owen's late preceptor. She stood before him a moment, smiling while she opened and shut her fan, and then said abruptly, raising her strange eyes: "I know what you've come for, but it isn't any use."

"I've come to look after *you* a little. Isn't *that* any use?"

"It's very kind. But I'm not the question of the hour. You won't do anything with Owen."

Spencer Coyle hesitated a moment. "What will *you* do with his young friend?"

She stared, looked round her. "Mr. Lechmere? Oh poor little lad! We've been talking about Owen. He admires him so."

"So do I. I should tell you that."

"So do we all. That's why we're in such despair."

"Personally then you'd *like* him to be a soldier?" the visitor asked.

"I've quite set my heart on it. I adore the army and I'm awfully fond of my old playmate," said Miss Julian.

Spencer recalled the young man's own different version of her attitude; but he judged it loyal not to challenge her. "It's not conceivable that your old playmate shouldn't be fond of you. He must therefore wish to please you; and I don't see why—between you, such clever young people as you are!—you don't set the matter right."

"Wish to please me!" Miss Julian echoed. "I'm sorry to say he shows no such desire. He thinks me an impudent wretch. I've told him what I think of *him*, and he simply hates me."

"But you think so highly! You just told me you admire him."

"His talents, his possibilities, yes; even his personal appearance, if I may allude to such a matter. But I don't admire his present behaviour."

"Have you had the question out with him?" Spencer asked.

"Oh yes, I've ventured to be frank—the occasion seemed to excuse it. He couldn't like what I said."

"What did you say?"

The girl, thinking a moment, opened and shut her fan again. "Why—as we're such good old friends—that such conduct doesn't begin to be that of a gentleman!"

After she had spoken her eyes met Mr. Coyle's, who looked into their ambiguous depths. "What then would you have said without that tie?"

"How odd for *you* to ask that—in such a way!" she returned with a laugh. "I don't understand your position: I thought your line was to *make* soldiers!"

"You should take my little joke. But, as regards Owen Wingrave, there's no 'making' needed," he declared. "To my sense"—and the little crammer paused as with a consciousness of responsibility for his paradox—"to my sense he *is*, in a high sense of the term, a fighting man."

"Ah let him prove it!" she cried with impatience and turning short off.

Spencer Coyle let her go; something in her tone annoyed and even not a little shocked him. There had evidently been a violent passage between these young persons, and the reflexion that such a matter was after all none of his business but troubled him the more. It was indeed a military house, and she was at any rate a damsel who placed her ideal of manhood—damsels doubtless always had their ideals of manhood—in the type of the belted warrior. It was a taste like another; but even a quarter of an hour later, finding himself near young Lechmere, in whom this type was embodied, Spencer Coyle was still so ruffled that he addressed the innocent lad with a certain magisterial dryness. "You're under no pressure to sit up late, you know. That's not what I brought you down for." The dinner-guests were taking leave and the bedroom candles twinkled in a monitory row. Young Lechmere however was too agreeably agitated to be accessible to a snub; he had a happy preoccupation which almost engendered a grin.

"I'm only too eager for bedtime. Do you know there's an awfully jolly room?"

Coyle debated a moment as to whether he should take the allusion—then spoke from his general tension. "Surely they haven't put you there?"

"No indeed: no one has passed a night in it for ages. But that's exactly what I want to do—it would be tremendous fun."

"And have you been trying to get Miss Julian's leave?"

'Oh *she* can't give it she says. But she believes in it, and she maintains that no man has ever dared."

"No man *shall* ever!" said Spencer with decision. "A fellow in your critical position in particular must have a quiet night."

Young Lechmere gave a disappointed but reasonable sigh. "Oh all right. But mayn't I sit up for a little go at Wingrave? I haven't had any yet."

Mr. Coyle looked at his watch. "You may smoke *one* cigarette."

He felt a hand on his shoulder and turned round to see his wife tilting candle-grease upon his coat. The ladies were going to bed and it was Sir Philip's inveterate hour; but Mrs. Coyle confided to her husband that after the dreadful things he had told her she positively declined to be left alone, for no matter how short an interval, in any part of the house. He promised to follow her within three minutes, and after the orthodox handshakes the ladies rustled away. The forms were kept up at Paramore as bravely as if the old house had no present intensity of heartache. The only one of which Coyle noticed the drop was some salutation to himself from Kate Julian. She gave him neither a word nor a glance, but he saw her look hard at Owen. Her mother, timid and pitying, was apparently the only person from whom this young man caught an inclination of the head. Miss Wingrave marshalled the three ladies—her little procession of twinkling tapers—up the wide oaken stairs and past the watching portrait of her ill-fated ancestor. Sir Philip's servant appeared and offered his arm to the old man, who turned a perpendicular back on poor Owen when the boy made a vague movement to anticipate this office. Mr. Coyle learned later that before Owen had forfeited favour it had always, when he was at home, been his privilege at bedtime to conduct his grandfather ceremoniously to rest. Sir Philip's habits were contemptuously different now. His apartments were on the lower floor and he shuffled stiffly off to them with his valet's help, after fixing for a moment significantly on the most responsible of his visitors the thick red ray, like the glow of stirred embers, that always made his eyes conflict oddly with his mild manners. They seemed to say to poor Spencer "We'll let the young scoundrel have it to-morrow!" One might have gathered from them that the young scoundrel, who had now strolled to the other end of the hall, had at least forged a cheque. His friend watched him an instant, saw him drop nervously into a chair and then with a restless movement get up. The same movement brought him back to where Mr. Coyle stood addressing a last injunction to young Lechmere.

"I'm going to bed and I should like you particularly to conform to what I said to you a short time ago. Smoke a single cigarette with our host here and then go to your room. You'll have me down on you if I hear of your having, during the night, tried any preposterous games." Young Lechmere, looking down with his hands in his pockets, said nothing—he only poked at the corner of a rug with his toe; so that his fellow visitor, dissatisfied with so tacit a pledge, presently went on to Owen: "I must request you, Wingrave, not to keep so sensitive a subject sitting up—and indeed to put him to bed and turn his key in the door." As Owen stared an instant, apparently not understanding the motive of so much solicitude, he added: "Lechmere has a morbid curiosity about one of your legends—of your historic rooms. Nip it in the bud."

"Oh the legend's rather good, but I'm afraid the room's an awful sell!" Owen laughed.

"You know you don't *believe* that, my boy!" young Lechmere returned.

"I don't think he does"—Mr. Coyle noticed Owen's mottled flush.

"He wouldn't try a night there himself!" their companion pursued.

"I know who told you that," said Owen, lighting a cigarette in an embarrassed way at the candle, without offering one to either of his friends.

"Well, what if she did?" asked the younger of these gentlemen, rather red. "Do you want them *all* yourself?" he continued facetiously, fumbling in the cigarette-box.

Owen Wingrave only smoked quietly; then he brought out: "Yes—what if she did? But she doesn't know," he added.

"She doesn't know what?"

"She doesn't know anything!—I'll tuck him in!" Owen went on gaily to Mr. Coyle, who saw that his presence, now a certain note had been struck, made the young men uncomfortable. He was curious, but there were discretions and delicacies, with his pupils, that he had always pretended to practise; scruples which however didn't prevent, as he took his way upstairs, his recommending them not to be donkeys.

At the top of the staircase, to his surprise, he met Miss Julian, who was apparently going down again. She hadn't begun to undress, nor was she perceptibly disconcerted at seeing him. She nevertheless, in a manner slightly at variance with the rigour with which she had overlooked him ten minutes before, dropped the words: "I'm going down to look for something. I've lost a jewel."

"A jewel?"

"A rather good turquoise, out of my locket. As it's the only *real* ornament I've the honour to possess—!" And she began to descend.

"Shall I go with you and help you?" asked Spencer Coyle.

She paused a few steps below him, looking back with her Oriental eyes. "Don't I hear our friends' voices in the hall?"

"Those remarkable young men are there."

"*They'll* help me." And Kate Julian passed down.

Spencer Coyle was tempted to follow her, but remembering his standard of tact he rejoined his wife in their apartment. He delayed nevertheless to go to bed and, though he looked into his dressing-room, couldn't bring himself even to take off his coat. He pretended for half an hour to read a novel; after which, quietly, or perhaps I should say agitatedly, he stepped from the dressing-room into the corridor. He followed this passage to the door of the room he knew to have been assigned to young Lechmere and was comforted to see it closed. Half an hour earlier he had noticed it stand open; therefore he could take for granted the bewildered boy had come to bed. It was of this he had wished to assure himself, and having done so he was on the point of retreating. But at the same instant he heard a sound in the room—the occupant was doing, at the window, something that showed him he might knock without the reproach of waking his pupil up. Young Lechmere came in fact to the door in his shirt and trousers. He admitted his visitor in some surprise, and when the door was closed again the latter said: "I don't want to make your life a burden, but I had it on my conscience to see for myself that you're not exposed to undue excitement."

"Oh there's plenty of that!" said the ingenuous youth. "Miss Julian came down again."

"To look for a turquoise?"

"So she said."

"Did she find it?"

"I don't know. I came up. I left her with poor Owen."

"Quite the right thing," said Spencer Coyle.

"I don't know," young Lechmere repeated uneasily. "I left them quarrelling."

"What about?"

"I don't understand. They're a quaint pair!"

Spencer turned it over. He had, fundamentally, principles and high decencies, but what he had in particular just now was a curiosity, or rather, to recognise it for what it was, a sympathy, which brushed them away. "Does it strike you that *she's* down on him?" he permitted himself to enquire.

"Rather!—when she tells him he lies!"

"What do you mean?"

"Why before *me*. It made me leave them; it was getting too hot. I stupidly brought up the question of that bad room again, and said how sorry I was I had to promise you not to try my luck with it."

"You can't pry about in that gross way in other people's houses—you can't take such liberties, you know!" Mr. Coyle interjected.

"I'm all right—see how good I am. I don't want to go *near* the place!" said young Lechmere confidingly. "Miss Julian said to me 'Oh I dare say *you'd* risk it, but'—and she turned and laughed at poor Owen—'that's more than we can expect of a gentleman who has taken *his* extraordinary line.' I could see that something had already passed between them on the subject—some teasing or challenging of hers. It may have been only chaff, but his chucking the profession had evidently brought up the question of the white feather—I mean of his pluck."

"And what did Owen say?"

"Nothing at first; but presently he brought out very quietly: 'I spent all last night in the confounded place.' We both stared and cried out at this and I asked him what he had seen there. He said he had seen nothing, and Miss Julian replied that he ought to tell his story better than that—he ought to make something good of it. 'It's not a story—it's a simple fact,' said he; on which she jeered at him and wanted to know why, if he had done it, he hadn't told her in the morning, since he knew what she thought of him. 'I know, my dear, but I don't care,' the poor devil said. This made her angry, and she asked him quite seriously whether he'd care if he should know she believed him to be trying to deceive us."

"Ah what a brute!" cried Spencer Coyle.

"She's a most extraordinary girl—I don't know what she's up to," young Lechmere quite panted.

"Extraordinary indeed—to be romping and bandying words at that hour of the night with fast young men!"

But young Lechmere made his distinction. "I mean because I think she likes him."

Mr. Coyle was so struck with this unwonted symptom of subtlety that he flashed out: "And do you think he likes *her*?"

It produced on his pupil's part a drop and a plaintive sigh. "I don't know—I give it up!—But I'm sure he *did* see something or hear something," the youth added.

"In that ridiculous place? What makes you sure?"

"Well, because he looks as if he had. I've an idea you can tell—in such a case. He behaves as if he had."

"Why then shouldn't he name it?"

Young Lechmere wondered and found. "Perhaps it's too bad to mention."

Spencer Coyle gave a laugh. "Aren't you glad then *you're* not in it?"

"Uncommonly!"

"Go to bed, you goose," Spencer said with renewed nervous derision. "But before you go tell me how he met her charge that he was trying to deceive you."

" 'Take me there yourself then and lock me in!' "

"And *did* she take him?"

"I don't know—I came up."

He exchanged a long look with his pupil. "I don't think they're in the hall now. Where's Owen's own room?"

"I haven't the least idea."

Mr. Coyle was at a loss; he was in equal ignorance and he couldn't go about trying doors. He bade young Lechmere sink to slumber; after which he came out into the passage. He asked himself if he should be able to find his way to the room Owen had formerly shown him, remembering that in common with many of the others it had its ancient name painted on it. But the corridors of Paramore were intricate; moreover some of the servants would still be up, and he didn't wish to appear unduly to prowl. He went back to his own quarters, where Mrs. Coyle soon noted the continuance of his inability to rest. As she confessed for her own part, in the dreadful place, to an increased sense of "creepiness," they spent the early part of the night in conversation, so that a portion of their vigil was inevitably beguiled by her husband's account of his colloquy with little Lechmere and by their exchange of opinions upon it. Toward two o'clock Mrs. Coyle became so nervous about their persecuted young friend, and so possessed by the fear that that wicked girl had availed herself of his invitation to put him to an abominable test, that she begged her husband to go and look into the matter as whatever cost to his own tranquillity. But Spencer, perversely, had ended, as the perfect stillness of the night settled upon them, by charming himself into a pale acceptance of Owen's readiness to face God knew what unholy strain—an exposure the more trying to excited sensibilities as the poor boy had now learned by the ordeal of the previous night how resolute an effort he should have to make. "I hope he *is* there," he said to his wife: "it puts them all so hideously in the wrong!" At any rate he couldn't take on himself to explore a house he knew so little. He was inconsequent—he didn't prepare for bed. He sat in the dressing-room with his light and his novel—he waited to find himself nod. At last however Mrs. Coyle turned over and ceased to talk, and at last too he fell asleep in his chair. How long he slept he only knew afterwards by computation; what he knew to begin with was that he had started up in confusion and under the shock of an appalling sound. His consciousness cleared itself fast, helped doubtless by a confirmatory cry of horror from his wife's room. But he gave no heed to his wife; he had already bounded into the passage. There the sound was repeated—it was the "Help! help!" of a woman in agonised terror. It came from a distant quarter of the house, but the quarter was sufficiently indicated. He rushed straight before him, the sound of opening doors and alarmed voices in his ears and the faintness of the early dawn in his eyes. At a turn of one of the passages he came upon the white figure of a girl in a swoon on a bench, and in the vividness of the revelation he read as he went that Kate Julian, stricken in her pride too late with a chill of compunction for what she had mockingly done, had, after coming to release the victim of her derision, reeled away, overwhelmed, from the catastrophe that was her work—the catastrophe that the next moment he found himself aghast at on the threshold of an open door. Owen Wingrave, dressed as he had last seen him, lay dead on the spot on which his ancestor had been found. He was all the young soldier on the gained field.

Questions for Study

1. *What turns Owen Wingrave against the military life?*
2. *What causes his death?*
3. *What ultimate victory does he achieve?*
4. *What is the role of Spencer Coyle? What makes him appropriate for this role?*
5. *What disturbs Jane Wingrave about Owen's decision, other than the fact that he is deserting the family tradition?*
6. *What is ironic about Coyle asking Lechmere to "save" Owen?*
7. *To what extent is Kate Julian responsible for Owen's death?*
8. *Why is the room Owen dies in a fitting place for his end?*

Topics for Discussion and Writing

1. *Discuss the main irony that, although Owen renounces a military career, he lives and dies like a soldier.*
2. *Discuss Owen's conflicts and show how they lead to his tragic death. In this connection consider two opposing views of the ending. George Bernard Shaw accused James of allowing a ghost to kill off Owen against all common sense. James replied, "We would have howled at a surviving Owen Wingrave who would have embodied for us a failure . . . and an ineptitude."*
3. *Discuss how the characterization of Owen makes the story more than a ghost story.*
4. *Contrast Owen and Lechmere and indicate the purpose of this contrast.*
5. *Discuss Owen's relationship with one of the flat characters in the story such as Spencer Coyle, Jane Wingrave, or Kate Julian.*

ALEXANDER SOLZHENITSYN

Matryona's House

A hundred and eighty-four kilometers from Moscow trains were still slowing down to a crawl a good six months after it happened. Passengers stood glued to the windows or went out to stand by the doors. Was the line under repair, or what? Would the train be late?

It was all right. Past the crossing the train picked up speed again and the passengers went back to their seats.

Only the engine-drivers knew what it was all about.

The engine-drivers and I.

In the summer of 1956 I was coming back from the hot and dusty desert, just following my nose—so long as it led me back to Russia. Nobody waited or wanted me at any particular place, because I was a little matter of ten years overdue. I just wanted to get to the central belt, away from the great heats, close to the leafy muttering of forests. I wanted to efface myself, to lose myself in deepest Russia . . . if it was still anywhere to be found.

A year earlier I should have been lucky to get a job carrying a hod this side of the Urals. They wouldn't have taken me as an electrician on a decent construction job. And I had an itch to teach. Those who knew told me that it was a waste of money buying a ticket, that I should have a journey for nothing.

But things were beginning to move. When I went up the stairs of the N—— Oblast Education Department and asked for the Personnel Section, I was surprised to find Personnel sitting behind a glass partition, like in a chemist's shop, instead of the usual black leather-padded door. I went timidly up to the window, bowed, and asked, "Please, do you need any mathematicians somewhere where the trains don't run? I should like to settle there for good."

They passed every dot and comma in my documents through a fine comb, went from one room to another, made telephone calls. It was something out of the ordinary for them too—people always wanted the towns, the bigger the better. And lo and behold, they found just the place for me—Vysokoe Polye. The very sound of it gladdened my heart.

Vysokoe Polye did not belie its name. It stood on rising ground, with gentle hollows and other little hills around it. It was enclosed by an unbroken ring of forest. There was a pool behind a weir. Just the place where I wouldn't mind living and dying. I spent a long time sitting on a stump in a coppice and wishing with all my heart that I didn't need breakfast and dinner every day but could just stay here and listen to the branches brushing against the roof in the night, with not a wireless anywhere to be heard and the whole world silent.

Alas, nobody baked bread in Vysokoe Polye. There was nothing edible on sale. The whole village lugged its victuals in sacks from the big town.

I went back to Personnel Section and raised my voice in prayer at the little window. At first they wouldn't even talk to me. But then they started going from one room to another, made a telephone call, scratched with their pens, and stamped on my orders the word *"Torfoprodukt."*

Torfoprodukt? Turgenev never knew that you can put words like that together in Russian.

On the station building at Torfoprodukt, an antiquated temporary hut of gray wood, hung a stern notice, BOARD TRAINS ONLY FROM THE PASSENGERS' HALL. A further message had been scratched on the boards with a nail, *And Without Tickets.* And by the booking-office, with the same melancholy wit, somebody had carved for all time the words, *No Tickets.* It was only later that I fully appreciated the meaning of these addenda. Getting to Torfoprodukt was easy. But not getting away.

Here too, deep and trackless forests had once stood, and were still standing after the Revolution. Then they were chopped down by the peatcutters and the neighboring kolkhoz. Its chairman, Shashkov, had razed quite a few hectares of timber and sold it at a good profit down in Odessa oblast.

The workers' settlement sprawled untidily among the peat bogs—monotonous shacks from the 'thirties, and little houses with carved façades and glass verandas, put up in the 'fifties. But inside these houses I could see no partitions reaching up to the ceilings, so there was no hope of renting a room with four real walls.

Over the settlement hung smoke from the factory chimney. Little locomotives ran this way and that along narrow-gauge railway lines, giving out more thick smoke and piercing whistles, pulling loads of dirty brown peat in slabs and briquettes. I could safely assume that in the evening a loudspeaker would be crying its heart out over the door of the club and there would be drunks roaming the streets and, sooner or later, sticking knives in each other.

This was what my dream about a quiet corner of Russia had brought me to . . . when I could have stayed where I was and lived in an adobe hut looking out on the desert, with a fresh breeze at night and only the starry dome of the sky overhead.

I couldn't sleep on the station bench, and as soon as it started getting light I went for another stroll around the settlement. This time I saw the tiny market-place. Only one woman stood there at that early hour, selling milk, and I took a bottle and started drinking it on the spot.

I was struck by the way she talked. Instead of a normal speaking voice she used an ingratiating singsong, and her words were the ones I was longing to hear when I left Asia for this place.

"Drink, and God bless you. You must be a stranger round here?"

"And where are you from?" I asked, feeling more cheerful.

I learned that the peat workings weren't the only thing, that over the railway lines there was a hill, and over the hill a village, that this village was Talnovo, and it had been there ages ago, when the "gypsy woman" lived in the big house and the wild woods stood all round. And farther on there was a whole countryside full of villages—Chaslitsy, Ovintsy, Spudni, Shevertni, Shestimirovo, deeper and deeper into the woods, farther and farther from the railway, up towards the lakes.

The names were like a soothing breeze to me. They held a promise of backwoods Russia. I asked my new acquaintance to take me to Talnovo after the market was over, and find a house for me to lodge in.

It appeared that I was a lodger worth having: in addition to my rent, the school offered a lorry-load of peat for the winter to whoever took me. The woman's ingratiating smile gave way to a thoughtful frown. She had no room herself, because she and her husband were "keeping" her aged mother, so she took me first to one lot of relatives, then to another. But there wasn't a separate room to be had and both places were crowded and noisy.

We had come to a dammed-up stream that was short of water and had a little bridge over it. No other place in all the village took my fancy as this did: there were two or three willows, a lop-sided house, ducks swimming on the pond, geese shaking themselves as they stepped out of the water.

"Well, perhaps we might just call on Matryona," said my guide, who was getting tired of me by now. "Only it isn't so neat and cozylike in her house, neglects things she does. She's unwell."

Matryona's house stood quite nearby. Its row of four windows looked out on the cold backs, the two slopes of the roof were covered with shingles, and a little attic window was decorated in the old Russian style. But the shingles were rotting, the beam-ends of the house and the once mighty gates had turned gray with age, and there were gaps in the little shelter over the gate.

The small door let into the gate was fastened, but instead of knocking my companion just put her hand under and turned the catch, a simple device to prevent animals from straying. The yard was not covered, but there was a lot under the roof of the house. As you went through the outer door a short flight of steps rose to a roomy landing, which was open to the roof high overhead. To the left, other steps led up to the top room, which was a separate structure with no stove, and yet another flight down to the basement. To the right lay the house proper, with its attic and its cellar.

It had been built a long time ago, built sturdily, to house a big family, and now one lonely woman of nearly sixty lived in it.

When I went into the cottage she was lying on the Russian stove under a heap of those indeterminate dingy rags which are so precious to a working man or woman.

The spacious room, and especially the best part near the windows, was full of rubber-plants in pots and tubs standing on stools and benches. They peopled the householder's loneliness like a speechless but living crowd. They had been allowed to run wild, and they took up all the scanty light on the north side. In what was left of the light, and half-hidden by the stove-pipe, the mistress of the house looked yellow and weak. You could see from her clouded eyes that illness had drained all the strength out of her.

While we talked she lay on the stove face downwards, without a pillow, her head towards the door, and I stood looking up at her. She showed no pleasure at getting a lodger, just complained about the wicked disease she had. She was just getting over an attack; it didn't come upon her every month; but when it did, "It hangs on two or three days so as I shan't manage to get up and wait on you. I've room and to spare, you can live here if you like."

Then she went over the list of other housewives with whom I should be quieter and cozier, and wanted me to make the round of them. But I had already seen that I was destined to settle in this dimly lit house with the tarnished mirror in which you couldn't see yourself, and the two garish posters (one advertising books, the other about the harvest), bought for a ruble each to brighten up the walls.

Matryona Vasilyevna made me go off round the village again, and when I called on her the second time she kept trying to put me off. "We're not clever, we can't cook, I don't know how we shall suit. . . ." But this time she was on her feet when I got there, and I thought I saw a glimmer of pleasure in her eyes to see me back. We reached agreement about the rent and the load of peat which the school would deliver.

Later on I found out that, year in year out, it was a long time since Matryona Vasilyevna had earned a single ruble. She didn't get a pension. Her relatives gave her very little help. In the kolkhoz she had worked not for money but for credits, the marks recording her labor days in her well-thumbed workbook.

So I moved in with Matryona Vasilyevna. We didn't divide the room. Her bed was in the corner between the door and the stove, and I unfolded my camp-bed by one window and pushed Matryona's beloved rubber-plants out of the light to make room for a little table by another. The village had electric light, laid on back in the 'twenties, from Shatury. The newspapers were writing about "Ilyich's little lamps," but the peasants talked wide-eyed about "Tsar Fire."

Some of the better-off people in the village might not have thought Matryona's house much of a home, but it kept us snug enough that autumn and winter. The roof still held the rain out, and the freezing winds could not blow the warmth of the stove away all at once, though it was cold by morning, especially when the wind blew on the shabby side.

In addition to Matryona and myself, a cat, some mice, and some cockroaches lived in the house.

The cat was no longer young, and gammy-legged as well. Matryona had taken her in out of pity, and she had stayed. She walked on all four feet but with a heavy limp: one of her feet was sore and she favored it. When she jumped from the stove she didn't land with the soft sound a cat usually makes, but with a heavy thud as three of her feet struck the floor at once—such a heavy thud that until I got used to it, it gave me a start. This was because she stuck three feet out together to save the fourth.

It wasn't because the cat couldn't deal with them that there were mice in the cottage: she would pounce into the corner like lightning, and come back with a mouse between her teeth. But the mice were usually out of reach because somebody, back in the good old days, had stuck embossed wallpaper of a greenish color on Matryona's walls, and not just one layer of it but five. The layers held together all right, but in many places the whole lot had come away from the wall, giving the room a sort of inner skin. Between the timber of the walls and the skin of wallpaper the mice had made themselves runs where they impudently scampered about, running at times right up to the ceiling. The cat followed their scamperings with angry eyes, but couldn't get at them.

Sometimes the cat ate cockroaches as well, but they made her sick. The only thing the cockroaches respected was the partition which screened the mouth of the Russian stove and the kitchen from the best part of the room.

They did not creep into the best room. But the kitchen at night swarmed with them, and if I went in late in the evening for a drink of water and switched on the light the whole floor, the big bench, and even the wall would be one rustling brown mass. From time to time I brought home some borax from the school laboratory and we mixed it with dough to poison them. There would be fewer cockroaches for a while, but Matryona was afraid that we might poison the cat as well. We stopped putting down poison and the cockroaches multiplied anew.

At night, when Matryona was already asleep and I was working at my table, the occasional rapid scamper of mice behind the wallpaper would be drowned in the sustained and ceaseless rustling of cockroaches behind the screen, like the sound of the sea in the distance. But I got used to it because there was nothing evil in it; nothing dishonest. Rustling was life to them.

I even got used to the crude beauty on the poster, forever reaching out from the wall to offer me Belinsky, Panferov, and a pile of other books—but never saying a word. I got used to everything in Matryona's cottage.

Matryona got up at four or five in the morning. Her wall-clock was twenty-seven years old, and had been bought in the village shop. It was always fast, but Matryona didn't worry about that—just so long as it didn't lose and make her late in the morning. She switched on the light behind the kitchen screen and moving quietly, considerately, doing her best not to make a noise, she lit the stove, went to milk the goat (all the livestock she had was this one dirty-white goat with twisted horns), fetched water and boiled it in three iron pots; one for me, one for herself, and one for the goat. She fetched potatoes from the cellar, picking out the littlest for the goat, little ones for herself and egg-sized ones for me. There were no big ones, because her garden was sandy, had not been manured since the war and was always planted with potatoes, potatoes, and potatoes again, so that it wouldn't grow big ones.

I scarcely heard her about her morning tasks. I slept late, woke up in the wintry daylight, stretched a bit and stuck my head out from under my blanket and my sheep-skin. These, together with the prisoner's jerkin round my legs and a sack stuffed with straw underneath me, kept me warm in bed even on nights when the cold wind rattled our wobbly windows from the north. When I heard the discreet noises on the other side of the screen I spoke to her, slowly and deliberately.

"Good morning, Matryona Vasilyevna!"

And every time the same good-natured words came to me from behind the screen. They began with a warm, throaty gurgle, the sort of sound grandmothers make in fairy-tales.

"M-m-m . . . same to you too!"

And after a little while, "Your breakfast's ready for you now."

She didn't announce what was for breakfast, but it was easy to guess: taters in their jackets or tatty soup (as everybody in the village called it), or barley gruel (no other grain could be bought in Torfoprodukt that year, and even the barley you had to fight for, because it was the cheapest and people bought it up by the sack to fatten their pigs on it). It wasn't always salted as it should be, it was often slightly burnt, it furred the palate and the gums, and it gave me heartburn.

But Matryona wasn't to blame: there was no butter in Torfoprodukt either, margarine was desperately short, and only mixed cooking fat was plentiful, and when I got to know it I saw that the Russian stove was not convenient for cooking: the cook cannot see the pots and they are not heated evenly all round. I suppose the stove came down to our ancestors from the Stone Age because you can stoke it up once before daylight, and food and water, mash and swill, will keep warm in it all day long. And it keeps you warm while you sleep.

I ate everything that was cooked for me without demur, patiently putting aside anything uncalled-for that I came across: a hair, a bit of peat, a cockroach's leg. I hadn't the heart to find fault with Matryona. After all, she had warned me herself.

"We aren't clever, we can't cook—I don't know how we shall suit. . . ."

"Thank you," I said quite sincerely.

"What for? For what is your own?" she answered, disarming me with a radiant smile. And, with a guileless look of her faded blue eyes, she would ask, "And what shall I cook you for just now?"

For just now meant for supper. I ate twice a day, like at the front. What could I order for just now? It would have to be one of the same old things, taters or tatty soup.

I resigned myself to it, because I had learned by now not to look for the meaning of life in food. More important to me was the smile of her roundish face, which I tried in vain to catch when at last I had earned enough to buy a camera. As soon as she saw the cold eye of the lens upon her Matryona assumed a strained or else an exaggeratedly severe expression.

Just once I did manage to get a snap of her looking through the window into the street and smiling at something.

Matryona had a lot of worries that winter. Her neighbors put it into her head to try and get a pension. She was all alone in the world, and when she began to be seriously ill she had been dismissed from the kolkhoz as well. Injustices had piled up, one on top of another. She was ill, but not regarded as a disabled person. She had worked for a quarter of a century in the kolkhoz, but it was a kolkhoz and not a factory, so she was not entitled to a pension for herself. She could only try and get one for her husband, for the loss of her bread-winner. But she had had no husband for twelve years now, not since the beginning of the war, and it wasn't easy to obtain all the particulars from different places about his length of service and how much he had earned. What a bother it was getting those forms through! Getting somebody to certify that he'd earned say, 300 rubles a month; that she lived alone and nobody helped her; what year she was born in. Then all this had to be taken to the pensions office. And taken somewhere else to get all the mistakes corrected. And taken back again. Then you had to find out whether they would give you a pension.

To make it all more difficult the Pensions Office was twenty kilometers east of Talnovo, the Rural Council Offices ten kilometers to the west, the Factory District Council an hour's walk to the north. They made her run around from office to office for two months on end, to get an *i* dotted or a *t* crossed. Every trip took a day. She goes down to the rural district council—and the secretary isn't there today. Secretaries of rural councils often aren't here today. So come in tomorrow. Tomorrow the secretary is in, but he hasn't got his rubber stamp. So come again the next day. And the day after that back she goes yet again, because all her papers are pinned together and some cock-eyed clerk has signed the wrong one.

"They shove me around, Ignatich," she used to complain to me after these fruitless excursions. "Worn out with it I am."

But she soon brightened up. I found that she had a sure means of putting herself in a good humor. She worked. She would grab a shovel and go off to lift potatoes. Or she would tuck a sack under her arm and go after peat. Or take a wicker basket and look for berries deep in the woods. When she's been bending her back to bushes instead of office desks for a while, and her shoulders were aching from a heavy load, Matryona would come back cheerful, at peace with the world and smiling her nice smile.

"I'm on to a good thing now, Ignatich. I know where to go for it" (peat she meant), "a lovely place it is."

"But surely my peat is enough, Matryona Vasilyevna? There's a whole lorry-load of it."

"Pooh! Your peat! As much again, and then as much again, that might be enough. When the winter gets really stiff and the wind's battling at the windows, it blows the heat out of the house faster than you can make the stove up. Last year we got heaps and heaps of it. I'd have had three loads in by now. But they're out to catch us. They've summoned one woman from our village already."

That's how it was. The frightening breath of winter was already in the air. There were forests all round, and no fuel to be had anywhere. Excavators roared away in the bogs, but there was no peat on sale to the villagers. It was delivered, free, to the bosses and to the people round the bosses, and teachers, doctors, and workers got a load each. The people of Talnovo were not supposed to get any peat, and they weren't supposed to ask about it. The chairman of the kolkhoz walked about the village looking people in the eye while he gave his orders or stood chatting, and talked about anything you liked except fuel. He was stocked-up. Who said anything about winter coming?

So just as in the old days they used to steal the squire's wood, now they pinched peat from the trust. The women went in parties of five or ten so that they would be less frightened. They went in the daytime. The peat cut during the summer had been stacked up all over the place to dry. That's the good thing about peat, it can't be carted off as soon as it's cut. It lies around drying till autumn, or, if the roads are bad, till the snow starts falling. This was when the women used to come and take it. They could get six peats in a sack if it was damp, or ten if it was dry. A sackful weighed about two poods and it sometimes had to be carried over three kilometers. This was enough to make the stove up once. There were two hundred days in the winter. The

Russian stove had to be lit in the mornings, and the "Dutch" stove in the evenings.

"Why beat about the bush?" said Matryona angrily to someone invisible. "Since there've been no more horses, what you can't heave around yourself you haven't got. My back never heals up. Winter you're pulling sledges, summer it's bundles on your back, it's God's truth I'm telling you."

The women went more than once in a day. On good days Matryona brought six sacks home. She piled my peat up where it could be seen, and hid her own under the passageway, boarding up the hole every night.

"If they don't just happen to think of it, the devils will never find it in their born days," said Matryona smiling and wiping the sweat from her brow.

What could the peat trust do? Its establishment didn't run to a watchman for every bog. I suppose they had to show a rich haul in their returns, and then write off so much for crumbling, so much washed away by the rain. . . . Sometimes they would take it into their heads to put out patrols and try to catch the women as they came into the village. The women would drop their sacks and scatter. Or somebody would inform and there would be a house-to-house search. They would draw up a report on the stolen peat, and threaten a court action. The women would stop fetching it for a while, but the approach of winter drove them out with sledges in the middle of the night.

When I had seen a little more of Matryona I noticed that apart from cooking and looking after the house, she had quite a lot of other jobs to do every day. She kept all her jobs, and the proper times for them, in her head and always knew when she woke up in the morning how her day would be occupied. Apart from fetching peat, and stumps which the tractors unearthed in the bogs, apart from the cranberries which she put to soak in big jars for the winter ("Give your teeth an edge, Ignatich," she used to say when she offered me some), apart from digging potatoes and all the coming and going to do with her pension, she had to get hay from somewhere for her one and only dirty-white goat.

"Why don't you keep a cow, Matryona?"

Matryona stood there in her grubby apron, by the opening in the kitchen screen, facing my table, and explained to me.

"Oh, Ignatich, there's enough milk from the goat for me. And if I started keeping a cow she'd eat me out of house and home in no time. You can't cut the grass by the railway track, because it belongs to the railway, and you can't cut any in the woods, because it belongs to the foresters, and they won't let me have any at the kolkhoz because I'm not a member any more, they reckon. And those who are members have to work there every day till the white flies swarm, and make their own hay when there's snow on the ground—what's the good of grass like that? In the old days they used to be sweating to get the hay in at midsummer, between the end of June and the end of July, while the grass was sweet and juicy. . . ."

So it meant a lot of work for Matryona to gather enough hay for one skinny little goat. She took her sickle and a sack and went off early in the morning to places where she knew there was grass growing—round the edges of fields, on the roadside, on hummocks in the bog. When she had stuffed her sack with heavy fresh grass she dragged it home and spread it out in her yard to dry. From a sackful of grass she got one forkload of dry hay.

The farm had a new chairman, sent down from the town not long ago, and the first thing he did was to cut down the garden-plots for those who were not fit to work. He left Matryona fifteen hundredths of sand—when there were ten hundredths just lying idle on the other side of the fence. Yet when they were short of working hands, when the women dug in their heels and wouldn't budge, the chairman's wife would come to see Matryona. She was from the town as well, a determined woman whose short gray overcoat and intimidating glare gave her a somewhat military appearance. She walked into the house without so much as a good morning and looked sternly at Matryona. Matryona was uneasy.

"Well now, Comrade Vasilyevna," said the chairman's wife, drawing out her words. "You will have to help the kolkhoz! You will have to go and help cart muck out tomorrow!"

A little smile of forgiveness wrinkled Matryona's face—as though she understood the embarrassment which the chairman's wife must feel not being able to pay her for her work.

"Well—er," she droned, "I'm not well, of course, and I'm not attached to you any more. . . ." Then she hurried to correct herself. "What time should I come, then?"

"And bring your own fork!" the chairman's wife instructed her. Her stiff skirt crackled as she walked away.

"Think of that!" grumbled Matryona as the door closed. "Bring your own fork! They've got neither forks nor shovels on the kolkhoz. And I don't have a man who'll put a handle on for me!"

She went on thinking about it out loud all evening.

"What's the good of talking, Ignatich. I must help, of course. Only the way they work it's all a waste of time—don't know whether they're coming or going. The women stand propped up on their shovels and waiting for the factory hooter to blow twelve o'clock. Or else they get on to adding up who's earned what and who's turned up for work and who hasn't. Now what I call work, there isn't a sound out of anybody, only . . . oh dear, dear, dinner time's soon rolled round—what, getting dark already. . . ."

In the morning she went off with her fork.

But it wasn't just the kolkhoz—any distant relative, or just a neighbor, could come to Matryona of an evening and say, "Come and give me a hand tomorrow, Matryona. We'll finish lifting the potatoes."

Matryona couldn't say no. She gave up what she should be doing next and went to help her neighbor, and when she came back she would say without a trace of envy, "Ah, you should see the size of her potatoes, Ignatich! It was a joy to dig them up. I didn't want to leave the allotment, God's truth I didn't."

Needless to say, not a garden could be plowed without Matryona's help. The women of Talnovo had got it neatly worked out that it was a longer and harder job for one woman to dig her garden with a spade than for six of them to put themselves in harness and plow six gardens. So they sent for Matryona to help them.

"Well—did you pay her?" I asked sometimes.

"She won't take money. You have to try and hide it on her when she's not looking."

Matryona had yet another troublesome chore when her turn came to feed the herdsmen. One of them was a hefty deaf mute, the other a boy who was never without a cigarette in his drooling mouth. Matryona's turn only came round every six weeks, but it put her to great expense. She went to the shop to buy tinned fish, and was lavish with sugar and butter, things she never ate herself. It seems that the housewives showed off in this way, trying to outdo each other in feeding the herdsmen.

"You've got to be careful with tailors and herdsmen," Matryona explained. "They'll spread your name all round the village if something doesn't suit them."

And every now and then attacks of serious illness broke in on this life that was already crammed with troubles. Matryona would be off her feet for a day or two, lying flat out on the stove. She didn't complain, and didn't groan, but she hardly stirred either. On these days, Masha, Matryona's closest friend from her earliest years, would come to look after the goat and light the stove. Matryona herself ate nothing, drank nothing, asked for nothing. To call in the doctor from the clinic at the settlement would have seemed strange in Talnovo, and would have given the neighbors something to talk about—what does she think she is, a lady? They did call her in once, and she arrived in a real temper and told Matryona to come down to the clinic when she was on her feet again. Matryona went, although she didn't really want to; they took specimens and sent them off to the district hospital—and that's the last anybody heard about it. Matryona was partly to blame herself.

But there was work waiting to be done, and Matryona soon started getting up again, moving slowly at first and then as briskly as ever.

"You never saw me in the old days, Ignatich. I'd lift any sack you liked, I didn't think five poods was too heavy. My father-in-law used to say, 'Matryona, you'll break your back.' And my brother-in-law didn't have to come and help me lift on the cart. Our horse was a war-horse, a big strong one. . . ."

"What do you mean, a war-horse?"

"They took ours for the war and gave us this one instead—he'd been wounded. But he turned out a bit spirited. Once he bolted with the sledge right into the lake, the men-folk hopped out of the way, but I grabbed the bridle, as true as I'm here, and stopped him. . . . Full of oats that horse was. They liked to feed their horses well in our village. If a horse feels his oats he doesn't know what heavy means."

But Matryona was a long way from being fearless. She was afraid of fire, afraid of "the lightning," and most of all she was for some reason afraid of trains.

"When I had to go to Cherusti the train came up from Nechaevka way with its great big eyes popping out and the rails humming away—put me in a proper fever. My knees started knocking. God's truth I'm telling you!" Matryona raised her shoulders as though she surprised herself.

"Maybe it's because they won't give people tickets, Matryona Vasilyevna?"

"At the window? They try to shove first-class tickets on to you. And the train was starting to move. We dashed about all over the place. 'Give us tickets, for pity's sake.'

"The men-folk had climbed on top of the carriages. Then we found a door that wasn't locked and shoved straight in without tickets . . . and all the carriages were empty, they were all empty, you could stretch out on the seat if you wanted to. Why they wouldn't give us tickets, the hard-hearted parasites, I don't know. . . ."

Still, before winter came Matryona's affairs were in a better state than ever before. They started paying her at last a pension of eighty rubles. Besides this she got just over a hundred from the school and me.

Some of her neighbors began to be envious.

"Hm! Matryona can live forever now! If she had any more money she wouldn't know what to do with it at her age."

Matryona had herself some new felt boots made. She bought a new jerkin. And she had an overcoat made out of the worn-out railway-man's greatcoat given to her by the engine-driver from Cherusti who had married Kira, her foster-daughter. The humped-backed village tailor put a padded lining under the cloth and it made a marvelous coat, such as Matryona had never worn before in all her sixty years.

In the middle of winter Matryona sewed two hundred rubles into the lining of this coat for her funeral. This made her quite cheerful.

"Now my mind's a bit easier, Ignatich."

December went by, January went by—and in those two months Matryona's illness held off. She started going over to Masha's house more often in the evening, to sit chewing sunflower seeds with her. She didn't invite guests herself in the evening out of consideration for my work. Once, on the feast of the Epiphany, I came back from school and found a party going on and was introduced to Matryona's three sisters, who called her "nan-nan" or "nanny" because she was the oldest. Until then not much had been heard of the sisters in our cottage—perhaps they were afraid that Matryona might ask them for help.

But one ominous event cast a shadow on the holiday for Matryona. She went to the church five versts away for the blessing of the water, and put her pot down among the others. When the blessing was over the women went rushing and jostling to get their pots back again. There were a lot of women in front of Matryona and when she got there her pot was missing, and no other vessel had been left behind. The pot had vanished as though the devil had run off with it.

Matryona went around the worshipers asking them, "Has any of you girls accidentally mistook somebody else's holy water? In a pot?"

Nobody owned up. There had been some boys there, and boys got up to mischief sometimes. Matryona came home sad.

No one could say that Matryona was a devout believer. If anything, she was a heathen, and her strongest beliefs were superstitious. You mustn't go into the garden on the fast of St. John or there would be no harvest next year. A blizzard meant that somebody had hanged himself. If you pinched your foot in the door you could expect a guest. All the time I lived with her I didn't once see her say her prayers or even cross herself. But, whatever job she was doing, she began with a "God bless us," and she never failed to say "God bless you," when I set out for school. Perhaps she did say her prayers, but on the quiet, either because she was shy or because she didn't want to embarrass me. There were icons on the walls. Ordinary days they were left in darkness, but for the vigil of a great feast, or on the morning of a holiday, Matryona would light the little lamp.

She had fewer sins on her conscience than her gammy-legged cat. The cat did kill mice. . . .

Now that her life was running more smoothly, Matryona started listening more carefully to my radio. (I had, of course, installed a speaker, or as Matryona called it, a peeker.)

When they announced on the radio that some new machine had been invented, I heard Matryona grumbling out in the kitchen, "New ones all the time, nothing but new ones. People don't want to work with the old ones any more, where are we going to store them all?"

There was a program about the seeding of clouds from airplanes. Matryona, listening up on the stove, shook her head, "Oh dear, dear, dear, they'll do away with one of the two—summer or winter."

Once Chaliapin was singing Russian folk songs. Matryona stood listening for a long time before she gave her emphatic verdict, "Queer singing, not our sort of singing."

"You can't mean that, Matryona Vasilyevna . . . just listen to him."

She listened a bit longer, and pursed her lips. "No, it's wrong. It isn't our sort of tune, and he's tricky with his voice."

She made up for this another time. They were broadcasting some of Glinka's songs. After half a dozen of these drawing-room ballads, Matryona suddenly came from behind the screen clutching her apron, with a flush on her face and a film of tears over her dim eyes. "That's our sort of singing," she said in a whisper.

So Matryona and I got used to each other and took each other for granted. She never pestered me with questions about myself. I don't know whether she was lacking in normal female curiosity or just tactful, but she never once asked if I had been married. All the Talnovo women kept at her to find out about me. Her answer was, "You want to know—you ask him. All I know is he's from distant parts."

And when I got round to telling her that I had spent a lot of time in prison she said nothing but just nodded, as though she had already suspected it.

And I thought of Matryona only as the helpless old woman she was now, and didn't try to rake up her past, didn't even suspect that there was anything to be found there.

I knew that Matryona had got married before the Revolution and come to live in the house I now shared with her, that she had gone "to the stove" immediately. (She had no mother-in-law and no older sister-in-law, so it was her job to put the pots in the oven on the very first morning of her married life.) I knew that she had had six children and that they had all died very young, so that there were never two of them alive at once. Then there was a sort of foster-daughter, Kira. Matryona's husband had not come back from the last war. She received no notification of his death. Men from the village who had served in the same company said that he might have been taken prisoner, or he might have been killed and his body not found. In the eight years that had gone by since the war Matryona had decided that he was not alive. It was a good thing that she thought so. If he was still alive he was probably in Brazil or Australia, and married again. The village of Talnovo, and the Russian language, would be fading from his memory.

One day, when I got back from school, I found a guest in the house. A tall, dark man, with his hat on his lap, was sitting on a chair which Matryona had moved up to the Dutch stove in the middle of the room. His face was completely surrounded by bushy black hair with hardly a trace of gray in it. His thick black mustaches ran into his full black beard, so that his mouth could hardly be seen. Black side-whiskers merged with the black locks which hung down from his crown, leaving only the tips of his ears visible; and broad black eyebrows met in a wide double span. But the front of his head as far as the crown was a spacious bald dome. His whole appearance made an impression of wisdom and dignity. He sat squarely on his chair, with his hands folded on his stick, and his stick resting vertically on the floor, in an attitude of patient expectation, and he obviously hadn't much to say to Matryona, who was busy behind the screen.

When I came in he eased his majestic head round towards me and suddenly addressed me, "Master, I can't see you very well. My son goes to your school. Grigoriev, Antoshka . . ."

There was no need for him to say any more. . . . However strongly inclined I felt to help this worthy old man I knew and dismissed in advance all the pointless things he was going to say. Antoshka Grigoriev was a plump, red-faced lad in 8-D who looked like a cat that's swallowed the cream. He seemed to think that he came to school for a rest and sat at his desk with a lazy smile on his face. Needless to say, he never did his homework. But the worst of it was that he had been put up into the next class from year to year because our district, and indeed the whole oblast and the neighboring oblasts, were famous for the high percentage of passes they obtained, and the school had to make an effort to keep its record up. So Antoshka had got it clear in his mind that however much the teachers threatened him they would put him up in the end, and there was no need for him to learn anything. He just laughed at us. There he sat in the eighth class, and he hadn't even mastered his decimals and didn't know one triangle from another. In the first two terms of the school year I had kept him firmly below the pass line and the same treatment awaited him in the third.

But now this half-blind old man, who should have been Antoshka's grandfather rather than his father, had come to humble himself before me—how could I tell him that the school had been deceiving him for years, and that I couldn't go on deceiving him, because I didn't want to ruin the whole class, to become a liar and a fake, to start despising my work and my profession.

For the time being I patiently explained that his son had been very slack, that he told lies at school and at home, that his mark-book must be checked frequently, and that we must both take him severely in hand.

"Severe as you like, master," he assured me, "I beat him every week now.

And I've got a heavy hand."

While we were talking I remembered that Matryona had once interceded for Antoshka Grigoriev, but I hadn't asked what relation of hers he was and I had refused to do what she wanted. Matryona was standing in the kitchen doorway like a mute suppliant on this occasion too. When Faddei Mironovich left saying that he would call on me to see how things were going, I asked her, "I can't make out what relation this Antoshka is to you, Matryona Vasilyevna."

"My brother-in-law's son," said Matryona shortly, and went out to milk the goat.

When I'd worked it out I realized that this determined old man with the black hair was the brother of the missing husband.

The long evening went by, and Matryona didn't bring up the subject again. But late at night, when I had stopped thinking about the old man and was working in a silence broken only by the rustling of the cockroaches and the heavy tick of the wall-clock, Matryona suddenly spoke from her dark corner, "You know, Ignatich, I nearly married him once."

I had forgotten that Matryona was in the room. I hadn't heard a sound from her—and suddenly her voice came out of the darkness, as agitated as if the old man were still trying to win her.

I could see that Matryona had been thinking about nothing else all evening.

She got up from her wretched rag bed and walked slowly towards me, as though she were following her own words. I sat back in my chair and caught my first glimpse of a quite different Matryona.

There was no overhead light in our big room with its forest of rubber-plants. The table lamp cast a ring of light round my exercise books, and when I tore my eyes away from it the rest of the room seemed to be half-dark and faintly tinged with pink. I thought I could see the same pinkish glow in her usually sallow cheeks.

"He was the first one who came courting me, before Yefim did . . . he was his brother . . . the older one . . . I was nineteen and Faddei was twenty-three. . . . They lived in this very same house. Their house it was. Their father built it."

I looked round the room automatically. Instead of the old gray house rotting under the faded green skin of wallpaper where the mice had their playground, I suddenly saw new timbers, freshly trimmed, and not yet discolored, and caught the cheerful smell of pine-tar.

"Well, and what happened then?"

"That summer we went to sit in the coppice together," she whispered. "There used to be a coppice where the stable-yard is now. They chopped it down. . . . I was just going to marry him, Ignatich. Then the German war started. They took Faddei in the army."

She let fall these few words—and suddenly the blue and white and yellow July of the year 1914 burst into flower before my eyes: the sky still peaceful, the floating clouds, the people sweating to get the ripe corn in. I imagined them side by side, the black-haired Hercules with a scythe over his shoulder, and the red-faced girl clasping a sheaf. And there was singing out under the open sky, such songs as nobody can sing nowadays, with all the machines in the fields.

"He went to the war—and vanished. For three years I kept to myself and waited. Never a sign of life did he give. . . ."

Matryona's round face looked out at me from an elderly threadbare head-scarf. As she stood there in the gentle reflected light from my lamp her face seemed to lose its slovenly workaday covering of wrinkles, and she was a scared young girl again with a frightening decision to make.

Yes. . . . I could see it. . . . The trees shed their leaves, the snow fell and melted. They plowed and sowed and reaped again. Again the trees shed their leaves, and snow fell. There was a revolution. Then another revolution. And the whole world was turned upside down.

"Their mother died and Yefim came to court me. You wanted to come to our house, he says, so come. He was a year younger than me, Yefim was. It's a saying with us—sensible girls get married after Michaelmas, and silly ones at midsummer. They were short-handed. I got married. . . . The wedding was on St. Peter's day, and then about St. Nicholas' day in the winter he came back . . . Faddei, I mean, from being a prisoner in Hungary."

Matryona covered her eyes.

I said nothing.

She turned towards the door as though somebody were standing there. "He stood there at the door. What a scream I let out! I wanted to throw myself at his feet! . . . But I couldn't. If it wasn't my own brother, he says, I'd take my axe to the both of you."

I shuddered. Matryona's despair, or her terror, conjured up a vivid picture of him standing in the dark doorway and raising his axe to her.

But she quieted down and went on with her story in a singsong voice, leaning on a chairback, "Oh dear, dear me, the poor dear man! There were so many girls in the village—but he wouldn't marry. I'll look for one with the same name as you, a second Matryona, he said. And that's what he did—fetched himself a Matryona from Lipovka. They built themselves a house of their own and they're still living in it. You pass their place every day on your way to school."

So that was it. I realized that I had seen the other Matryona quite often. I didn't like her. She was always coming to my Matryona to complain about her husband—he beat her, he was stingy, he was working her to death. She would weep and weep, and her voice always had a tearful note in it. As it turned out, my Matryona had nothing to regret, with Faddei beating his Matryona every day of his life and being so tight-fisted.

"Mine never beat me once," said Matryona of Yefim. "He'd pitch into another man in the street, but me he never hit once. . . . Well, there was one time . . . I quarreled with my sister-in-law and he cracked me on the forehead with a spoon. I jumped up from the table and shouted at them, 'Hope it sticks in your gullets, you idle lot of beggars, hope you choke!' I said. And off I went into the woods. He never touched me any more."

Faddei didn't seem to have any cause for regret either. The other Matryona had borne him six children (my Antoshka was one of them, the littlest, the runt) and they had all lived, whereas the children of Matryona and Yefim had died, everyone of them, before they reached the age of three months, without any illness.

"One daughter, Elena, was born and was alive when they washed her, and then she died right after. . . . My wedding was on St. Peter's day, and it was St. Peter's day I buried my sixth, Alexander.

The whole village decided that there was a curse on Matryona.

Matryona still nodded emphatic belief when she talked about it. "There was a *course* on me. They took me to a woman as used to be a nun to get cured, she set me off coughing and waited for the *course* to jump out of me like a frog. Only nothing jumped out. . . ."

And the years had run by like running water. . . . In 1941 they didn't take Faddei into the army because of his poor sight, but they took Yefim. And what had happened to the elder brother in the first war happened to the younger in the second . . . he vanished without trace. Only he never came back at all. The once noisy cottage was deserted, it became old and rotten, and Matryona, all alone in the world, grew old in it.

So she begged from the other Matryona, the cruelly beaten Matryona, a child of her womb (or was it a spot of Faddei's blood?), the youngest daughter, Kira.

For ten years she brought the girl up in her own house, in place of the children who had not lived. Then, not long before I arrived, she had married her off to a young engine-driver from Cherusti. The only help she got from anywhere came in dribs and drabs from Cherusti: a bit of sugar from time to time, or some of the fat when they killed a pig.

Sick and suffering, and feeling that death was not far off, Matryona had made known her will: the top room, which was a separate frame joined by tie-beams to the rest of the house, should go to Kira when she died. She said nothing about the house itself. Her three sisters had their eyes on it too.

That evening Matryona opened her heart to me. And, as often happens, no sooner were the hidden springs of her life revealed to me than I saw them in motion.

Kira arrived from Cherusti. Old Faddei was very worried. To get and keep a plot of land in Cherusti the young couple had to put up some sort of building. Matryona's top room would do very well. There was nothing else they could put up, because there was no timber to be had anywhere. It wasn't Kira herself so much, and it wasn't her husband, but old Faddei who was consumed with eagerness for them to get their hands on the plot at Cherusti.

He became a frequent visitor, laying down the law to Matryona and insisting that she should hand over the top room right away, before she died. On these occasions I saw a different Faddei. He was no longer an old man propped up by a stick, whom a push or a harsh word would bowl over. Although he was slightly bent by backache, he was still a fine figure; he had kept the vigorous black hair of a young man in his sixties; he was hot and urgent.

Matryona had not slept for two nights. It wasn't easy for her to make up her mind. She didn't grudge them the top room, which was standing there idle, any more than she ever grudged her labor or her belongings. And the top room was willed to Kira in any case. But the thought of breaking up the roof she had lived under for forty years was torture to her. Even I, a mere lodger, found it painful to think of them stripping away boards and wrenching out beams. For Matryona it was the end of everything.

But the people who were so insistent knew that she would let them break up her house before she died.

So Faddei and his sons and sons-in-law came along one February morning, the blows of five axes were heard and boards creaked and cracked as they were wrenched out. Faddei's eyes twinkled busily. Although his back wasn't quite straight yet he scrambled nimbly up under the rafters and bustled about down below, shouting at his assistants. He and his father had built this house when he was a lad, a long time ago. The top room had been put up for him, the oldest son, to move in with his bride. And now he was furiously taking it apart, board by board, to carry it out of somebody else's yard.

After numbering the beam-ends and the ceiling boards they dismantled the top room and the storeroom underneath it. The living room, and what was left of the landing, they boarded up with a thin wall of deal. They did nothing about the cracks in the wall. It was plain to see that they were wreckers, not builders, and that they did not expect Matryona to be living there very long.

While the men were busy wrecking, the women were getting the drink ready for moving day—vodka would cost a lot too much. Kira brought a pood of sugar from Moscow oblast, and Matryona carried the sugar and some bottles to the distiller under cover of night.

The timbers were carried out and stacked in front of the gates, and the engine-driver son-in-law went off to Cherusti for the tractor.

But the very same day a blizzard, or "a blower" as Matryona called it, began. It howled and whirled for two days and nights and buried the road under enormous drifts. Then, no sooner had they made the road passable and a couple of lorries gone by, than it got suddenly warmer. Within a day everything was thawing out, damp mist hung in the air and rivulets gurgled as they burrowed into the snow, and you could get stuck up to the top of your knee-boots.

Two weeks passed before the tractor could get at the dismantled top room. All this time Matryona went around like someone lost. What particularly upset her was that her three sisters came and with one voice called her a fool for giving the top room away, said they didn't want to see her anymore, and went off. At about the same time the lame cat strayed and was seen no more. It was just one thing after another. This was another blow to Matryona

At last the frost got a grip on the slushy road. A sunny day came along and everybody felt more cheerful. Matryona had had a lucky dream the night before. In the morning she heard that I wanted to take a photograph of somebody at an old-fashioned hand-loom. (There were looms still standing in two cottages in the village; they wove coarse rugs on them.) She smiled shyly and said, "You just wait a day or two, Ignatich, I'll just send the top room there off and I'll put my loom up, I've still got it, you know, and then you can snap me. Honest to God!"

She was obviously attracted by the idea of posing in an old-fashioned setting. The red, frosty sun tinged the window of the curtailed passageway with a faint pink, and this reflected light warmed Matryona's face. People who are at ease with their consciences always have nice faces.

Coming back from school before dusk I saw some movement near our house. A big new tractor-drawn sledge was already fully loaded, and there was no room for a lot of the timbers, so old Faddei's family and the helpers they had called in had nearly finished knocking together another home-made sledge. They were all working like madmen, in the frenzy that comes upon people when there is a smell of good money in the air or when they are looking forward to some treat. They were shouting at one another and arguing.

They could not agree whether the sledges should be hauled separately or both together. One of Faddei's sons (the lame one) and the engine-driver son-in-law reasoned that the sledges couldn't both be taken at once because the tractor wouldn't be able to pull them. The man in charge of the tractor, a hefty fat-faced fellow who was very sure of himself, said hoarsely that he knew best, he was the driver, and he would take both at once. His motives were obvious: according to the agreement the engine-driver was paying him for the removal of the upper room, not for the number of trips he had to make. He could never have made two trips in a night—twenty-five kilometers each way, and one return journey. And by morning he had to get the tractor back in the garage from which he had sneaked it out for this job on the side.

Old Faddei was impatient to get the top room moved that day, and at a nod from him his lads gave in. To the stout sledge in front they hitched the one which they had knocked together in such a hurry.

Matryona was running about amongst the men, fussing and helping them to heave the beams on to the sledge. Suddenly I noticed that she was wearing my jerkin and had dirtied the sleeves on the frozen mud round the beams. I was annoyed, and told her so. That jerkin held memories for me: it had kept me warm in the bad years.

This was the first time that I was ever angry with Matryona Vasilyevna.

Matryona was taken aback. "Oh dear, dear me," she said. "My poor head. I picked it up in a rush, you see, and never thought about it being yours. I'm sorry, Ignatich."

And she took it off and hung it up to dry.

The loading was finished, and all the men who had been working, about ten of them, clattered past my table and dived under the curtain into the kitchen. I could hear the muffled rattle of glasses and, from time to time, the clink of a bottle, the voices got louder and louder, the boasting more reckless. The biggest braggart was the tractor-driver. The stench of hooch floated in to me. But they didn't go on drinking long. It was getting dark and they had to hurry. They began to leave. The tractor-driver came out first, looking pleased with himself and fierce. The engine-driver son-in-law, Faddei's lame son and one of his nephews were going to Cherusti. The others went off home. Faddei was flourishing his stick, trying to overtake somebody and put him right about something. The lame son paused at my table to light up and suddenly started telling me how he loved Aunt Matryona, and that he had got married not long ago, and his wife had just had a son. Then they shouted for him and he went out. The tractor set up a roar outside.

After all the others had gone Matryona dashed out from behind the screen. She looked after them, anxiously shaking her head. She had put on her jerkin and her head-scarf. As she was going through the door she said to me, "Why ever couldn't they hire two? If one tractor had cracked up the other would have pulled them. What'll happen now, God only knows!"

She ran out after the others.

After the booze-up and the arguments and all the coming and going it was quieter than ever in the deserted cottage, and very chilly because the door had been opened so many times. I got into my jerkin and sat down to mark exercise books. The noise of the tractor died away in the distance.

An hour went by. And another. And a third. Matryona still hadn't come back, but I wasn't surprised. When she had seen the sledge off she must have gone round to her friend Masha.

Another hour went by. And yet another. Darkness and with it a deep silence had descended on the village. I couldn't understand at the time why it was so quiet. Later I found out that it was because all evening not a single train had gone along the line half a verst from the house. No sound was coming from my radio and I noticed that the mice were wilder than ever. Their scampering and scratching and squeaking behind the wallpaper was getting noisier and more defiant all the time.

I woke up. It was one o'clock in the morning and Matryona still hadn't come home.

Suddenly I heard several people talking loudly. They were still a long way off, but something told me that they were coming to our house. And sure enough I heard soon afterwards a heavy knock at the gate. A commanding voice, strange to me, yelled out an order to open up. I went out into the thick darkness with a torch. The whole village was asleep, there was no light in the windows, and the snow had started melting in the last week so that it gave no reflected light. I turned the catch and let them in. Four men in greatcoats went on towards the house. It's a very unpleasant thing to be visited at night by noisy people in greatcoats.

When we got into the light, though, I saw that two of them were wearing railway uniforms. The older of the two, a fat man with the same sort of face as the tractor-driver, asked, "Where's the woman of the house?"

"I don't know."

"This is the place the tractor with a sledge came from?"

"This is it."

"Had they been drinking before they left?"

All four of them were looking around them, screwing up their eyes in the dim light from the table-lamp. I realized that they had either made an arrest or wanted to make one.

"What's happened, then?"

"Answer the question!"

"But . . ."

"Were they drunk when they went?"

"Were they drinking here?"

Had there been a murder? Or hadn't they been able to move the top room? The men in greatcoats had me off balance. But one thing was certain: Matryona could do time for making hooch.

I stepped back to stand between them and the kitchen door. "I honestly didn't notice. I didn't see anything." (I really hadn't seen anything—only heard.) I made what was supposed to be a helpless gesture, drawing attention to the state of the cottage: a table-lamp shining peacefully on books and exercises, a crowd of frightened rubber-plants, the austere couch of a recluse, not a sign of debauchery.

They had already seen for themselves, to their annoyance, that there had been no drinking in that room. They turned to leave, telling each other this wasn't where the drinking had been then, but it would be a good thing to put in that it was. I saw them out and tried to discover what had happened. It was only at the gate that one of them growled, "They've all been cut to bits. Can't find all the pieces."

"That's a detail. The express at 21:00 hours nearly went off the rails. That would have been something." And they walked briskly away.

I went back to the hut in a daze. Who were "they"? What did "all of them" mean? And where was Matryona?

I moved the curtain aside and went into the kitchen. The stink of hooch rose and hit me. It was a deserted battlefield: a huddle of stools and benches, empty bottles lying around, one bottle half-full, glasses, the remains of pickled herring, onion, and sliced fat pork.

Everything was deathly still. Just cockroaches creeping unperturbed about the field of battle.

They had said something about the express at 21:00. Why? Perhaps I should have shown them all this? I began to wonder whether I had done right. But what a damnable way to behave—keeping their explanations for official persons only.

Suddenly the small gate creaked. I hurried out on to the landing. "Matryona Vasilyevna?"

The yard door opened and Matryona's friend Masha came in, swaying and wringing her hands. "Matryona . . . our Matryona, Ignatich . . ."

I sat her down and through her tears she told me the story.

The approach to the crossing was a steep rise. There was no barrier. The tractor and the first sledge went over, but the tow-rope broke and the second sledge, the home-made one, got stuck on the crossing and started falling apart—the wood Faddei had given them to make the second sledge was no good. They towed the first sledge out of the way and went back for the second. They were fixing the tow-rope—the tractor-driver and Faddei's lame son, and Matryona, heaven knows what brought her there, was with them, between the tractor and the sledge. What help did she think she could be to the men? She was forever meddling in men's work. Hadn't a bolting horse nearly tipped her into the lake once, through a hole in the ice?

Why did she have to go to the damned crossing? She had handed over the top room, and owed nothing to anybody. . . . The engine-driver kept a look-out in case the train from Cherusti rushed up on them. Its head-lamps would be visible a long way off. But two engines coupled together came from the other direction, from our station, backing without lights. Why they were without lights nobody knows. When an engine is backing, coal-dust blows into the driver's eyes from the tender and he can't see very well. The two engines flew into them and crushed the three people between the tractor and the sledge to pulp. The tractor was wrecked, the sledge was matchwood, the rails were buckled, and both engines turned over.

"But how was it they didn't hear the engines coming?"

"The tractor engine was making such a din."

"What about the bodies?"

"They won't let anybody in. They've roped them off."

"What was that somebody was telling me about the express?"

"The nine o'clock express goes through our station at a good speed and on to the crossing. But the two drivers weren't hurt when their engines crashed, they jumped out and ran back along the line waving their hands and they managed to stop the train. . . . The nephew was hurt by a beam as well. He's hiding at Klavka's now so that they won't know he was at the crossing. If they find out they'll drag him in as a witness. . . . Don't know lies up, and do know gets tied up. Kira's husband didn't get a scratch. He tried to hang himself, they had to cut him down. It's all because of me, he says, my auntie's killed and my brother. Now he's gone and given himself up. But the madhouse is where he'll be going, not prison. Oh, Matryona, my dearest Matryona. . . ."

Matryona was gone. Someone close to me had been killed. And on her last day I had scolded her for wearing my jerkin.

The lovingly drawn red and yellow woman in the book advertisement smiled happily on.

Old Masha sat there weeping a little longer. Then she got up to go. And suddenly she asked me, "Ignatich, you remember, Matryona had a gray shawl. She meant it to go to my Tanya when she died, didn't she?"

She looked at me hopefully in the half-darkness . . surely I hadn't forgotten?

No, I remembered. "She said so, yes."

"Well, listen, maybe you could let me take it with me now. The family will be swarming in tomorrow and I'll never get it then." And she gave me another hopeful, imploring look. She had been Matryona's friend for half a century, the only one in the village who truly loved her.

No doubt she was right.

"Of course . . . take it."

She opened the chest, took out the shawl, tucked it under her coat and went out.

The mice had gone mad. They were running furiously up and down the walls, and you could almost see the green wallpaper rippling and rolling over their backs.

In the morning I had to go to school. The time was three o'clock. The only thing to do was to lock up and go to bed.

Lock up, because Matryona would not be coming.

I lay down, leaving the light on. The mice were squeaking, almost moaning, racing and running. My mind was weary and wandering, and I couldn't rid myself of an uneasy feeling that an invisible Matryona was flitting about and saying good-bye to her home.

And suddenly I imagined Faddei standing there, young and black-haired, in the dark patch by the door, with his axe uplifted. "If it wasn't my own brother I'd chop the both of you to bits."

The threat had lain around for forty years, like an old broadsword in a corner, and in the end it had struck its blow.

When it was light the women went to the crossing and brought back all that was left of Matryona on a hand-sledge with a dirty sack over it. They threw off the sack to wash her. There was just a mess . . . no feet, only half a body, no left hand. One woman said, "The Lord has left her her right hand. She'll be able to say her prayers where she's going. . . ."

Then the whole crowd of rubber-plants was carried out of the cottage . . . these plants that Matryona had loved so much that once when smoke woke her up in the night she didn't rush to save her house but to tip the plants on to the floor in case they were suffocated. The women swept the floor clean. They hung a wide towel of old homespun over Matryona's dim mirror. They took down the jolly posters. They moved my table out of the way. Under the icons, near the windows, they stood a rough unadorned coffin on a row of stools.

In the coffin lay Matryona. Her body, mangled and lifeless, was covered with a clean sheet. Her head was swathed in a white kerchief. Her face was almost undamaged, peaceful, more alive than dead.

The villagers came to pay their last respects. The women even brought their small children to take a look at the dead. And if anyone raised a lament, all the women, even those who had looked in out of idle curiosity, always joined in, wailing where they stood by the door or the wall, as though they were providing a choral accompaniment. The men stood stiff and silent with their caps off.

The formal lamentation had to be performed by the women of Matryona's family. I observed that the lament followed a coldly calculated age-old ritual. The more distant relatives went up to the coffin for a short while and made low wailing noises over it. Those who considered themselves closer kin to the dead woman began their lament in the doorway and when they got as far as the coffin, bowed down and roared out their grief right in the face of the departed. Every lamenter made up her own melody. And expressed her own thoughts and feelings.

I realized that a lament for the dead is not just a lament, but a kind of politics. Matryona's three sisters swooped, took possession of the cottage, the goat, and the stove, locked up the chest, ripped the two hundred rubles for the funeral out of the coat lining, and drummed it into everybody who came that only they were near relatives. Their lament over the coffin went like this, "*Oh nanny, nanny! Oh nan-nan!* All we had in the world was you! You could have lived in peace and quiet, you could. And we should always have been kind and loving to you. Now your top room's been the death of you. Finished you off it has, the cursed thing! Oh why did you have to take it down? Why didn't you listen to us?"

Thus the sisters' laments were indictments of Matryona's husband's family: they shouldn't have made her take the top room down. (There was an underlying meaning too: you've taken the top room all right but we won't let you have the house itself!)

Matryona's husband's family, her sisters-in-law, Yefim and Faddei's sisters, and various nieces lamented like this, "*Oh poor auntie, poor auntie!* Why didn't you take better care of yourself! Now they're angry with us for sure. Our own dear Matryona you were, and it's your own fault! The top room has nothing to do with it. Oh why did you go where death was waiting for you? Nobody asked you to go there. And what a way to die! Oh why didn't you listen to us?" (Their answer to the others showed through these laments: we are not to blame for her death, and the house we'll talk about later.)

But the "second" Matryona, a coarse, broad-faced woman, the substitute Matryona whom Faddei had married so long ago for the sake of her name, got out of step with family policy, wailing and sobbing over the coffin in her simplicity, "*Oh my poor dear sister!* You won't be angry with me, will you now? Oh-oh-oh! How we used to talk and talk, you and me! Forgive a poor miserable woman! You've gone to be with your dear mother, and you'll come for me some day for sure! Oh-oh-oh-oh! . . ."

At every "oh-oh-oh" it was as though she were giving up the ghost. She writhed and gasped, with her breast against the side of the coffin. When her lament went beyond the ritual prescription the women, as though acknowledging its success, all started saying, "Come away now, come away."

Matryona came away, but back she went again, sobbing with even greater abandon. Then an ancient woman came out of a corner, put her hand on Matryona's shoulder, and said, "There are two riddles in this world: how I was born I don't remember, how I shall die I don't know."

And Matryona fell silent at once, and all the others were silent, so that there was an unbroken hush.

But the old woman herself, who was much older than all the other old women there and didn't seem to belong to Matryona at all, after a while started wailing, "Oh my poor sick Matryona! Oh my poor Vasilyevna! Oh what a weary thing it is to be seeing you into your grave!"

There was one who didn't follow the ritual, but wept straightforwardly, in the fashion of our age, which has had plenty of practice at it. This was Matryona's unfortunate foster-daughter, Kira, from Cherusti, for whom the top room had been taken down and moved. Her ringlets were pitifully out of curl. Her eyes looked red and bloodshot. She didn't notice that her red-scarf was slipping off out in the frosty air and that her arm hadn't found the sleeve of her coat. She walked in a stupor from her foster-mother's coffin in one house to her brother's in another. They were afraid she would lose her mind, because her husband had to go for trial as well.

It looked as if her husband was doubly at fault: not only was he moving the top room, but as an engine-driver he knew the regulations about unprotected crossings, and should have gone down to the station to warn them about the tractor. There were a thousand people on the Urals express that night, peacefully sleeping in the upper and lower berths of their dimly lit carriages, and all those lives were nearly cut short. All because of a few greedy people, wanting to get their hands on a plot of land, or not wanting to make a second trip with a tractor.

All because of the top room, which had been under a curse ever since Faddei's hands had started itching to take it down.

The tractor-driver was already beyond human justice. And the railway authorities were also at fault, both because a busy crossing was unguarded and because the coupled engines were traveling without lights. That was why they had tried at first to blame it all on the drink, and then to keep the case out of court.

The rails and the track were so twisted and torn that for three days, while the coffins were still in the house, no trains ran—they were diverted on to another line. All Friday, Saturday, and Sunday, from the end of the investigation until the funeral, the work of repairing the line went on day and night. The repair gang was frozen, and they made fires to warm themselves and to light their work at night, using the boards and beams from the second sledge which were there for the taking, scattered around the crossing.

The first sledge just stood there, undamaged and still loaded, a little way beyond the crossing.

One sledge, tantalizingly ready to be towed away, and the other perhaps still to be plucked from the flames—that was what harrowed the soul of black-bearded Faddei all day Friday and all day Saturday. His daughter was going out of her mind, his son-in-law had a criminal charge hanging over him, in his own house lay the son he had killed, and along the street the woman he had killed and whom he had once loved. But Faddei stood by the coffins clutching his beard only for a short time, and went away again. His tall brow was clouded by painful thoughts, but what he was thinking about was how to save the timbers of the top room from the flames and from Matryona's scheming sisters.

Going over the people of Talnovo in my mind I realized that Faddei was not the only one like that.

Property, the people's property, or my property, is strangely called our "goods." If you lose your goods, people think you disgrace yourself and make yourself look foolish.

Faddei dashed about, never stopping for a sit-down, from the settlement to the station, from one official to another, stood there with his bent back, leaning heavily on his stick; and begged them all to take pity on an old man and give him permission to recover the top room.

Somebody gave permission. And Faddei gathered together his surviving sons, sons-in-law and nephews, got horses from the kolkhoz and from the other side of the wrecked crossing, by a roundabout way that led through three villages, brought the remnants of the top room home to his yard. He finished the job in the early hours of Sunday morning.

On Sunday afternoon they were buried. The two coffins met in the middle of the village, and the relatives argued about which of them should go first. Then they put them side by side on an open sledge, the aunt and the nephew, and carried the dead over the damp snow, with a gloomy February sky above, to the churchyard two villages away. There was an unkind wind, so the priest and the deacon waited inside the church and didn't come out to Talnovo to meet them.

A crowd of people walked slowly behind the coffins, singing in chorus. Outside the village they fell back.

When Sunday came the women were still fussing around the house.

An old woman mumbled psalms by the coffin, Matryona's sisters flitted about, popping things into the oven, and the air round the mouth of the stove trembled with the heat of red-hot peats, those which Matryona had carried in a sack from a distant bog. They were making unappetizing pies with poor flour.

When the funeral was over and it was already getting on towards evening, they gathered for the wake. Tables were put together to make a long one, which hid the place where the coffin had stood in the morning. To start with they all stood round the table, and an old man, the husband of a sister-in-law, said the Lord's Prayer. Then they poured everybody a little honey and warm water, just enough to cover the bottom of the bowl. We spooned it up without bread or anything, in memory of the dead. Then we ate something and drank vodka and the conversation became more animated. Before the jelly they all stood up and sang "Eternal Remembrance" (they explained to me that it had to be sung before the jelly). There was more drinking. By now they were talking louder than ever, and not about Matryona at all. The sister-in-law's husband started boasting, "Did you notice, brother Christians, that they took the funeral service slowly today? That's because Father Mikhail noticed me. He knows I know the service. Other times it's saints defend us, homeward wend us, and that's all."

At last the supper was over. They all rose again. They sang "Worthy Is She." Then again, with a triple repetition of "Eternal Remembrance." But the voices were hoarse and out of tune, their faces drunken, and nobody put any feeling into this "eternal memory."

Then the main guests went away, and only the near relatives were left. They pulled out their cigarettes and lit up, there were jokes and laughter. There was some mention of Matryona's husband and his disappearance. The sister-in-law's husband, striking himself on the chest, assured me and the cobbler who was married to one of Matryona's sisters, "He was dead, Yefim was dead! What could stop him coming back if he wasn't? If I knew they were going to hang me when I got to the old country I'd come back just the same!"

The old cobbler nodded in agreement. He was a deserter and had never left the old country. All through the war he was hiding in his mother's cellar.

The stern and silent old woman who was more ancient than all the ancients was staying the night and sat high up on the stove. She looked down in mute disapproval on the indecently animated youngsters of fifty and sixty.

But the unhappy foster-daughter, who had grown up within these walls, went away behind the kitchen screen to cry.

Faddei didn't come to Matryona's wake—perhaps because he was holding a wake for his son. But twice in the next few days he walked angrily into the house for discussions with Matryona's sisters and the deserting cobbler.

The argument was about the house. Should it go to one of the sisters or to the foster-daughter? They were on the verge of taking it to court, but they made peace because they realized that the court would hand over the house to neither side, but to the rural district council. A bargain was struck. One sister took the goat, the cobbler and his wife got the house, and to make up Faddei's share, since he had "nursed every bit of timber here in his arms," in addition to the top room which had already been carried away, they let him have the shed which had housed the goat, and the whole of the inner fence between the yard and the garden.

Once again the insatiable old man got the better of sickness and pain and became young and active. Once again he gathered together his surviving sons and sons-in-law, and they dismantled the shed and the fence, and he hauled the timbers himself, sledge by sledge, and only towards the end did he have Antoshka of 8-D, who didn't slack this time, to help him.

They boarded Matryona's house up till the spring, and I moved in with one of her sisters-in-law, not far away. This sister-in-law on several occasions came out with some recollection of Matryona, and made me see the dead woman in a new light. "Yefim didn't love her. He used to say, 'I like to dress in an educated way, but she dresses any old way, like they do in the country.' Well then, he thinks, if she doesn't want anything, he might as well drink whatever's to spare. One time I went with him to the town to work, and he got himself a madam there and never wanted to come back to Matryona."

Everything she said about Matryona was disapproving. She was slovenly, she made no effort to get a few things about her. She wasn't the saving kind. She didn't even keep a pig, because she didn't like fattening them up for some reason. And the silly woman helped other people without payment. (What brought Matryona to mind this time was that the garden needed plowing and she couldn't find enough helpers to pull the plow.)

Matryona's sister-in-law admitted that she was warm-hearted and straightforward, but pitied and despised her for it.

It was only then, after these disapproving comments from her sister-in-law, that a true likeness of Matryona formed itself before my eyes, and I understood her as I never had when I lived side by side with her.

Of course! Every house in the village kept a pig. But she didn't. What can be easier than fattening a greedy piglet that cares for nothing in the world but food! You warm his swill three times a day, you live for him—then you cut his throat and you have some fat.

But she had none. . . .

She made no effort to get things round her. . . . She didn't struggle and strain to buy things and then care for them more than life itself.

She didn't go all out after fine clothes. Clothes, that beautify what is ugly and evil.

She was misunderstood and abandoned even by her husband. She had lost six children, but not her social ways. She was a stranger to her sisters and sisters-in-law, a ridiculous creature who stupidly worked for others without pay. She didn't accumulate property against the day she died. A dirty-white goat, a gammy-legged cat, some rubber-plants. . . .

We had all lived side by side with her and never understood that she was that righteous one without whom, as the proverb says, no village can stand.

Nor any city.

Nor our whole land.

Questions for Study

1. Why is Ignatich an appropriate narrator for the story?
2. What does Ignatich mean when he says early in the story, "I was destined to settle in this dimly lit house"?
3. What is the attitude of the family toward Matryona before and after her death?
4. What is significant about the reaction of the mourners toward her death?
5. Why is it appropriate that Kira's husband assume the guilt for Matryona's death?
6. Why does Faddei marry another Matryona and mistreat her?
7. How do the objects in Matryona's house, such as the cat, the wallpaper, and the stove, reveal her character?
8. What part does the collective farm play in Matryona's life?

Topics for Discussion and Writing

1. Explain what Matryona signifies for Ignatich.
2. Although Matryona is depicted throughout as a virtuous woman and a martyr, explain how the author makes her a credible human being.
3. Discuss the narrator's statement at the end of the story to the effect that Matryona is "that one righteous person without whom . . . no village can stand. . . . Nor our whole land."
4. Contrast the part Paramore plays in Owen Wingrave's life with the part her house plays in Matryona's life.
5. Write a character analysis of Faddei, explaining his function in the story as a flat character.

POINT OF VIEW: THE ANGLE OF NARRATION

Point of view is the position an author takes in presenting a story. It answers the question who is speaking. It indicates through whose eyes you are seeing what happens. In many ways it is the most important element of fiction for a writer because he or she must decide at the start how to employ the narrator to reveal everything in a consistent and credible manner. Should the first-person point of view be used? The third-person omniscient or third-person limited omniscient? Should the story follow the format of a play, in which an effaced narrator (one who appears not to exist) describes what happens and records what the characters say without any commentary? The writer must consider not only how the story is being told, but also how involved or detached the narrator will be. Should the narrator become a full participant in the action or remain a spectator? Should he or she refrain from commenting on what goes on or interject personal observations? The writer's decisions, of course, will ultimately determine your own degree of involvement or detachment.

The **first-person** point of view is one of the most compatible with the short story. It has immediacy, authority, and naturalness. The speaker, who can be an observer or a participant, a major or a minor character, persuades you of the truth of the story because he or she is an eyewitness and thus thrusts you directly into the action. Jinny Wiley narrating her capture, imprisonment, and escape from the Indians in Caroline Gordon's "The Captive" (p. 120) provides a first-hand account which makes her fantastic experiences convincing in a manner no other method could accomplish so well. In fact, the author has said she chose the device instinctively because "I just think it's better told that way." She recognized an organic relationship between her material and her presentation of it. As you read, you share Jinny's life and trust what the narrator says.

Even with stories in the first person, however, you should not assume that what the narrator reveals is an accurate reflection of either the narrator's or the author's real attitudes or ideas. In some cases the author deliberately creates a narrator who is unreliable or unsympathetic and opposed to the values implicit in the story. One of the most famous examples in literature is the narrator of Dostoevsky's *Notes from the Underground.* The more he makes himself repulsive and untrustworthy, the more you realize how desperately he wants to be loved and trusted. His actual conduct and confession are opposed to the Christian concepts of suffering and humility which underlie the story. Such irony complicating the narrative is a favorite technique of the modern writer. You must determine to what extent narrators are telling the truth and to what extent they are misrepresenting their actions and themselves and why they are doing so. Another famous example of the first person unreliable narrator is the governess in Henry James's *The Turn of the Screw.* The reader is faced with the question of her dependability and truthfulness. Is she a heroine protecting the innocent children under her care from corruption, or is she the corrupting influence herself?

Still another type of irony concerns not an unreliable narrator, but one who is unaware of the full significance of what he or she is reporting. For example, Jinny Wiley in "The Captive" gives a detailed but narrow account of what happens to her. Although she is a reliable narrator, she does not appear to be aware of all the implications of her situation. Her comment at the end, "Lord God, I was lucky to git away from them Indians," reveals the gap between what this simple heroic woman endured and her matter-of-fact acceptance of the nightmare, between the reader's broad understanding of her situation and her own local one. We believe everything she reports, but we see more significance in her narration than she does.

There are disadvantages to first-person narrators as well as advantages, however. They can ramble too much. They can fail to establish themselves as characters or authentic voices. They can become mere mouthpieces for authors' ideas. They can be biased observers or participants who reveal only one aspect of situations, despite perceptive comments on what is happening.

The **third-person omniscient** point of view is just the opposite. The narrator speaks in a neutral fashion from outside the action, analyzing and summarizing, moving in and out of the minds of the characters at will, going back and forth in time, providing a panoramic sweep of a scene when necessary. This method is used to good effect in novels such as *War and Peace,* in which there are many characters, scenes, and opportunities for authorial comment, and in which intensity and economy are not so necessary as they are in the short story. The advantages of this method are variety, trustworthiness, and flexibility; and in most instances it gives a more detailed presentation of the action than the first-person.

The weakness of this method is that the author or narrator reports everything at second-hand in an expository manner much of the time and does not always reveal people acting and conversing in a direct way. The author tells rather than shows, editorializes rather than dramatizes, filters everything through the general godlike voice of the narrator. Isaac Babel in "The Sin of Jesus" (p. 116), however, avoids such detachment by giving his third-person narrator a distinct voice and a definite role. His all-knowing speaker shares the hotel world of his characters, not as a participant but as their chronicler. He comments on their lives in a familiar way. Near the conclusion he announces, "And that is the end of my tale." His omniscience thus is restricted. Behind him lurks another narrator who finishes the story without seeming to be part of it, merely recording what is happening and being said.

A technique which combines the first-person with the third-person omniscient point of view and which is favored by the majority of short story writers today is **limited omniscience.** The narrators tell their stories through the eyes of the protagonists, but at the same time they remain outside the action. In this fashion they achieve intimacy while maintaining detachment. They speak in their own voices yet present much of the story from the perspective of the central characters. Nick in Hemingway's "Indian Camp" (p. 110) is the medium through which all the action is presented. He registers the sights and sounds of the birth of the baby and the death of the father and conveys the impact of the whole experience. We, as readers, identify with him from the very beginning. At the same time we remain outside him.

The advantages of this method are those of the first-person narrator—immediacy, authority, convincing realism—combined with those of the omniscient narrator—variety, flexibility, and total access to the main character's mind and background. The author can still analyze, summarize, and explain in the manner of an omniscient narrator, but now in a dramatic instead of a static way. Expository passages are enlivened by indirect recordings of the protagonist's thoughts. The disadvantage is the narrowness of scope. The narrator cannot range too far or reveal too much. He or she has to stay close to the central character, reporting only what concerns that character. In a short story, however, this can work in the narrator's favor since the stress is on the intensity of a single person or moment and there is no question of capturing a whole society or covering many events. The narrator can concentrate on one consciousness without making you aware of the constriction, and can dramatize that consciousness as either reliable or unreliable, sympathetic or unsympathetic, depending on his or her purpose.

The **dramatic** point of view is rarely used for a whole short story or novel. The presentation of the action and the characters scenically, as in a play on a stage, permits no interpretation or analysis. The voice of the effaced narrator is strictly neutral and objective. The advantage is that you plunge immediately into the situation with a minimum of description and the characters take over. You become caught up in the dramatization, focusing only on what is happening and being said. "Indian Camp" combines this method with limited omniscience. Although everything Nick sees is recorded, it is recorded in a seemingly neutral manner with little narrative comment. The dramatic point of view also appears toward the end of "The Sin of Jesus," after the narrator announces his tale is finished.

Closely connected with point of view is **tone,** the narrator's attitude toward the story, the way the narrator looks at the characters and their world. The narrator may view them as foolish or admirable, unhappy or gay. He or she may see their situation as satiric or comic, pathetic or tragic. Occasionally you will find that, although a story has a dominant tone, such as grimness or sadness as in "Indian Camp," there are subtle variations. Nick's contentment and confidence while rowing back across the lake and his reactions to the warm water contrast with his shock at the screams of the Indian mother and his bewilderment at the father's suicide. Furthermore, the narrator takes an ironic attitude toward him, seeing Nick as still basically naive and ignorant of the true meaning of the experience he has gone through. Like all young people, Nick thinks he will never die.

How do you discover what the tone of a story is? First you examine the language used to describe the characters and their actions. You study the connotations of the words to find their emotional nuances. You look at the context of these words. Dialogue is another clue to tone—what is being said and how it is being said and to whom. What characters do and how they do it also is important. In fact, almost everywhere you turn in a story you find evidence of tone. The main thing is to come to a conclusion about the dominant tone, to make up your mind about how it is established and the way it controls the story.

The best approach to analyzing tone is to look at a particular passage. Ask yourself what the words convey—violence, happiness, fear, disgust, humor? Next see how this specific tone fits the rest of the story. The last two paragraphs of "Indian Camp" create a tone of ease and security. The sun is coming up, the bass are jumping, the water is warm against the chill air. After a terrible night everything seems right with the world for Nick. But the passage is set against the tragic events of the past and suggest the boy's limited awareness of what he has seen and what it means. The tone is really ironic. The narrator, speaking through Nick's consciousness, appears to be saying one thing in terms of the scene yet implying another almost the opposite in terms of the whole story. Although humans are mortal, Nick is affirming his immortality in defiance of reality. The point of view, then, controls the tone. The narrator recognizes how narrow the boy's outlook is, yet does not announce this point. Instead, Nick is allowed to express his feelings through limited omniscience. Simultaneously you have Nick's ideas and the narrator's sympathetic yet firm judgment of them. Ultimately it is the point of view of the narrator that decides the tone of the story.

ERNEST HEMINGWAY

Indian Camp

At the lake shore there was another rowboat drawn up. The two Indians stood waiting.

Nick and his father got in the stern of the boat and the Indians shoved it off and one of them got in to row. Uncle George sat in the stern of the camp rowboat. The young Indian shoved the camp boat off and got in to row Uncle George.

The two boats started off in the dark. Nick heard the oar-locks of the other boat quite a way ahead of them in the mist. The Indians rowed with quick choppy strokes. Nick lay back with his father's arm around him. It was cold on the water. The Indian who was rowing them was working very hard, but the other boat moved further ahead in the mist all the time.

"Where are we going, Dad?" Nick asked.

"Over to the Indian camp. There is an Indian lady very sick."

"Oh," said Nick.

Across the bay they found the other boat beached. Uncle George was smoking a cigar in the dark. The young Indian pulled the boat way up the beach. Uncle George gave both the Indians cigars.

They walked up from the beach through a meadow that was soaking wet with dew, following the young Indian who carried a lantern. Then they went into the woods and followed a trail that led to the logging road that ran back into the hills. It was much lighter on the logging road as the timber was cut away on both sides. The young Indian stopped and blew out his lantern and they all walked on along the road.

They came around a bend and a dog come out barking. Ahead were the lights of the shanties where the Indian bark-peelers lived. More dogs rushed out at them. The two Indians sent them back to the shanties. In the shanty nearest the road there was a light in the window. An old woman stood in the doorway holding a lamp.

Inside on a wooden bunk lay a young Indian woman. She had been trying to have her baby for two days. All the old women in the camp had been helping her. The men had moved off up the road to sit in the dark and smoke out of range of the noise she made. She screamed just as Nick and the two Indians followed his father and Uncle George into the shanty. She lay in the lower bunk, very big under a quilt. Her head was turned to one side. In the upper bunk was her husband. He had cut his foot very badly with an axe three days before. He was smoking a pipe. The room smelled very bad.

Nick's father ordered some water to be put on the stove, and while it was heating he spoke to Nick.

"This lady is going to have a baby, Nick," he said.

"I know," said Nick.

"You don't know," said his father. "Listen to me. What she is going through is called being in labor. The baby wants to be born and she wants it to be born. All her muscles are trying to get the baby born. That is what is happening when she screams."

"I see," Nick said.

Just then the woman cried out.

"Oh, Daddy, can't you give her something to make her stop screaming?" asked Nick.

"No. I haven't any anæsthetic," his father said. "But her screams are not important. I don't hear them because they are not important."

The husband in the upper bunk rolled over against the wall.

The woman in the kitchen motioned to the doctor that the water was hot. Nick's father went into the kitchen and poured about half of the water out of the big kettle into a basin. Into the water left in the kettle he put several things he unwrapped from a handkerchief.

"Those must boil," he said, and began to scrub his hands in the basin of hot water with a cake of soap he had brought from the camp. Nick watched his father's hands scrubbing each other with the soap. While his father washed his hands very carefully and thoroughly, he talked.

"You see, Nick, babies are supposed to be born head first but sometimes they're not. When they're not they make a lot of trouble for everybody. Maybe I'll have to operate on this lady. We'll know in a little while."

When he was satisfied with his hands he went in and went to work.

"Pull back that quilt, will you, George?" he said. "I'd rather not touch it."

Later when he started to operate Uncle George and three Indian men held the woman still. She bit Uncle George on the arm and Uncle George said, "Damn squaw bitch!" and the young Indian who had rowed Uncle George over laughed at him. Nick held the basin for his father. It all took a long time.

His father picked the baby up and slapped it to make it breathe and handed it to the old woman.

"See, it's a boy, Nick," he said. "How do you like being an interne?"

Nick said, "All right." He was looking away so as not to see what his father was doing.

"There. That gets it," said his father and put something into the basin.

Nick didn't look at it.

"Now," his father said, "there's some stitches to put in. You can watch this or not, Nick, just as you like. I'm going to sew up the incision I made."

Nick did not watch. His curiosity had been gone for a long time.

His father finished and stood up. Uncle George and the three Indian men stood up. Nick put the basin out in the kitchen.

Uncle George looked at his arm. The young Indian smiled reminiscently.

"I'll put some peroxide on that, George," the doctor said.

He bent over the Indian woman. She was quiet now and her eyes were closed. She looked very pale. She did not know what had become of the baby or anything.

"I'll be back in the morning," the doctor said, standing up. "The nurse should be here from St. Ignace by noon and she'll bring everything we need."

He was feeling exalted and talkative as football players are in the dressing room after a game.

"That's one for the medical journal, George," he said. "Doing a Cæsarian with a jack-knife and sewing it up with nine-foot, tapered gut-leaders."

Uncle George was standing against the wall, looking at his arm.

"Oh, you're a great man, all right," he said.

"Ought to have a look at the proud father. They're usually the worst sufferers in these little affairs," the doctor said. "I must say he took it all pretty quietly."

He pulled back the blanket from the Indian's head. His hand came away wet. He mounted on the edge of the lower bunk with the lamp in one hand and looked in. The Indian lay with his face toward the wall. His throat had been cut from ear to ear. The blood had flowed down into a pool where his body sagged the bunk. His head rested on his left arm. The open razor lay, edge up, in the blankets.

"Take Nick out of the shanty, George," the doctor said.

There was no need of that. Nick, standing in the door of the kitchen, had a good view of the upper bunk when his father, the lamp in one hand, tipped the Indian's head back.

It was just beginning to be daylight when they walked along the logging road back toward the lake.

"I'm terribly sorry I brought you along, Nickie," said his father, all his post-operative exhilaration gone. "It was an awful mess to put you through."

"Do ladies always have such a hard time having babies?" Nick asked.

"No, that was very, very exceptional."

"Why did he kill himself, Daddy?"

"I don't know, Nick. He couldn't stand things, I guess."

"Do many men kill themselves, Daddy?"

"Not very many, Nick."

"Do many women?"

"Hardly ever."

"Don't they ever?"

"Oh, yes. They do sometimes."

"Daddy?"

"Yes."

"Where did Uncle George go?"

"He'll turn up all right."

"Is dying hard, Daddy?"

"No, I think it's pretty easy, Nick. It all depends."

They were seated in the boat, Nick in the stern, his father rowing. The sun was coming up over the hills. A bass jumped, making a circle in the water. Nick trailed his hand in the water. It felt warm in the sharp chill of the morning.

In the early morning on the lake sitting in the stern of the boat with his father rowing, he felt quite sure that he would never die.

Writing About Point of View

Before you begin to write on point of view, you need to ask yourself a series of questions. The first and most important one concerns what point of view is used. Who is the speaker, a third-person or a first-person narrator? Is the narrator reliable, naive, ironic, detached? What is the dominant tone? What is the narrator's relationship to the action, to the characters, to the author, to the reader? How appropriate is the point of view to the material? To what degree does it determine the tone of the story? Is there more than one point of view?

These questions should start you looking at the story strictly in terms of point of view. You must be wary of straying from the subject and discussing a scene, an idea, or a character. Also you must avoid plot summaries as you describe the point of view. One other danger to watch out for is attributing the author's philosophy and personality to the narrator, whether third- or first-person. In some cases the views will be identical to the narrator's, but most of the time they will not be. The narrator is not the same person as the writer of the story. Fiction is not autobiography, though it can contain autobiographical elements.

In choosing a topic on point of view, it is important to select one appropriate to the nature of the story. Possible subjects are the objectivity of the narrator, the use of editorializing both directly and indirectly, and the unreliable narrator. With regard to the first-person you might analyze, for example, the way in which the narrator's apparent innocence achieves ironic effects. With the third-person there is the question of what strategy the author, through the narrator, uses to bring the reader into the story or how the author manages to shift from character to character, scene to scene, and yet retain unity. A very general topic might be the effect of the point of view on the story. What are its strengths and weaknesses? Why do you think it was chosen?

A good topic for almost any story is the appropriateness of the point of view. This has several advantages. It forces you to decide exactly which point of view is used, how it fits the story, and what its strengths and weaknesses are. Immediately you have restricted your subject. There is little chance of your straying into a straight plot summary or character analysis.

Writing on "Indian Camp," however, presents a problem. At first glance the point of view appears to be either omniscient or dramatic. The third-person narrator is either an impersonal voice reporting everything or an effaced narrator dramatizing the scene with no comment. The further you go into the story, however, the more you become aware of the use of the limited omniscient point of view because Nick dominates the action and most of it is seen through his eyes.

The next task is to formulate a thesis sentence about the limited omniscience of the story. One way to do this is to ask yourself why Hemingway chose to tell his story the way he did. Once you have answered this question you should be ready to establish the central idea in a thesis sentence: Hemingway uses limited omniscience in "Indian Camp" because it dramatizes effectively Nick's passage from innocence to experience. Such a broad generalization, of course, must be broken down into several parts. First, there is the reason why Hemingway chose limited omniscience. Second, there is the use of it throughout the story. Finally, there is the evaluation of its success in dramatizing Nick's situation. Here, then, are the main divisions of your essay.

In selecting evidence to support your thesis, you must above all stay clear of retelling the story, although obviously you will do a great deal of summing up to support the points you make. You must keep uppermost in mind the fact that you are analyzing how the author handles point of view. To do this you must recognize that the story moves from the innocence of Nick to his baptism in experience, from a naive acceptance of what his father tells him to a questioning of his father about what they both have witnessed. The point of view records this progress toward initiation very precisely. Hence you will use only those details that are immediately relevant to your analysis.

Nick's Initiation

The limited omniscient point of view of "Indian Camp" is different from that found in most stories. Hemingway does not enter the mind of his protagonist directly, indicate what he is thinking, or probe his past. Instead he reports what Nick sees and feels at the moment. He does this to remain true to the mind of a sensitive boy going through a traumatic experience. He records without comment what is seen and heard. Occasionally he switches to omniscience, as when he says, "She had been trying to have a baby for days." Still Nick is the main medium through whom most of the action passes and on whom the significance of what happens registers.

The story begins with Nick knowing very little. As he rides across the lake and walks through the woods, he responds to the various sights and sounds without attaching any particular meaning to them. He is merely following his father trustingly into a new world and reacting instinctively to it. Even in the shanty he still does not really grasp why he is there or what is happening to the woman in labor. Stubbornly he insists, however, he does know the truth. But his father tells him, "You don't know," and proceeds to explain what labor is. Their relationship is changing from the son–father security of the boat to the intern–doctor training of a profession, but changing slowly. Nick asks his father to stop the woman from screaming, proving he does not truly understand the full import of what is happening. His father, accustomed to such suffering, says that he does not hear the screams and continues the initiation of his son into the hard realities of birth and, ultimately, of life. The process is not complete, for Nick shrinks from looking at what is in the basin, the placenta never mentioned by name. He still has much to learn. Ironically, so does his father, despite his professional pose and his "post-operative exhilaration."

It is this second aspect of the experience, the discovery of the Indian's suicide, that completes Nick's apprenticeship and shakes up the doctor's confidence. He had not intended his son to go through such "an awful mess," only to see what a birth was like. His answers to his son's questions about the suicide are curt and oversimplified. They serve the purpose of comforting the boy so that he feels, if death is like this, he will never die, never commit suicide. Yet they open up to him a whole new world beyond the warm water and the reassuring presence of his father as the two of them row back across the lake, the doctor's arm no longer around his son.

The advantages of telling the story through Nick's eyes are clear. He acts like a first-person narrator in that what he sees and perceives has an immediacy and authenticity that are unmistakeable. You share his experiences and his discoveries the moment they take place. At the same time the limited omniscience of the third-person narrator gives you an ironic, detached view of him. You see Nick as part of a wider and more complex world than he himself could possibly be aware of or express. You see him avoiding realities and simplifying complexities. No other point of view would work so well in conveying the initiation process and its effect on the consciousness of a young boy. You are inside as well as outside Nick at the same time.

ISAAC BABEL

The Sin of Jesus

Arina was a servant at the hotel. She lived next to the main staircase, while Seryoga, the janitor's helper, lived over the back stairs. Between them there was shame. On Palm Sunday Arina gave Seryoga a present—twins. Water flows, stars shine, a man lusts, and soon Arina was big again, her sixth month was rolling by—they're slippery, a woman's months. And now, Seryoga must go into the army. There's a mess for you!

So Arina goes and says: "No sense, Seryoga. There's no sense in my waiting for you. For four years we'll be parted, and in four years, whichever way you look at it, I'll be sure to bring two or three more into this world. It's like walking around with your skirt turned up, working at the hotel. Whoever stops here, he's your master, let him be a Jew, let him be anybody at all. By the time you come home, my insides will be no good any more. I'll be a used-up woman, no match for you."

"That's so," Seryoga nodded.

"There's many that want me. Trofimych the contractor—but he's no gentleman. And Isai Abramych, the warden of Nikolo-Svyatsky Church, a feeble old man, but anyway I'm sick to the stomach of your murderous strength. I tell you this now, and I say it like I would at confession, I've got the wind plain knocked out of me. I'll spill my load in three months, then I'll take the baby to the orphange and marry the old man."

When Seryoga heard this, he took off his belt and beat her like a hero, right on the belly.

"Look out there," Arina says to him, "go soft on the belly. It's your stuffing, no one else's."

There was no end to the beating, no end to the man's tears and the woman's blood, but that is neither here nor there.

Then the woman came to Jesus Christ.

"So on and so forth," she says, "Lord Jesus, I am the woman from the Hotel Madrid and Louvre, the one on Tverskaya Street. Working at the hotel, it's just like going around with your skirt up. Just let a man stop there, and he's your lord and master, let him be a Jew, let him be anyone at all. There is another slave of yours walking the earth, the janitor's helper, Seryoga. Last year on Palm Sunday I bore him twins."

And so she described it all to the Lord.

"And what if Seryoga were not to go into the army after all?" the Savior suggested.

"Try and get away with it—not with the policeman around. He'll drag him off as sure as daylight."

"Oh yes, the policeman," the Lord bowed His head, "I never thought of him. Then perhaps you ought to live in purity for a while?"

"For four years?" the woman cried. "To hear you talk, all people should deny their animal nature. That's just your old ways all over again. And where will the increase come from? No, you'd better give me some sensible advice."

The Lord's cheeks turned scarlet, the woman's words had touched a tender spot. But He said nothing. You cannot kiss your own ear—even God knows that.

"I'll tell you what, God's servant, glorious sinner, maiden Arina," the Lord proclaimed in all His glory, "I have a little angel here in heaven, hanging around uselessly. His name is Alfred. Lately he's gotten out of hand altogether, keeps crying and nagging all the time: 'What have you done to me, Lord? Why do you turn me into an angel in my twentieth year, and me a hale young fellow?' So I'll give you Alfred the angel as a husband for four years. He'll be your prayer, he'll be your protection, and he'll be your solace. And as for offspring, you've nothing to worry about—you can't bear a duckling from him, let alone a baby, for there's a lot fun in him, but no seriousness."

"That's just what I need," the maid Arina wept gratefully. "Their seriousness takes me to the doorstep of the grave three times every two years.

"You'll have a sweet respite, God's child Arina. May your prayer be light as a song. Amen."

And so it was decided. Alfred was brought in—a frail young fellow, delicate, two wings fluttering behind his pale-blue shoulders, rippling with rosy light like two doves playing in heaven. Arina threw her hefty arms about him, weeping out of tenderness, out of her woman's soft heart.

"Alfred, my soul, my consolation, my bridegroom . . ."

In parting, the Lord gave her strict instructions to take off the angel's wings every night before he went to bed. His wings were attached to hinges, like a door, and every night she was to take them off and wrap them in a clean sheet, because they were brittle, his wings, and could snap as he tossed in bed—for what were they made of but the sighs of babes, no more than that.

For the last time the Lord blessed the union, while the choir of bishops, called in for the occasion, rendered thunderous praises. No food was served—not a crumb—that wasn't the style in heaven—and then Arina and Alfred, their arms about each other, ran down a silken ladder, straight back to earth. They came to Petrovka, the street where nothing but the best is sold. The woman would do right by her Alfred for he, if one might say so, not only lacked socks, but was altogether as natural as when his mother bore him. And she bought him patent-leather half-boots, checked jersey trousers, a fine hunting jacket, and an electric-blue vest.

"The rest," she says, "we'll find at home."

That day Arina begged off from work. Seryoga came and raised a fuss, but she did not even come out to him, only said from behind her locked door:

"Sergey Nifantyich, I am at present a-washing my feet and beg you to retire without further noise."

He went away without a word—the angel's power was already beginning to manifest itself!

In the evening Arina set out a supper fit for a merchant—the woman had devilish vanity! A half-pint of vodka, wine on the side, a Danube herring with potatoes, a samovar of tea. When Alfred had partaken of all these earthly blessings, he keeled over in a dead sleep. Quick as a wink, Arina lifted off his wings from the hinges, packed them away, and carried him to bed in her arms.

There it lies, the snowy wonder on the eiderdown pillows of her tattered, sinful bed, sending forth a heavenly radiance: moon-silver shafts of light pass and repass, alternate with red ones, float across the floor, sway over his shining feet. Arina weeps and rejoices, sings and prays. Arina, thou hast been granted a happiness unheard of on this battered earth. Blessed art thou among women!

They had drunk the vodka to the last drop, and now it took effect. As soon as they fell asleep, she went and rolled on top of Alfred with her hot, six-months-big belly. Not enough for her to sleep with an angel, not enough that nobody beside her spat at the wall, snored and snorted—that wasn't enough for the clumsy, ravening slut. No, she had to warm her belly too, her burning belly big with Seryoga's lust. And so she smothered him in her fuddled sleep, smothered him like a week-old babe in the midst of her rejoicing, crushed him under her bloated weight, and he gave up the ghost, and his wings, wrapped in her sheet, wept pale tears.

Dawn came—and all the trees bowed low to the ground. In distant northern forests each fir tree turned into a priest, each fir tree bent its knees in silent worship.

Once more the woman stands before the Lord's throne. She is broad in the shoulders, mighty, the young corpse drooping in her huge red arms.

"Behold, Lord . . ."

But here the gentle heart of Jesus could endure no more, and He cursed the woman in His anger:

"As it is on earth, so shall it be with you, Arina, from this day on."

"How is it then, Lord?" the woman replied in a scarcely audible voice. "Was it I who made my body heavy, was it I that brewed vodka on earth, was it I that created a woman's soul, stupid and lonely?"

"I don't wish to be bothered with you," exclaimed the Lord Jesus. "You've smothered my angel, you filthy scum."

And Arina was thrown back to earth on a putrid wind, straight down to Tverskaya Street, to the Hotel Madrid and Louvre, where she was doomed to spend her days. And once there, the sky was the limit. Seryoga was carousing, drinking away his last days, seeing as he was a recruit. The contractor Trofimych, just come from Kolomna, took one look at Arina, hefty and red-cheeked: "Oh, you cute little belly," he said, and so on and so forth.

Isai Abramych, the old codger, heard about this cute little belly, and he was right there too, wheezing toothlessly:

"I cannot wed you lawfully," he said, "after all that happened. However, I can lie with you the same as anyone."

The old man ought to be lying in cold mother earth instead of thinking of such things, but no, he too must take his turn at spitting into her soul. It was as though they had all slipped the chain—kitchen-boys, merchants, foreigners. A fellow in trade—he likes to have his fun.

And that is the end of my tale.

Before she was laid up, for three months had rolled by in the meantime, Arina went out into the back yard, behind the janitor's rooms, raised her monstrous belly to the silken sky, and said stupidly:

"See, Lord, what a belly! They hammer at it like peas falling in a colander. And what sense there's in it I just can't see. But I've had enough."

With His tears Jesus laved Arina when he heard these words. The Savior fell on His knees before her.

"Forgive me, little Arina. Forgive your sinful God for all He has done to you . . ."

But Arina shook her head and would not listen.

"There's no forgiveness for you, Jesus Christ," she said. "No forgiveness, and never will be."

Questions for Study

1. *What is the point of view of the story? Why do you think it was chosen?*
2. *Is the narrator personal or impersonal?*
3. *What is the narrator's attitude toward the characters, especially Arina?*
4. *Why does the narrator remark before the story is completed, "And that is the end of my tale"? Who narrates the remainder of the story and why?*
5. *Are Arina's scenes with the Lord inconsistent with the point of view of the story? Why or why not?*
6. *How does the point of view make credible Arina's smothering of Alfred?*
7. *What is the tone of the story? How is it established?*

Topics for Discussion and Writing

1. *Discuss the reasons why someone else takes over the story at the end and analyze the narration of the final scene.*
2. *Discuss Arina's immorality and the way in which the point of view makes it acceptable and believable.*
3. *Discuss the appropriateness of the point of view for the story.*
4. *Discuss the tone of the story and the various ways it is conveyed.*

CAROLINE GORDON

The Captive

I

We were up long before day and were loading the horses at first dawn streak. Even then Tom didn't want to go.

"This ginseng don't have to get to the station," he said, "and as for the money it'll bring, we can get along without that."

"We've been without salt for three weeks now," I told him.

"There's worse things than doing without salt," Tom said.

I knew if he got to studying about it he wouldn't go and I was bound he should make the trip, Indians or no Indians. I slapped the lead horse on the rump. "Go along," I said. "I'd as soon be scalped now and have done with it as keep on thinking about it all the time."

Tom rode off without saying anything more, and I went on in the house and set about my morning work. The children were all stirring by that time. Joe felt mighty big to be the only man on the place. He was telling them what he'd do if Indians came.

"You'd better hush that up," I said. "Can't you get your mind off Indians a minute?"

All that morning, though, I was thinking about what Tom had said and wishing he hadn't had to go. It seemed like I was riding with him most of the day.

"Now he's at West Fork," I'd say to myself, and then after I'd done some more chores, "He'll be about at the crossroads now or maybe Sayler's Tavern." I knew, though, it wasn't much use to be following him that way in my mind. It'd be good dark before he could get home, and my thinking about it wouldn't hurry him.

It was around ten o'clock that I heard the first owl hooting. Over on the mountain, it seemed. Joe was in the yard feeding the chickens and he stopped stock still and threw his head back.

"You hear that, Mammy?" he asked.

I knew then that there must be something wrong with the call, or a boy like Joe wouldn't have noticed it.

I spoke up sharp, though. "I heard it," I said, "and I could hear a heap of other things if I had time to stand around with my ears open. How long you reckon it's going to take you to get those chickens fed?"

We both went on about our business without more talk, but all the time I was saying to myself that if I could get through this and see Tom Wiley riding in at the gate one more time I'd be content to bide without salt the rest of my natural life. I knew it wouldn't do to let down before the children, though, and I kept them busy doing one thing and another till dinner time. It began to rain while we were eating and it rained a long time. After it stopped raining the fog settled down, so thick you could hardly see your hand before you. And all the time the owls were calling. Calling back and forth from one mountain to another. My littlest girl, Martha, got scared, so I made all the children stay in the house and play by the fire whilst I started in on a piece of cloth I'd had in the loom a long time and never could seem to finish. I'd put a sripe through it and I was going to dye it red and make both the girls a dress out of that piece before the winter set in.

By that time he fog had risen as high as the top of the ridges and the whole house was swallowed up in it. The children kept teasing, saying it was good dark now and couldn't they have a candle.

"Yes," I said, "we're here all by ourselves and you want to go lighting candles, so they can't help finding the house."

One of the girls got to crying. "Who's coming?" she said. "Mammy, who you think's coming?"

I saw I'd got them stirred up and I'd have to settle them, for I couldn't stand to be worrying like I was and have the children crying. I gave them all a lump of sugar around and got them started on a play-party. I made out that I had the headache and if they were going to sing they'd have to sing low. It was "Hog Drovers" they were playing.

> "Hog-drovers, hog-drovers, hog-drovers we air,
> A-courtin' your daughter so sweet and so fair.
> Kin we git lodgin' here, O here,
> Kin we git lodgin' here?"

I got them started to frolicking and went back to my work. But I couldn't get my mind off something a man said to me once when we were out hunting on the Hurricane, and I made him to go right in on a bear without waiting for the other menfolks to come up.

"You're brash, Jinny," he said, "and you always been lucky, but one of these times you going to be too brash."

Sitting there listening to them owls calling, and wondering how much longer it would be before Tom got home, I got to thinking that maybe this was the time I was too brash. For I knew well there wasn't another woman in the settlements would have undertaken to stay on that place all day with nothing but a parcel of children. Still, I said to myself, it's done now and there's no undoing it. And the first thing I know, Tom will be back, and tomorrow morning it'll fair up, and I'll be thinking what a goose I was to get scared over nothing.

The children were still singing:

> "Oh, this is my daughter that sets by my lap.
> No pig-stealing drover kin git her from Pap.
> You can't git lodgin' here, O here,
> You can't git lodgin' here."

I got up and looked out of the window. It seemed to me that the fog was lifting a little. A man was coming up the path. I knew it was a white man by the walk, but I didn't know it was John Borders till he stepped up to the door.

The first thing he asked was where was Tom.

"Gone to the station with a load of ginseng," I told him. "I'm looking for him back now any minute."

He stood looking off towards the mountain. "How long them owls been calling?" he asked.

"Off and on all evening," I said, "but owls'll hoot, dark days like this."

"Yes," he said, "and some owls'll holler like wolves and gobble like turkeys and every other kind of varmint. Jinny, you better git them children and come over to our house. Ain't no telling when Tom'll be back."

Just then an owl hooted and another one answered him from somewhere on top of the ridge. We both listened hard. It sounded like a real owl calling to his mate, but I was good and scared by that time and I thought I'd best go over to the Borderses'. It was my judgment, though, that there wasn't any hurry. Indians hardly ever come round before nightfall.

I told John that if he'd wait till I'd fastened up the stock I'd go back with him. He said that while I was doing that he'd walk out in the woods a little way. He'd been looking all day for some strayed sheep and hadn't found trace of them, but he thought they might be herded up in that gully by the spring. He went off down the path and I fastened the front door and went out the back way. I didn't fasten the back door, but I kept my eye on it all the time I was worrying with the cattle. Joe was along helping me. The cow was standing there at the pen; so I stopped and milked her while Joe went up in the triangle to look for the heifer. He found her and brought her up to the cowpen just as I finished milking. We fastened both cows up in the stable and Joe went over and saw that all the chickens were up and fastened the door on them. Then we started back to the house with the milk.

We were halfway up the path when we heard the Indians holler. We started for the house on a dead run. I could see Indians in the yard, and one Indian was coming around the house to the back door. I ran faster and slipped in the door ahead of him. Joe was right behind me. The room was so full of Indians that at first I couldn't see any of my children. The Indians was dancing around and hollering and hacking with their tomahawks. I heard one of the children screaming but I didn't know which one it was. An Indian caught me around the waist but I got away from him. I thought, I have got to do something. I fell down on my knees and crawled around between the Indians' legs, they striking at me all the time, till I found Martha, my littlest one, in the corner by the loom. She was dead and I crawled on a little way and found Sadie. She was dead, too, with her skull split open. The baby was just sitting there holding on to the bar of the loom. I caught him in my bosom and held him up to me tight; then I got to my feet. Joe was right behind me all the time and he stood up when I did. But an Indian come up and brained him with a tomahawk. I saw him go down and I knew I couldn't get any more help from him. I couldn't think of anything to do; so I worked my way over towards the door, but there was two or three Indians standing on the porch and I knew there was no use running for it. I just stood there holding the baby while the Indians pulled burning logs out of the fire onto the floor. When the blaze had sprung up they all come out onto the porch.

I made a break and got some way down the path, but an Indian run after me and caught me. He stood there, holding me tight till the other Indians come up; then he laid his hand on my head and he touched the baby too. It seemed he was claiming me for his prisoner. He had rings on his arms and ankles, and trinkets in his ears. I knew he was a chief and I thought he must be a Shawnee. I could understand some of what he said.

He was telling them they better hurry and get away before Tice Harman come home. Another Indian stepped up. I knew him—a Cherokee that come sometimes to the station. Mad Dog they called him. Tice Harman had killed his son. It come to me that they had been thinking all along that they was at Tice Harman's. I jerked my arm away from the Shawnee chief.

"You think you're burning Tice Harman's house," I said. "This ain't Tice Harman's house. It's Tom Wiley's. Tom Wiley. Tom Wiley never killed any Indians."

They looked at each other and I think they was feared. Feared because they had burned the wrong house, but feared too of Tice Harman. Mad Dog said something and laid his hand on his tomahawk, but the old chief shook his head and took hold of my arm again. He spoke, too, but so fast I couldn't tell what he was saying. The Cherokee looked mad but he turned around after a minute and called to the other Indians, and they all left the house and started off through the woods. Mad Dog went first and half a dozen young Indians after him. The old chief and I came last. He had hold of my arm and was hurrying me along, and all the time he kept talking, telling me that he had saved my life, that I was to go with him to his town to be a daughter to him to take the place of a daughter that had died.

I didn't take in much that he was saying. I kept looking back towards the burning house, thinking maybe they wasn't all dead before the Indians set fire to it. Finally I couldn't stand it no longer and I asked the old Shawnee. He pointed to one of the young Indians who was going up the ridge ahead of us. I saw something dangling from his belt and I looked away quick. I knew it was the scalps of my children.

II

We went up over the ridge and then struck north through the woods. I didn't take much notice of where we was going. I had all I could do to keep Dinny quiet—he warn't but ten months old. I let him suck all the way but it didn't do much good. We went so fast it'd jolt out of his mouth and he'd cry louder than ever. The Shawnee would grab my arm and say that the other Indians would kill him sure if he kept that up. Finally I go his head down inside the waist of my dress and I held him up against me so tight he couldn't cry, and then I was scared he'd smother, but the Shawnee wouldn't let me stop to find out.

We went on, up one valley and down another, till finally we come out on level land at the foot of a mountain. The old chief made me go first, right up the mountainside. It was worse there than it was in the woods. The laurel and the ivy was so thick that sometimes he'd have to reach ahead of me and break a way through. My arms got numb and wouldn't hold the baby up. It was lucky for me I was crawling up a mountain. I would put him up ahead of me and then crawl up to him, and in this way my arms would get a little ease of the burden. The old chief didn't like this, though, and every time it happened he'd slap me and tell me to go faster, go faster or they would surely kill the baby.

We got to the top of the mountain, somehow, and started down. My legs were hurting me now worse than my arms. It was going so straight down the mountainside. The back of my legs got stiff and would jerk me up every time I set my foot down, what they call stifled in a horse. I got on, somehow, though, all through that night and for most of the next day. It was near sundown when we stopped, in a rockhouse at the head of a creek. The Indians must have thought they were too far for any white men to follow them. They made up a big fire and walked around it pretty careless. Two of the young Indians went off in the woods. I heard a shot and they come back dragging a little deer. They butchered it and sliced it down the middle, and slung the two haunches over the fire on forked sticks. The tenderer parts they broiled on rocks that they heated red-hot in the coals. A young buck squatted down by the fire and kept the venison turning. Soon the smell of rich meat cooking rose up in the air. The juices begun dripping down into the blaze and I thought it was a shame for all that gravy to go to waste. I asked the Shawnee to lend me a little kettle he had, and I hung it on a forked stick and caught the juices as they fell, and then poured them back over the meat. When they turned brown and rich I caught the gravy in the little kettle and sopped my fingers in it and let the baby suck them.

The old chief Crowmocker, smiled like he thought a lot of me. "White woman know," he said. "White woman teach Indian women. You make rum?"

I said I didn't know how to make rum, but there was plenty in the settlements and if he would take me back, take me just within a mile or two of the clearing, I'd undertake to furnish him and his men with all the rum they could drink.

He laughed. "White people promise," he said. "You in your cabin you forget poor Indian."

The Cherokee, Mad Dog, had been sitting there broiling the deer nose on a rock that he had got red-hot in the flames. When it was brown he brought it over and gave it to me. Then he went back and sat down, sullen like, not saying anything. The fire shone on his black eyes and on his long beak of a nose. When he moved, you could see the muscles moving, too, in his big chest and up and down his naked legs. An Indian woman would have thought him a fine-looking man, tall and well formed in every way, but it frightened me to look at him. I was glad it was the old chief and not him that had taken me prisoner. I was glad, too, that the chief was old. I'd heard tell how particular the Indians are about things like that. I thought the old chief would likely do what he said and keep me for his daughter, but if it was Mad Dog he would have me for his wife.

I thought the meat never would get done, but it finally did. The Indians give me a good-size piece off the haunch and I ate it all, except a little piece I put in Dinny's mouth. He spit it out, but I kept putting it back till he got some good of it. Then I took him down to the creek and scooped up water in my hands for him. He'd been fretting because my milk was giving out, but the water and the juice from the meat quieted him a little. After we'd both had all the water we could drink I went back up the hill and sat down on a log with Dinny laying across my knees. It felt good to have his weight off my arms, but I was afraid to take my hands off him. I was feared one of them might come up and snatch him away from me any minute.

He laid there a while a-fretting and then he put his little hand up and felt my face.

"Sadie . . . ," he said. "Sadie . . ."

Sadie was the oldest girl. She played with him a lot and fondled him. He'd go to her any time out of my arms.

I hugged him up close and sang him the song Sadie used to get him to sleep by. "Lord Lovell, he stood at the castle gate," I sang and the tears a-running down my face.

"Hush, my pretty," I said, "hush. Sadie's gone, but Mammy's here. Mammy's here with Baby."

He cried, though, for Sadie and wouldn't nothing I could do comfort him. He cried himself hoarse and then he'd keep opening his little mouth but wouldn't no sound come. I felt him and he was hot to the touch. I was feared he'd fret himself into a fever, but there wasn't nothing I could do. I held his arms and legs to the blaze and got him as warm as I could, and then I went off from the fire a little way and laid down with him in my arms.

The Indians kept putting fresh wood to the fire till it blazed up and lit the whole hollow. They squatted around it, talking. After a while half a dozen of them got up and went off in the woods. The light fell far out through the trees. I could see their naked legs moving between the black trunks. Some of them was dragging up down timber for the fire and some kept reaching up and tearing boughs off the trees. They came back trailing the green boughs behind them. Two or three other Indians come over and they all squatted down and began stripping the leaves off the switches and binding them into hoops. An Indian took one of the scalps off his belt—Sadie's light hair, curling a little at the ends and speckled now all over with blood. I watched it fall across the bough of maple. I watched till they began stretching the scalp on the hoop and then I shut my eyes.

After a while Crowmocker come over and tied me with some rawhide thongs that he took off his belt. He tied me up tight and it felt good to have the keen thongs cutting into me. I strained against them for a while and then I must have dropped off to sleep. I woke myself up hollering. I thought at first it was the Indians hollering, and then I knew it was me. I tried to stop but I couldn't. It would start way down inside me and I would fight to hold it in, but before I knew it my mouth would be wide open and as soon as I'd loose one shriek another would start working its way up and there wasn't nothing I could do to hold it back. I was shaking, too, so hard that the baby rolled out of my arms and started crying.

The old chief got up from where he was sleeping and come over. He stood there looking down at me and then he lighted a torch and went off in the woods a little way. He brought some leaves back with him and he put them to boil in his little kettle. He made me drink some tea from the leaves and he gave the baby some too, and after a while we both went off to sleep.

III

I woke with the old chief shaking me by the arm and telling me it was time to get up. I was still sort of lightheaded and for a minute I didn't know where I was. It was raining hard and so dark you couldn't tell whether it was good day. The Indians had built a fire up under the ledge and were broiling the rest of the venison. I laid there and I saw the light shine on their naked legs and the tomahawks hanging from their belts, and I knew where I was and all that had happened.

The old chief untied the thongs and I stood up with Dinny in my arms. They gave me a little piece of venison and some parched corn. My lips were so swelled I couldn't chew, but I swallowed the corn and I put the meat in my mouth and sucked it till it went away. I felt milk in my breasts and I was glad for the baby. I gave him his dinny but he wouldn't suck. He wouldn't hardly open his eyes. I thought that was from the tea the old Indian had given us and I feared he'd got too much. He was still hot to the touch and I thought he might have got a fever from laying out all night in the rain. I tore off part of my top skirt and I made a sort of sling that I put around my shoulders to carry him in; and I made a cover, too, out of part of the cloth to keep the rain off his little face.

Soon as we had finished eating, the Indians stomped out the fire and scattered the ashes so you couldn't have told there had ever been a camp there, and we started off through the woods.

We hadn't gone far before two of the young Indians left us. I thought they was most likely going back over the trail to watch if anybody was following us. I heard them saying that the folks at the settlement would be sure to send out a party. Some of the Indians thought it wouldn't do no good because the heavy rains had washed out the trail so nobody could find it. But Mad Dog said Tice Harman could follow any trail. I never knew before the Indians was so feared of Harman. They said he was the best hunter among the Long Knives, that he could go as far and stand as much as any Indian, and that they would like for him to come and live with them and be one of their warriors. Mad Dog said now that the only thing was to go so fast and go so far that even Tice Harman couldn't come up with us. He said "O-hi-yo" several times and I judged they meant to make for one of the towns on the river.

It stopped raining after a while but it didn't do much good. It was level ground we was traveling over and the water was standing everywhere, so that half the time you was wading. I knew we was some place high up in the hills, but afterwards I couldn't have told what country I had passed over. I went with my head down most of the time, not seeing anything but the black trunks of the trees going by and the yellow leaves floating in the puddles. Beech woods we must have been in because the leaves was all yellow and little.

We went on like that all day, not stopping to eat anything except some parched corn that the old chief took out of his bag and handled around to us still traveling. Late that evening we come to a water hole. One of the Indians shot a bear and we stopped and built a fire under a cliff. The Indians hadn't no more'n butchered the meat when two scouts come running into camp. They said that white men were following us, on horseback. The Indians all looked scared at this. Crowmocker stood there talking to Mad Dog about what we had best do. I went over and stood by them. Mad Dog said that they ought to kill the child and change the course, that they would have to go faster than ever now and I couldn't keep up, carrying the baby. Crowmocker showed him the sling I had made and said the baby wasn't no burden to me now. He said he had brought me this far and was going to carry me on to his town to teach his women how to weave cloth like the dress I had on.

He told Mad Dog that and then he motioned to me and said, "Go!" I started off, top speed, through the trees. Behind me I could hear the Indians stomping around in the leaves to cover up the signs of the fire. I went on as fast as I could, but every now and then an Indian would shoot past me. Pretty soon they was all ahead except the old chief.

We went down hill towards a hollow that had a little branch running through it. Mad Dog was in the lead, the other Indians right on his heels, jumping over down logs and bushes quick as cats. The old chief stayed by me, and when I'd slow up getting over a log or fall down in the bushes he'd jerk me onto my feet again.

The branch was narrow but running deep with the rains. Mad Dog started wading downstream and the other Indians after him, single file. They hadn't slowed up much and water splashed high. I could see their legs moving through the splashing water. The old chief by my side was breathing hard. I knew he was winded but I thought he would wind quicker than the others. I thought I would keep moving as long as I saw the Indians' legs going on.

The Indian that was in front of me stepped in a hole up to his waist. When he come out of it he took two, three steps and stood still. I knew then that Mad Dog had stopped and I knew he would be coming back down the line. I looked up, but the sides of the gully was too steep. I turned and ran back upstream fast as I could. I heard the breathing close behind me and I knew it was the old chief, and then there was a big splashing. Mad Dog was after me.

I left the water and ran sideways up the gully. The breathing was closer now. I tried to run faster and I caught my foot in a root. They were on me as soon as I went down. Mad Dog grabbed me by both arms. Crowmocker got there a second after, but Mad Dog already had hold of Dinny. I caught at his legs and tried to push them out from under him but he kicked me away. I got up and went at him again but he kicked me down. He kicked me again and then he went on up the side of the gully till he came to a big tree and he held the baby by the feet and dashed his brains out.

I rolled over on my face and I laid there flat on the ground till the old chief come up. He pulled me to my feet and said we would have to run on fast, that the white men were following us on horses. I said no, I wouldn't go, I would stay there with my baby; but he and another Indian took me by the arms and drug me down the stream spite of all I could do.

We went on down the branch a good way. Towards dark we came out on the banks of a river. Water was standing halfway up the trunks of big trees. I saw the current, running fast and covered with black drift, and I didn't believe even an Indian could get across that raging river. But they didn't stop a minute. Crowmocker fell back and two young Indians took hold of my arms and carried me out into the water. The current caught us and swept us off our feet. I couldn't swim much on account of my clothes, but the two young Indians held on to my wrists and carried me on between them. The other Indians come right in after us. They held their guns up high over their heads and swum like boys treading water. I could see their heads bobbing all around me through the black drift and I couldn't see nothing to keep all of us from drowning. They managed to keep out of the drift somehow, though, and all the time they were working towards the other bank till finally we come out in dead water at the mouth of a creek. The Indians that were holding me up stopped swimming all of a sudden, and I knew that we must have got across. It was so dark by that time I couldn't see anything. I got out of the water as best I could and a little way up the creek bank. I fell down there 'mongst some willows. I saw the Indians come up out of the water shaking themselves like dogs, and I saw them falling down all around me, and then my eyes went shut.

IV

The old chief woke me up at the first dawn streak. I heard him and I felt him shaking me, but I didn't get up. As soon as I opened my eyes the pain in my feet started up. I touched one foot to the ground and it throbbed worse'n toothache. I knew I couldn't travel any that day and I didn't care. I turned over on my back and laid there looking up at the sky. It had cleared off during the night and the stars were shining. The sky was all a pale gray except for one long sulpher-colored streak where day was getting ready to break. Behind me the Indians was looking to their guns and settling their tomahawks in their belts. I watched their heads and shoulders moving against that yellow light, and I saw one of them take his tomahawk out and heft it and then try the blade with his finger. I thought that if I just kept on laying there that maybe he would be the one to finish me off, and then I thought Mad Dog was quicker and would beat him to it.

The old chief was still shaking me. "Get up, Jinny. Day come."

"No," I said, "I ain't going to get up."

He took me by the shoulders and tried to pull me to my feet but I slumped back on the ground. I spoke to him in Shawnee.

"My feet bleed and I cannot travel. Let me die."

He leaned over and looked at my feet and then he called to one of the young Indians to bring him some white oak bark. When the bark come he boiled it over the fire and then he took the liquor from the bark and cooled it with more water and poured it over my feet.

The other Indians had finished scattering the fire and was starting out through the willows, but Crowmocker just sat there pouring that stuff on my feet. I could feel the swelling going down and after a while I touched my feet to the ground. It didn't hurt like it had, and I got up and we started off. He give me some parched corn and I ate it, walking. He said we would have to travel fast to catch up with the other Indians. I asked him if the white people were still following us and he laughed and said no white men could get across the river. I owned to myself that they couldn't and I didn't think any more about them coming after me. I thought the Indians would probably take me so far away that I'd never again see a white face.

We caught up with the other Indians towards dark. That night we slept in a canebrake by a little river. A buffalo was wallowing in the river as we come up. One of the Indians shot him. They butchered him there in the water and drug big slabs of the meat up the bank with ropes cut from the hide. We must have been in Indian country by this time. They didn't seem to think it made any different how much noise they made. They made up a big fire to one side of the brake and they were half the night cooking the meat and eating. I went to sleep under a tree with them singing and yelling all around me.

When I woke up the next morning they were having a council. They talked till the sun was high and then they split up into two parties. Mad Dog and three of the young bucks left us and swum across the river. The rest of us kept on up the bank. We traveled all that day through the cane and then we struck a divide and followed it into another valley. We had run out of everything to eat by this time except the strings of jerked meat that they all carried slung around their necks. We stayed two, three days at a buffalo lick, hoping to kill some game, but none came and we went on.

Most of the leaves were off the trees by this time and the nights were cold. I knew it was some time in October that the Indians come and burned our house, but I didn't know how long we'd been on the trail and I didn't have any idea what country we were in.

One morning we come out in some deep narrows just above where two creeks flowed together. A wild-looking place with tumbling falls and big rocks laying around everywhere. I looked up at the cliffs over our heads and I couldn't believe my eyes. They were *painted*: deer and buffalo and turtles big as a man, painted in red and in black on the rock. Some of the young Indians acted like they had never been there before either. They would keep walking around looking at things and sometimes stand and stare at the pictures of wild beasts that were painted everywhere on the smooth rock.

The old chief took a way up the side of the cliffs, the rest of us following. The young Indians went up like deer, but I had to pull myself up by the laurel that grew down in between the rocks. We walked along a narrow ledge and come to a rockhouse. It was the biggest rockhouse ever I saw, run all along one side of the cliff. The old chief uncovered an iron pot from where it was hid in a lot of trash in one corner of the cave and showed me how to set it up on forked sticks. He said that I would have to do all the work around the camp from now on, the way Indian women did, and when the spring rains come and melted the snows he would take me to his town on the Tenassee and I would learn more about Indian ways and be adopted into the tribe in place of his dead daughter.

I thought if he took me there I would never get away and I had it in mind to make a break for it first chance I got. I got hold of two strings of jerked meat and I kept them tied around my waist so I'd be ready when the time came. I thought I would wait, though, and maybe I would find out how far it was to the settlements. I would lie there in my corner of the cave at night, making out I was asleep, and listen to them talking around the fire.

I heard them call the names of the creeks that flowed through that valley—Big Paint and Little Mudlick; and further off was another creek, Big Mudlick, where they went sometimes to hunt. The names were strange to me and I never could tell from their talk how far it was to the settlements or even which way to go. I had an idea that the place I was in was secret to the Indians, for it was a wonder to see and yet I had never heard any white body tell of it. I asked Crowmocker what the pictures of deer and buffalo and bear were for and he said they were the Indians' fathers and that I would learn about them when I was adopted into the tribe. Once he pointed some mounds out to me and said they were graves. He said that he and his people always stopped when they come this way to visit the graves of their fathers that was all over the valley.

A spell of fine weather come, late in the fall. Indian summer they call it. We looked out one day and bees were swarming on the cliffside. Crowmocker was mad when he saw them. He said it meant that the white people were coming; that when bees swarmed out of season they were running away from the white people who had scared all the game out of the country and made it so that even bees couldn't live in it. I asked would the white people find their way into this valley and he said they couldn't—that it was a way known only to Indians; that if a white man ever set foot in it the great bear would come down off the wall and crush him in his paws. He said, though, that there would be fighting soon over all the land and a lot of bloodshed.

I knew that was all foolishness about the bear, but I thought likely as not there would be fighting and I wanted to get away worse than ever. One morning I was down in the hollow by myself, gathering wood, and I thought that was the time. Three of the Indians had gone off hunting and I knew the others were laying up in the cave asleep. I didn't think anybody would be following me, for a while, anyhow. I started off, slipping from tree to tree, and I got quite a way up the hollow. I knew nobody was following me, but I would keep looking back over my shoulder all the time. I got to thinking. I didn't have any way to kill game, and nothing to eat but two strings of jerked meat. I didn't even know how far I'd have to go before I came to any settlement. Worst of all, I didn't even know which way to take. Likely as not I'd starve to death in the woods, or freeze if the weather turned. I'd better stay with the Indians, where at least I could sleep warm and eat, if it wasn't anything but parched corn. I picked up my load of wood and got back to camp quick as I could, and didn't none of them ever know I'd been away.

I never tried it again, but sometimes I'd sit there on the edge of the cliff and pick out the way I'd take if I did go. There was a ridge covered with black pines rose up right in front of the rockhouse. I thought if I could once get up there I could get down into the valley easy. I hadn't ever been over there, but I knew what the country would be like. I saw myself slipping along through that divide, around the foot of the mountain and over some more mountains till I'd come out on a clearing. I'd slip up to some cabin, towards dark. They'd think I was an Indian at first, maybe, and then they'd see my eyes was light and they'd take me in and keep me till I could get back to my own folks again.

We stayed in that rockhouse a long time. The leaves all fell off the trees, and one or two light snows fell, but the real cold weather was late coming. The Indians hunted just enough to keep us in meat. They said the pelts were thin that year and not worth taking. Sometimes they would take me along to bring in the game, but mostly they left me to work by myself. When cold weather set in we built big fires in the cave and it was warm inside like a house. When the Indians weren't hunting they would lie around on buffalo skins and sleep. The smoke was terrible and the smell of Indians was all over everything. At first it bothered me, but after a while I got so I didn't notice it.

I wasn't in the cave much, even in bad weather. I had to gather all the firewood. The Indians didn't have an axe and I couldn't get anything but dead branches. There wasn't much down timber on the cliffside; so I'd mostly go up over the cliffs when I was hunting wood. There was a barren there, flat as the palm of your hand and covered with a thin kind of grass. It had plenty of trees on it but they were all twisty and stunted by the wind. The only sizeable tree was a big elm. It was peeled for thirty or forty feet and had a rattlesnake painted on it—a monster snake coiling up around the trunk. You could see that snake from everywhere on the barren. I was feared to look at it. The Indians seemed to think a lot of it. Sometimes they would go up there at night and I would hear them singing and dancing and calling to the snake.

Somewhere on the barren there were lead mines. The Indians never let me go to them, but they would go off and stay two, three hours and come back with big balls of lead. They made me smelt it out for bullets. I had to have a mighty fire. It would take me days and days to get up enough wood. I would heap it up in a big pile and then I would kindle the fire and keep it going for hours. When the lead melted, it ran down through little ditches into holes that I had dug to form the bullets. It would take the lead a long time to melt. Sometimes I would be up on the barren from sunup to sundown.

I would sit there and think about my husband and my children. I would wonder whether Tom went out in the woods hunting ginseng the way he used to do, and was he still looking for me or had give me up for dead. When I thought of Tom the house would be there, too, not burning down the way it was last time I saw it, but standing with the rooms just the way they always were. I could see both rooms plain, even to the hole that was burnt in the floor when a big log fell out one night. The children would be playing in and out of the house like they did. It was like they were all living; it was only me that was gone away.

I would think back, too, over things that happened long before ever I was grown and married to Tom Wiley. There was a man named Rayburn stayed at the settlement one winter. Lance Rayburn. A big, strong man and a mighty hunter. We ate bear of his shooting all that fall. He was handy with snares too, and took over a hundred beaver down in the bottom. He courted me some that winter, sitting in front of the fire after the old folks were in bed. I laughed and went on with him, but Tom Wiley had just started a-courting me and all the time my mind was on him more'n it was on the stranger.

Come time for Rayburn to pack up his pelts to take to the station, he saved one out for me. Beaver, and extra fine and soft. He give it to my sister, Sarah, and told her to hand it to me when I come to the house. She made one of the children bring it down to the creek where I was boiling clothes. I laid it there on the grass and I would stop and look at it as I went back and forth with my clothes, and sometimes I would wipe my hands dry and lay them on the soft fur for pleasure in the feel. But all the time I knew I wasn't going to keep it. When Rayburn come towards me through the willows I went to meet him with the pelt in my hands.

"Keep this," I said, "and give it to some girl where you're going."

"Don't you want it?" he asked.

"I ain't taking nothing from you."

He stood there looking at me and all of a sudden his eyes narrowed up like a cat's. "You're full young to be marrying," he said.

"I ain't too young to know my own mind," I told him and before I thought I laughed.

He come towards me, and before I knowed what he was up to he was on me and trying to bear me to the ground. He was a strong man but I was stout, too, and I stood up to him. We was rassling around in the bushes quite some while before he got me down, and then he had to keep both his hands on my chest. I laid there right still, looking up at him.

"What you reckon my pappy'll say when I tell him about this?" I asked.

He laughed, "I ain't a-feared of no Sellards that ever walked," he said, "but that Tom Wiley ain't no manner of man for you," he said.

"You can talk against Tom Wiley and you can hold me here till Doomsday," I told him, "but it ain't going to do you no good. I ain't going to have none of you no matter what happens."

His face kind of changed. Looked like it hurt him to hear me say it. He got up off me right away and he picked the beaver pelt up from where it lay in the grass and he throwed it hard as he could into the creek.

"It'll git to my girl that way fast as any other," he said.

I watched the pelt floating down the water and onto a rock and then off again. When I turned around he was out of sight and he was gone when I got back to the house. He stayed at the station a while and then he went off in the mountains hunting bear and wasn't ever heard of again. Some said he was killed by wild beasts. A rifle and a cap that they said was his was found up in the hills. The man that found the rifle kept it, but they give the cap to the Borderses. Wouldn't anybody wear it, and Sally hung it up in the dog alley. I used to look at it every time I passed and wonder whether it had ever been on Lance Rayburn's head and was he dead or still living. And sometimes I'd wonder how it'd been if I'd married him instead of Tom, but I knew all the time I wouldn't ever have married anybody but Tom because he was the one I fancied from the time I was a chap, living neighbor to the Wileys, back in the Roanoke country.

I thought about Lance Rayburn and I thought about a lot of other folks that had come to the settlement and stayed and then gone on and wouldn't anybody know whether they were living still or dead. And I thought about people dead long ago, my old granny back in Carolina, ninety-eight years old and turned simple. She'd sit in the chimney corner all day long, singing the likeliest tunes!

"Pa'tridge in the pea patch," she'd sing and call me to her and fondle me, liking gals, she said, always better than boys.

"Pa'tridge in the pea patch
Pickin' up the peas.
'Long comes the bell cow
Kickin' up her heels . . ."

"Oh . . . h, the bell cow," she'd sing and catch me by my little shimmy tail. "O . . . O . . . hh, the bell cow . . ." and hist me up over the arm of her chair. "O . . . O . . . hh, the bell cow, kickin' up her heels. Call the little gal to milk her in the pail."

I used to call those songs to mind when I had to go down to the lick for salt. It was a place I didn't like to go. A deep hollow with three sulphur springs and a lick that covered nigh an acre of ground. The biggest lick ever I saw in my life. The way was white with the bones of beasts, and in between the piled up bones the long furrows that the buffalo made licking the ground for salt. I would walk down those furrows to the spring and fill my bucket with the salty water and go back up the hill to where my kettle was slung between two little birches. Sitting there waiting for the water to boil, I couldn't keep my eyes off the bones. I would take them up in my hand and turn them over and over, wondering what manner of beasts they had belonged to.

Once I made myself a little beast, laying all the bones out on some lacy moss, the front feet stiff like it was galloping off in the woods, the hind legs drawn up under him. A hare it might have been or a little fawn. Or maybe a beast that nobody ever heard of before.

There were beasts come to that lick one time or another not known to man. Bigger'n buffalo they must have been. One thigh-bone, I mind, longer'n I was and twice as big around as two good-sized men.

I thought of a man used to be around the station, Vard Wiley, second cousin to Tom. Folks said he was the biggest liar in the settlements. He would stay off in the woods hunting day after day and never bring in any game except maybe a brace of wild turkeys. And he told tall tales about a lick bigger'n any lick around those parts, where the beasts come up in tens of thousands. He would lay up in a tree all day and watch 'em, he said, and not take a shot for wonder. There were beasts used there, he said, ten times the size of buffalo. He offered to take anybody there and show them the bones, and when they asked him why he didn't bring them back to the settlement he said couldn't no man carry them, nor no two horses.

Folks laughed at him, and the children round the settlement used to sing a song:

"Vard Wiley's gone west, Vard Wiley's gone east,
A-huntin' the woods for a monster beast.

"He'll make him a tent out of the wild beast's hide
And all the king's horses can stable inside.

"He'll make him a wagon out of solid bone
And it'll take ten oxen to draw it home."

I called that song to mind and I thought how if I ever saw Vard Wiley again I'd go up to him and say I knew him to be a truth-teller, and all the people would laugh at me maybe, the way they did Vard Wiley, but all the time I would be knowing it was the truth.

I thought, too, of other tales he told and of jokes he played. Of the time he borrowed my dress and sunbonnet and shawl and went and sat on the creek bank when the schoolmaster was in swimming. He sat there all evening with the sunbonnet hiding his face and old Mister Daugherty shaking his fist at him. "You hussy! You brazen hussy! Don't you know I'm naked?" and finally when he come up out of the water naked as the day he was born Vard took out after him and run him clean to the house. Old Mister Daugherty went around saying there was a woman ought to be run out of the settlements, and Vard would talk to him and make out it was me. But Old Man Daugherty knew wouldn't none of Hezekiah Sellards' daughters be carrying on like that. He was bound it was a woman from Ab's Valley.

I would think about 'em sitting there and arguing about how the hussy ought to be run out of the settlements, and I would laugh all by myself there in the woods. Throw back my head and laugh and then feel silly when the woods give back the echo.

I did a lot of work while I was with the Indians. It was hard on me at first but I got used to it. It was better after Mad Dog left us. The old chief was like a father to me, and the young ones knew I belonged to him and didn't bother me. I slept off by myself in a far corner of the cave and he would wake me up at daybreak and tell me what there was to do that day. He took pains to show me how to flesh pelts and cure them, and he showed me how to split a deer sinew for thread and how to make a whistle to call deer out of birch bark and sticks. And after I got so I could sew skins good he had me make him a pair of leggings and trim them with porcupine quills—porcupine quills colored with some roots he got out of the woods.

It bothered him the way I looked and he made me paint my face the way the Indians did. Fixed me up some of the red root mixed with bear's grease, and after I'd been putting it on my face for a while you couldn't told me from an Indian woman, except for my light eyes.

He'd stay in the cave with me sometimes all day, his buffalo hide wrapped around him so tight that his knees were up against him like a chair. He'd sit there and rock back and forth on his heels and talk while I worked. Down in the hollow the young braves would be practicing their war whoops. He would listen to them and laugh.

"Our young men give the war whoop loudly to cover up their fear of the enemy. It was not so when I was young. There was joy in the war whoop then."

He said he was a chief but he might have been something better. He might have been a medicine man. He had the gift of it from his grandmother. His own mother died when he was born, he said, and his old granny raised him. He told me about how she would take him into the woods with her looking for yarbs and roots, and how she knew where everything grew and which roots would be good to take and which had no strength in them. He said that after I was adopted into the tribe he would tell some of her secrets to me, but the Spirit would be angry if a white woman knew them.

I asked him wouldn't I still be a white woman after I was adopted into the tribe but he said no, the white blood would go out of me and the Spirit would send Indian blood to take its place, and then I would feel like an Indian and know all the Indian ways and maybe get to be a wise woman like his old granny.

He told me about his youngest daughter and how she come by her death, following what she thought was a fawn bleating. They found her days afterward, three enemy arrows in her. Her death had been paid for with three scalps of warriors, and he would say that he didn't grieve over her, but I knew he did. I got to feeling sorry for him sometimes to have lost his daughter that meant so much to him, and then I would think how I had lost all my children and my husband and I would cry, dropping tears on the skin I was sewing.

I got so after a while that the Indian way of doing things seemed natural to me. I thought nothing of seeing dark faces around me all the time, but in the night sometimes I would dream of white faces. White faces coming towards me through the trees. Or sometimes I would be in a house again and look up all of a sudden and all the faces in the room would be white.

One white face was always coming to me in my dreams: Tice Harman, the man whose house the Indians thought they were burning the day they burned ours. I always thought that if anybody came to save me it would be Tice Harman. I could see him plain in my dreams. A little man, wouldn't weigh more'n a hundred and twenty pounds, but he had a big head. A big head and a big beak of a nose and long yellow hair down to his shoulders. His eyes were blue and in my dreams they glittered like ice. I would dream about Tice Harman and when I waked I would think what I'd heard said of him—how he could go further and stand more than any man in the settlements, and how he loved to fight Indians better'n eat when he was hungry. I would think, too, of how folks said he would bring trouble on the settlements shooting that Indian down when there warn't really any use in it; and I would think that since it was him that brought all my trouble on me, maybe it would be him that would get me away from the Indians. But time went on and nobody came, and after a while I got so I didn't think much about it.

One evening I was gathering wood on the cliffside and I heard a lot of whooping and hollering down near the mouth of the creek. The Indians come out from where they were sleeping back in the cave and stood looking over the falls. A long whoop came and the old chief put his hands to his mouth and answered it. There was more whooping back and forth, and then Mad Dog came up the trail by the falls with about twenty Indians following him. They were painted for war and marched single file, all except the last six or eight. They were in pairs and in the middle of them a white man, walking with his hands tied behind him. A white man? A boy. Couldn't have been more than eighteen years old.

I had to step out of the path to let them by. The dead branches rustled in my hands. The prisoner turned his head. He looked straight into my eyes. It was like he didn't know I was there. I spoke to him.

"I can't do nothing," I said. "I'm a white woman, but I can't do nothing. Christ!" I said, "there ain't nothing I can do."

He kept on looking at me but he didn't speak. They were hurrying him past. I dropped the branches and run after them. Mad Dog called to one of the young bucks and he caught me and held me. I fought him, but he held me till they had all gone up the path.

I went on to the rockhouse and kindled up the fire. After a while Mad Dog come down and told me to cook up some meat quick as I could. There would be singing and dancing, he said; they would want meat all night long.

I looked at him. "A present," I said. "A present for Kagahye-liske's daughter. Give me this boy. He is not good for anything but to gather wood."

His eyes were fierce. "Boy?" he said. "He has this day killed my brother." Then he laughed and smoothed my hair. "Jinny," he said, "pretty Jinny."

I made out I had to see to the fire and walked away. I put some bear meat on to boil and I told him I would call him when it was done, and he went on back up the path.

There was a moon coming. I sat there waiting for the meat to boil and watched it rise over the pines. Up on the barren the Indians were dragging up all the dead branches they could find into one pile. After a while I looked up over the rockhouse and saw the sky all light and knew they had kindled the fire.

The stamping and yelling went on, and every now and then a gun would go off. Then there was running around the tree. You could hear the feet pounding and the long calls. "Ai . . . yi . . . Ai . . . yi . . . Ai . . . yi . . ." One for each man that had died that day. And the sharp cry for the scalp taking. They would act it all out and the boy standing there watching. He was dazed, though; he wouldn't see it for what it was. He wouldn't know what they were doing, might not know what they were going to do. There on the path he looked at me and didn't know me for a white woman. I ought to have found out his name and where he come from. I ought to have done that much. But he wouldn't have answered. And what good would it do his folks . . . if I ever saw white folks again. Then Mad Dog's hand on my hair. "Pretty Jinny . . . pretty Jinny . . ."

The flames shot up and lit the whole valley. The moon looked cold where it hung over the pines. I kept the fire up under the kettle but I couldn't sit still. I walked back and forth in the rockhouse, back and forth, back and forth, waiting for the shrieks to start.

They were a long time coming. I thought maybe it was already going on. Indians can stand there burning and not make a sound, and there have been white men that could. But this was just a boy . . .

The first shriek was long and then they come short and quick, one right after the other. I got over in a corner of the rockhouse and held on tight to a big rock. After a while I let go of the rock and put both fingers in my ears and then I was feared to take them out, thinking it might not be over yet. The Indians were still yelling and stamping. The young ones kept running down and grabbing up chunks of meat from the boiling pot and carrying them up to the barren. I could see the old chief's shadow where he stood on the edge of the cliff calling to the new moon.

When he came down to the rockhouse Mad Dog was with him. They stood there dipping meat up out of the kettle. Mad Dog talked.

"It is too much. For five hundred brooches I could buy a girl of the Wild-Cats, young and swift, a fine worker in beads. A girl like a moonbeam, daughter of a mighty warrior."

His eyes were black in the circles of paint. His tongue showed bright between his painted lips. The red lines ran from his forehead down the sides of his cheeks to make gouts of blood on his chin.

A devil. A devil come straight from hell to burn and murder. Three white men killed that day and the boy brought back to torture. It was him that killed them, him that yelled loudest when the boy was burning. Him that set fire to my house and burned my children . . .

I saw him running through the woods, white men after him. I saw him fall, a dozen bullets in him. But he wouldn't be dead. He would lie there bleeding and look at me out of his painted eyes, and I would go up and stomp on him, stomp him into the dirt . . .

My hands shook so I dropped the sticks I was carrying. I was near enough now to hear all they were saying. Mad Dog was taking little silver brooches out of a buckskin. He poured them out in a pile on a rock and then counted them. The old chief stood there till he got through counting; then he swept them all up into a bag he took from around his neck.

"Brother," he said, "the woman is yours."

Mad Dog had left the fire and was coming towards me. I ran over and caught hold of the old chief's arm. I called him by his Indian name.

"Kagahye-liske, do not give me to this man. He has killed my children and burned my house."

He looked down at me and it was like he'd never seen me before. His face, not painted, was as cruel as the Cherokee's, the eyes bloodshot and the whole face swollen from the meat he had eaten.

"The war whoop drowns sorrow," he said. "This chief is my brother and a mighty warrior. He has this day killed three white men."

I hung on to his arm. "Keep me for one of the young men of your village," I said. "The Cherokee are old women. You have said so and you have promised. You have promised to take me with you wherever you go."

He shook my hands off. "A promise," he said, "to a white coward! Go to your work."

He turned around like he was going to leave the cave. I run after him and caught hold of his knees, but he broke away. Mad Dog come and tied me up tight with thongs that he cut from buffalo hide, and then they both went on up to the barren where the other Indians was still screeching and stamping.

The screeching and stamping went on far into the night. The fire under the kettle went out and it was dark except for a little light from the moon. I laid there on the floor, listening to the Indians and thinking about how it would be when Mad Dog came down to take me for his wife. I laid there, expecting him to come any minute, but the singing and dancing went on and he didn't come, and after a while I went to sleep.

V

The white boy that they had burned came to me while I was asleep. He came carrying a lamp that was made from the bleached skull of a sheep. The brain hollow was filled with buffalo fat and there was a wick in it burning bright. He came walking between the trees like he didn't have need to look where he was going. His hair was light like I had seen it when he passed me there on the path, but it was long, too, like Tice Harman's. His eyes were the same eyes that had looked at me there on the path.

I said to him what I had said there. "I couldn't do nothing," I said. "There wasn't nothing I could do."

He didn't speak—only made signs for me to follow him. I got up and walked after him. The rawhide thongs were still on me but they didn't bind any more and I moved as easy and as light as he did. He went down by the falls and clomb up over the hill to where the elm tree stood that had the big rattlesnake painted on it. He walked past the elm tree and struck out through the black pines that were all over that ridge. Sometimes he would go so fast that I couldn't keep up with him, and then I would stand still and after a while I would see the light flickering through the trees and I would go on to where he was waiting for me. We went on through the pine woods and started down the side of the ridge. I heard water running somewhere far down below. I thought that would be Mudlick Creek, but when I got to it it was a branch I'd never seen before. We crossed it and went on up a path through a clearing. There were little shrubs all around like the ones up on the barren, and in the middle of them was a house. It was my house and yet it wasn't. White all over and the walls so thin you could see the light from the lamp shining through the logs.

People were walking around in the yard and sitting on the doorstep. They moved to let me go through the door, but they didn't speak to me and I didn't speak to them.

The men that were sitting in front of the fire playing draughts didn't even look up when I came in. I went over to the hearth and tried to dry out my clothes. I stood there holding out my hands but no heat came. I looked at the logs and they were white like the timbers of the house, and the same light came from them. I saw that the men playing didn't have a lamp and yet there was light all around them.

People kept walking in and out of the cabin, men and women and little children. I would go up to them and look in their faces, but there wasn't anybody there I knew. I walked round and round the room. Every now and then the people would move out of the way and I would catch sight of the walls. White, with patches of green on them. I put my hand up and felt one of the logs. It was round and cold to the touch. No log at all, but bleached bone. I knew then that all the house was bone, the floor and the walls and the chimney, even the table that the men were playing on, all made from the big bones down at the lick.

One of the men at the table stretched his arm out and pulled me over to him. He had on a beaver cap and his face under it was pale like he'd been in the woods a long time. He looked at me and I saw it was Lance Rayburn. He sang, pulling me up over the arm of his chair:

"Oh . . . the bell cow, kicking up her heels,
Call the little gal to milk her in the pail . . ."

Fiddling started up somewhere and all fell to dancing. They danced to one of my old granny's tunes:

"There was an old lord lived in a northern countree,
Bowee down, bowee down . . ."

There was bowing back and forth and balancing, and there were figures called, but wasn't any women dancing. I would see something going by and think it was a woman's skirt, but when I got up to it it would be fur or feathers dangling from a belt and all the faces around were dark, not like they were at first.

The great flames went leaping up the chimney, and all of a sudden I knew that they had built that fire to burn somebody by. I looked around for the one they were going to burn but he wasn't there. I said, "They will burn me next," and I saw what they would tie me to—the rattlesnake tree, going straight up from the table through the roof.

I went to the door and I saw through the black trunks a light flickering. I run and Mad Dog and the old chief were after me the way they were that day in the hollow. I thought, "They will kill me now when I go down," and I run faster and then they were both gone away and I was walking through pine woods, the light flickering on ahead of me.

I walked on and come to a creek that run along between wide banks of cane. The light shone on the water and made it light as mist. I stepped in, not knowing whether it was water or mist, and I could feel it coming up around my knees, water and yet not water. I moved along through it light as the wind till I come to where the creek forked. I could see the two forks and the white trunks of the sycamores along the bank, but I didn't know which way to go.

The light was all around me. I could see it shining on the reeds and on the little leaves of the cane and on the water where it broke on the rocks. Behind me there were voices talking.

"Jinny Wiley . . . Jinny Wiley, that was stolen and lived with the Indians . . ."

And then it was the old chief talking to the new moon:

"The white people . . . The white people are all over the land. The beaver makes no more dams and the buffalo does not come to the lick. And bees swarm here in the ancient village. Bees swarm on the graves of our fathers . . ."

The light that had been around me was gone. It was shining now through the tree trunks down a fork of the creek. I waded towards it through the light water, the voices following, and then they were gone and I was standing at the foot of a high mountain. I looked up and saw the light flickering at the top and I clomb towards it, pulling myself up by the scrubs and holly bushes.

I got up on the mountaintop but the young man wasn't there. I walked out onto the edge of a cliff and he was by my side. He said, "Look, Jinny!" and the flame of his lamp leaped up and lighted the whole valley and I looked across a river and saw a fort. I saw the roofs of the houses and the stockade and the timber burned back over the rifle range, and I saw men and women walking around inside the stockade.

I said, "I'm a-going over there," but the young man wasn't with me any more, and the dark that was all around was the inside of the rockhouse.

VI

When I woke up the next morning the Indians had a big fire going and were all sitting around eating. I laid there and made out I was still asleep. They had found trace of buffalo down at the lick and were making ready for a big hunt. I thought maybe they would take me along to bring in the game the way they did sometimes, and then I heard Mad Dog say they would leave me tied up in the cave till they got ready to start for their town.

I was laying with my face turned up and I was feared they could tell by my eyes that I wasn't asleep. I give a kind of groan and rolled over on my side. I laid there not moving while the talking went on all around me. Once footsteps come over to the corner where I was laying and I heard something slap down on the ground right by me but I didn't give any sign and the footsteps went away.

I laid there so still that I went to sleep again with the talking and the making ready for the hunt still going on. I was waked up by a kind of roaring sound. At first I thought it was the falls and then I knew the falls wouldn't sound that loud. I opened my eyes. The Indians were all gone and there was a big storm blowing up.

I laid there watching the pine tops lash back and forth in the wind, and the dream I'd had come back into my mind as plain as if it was something that had happened. I thought it was sent to me on purpose to tell me that now was the chance to get away. I knew that if the Indians come back with any game that night they'd feast high again and were more than likely to take me up on the barren and burn me like they done that boy.

I sat up. A piece of meat was lying on the floor right by me. That meant that the Indians would be gone all day and maybe another day. If I could only get free of the thongs I might get a long way off before they knew I was gone.

There was a knife stuck in a crack of the rock where they laid the meat. If I could only get hold of that! I rolled over and over till I got to the rock and managed to get up on my knees, though the thongs cut into me bad. I could see the handle of the knife sticking up out of the crack and I laid my face down flat on the rock and tried to catch hold of it with my teeth. But it was too far down and all I did was get my mouth full of grit and sand. I gave up and laid down again. The wind wasn't as high as it had been, but the rain was coming down hard. It blew way back into the cave. I laid there with the big drops spattering in my face and a thought came to me. I rolled over to where the rain was pouring down off the roof and I laid there till I was soaked through. All the time I kept straining at the thongs and I could feel them giving a little, the way leather does when it's wet. I kept on, getting them looser and looser till finally I worked my way out of them and stood up free.

I listened and I couldn't hear anything but the roaring of the wind and the beating of the rain on the ledge. I tiptoed to the end of the cave and looked down the path. But I couldn't see any sign of living creature. I dug the knife out from between the rocks and I took the piece of cooked meat and a little kettle that the old chief had left laying around, and went off out of the other end of the cave and along the cliffside.

I kept to the path a little way and then I struck off through the trees down the hillside. The ground was wet and slid from under my feet in big chunks. I caught on to the trees all the way to keep myself from falling. When I got to the bottom I could look back and see where I'd come, as plain as if I'd blazed a trail. I knew I'd have to strike water. I run in among some pines and come to a wet weather branch. I waded right in. It was swift water and full of holes. I would step in one every now and then and go down, but I kept on as fast as I could. I felt all the time like the Indians were after me. I knew they had gone south towards the salt lick and I knew the whole cliffside and the barren was between me and them, but all the time I felt like they were right behind me. When I looked over my shoulder the top boughs of the rattlesnake tree showed from the barren. I was glad when I rounded a bend and it was out of sight.

When I come out to where the branch flowed into the creek I didn't know which way to go, and then I thought that in my dream I was following water and I struck right down the stream. It was harder going here than it was in the branch. The snows melting had filled all the dry weather branches, and muddy water kept running in till you couldn't tell anything about the depth. It was well I was going downstream, but even then the current was a hindrance to me, reaching in and sweeping me off my feet sometimes into a hole that I would have a time getting out of. More than once I was in danger of drowning.

I kept on like this all day. When it was drawing towards dark I crawled up on the bank under some cedars and I laid there and I ate a good-sized piece of the cooked meat I had brought with me. The rain had fallen off to a light drizzle and there was some color in the sky, sign of a clear day tomorrow. There was a flight of little birds over the water and then round and round the tops of the cedars. Some of them lit in the boughs of the tree I was laying under. I could hear them flying in and out and the quick cries and then the twittering as they settled down to roost. It was dark under the trees but the streak of light stayed on the water. I laid here and watched it fade and I wished I could stay there where the cedar boughs were like a little house. I wished I could stay there and not run any more. I thought I would maybe sleep a few minutes and then I could go on faster. But when I shut my eyes I would think I heard the Indians coming through the trees and after a little I got up and went on again.

I tried wading some more but I couldn't make it in the pitch dark. I got up on the bank of the creek and pushed my way through the bushes as best I could. Sometimes the undergrowth would be so thick I couldn't make it, and then I would have to get down in the water again. All the way I was worrying about losing time following the bending and twisting of the creek, and then I would think that was the only sure way to get out of the hill country and I had best stick to water, spite of all the bending.

Sometime during the night I lost my way from the creek and wandered in the pitch dark into a marsh that was all along the creek bottom. More like a bog it was. I couldn't seem to get out of it no matter what I did. I stood there bogged to the knees and couldn't even hear the creek running—nothing but the wind soughing in the trees. And I thought what a lone place it was and if I came on quicksand, as was more than likely, I could go down and even my bones never be found. And I thought of how Lance Rayburn's bones might have been laying all this time in some hollow of the mountain and nothing maybe but squirrels or deer ever going near the place, and it seemed to me I might better have stayed with the Indians. But I knew it wouldn't be any use going back now. They would put the fire to me sure.

I stood there and I heard some wild thing passing. Pit pat pit pat it went; feet falling on dry ground. I pulled out of the muck and made towards the sound, and a deer or something broke through the thicket and went off through the woods.

I followed and come out on high ground, a slope covered with pine needles. I threw myself down flat on my face. I must have gone off to sleep. When I come to myself light was growing through the trees, and all around me I could hear twigs snapping and little rustlings. I got up quick, thinking it was the Indians coming, and then I felt foolish, knowing it was only game stirring at break of day. I saw two deer go by, moving slow over the brown pine needles. The air was so still they didn't get a whiff of me until they were out of the thicket. The buck wheeled so quick he almost knocked the doe over, and then they were both clattering off over the hill.

I went down to the creek bank and washed my face and let the water run over my wrists where they were scratched by the branches. I ate the last of my meat sitting there on a rock. When I got ready to go I found out that one of my strings of jerked meat had slipped off during the night. I couldn't hardly believe it at first. I stood up and felt all over my clothes time and again but it warn't there.

"Well," I said, "it's gone and they ain't no use crying over it, but I wish to God it'd a been the little piece."

I got in the water and started wading again. The creek was shallow for about half a mile and then it run into a bigger creek. The two of them run on before me and I didn't know which way to go. I stood there looking. The sun was up and it shone on the water. I watched the riffles break on the black rocks when the sun caught them, and the place was not the same place I had seen in the dream and yet it was the same because of the light that was over everything.

I remembered the way I took in the dream. "Left I'll go," I said, "like it was in the dream, and if it don't turn out right it's no fault of mine."

I went on, wading half the time. All that day I was thinking about something to eat. Seems like everything good I ever had to eat in my life come back to torment me that day. The smell of herring, cooking, bothered me most. I would see myself, a chap, back in the Roanoke country, broiling herrings over the coals the way children did when their mammy wouldn't give them anything else to eat between meals. I would go over it all, time and again, the herrings hanging in rows in the smokehouse, like tobacco in a barn, and us climbing up on a slab of wood to get at them.

"Three," Dinny, that's my oldest brother, 'd say every time. "Three. You might as well get one apiece while you're at it."

I thought, too, about people wasting things, of a woman I knew used to give all her buttermilk to her pig, and I thought how it was shameful to have no mind for them that might be starving. And I thought how if I could have that pig's dinner one time, or even a moldy piece of bread, the kind I'd thrown away many a time as not good enough for the dogs. And yet I'd been as wasteful as any of them in my day—worse, even, with game. I used to go hunting just for the fun of it. Seemed like there warn't nothing I liked better than sighting down a rifle. Warn't none of the Sellards or Damron boys a better shot than I was, and I could throw a knife with the best of them. That time John and Dick and me and the two Damrons went to Sinking Fork on a big hunt I shot eighteen wild gobblers, and when we loaded up and there were more'n we could carry it was me that said to leave them laying, that there warn't no use in breaking yourself down and the woods full of gobblers. I thought about them gobblers more'n once that day and, Lord, how I wished I could git my hands on a rifle butt just one more time.

I threw my knife once or twice at some small game, mostly rabbits, but it was a rusty old thing and not fitted to the hand the way a knife has to be to turn proper. One rabbit that I hit square in the middle got up and skittered off like nothing had happened, and I saw then it was a waste of time to throw at them.

Late that evening I come on some forward wild greens in a sheltered place on the creek bank. I went down on my knees and gathered every shoot. I found some punk and went up to a rockhouse on the side of the hill and built a little fire way in under the ledge the way I'd seen the Indians do. I knew it was craziness to build a fire, but it might be days before I'd come on any wild greens again. "I'll eat," I said, "varmints or no varmints."

I put my greens on to boil in the little kettle with a piece of the jerked meat and sat there, thinking about how Indians would go up on a cliff to sight over the country and how the least little smoke curling up would be a sign to them. Once I was on the point of putting the fire out but I couldn't bring myself to do it. I feared to feed it much and yet I'd catch myself putting dead twigs to it. It was a long time before the bubbles started rising up in that little old kettle. I sat there rocking on my heels and talking to them.

"Boil," I said, "boil. God's sake, can't you boil no faster'n that? And me setting here starving."

I ate up every mite of the greens and drank the pot liquor and licked the kettle and then I put out down the hill as fast as I could. I could feel my stomach tight under my waistband and strength coming up in me from the vittles and I run faster than I'd ever run before. It was dark under the trees but there was still light down the water courses. I thought how in some cleared place or in a town it wouldn't be dark for two or three hours yet and I saw myself in such a place, moving around and talking to people but staying always in the light. And I said to myself, if I ever got into such a cleared place again it'd be hard to get me to set foot in the woods.

The creek I was following was a master tumbler. Straight down it went over big rocks and the water white everywhere with its dashing. Once I thought I would leave it and strike out through the woods again, and then I thought falling water'd take me out of the hills quicker'n anything else and I'd best stick to it long as I could.

I went on and then all of a sudden I come upon something that froze my guts cold: the print of a foot by the water. I knew it would be a moccasin but I stooped down and looked at it good. I told myself it might be a white man—might be a hunter wearing moccasins like most of 'em did; but I went on a little way and there were three, four footprints in some wet sand and all of them were moccasins. I thought then the game was up or would be directly, but I run on. I run on. I couldn't think of anything else to do.

It was still light when I come out on a big rock by some little falls. I stood there looking and I couldn't believe my eyes. A broad river ran there before me with clearings here and there on the bank and, right across from the rock I was standing on, a fort: a blockhouse with a stockade fence around it and the timber burned back over the rifle range.

I got off the rock and run down towards the water. A woman and some children were walking along outside the stockade. I called to the woman. She give one look at me and turned and run inside the fort, the children after her. I saw the gate swing to behind them and I knew they had shot the bolt.

I tore off my petticoat and waved it over my head and yelled loud as I could:

"Let me in! Let me in, I tell you!"

I could see heads at the upper story and one somebody standing up on a stump to look over the stockade. But nobody answered and there wasn't no sign of the gate opening.

I looked over my shoulder. The woods were dark behind me and there wasn't any sign of Indians, but I knew they'd be coming any minute. I felt like I knew the place in the woods they were at now. I saw them trotting, trotting through the trees, one after another, the way they went.

I thought, "I'll have to do something quick or they'll get me sure, after all my trouble." I started in to swim it but I couldn't make headway against that current. I saw I would be drowning in a minute, and I swum hard and got back to shallow water. It come to me then that the folks in the fort didn't know who I was. I stood up in the water and yelled, loud as I could:

"I'm Jinny Wiley . . . Jinny Wiley that the Indians stole."

The echo come back to me from the woods, but there wasn't any sound from the fort. Then the gate opened a little way and an old man come out with a gun in his hand. He stood there looking at me and he turned around and said something to the folks in the fort and then he started down the path. I watched him coming down over the rifle range, an old man, gray-haired and feeble enough to a been my grandsire. I shouted at him.

"You can't do it. Send some young body over."

He stood on the bank and shouted back at me, his old voice quavering across the water:

"Where'd you come from?"

I jumped up and down and shrieked, top of my voice:

"God's sakes, man, you going to let me die right here before your eyes?

I'm white! White, I tell you."

"All of 'em's gone but me," he said, "and they ain't no canoe."

"Make a raft," I told him.

He nodded his head up and down. I could see his old gray beard a-shaking. "You better be ready to swim for it," he said. "I don't know as I can git across."

He called to the women in the fort and they come and brought an axe. There was a dead mulberry tree on the bank and they went to work felling it. The old man went off in the woods and come back with some grapevine. When the tree fell it split into three logs and he tied them together with a grapevine and then he and the women rolled them down to the water. They handed him two rifles and he laid them on the raft and started poling. The current caught him and he was going downstream. Yelling had started behind me somewhere in the woods. The Indians were coming.

I run down the bank till I got even with the raft and I swum out and clomb aboard. The old man poled hard. We got halfway out in the river and then the vines begun to come loose and the raft was spreading apart. I knelt down and held the logs together with my hands the best I could. The old man fell down on his knees and started praying.

" 'Tain't no use," he said; "we can't make it."

I looked over my shoulder. The Indians were swarming down to the water. I knew they'd be swimming directly. The old man was still praying. I took the pole away from him.

"Go on and pray, you old fool," I said. "I'm a-going to git across this river."

I put all the strength I had into it, and we made some headway. The yelling was closer now. The Indians were in the water. A shot rung out. I hoped to God one of 'em was hit. I poled harder and I saw some willow boughs ahead of me. I reached out and grabbed hold of 'em and we pulled ourselves to shore.

We went up over the rifle range fast as we could. I looked back once. The Indians had left the water and were standing on the bank. I heard Mad Dog calling:

"Whoopee! . . . whoopee! . . . pretty Jinny!"

We went through the gate. I heard the bolt shoot home and I knew I was inside the fort. I fell down on the ground and the women and children come crowding. The Indians were still yelling. I sat up and the high stockade fence was all around me.

"Lord God," I said, "I was lucky to git away from them Indians!"

Questions for Study

1. *What is the point of view of the story? What advantages are there in using it?*
2. *The story is based on an historical document,* The Founding of Harman's Station with an Account of the Indian Captivity of Mrs. Jennie Wiley, *by William Esley Connelley. Is there any evidence that the tale*

is from such a source? How is the point of view affected by this fact?
3. How does the point of view contribute to dramatizing Jinny's character? Could she have been presented differently and made just as vivid and heroic?
4. What is the purpose of the dream episode in Section V? How is the point of view suitable for it?
5. What is the tone of the story? How does the point of view contribute to this tone?
6. At first the author began the story with the tomahawking of the children. Why did she add material leading up to this action?
7. Why is the last sentence of the story a fitting conclusion?

Topics for Discussion and Writing

1. Discuss how the first-person point of view is successful in recreating a picture of pioneer life.
2. Contrast the story with conventional Indian and frontier movies and novels and indicate why "The Captive" succeeds where so many of them fail.
3. Discuss Jinny as a reliable narrator.
4. Discuss the courtship episode with Lance Rayburn, which the author says she added to the original tale. In your essay indicate why such an episode was necessary and what it contributes to the total story.
5. Discuss Jinny as a naive narrator. In your essay analyze her narrative tone and indicate how it affects the reader's response.

SETTING: WHERE AND WHEN

Setting concerns both time and place. It is the hour or day or year the action takes place, as well as the scenery and all the details that compose it. Even the clothes described and the objects mentioned, no matter how trivial, belong to the setting. Without such a temporal, spatial, and physical environment the characters would live in a vacuum, and you would be unable to experience their world. You would also have difficulty in discovering the mood of the story, the emotional climate, all so dependent on the creation of a setting.

In John Cheever's "The Swimmer" (p. 149), setting includes a Sunday afternoon in midsummer, Westchester County outside New York City, and a series of swimming pools that form in the hero's mind a "quasi-subterranean stream" curving across the county for eight miles from the Westerhazys' residence to his own in Bullet Park. The day and the season make plausible the parties at poolside, establish a falsely festive mood, prepare for the emptiness and darkness that greet Neddy Merrill as he reaches home. He is an integral part of the whole suburban scene which once molded his life and now has undermined it. In a similar way the harsh, primitive Mexican region where the heroine in Katherine Anne Porter's "María Concepción" (p. 167) lives, the thorny roads she walks, the beehives and honey she delights in, the sinister wind she hears whimpering through the cactus leaves all contribute to making her actions and her character convincing. She is inseparable from such a rural world with its swift cruelties and profound rhythms that move in harmony with the earth. More than a background for her story, this world is an integral part of her nature. It creates her. One could not conceive of the grim situation existing outside this Indian community.

Not only does setting furnish the environment for a story, but it also helps develop the structure and influence the characters. The pools and their parties set up the incidents that reveal Merrill's plight in "The Swimmer," each one progressively more uncomfortable for him as he moves closer to the truth about himself. In "María Concepción" Katherine Anne Porter uses a technique similar to a **framing device**, the presentation of the same setting at the beginning and end of the story. Only here, instead of two similar settings, there are two similar moods. In both María feels at peace with the life around her.

As if to dramatize the importance of this device in a thematic as well as a structural way, the narrator in the conclusion points to María's maternal state and her domestic happiness, which were highlighted in the beginning as she walked to market pregnant and contented. Whereas in the first scene María thinks her husband is at work, in the last she is certain he is returning to his job. Order once more reigns in her home as well as in the universe. While the action of the story between these two episodes is not focused, as in "The Swimmer," on a single object, the cactus serves to stress the cruelty of María's situation.

The influence of setting on the characters is often crucial. Just as the suburb Neddy Merrill lives in intensifies his sense of isolation, so the backward region María Concepción lives in intensifies her sense of the good life and what she as a Christian and a woman must do to preserve it. Neddy is the victim of the rootlessness, fast living, and expensive tastes of his social set. His imagining himself as an explorer and the pools an unknown river indicates not only his boyish naiveté but also his vague dissatisfaction with this world and his longing to transcend it. María Concepción adheres to the code of her culture and her religion in defending her home. Like Merrill she struggles to rise above her milieu, but unlike him she is victorious in her own savage way. Instead of succumbing to loneliness and bitterness after the desertion of her husband and the death of her baby, she overcomes these misfortunes to find once again her true place in the natural scheme of things.

What is more, these locales become characters in their own right. The pools, with their different construction and water color and their different kinds of people drinking around them, introduce a variety of moods that correspond to those of the protagonist. Likewise the area María lives in, with its bristling cacti and pungent pepper-trees, its dusty roads and ripening fruits, reflect the dual sides of her character as she moves from delight in dabbling her feet in the stream to sorrowful meditation under a "thorny bush" just before she decides to kill her rival. In fact, so closely related are María and her environment that a hedge of cactus is compared to "bared knife blades," the very instruments she uses in her trade and in her crime.

Thus setting in these two stories, as in so many others in which description dominates, is functional, evocative, and significant. It links the plot to a specific time and place, gives substance to the characters, and suggests the meaning of much that occurs. With regard to this last point, you should note the imaginative use of language in dramatizing and making vivid the setting so that it does not remain static background material, but plays an active part in presenting the whole story, establishing mood, and revealing aspects of the protagonist's character. The cumulus clouds at the beginning of "The Swimmer" are compared to a "city seen from a distance." They are part of the hero's happy illusions about himself and his world and create a pleasant atmosphere. Later, as his problems mount, a storm threatens and the cumulus city darkens. Now he understands the disaster that is overwhelming himself and his world. The "sharp staccato whimper of wind through the cactus leaves" that springs up after María's crime underscores the feeling of terror that fills her and her husband as they wait in the "hostile darkness" for the gendarmes. The words bring the scene to life in an emotional as well as a pictorial way. At the end Juan's and her breathing blend with that of the child, whose "faint breath was a mere shadowy moth of sound in the silver air." Together their breathing becomes part of the earth's "limitless, unhurried, benign breathing." Such imaginative description reflects the mental state of the protagonist and those around her and offers an interpretation of the events.

Not all stories depend so heavily on setting as those mentioned above. In some it is scarcely a factor. In others it tends to be decorative or necessary only for establishing background atmosphere. In still others it is unobtrusive and has no evocative quality. It has no meaning beyond itself. Much depends on the kind of story and the kind of point of view introduced. Generally in stories that use the dramatic point of view the setting is briefly and objectively outlined. Both "Indian Camp" and "In Trouble" are examples. In those with an unlimited omniscience it is recorded fully, as in "The Sin of Jesus." First-person narration relies heavily on impressions, as in "The Captive." Limited omniscience also emphasizes setting, yet tends to be more objective than the first-person. For instance, in "A Sunrise on the Veld" (p. 161) setting has both the detachment of the dramatic point of view and the involved self-consciousness of the first-person point of view. You not only visualize with clarity the grassy open country just before and after dawn, but you also see it through the mental prism of the eager fifteen-year-old boy and thus get his strong reactions. He rushes to the hunt through the brush "under a tumult of crimson and gold light." The brisk air smells to him "like a challenge." Suddenly he hears a "sound of pain," which turns out to be as much his own as that of the wounded buck. The setting becomes internalized. You see it from both within and without the main character as he first exalts in nature and then grows grimly aware of its "fatality" upon viewing the ants picking clean the dying animal. You note the contrast between how the earth looks to him when he starts out on his hunt full of joy and confidence and how it appears to him after he discovers the cruel scene and resigns himself to the fact "ants must eat too." In this fashion setting becomes psychological as well as physical. It is not a stage with props, but a living world that is an essential part of the characters and their actions.

JOHN CHEEVER

The Swimmer

It was one of those midsummer Sundays when everyone sits around saying: "I *drank* too much last night." You might have heard it whispered by the parishioners leaving church, heard it from the lips of the priest himself, struggling with his cassock in the *vestiarium*, heard it from the golf links and the tennis courts, heard it from the wildlife preserve where the leader of the Audubon group was suffering from a terrible hangover. "I *drank* too much," said Donald Westerhazy. "We all *drank* too much," said Lucinda Merrill. "It must have been the wine," said Helen Westerhazy. "I *drank* too much of that claret."

This was at the edge of the Westerhazys' pool. The pool, fed by an artesian well with a high iron content, was a pale shade of green. It was a fine day. In the west there was a massive stand of cumulus cloud so like a city seen from a distance—from the bow of an approaching ship—that it might have had a name. Lisbon. Hackensack. The sun was hot. Neddy Merrill sat by the green water, one hand in it, one around a glass of gin. He was a slender man—he seemed to have the especial slenderness of youth—and while he was far from young he had slid down his banister that morning and given the bronze backside of Aphrodite on the hall table a smack, as he jogged toward the smell of coffee in his dining room. He might have been compared to a summer's day, particularly the last hours of one, and while he lacked a tennis racket or a sail bag the impression was definitely one of youth, sport, and clement weather. He had been swimming and now he was breathing deeply, stertorously as if he could gulp into his lungs the components of that moment, the heat of the sun, the intenseness of his pleasure. It all seemed to flow into his chest. His own house stood in Bullet Park, eight miles to the south, where his four beautiful daughters would have had their lunch and might be playing tennis. Then it occurred to him that by taking a dogleg to the southwest he could reach his home by water.

His life was not confining and the delight he took in this observation could not be explained by its suggestion of escape. He seemed to see, with a cartographer's eye, that string of swimming pools, that quasi-subterranean stream that curved across the county. He had made a discovery, a contribution to modern geography; he would name the stream Lucinda after his wife. He was not a practical joker nor was he a fool but he was determinedly original and had a vague and modest idea of himself as a legendary figure. The day was beautiful and it seemed to him that a long swim might enlarge and celebrate its beauty.

He took off a sweater that was hung over his shoulders and dove in. He had an inexplicable contempt for men who did not hurl themselves into pools. He swam a choppy crawl, breathing either with every stroke or every fourth stroke and counting somewhere well in the back of his mind the one-two one-two of a flutter kick. It was not a serviceable stroke for long distances but the domestication of swimming had saddled the sport with some customs and in his part of the world a crawl was customary. To be embraced and sustained by the light green water was less a pleasure, it seemed, than the resumption of a natural condition, and he would have liked to swim without trunks, but this was not possible, considering his project. He hoisted himself up on the far curb—he never used the ladder—and started across the lawn. When Lucinda asked where he was going he said he was going to swim home.

The only maps and charts he had to go by were remembered or imaginary but these were clear enough. First there were the Grahams, the Hammers, the Lears, the Howlands, and the Crosscups. He would cross Ditmar Street to the

Bunkers and come, after a short portage, to the Levys, the Welchers, and the public pool in Lancaster. Then there were the Hallorans, the Sachses, the Biswangers, Shirley Adams, the Gilmartins, and the Clydes. The day was lovely, and that he lived in a world so generously supplied with water seemed like a clemency, a beneficence. His heart was high and he ran across the grass. Making his way home by an uncommon route gave him the feeling that he was a pilgrim, an explorer, a man with a destiny, and he knew that he would find friends all along the way; friends would line the banks of the Lucinda River.

He went through a hedge that separated the Westerhazys' land from the Grahams', walked under some flowering apple trees, passed the shed that housed their pump and filter, and came out at the Grahams' pool. "Why, Neddy," Mrs. Graham said, "what a marvelous surprise. I've been trying to get you on the phone all morning. Here, let me get you a drink." He saw then, like any explorer, that the hospitable customs and traditions of the natives would have to be handled with diplomacy if he was ever going to reach his destination. He did not want to mystify or seem rude to the Grahams nor did he have the time to linger there. He swam the length of their pool and joined them in the sun and was rescued, a few minutes later, by the arrival of two carloads of friends from Connecticut. During the uproarious reunions he was able to slip away. He went down by the front of the Grahams' house, stepped over a thorny hedge, and crossed a vacant lot to the Hammers'. Mrs. Hammer, looking up from her roses, saw him swim by although she wasn't quite sure who it was. The Lears heard him splashing past the open windows of their living room. The Howlands and the Crosscups were away. After leaving the Howlands' he crossed Ditmar Street and started for the Bunkers', where he could hear, even at that distance, the noise of a party.

The water refracted the sound of voices and laughter and seemed to suspend it in midair. The Bunkers' pool was on a rise and he climbed some stairs to a terrace where twenty-five or thirty men and women were drinking. The only person in the water was Rusty Towers, who floated there on a rubber raft. Oh how bonny and lush were the banks of the Lucinda River! Prosperous men and women gathered by the sapphire-colored waters while caterer's men in white coats passed them cold gin. Overhead a red de Haviland trainer was circling around and around and around in the sky with something like the glee of a child in a swing. Ned felt a passing affection for the scene, a tenderness for the gathering, as if it was something he might touch. In the distance he heard thunder. As soon as Enid Bunker saw him she began to scream: "Oh look who's here! What a marvelous surprise! When Lucinda said that you couldn't come I thought I'd *die*." She made her way to him through the crowd, and when they had finished kissing she led him to the bar, a progress that was slowed by the fact that he stopped to kiss eight or ten other women and shake the hands of as many men. A smiling bartender he had seen at a hundred parties gave him a gin and tonic and he stood by the bar for a moment, anxious not to get stuck in any conversation that would delay his voyage. When he seemed about to be surrounded he dove in and swam close to the side to avoid colliding with Rusty's raft. At the far end of the pool he bypassed the Tomlinsons with a broad smile and jogged up the garden path. The gravel cut his feet but this was the only unpleasantness. The party was confined to the pool, and as he went toward the house he heard the brilliant, watery sound of voices fade, heard the noise of a radio from the Bunkers' kitchen, where someone was listening to a ballgame. Sunday afternoon. He made his way through the parked cars and down the grassy border of their driveway to Alewives' Lane. He did not want to be seen on the road in his bathing trunks but there was no traffic and he made the short distance to the Levys' driveway, marked with a private property sign and a green tube for the *New York Times*. All the doors and windows of the big house were open but there were no signs of life; not even a dog barked. He went around the side of the house to the pool and saw that the Levys had only recently left. Glasses and bottles and dishes of nuts were on a table at the deep end, where there was a bathhouse or gazebo, hung with Japanese lanterns. After swimming the pool he got himself a glass and poured a drink. It was his fourth or fifth drink and he had swum nearly half the length of the Lucinda River. He felt tired, clean, and pleased at that moment to be alone; pleased with everything.

It would storm. The stand of cumulus cloud—that city—had risen and darkened, and while he sat there he heard the percussiveness of thunder again. The de Haviland trainer was still circling overhead and it seemed to Ned that he could almost hear the pilot laugh with pleasure in the afternoon; but when there was another peal of thunder he took off for home. A train whistle blew and he wondered what time it had gotten to be. Four? Five? He thought of the provincial station at that hour, where a waiter, his tuxedo concealed by a raincoat, a dwarf with some flowers wrapped in newspaper, and a woman who had been crying would be waiting for the local. It was suddenly growing dark; it was that moment when the pin-headed birds seem to organize their song into some acute and knowledgeable recognition of the storm's approach. Then there was a fine noise of rushing water from the crown of an oak at his back, as if a spigot there had been turned. Then the noise of fountains came from the crowns of all the tall trees. Why did he love storms, what was the meaning of his excitement when the door sprang open and the rain wind fled rudely up the stairs, why had the simple task of shutting the windows of an old house seemed fitting and urgent, why did the first watery notes of a storm wind have for him the unmistakable sound of good news, cheer, glad tidings? Then there was an explosion, a smell of cordite, and rain lashed the Japanese lanterns that Mrs. Levy had bought in Kyoto the year before last, or was it the year before that?

He stayed in the Levys' gazebo until the storm had passed. The rain had cooled the air and he shivered. The force of the wind had stripped a maple of its red and yellow leaves and scattered them over the grass and the water. Since it was midsummer the tree must be blighted, and yet he felt a peculiar sadness at this sign of autumn. He braced his shoulders, emptied his glass, and started for the Welchers' pool. This meant crossing the Lindleys' riding ring and he was surprised to find it overgrown with grass and all the jumps dismantled. He wondered if the Lindleys had sold their horses or gone away for the summer and put them out to board. He seemed to remember having heard something about the Lindleys and their horses but the memory was unclear. On he went, barefoot through the wet grass, to the Welchers', where he found their pool was dry.

This breach in his chain of water disappointed him absurdly, and he felt like some explorer who seeks a torrential headwater and finds a dead stream. He was disappointed and mystified. It was common enough to go away for the summer but no one ever drained his pool. The Welchers had definitely gone away. The pool furniture was folded, stacked, and covered with a tarpaulin. The bathhouse was locked. All the windows of the house were shut, and when he went around to the driveway in front he saw a for-sale sign nailed to a tree. When had he last heard from the Welchers—when, that is, had he and Lucinda last regretted an invitation to dine with them. It seemed only a week or so ago. Was his memory failing or had he so disciplined it in the repression of unpleasant facts that he had damaged his sense of the truth? Then in the distance he heard the sound of a tennis game. This cheered him, cleared away all his apprehensions and let him regard the overcast sky and the cold air with indifference. This was the day that Neddy Merrill swam across the county. That was the day! He started off then for his most difficult portage.

Had you gone for a Sunday afternoon ride that day you might have seen him, close to naked, standing on the shoulders of route 424, waiting for a chance to cross. You might have wondered if he was the victim of foul play, had his car broken down, or was he merely a fool. Standing barefoot in the deposits of the highway—beer cans, rags, and blowout patches—exposed to all kinds of ridicule, he seemed pitiful. He had known when he started that this was a part of his journey—it had been on his maps—but confronted with the lines of traffic, worming through the summery light, he found himself unprepared. He was laughed at, jeered at, a beer can was thrown at him, and he had no dignity or humor to bring to the situation. He could have gone back, back to the Westerhazys', where Lucinda would still be sitting in the sun. He had signed nothing, vowed nothing, pledged nothing not even to himself. Why, believing as he did, that all human obduracy was susceptible to common sense, was he unable to turn back? Why was he determined to complete his journey even if it meant putting his life in danger? At what point had this prank, this joke, this piece of horseplay become serious? He could not go back, he could not even recall with any clearness the green water at the Westerhazys', the sense of inhaling the day's components, the friendly and relaxed voices saying that they had *drunk* too much. In the space of an hour, more or less, he had covered a distance that made his return impossible.

An old man, tooling down the highway at fifteen miles an hour, let him get to the middle of the road, where there was a grass divider. Here he was exposed to the ridicule of the northbound traffic, but after ten or fifteen minutes he was able to cross. From here he had only a short walk to the Recreation Center at the edge of the Village of Lancaster, where there were some handball courts and a public pool.

The effect of the water on voices, the illusion of brilliance and suspense, was the same here as it had been at the Bunkers' but the sounds here were louder, harsher, and more shrill, and as soon as he entered the crowded enclosure he was confronted with regimentation. "ALL SWIMMERS MUST TAKE A

SHOWER BEFORE USING THE POOL. ALL SWIMMERS MUST USE THE FOOTBATH. ALL SWIMMERS MUST WEAR THEIR IDENTIFICATION DISKS." He took a shower, washed his feet in a cloudy and bitter solution and made his way to the edge of the water. It stank of chlorine and looked to him like a sink. A pair of lifeguards in a pair of towers blew police whistles at what seemed to be regular intervals and abused the swimmers through a public address system. Neddy remembered the sapphire water at the Bunkers' with longing and thought that he might contaminate himself—damage his own prosperousness and charm—by swimming in this murk, but he reminded himself that he was an explorer, a pilgrim, and that this was merely a stagnant bend in the Lucinda River. He dove, scowling with distaste, into the chlorine and had to swim with his head above water to avoid collisions, but even so he was bumped into, splashed and jostled. When he got to the shallow end both lifeguards were shouting at him: "Hey, you, you without the identification disk, get outa the water." He did, but they had no way of pursuing him and he went through the reck of suntan oil and chlorine out through the hurricane fence and passed the handball courts. By crossing the road he entered the wooded part of the Halloran estate. The woods were not cleared and the footing was treacherous and difficult until he reached the lawn and the clipped beech hedge that encircled their pool.

The Hallorans were friends, an elderly couple of enormous wealth who seemed to bask in the suspicion that they might be Communists. They were zealous reformers but they were not Communists, and yet when they were accused, as they sometimes were, of subversion, it seemed to gratify and excite them. Their beech hedge was yellow and he guessed this had been blighted like the Levy's maple. He called hullo, hullo, to warn the Hallorans of his approach, to palliate his invasion of their privacy. The Hallorans, for reasons that had never been explained to him, did not wear bathing suits. No explanations were in order, really. Their nakedness was a detail in their uncompromising zeal for reform and he stepped politely out of his trunks before he went through the opening in the hedge.

Mrs. Halloran, a stout woman with white hair and a serene face, was reading the *Times*. Mr. Halloran was taking beech leaves out of the water with a scoop. They seemed not surprised or displeased to see him. Their pool was perhaps the oldest in the county, a fieldstone rectangle, fed by a brook. It had no filter or pump and its waters were the opaque gold of the stream.

"I'm swimming across the county," Ned said.

"Why, I didn't know one could," exclaimed Mrs. Halloran.

"Well, I've made it from the Westerhazys'," Ned said. "That must be about four miles."

He left his trunks at the deep end, walked to the shallow end, and swam this stretch. As he was pulling himself out of the water he heard Mrs. Halloran say: "We've been *terribly* sorry to hear about all your misfortunes, Neddy."

"My misfortunes?" Ned asked. "I don't know what you mean."

"Why, we heard that you'd sold the house and that your poor children . . ."

"I don't recall having sold the house," Ned said, "and the girls are at home."

"Yes," Mrs. Halloran sighed. "Yes . . ." Her voice filled the air with an unseasonable melancholy and Ned spoke briskly. "Thank you for the swim."

"Well, have a nice trip," said Mrs. Halloran.

Beyond the hedge he pulled on his trunks and fastened them. They were loose and he wondered if, during the space of an afternoon, he could have lost some weight. He was cold and he was tired and the naked Hallorans and their dark water had depressed him. The swim was too much for his strength but how could he have guessed this, sliding down the banister that morning and sitting in the Westerhazys' sun? His arms were lame. His legs felt rubbery and ached at the joints. The worst of it was the cold in his bones and the feeling that he might never be warm again. Leaves were falling down around him and he smelled woodsmoke on the wind. Who would be burning wood at this time of year?

He needed a drink. Whiskey would warm him, pick him up, carry him through the last of his journey, refresh his feeling that it was original and valorous to swim across the county. Channel swimmers took brandy. He needed a stimulant. He crossed the lawn in front of the Hallorans' house and went down a little path to where they had built a house for their only daughter Helen and her husband Eric Sachs. The Sachses' pool was small and he found Helen and her husband there.

"Oh, *Neddy*," Helen said. "Did you lunch at Mother's?"

"Not *really*," Ned said. "I *did* stop to see your parents." This seemed to be explanation enough. "I'm terribly sorry to break in on you like this but I've taken a chill and I wonder if you'd give me a drink."

"Why, I'd *love* to," Helen said, "but there hasn't been anything in this house to drink since Eric's operation. That was three years ago."

Was he losing his memory, had his gift for concealing painful facts let him forget that he had sold his house, that his children were in trouble, and that his friend had been ill? His eyes slipped from Eric's face to his abdomen, where he saw three pale, sutured scars, two of them at least a foot long. Gone was his navel, and what, Neddy thought, would the roving hand, bed-checking one's gifts at 3 A.M., make of a belly with no navel, no link to birth, this breach in the succession?

"I'm sure you can get a drink at the Biswangers'," Helen said. "They're having an enormous do. You can hear it from here. Listen!"

She raised her head and from across the road, the lawns, the gardens, the woods, the fields, he heard again the brilliant noise of voices over water. "Well, I'll get wet," he said, still feeling that he had no freedom of choice about his means of travel. He drove into the Sachses' cold water and, gasping, close to drowning, made his way from one end of the pool to the other. "Lucinda and I want *terribly* to see you," he said over his shoulder, his face set toward the Biswangers'. "We're sorry it's been so long and we'll call you *very* soon."

He crossed some fields to the Biswangers' and the sounds of revelry there. They would be honored to give him a drink, they would be happy to give him a drink, they would in fact be lucky to give him a drink. The

Biswangers invited him and Lucinda for dinner four times a year, six weeks in advance. They were always rebuffed and yet they continued to send out their invitations, unwilling to comprehend the rigid and undemocratic realities of their society. They were the sort of people who discussed the price of things at cocktails, exchanged market tips during dinner, and after dinner told dirty stories to mixed company. They did not belong to Neddy's set—they were not even on Lucinda's Christmas card list. He went toward their pool with feelings of indifference, charity, and some unease, since it seemed to be getting dark and these were the longest days of the year. The party when he joined it was noisy and large. Grace Biswanger was the kind of hostess who asked the optometrist, the veterinarian, the real-estate dealer and the dentist. No one was swimming and the twilight, reflected on the water of the pool, had a wintry gleam. There was a bar and he started for this. When Grace Biswanger saw him she came toward him, not affectionately as he had every right to expect, but bellicosely.

"Why, this party has everything," she said loudly, "including a gate crasher."

She could not deal him a social blow—there was no question about this and he did not flinch. "As a gate crasher," he asked politely, "do I rate a drink?"

"Suit yourself," she said. "You don't seem to pay much attention to invitations."

She turned her back on him and joined some guests, and he went to the bar and ordered a whiskey. The bartender served him but he served him rudely. His was a world in which the caterer's men kept the social score, and to be rebuffed by a part-time barkeep meant that he had suffered some loss of social esteem. Or perhaps the man was new and uninformed. Then he heard Grace at his back say: "They went for broke overnight—nothing but income—and he showed up drunk one Sunday and asked us to loan him five thousand dollars. . . ." She was always talking about money. It was worse than eating your peas off a knife. He dove into the pool, swam its length and went away.

The next pool on his list, the last but two, belonged to his old mistress, Shirley Adams. If he had suffered any injuries at the Biswangers' they would be cured here. Love—sexual roughhouse in fact—was the supreme elixir, the painkiller, the brightly colored pill that would put the spring back into his step, the joy of life in his heart. They had had an affair last week, last month, last year. He couldn't remember. It was he who had broken it off, his was the upper hand, and he stepped through the gate of the wall that surrounded her pool with nothing so considered as self-confidence. It seemed in a way to be his pool as the lover, particularly the illicit lover, enjoys the possessions of his mistress with an authority unknown to holy matrimony. She was there, her hair the color of brass, but her figure, at the edge of the lighted, cerulean water, excited in him no profound memories. It had been, he thought, a lighthearted affair, although she had wept when he broke it off. She seemed confused to see him and he wondered if she was still wounded. Would she, God forbid, weep again?

"What do you want?" she asked.

"I'm swimming across the county."

"Good Christ. Will you ever grow up?"

"What's the matter?"

"If you've come here for money," she said, "I won't give you another cent."

"You could give me a drink."

"I could but I won't. I'm not alone."

"Well, I'm on my way."

He dove in and swam the pool, but when he tried to haul himself up onto the curb he found that the strength in his arms and his shoulders had gone, and he paddled to the ladder and climbed out. Looking over his shoulder he saw, in the lighted bathhouse, a young man. Going out onto the dark lawn he smelled chrysanthemums or marigolds—some stubborn autumnal fragrance—on the night air, strong as gas. Looking overhead he saw that the stars had come out, but why should he seem to see Andromeda, Cepheus, and Cassiopeia? What had become of the constellations of midsummer? He began to cry.

It was probably the first time in his adult life that he had ever cried, certainly the first time in his life that he had ever felt so miserable, cold, tired, and bewildered. He could not understand the rudeness of the caterer's barkeep or the rudeness of a mistress who had come to him on her knees and showered his trousers with tears. He had swum too long, he had been immersed too long, and his nose and his throat were sore from the water. What he needed then was a drink, some company, and some clean dry clothes, and while he could have cut directly across the road to his home he went on to the Gilmartins' pool. Here, for the first time in his life, he did not dive but went down the steps into the icy water and swam a hobbled side stroke that he might have learned as a youth. He staggered with fatigue on his way to the Clydes' and paddled the length of their pool, stopping again and again with his hand on the curb to rest. He climbed up the ladder and wondered if he had the strength to get home. He had done what he wanted, he had swum the county, but he was so stupefied with exhaustion that his triumph seemed vague. Stooped, holding onto the gateposts for support, he turned up the driveway of his own house.

The place was dark. Was it so late that they had all gone to bed? Had Lucinda stayed at the Westerhazys' for supper? Had the girls joined her there or gone someplace else? Hadn't they agreed, as they usually did on Sunday, to regret all their invitations and stay at home? He tried the garage doors to see what cars were in but the doors were locked and rust came off the handles onto his hands. Going toward the house, he saw that the force of the thunderstorm had knocked one of the rain gutters loose. It hung down over the front door like an umbrella rib, but it could be fixed in the morning. The house was locked, and he thought that the stupid cook or the stupid maid must have locked the place up until he remembered that it had been some time since they had employed a maid or a cook. He shouted, pounded on the door, tried to force it with his shoulder, and then, looking in at the windows, saw that the place was empty.

Writing About Setting

Most essays on setting concern themselves with the mood of the story, character, ideas, or a combination of these. They reveal how setting establishes the background of the story, develops character, or highlights a basic point. Obviously, you cannot deal with all these topics in one paper. You have to find the one that best suits the story you are reading. To do this you should first make sure you understand what the setting is and how it is related to other features of the story. You should ask yourself questions about how specific and vivid it is, how realistic and convincing. Next, there is the matter of how it fits the main idea of the story. What is its connection to the central character? What points does it make? What effect does it have? Finally, you should decide what parts of the setting you wish to concentrate on, especially if it is a complex and varied fictional world you are concerned with and there are numerous possible approaches. Some stories contain too rich and varied a setting to write about in a short paper.

Writing on setting in "María Concepción," for instance, you could focus on the framing device. This would lead you into an analysis of María's relationship with the land she lives on, its starkness and its sweetness and the way in which her determination and her passion spring from it. Or you could concentrate specifically on the cactus that is so representative of the country, revealing how its hardiness and sharpness are reflective of María and her world. It creates the mood of the story and defines her character better than any other single object. The beehives and the buried city being unearthed by the archeologist Givens are other subjects that you could write about, limited as they are. They help develop the atmosphere, indicate changes in the action, and supply contrasting scenes essential to the full meaning of the story. To narrow the scope of your paper even further, you could dwell on the shifting attitude of the townspeople toward María and her plight or on Juan's clothes and how they characterize him. Finally there are the innumerable details that convince you of the reality of María's world and lead you to believe in her, sympathize with her, and accept her barbarous action and her husband's and friends' tolerance of it.

The most important thing to do is to find an approach which is relevant and which works for you. Next, you should determine the kind of organization you are going to follow. And last you need to make sure that, in dealing with the particular aspect of setting you have chosen, you are not merely cataloguing and quoting but analyzing and interpreting.

The setting of "The Swimmer" offers many possible topics to write on, from the accurate description of suburbia to the false values of suburban society, from the pools as representative of the different aspects of this society to the significance of the weather. An even more fitting subject is the use of setting to portray Neddy Merrill. After all, the main concern of John Cheever is the protagonist and the way the details of the story relate to him. What happens to him, the kind of man he is, and the things he stands for are bound up with the day, the season, and the pools he swims. Hence you can write an essay that shows the relationship between his environment and him.

The topic is a general one, however, and must be made specific. The way to do this is, first, to go over the setting to discover which elements seem to be the most important with respect to Merrill. In the broadest sense they are time and place. In a more definite sense they are midsummer and Sunday, suburbia and swimming pools. In fact, the more closely you look at the story, the more you realize how precisely Cheever ties in his central character to these two fundamental aspects of setting. A thesis sentence would be as follows: Time and place in "The Swimmer" have a direct relationship to the character of Neddy Merrill. Although this might still seem too general, once you begin organizing it you will discover how very specific it actually becomes.

The first step to take in developing your essay is to divide it into three basic parts: time and Neddv Merrill, place and Neddy Merrill, and an evaluation of the author's achievement in rendering these two elements of setting. The next step is to divide further the two main areas into smaller units. Time has two parts, summer and Sunday. Place concerns first the pools and second the people who own them and their relationship to Merrill. The conclusion is an evaluation of the effectiveness of the setting.

Take care to avoid paraphrases of descriptions, lists of objects that appear in the story, and long quotations. You must remember that your primary purpose is to analyze and interpret and reach a decision about the author's handling of his materials. On the other hand, you must be careful not to depend on abstractions and vague generalizations. You must constantly refer to the scenes of the story.

The Loneliness of the Long-Distance Swimmer

Time and place in "The Swimmer" are not merely background for the actions of Neddy Merrill, but are an integral part of his characterization. What happens to him, the kind of man he is, and the things he represents are bound up with the season, the day, the pools he swims, and the people he meets. In the beginning he is in harmony with the bright day, seeing himself as "a pilgrim, an explorer, a man of destiny" seeking an excitingly new route home. In the end he discovers himself facing what the day and midsummer face in the future, darkness and a fall full of leaves.

First there is the importance of time. The fact that the action takes place on a midsummer day is no accident. The author compares his protagonist to a "summer's day, particularly the last hours of one." Like it he starts out full of vigor and eager for pleasure. He gives the impression of "youth, sport, and clement weather." But as the day wanes, so do his illusions about his strength and prosperous condition. The later it becomes the more unpleasantness he encounters from his friends until finally he reaches a home locked up and lightless. Here he must face the reality of what he is and what has become of him. The thundershower is the turning point. Before it he exults in his escapade and is warmly received by the people whose pools he swims. Even during the storm he pities the lonely souls at the station waiting for the local to take them into the city. But after the rain passes, the air becomes cool and he shivers. He notices blighted trees that resemble those of autumn. Midsummer is turning to autumn, middle-age to old age.

Another aspect of time is the particular day, Sunday, when everyone in suburbia sits around and talks about how much he drank last night. The holy day is given over to reminiscences of the weekend and to more drinking parties. It is an occasion for socializing and relaxing, not nuturing the spiritual life. A perfect day for Merrill, or so he thinks. He sets out on the pilgrimage to his home full of hope, at peace with his world. He ends it with a realization of his isolation. The good life he once knew is gone and there is nothing to replace it, only exhaustion and disillusionment.

Like all good writers Cheever has a strong sense of place. He knows thoroughly suburban living. He uses this knowledge not just to document the suburban scene, but to reveal something about Merrill's character. This is evident in his description of the various pools his hero swims and the actions around them. They vary with his mood, with the kind of people who surround them, and with the progress he is making on his journey homeward. The Westerhazys' pool he starts out in is fresh and green. He takes great delight in his friends. He is at the start of a great exploration. But as he moves on, each pool becomes a little less inviting, each group of neighbors a little less friendly, until he reaches the home of his former mistress, Shirley Adams. Here he sees the new lover who has replaced him and smells the flowers of autumn.

How precisely Cheever fits his settings to his characters and to the development of his protagonist is evident in the scene with the Hallorans, the wealthy liberals who sit around their pool naked. Their blighted beech hedge is symbolic of their age and their separation from the rest of his friends and the summer. Their pool, like them, is old-fashioned and natural, made of fieldstone and fed by a brook. The water is golden, not green or blue. It is they who express the most sincere sorrow for Merrill's misfortunes "with an unseasonable melancholy."

The author has created an effective setting. It is realistic and recognizable, true to suburbia and those who live in it. Furthermore, every detail suggests some larger meaning. Finally, setting expresses the protagonist. He is one with his world, though trying to transcend it. What happens to him stems from his environment. His only triumph is that gradually he realizes this fact. Upon reaching home and trying to deny to himself that the house has been abandoned, he comes to the full realization that it and his own life too are "empty."

DORIS LESSING

A Sunrise on the Veld

Every night that winter he said aloud into the dark of the pillow: Half-past four! Half-past four! till he felt his brain had gripped the words and held them fast. Then he fell asleep at once, as if a shutter had fallen; and lay with his face turned to the clock so that he could see it first thing when he woke.

It was half-past four to the minute, every morning. Triumphantly pressing down the alarm-knob of the clock, which the dark half of his mind had outwitted, remaining vigilant all night and counting the hours as he lay relaxed in sleep, he huddled down for a last warm moment under the clothes, playing with the idea of lying abed for this once only. But he played with it for the fun of knowing that it was a weakness he could defeat without effort; just as he set the alarm each night for the delight of the moment when he woke and stretched his limbs, feeling the muscles tighten, and thought: Even my brain—even that! I can control every part of myself.

Luxury of warm rested body, with the arms and legs and fingers waiting like soldiers for a word of command! Joy of knowing that the precious hours were given to sleep voluntarily!—for he had once stayed awake three nights running, to prove that he could, and then worked all day, refusing even to admit that he was tired; and now sleep seemed to him a servant to be commanded and refused.

The boy stretched his frame full-length, touching the wall at his head with his hands, and the bedfoot with his toes; then he sprung out, like a fish leaping from water. And it was cold, cold.

He always dressed rapidly, so as to try and conserve his night-warmth till the sun rose two hours later; but by the time he had on his clothes his hands were numbed and he could scarcely hold his shoes. These he could not put on for fear of waking his parents, who never came to know how early he rose.

As soon as he stepped over the lintel, the flesh of his soles contracted on the chilled earth, and his legs began to ache with cold. It was night: the stars were glittering, the trees standing black and still. He looked for signs of day, for the greying of the edge of a stone, or a lightening in the sky where the sun would rise, but there was nothing yet. Alert as an animal he crept past the dangerous window, standing poised with his hand on the sill for one proudly fastidious moment, looking in at the stuffy blackness of the room where his parents lay.

Feeling for the grass-edge of the path with his toes, he reached inside another window further along the wall, where his gun had been set in readiness the night before. The steel was icy, and numbed fingers slipped along it, so that he had to hold it in the crook of his arm for safety. Then he tiptoed to the room where the dogs slept, and was fearful that they might have been tempted to go before him; but they were waiting, their haunches crouched in reluctance at the cold, but ears and swinging tails greeting the gun ecstatically. His warning undertone kept them secret and silent till the house was a hundred yards back: then they bolted off into the bush, yelping excitedly. The boy imagined his parents turning in their beds and muttering: Those dogs again! before they were dragged back in sleep; and he smiled scornfully. He always looked back over his shoulder at the house before he passed a wall of trees that shut it from sight. It looked so low and small, crouching there under a tall and brilliant sky. Then he turned his back on it, and on the frowsting sleepers, and forgot them.

He would have to hurry. Before the light grew strong he must be four miles away; and already a tint of green stood in the hollow of a leaf, and the air smelled of morning and the stars were dimming.

He slung the shoes over his shoulder, veld *skoen* that were crinkled and hard with the dews of a hundred mornings. They would be necessary when the ground became too hot to bear. Now he felt the chilled dust push up between his toes, and he let the muscles of his feet spread and settle into the shapes of the earth; and he thought: I could walk a hundred miles on feet like these! I could walk all day, and never tire!

He was walking swiftly through the dark tunnel of foliage that in day-time was a road. The dogs were invisibly ranging the lower travelways of the bush, and he heard them panting. Sometimes he felt a cold muzzle on his leg before they were off again, scouting for a trail to follow. They were not trained, but free-running companions of the hunt, who often tired of the long stalk before the final shots, and went off on their own pleasure. Soon he could see them, small and wild-looking in a wild strange light, now that the bush stood trembling on the verge of colour, waiting for the sun to paint earth and grass afresh.

The grass stood to his shoulders; and the trees were showering a faint silvery rain. He was soaked; his whole body was clenched in a steady shiver.

Once he bent to the road that was newly scored with animal trails, and regretfully straightened, reminding himself that the pleasure of tracking must wait till another day.

He began to run along the edge of a field, noting jerkily how it was filmed over with fresh spiderweb, so that the long reaches of great black clods seemed netted in glistening grey. He was using the steady lope he had learned by watching the natives, the run that is a dropping of the weight of the body from one foot to the next in a slow balancing movement that never tires, nor shortens the breath; and he felt the blood pulsing down his legs and along his arms, and the exultation and pride of body mounted in him till he was shutting his teeth hard against a violent desire to shout his triumph.

Soon he had left the cultivated part of the farm. Behind him the bush was low and black. In front was a long vlei, acres of long pale grass that sent back a hollowing gleam of light to a satiny sky. Near him thick swathes of grass were bent with the weight of water, and diamond drops sparkled on each frond.

The first bird woke at his feet and at once a flock of them sprang into the air calling shrilly that day had come; and suddenly, behind him, the bush woke into song, and he could hear the guinea fowl calling far ahead of him. That meant they would now be sailing down from their trees into thick grass, and it was for them he had come: he was too late. But he did not mind. He forgot he had come to shoot. He set his legs wide, and balanced from foot to foot, and swung his gun up and down in both hands horizontally, in a kind of improvised exercise, and let his head sink back till it was pillowed in his neck muscles, and watched how above him small rosy clouds floated in a lake of gold.

Suddenly it all rose in him: it was unbearable. He leapt up into the air, shouting and yelling wild, unrecognisable noises. Then he began to run, not carefully, as he had before, but madly, like a wild thing. He was clean crazy, yelling mad with the joy of living and a superfluity of youth. He rushed down the vlei under a tumult of crimson and gold, while all the birds of the world sang about him. He ran in great leaping strides, and shouted as he ran, feeling his body rise into the crisp rushing air and fall back surely on to sure feet; and thought briefly, not believing that such a thing could happen to him, that he could break his ankle any moment, in this thick tangled grass. He cleared bushes like a duiker, leapt over rocks; and finally came to a dead stop at a place where the ground fell abruptly away below him to the river. It was a two-mile-long dash through waist-high growth, and he was breathing hoarsely and could no longer sing. But he poised on a rock and looked down at stretches of water that gleamed through stooping trees, and thought suddenly, I am fifteen! Fifteen! The words came new to him; so that he kept repeating them wonderingly, with swelling excitement; and he felt the years of his life with his hands, as if he were counting marbles, each one hard and separate and compact, each one a wonderful shining thing. That was what he was: fifteen years of this rich soil, and this slow-moving water, and air that smelt like a challenge whether it was warm and sultry at noon, or as brisk as cold water, like it was now.

There was nothing he couldn't do, nothing! A vision came to him, as he stood there, like when a child hears the word "eternity" and tries to understand it, and time takes possession of the mind. He felt his life ahead of him as a great and wonderful thing, something that was his; and he said aloud, with the blood rising to his head: all the great men of the world have been as I am now, and there is nothing I can't become, nothing I can't do; there is no country in the world I cannot make part of myself, if I choose. I contain the world. I can make of it what I want. If I choose, I can change everything that is going to happen: it depends on me, and what I decide now.

The urgency, and the truth and the courage of what his voice was saying exulted him so that he began to sing again, at the top of his voice, and the sound went echoing down the river gorge. He stopped for the echo, and sang again: stopped and shouted. That was what he was!—he sang, if he chose; and the world had to answer him.

And for minutes he stood there, shouting and singing and waiting for the lovely eddying sound of the echo; so that his own new strong thoughts came back and washed round his head, as if someone were answering him and encouraging him; till the gorge was full of soft voices clashing back and forth from rock to rock over the river. And then it seemed as if there was a new voice. He listened, puzzled, for it was not his own. Soon he was leaning forward, all his nerves alert, quite still: somewhere close to him there was a noise that was no joyful bird, nor tinkle of falling water, nor ponderous movement of cattle.

There it was again. In the deep morning hush that held his future and his past, was a sound of pain, and repeated over and over: it was a kind of shortened scream, as if someone, something, had no breath to scream. He came to himself, looked about him, and called for the dogs. They did not appear: they had gone off on their own business, and he was alone. Now he was clean sober, all the madness gone. His heart beating fast, because of that frightened screaming, he stepped carefully off the rock and went towards a belt of trees. He was moving cautiously, for not so long ago he had seen a leopard in just this spot.

At the edge of the trees he stopped and peered, holding his gun ready; he advanced, looking steadily about him, his eyes narrowed. Then, all at once, in the middle of a step, he faltered, and his face was puzzled. He shook his head impatiently, as if he doubted his own sight.

There, between two trees, against a background of gaunt black rocks, was a figure from a dream, a strange beast that was horned and drunken-legged, but like something he had never even imagined. It seemed to be ragged. It looked like a small buck that had black ragged tufts of fur standing up irregularly all over it, with patches of raw flesh beneath . . . but the patches of rawness were disappearing under moving black and came again elsewhere; and all the time the creature screamed, in small gasping screams, and leaped drunkenly from side to side, as if it were blind.

Then the boy understood: it *was* a buck. He ran closer, and again stood still, stopped by a new fear. Around him the grass was whispering and alive. He looked wildly about, and then down. The ground was black with ants, great energetic ants that took no notice of him, but hurried and scurried towards the fighting shape, like glistening black water flowing through the grass.

And, as he drew in his breath and pity and terror seized him, the beast fell and the screaming stopped. Now he could hear nothing but one bird singing, and the sound of the rustling, whispering ants.

He peered over at the writhing blackness that jerked convulsively with the jerking nerves. It grew quieter. There were small twitches from the mass that still looked vaguely like the shape of a small animal.

It came into his mind that he should shoot it and end its pain; and he raised the gun. Then he lowered it again. The buck could no longer feel; its fighting was a mechanical protest of the nerves. But it was not that which made him put down the gun. It was a swelling feeling of rage and misery and protest that expressed itself in the thought: if I had not come it would have died like this: so why should I interfere? All over the bush things like this happen; they happen all the time; this is how life goes on, by living things dying in anguish. He gripped the gun between his knees and felt in his own limbs the myriad swarming pain of the twitching animal that could no longer feel, and set his teeth, and said over and over again under his breath: I can't stop it. I can't stop it. There is nothing I can do.

He was glad that the buck was unconscious and had gone past suffering so that he did not have to make a decision to kill it even when he was feeling with his whole body: this is what happens, this is how things work.

It was right—that was what he was feeling. *It was right and nothing could alter it.*

The knowledge of fatality, of what has to be, had gripped him and for the first time in his life; and he was left unable to make any movement of brain or body, except to say: "Yes, yes. That is what living is." It had entered his flesh and his bones and grown in to the furthest corners of his brain and would never leave him. And at that moment he could not have performed the smallest action of mercy, knowing as he did, having lived on it all his life, the vast unalterable, cruel veld, where at any moment one might stumble over a skull or crush the skeleton of some small creature.

Suffering, sick, and angry, but also grimly satisfied with his new stoicism, he stood there leaning on his rifle, and watched the seething black mound grow smaller. At his feet, now, were ants trickling back with pink fragments in their mouths, and there was a fresh acid smell in his nostrils. He sternly controlled the uselessly convulsing muscles of his empty stomach, and reminded himself: the ants must eat too! At the same time he found that the tears were streaming down his face, and his clothes were soaked with the sweat of that other creature's pain.

The shape had grown small. Now it looked like nothing recognisable. He did not know how long it was before he saw the blackness thin, and bits of white showed through, shining in the sun—yes, there was the sun, just up, glowing over the rocks. Why, the whole thing could not have taken longer than a few minutes.

He began to swear, as if the shortness of the time was in itself unbearable, using the words he had heard his father say. He strode forward, crushing ants with each step, and brushing them off his clothes, till he stood above the skeleton, which lay sprawled under a small bush. It was clean-picked. It might have been lying there years, save that on the white bone were pink fragments of gristle. About the bones ants were ebbing away, their pincers full of meat.

The boy looked at them, big black ugly insects. A few were standing and gazing up at him with small glittering eyes.

"Go away!" he said to the ants, very coldly. "I am not for you—not just yet, at any rate. Go away." And he fancied that the ants turned and went away.

He bent over the bones and touched the sockets in the skull; that was where the eyes were, he thought incredulously, remembering the liquid dark eyes of a buck. And then he bent the slim foreleg bone, swinging it horizontally in his palm.

That morning, perhaps an hour ago, this small creature had been stepping proud and free through the bush, feeling the chill on its hide even as he himself had done, exhilarated by it. Proudly stepping the earth, tossing its horns, frisking a pretty white tail, it had sniffed the cold morning air. Walking like kings and conquerors it had moved through this free-held bush, where each blade of grass grew for it alone, and where the river ran pure sparkling water for its slaking.

And then—what had happened? Such a swift surefooted thing could surely not be trapped by a swarm of ants?

The boy bent curiously to the skeleton. Then he saw that the back leg that lay uppermost and strained out in the tension of death, was snapped midway in the thigh, so that broken bones jutted over each other uselessly. So that was it! Limping into the ant-masses it could not escape, once it had sensed the danger. Yes, but how had the leg been broken? Had it fallen, perhaps? Impossible, a buck was too light and graceful. Had some jealous rival horned it?

What could possibly have happened? Perhaps some Africans had thrown stones at it, as they do, trying to kill it for meat, and had broken its leg. Yes, that must be it.

Even as he imagined the crowd of running, shouting natives, and the flying stones, and the leaping buck, another picture came into his mind. He saw himself, on any one of these bright ringing mornings, drunk with excitement, taking a snap shot at some half-seen buck. He saw himself with the gun lowered, wondering whether he had missed or not; and thinking at last that it was late, and he wanted his breakfast, and it was not worth while to track miles after an animal that would very likely get away from him in any case.

For a moment he would not face it. He was a small boy again, kicking sulkily at the skeleton, hanging his head, refusing to accept the responsibility.

Then he straightened up, and looked down at the bones with an odd expression of dismay, all the anger gone out of him. His mind went quite empty: all around him he could see trickles of ants disappearing into the grass. The whispering noise was faint and dry, like the rustling of a cast snakeskin.

At last he picked up his gun and walked homewards. He was telling himself half defiantly that he wanted his breakfast. He was telling himself that it was getting very hot, much too hot to be out roaming the bush.

Really, he was tired. He walked heavily, not looking where he put his feet. When he came within sight of his home he stopped, knitting his brows. There was something he had to think out. The death of that small animal was a thing that concerned him, and he was by no means finished with it. It lay at the back of his mind uncomfortably.

Soon, the very next morning, he would get clear of everybody and go to the bush and think about it.

Questions for Study

1. *Why does the story begin in the boy's bedroom instead of on the veld?*
2. *Why does the author stress so strongly the boy's body and its movements?*
3. *What besides the "joy of living" causes the boy to begin shouting madly?*
4. *How does the setting prepare for the discovery of the dying buck?*
5. *What is the boy's final attitude toward the ants?*
6. *Why does he brood over what caused the buck to become helpless?*
7. *Why does he decide to return to the bush to think about the death of the animal?*

Topics for Discussion and Writing

1. *Show how the setting changes as the protagonist's attitude changes, indicating how the author uses natural detail to reveal the boy's thinking and feeling.*
2. *Discuss the paragraph on p. 165 beginning "That morning, perhaps an hour ago, this small creature had been stepping proud and free through the bush . . ." as a mirror of the natural as well as the human world in the story. In your essay show how the boy thinks of himself in terms of the buck.*
3. *Discuss the relationship of the boy to the bush, his exaltation in it, his acceptance of its grim reality, and his decision at the end of the story to return to it to think about what he has seen.*
4. *Discuss the veld as representing both the joy of living and the terror of death for the protagonist.*

KATHERINE ANNE PORTER

María Concepción

María Concepción walked carefully, keeping to the middle of the white dusty road, where the maguey thorns and the treacherous curved spines of organ cactus had not gathered so profusely. She would have enjoyed resting for a moment in the dark shade by the roadside, but she had no time to waste drawing cactus needles from her feet. Juan and his chief would be waiting for their food in the damp trenches of the buried city.

She carried about a dozen living fowls slung over her right shoulder, their feet fastened together. Half of them fell upon the flat of her back, the balance dangled uneasily over her breast. They wriggled their benumbed and swollen legs against her neck, they twisted their stupefied eyes and peered into her face inquiringly. She did not see them or think of them. Her left arm was tired with the weight of the food basket, and she was hungry after her long morning's work.

Her straight back outlined itself strongly under her clean bright blue cotton rebozo. Instinctive serenity softened her black eyes, shaped like almonds, set far apart, and tilted a bit endwise. She walked with the free, natural, guarded ease of the primitive woman carrying an unborn child. The shape of her body was easy, the swelling life was not a distortion, but the right inevitable proportions of a woman. She was entirely contented. Her husband was at work and she was on her way to market to sell her fowls.

Her small house sat half-way up a shallow hill, under a clump of pepper-trees, a wall of organ cactus enclosing it on the side nearest to the road. Now she came down into the valley, divided by the narrow spring, and crossed a bridge of loose stones near the hut where María Rosa the beekeeper lived with her old godmother, Lupe the medicine woman. María Concepción had no faith in the charred owl bones, the singed rabbit fur, the cat entrails, the messes and ointments sold by Lupe to the ailing of the village. She was a good Christian, and drank simple herb teas for headache and stomachache, or bought her remedies bottled, with printed directions that she could not read, at the drugstore near the city market, where she went almost daily. But she often bought a jar of honey from young María Rosa, a pretty, shy child only fifteen years old.

María Concepción and her husband, Juan Villegas, were each a little past their eighteenth year. She had a good reputation with the neighbors as an energetic religious woman who could drive a bargain to the end. It was commonly known that if she wished to buy a new rebozo for herself or a shirt for Juan, she could bring out a sack of hard silver coins for the purpose.

She had paid for the license, nearly a year ago, the potent bit of stamped paper which permits people to be married in the church. She had given money to the priest before she and Juan walked together up to the altar the Monday after Holy Week. It had been the adventure of the villagers to go, three Sundays one after another, to hear the banns called by the priest for Juan de Dios Villegas and María Concepción Manríquez, who were actually getting married in the church, instead of behind it, which was the usual custom, less expensive, and as binding as any other ceremony. But María Concepción was always as proud as if she owned a hacienda.

She paused on the bridge and dabbled her feet in the water, her eyes resting themselves from the sun-rays in a fixed gaze to the far-off mountains, deeply blue under their hanging drift of clouds. It came to her that she would like a fresh crust of honey. The delicious aroma of bees, their slow thrilling hum, awakened a pleasant desire for a flake of sweetness in her mouth.

"If I do not eat it now, I shall mark my child," she thought, peering through the crevices in the thick hedge of cactus that sheered up nakedly, like bared knife blades set protectingly around the small clearing. The place was so silent she doubted if María Rosa and Lupe were at home.

The leaning jacal of dried rush-withes and corn sheaves, bound to tall saplings thrust into the earth, roofed with yellow maguey leaves flattened and overlapping like shingles, hunched drowsy and fragrant in the warmth of noonday. The hives, similarly made, were scattered towards the back of the clearing, like small mounds of clean vegetable refuse. Over each mound there hung a dusty golden shimmer of bees.

A light gay scream of laughter rose from behind the hut; a man's short laugh joined in. "Ah, hahahaha!" went the voices together high and low, like a song.

"So María Rosa has a man!" María Concepción stopped short, smiling, shifted her burden slightly, and bent forward shading her eyes to see more clearly through the spaces of the hedge.

María Rosa ran, dodging between beehives, parting two stunted jasmine bushes as she came, lifting her knees in swift leaps, looking over her shoulder and laughing in a quivering, excited way. A heavy jar, swung to her wrist by the handle, knocked against her thighs as she ran. Her toes pushed up sudden spurts of dust, her half-raveled braids showered around her shoulders in long crinkled wisps.

Juan Villegas ran after her, also laughing strangely, his teeth set, both rows gleaming behind the small soft black beard growing sparsely on his lips, his chin, leaving his brown cheeks girl-smooth. When he seized her, he clenched so hard her chemise gave way and ripped from her shoulder. She stopped laughing at this, pushed him away and stood silent, trying to pull up the torn sleeve with one hand. Her pointed chin and dark red mouth moved in an uncertain way, as if she wished to laugh again; her long black lashes flickered with the quick-moving lights in her hidden eyes.

María Concepción did not stir nor breathe for some seconds. Her forehead was cold, and yet boiling water seemed to be pouring slowly along her spine. An unaccountable pain was in her knees, as if they were broken. She was afraid Juan and María Rosa would feel her eyes fixed upon them and would find her there, unable to move, spying upon them. But they did not pass beyond the enclosure, nor even glance towards the gap in the wall opening upon the road.

Juan lifted one of María Rosa's loosened braids and slapped her neck with it playfully. She smiled softly, consentingly. Together they moved back through the hives of honey-comb. María Rosa balanced her jar on one hip and swung her long full petticoats with every step. Juan flourished his wide hat back and forth, walking proudly as a game-cock.

María Concepción came out of the heavy cloud which enwrapped her head and bound her throat, and found herself walking onward, keeping the road without knowing it, feeling her way delicately, her ears strumming as if all María Rosa's bees had hived in them. Her careful sense of duty kept her moving toward the buried city where Juan's chief, the American archeologist, was taking his midday rest, waiting for his food.

Juan and María Rosa! She burned all over now, as if a layer of tiny fig-cactus bristles, as cruel as spun glass, had crawled under her skin. She wished to sit down quietly and wait for her death, but not until she had cut the throats of her man and that girl who were laughing and kissing under the cornstalks. Once when she was a young girl she had come back from market to find her jacal burned to a pile of ash and her few silver coins gone. A dark empty feeling had filled her; she kept moving about the place, not believing her eyes, expecting it all to take shape again before her. But it was gone, and though she knew an enemy had done it, she could not find out who it was, and could only curse and threaten the air. Now here was a worse thing, but she knew her enemy. María Rosa, that sinful girl, shameless! She heard herself saying a harsh, true word about María Rosa, saying it aloud as if she expected someone to agree with her: "Yes, she is a whore! She has no right to live."

At this moment the gray untidy head of Givens appeared over the edges of the newest trench he had caused to be dug in his field of excavations. The long deep crevasses, in which a man might stand without being seen, lay criss-crossed like orderly gashes of a giant scalpel. Nearly all of the men of the community worked for Givens, helping him to uncover the lost city of their ancestors. They worked all the year through and prospered, digging every day for those small clay heads and bits of pottery and fragments of painted walls for which there was no good use on earth, being all broken and encrusted with clay. They themselves could make better ones, perfectly stout and new, which they took to town and peddled to foreigners for real money. But the unearthly delight of the chief in finding these worn-out things was an endless puzzle. He would fairly roar for joy at times, waving a shattered pot or a human skull above his head, shouting for his photographer to come and make a picture of this!

Now he emerged, and his young enthusiast's eyes welcomed María Concepción from his old-man face, covered with hard wrinkles and burned to the color of red earth. "I hope you've brought me a nice fat one." He selected a fowl from the bunch dangling nearest him as María Concepción, wordless, leaned over the trench. "Dress it for me, there's a good girl. I'll broil it."

María Concepción took the fowl by the head, and silently, swiftly drew her knife across its throat, twisting the head off with the casual firmness she might use with the top of a beet.

"Good God, woman, you do have nerve," said Givens, watching her. "I can't do that. It gives me the creeps."

"My home country is Gualalajara," exclaimed María Concepción, without bravado, as she picked and gutted the fowl.

She stood and regarded Givens condescendingly, that diverting white man who had no woman of his own to cook for him, and moreover appeared not to feel any loss of dignity in preparing his own food. He squatted now, eyes squinted, nose wrinkled to avoid the smoke, turning the roasting fowl busily on a stick. A mysterious man, undoubtedly rich, and Juan's chief, therefore to be respected, to be placated.

"The tortillas are fresh and hot, señor," she murmured gently. "With your permission I will now go to market."

"Yes, yes, run along; bring me another of these tomorrow." Givens turned his head to look at her again. Her grand manner sometimes reminded him of royalty in exile. He noticed her unnatural paleness. "The sun is too hot, eh?" he asked.

"Yes, sir. Pardon me, but Juan will be here soon?"

"He ought to be here now. Leave his food. The others will eat it."

She moved away; the blue of her rebozo became a dancing spot in the heat waves that rose from the gray-red soil. Givens liked his Indians best when he could feel a fatherly indulgence for their primitive childish ways. He told comic stories of Juan's escapades, of how often he had saved him, in the past five years, from going to jail, and even from being shot, for his varied and always unexpected misdeeds.

"I am never a minute too soon to get him out of one pickle or another," he would say. "Well, he's a good worker, and I know how to manage him."

After Juan was married, he used to twit him, with exactly the right shade of condescension, on his many infidelities to María Concepción. "She'll catch you yet, and God help you!" he was fond of saying, and Juan would laugh with immense pleasure.

It did not occur to María Concepción to tell Juan she had found him out. During the day her anger against him died, and her anger against

María Rosa grew. She kept saying to herself, "When I was a young girl like María Rosa, if a man had caught hold of me so, I would have broken my jar over his head." She forgot completely that she had not resisted even so much as María Rosa, on the day that Juan had first taken hold of her. Besides she had married him afterwards in the church, and that was a very different thing.

Juan did not come home that night, but went away to war and María Rosa went with him. Juan had a rifle at his shoulder and two pistols at his belt. María Rosa wore a rifle also, slung on her back along with the blankets and the cooking pots. They joined the nearest detachment of troops in the field, and María Rosa marched ahead with the battalion of experienced women of war, which went over the crops like locusts, gathering provisions for the army. She cooked with them, and ate with them what was left after the men had eaten. After battles she went out on the field with the others to salvage clothing and ammunition and guns from the slain before they should begin to swell in the heat. Sometimes they would encounter the women from the other army, and a second battle as grim as the first would take place.

There was no particular scandal in the village. People shrugged, grinned. It was far better that they were gone. The neighbors went around saying that María Rosa was safer in the army than she would be in the same village with María Concepción.

María Concepción did not weep when Juan left her; and when the baby was born, and died within four days, she did not weep. "She is mere stone," said old Lupe, who went over and offered charms to preserve the baby.

"May you rot in hell with your charms," said María Concepción.

If she had not gone so regularly to church, lighting candles before the saints, kneeling with her arms spread in the form of a cross for hours at a time, and receiving holy communion every month, there might have been talk of her being devil-possessed, her face was so changed and blind-looking. But this was impossible when, after all, she had been married by the priest. It must be, they reasoned, that she was being punished for her pride. They decided that this was the true cause for everything: she was altogether too proud. So they pitied her.

During the year that Juan and María Rosa were gone María Concepción sold her fowls and looked after her garden and her sack of hard coins grew. Lupe had no talent for bees, and the hives did not prosper. She began to blame María Rosa for running away, and to praise María Concepción for her behavior. She used to see María Concepción at the market or at church, and she always said that no one could tell by looking at her now that she was a woman who had such a heavy grief.

"I pray God everything goes well with María Concepción from this out," she would say, "for she has had her share of trouble."

When some idle person repeated this to the deserted woman, she went down to Lupe's house and stood within the clearing and called to the medicine woman, who sat in her doorway stirring a mess of her infallible cure for sores: "Keep your prayers to yourself, Lupe, or offer them for others who need them. I will ask God for what I want in this world."

"And will you get it, you think, María Concepción?" asked Lupe, tittering cruelly and smelling the wooden mixing spoon. "Did you pray for what you have now?"

Afterward everyone noticed that María Concepción went oftener to church, and even seldomer to the village to talk with the other women as they sat along the curb, nursing their babies and eating fruit, at the end of the market-day.

"She is wrong to take us for enemies," said old Soledad, who was a thinker and a peace-maker. "All women have these troubles. Well, we should suffer together."

But María Concepción lived alone. She was gaunt, as if something were gnawing her away inside, her eyes were sunken, and she would not speak a word if she could help it. She worked harder than ever, and her butchering knife was scarcely ever out of her hand.

Juan and María Rosa, disgusted with military life, came home one day without asking permission of anyone. The field of war had unrolled itself, a long scroll of vexations, until the end had frayed out within twenty miles of Juan's village. So he and María Rosa, now lean as a wolf, burdened with a child daily expected, set out with no farewells to the regiment and walked home.

They arrived one morning about daybreak. Juan was picked up on sight by a group of military police from the small barracks on the edge of town, and taken to prison, where the officer in charge told him with impersonal cheerfulness that he would add one to a catch of ten waiting to be shot as deserters the next morning.

María Rosa, screaming and falling on her face in the road, was taken under the armpits by two guards and helped briskly to her jacal, now sadly run down. She was received with professional importance by Lupe, who helped the baby to be born at once.

Limping with foot soreness, a layer of dust concealing his fine new clothes got mysteriously from somewhere, Juan appeared before the captain at the barracks. The captain recognized him as head digger for his good friend Givens, and dispatched a note to Givens saying: "I am holding the person of Juan Villegas awaiting your further disposition."

When Givens showed up Juan was delivered to him with the urgent request that nothing be made public about so humane and sensible an operation on the part of military authority.

Juan walked out of the rather stifling atmosphere of the drumhead court, a definite air of swagger about him. His hat, of unreasonable dimensions and embroidered with silver thread, hung over one eyebrow, secured at the back by a cord of silver dripping with bright blue tassels. His shirt was of a checkerboard pattern in green and black, his white cotton trousers were bound by a belt of yellow leather tooled in red. His feet were bare, full of stone bruises, and sadly ragged as to toenails. He removed his cigarette from the corner of his full-lipped wide mouth. He removed the splendid hat. His black dusty hair, pressed moistly to his forehead, sprang up suddenly in a cloudy thatch on his crown. He bowed to the officer, who appeared to be gazing at a vacuum. He swung his arm wide in a free circle upsoaring towards the prison window, where forlorn heads poked over the window sill, hot eyes following after the lucky departing one. Two or three of the heads nodded, and a half dozen hands were flipped at him in an effort to imitate his own casual and heady manner.

Juan kept up this insufferable pantomime until they rounded the first clump of fig-cactus. Then he seized Givens' hand and burst into oratory. "Blessed be the day your servant Juan Villegas first came under your eyes. From this day my life is yours without condition, ten thousand thanks with all my heart!"

"For God's sake stop playing the fool," said Givens irritably. "Some day I'm going to be five minutes too late."

"Well, it is nothing much to be shot, my chief—certainly you know I was not afraid—but to be shot in a drove of deserters, against a cold wall, just in the moment of my home-coming, by order of that . . ."

Glittering epithets tumbled over one another like explosions of a rocket. All the scandalous analogies from the animal and vegetable worlds were applied in a vivid, unique and personal way to the life, loves, and family history of the officer who had just set him free. When he had quite cursed himself dry, and his nerves were soothed, he added: "With your permission, my chief!"

"What will María Concepción say to all this?" asked Givens. "You are very informal, Juan, for a man who was married in the church."

Juan put on his hat.

"Oh, María Concepción! That's nothing. Look, my chief, to be married in the church is a great misfortune for a man. After that he is not himself any more. How can that woman complain when I do not drink even at fiestas enough to be really drunk? I do not beat her; never, never. We were always at peace. I say to her, Come here, and she comes straight. I say, Go there, and she goes quickly. Yet sometimes I looked at her and thought, Now I am married to that woman in the church, and I felt a sinking inside, as if something were lying heavy on my stomach. With María Rosa it is all different. She is not silent; she talks. When she talks too much, I slap her and say, Silence, thou simpleton! and she weeps. She is just a girl with whom I do as I please. You know how she used to keep those clean little bees in their hives? She is like their honey to me. I swear it. I would not harm María Concepción because I am married to her in the church; but also, my chief, I will not leave María Rosa, because she pleases me more than any other woman."

"Let me tell you, Juan, things haven't been going as well as you think. You be careful. Some day María Concepción will just take your head off with that carving knife of hers. You keep that in mind."

Juan's expression was the proper blend of masculine triumph and sentimental melancholy. It was pleasant to see himself in the role of hero to two such desirable women. He had just escaped from the threat of a disagreeable end. His clothes were new and handsome, and they had cost him just nothing. María Rosa had collected them for him here and there after battles. He was walking in the early sunshine, smelling the good smells of ripening cactus-figs, peaches, and melons, of pungent berries dangling from the pepper-trees, and the smoke of his cigarette under his nose. He was on his way to civilian life with his patient chief. His situation was ineffably perfect, and he swallowed it whole.

"My chief," he addressed Givens handsomely, as one man of the world to another, "women are good things, but not at this moment. With your permission, I will now go to the village and eat. My God, *how* I shall eat! Tomorrow morning very early I will come to the buried city and work like seven men. Let us forget María Concepción and María Rosa. Each one in her place. I will manage them when the time comes."

News of Juan's adventure soon got abroad, and Juan found many friends about him during the morning. They frankly commended his way of leaving the army. It was in itself the act of a hero. The new hero ate a great deal and drank somewhat, the occasion being better than a feastday. It was almost noon before he returned to visit María Rosa.

He found her sitting on a clean straw mat, rubbing fat on her three-hour-old son. Before this felicitous vision Juan's emotions so twisted him that he returned to the village and invited every man in the "Death and Resurrection" pulque shop to drink with him.

Having thus taken leave of his balance, he started back to María Rosa, and found himself unaccountably in his own house, attempting to beat María Concepción by way of re-establishing himself in his legal household.

María Concepción, knowing all the events of that unhappy day, was not in a yielding mood, and refused to be beaten. She did not scream nor implore; she stood her ground and resisted; she even struck at him. Juan, amazed, hardly knowing what he did, stepped back and gazed at her inquiringly through a leisurely whirling film which seemed to have lodged behind his eyes. Certainly he had not even thought of touching her. Oh, well, no harm done. He gave up, turned away, half-asleep on his feet. He dropped amiably in a shadowed corner and began to snore.

María Concepción, seeing that he was quiet, began to bind the legs of her fowls. It was market-day and she was late. She fumbled and tangled the bits of cord in her haste, and set off across the plowed fields instead of taking the accustomed road. She ran with a crazy panic in her head, her stumbling legs. Now and then she would stop and look about her, trying to place herself, then go on a few steps, until she realized that she was not going towards the market.

At once she came to her senses completely, recognized the thing that troubled her so terribly, was certain of what she wanted. She sat down quietly under a sheltering thorny bush and gave herself over to her long devouring sorrow. The thing which had for so long squeezed her whole body into a tight dumb knot of suffering suddenly broke with shocking violence. She jerked with the involuntary recoil of one who receives a blow, and the sweat poured from her skin as if the wounds of her whole life were shedding their salt ichor. Drawing her rebozo over her head, she bowed her forehead on her updrawn knees, and sat there in deadly silence and immobility. From time to time she lifted her head where the sweat formed steadily and poured down her face, drenching the front of her chemise, and her mouth had the shape of crying, but there were no tears and no sound. All her being was a dark confused memory of grief burning in her at night, of deadly baffled anger eating at her by day, until her very tongue tasted bitter, and her feet were as heavy as if she were mired in the muddy roads during the time of rains.

After a great while she stood up and threw the rebozo off her face, and set out walking again.

Juan awakened slowly, with long yawns and grumblings, alternated with short relapses into sleep full of visions and clamors. A blur of orange light seared his eyeballs when he tried to unseal his lids. There came from somewhere a low voice weeping without tears, saying meaningless phrases over and over. He began to listen. He tugged at the leash of his stupor, he strained to grasp those words which terrified him even though he could not quite hear them. Then he came awake with frightening suddenness, sitting up and staring at the long sharpened streak of light piercing the corn-husk walls from the level disappearing sun.

María Concepción stood in the doorway, looming colossally tall to his betrayed eyes. She was talking quickly, and calling his name. Then he saw her clearly.

"God's name!" said Juan, frozen to the marrow, "here I am facing my death!" for the long knife she wore habitually at her belt was in her hand. But instead, she threw it away, clear from her, and got down on her knees, crawling toward him as he had seen her crawl many times toward the shrine at Guadalupe Villa. He watched her approach with such horror that the hair of his head seemed to be lifting itself away from him. Falling forward upon her face, she huddled over him, lips moving in a ghostly whisper. Her words became clear, and Juan understood them all.

For a second he could not move nor speak. Then he took her head between both his hands, and supported her in this way, saying swiftly, anxiously reassuring, almost in a babble:

"Oh, thou poor creature! Oh, madwoman! Oh, my María Concepción, unfortunate! Listen. . . . Don't be afraid. Listen to me! I will hide thee away, I thy own man will protect thee! Quiet! Not a sound!"

Trying to collect himself, he held her and cursed under his breath for a few moments in the gathering darkness. María Concepción bent over, face almost on the ground, her feet folded under her, as if she would hide behind him. For the first time in his life Juan was aware of danger. This was danger. María Concepción would be dragged away between two gendarmes, with him following helpless and unarmed, to spend the rest of her days in Belén Prison, maybe. Danger! The night swarmed with threats. He stood up and dragged her up with him. She was silent and perfectly rigid, holding to him with resistless strength, her hands stiffened on his arms.

"Get me the knife," he told her in a whisper. Shc obeyed, her feet slipping along the hard earth floor, her shoulders straight, her arms close to her side. He lighted a candle. María Concepción held the knife out to him. It was stained and dark even to the handle with drying blood.

He frowned at her harshly, noting the same stains on her chemise and hands.

"Take off thy clothes and wash thy hands," he ordered. He washed the knife carefully, and threw the water wide of the doorway. She watched him and did likewise with the bowl in which she had bathed.

"Light the brasero and cook food for me," he told her in the same peremptory tone. He took her garments and went out. When he returned, she was wearing an old soiled dress, and was fanning the fire in the charcoal burner. Seating himself cross-legged near her, he stared at her as at a creature unknown to him, who bewildered him utterly, for whom there was no possible explanation. She did not turn her head, but kept silent and still, except for the movements of her strong hands fanning the blaze which cast sparks and small jets of white smoke, flaring and dying rhythmically with the motion of the fan lighting her face and darkening it by turns.

Juan's voice barely disturbed the silence: "Listen to me carefully, and tell me the truth, and when the gendarmes come here for us, thou shalt have nothing to fear. But there will be something for us to settle between us afterward."

The light from the charcoal burner shone in her eyes; a yellow phosphorescence, glimmered behind the dark iris.

"For me everything is settled now," she answered, in a tone so tender, so grave, so heavy with suffering, that Juan felt his vitals contract. He wished to repent openly, not as a man, but as a very small child. He could not fathom her, nor himself, nor the mysterious fortunes of life grown so instantly confused where all had seemed so gay and simple. He felt too that she had become invaluable, a woman without equal among a million women, and he could not tell why. He drew an enormous sigh that rattled in his chest.

"Yes, yes, it is all settled. I shall not go away again. We must stay here together."

Whispering, he questioned her and she answered whispering, and he instructed her over and over until she had her lesson by heart. The hostile darkness of the night encroached upon them, flowing over the narrow threshold, invading their hearts. It brought with it sighs and murmurs, the pad of secretive feet in the near-by road, the sharp staccato whimper of wind through the cactus leaves. All these familiar, once friendly cadences were now invested with sinister terrors; a dread, formless and uncontrollable, took hold of them both.

"Light another candle," said Juan, loudly, in too resolute, too sharp a tone. "Let us eat now."

They sat facing each other and ate from the same dish, after their old habit. Neither tasted what they ate. With food half-way to his mouth, Juan listened. The sound of voices rose, spread, widened at the turn of the road along the cactus wall. A spray of lantern light shot through the hedge, a single voice slashed the blackness, ripped the fragile layer of silence suspended above the hut.

"Juan Villegas!"

"Pass, friends!" Juan roared back cheerfully.

They stood in the doorway, simple cautious gendarmes from the village, mixed-bloods themselves with Indian sympathies, well known to all the community. They flashed their lanterns almost apologetically upon the pleasant, harmless scene of a man eating supper with his wife.

"Pardon, brother," said the leader. "Someone has killed the woman María Rosa, and we must question her neighbors and friends." He paused, and added with an attempt at severity, "Naturally!"

"Naturally," agreed Juan. "You know that I was a good friend of María Rosa. This is bad news."

They all went away together, the men walking in a group, María Concepción following a few steps in the rear, near Juan. No one spoke.

The two points of candlelight at María Rosa's head fluttered uneasily; the shadows shifted and dodged on the stained darkened walls. To María Concepción everything in the smothering enclosing room shared an evil restlessness. The watchful faces of those called as witnesses, the faces of old friends, were made alien by the look of speculation in their eyes. The ridges of the rose-colored rebozo thrown over the body varied continually, as though the thing it covered was not perfectly in repose. Her eyes swerved over the body in the open painted coffin, from the candle tips at the head to the feet, jutting up thinly, the small scarred soles protruding, freshly washed, a mass of crooked, half-healed wounds, thornpricks and cuts of sharp stones. Her gaze went back to the candle flame, to Juan's eyes warning her, to the gendarmes talking among themselves. Her eyes would not be controlled.

With a leap that shook her her gaze settled upon the face of María Rosa. Instantly her blood ran smoothly again: there was nothing to fear. Even the restless light could not give a look of life to that fixed countenance. She was dead. María Concepción felt her muscles give way softly; her heart began beating steadily without effort. She knew no more rancor against that pitiable thing, lying indifferently in its blue coffin under the fine silk rebozo. The mouth drooped sharply at the corners in a grimace of weeping arrested half-way. The brows were distressed; the dead flesh could not cast off the shape of its last terror. It was all finished. María Rosa had eaten too much honey and had had too much love. Now she must sit in hell, crying over her sins and her hard death forever and ever.

Old Lupe's cackling voice arose. She had spent the morning helping María Rosa, and it had been hard work. The child had spat blood the moment it was born, a bad sign. She thought then that bad luck would come to the house. Well, about sunset she was in the yard at the back of the house grinding tomatoes and peppers. She had left mother and babe asleep. She heard a strange noise in the house, a choking and smothered calling, like someone wailing in sleep. Well, such a thing is only natural. But there followed a light, quick, thudding sound—

"Like the blows of a fist?" interrupted an officer.

"No, not at all like such a thing."

"How do you know?"

"I am well acquainted with that sound, friends," retorted Lupe. "This was something else."

She was at a loss to describe it exactly. A moment later, there came the sound of pebbles rolling and slipping under feet; then she knew someone had been there and was running away.

"Why did you wait so long before going to see?"

"I am old and hard in the joints," said Lupe. "I cannot run after people. I walked as fast as I could to the cactus hedge, for it is only by this way that anyone can enter. There was no one in the road, sir, no one. Three cows, with a dog driving them; nothing else. When I got to María Rosa, she was lying all tangled up, and from her neck to her middle she was full of knife-holes. It was a sight to move the Blessed Image Himself! Her eyes were—"

"Never mind. Who came oftenest to her house before she went away? Did you know her enemies?"

Lupe's face congealed, closed. Her spongy skin drew into a network of secretive wrinkles. She turned withdrawn and expressionless eyes upon the gendarmes.

"I am an old woman. I do not see well. I cannot hurry on my feet. I know no enemy of María Rosa. I did not see anyone leave the clearing."

"You did not hear splashing in the spring near the bridge?"

"No, sir."

"Why, then, do our dogs follow a scent there and lose it?"

"God only knows, my friend. I am an old wo—"

"Yes. How did the footfalls sound?"

"Like the tread of an evil spirit!" Lupe broke forth in a swelling oracular tone that startled them. The Indians stirred uneasily, glanced at the dead, then at Lupe. They half expected her to produce the evil spirit among them at once.

The gendarme began to lose his temper.

"No, poor unfortunate; I mean, were they heavy or light? The footsteps of a man or of a woman? Was the person shod or barefoot?"

A glance at the listening circle assured Lupe of their thrilled attention. She enjoyed the dangerous importance of her situation. She could have ruined that María Concepción with a word, but it was even sweeter to make fools of these gendarmes who went about spying on honest people. She raised her voice again. What she had not seen she could not describe, thank God! No one could harm her because her knees were stiff and she could not run even to seize a murderer. As for knowing the difference between footfalls, shod or bare, man or woman, nay, between devil and human, who ever heard of such madness?

"My eyes are not ears, gentlemen," she ended grandly, "but upon my heart I swear those footsteps fell as the tread of the spirit of evil!"

"Imbecile!" yapped the leader in a shrill voice. "Take her away, one of you! Now, Juan Villegas, tell me—"

Juan told his story patiently, several times over. He had returned to his wife that day. She had gone to market as usual. He had helped her prepare her fowls. She had returned about mid-afternoon, they had talked, she had cooked, they had eaten, nothing was amiss. Then the gendarmes came with the news about María Rosa. That was all. Yes, María Rosa had run away with him, but there had been no bad blood between him and his wife on this account, nor between his wife and María Rosa. Everybody knew that his wife was a quiet woman.

María Concepción heard her own voice answering without a break. It was true at first she was troubled when her husband went away, but after that she had not worried about him. It was the way of men, she believed. She was a church-married woman and knew her place. Well, he had come home at last. She had gone to market, but had come back early, because now she had her man to cook for. That was all.

Other voices broke in. A toothless old man said: "She is a woman of good reputation among us, and María Rosa was not." A smiling young mother, Anita, baby at breast, said: "If no one thinks so, how can you accuse her? It was the loss of her child and not of her husband that changed her so." Another: "María Rosa had a strange life, apart from us. How do we know who might have come from another place to do her evil?" And old Soledad spoke up boldly: "When I saw María Concepción in the market today, I said, 'Good luck to you, María Concepción, this is a happy day for you!' " and she gave María Concepción a long easy stare, and the smile of a born wise-woman.

María Concepción suddenly felt herself guarded, surrounded, upborne by her faithful friends. They were around her, speaking for her, defending her, the forces of life were ranged invincibly with her against the beaten dead. María Rosa had thrown away her share of strength in them, she lay forfeited among them. María Concepción looked from one to the other of the circling, intent faces. Their eyes gave back reassurance, understanding, a secret and mighty sympathy.

The gendarmes were at a loss. They, too, felt that sheltering wall cast impenetrably around her. They were certain she had done it, and yet they could not accuse her. Nobody could be accused; there was not a shred of true evidence. They shrugged their shoulders and snapped their fingers and shuffled their feet. Well, then, good night to everybody. Many pardons for having intruded. Good health!

A small bundle lying against the wall at the head of the coffin squirmed like an eel. A wail, a mere sliver of sound, issued. María Concepción took the son of María Rosa in her arms.

"He is mine," she said clearly, "I will take him with me."

No one assented in words, but an approving nod, a bare breath of complete agreement, stirred among them as they made way for her.

María Concepción, carrying the child, followed Juan from the clearing. The hut was left with its lighted candles and a crowd of old women who would sit up all night, drinking coffee and smoking and telling ghost stories.

Juan's exaltation had burned out. There was not an ember of excitement left in him. He was tired. The perilous adventure was over. María Rosa had vanished, to come no more forever. Their days of marching, of eating, of quarreling and making love between battles, were all over. Tomorrow he would go back to dull and endless labor, he must descend into the trenches of the buried city as María Rosa must go into her grave. He felt his veins fill up with bitterness, with black unendurable melancholy. Oh, Jesus! what bad luck overtakes a man!

Well, there was no way out of it now. For the moment he craved only to sleep. He was so drowsy he could scarcely guide his feet. The occasional light touch of the woman at his elbow was as unreal, as ghostly as the brushing of a leaf against his face. He did not know why he had fought to save her, and now he forgot her. There was nothing in him except a vast blind hurt like a covered wound.

He entered the jacal, and without waiting to light a candle, threw off his clothing, sitting just within the door. He moved with lagging, half-awake hands, to strip his body of its heavy finery. With a long groaning sigh of relief he fell straight back on the floor, almost instantly asleep, his arms flung up and outward.

María Concepción, a small clay jar in her hand, approached the gentle little mother goat tethered to a sapling, which gave and yielded as she pulled at the rope's end after the farthest reaches of grass about her. The kid, tied up a few feet away, rose bleating, its feathery fleece shivering in the fresh wind. Sitting on her heels, holding his tether, she allowed him to suckle a few moments. Afterward—all her movements very deliberate and even—she drew a supply of milk for the child.

She sat against the wall of her house, near the doorway. The child, fed and asleep, was cradled in the hollow of her crossed legs. The silence overfilled the world, the skies flowed down evenly to the rim of the valley, the stealthy moon crept slantwise to the shelter of the mountains. She felt soft and warm all over; she dreamed that the newly born child was her own, and she was resting deliciously.

María Concepción could hear Juan's breathing. The sound vapored from the low doorway, calmly; the house seemed to be resting after a burdensome day. She breathed, too, very slowly and quietly, each inspiration saturating her with repose. The child's light, faint breath was a mere shadowy moth of sound in the silver air. The night, the earth under her, seemed to swell and recede together with a limitless, unhurried, benign breathing. She drooped and closed her eyes, feeling the slow rise and fall within her own body. She did not know what it was, but it eased her all through. Even as she was falling asleep, head bowed over the child, she was still aware of a strange, wakeful happiness.

Questions for Study

1. *What is the significance of the fowls María Concepción is carrying in the beginning of the story? What do they tell us about her?*
2. *What does María's stopping at Lupe's house for honey reveal about her?*
3. *What are the various attitudes of the community toward María Concepción?*
4. *In what sense do "the long deep crevasses" of the buried city indicate the function of Givens in the story?*
5. *What does María mean, when she replies to Givens' question about how she can kill fowls so easily, "My home country is Guadalajara"?*
6. *How do Juan's clothes indicate the kind of person he is?*
7. *How does the author use light and dark to signal changes in the mood of the story?*

Topics for Discussion and Writing

1. Discuss the character of María Concepción in terms of the setting and show how it makes her believable.
2. Indicate how the beginning and end of the story are alike and how they are different and what these similarities and differences signify in terms of the meaning of the story.
3. Discuss the significance of the buried city and explain the part it plays in the story.
4. Contrast the world of Juan and María Rosa and that of María Concepción. Explain how this contrast is basic to an understanding of the story.

THEME: IDEAS IN ACTION

Theme is the total meaning of the story, the complex of ideas that make up the author's main point. In essence it answers the question what the story is all about, what it signifies. However, it should not be confused with a moral or a message, a broad topic like love or death, or some aspect of the writer's philosophy except where warranted. The problem is how to find the theme, for it is not so easy to identify as plot, character, point of view, and setting. In fact, it is a part of each of them, or, more precisely, each element of fiction contributes to it.

The best way to proceed in locating the theme is to examine several aspects of the story: the author's statements, the narrator's statements, statements made by the characters, and the overall impression the story conveys through its plot, characters, setting, and symbolism. Let us look at each of these sources in turn.

Most authors do not come right out and tell you what their story means. Instead they dramatize their meaning indirectly through characters and scenes, letting you discover for yourself the central point through the gradual unfolding of the action. Authors use various methods to present subtly their views and themes. One device is a favorite kind of character that appears in story after story by a particular writer. Hemingway, for instance, expresses his stoical attitude toward life much of the time through a bullfighter, soldier, or hunter who, though fated to fail, accepts his defeat in a brave and disciplined manner.

More frequently the theme is found in the comments of a first-person or third-person narrator. First-person narrators, characters themselves and not to be confused with the author, occasionally reflect the author's meaning. Jinny Wiley in "The Captive" is a good example: she personifies courage in the face of adversity. Sometimes they represent a position opposite the author's, such as the narrator of "Spotted Horses," whose admiration of Flem Snopes is not shared by Faulkner. Third-person narrators like the one in Stephen Crane's "The Blue Hotel" (p. 200) offer strong judgments on characters and what happens to them. Their ideas often coincide with those of their creator and should be examined closely to see if they form a consistent attitude toward the events of the story.

Remarks made by a character are another source of the theme. Again this character may or may not speak for the author. You can usually tell by looking at the whole story. For instance, Mrs. Littlejohn's comment in "Spotted Horses," "See if you can't find something else to play with that will kill some more of you," seems to reflect Faulkner's attitude. Like the chorus in a Greek tragedy, she stands aside from the furor caused by the horses to offer her commonsense observations on the foolishness of those caught up in the excitement. Characters not only make remarks you should pay attention to, but also stand for certain ideas. This is especially true of flat characters. Lucy Nelson's mother and father in "In Trouble" represent respectively the submissiveness and irresponsibility that Lucy is rebelling against. The actions of characters are important also. María Concepción's killing of María Rosa in "María Concepción" and adopting of her baby suggest her determination to see order restored in her own life.

Finally, there is the impression that the story makes as a whole. This comes from your experience with all the fictional elements and the way in which they are bound together. You read a story such as "Owen Wingrave" and you conclude from the action, the characters, and the setting that the theme is one man's heroic struggle against the military life his family has determined for him.

To be more specific about how to find the theme of a story let us take another look at "Indian Camp" (p. 110). The author is not clearly present, and the effaced narrator serves mainly as a stage director rather than as a commentator. Hence you need to examine the characters, especially the protagonist, his actions, and what he says and thinks. As you do, you come to realize the story concerns Nick's initiation into the bitter experiences of life. He begins to question why people take their own lives and decides he will never die. On the other hand, his doctor-father learns he is neither as knowledgeable about death nor as unaffected by it as he once thought. Furthermore, he cannot answer confidently or fully his son's questions about why men kill themselves. Another facet of the theme is the primitive setting of the camp and the Indians themselves. They represent an alien world the white men do not understand and act superior to. In the broadest sense you could say that the theme is what Nick learns from his father, from the woman who has the baby, from the man who kills himself, and most of all from his visit to the Indian camp itself.

Hemingway does not deal with these large issues in an abstract way that can be easily summarized. He dramatizes them in a concrete and subtle way that requires interpretation on the part of the reader. The ideas are implied in the action, the characters, and the setting. He lets you experience them and come to your own conclusion about what they all mean.

Stephen Crane in "The Blue Hotel" is more explicit than Hemingway in stating his theme. The narrator makes numerous statements about the characters that you come to accept. Most of them concern the individual's futile struggle against the overwhelming power of nature. The protagonist, the Swede, though defiant and proud, is the victim of a chaotic and indifferent universe, a louse on this "space-lost bulb." But this is scarcely the sole meaning of the story, although it is one of the most important. Others include the collaboration of society in a crime against an individual, the individual's relationship to fate, and misunderstandings that lead to tragedy. But again it is best, when confronted with several possible themes, to choose the one you think is dominant and to see how the others relate to it.

The theme in Jorge Luis Borges' "The Gospel According to Mark" (p. 196) is more elusive than that in "The Blue Hotel." You need to examine carefully the narrator's comments, the Indians' actions and motives, and the significance of the crucifixion at the end. The several ideas, though related, concern the aimlessness of an educated man, primitive culture versus the civilized world, and an ordinary and not particularly religious man being mistaken for Christ and forced to suffer like Him. The irony of this last idea comes closer to expressing the main theme than the others.

D. H. Lawrence's "Things" (p. 186) is different from the three stories mentioned above in that the author's views are expressed so clearly you know not only what they are, but also how he wants you to feel about them. Lawrence expresses a strong personal conviction, and he does not use much subtlety in presenting it. He is, in a sense, the narrator. His characters are mouthpieces for the different viewpoints he puts forth. What they stand for means more than what they do or who they are. The Melvilles represent over-intellectualized, over-cultured middle-class Americans who repudiate their materialistic country to pursue art and philosophy in Europe. However, they find there the same crass interests they knew in America and return home to live dull and empty lives. Lawrence attacks their dullness and their emptiness, their hypocrisy and arrogance, their lack of roots and commitment to anything but themselves. They waste their lives collecting useless "things." Still the story is not strictly a sermon or a moral tract. There is dramatization and characterization. The ideas, because of the forceful way Lawrence presents them, are convincing. What makes them so convincing, in addition to the vigor of his expression, is the persuasiveness of his symbols.

Since most writers use symbols to develop their meaning, it is important to be able to recognize them and understand how they work. A **symbol** is an action, a character, an object, a setting, an image that signifies something greater than itself. It stands for a number of ideas or emotions. We are all familiar with common symbols like money and home, the flag and the cross. In literature there are two types of symbols, the **conventional** and the **created.** The first is an object, such as the sun, that stands immediately and universally for certain recognizable values or ideas, such as warmth, fertility, illumination. The blizzard in "The Blue Hotel," for example, represents the vast forces of nature indifferent to the struggles and problems of individuals. The created symbol stands for a number of ideas and feelings peculiar to the context of a particular story, such as the vine in "Things." The young couple, like a vine, are searching for something to cling to and climb during their search for freedom and beauty. Lawrence is very explicit about this: "And human beings are all vines. But especially the idealist." However, outside the story the vine is not necessarily used in this fashion. It can symbolize all sorts of things, from a choker of life to someone searching for something to cling to. Lawrence makes it work for him in a special way, and you accept his meaning because of the forceful, consistent, and relevant way he uses it.

The function of a symbol, then, is to permit the author to establish a point concretely and dramatically, to suggest ideas, attitudes, beliefs without using general statements of low intensity and restricted meaning. Almost any object can become a symbol. All that is necessary is that it possess a meaning that transcends the literal and the physical. For instance, you would not classify the cards in "The Blue Hotel" as symbols by themselves, though the card game taken as a whole symbolizes chance and the rules people live by and is one cause of the violence that erupts.

Another way of looking at symbols is to consider them in terms of the mythical and natural worlds. The hero of "The Gospel According to Mark," though a student living in the everyday world, becomes a mythical figure to the Gutre family in the sense that he suggests Christ to them as he reads the Gospel and performs what they consider miracles. Natural symbols, on the other hand, relate to environment. The rain in Borges' story signifies impending disaster as well as the isolation of Espinosa from the outside world and his closer communication with the illiterate country people on the ranch. When the rain turns into a flood and becomes associated with the Bible, mythical and natural symbols join together to prepare for the climax of the story and for the sacrifice of Espinosa by the primitive family in order "to save all other men on earth."

Sometimes stories steeped in myth, such as "The Gospel According to Mark," are told along the lines of a parable or fable. They illustrate a fundamental truth. Others, such as "Things," border on allegory, that is, they become narratives in which the action, characters, setting, and objects represent specific philosophical or religious ideas. Bunyan's *Pilgrim's Progress* is the best-known example of a prose allegory in English. The hero is Christian. On the way to the Celestial City he encounters people such as Faith and Despair and visits a place called Vanity Fair. "The Blue Hotel" approaches allegory in that the characters are representative of certain common human traits and the Swede's death is symbolic of collective as well as individual irresponsibility. The difference is that, whereas a clear-cut abstraction stands behind each of Bunyan's scenes and characters, modern authors rarely offer such a point-by-point correspondence between the situation, person, and action and their significance. Nor do they develop explicit patterns that are so obvious to discern and easy to interpret.

Once you have determined the theme you have to be careful, in treating it, of your own biases. You may disagree with the type of experience depicted and the interpretation put upon it, but you should not judge the truth or falsity of the theme detached from the story. If it is in harmony with the whole fictional world, action and character and setting, then it has artistic validity. A poor fictional theme is one that is weakly, obscurely, or incoherently developed, one without point or power, not one you feel is unworthy of writing about, inadmissible in literature, or alien to your set of values. An author is saying something to you he or she considers important. It is your responsibility to find out what it is, first in terms of the story and then in terms of the life around you. Hence the difficulty and the fascination of analyzing this most elusive element of fiction.

D. H. LAWRENCE

Things

They were true idealists from New England. But that is some time ago: before the war. Several years before the war, they met and married; he a tall, keen-eyed young man from Connecticut, she a smallish, demure, Puritan-looking young woman from Massachusetts. They both had a little money. Not much, however. Even added together, it didn't make three thousand dollars a year. Still—they were free. Free!

Ah! Freedom! To be free to live one's own life! To be twenty-five and twenty-seven, a pair of true idealists with a mutual love of beauty, and an inclination towards "Indian thought"—meaning, alas, Mrs. Besant—and an income a little under three thousand dollars a year! But what is money? All one wishes to do is to live a full and beautiful life. In Europe, of course, right at the fountain-head of tradition. It might possibly be done in America: in New England, for example. But at a forfeiture of a certain amount of "beauty." True beauty takes a long time to mature. The baroque is only half-beautiful, half-matured. No, the real silver bloom, the real golden-sweet bouquet of beauty had its roots in the Renaissance, not in any later or shallower period.

Therefore the two idealists, who were married in New Haven, sailed at once to Paris: Paris of the old days. They had a studio apartment on the Boulevard Montparnasse, and they became real Parisians, in the old, delightful sense, not in the modern, vulgar. It was the shimmer of the pure impressionists, Monet and his followers, the world seen in terms of pure light, light broken and unbroken. How lovely! How lovely the nights, the river, the mornings in the old streets and by the flower-stalls and the book-stalls, the afternoons up on Montmartre or in the Tuileries, the evenings on the boulevards!

They both painted, but not desperately. Art had not taken them by the throat, and they did not take Art by the throat. They painted: that's all. They knew people—nice people, if possible, though one had to take them mixed. And they were happy.

Yet it seems as if human beings must set their claws in *something*. To be "free," to be "living a full and beautiful life," you must, alas, be attached to something. A "full and beautiful life" means a tight attachment to *something*—at least, it is so for all idealists—or else a certain boredom supervenes; there is a certain waving of loose ends upon the air, like the waving, yearning tendrils of the vine that spread and rotate, seeking something to clutch, something up which to climb towards the necessary sun. Finding nothing, the vine can only trail, half-fulfilled, upon the ground. Such is freedom!—a clutching of the right pole. And human beings are all vines. But especially the idealist. He is a vine, and he needs to clutch and climb. And he despises the man who is a mere *potato*, or turnip, or lump of wood.

Our idealists were frightfully happy, but they were all the time reaching out for something to cotton on to. At first, Paris was enough. They explored Paris *thoroughly*. And they learned French till they almost felt like French people, they could speak it so glibly.

Still, you know, you never talk French with your *soul*. It can't be done. And though it's very thrilling, at first, talking in French to clever Frenchmen—they seem *so* much cleverer than oneself—still, in the long run, it is not satisfying. The endlessly clever *materialism* of the French leaves you cold, in the end, gives a sense of barrenness and incompatibility with true New England depth. So our two idealists felt.

They turned away from France—but ever so gently. France had disappointed them. "We've loved it, and we've got a great deal out of it. But after a while, after a considerable while, several years, in fact, Paris leaves one feeling disappointed. It hasn't quite got what one wants."

"But Paris isn't France."

"No, perhaps not. France is quite different from Paris. And France is lovely—quite lovely. But to *us*, though we love it, it doesn't say a great deal."

So, when the war came, the idealists moved to Italy. And they loved Italy. They found it beautiful, and more poignant than France. It seemed much nearer to the New England conception of beauty: something pure, and full of sympathy, without the *materialism* and the *cynicism* of the French. The two idealists seemed to breathe their own true air in Italy.

And in Italy, much more than in Paris, they felt they could thrill to the teachings of the Buddha. They entered the swelling stream of modern Buddhistic emotion, and they read the books, and they practised meditation, and they deliberately set themselves to eliminate from their own souls greed, pain, and sorrow. They did not realise—yet—that Buddha's very eagerness to free himself from pain and sorrow is in itself a sort of greed. No, they dreamed of a perfect world, from which all greed, and nearly all pain, and a great deal of sorrow, were eliminated.

But America entered the war, so the two idealists had to help. They did hospital work. And though their experience made them realise more than ever that greed, pain, and sorrow *should* be eliminated from the world, nevertheless the Buddhism, or the theosophy, didn't emerge very triumphant from the long crisis. Somehow, somewhere, in some part of themselves, they felt that greed, pain, and sorrow would never be eliminated, because most people don't care about eliminating them, and never will care. Our idealists were far too Western to think of abandoning all the world to damnation, while they saved their two selves. They were far too unselfish to sit tight under a bho tree and reach Nirvana in a mere couple.

It was more than that, though. They simply hadn't enough *Seitzfleisch* to squat under a bho tree and get to Nirvana by contemplating anything, least of all their own navel. If the whole wide world was not going to be saved, they, personally, were not so very keen on being saved just by themselves. No, it would be so lonesome. They were New Englanders, so it must be all or nothing. Greed, pain, and sorrow must either be eliminated from *all the world*, or else, what was the use of eliminating them from oneself? No use at all! One was just a victim.

And so, although they still *loved* "Indian thought," and felt very tender about it: well, to go back to our metaphor, the pole up which the green and anxious vines had clambered so far now proved dry-rotten. It snapped, and the vines came slowly subsiding to earth again. There was no crack and crash. The vines held themselves up by their own foliage, for a while. But they subsided. The beanstalk of "Indian thought" had given way before Jack and Jill had climbed off the tip of it to a further world.

They subsided with a slow rustle back to earth again. But they made no outcry. They were again "disappointed." But they never admitted it. "Indian thought" had let them down. But they never complained. Even to one another, they never said a word. They were disappointed, faintly but deeply disillusioned, and they both knew it. But the knowledge was tacit.

And they still had so much in their lives. They still had Italy—dear Italy. And they still had freedom, the priceless treasure. And they still had so much "beauty." About the fullness of their lives they were not quite so sure. They had one little boy, whom they loved as parents should love their children, but whom they wisely refrained from fastening upon, to build their lives on him. No, no, they must live their own lives! They still had strength of mind to know that.

But they were now no longer very young. Twenty-five and twenty-seven had become thirty-five and thirty-seven. And though they had had a very wonderful time in Europe, and though they still loved Italy—dear Italy!—yet: they were disappointed. They had got a lot out of it: oh, a very great deal indeed! Still, it hadn't given them quite, not *quite*, what they had expected. Europe was lovely, but it was dead. Living in Europe, you were living on the past. And Europeans, with all their superficial charm, were not *really* charming. They were materialistic, they had no *real* soul. They just did not understand the inner urge of the spirit, because the inner urge was dead in them, they were all survivals. There, that was the truth about Europeans: they were survivals, with no more getting ahead in them.

It was another bean-pole, another vine-support crumbled under the green life of the vine. And very bitter it was, this time. For up the old tree-trunk of Europe the green vine had been clambering silently for more than ten years, ten hugely important years, the years of real living. The two idealists had *lived* in Europe, lived on Europe and on European life and European things as vines in an everlasting vineyard.

They had made their home here: a home such as you could never make in America. Their watchword had been "beauty." They had rented, the last four years, the second floor of an old palazzo on the Arno, and here they had all their "things." And they derived a profound, profound satisfaction from their apartment: the lofty, silent, ancient rooms with windows on the river, with glistening, dark-red floors, and the beautiful furniture that the idealists had "picked up."

Yes, unknown to themselves, the lives of the idealists had been running with a fierce swiftness horizontally, all the time. They had become tense, fierce, hunters of "things" for their home. While their souls were climbing up to the sun of old European culture or old Indian thought, their passions were running horizontally, clutching at "things." Of course they did not buy the things for the things' sakes, but for the sake of "beauty." They looked upon their home as a place entirely furnished by loveliness, not by "things" at all. Valerie had some very lovely curtains at the windows of the long *salotto*, looking on the river: curtains of queer ancient material that looked like finely-knitted silk, most beautifully faded down from vermilion and orange, and gold, and black, down to a sheer soft glow. Valerie hardly ever came into the *salotto* without mentally falling on her knees before the curtains. "Chartres!" she said. "To me they are Chartres!" And Melville never turned and looked at his sixteenth-century Venetian bookcase, with its two or three dozen of choice books, without feeling his marrow stir in his bones. The holy of holies!

The child silently, almost sinisterly, avoided any rude contact with these ancient monuments of furniture, as if they had been nests of sleeping cobras, or that "thing" most perilous to the touch, the Ark of the Covenant. His childish awe was silent and cold, but final.

Still, a couple of New England idealists cannot live merely on the bygone glory of their furniture. At least, one couple could not. They got used to the marvelous Bologna cupboard, they got used to the wonderful Venetian bookcase, and the books, and the Siena curtains and bronzes, and the lovely sofas and side-tables and chairs they had "picked up" in Paris. Oh, they had been picking things up since the first day they landed in Europe. And they were still at it. It is the last interest Europe can offer to an outsider: or to an insider either.

When people came, and were thrilled by the Melville interior, then Valerie and Erasmus felt they had not lived in vain: that they still were living. But in the long mornings, when Erasmus was desultorily working at Renaissance Florentine literature, and Valerie was attending to the apartment: and in the long hours after lunch; and in the long, usually very cold and oppressive evenings in the ancient palazzo: then the halo died from around the furniture, and the things became things, lumps of matter that just stood there or hung there, *ad infinitum*, and said nothing; and Valerie and Erasmus almost hated them. The glow of beauty, like every other glow, dies down unless it is fed. The idealists still dearly loved their things. But they had got them. And the sad fact is, things that glow vividly while you're getting them, go almost quite cold after a year or two. Unless, of course, people envy them very much, and the museums are pining for them. And the Melvilles' "things," though very good, were not quite so good as that.

So, the glow gradually went out of everything, out of Europe, out of Italy —"the Italians are *dears*"—even out of that marvellous apartment on the Arno. "Why, if I had this apartment, I'd never, never even want to go out of doors! It's too lovely and perfect." That was something, of course—to hear that.

And yet Valerie and Erasmus went out of doors: they even went out to get away from its ancient, cold-floored, stone-heavy silence and dead dignity. "We're living on the past, you know, Dick," said Valerie to her husband. She called him Dick.

They were grimly hanging on. They did not like to give in. They did not like to own up that they were through. For twelve years, now, they had been "free" people living a "full and beautiful life." And America for twelve years had been their anathema, the Sodom and Gomorrah of industrial materialism.

It wasn't easy to own that you were "through." They hated to admit that they wanted to go back. But at last, reluctantly, they decided to go, "for the boy's sake."—"We can't *bear* to leave Europe. But Peter is an American, so he had better look at America while he's young." The Melvilles had an entirely English accent and manner; almost; a little Italian and French here and there.

They left Europe behind, but they took as much of it along with them as possible. Several van-loads, as a matter of fact. All those adorable and irreplaceable "things." And all arrived in New York, idealists, child, and the huge bulk of Europe they had lugged along.

Valerie had dreamed of a pleasant apartment, perhaps on Riverside Drive, where it was not so expensive as east of Fifth Avenue, and where all their wonderful things would look marvellous. She and Erasmus house-hunted. But alas! their income was quite under three thousand dollars a year. They found—well, everybody knows what they found. Two small rooms and a kitchenette, and don't let us unpack a *thing!*

The chunk of Europe which they had bitten off went into a warehouse, at fifty dollars a month. And they sat in two small rooms and a kitchenette, and wondered why they'd done it.

Erasmus, of course, ought to get a job. This was what was written on the wall, and what they both pretended not to see. But it had been the strange, vague threat that the Statue of Liberty had always held over them: "Thou shalt get a job!" Erasmus had the tickets, as they say. A scholastic career was still possible for him. He had taken his exams brilliantly at Yale, and had kept up his "researches" all the time he had been in Europe.

But both he and Valerie shuddered. A scholastic career! The scholastic world! The *American* scholastic world! Shudder upon shudder! Give up their freedom, their full and beautiful life? Never! Never! Erasmus would be forty next birthday.

The "things" remained in warehouse. Valerie went to look at them. It cost her a dollar an hour, and horrid pangs. The "things," poor things, looked a bit shabby and wretched, in that warehouse.

However, New York was not all America. There was the great clean West. So the Melvilles went West, with Peter, but without the things. They tried living the simple life, in the mountains. But doing their own chores became almost a nightmare. "Things" are all very well to look at, but it's awful handling them, even when they're beautiful. To be the slave of hideous things, to keep a stove going, cook meals, wash dishes, carry water and clean floors: pure horror of sordid anti-life!

In the cabin on the mountains, Valerie dreamed of Florence, the lost apartment; and her Bologna cupboard and Louis-Quinze chairs, above all, her "Chartres" curtains, stood in New York and costing fifty dollars a month.

A millionaire friend came to the rescue, offering them a cottage on the Californian coast—California! Where the new soul is to be born in man. With joy the idealists moved a little farther west, catching at new vine-props of hope.

And finding them straws! The millionaire cottage was perfectly equipped. It was perhaps as labour-savingly perfect as is possible: electric heating and cooking, a white-and-pearl-enamelled kitchen, nothing to make dirt except the human being himself. In an hour or so the idealists had got through their chores. They were "free"—free to hear the great Pacific pounding the coast, and to feel a new soul filling their bodies.

Alas! the Pacific pounded the coast with hideous brutality, brute force itself! And the new soul, instead of sweetly stealing into their bodies, seemed only meanly to gnaw the old soul out of their bodies. To feel you are under the fist of the most blind and crunching brute force: to feel that your cherished idealist's soul is being gnawed out of you, and only irritation left in place of it: well, it isn't good enough.

After about nine months, the idealists departed from the Californian west. It had been a great experience, they were glad to have had it. But, in the long run, the West was not the place for them, and they knew it. No, the people who wanted new souls had better get them. They, Valerie and Erasmus Melville, would like to develop the old soul a little further. Anyway, they had not felt any influx of new soul on the Californian coast. On the contrary.

So, with a slight hole in their material capital, they returned to Massachusetts and paid a visit to Valerie's parents, taking the boy along. The grandparents welcomed the child—poor expatriated boy—and were rather cold to Valerie, but really cold to Erasmus. Valerie's mother definitely said to Valerie, one day, that Erasmus ought to take a job, so that Valerie could live decently. Valerie haughtily reminded her mother of the beautiful apartment on the Arno, and the "wonderful" things in store in New York, and of the "marvelous and satisfying life" she and Erasmus had led. Valerie's mother said that she didn't think her daughter's life looked so very marvellous at present: homeless, with a husband idle at the age of forty, a child to educate, and a dwindling capital: looked the reverse of marvellous to *her*. Let Erasmus take some post in one of the universities.

"What post? What university?" interrupted Valerie.

"That could be found, considering your father's connections and Erasmus's qualifications," replied Valerie's mother. "And you could get all your valuable things out of store, and have a really lovely home, which everybody in America would be proud to visit. As it is, your furniture is eating up your income, and you are living like rats in a hole, with nowhere to go to."

This was very true. Valerie was beginning to pine for a home, with her "things." Of course, she could have sold her furniture for a substantial sum. But nothing would have induced her to. Whatever else passed away, religions, cultures, continents, and hopes, Valerie would *never* part from the "things" which she and Erasmus had collected with such passion. To these she was nailed.

But she and Erasmus still would not give up that freedom, that full and beautiful life they had so believed in. Erasmus cursed America. He did not *want* to earn a living. He panted for Europe.

Leaving the boy in charge of Valerie's parents, the two idealists once more set off for Europe. In New York they paid two dollars and looked for a brief, bitter hour at their "things." They sailed "student class"—that is, third. Their income now was less than two thousand dollars instead of three. And they made straight for Paris—cheap Paris.

They found Europe, this time, a complete failure. "We have returned like dogs to our vomit," said Erasmus; "but the vomit has staled in the meantime."

He found he couldn't stand Europe. It irritated every nerve in his body. He hated America too. But America at least was a darn sight better than this miserable, dirt-eating continent; which was by no means cheap any more, either.

Valerie, with her heart on her things—she had really burned to get them out of that warehouse, where they had stood now for three years, eating up two thousand dollars—wrote to her mother she thought Erasmus would come back if he could get some suitable work in America. Erasmus, in a state of frustration bordering on rage and insanity, just went round Italy in a poverty-stricken fashion, his coat-cuffs frayed, hating everything with intensity. And when a post was found for him in Cleveland University, to teach French, Italian, and Spanish literature, his eyes grew more beady, and his long, queer face grew sharper and more rat-like with utter baffled fury. He was forty, and the job was upon him.

"I think you'd better accept, dear. You don't care for Europe any longer. As you say, it's dead and finished. They offer us a house on the college lot, and mother says there's room in it for all our things. I think we'd better cable 'Accept.' "

He glowered at her like a cornered rat. One almost expected to see rat's whiskers twitching at the sides of the sharp nose.

"Shall I send the cablegram?" she asked.

"Send it!" he blurted.

And she went out and sent it.

He was a changed man, quieter, much less irritable. A load was off him. He was inside the cage.

But when he looked at the furnaces of Cleveland, vast and like the greatest of black forests, with red and white-hot cascades of gushing metal, and tiny gnomes of men, and terrific noises, gigantic, he said to Valerie:

"Say what you like, Valerie, this is the biggest thing the modern world has to show."

And when they were in their up-to-date little house on the college lot of Cleveland University, and that woebegone débris of Europe: Bologna cupboard, Venice book-shelves, Ravenna bishop's chair, Louis-Quinze side-tables, "Chartres" curtains, Siena bronze lamps, all were arrayed, and all looked perfectly out of keeping, and therefore very impressive; and when the idealists had had a bunch of gaping people in, and Erasmus had showed off in his best European manner, but still quite cordial and American; and Valerie had been most ladylike, but for all that, "we prefer America"; then Erasmus said, looking at her with queer, sharp eyes of a rat:

"Europe's the mayonnaise all right, but America supplies the good old lobster—what?"

"Every time!" she said, with satisfaction.

And he peered at her. He was in the cage: but it was safe inside. And she, evidently, was her real self at last. She had got the goods. Yet round his nose was a queer, evil scholastic look of pure scepticism. But he liked lobster.

Writing About Theme

When you write about theme, you should first decide what the main ideas are. Once you have chosen them, you need to come to a conclusion about how these ideas compose what you consider the theme. Of course, you should realize no two people look at any piece of literature in the same light. Your responsibility is simply to prove that your version has validity and can be supported by analysis and citation. You should also consider the effectiveness of the author's presentation of the theme.

Your approach naturally depends on the kind of story you are writing about. "The Blue Hotel" contains a number of powerful ideas, such as the collective guilt of society in a murder versus individual responsibility, the position of a man whose fate is beyond his control, the thin veneer of civilization which covers people's primitive aggressiveness. Since the Swede and the storm are the most significant elements in the story, you might examine them to find out what each contributes to Crane's depiction of the individual against nature. This will require an analysis of the Swede's remarks and actions and an analysis of what Crane says about nature and people's relationships to it.

"The Gospel According to Mark" requires a different approach. It offers a parable-like situation for interpretation. You do not have any clear authorial commentary to guide you. The voice, the characters, and the action are quite ambiguous. But if you center on the symbol of the crucifixion and the relationship of the main character to it, his background and ideas, and the ignorant worshipers of the ranch who are planning to put him to death in order to save themselves, you have the essence of a theme-oriented essay. The important thing is to study the story to see how the sacrifice pattern emerges and what Borges does with it to develop a story about a man who unwittingly becomes an ironic savior.

"Things" requires still another approach since it deals with so many ideas in an abstract way. Just to list them is to see what you face in trying to write on the story: commitment, freedom, materialism, artistic beauty, European versus American culture. The temptation is to take one of these abstractions and write about it, ignoring the story for the most part. Although this might seem profitable at first, you will soon find yourself running out of things to say or composing essays on topics over your head. Thus it is best to select a specific point you consider the most revealing one in the whole story. A good topic that is both general enough to discuss and definite enough to analyze in terms of the particulars of the story is the Melvilles' hypocritical idealism. It embraces all the large abstractions listed above and is consistent with the hostile attitude Lawrence expresses toward his characters and their rootless lives.

The next step is to formulate a thesis sentence which will help you control such a comprehensive subject. Ask yourself what they are hypocritical about. Your answer might be their view of America and Europe, their view toward collecting "things," and their view of themselves. A possible controlling thesis sentence could be as follows: The theme of "Things" is the hypocritical view the Melvilles assume toward the countries they live in, the objects they collect, and the lives they lead. Such a sentence sets forth your organization. Your task is to search for material to support the points you plan to make about their hypocrisy.

In the first paragraph you should announce your topic and indicate Lawrence's approach to it. As you go over the story, look for material to substantiate the points you make, concentrating on the author's blunt comments on his characters and how he wishes us to view them. His remarks are not so ambiguous as those of Borges or so philosophically weighty as those of Crane. They seem to have a personal bias to them, and you have to take this into consideration. The second paragraph should deal with the Melvilles' travel at home and abroad and how their search for a cultural home masks their empty lives. In your third and fourth paragraphs you could discuss art collecting and narcissism respectively. The conclusion should dwell on how convincingly you think Lawrence presents his theme.

The principal danger in writing on theme is getting carried away with your generalizations, allowing them to take over and become your whole paper, forgetting that you are writing about a story, not a philosophical treatise. You must stick to the elements of fiction before you. Of course, if you know something about the author's ideas that have a bearing on the story, you should introduce them. Lawrence is a writer who speaks out boldly in his fiction, and his stories are sometimes obvious reflections of his personal beliefs. He clearly indicates in "Things," as he says elsewhere, that he hates "the beastly bourgeoisie." He dislikes too the abstract, the uncommitted, the insincere, and the story shows his bias dramatically. However, not very many writers are so forthright in stating a theme. They prefer to let it emerge of its own accord from the situation and the characters.

Phony Idealism in "Things"

"Things" is a story about middle-class values with respect to travel abroad, art collecting, and the good life. The two central characters, Valerie and Erasmus Melville, are New England idealists who scorn money and work and their native land and go off to Europe in search of freedom and high culture. The irony is that their commitment to idealism is shallow and hypocritical. They end up becoming more attached to comfort and security than to beauty and philosophy.

The pattern of the Melvilles' travel from America to Europe and back again reveals how false is their desire to escape from the materialism they first scorn. In the beginning they announce they are fleeing from the provincialism of their own country to seek the freedom and beauty of the Old World. However, they become disillusioned with conditions abroad and settle for the creature comforts of the United States. Europe may be the "mayonnaise," but "America supplies the good old lobster." The idealist becomes the "perfect materialist," which is how Lawrence once defined an idealist. Although proclaiming their desire to be free and to praise the beautiful, the Melvilles settle in Cleveland, a midwestern inferno. To Erasmus, Cleveland is a cage, though a secure one, and to Valerie an awesome spectacle, "the biggest thing the modern world has to show," and the perfect place to exhibit the "things" she has purchased abroad.

Collecting "things" is another phase of the Melvilles' misguided idealism. The higher they climb toward their goals of freedom and beauty during their travels, the wider they spread out to grasp "things" which, once possessed, grow cold and ornamental, abstract and useless. Hence, while they want to absorb "European culture or old Indian thought," their desire for grabbing objects moves them in the opposite direction. The point is that they are dedicated to nothing very high and noble, although they pretend to be. Their real goal is objects. As the narrator says, "Art had not taken them by the throat, and they did not take Art by the throat." Consequently, they travel and collect and dream of the good life without sinking their claws into anything solid and meaningful. They live bored, superfluous lives. Genuine freedom is not groping in the air like a vine but "clutching the right pole," and that they never seem to do.

What the Melvilles finally settle for are meals, money, and a job. Erasmus, although he disdains the materialistic life at the university, prefers it to living for his ideals in poverty. He and his wife insist they must abandon their fight against "greed, pain, and sorrow" because it never could be won, and they do not want to save themselves while the rest of the world is damned. They would be too lonely. Their unselfish idealism turns into a form of narcissism, a love of themselves and their own pleasures. Travelling, collecting, displaying "things" is a form of self-indulgence.

Lawrence sets in opposition to the Melvilles the primitive and the deeply committed and thus expresses his own views. The contrast between the "brute force" represented by the ocean and the Melvilles' idealism represented by the vine reflects his own bias. So is his comment that "human beings must set their claws in something. To be 'free,' to be 'living a full and beautiful life,' you must, alas, be attached to something." He has nothing but contempt for those who, like the vine, are constantly at loose ends and do not understand that a " 'full and beautiful life' means a tight attachment to something." In most stories such outspoken commentary and heavy-handed satire by the author would seem blatant editorializing. But here it suits the savage thrust of the narrative because the voice of Lawrence is a vital part of the story. He almost becomes a character, ridiculing the Melvilles and exposing their phony idealism. The reader identifies with him and thus is brought dramatically into the story to share his attitude toward the theme.

JORGE LUIS BORGES

The Gospel According to Mark

These events took place at La Colorada ranch, in the southern part of the township of Junín, during the last days of March, 1928. The protagonist was a medical student named Baltasar Espinosa. We may describe him, for now, as one of the common run of young men from Buenos Aires, with nothing more noteworthy about him than an almost unlimited kindness and a capacity for public speaking that had earned him several prizes at the English school in Ramos Mejía. He did not like arguing, and preferred having his listener rather than himself in the right. Although he was fascinated by the probabilities of chance in any game he played, he was a bad player because it gave him no pleasure to win. His wide intelligence was undirected; at the age of thirty-three, he still lacked credit for graduation, by one course—the course to which he was most drawn. His father, who was a freethinker (like all the gentlemen of his day), had introduced him to the lessons of Herbert Spencer, but his mother, before leaving on a trip to Montevideo, once asked him to say the Lord's Prayer and make the sign of the cross every night. Through the years, he had never gone back on that promise.

Espinosa was not lacking in spirit; one day, with more indifference than anger, he had exchanged two or three punches with a group of fellow-students who were trying to force him to take part in a university demonstration. Owing to an acquiescent nature, he was full of opinions, or habits of mind, that were questionable: Argentina mattered less to him than a fear that in other parts of the world people might think of us as Indians; he worshiped France but despised the French; he thought little of Americans but approved the fact that there were tall buildings, like theirs, in Buenos Aires; he believed the gauchos of the plains to be better riders than those of hill or mountain country. When his cousin Daniel invited him to spend the summer months out at La Colorada, he said yes at once—not because he was really fond of the country, but more out of his natural complacency and also because it was easier to say yes than to dream up reasons for saying no.

The ranch's main house was big and slightly run-down; the quarters of the foreman, whose name was Gutre, were close by. The Gutres were three: the father, an unusually uncouth son, and a daughter of uncertain paternity. They were tall, strong, and bony, and had hair that was on the reddish side and faces that showed traces of Indian blood. They were barely articulate. The foreman's wife had died years before.

There in the country, Espinosa began learning things he never knew, or even suspected—for example, that you do not gallop a horse when approaching settlements, and that you never go out riding except for some special purpose. In time, he was to come to tell the birds apart by their calls.

After a few days, Daniel had to leave for Buenos Aires to close a deal on some cattle. At most, this bit of business might take him a week. Espinosa, who was already somewhat weary of hearing about his cousin's incessant luck with women and his tireless interest in the minute details of men's fashion, preferred staying on at the ranch with his textbooks. But the heat was unbearable, and even the night brought no relief. One morning at daybreak, thunder woke him. Outside, the wind was rocking the Australian pines. Listening to the first heavy drops of rain, Espinosa thanked God. All at once, cold air rolled in. That afternoon, the Salado overflowed its banks.

The next day, looking out over the flooded fields from the gallery of the main house, Baltasar Espinosa thought that the stock metaphor comparing the pampa to the sea was not altogether false—at least, not that morning—though W. H. Hudson had remarked that the sea seems wider because we view it from a ship's deck and not from a horse or from eye level.

The rain did not let up. The Gutres, helped or hindered by Espinosa, the town dweller, rescued a good part of the livestock, but many animals were drowned. There were four roads leading to La Colorada; all of them were under water. On the third day, when a leak threatened the foreman's house, Espinosa gave the Gutres a room near the tool shed, at the back of the main house. This drew them all closer; they ate together in the big dining room. Conversation turned out to be difficult. The Gutres, who knew so much about country things, were hard put to it to explain them. One night, Espinosa asked them if people still remembered the Indian raids from back when the frontier command was located there in Junín. They told him yes, but they would have given the same answer to a question about the beheading of Charles I. Espinosa recalled his father's saying that almost every case of longevity that was cited in the country was really a case of bad memory or of a dim notion of dates. Gauchos are apt to be ignorant of the year of their birth or of the name of the man who begot them.

In the whole house, there was apparently no other reading matter than a set of the *Farm Journal*, a handbook of veterinary medicine, a deluxe edition of the Uruguayan epic *Tabaré*, a *History of Shorthorn Cattle in Argentina*, a number of erotic or detective stories, and a recent novel called *Don Segundo Sombra*. Espinosa, trying in some way to bridge the inevitable after-dinner gap, read a couple of chapters of this novel to the Gutres, none of whom could read or write. Unfortunately, the foreman had been a cattle drover, and the doings of the hero, another cattle drover, failed to whet his interest. He said that the work was light, that drovers always traveled with a packhorse that carried everything they needed, and that, had he not been a drover, he would never have seen such far-flung places as the Laguna de Gómez, the town of Bragado, and the spread of the Núñez family in Chacabuco. There was a guitar in the kitchen; the ranch hands, before the time of the events I am describing, used to sit around in a circle. Someone would tune the instrument without ever getting around to playing it. This was known as a guitarfest.

Espinosa, who had grown a beard, began dallying in front of the mirror to study his new face, and he smiled to think how, back in Buenos Aires, he would bore his friends by telling them the story of the Salado flood. Strangely enough, he missed places he never frequented and never would: a corner of

Cabrera Street on which there was a mailbox; one of the cement lions of a gateway on Jujuy Street, a few blocks from the Plaza del Once; an old barroom with a tiled floor, whose exact whereabouts he was unsure of. As for his brothers and his father, they would already have learned from Daniel that he was isolated—etymologically, the word was perfect—by the floodwaters.

Exploring the house, still hemmed in by the watery waste, Espinosa came across an English Bible. Among the blank pages at the end, the Guthries—such was their original name—had left a handwritten record of their lineage. They were natives of Inverness; had reached the New World, no doubt as common laborers, in the early part of the nineteenth century; and had intermarried with Indians. The chronicle broke off sometime during the eighteen-seventies, when they no longer knew how to write. After a few generations, they had forgotten English; their Spanish, at the time Espinosa knew them, gave them trouble. They lacked any religious faith, but there survived in their blood, like faint tracks, the rigid fanaticism of the Calvinist and the superstitions of the pampa Indian. Espinosa later told them of his find, but they barely took notice.

Leafing through the volume, his fingers opened it at the beginning of the Gospel according to St. Mark. As an exercise in translation, and maybe to find out whether the Gutres understood any of it, Epinosa decided to begin reading them that text after their evening meal. It surprised him that they listened attentively, absorbed. Maybe the gold letters on the cover lent the book authority. It's still there in their blood, Espinosa thought. It also occurred to him that the generations of men, throughout recorded time, have always told and retold two stories—that of a lost ship which searches the Mediterranean seas for a dearly loved island, and that of a god who is crucified on Golgotha. Remembering his lessons in elocution from his schooldays in Ramos Mejía, Espinosa got to his feet when he came to the parables.

The Gutres took to bolting their barbecued meat and their sardines so as not to delay the Gospel. A pet lamb that the girl adorned with a small blue ribbon had injured itself on a strand of barbed wire. To stop the bleeding, the three had wanted to apply a cobweb to the wound, but Espinosa treated the animal with some pills. The gratitude that this treatment awakened in them took him aback. (Not trusting the Gutres at first, he'd hidden away in one of his books the two hundred and forty pesos he had brought with him.) Now, the owner of the place away, Espinosa took over and gave timid orders, which were immediately obeyed. The Gutres, as if lost without him, liked following him from room to room and along the gallery that ran around the house. While he read to them, he noticed that they were secretly stealing the crumbs he had dropped on the table. One evening, he caught them unawares, talking about him respectfully, in very few words.

Having finished the Gospel according to St. Mark, he wanted to read another of the three Gospels that remained, but the father asked him to repeat the one he had just read, so that they could understand it better. Espinosa felt that they were like children, to whom repetition is more pleasing than variations or novelty. That night—this is not to be wondered at—he dreamed of the Flood; the hammer blows of the building of the Ark woke him up, and he thought that perhaps they were thunder. In fact, the rain, which had let up, started again. The cold was bitter. The Gutres had told him that the storm had damaged the roof of the tool shed, and that they would show it to him when the beams were fixed. No longer a stranger now, he was treated by them with special attention, almost to the point of spoiling him. None of them liked coffee, but for him there was always a small cup into which they heaped sugar.

The new storm had broken out on a Tuesday. Thursday night, Espinosa was awakened by a soft knock at his door, which—just in case—he always kept locked. He got out of bed and opened it; there was the girl. In the dark he could hardly make her out, but by her footsteps he could tell she was barefoot, and moments later, in bed, that she must have come all the way from the other end of the house naked. She did not embrace him or speak a single word; she lay beside him, trembling. It was the first time she had known a man. When she left, she did not kiss him; Espinosa realized that he didn't even know her name. For some reason that he did not want to pry into, he made up his mind that upon returning to Buenos Aires he would tell no one about what had taken place.

The next day began like the previous ones, except that the father spoke to Espinosa and asked him if Christ had let Himself be killed so as to save all other men on earth. Espinosa, who was a freethinker but who felt committed to what he had read to the Gutres, answered, "Yes, to save everyone from Hell."

Gutre then asked, "What's Hell?"

"A place under the ground where souls burn and burn."

"And the Roman soldiers who hammered in the nails—were they saved, too?"

"Yes," said Espinosa, whose theology was rather dim.

All along, he was afraid that the foreman might ask him about what had gone on the night before with his daughter. After lunch, they asked him to read the last chapters over again.

Espinosa slept a long nap that afternoon. It was light sleep, disturbed by persistent hammering and by vague premonitions. Toward evening, he got up and went out onto the gallery. He said, as if thinking aloud, "The waters have dropped. It won't be long now."

"It won't be long now," Gutre repeated, like an echo.

The three had been following him. Bowing their knees to the stone pavement, they asked his blessing. Then they mocked at him, spat on him, and shoved him toward the back part of the house. The girl wept. Espinosa understood what awaited him on the other side of the door. When they opened it, he saw a patch of sky. A bird sang out. A goldfinch, he thought. The shed was without a roof; they had pulled down the beams to make the cross.

Questions for Study

1. *Why is Espinosa described as undistinguished and undirected?*
2. *What is significant about his religious background?*
3. *How are his questionable opinions related to his eventual role in the story?*
4. *Why does Espinosa agree to go to the ranch?*

5. *Why does he think the stories of the lost ship and the crucifixion have been told over and over throughout history?*
6. *Why do the Gutres ask him about Hell and the Roman soldiers?*
7. *How is the flood used to prepare for the sacrifice?*
8. *Why do you think the Gospel of St. Mark is used? Why do the Gutres insist he read only it?*
9. *What is the significance of the girl who lies with Espinosa?*

Topics for Discussion and Writing

1. *Discuss the story as a parable. In your essay consider Borges' statement to the effect that he writes "straightforward stories" and is no "preacher of parables," that he is realistic, and that he sets his stories "some distance off in time and space" in order to allow his imagination greater freedom.*
2. *Discuss the hero as a Christ figure, indicating which traits are similar to those of the Savior and which are different.*
3. *Discuss the religion of the Gutres.*
4. *Discuss Espinosa's relationship with the Gutres in terms of a man from the city invading the culture of a semiprimitive people.*

STEPHEN CRANE

The Blue Hotel

I

The Palace Hotel at Fort Romper was painted a light blue, a shade that is on the legs of a kind of heron, causing the bird to declare its position against any background. The Palace Hotel, then, was always screaming and howling in a way that made the dazzling winter landscape of Nebraska seem only a gray swampish hush. It stood alone on the prairie, and when the snow was falling the town two hundred yards away was not visible. But when the traveler alighted at the railway station he was obliged to pass the Palace Hotel before he could come upon the company of low clapboard houses which composed Fort Romper, and it was not to be thought that any traveler could pass the Palace Hotel without looking at it. Pat Scully, the proprietor, had proved himself a master of strategy when he chose his paints. It is true that on clear days, when the great transcontinental expresses, long lines of swaying Pullmans, swept through Fort Romper, passengers were overcome at the sight, and the cult that knows the brown-reds and the subdivisions of the dark greens of the East expressed shame, pity, horror, in a laugh. But to the citizens of this prairie town and to the people who would naturally stop there, Pat Scully had performed a feat. With this opulence and splendor, these creeds, classes, egotisms, that streamed through Romper on the rails day after day, they had no color in common.

As if the displayed delights of such a blue hotel were not sufficiently enticing, it was Scully's habit to go every morning and evening to meet the leisurely trains that stopped at Romper and work his seductions upon any man that he might see wavering, gripsack in hand.

One morning, when a snow-crusted engine dragged its long string of freight cars and its one passenger coach to the station, Scully performed the marvel of catching three men. One was a shaky and quick-eyed Swede, with a great shining cheap valise; one was a tall bronzed cowboy, who was on his way to a ranch near the Dakota line; one was a little silent man from the East, who didn't look it, and didn't announce it. Scully practically made them prisoners. He was so nimble and merry and kindly that each probably felt it would be the height of brutality to try to escape. They trudged off over the creaking board sidewalks in the wake of the eager little Irishman. He wore a heavy fur cap squeezed tightly down on his head. It caused his two red ears to stick out stiffly, as if they were made of tin.

At last, Scully, elaborately, with boisterous hospitality, conducted them through the portals of the blue hotel. The room which they entered was small. It seemed to be merely a proper temple for an enormous stove, which, in the center, was humming with godlike violence. At various points on its surface the iron had become luminous and glowed yellow from the heat. Beside the stove Scully's son Johnnie was playing High-Five with an old farmer who had whiskers both gray and sandy. They were quarreling. Frequently the old farmer turned his face toward a box of sawdust—colored brown from tobacco juice—that was behind the stove, and spat with an air of great impatience and irritation. With a loud flourish of words Scully destroyed the game of cards, and bustled his son upstairs with part of the baggage of the new guests. He himself conducted them to three basins of the coldest water in the world. The cowboy and the Easterner burnished themselves fiery red with this water, until it seemed to be some kind of metalpolish. The Swede, however, merely dipped his fingers gingerly and with trepidation. It was notable that throughout this series of small ceremonies the three travelers were made to feel that Scully was very benevolent. He was conferring great favors upon them. He handed the towel from one to another with an air of philanthropic impulse.

Afterward they went to the first room, and, sitting about the stove, listened to Scully's officious clamor at his daughters, who were preparing the midday meal. They reflected in the silence of experienced men who tread carefully amid new people. Nevertheless, the old farmer, stationary, invincible in his chair near the warmest part of the stove, turned his face from the sawdust-box frequently and addressed a glowing commonplace to the strangers. Usually he was answered in short but adequate sentences by either the cowboy or the Easterner. The Swede said nothing. He seemed to be occupied in making furtive estimates of each man in the room. One might have thought that he had the sense of silly suspicion which comes to guilt. He resembled a badly frightened man.

Later, at dinner, he spoke a little, addressing his conversation entirely to Scully. He volunteered that he had come from New York, where for ten years he had worked as a tailor. These facts seemed to strike Scully as fascinating, and afterward he volunteered that he had lived at Romper for fourteen years. The Swede asked about the crops and the price of labor. He seemed barely to listen to Scully's extended replies. His eyes continued to rove from man to man.

Finally, with a laugh and a wink, he said that some of these Western communities were very dangerous; and after his statement he straightened his legs under the table, tilted his head, and laughed again, loudly. It was plain that the demonstration had no meaning to the others. They looked at him wondering and in silence.

II

As the men trooped heavily back into the front room, the two little windows presented views of a turmoiling sea of snow. The huge arms of the wind were making attempts—mighty, circular, futile—to embrace the flakes as they sped. A gate-post like a still man with a blanched face stood aghast amid this profligate fury. In a hearty voice Scully announced the presence of a blizzard. The guests of the blue hotel, lighting their pipes, assented with grunts of lazy masculine contentment. No island of the sea could be exempt in the degree of this little room with its humming stove. Johnnie, son of Scully, in a tone which defined his opinion of his ability as a card-player, challenged the old farmer of both gray and sandy whiskers to a game of High-Five. The farmer agreed with a contemptuous and bitter scoff. They sat close to the stove, and squared their knees under a wide board. The cowboy and the Easterner watched the game with interest. The Swede remained near the window, aloof, but with a countenance that showed signs of an inexplicable excitement.

The play of Johnnie and the gray-beard was suddenly ended by another quarrel. The old man arose while casting a look of heated scorn at his adversary. He slowly buttoned his coat, and then stalked with fabulous dignity from the room. In the discreet silence of all other men the Swede laughed. His laughter rang somehow childish. Men by this time had begun to look at him askance, as if they wished to inquire what ailed him.

A new game was formed jocosely. The cowboy volunteered to become the partner of Johnnie, and they all then turned to ask the Swede to throw in his lot with the little Easterner. He asked some questions about the game, and, learning that it wore many names, and that he had played it when it was under an alias, he accepted the invitation. He strode toward the men nervously, as if he expected to be assaulted. Finally, seated, he gazed from face to face and laughed shrilly. This laugh was so strange that the Easterner looked up quickly, the cowboy sat intent and with his mouth open, and Johnnie paused, holding the cards with still fingers.

Afterward there was a short silence. Then Johnnie said, "Well, let's get at it. Come on now!" They pulled their chairs forward until their knees were bunched under the board. They began to play, and their interest in the game caused the others to forget the manner of the Swede.

The cowboy was a board-whacker. Each time that he held superior cards he whanged them, one by one, with exceeding force, down upon the improvised table, and took the tricks with a glowing air of prowess and pride that sent thrills of indignation into the hearts of his opponents. A game with a board-whacker in it is sure to become intense. The countenances of the Easterner and the Swede were miserable whenever the cowboy thundered down his aces and kings, while Johnnie, his eyes gleaming with joy, chuckled and chuckled.

Because of the absorbing play none considered the strange ways of the Swede. They paid strict heed to the game. Finally, during a lull caused by a new deal, the Swede suddenly addressed Johnnie: "I suppose there have been a good many men killed in this room." The jaws of the others dropped and they looked at him.

"What in hell are you talking about?" said Johnnie.

The Swede laughed again his blatant laugh, full of a kind of false courage and defiance. "Oh, you know what I mean all right," he answered.

"I'm a liar if I do!" Johnnie protested. The card was halted, and the men stared at the Swede. Johnnie evidently felt that as the son of the proprietor, he should make a direct inquiry. "Now, what might you be drivin' at, mister?" he asked. The Swede winked at him. It was a wink full of cunning. His fingers shook on the edge of the board. "Oh, maybe you think I have been to nowheres. Maybe you think I'm a tenderfoot?"

"I don't know nothin' about you," answered Johnnie, "and I don't give a damn where you've been. All I got to say is that I don't know what you're driving at. There hain't never been nobody killed in this room."

The cowboy, who had been steadily gazing at the Swede, then spoke: "What's wrong with you, mister?"

Apparently it seemed to the Swede that he was formidably menaced. He shivered and turned white near the corners of his mouth. He sent an appealing glance in the direction of the little Easterner. During these moments he did not forget to wear his air of advanced pot-valor. "They say they don't know what I mean," he remarked mockingly to the Easterner.

The latter answered after prolonged and cautious reflection. "I don't understand you," he said, impassively.

The Swede made a movement then which announced that he thought he had encountered treachery from the only quarter where he had expected sympathy, if not help. "Oh, I see you are all against me, I see—"

The cowboy was in a state of deep stupefaction. "Say," he cried, as he tumbled the deck violently down upon the board, "say, what are you gittin' at, hey?"

The Swede sprang up with the celerity of a man escaping from a snake on the floor. "I don't want to fight!" he shouted. "I don't want to fight!"

The cowboy stretched his long legs indolently and deliberately. His hands were in his pockets. He spat into the sawdust-box. "Well, who the hell thought you did?" he inquired.

The Swede backed rapidly toward a corner of the room. His hands were out protectingly in front of his chest, but he was making an obvious struggle to control his fright. "Gentlemen," he quavered, "I suppose I am going to be killed before I can leave this house! I suppose I am going to be killed before I can leave this house!" In his eyes was the dying-swan look. Through the windows could be seen the snow turning blue in the shadow of dusk. The wind tore at the house, and some loose thing beat regularly against the clapboards like a spirit tapping.

A door opened, and Scully himself entered. He paused in surprise as he noted the tragic attitude of the Swede. Then he said, "What's the matter here?"

The Swede answered him swiftly and eagerly: "These men are going to kill me."

"Kill you!" ejaculated Scully. "Kill you! What are you talkin'?"

The Swede made the gesture of a martyr.

Scully wheeled sternly upon his son. "What is this, Johnnie?"

The lad had grown sullen. "Damned if I know," he answered. "I can't make no sense to it." He began to shuffle the cards, fluttering them together with an angry snap. "He says a good many men have been killed in this room, or something like that. And he says he's goin' to be killed here too. I don't know what ails him. He's crazy, I shouldn't wonder."

Scully then looked for explanation to the cowboy, but the cowboy simply shrugged his shoulders.

"Kill you?" said Scully again to the Swede. "Kill you? Man, you're off your nut."

"Oh, I know," burst out the Swede. "I know what will happen. Yes, I'm crazy—yes. Yes, of course, I'm crazy—yes. But I know one thing—" There was a sort of sweat of misery and terror upon his face. "I know I won't get out of here alive."

The cowboy drew a deep breath, as if his mind was passing into the last stages of dissolution. "Well, I'm doggoned," he whispered to himself.

Scully wheeled suddenly and faced his son. "You've been troublin' this man!"

Johnnie's voice was loud with its burden of grievance. "Why, good Gawd, I ain't done nothin' to 'im."

The Swede broke in. "Gentlemen, do not disturb yourselves. I will leave this house. I will go away, because"—he accused them dramatically with his glance—"because I do not want to be killed."

Scully was furious with his son. "Will you tell me what is the matter, you young divil? What's the matter, anyhow? Speak out!"

"Blame it!" cried Johnnie in despair, "don't I tell you I don't know? He—he says we want to kill him, and that's all I know. I can't tell what ails him."

The Swede continued to repeat: "Never mind. Mr. Scully; never mind. I will leave this house. I will go away, because I do not wish to be killed. Yes, of course, I am crazy—yes. But I know one thing! I will go away. I will leave this house. Never mind, Mr. Scully; never mind. I will go away."

"You will not go 'way," said Scully. "You will not go 'way until I hear the reason of this business. If anybody has troubled you I will take care of him. This is my house. You are under my roof, and I will not allow any peaceable man to be troubled here." He cast a terrible eye upon Johnnie, the cowboy, and the Easterner.

"Never mind, Mr. Scully; never mind. I will go away. I do not wish to be killed." The Swede moved toward the door which opened upon the stairs. It was evidently his intention to go at once for his baggage.

"No, no," shouted Scully peremptorily; but the white-faced man slid by him and disappeared. "Now," said Scully severely, "what does this mane?"

Johnnie and the cowboy cried together: "Why, we didn't do nothin' to 'im!"

Scully's eyes were cold. "No," he said, "you didn't?"

Johnnie swore a deep oath. "Why, this is the wildest loon I ever see. We didn't do nothin' at all. We were jest sittin' here playin' cards, and he—"

The father suddenly spoke to the Easterner, "Mr. Blanc," he asked, "what has these boys been doin'?"

The Easterner reflected again. "I didn't see anything wrong at all," he said at last, slowly.

Scully began to howl. "But what does it mane?" He stared ferociously at his son. "I have a mind to lather you for this, me boy."

Johnnie was frantic. "Well, what have I done?" he bawled at his father.

III

"I think you are tongue-tied," said Scully finally to his son, the cowboy, and the Easterner; and at the end of this scornful sentence he left the room.

Upstairs the Swede was swiftly fastening the straps of his great valise. Once his back happened to be half turned toward the door, and, hearing a noise there, he wheeled and sprang up, uttering a loud cry. Scully's wrinkled visage showed grimly in the light of the small lamp he carried. This yellow effulgence, streaming upward, colored only his prominent features, and left his eyes, for instance, in mysterious shadow. He resembled a murderer.

"Man! man!" he exclaimed, "have you gone daffy?"

"Oh, no! Oh, no!" rejoined the other. "There are people in this world who know pretty nearly as much as you do—understand?"

For a moment they stood gazing at each other. Upon the Swede's deathly pale cheeks were two spots brightly crimson and sharply edged, as if they had been carefully painted. Scully placed the light on the table and sat himself on the edge of the bed. He spoke ruminatively. "By cracky, I never heard of such a thing in my life. It's a complete muddle. I can't, for the soul of me, think how you ever got this idea into your head." Presently he lifted his eyes and asked: "And did you sure think they were going to kill you?"

The Swede scanned the old man as if he wished to see into his mind. "I did," he said at last. He obviously suspected that this answer might precipitate an outbreak. As he pulled on a strap his whole arm shook, the elbow wavering like a bit of paper.

Scully banged his hand impressively on the footboard of the bed. "Why, man, we're goin' to have a line of ilictric street-cars in this town next spring."

" 'A line of electric street-cars,' " repeated the Swede, stupidly.

"And," said Scully, "there's a new railroad goin' to be built down from Broken Arm to here. Not to mintion the four churches and the smashin' big brick schoolhouse. Then there's the big factory, too. Why, in two years Romper'll be a met-tro-*pol*-is."

Having finished the preparation of his baggage, the Swede straightened himself. "Mr. Scully," he said, with sudden hardihood, "how much do I owe you?"

"You don't owe me anythin'," said the old man, angrily.

"Yes, I do," retorted the Swede. He took seventy-five cents from his pocket and tendered it to Scully; but the latter snapped his fingers in disdainful refusal. However, it happened that they both stood gazing in a strange fashion at three silver pieces on the Swede's open palm.

"I'll not take your money," said Scully at last. "Not after what's been goin' on here." Then a plan seemed to strike him. "Here," he cried, picking up his lamp and moving toward the door. "Here! Come with me a minute."

"No," said the Swede, in overwhelming alarm.

"Yes," urged the old man. "Come on! I want you to come and see a picter—just across the hall—in my room."

The Swede must have concluded that his hour was come. His jaw dropped and his teeth showed like a dead man's. He ultimately followed Scully across the corridor, but he had the step of one hung in chains.

Scully flashed the light high on the wall of his own chamber. There was revealed a ridiculous photograph of a little girl. She was leaning against a balustrade of gorgeous decoration, and the formidable bang to her hair was prominent. The figure was as graceful as an upright sled-stake, and, withal, it was of the hue of lead. "There," said Scully, tenderly, "that's the picter of my little girl that died. Her name was Carrie. She had the purtiest hair you ever saw! I was that fond of her, she—"

Turning then, he saw that the Swede was not contemplating the picture at all, but, instead, was keeping keen watch on the gloom in the rear.

"Look, man!" cried Scully, heartily. "That's the picter of my little gal that died. Her name was Carrie. And then here's the picter of my oldest boy, Michael. He's a lawyer in Lincoln, an' doin' well. I gave that boy a grand eddication, and I'm glad for it now. He's a fine boy. Look at 'im now. Ain't he bold as blazes, him there in Lincoln, an honored an' respicted gintleman! An honored and respicted gintleman," concluded Scully with a flourish. And, so saying, he smote the Swede jovially on the back.

The Swede faintly smiled.

"Now," said the old man, "there's only one more thing." He dropped suddenly to the floor and thrust his head beneath the bed. The Swede could hear his muffled voice. "I'd keep it under me piller if it wasn't for that boy Johnnie. Then there's the old woman—Where is it now? I never put it twice in the same place. Ah, now come out with you!"

Presently he backed clumsily from under the bed, dragging with him an old coat rolled into a bundle. "I've fetched him," he muttered. Kneeling on the floor, he unrolled the coat and extracted from its heart a large yellow-brown whisky-bottle.

His first maneuver was to hold the bottle up to the light. Reassured, apparently, that nobody had been tampering with it, he thrust it with a generous movement toward the Swede.

The weak-kneed Swede was about to eagerly clutch this element of strength, but he suddenly jerked his hand away and cast a look of horror upon Scully.

"Drink," said the old man affectionately. He had risen to his feet, and now stood facing the Swede.

There was a silence. Then again Scully said: "Drink!"

The Swede laughed wildly. He grabbed the bottle, put it to his mouth; and as his lips curled absurdly around the opening and his throat worked, he kept his glance, burning with hatred, upon the old man's face.

IV

After the departure of Scully the three men, with the cardboard still upon their knees, preserved for a long time an astounded silence. Then Johnnie said: "That's the doddangedest Swede I ever see."

"He ain't no Swede," said the cowboy, scornfully.

"Well, what is he then?" cried Johnnie. "What is he then?"

"It's my opinion," replied the cowboy deliberately, "he's some kind of a Dutchman." It was a venerable custom of the country to entitle as Swedes all light-haired men who spoke with a heavy tongue. In consequence the idea of the cowboy was not without its daring. "Yes, sir," he repeated, "It's my opinion this feller is some kind of a Dutchman."

"Well, he says he's a Swede, anyhow," muttered Johnnie, sulkily. He turned to the Easterner: "What do you think, Mr. Blanc?"

"Oh, I don't know," replied the Easterner.

"Well, what do you think makes him act that way?" asked the cowboy.

"Why, he's frightened." The Easterner knocked his pipe against a rim of the stove. "He's clear frightened out of his boots."

"What at?" cried Johnnie and the cowboy together.

The Easterner reflected over his answer.

"What at?" cried the others again.

"Oh, I don't know but it seems to me this man has been reading dime novels, and he thinks he's right out in the middle of it—the shootin' and stabbin' and all."

"But," said the cowboy, deeply scandalized, "this ain't Wyoming, ner none of them places. This is Nebrasker."

"Yes," added Johnnie, "an' why don't he wait till he gits *out West?*"

The traveled Easterner laughed. "It isn't different there even—not in these days. But he thinks he's right in the middle of hell."

Johnnie and the cowboy mused long.

"It's awful funny," remarked Johnnie at last.

"Yes," said the cowboy, "This is a queer game. I hope we don't git snowed in, because then we'd have to stand this here man bein' around with us all the time. That wouldn't be no good."

"I wish pop would throw him out," said Johnnie.

Presently they heard a loud stamping on the stairs, accompanied by ringing jokes in the voice of old Scully, and laughter, evidently from the

Swede. The men around the stove stared vacantly at each other. "Gosh!" said the cowboy. The door flew open, and old Scully, flushed and anecdotal, came into the room. He was jabbering at the Swede, who followed him, laughing bravely. It was the entry of two roisterers from a banquet hall.

"Come now," said Scully sharply to the three seated men, "move up and give us a chance at the stove." The cowboy and the Easterner obediently sidled their chairs to make room for the new-comers. Johnnie, however, simply arranged himself in a more indolent attitude, and then remained motionless.

"Come! Git over, there," said Scully.

"Plenty of room on the other side of the stove," said Johnnie.

"Do you think we want to sit in the draught?" roared the father.

But the Swede here interposed with a grandeur of confidence. "No, no. Let the boy sit where he likes," he cried in a bullying voice to the father.

"All right! All right!" said Scully, deferentially. The cowboy and the Easterner exchanged glances of wonder.

The five chairs were formed in a crescent about one side of the stove. The Swede began to talk; he talked arrogantly, profanely, angrily. Johnnie, the cowboy, and the Easterner maintained a morose silence, while old Scully appeared to be receptive and eager, breaking in constantly with sympathetic ejaculations.

Finally the Swede announced that he was thirsty. He moved in his chair, and said that he would go for a drink of water.

"I'll git it for you," cried Scully at once.

"No," said the Swede, contemptuously. "I'll get it for myself." He arose and stalked with the air of of a owner off into the executive parts of the hotel.

As soon as the Swede was out of hearing Scully sprang to his feet and whispered intensely to the others: "Upstairs he thought I was tryin' to poison 'im."

"Say," said Johnnie, "this makes me sick. Why don't you throw 'im out in the snow?"

"Why, he's all right now," declared Scully. "It was only that he was from the East, and he thought this was a tough place. That's all. He's all right now."

The cowboy looked with admiration upon the Easterner. "You were straight," he said. "You were on to that there Dutchman."

"Well," said Johnnie to his father, "he may be all right now, but I don't see it. Other time he was scared, but now he's too fresh."

Scully's speech was always a combination of Irish brogue and idiom, Western twang and idiom, and scraps of curiously formal diction taken from the story-books and newspapers. He now hurled a strange mass of language at the head of his son. "What do I keep? What do I keep? What do I keep?" he demanded, in a voice of thunder. He slapped his knee impressively, to indicate that he himself was going to make reply, and that all should heed. "I keep a hotel," he shouted. "A hotel, do you mind? A guest under my roof has sacred privileges. He is to be intimidated by none. Not one word shall he hear that would prijudice him in favor of goin' away. I'll not have it. There's no place in this here town where they can say they iver took in a guest of mine because he was afraid to stay here." He wheeled suddenly upon the cowboy and the Easterner. "Am I right?"

"Yes, Mr. Scully," said the cowboy, "I think you're right."

"Yes, Mr. Scully," said the Easterner, "I think you're right."

V

At six-o'clock supper, the Swede fizzed like a firewheel. He sometimes seemed on the point of bursting into riotous song, and in all his madness he was encouraged by old Scully. The Easterner was encased in reserve; the cowboy sat in wide-mouthed amazement, forgetting to eat, while Johnnie wrathily demolished great plates of food. The daughters of the house, when they were obliged to replenish the biscuits, approached as warily as Indians, and, having succeeded in their purpose, fled with ill-concealed trepidation. The Swede domineered the whole feast, and he gave it the appearance of a cruel bacchanal. He seemed to have grown suddenly taller; he gazed brutally disdainful, into every face. His voice rang through the room. Once when he jabbed out harpoon-fashion with his fork to pinion a biscuit, the weapon nearly impaled the hand of the Easterner, which had been stretched quietly out for the same biscuit.

After supper, as the men filed toward the other room, the Swede smote Scully ruthlessly on the shoulder. "Well, old boy, that was a good, square meal." Johnnie looked hopefully at his father; he knew that shoulder was tender from an old fall; and, indeed, it appeared for a moment as if Scully was going to flame out over the matter, but in the end he smiled a sickly smile and remained silent. The others understood from his manner that he was admitting his responsibility for the Swede's new viewpoint.

Johnnie, however, addressed his parent in an aside. "Why don't you license somebody to kick you downstairs?" Scully scowled darkly by way of reply.

When they were gathered about the stove, the Swede insisted on another game of High-Five. Scully gently deprecated the plan at first, but the Swede turned a wolfish glare upon him. The old man subsided, and the Swede canvassed the others. In his tone there was always a great threat. The cowboy and the Easterner both remarked indifferently that they would play. Scully said that he would presently have to go to meet the 6:58 train, and so the Swede turned menacingly upon Johnnie. For a moment their glances crossed like blades, and then Johnnie smiled and said, "Yes, I'll play."

They formed a square, with the little board on their knees. The Easterner and the Swede were again partners. As the play went on, it was noticeable that the cowboy was not board-whacking as usual. Meanwhile, Scully, near the lamp, had put on his spectacles and, with an appearance curiously like an old priest, was reading a newspaper. In time he went out to meet the 6:58 train, and, despite his precautions, a gust of polar wind whirled into the room as he opened the door. Besides scattering the cards, it chilled the players to the marrow. The Swede cursed frightfully. When Scully returned, his entrance disturbed a cozy and friendly scene. The Swede again cursed. But presently they were once more intent, their heads bent forward and their hands moving swiftly. The Swede had adopted the fashion of board-whacking.

Scully took up his paper and for a long time remained immersed in matters which were extraordinarily remote from him. The lamp burned badly and once he stopped to adjust the wick. The newspaper, as he turned from page to page, rustled with a slow and comfortable sound. Then suddenly he heard three terrible words: "You are cheatin'!"

Such scenes often prove that there can be little of dramatic import in environment. Any room can present a tragic front; any room can be comic. This little den was now hideous as a torture-chamber. The new faces of the men themselves had changed it upon the instant. The Swede held a huge fist in front of Johnnie's face, while the latter looked steadily over it into the blazing orbs of his accuser. The Easterner had grown pallid; the cowboy's jaw had dropped in that expression of bovine amazement which was one of his important mannerisms. After the three words, the first sound in the room was made by Scully's paper as it floated forgotten to his feet. His spectacles had also fallen from his nose, but by a clutch he had saved them in air. His hand, grasping the spectacles, now remained poised awkwardly and near his shoulder. He stared at the card-players.

Probably the silence was while a second elapsed. Then, if the floor had been suddenly twitched out from under the men they could not have moved quicker. The five had projected themselves headlong toward a common point. It happened that Johnnie, in rising to hurl himself upon the Swede, had stumbled slightly because of his curiously instinctive care for the cards and the board. The loss of the moment allowed time for the arrival of Scully, and also allowed the cowboy time to give the Swede a great push which sent him staggering back. The men found tongue together, and hoarse shouts of rage, appeal, or fear burst from every throat. The cowboy pushed and jostled feverishly at the Swede, and the Easterner and Scully clung wildly to Johnnie; but through the smoky air, above the swaying bodies of the peace-compellers, the eyes of the two warriors ever sought each other in glances of challenge that were at once hot and steely.

Of course the board had been overturned, and now the whole company of cards was scattered over the floor, where the boots of the men trampled the fat and painted kings and queens as they gazed with their silly eyes at the war that was waging above them.

Scully's voice was dominating the yells. "Stop now! Stop, I say! Stop, now—"

Johnnie, as he struggled to burst through the rank formed by Scully and the Easterner, was crying, "Well, he says I cheated! He says I cheated! I won't allow no man to say I cheated! If he says I cheated, he's a——!"

The cowboy was telling the Swede, "Quit now! Quit, d'ye hear—"

The screams of the Swede never ceased: "He did cheat! I saw him! I saw him—"

As for the Easterner, he was importuning in a voice that was not heeded: "Wait a moment, can't you? Oh, wait a moment. What's the good of a fight over a game of cards? Wait a moment—"

In this tumult no complete sentences were clear. "Cheat"—"Quit"—"He says"—these fragments pierced the uproar and rang out sharply. It was remarkable that, whereas Scully undoubtedly made the most noise, he was the least heard of any of the riotous band.

Then suddenly there was a great cessation. It was as if each man had paused for breath; and although the room was still lighted with the anger of men, it could be seen that there was no danger of immediate conflict, and at once Johnnie, shouldering his way forward, almost succeeded in confronting the Swede. "What did you say I cheated for? What did you say I cheated for? I don't cheat, and I won't let any man say I do!"

The Swede said, "I saw you! I saw you!"

"Well," cried Johnnie, "I'll fight any man what says I cheat!"

"No, you won't," said the cowboy. "Not here."

"Ah, be still, can't you?" said Scully, coming between them.

The quiet was sufficient to allow the Easterner's voice to be heard. He was repeating, "Oh, wait a moment, can't you? What's the good of a fight over a game of cards? Wait a moment!"

Johnnie, his red face appearing above his father's shoulder, hailed the Swede again. "Did you say I cheated?"

The Swede showed his teeth. "Yes."

"Then," said Johnnie, "we must fight."

"Yes, fight," roared the Swede. He was like a demoniac. "Yes, fight! I'll show you what kind of a man I am! I'll show you who you want to fight! Maybe you think I can't fight! Maybe you think I can't! I'll show you, you skin, you card-sharp! Yes, you cheated! You cheated! You cheated!"

"Well, let's go at it, then, mister," said Johnnie, coolly.

The cowboy's brow was beaded with sweat from his efforts in intercepting all sorts of raids. He turned in despair to Scully. "What are you goin' to do now?"

A change had come over the Celtic visage of the old man. He now seemed all eagerness; his eyes glowed.

"We'll let them fight," he answered, stalwartly. "I can't put up with it any longer. I've stood this damned Swede till I'm sick. We'll let them fight."

VI

The men prepared to go out of doors. The Easterner was so nervous that he had great difficulty in getting his arms into the sleeves of his new leather coat. As the cowboy drew his fur cap down over his ears his hands trembled. In fact, Johnnie and old Scully were the only ones who displayed no agitation. These preliminaries were conducted without words.

Scully threw open the door. "Well, come on," he said. Instantly a terrific wind caused the flame of the lamp to struggle at its wick, while a puff of black smoke sprang from the chimney-top. The stove was in mid-current of the blast, and its voice swelled to equal the roar of the storm. Some of the scarred and bedabbled cards were caught up from the floor and dashed helplessly against the farther wall. The men lowered their heads and plunged into the tempest as into a sea.

No snow was falling, but great whirls and clouds of flakes, swept up from the ground by the frantic winds, were streaming southward with the speed of bullets. The covered land was blue with the sheen of an unearthly satin, and there was no other hue save where, at the low, black railway station—which seemed incredibly distant—one light gleamed like a tiny jewel. As the men floundered into a thigh-deep drift, it was known that the Swede was bawling out something. Scully went to him, put a hand on his shoulder, and projected an ear. "What's that you say?" he shouted.

"I say," bawled the Swede again, "I won't stand much show against this gang. I know you'll all pitch on me."

Scully smote him reproachfully on the arm. "Tut, man!" he yelled. The wind tore the words from Scully's lips and scattered them far alee.

"You are all a gang of—" boomed the Swede, but the storm also seized the remainder of this sentence.

Immediately turning their backs upon the wind, the men had swung around a corner to the sheltered side of the hotel. It was the function of the little house to preserve here, amid this great devastation of snow, an irregular V-shape of heavily encrusted grass, which crackled beneath the feet. One could imagine the great drifts piled against the windward side. When the party reached the comparative peace of this spot it was found that the Swede was still bellowing.

"Oh, I know what kind of a thing this is! I know you'll all pitch on me. I can't lick you all!"

Scully turned upon him panther-fashion. "You'll not have to whip all of us. You'll have to whip my son Johnnie. An' the man what troubles you durin' that time will have me to dale with."

The arrangements were swiftly made. The two men faced each other, obedient to the harsh commands of Scully, whose face, in the subtly luminous gloom, could be seen set in the austere impersonal lines that are pictured on the countenances of the Roman veterans. The Easterner's teeth were chattering, and he was hopping up and down like a mechanical toy. The cowboy stood rock-like.

The contestants had not stripped off any clothing. Each was in his ordinary attire. Their fists were up, and they eyed each other in a calm that had the elements of leonine cruelty in it.

During this pause, the Easterner's mind, like a film, took lasting impressions of three men—the iron-nerved master of the ceremony; the Swede, pale, motionless, terrible; and Johnnie, serene yet ferocious, brutish yet heroic. The entire prelude had in it a tragedy greater than the tragedy of action, and this aspect was accentuated by the long, mellow cry of the blizzard, as it sped the tumbling and wailing flakes into the black abyss of the south.

"Now!" said Scully.

The two combatants leaped forward and crashed together like bullocks. There was heard the cushioned sound of blows, and of a curse squeezing out from between the tight teeth of one.

As for the spectators, the Easterner's pent-up breath exploded from him with a pop of relief, absolute relief from the tension of the preliminaries. The cowboy bounded into the air with a yowl. Scully was immovable as from supreme amazement and fear at the fury of the fight which he himself had permitted and arranged.

For a time the encounter in the darkness was such a perplexity of flying arms that it presented no more detail than would a swiftly revolving wheel. Occasionally a face, as if illumined by a flash of light, would shine out, ghastly and marked with pink spots. A moment later, the men might have been known as shadows, if it were not for the involuntary utterance of oaths that came from them in whispers.

Suddenly a holocaust of warlike desire caught the cowboy, and he bolted forward with the speed of a broncho. "Go it, Johnnie! go it! Kill him! Kill him!"

Scully confronted him. "Kape back," he said; and by his glance the cowboy could tell that this man was Johnnie's father.

To the Easterner there was a monotony of unchangeable fighting that was an abomination. This confused mingling was eternal to his sense, which was concentrated in a longing for the end, the priceless end. Once the fighters lurched near him, and as he scrambled hastily backward he heard them breathe like men on the rack.

"Kill him, Johnnie! Kill him! Kill him! Kill him!" The cowboy's face was contorted like one of those agony masks in museums.

"Keep still," said Scully, icily.

Then there was a sudden loud grunt, incomplete, cut short, and Johnnie's body swung away from the Swede and fell with sickening heaviness to the grass. The cowboy was barely in time to prevent the mad Swede from flinging himself upon his prone adversary. "No, you don't," said the cowboy, interposing an arm. "Wait a second."

Scully was at his son's side. "Johnnie! Johnnie, me boy!" His voice had a quality of melancholy tenderness. "Johnnie! Can you go on with it?" He looked anxiously down into the bloody, pulpy face of his son.

There was a moment of silence, and then Johnnie answered in his ordinary voice, "Yes, I—it—yes."

Assisted by his father he struggled to his feet. "Wait a bit now till you git your wind," said the old man.

A few paces away the cowboy was lecturing the Swede. "No, you don't! Wait a second!"

The Easterner was plucking at Scully's sleeve. "Oh, this is enough," he pleaded. "This is enough! Let it go as it stands. This is enough!"

"Bill," said Scully, "git out of the road." The cowboy stepped aside. "Now." The combatants were actuated by a new caution as they advanced toward collision. They glared at each other, and then the Swede aimed a lightning blow that carried with it his entire weight. Johnnie was evidently half stupid from weakness, but he miraculously dodged, and his fist sent the overbalanced Swede sprawling.

The cowboy, Scully, and the Easterner burst into a cheer that was like a chorus of triumphant soldiery, but before its conclusion the Swede had scuffled agilely to his feet and come in beserk abandon at his foe. There was another perplexity of flying arms, and Johnnie's body again swung away and fell, even as a bundle might fall from a roof. The Swede instantly staggered to a little wind-waved tree and leaned upon it, breathing like an engine, while his savage and flame-lit eyes roamed from face to face as the men bent over Johnnie. There was a splendor of isolation in his situation at this time which the Easterner felt once when, lifting his eyes from the man on the ground, he beheld that mysterious and lonely figure, waiting.

"Are you any good yet, Johnnie?" asked Scully in a broken voice.

The son gasped and opened his eyes languidly. After a moment he answered, "No—I ain't—any good—any—more." Then, from shame and bodily ill, he began to weep, the tears furrowing down through the blood-stains on his face. "He was too—too—too heavy for me."

Scully straightened and addressed the waiting figure. "Stranger," he said, evenly, "it's all up with our side." Then his voice changed into that vibrant huskiness which is commonly the tone of the most simple and deadly announcements. "Johnnie is whipped."

Without replying, the victor moved off on the route to the front door of the hotel.

The cowboy was formulating new and unspellable blasphemies. The Easterner was startled to find that they were out in a wind that seemed to come direct from the shadowed arctic floes. He heard again the wail of the snow as it was flung to its grave in the south. He knew now that all this time the cold had been sinking into him deeper and deeper, and he wondered that he had not perished. He felt indifferent to the condition of the vanquished man.

"Johnnie, can you walk?" asked Scully.

"Did I hurt—hurt him any?" asked the son.

"Can you walk, boy? Can you walk?"

Johnnie's voice was suddenly strong. There was a robust impatience in it. "I asked you whether I hurt him any!"

"Yes, yes, Johnnie," answered the cowboy, consolingly; "he's hurt a good deal."

They raised him from the ground, and as soon as he was on his feet he went tottering off, rebuffing all attempts at assistance When the party rounded the corner they were fairly blinded by the pelting of the snow. It burned their faces like fire. The cowboy carried Johnnie through the drift to the door. As they entered, some cards again rose from the floor and beat against the wall.

The Easterner rushed to the stove. He was so profoundly chilled that he almost dared to embrace the glowing iron. The Swede was not in the room. Johnnie sank into a chair and, folding his arms on his knees, buried his face in them. Scully, warming one foot and then the other at a rim of the stove, muttered to himself with Celtic mournfulness. The cowboy had removed his fur cap, and with a dazed and rueful air he was running one hand through his tousled locks. From overhead they could hear the creaking of boards, as the Swede tramped here and there in his room.

The sad quiet was broken by the sudden flinging open of a door that led toward the kitchen. It was instantly followed by an inrush of women. They precipitated themselves upon Johnnie amid a chorus of lamentation. Before they carried their prey off to the kitchen, there to be bathed and harangued with that mixture of sympathy and abuse which is a feat of their sex, the mother straightened herself and fixed old Scully with an eye of stern reproach. "Shame be upon you, Patrick Scully!" she cried. "Your own son, too. Shame be upon you!"

"There, now! Be quiet, now!" said the old man, weakly.

"Shame be upon you, Patrick Scully!" The girls, rallying to this slogan, sniffed disdainfully in the direction of those trembling accomplices, the cowboy and the Easterner. Presently they bore Johnnie away, and left the three men to dismal reflection.

VII

"I'd like to fight this here Dutchman myself," said the cowboy, breaking a long silence.

Scully wagged his head sadly. "No, that wouldn't do. It wouldn't be right. It wouldn't be right."

"Well, why wouldn't it?" argued the cowboy. "I don't see no harm in it."

"No," answered Scully, with mournful heroism. "It wouldn't be right. It was Johnnie's fight, and now we mustn't whip the man just because he whipped Johnnie."

"Yes, that's true enough," said the cowboy; "but—he better not get fresh with me, because I couldn't stand no more of it."

"You'll not say a word to him," commanded Scully, and even then they heard the tread of the Swede on the stairs. His entrance was made theatric. He swept the door back with a bang and swaggered to the middle of the room. No one looked at him. "Well," he cried, insolently, at Scully, "I s'pose you'll tell me now how much I owe you?"

The old man remained stolid. "You don't owe me nothin'."

"Huh!" said the Swede, "huh! Don't owe 'im nothin'."

The cowboy addressed the Swede. "Stranger, I don't see how you come to be so gay around here."

Old Scully was instantly alert. "Stop!" he shouted, holding his hand forth, fingers upward. "Bill, you shut up!"

The cowboy spat carelessly into the sawdust-box. "I didn't say a word, did I?" he asked.

"Mr. Scully," called the Swede, "how much do I owe you?" It was seen that he was attired for departure, and that he had his valise in his hand.

"You don't owe me nothin'," repeated Scully in the same imperturbable way.

"Huh!" said the Swede. "I guess you're right. I guess if it was any way at all, you'd owe me somethin'. That's what I guess." He turned to the cowboy. " 'Kill him! Kill him! Kill him!' " he mimicked, and then guffawed victoriously. " 'Kill him!' " He was convulsed with ironical humor.

But he might have been jeering the dead. The three men were immovable and silent, staring with glassy eyes at the stove.

The Swede opened the door and passed into the storm, giving one derisive glance backward at the still group.

As soon as the door was closed, Scully and the cowboy leaped to their feet and began to curse. They trampled to and fro, waving their arms and smashing into the air with their fists. "Oh, but that was a hard minute!" wailed Scully. "That was a hard minute! Him there leerin' and scoffin'! One bang at his nose was worth forty dollars to me that minute! How did you stand it, Bill?"

"How did I stand it?" cried the cowboy in a quivering voice. "How did I stand it? Oh!"

The old man burst into sudden brogue. "I'd loike to take that Swade," he wailed, "and hould 'im down on a shtone flure and bate 'im to a jelly wid a shtick!"

The cowboy groaned in sympathy. "I'd like to git him by the neck and ha-ammer him"—he brought his hand down on a chair with a noise like a pistol-shot—"hammer that there Dutchman until he couldn't tell himself from a dead coyote!"

"I'd bate 'im until he—"

"I'd show *him* some things—"

And then together they raised a yearning, fanatic cry—"Oh-o-oh! if we only could—"

"Yes!"

"Yes!"

"And then I'd—"

"O-o-oh!"

VIII

The Swede, tightly gripping his valise, tacked across the face of the storm as if he carried sails. He was following a line of little naked, gasping trees which, he knew, must mark the way of the road. His face, fresh from the pounding of Johnnie's fists, felt more pleasure than pain in the wind and the driving snow. A number of square shapes loomed upon him finally, and he knew them as the houses of the main body of the town. He found a street and made travel along it, leaning heavily upon the wind whenever, at a corner, a terrific blast caught him.

He might have been in a deserted village. We picture the world as thick with conquering and elate humanity, but here, with the bugles of the tempest pealing, it was hard to imagine a peopled earth. One viewed the existence of man then as a marvel, and conceded a glamour of wonder to these lice which were caused to cling to a whirling, fire-smitten, ice-locked, disease-stricken, space-lost bulb. The conceit of man was explained by this storm to be the very engine of life. One was a coxcomb not to die in it. However, the Swede found a saloon.

In front of it an indomitable red light was burning, and the snowflakes were made blood-color as they flew through the circumscribed territory of the lamp's shining. The Swede pushed open the door of the saloon and entered. A sanded expanse was before him, and at the end of it four men sat about a table drinking. Down one side of the room extended a radiant bar, and its guardian was leaning upon his elbows listening to the talk of the men at the table. The Swede dropped his valise upon the floor and, smiling fraternally upon the barkeeper, said, "Gimme some whisky, will you?" The man placed a bottle, a whisky-glass, and a glass of ice-thick water upon the bar. The Swede poured himself an abnormal portion of whisky and drank it in three gulps. "Pretty bad night," remarked the bartender, indifferently. He was making the pretension of blindness which is usually a distinction of his class; but it could have been seen that he was furtively studying the half-erased blood-stains on the face of the Swede. "Bad night," he said again.

"Oh, it's good enough for me," replied the Swede, hardily, as he poured himself some more whisky. The barkeeper took his coin and maneuvered it through its reception by the highly nickeled cash-machine. A bell rang; a card labeled "20 cts." had appeared.

"No," continued the Swede, "this isn't too bad weather. It's good enough for me."

"So?" murmured the barkeeper, languidly.

The copious drams made the Swede's eyes swim, and he breathed a trifle heavier. "Yes, I like this weather. I like it. It suits me." It was apparently his design to impart a deep significance to these words.

"So?" murmured the bartender again. He turned to gaze dreamily at the scroll-like birds and bird-like scrolls which had been drawn with soap upon the mirrors in back of the bar.

"Well, I guess I'll take another drink," said the Swede, presently. "Have something?"

"No, thanks; I'm not drinkin'," answered the bartender. Afterward he asked, "How did you hurt your face?"

The Swede immediately began to boast loudly. "Why, in a fight. I thumped the soul out of a man down here at Scully's hotel."

The interest of the four men at the table was at last aroused.

"Who was it?" said one.

"Johnnie Scully," blustered the Swede. "Son of the man what runs it. He will be pretty near dead for some weeks, I can tell you. I made a nice thing of him, I did. He couldn't get up. They carried him in the house. Have a drink?"

Instantly the men in some subtle way encased themselves in reserve. "No, thanks," said one. The group was of curious formation. Two were prominent local business men; one was the district attorney; and one was a professional gambler of the kind known as "square." But a scrutiny of the group would not have enabled an observer to pick the gambler from the men of more reputable pursuits. He was, in fact, a man so delicate in manner, when among people of fair class, and so judicious in his choice of victims, that in the strictly masculine part of the town's life he had come to be explicitly trusted and admired. People called him a thoroughbred. The fear and contempt with which his craft was regarded were undoubtedly the reason why his quiet dignity shone conspicuous above the quiet dignity of men who might be merely hatters, billiard-markers, or grocery clerks. Beyond an occasional unwary traveler who came by rail, this gambler was supposed to prey solely upon reckless and senile farmers, who, when flush with good crops, drove into town in all the pride and confidence of an absolutely invulnerable stupidity. Hearing at times in circuitous fashion of the despoilment of such a farmer, the important men of Romper invariably laughed in contempt of the victim, and if they thought of the wolf at all, it was with a kind of pride at the knowledge that he would never dare think of attacking their wisdom and courage. Besides, it was popular that this gambler had a real wife and two real children in a neat cottage in a suburb, where he led an exemplary home life; and when anyone even suggested a discrepancy in his character, the crowd immediately vociferated descriptions of this virtuous family circle. Then men who led exemplary home lives, and men who did not lead exemplary home lives, all subsided in a bunch, remarking that there was nothing more to be said.

However, when a restriction was placed upon him—as, for instance, when a strong clique of members of the new Pollywog Club refused to permit him, even as a spectator, to appear in the rooms of the organization—the candor and gentleness with which he accepted the judgment disarmed many of his foes and made his friends more desperately partisan. He invariably distinguished between himself and a respectable Romper man so quickly and frankly that his manner actually appeared to be a continual broadcast compliment.

And one must not forget to declare the fundamental fact of his entire position in Romper. It is irrefutable that in all affairs outside his business, in all matters that occur eternally and commonly between man and man, this thieving card-player was so generous, so just, so moral, that, in a contest, he could have put to flight the consciences of nine tenths of the citizens of Romper.

And so it happened that he was seated in this saloon with the two prominent local merchants and the district attorney.

The Swede continued to drink raw whisky, meanwhile babbling at the barkeeper and trying to induce him to indulge in potations. "Come on. Have a drink. Come on. What—no? Well, have a little one, then. By gawd, I've whipped a man tonight, and I want to celebrate. I whipped him good, too. Gentlemen," the Swede cried to the men at the table, "have a drink?"

"Ssh!" said the barkeeper.

The group at the table, although furtively attentive, had been pretending to be deep in talk, but now a man lifted his eyes toward the Swede and said, shortly, "Thanks. We don't want any more."

At this reply the Swede ruffled out his chest like a rooster. "Well," he exploded, "it seems I can't get anybody to drink with me in this town. Seems so, don't it? Well!"

"Ssh!" said the barkeeper.

"Say," snarled the Swede, "don't you try to shut me up. I won't have it. I'm a gentleman, and I want people to drink with me. And I want 'em to drink with me now. *Now*—do you understand?" He rapped the bar with his knuckles.

Years of experience had calloused the bartender. He merely grew sulky. "I hear you," he answered.

"Well," cried the Swede, "listen hard then. See those men over there? Well, they're going to drink with me, and don't you forget it. Now you watch."

"Hi!" yelled the barkeeper, "this won't do!"

"Why won't it?" demanded the Swede. He stalked over to the table, and by chance laid his hand upon the shoulder of the gambler. "How about this?" he asked wrathfully. "I asked you to drink with me."

The gambler simply twisted his head and spoke over his shoulder. "My friend, I don't know you."

"Oh, hell!" answered the Swede, "come and have a drink."

"Now, my boy," advised the gambler, kindly, "take your hand off my shoulder and go 'way and mind your own business." He was a little, slim man, and it seemed strange to hear him use this tone of heroic patronage to the burly Swede. The other men at the table said nothing.

"What! You won't drink with me, you little dude? I'll make you, then! I'll make you!" The Swede had grasped the gambler frenziedly at the throat, and was dragging him from his chair. The other men sprang up. The barkeeper dashed around the corner of his bar. There was a great tumult, and then was seen a long blade in the hand of the gambler. It shot forward, and a human body, this citadel of virtue, wisdom, power, was pierced as easily as if it had been a melon. The Swede fell with a cry of supreme astonishment.

The prominent merchants and the district attorney must have at once tumbled out of the place backward. The bartender found himself hanging limply to the arm of a chair and gazing into the eyes of a murderer.

"Henry," said the latter, as he wiped his knife on one of the towels that hung beneath the bar rail, "you tell 'em where to find me. I'll be home, waiting for 'em." Then he vanished. A moment afterward the barkeeper was in the street dinning through the storm for help and, moreover, companionship.

The corpse of the Swede, alone in the saloon, had its eyes fixed upon a dreadful legend that dwelt atop of the cash-machine: "This registers the amount of your purchase."

IX

Months later, the cowboy was frying pork over the stove of a little ranch near the Dakota line, when there was a quick thud of hoofs outside, and presently the Easterner entered with the letters and the papers.

"Well," said the Easterner at once, "the chap that killed the Swede has got three years. Wasn't much, was it?"

"He has? Three years?" The cowboy poised his pan of pork, while he ruminated upon the news. "Three years. That ain't much."

"No. It was a light sentence," replied the Easterner as he unbuckled his spurs. "Seems there was a good deal of sympathy for him in Romper."

"If the bartender had been any good," observed the cowboy, thoughtfully, "he would have gone in and cracked that there Dutchman on the head with a bottle in the beginnin' of it and stopped all this here murderin'."

"Yes, a thousand things might have happened," said the Easterner, tartly.

The cowboy returned his pan of pork to the fire, but his philosophy continued. "It's funny, ain't it? If he hadn't said Johnnie was cheatin' he'd be alive this minute. He was an awful fool. Game played for fun, too. Not for money. I believe he was crazy."

"I feel sorry for that gambler," said the Easterner.

"Oh, so do I," said the cowboy. "He don't deserve none of it for killin' who he did."

"The Swede might not have been killed if everything had been square."

"Might not have been killed?" exclaimed the cowboy. "Everythin' square? Why, when he said that Johnnie was cheatin' and acted like such a jackass? And then in the saloon he fairly walked up to git hurt?" With these arguments the cowboy browbeat the Easterner and reduced him to rage.

"You're a fool!" cried the Easterner, viciously. "You're a bigger jackass than the Swede by a million majority. Now let me tell you one thing. Let me tell you something. Listen! Johnnie *was* cheating!"

" 'Johnnie,' " said the cowboy, blankly. There was a minute of silence, and then he said, robustly, "Why, no. The game was only for fun."

"Fun or not," said the Easterner, "Johnnie was cheating. I saw him. I know it. I saw him. And I refused to stand up and be a man. I let the Swede fight it out alone. And you—you were simply puffing around the place and wanting to fight. And then old Scully himself! We are all in it! This poor gambler isn't even a noun. He is kind of an adverb. Every sin is the result of a collaboration. We, five of us, have collaborated in the murder of this Swede. Usually there are from a dozen to forty women really involved in every murder, but in this case it seems to be only five men—you, I, Johnnie, old Scully; and that fool of an unfortunate gambler came merely as a culmination, the apex of a human movement, and gets all the punishment."

The cowboy, injured and rebellious, cried out blindly into this fog of mysterious theory: "Well, I didn't do anythin', did I?"

Questions for Study

1. *What aspects of Romper make it suitable for the scene of a murder?*
2. *What does the hotel symbolize? What is the significance of its color?*
3. *What do the five characters responsible for the Swede's death have in common?*
4. *Why does the Swede think he is going to be killed?*
5. *What does the heron mentioned in the first sentence symbolize?*
6. *During the fight, what is meant by the narrator's comment, "There was a splendor of isolation" in the Swede's situation?*
7. *Why is the gambler depicted as moral, generous, and a family man? Why is he called an "adverb?"*
8. *One critic believes the stove at the hotel represents "man's inner nature . . . burning with elemental aggressiveness." Explain this statement with reference to the narrator's comment in Section VI that the voice of the stove "swelled to equal the roar of the storm."*

Topics for Discussion and Writing

1. Discuss the Easterner's comment, "Every sin is the result of a collaboration."
2. Discuss the legend the Swede fixed on when he died: "This registers the amount of your purchase."
3. Discuss the story as a Western and indicate how it differs from and is similar to tales and movies about the West.
4. Discuss Crane's view of people as presented in the story with particular reference to the following statement: "One viewed the existence of man then as a marvel, and conceded a glamour of wonder to these lice which were caused to cling to a whirling, fire-smitten, ice-locked, disease-stricken, space-lost bulb."

STYLE: LANGUAGE IN ACTION

As you consider the elements of fiction—plot, character, point of view, setting, theme—you tend to forget the one thing that makes them all possible—language. Yet it is only through words that you receive a story and form an impression of it. If you stop and think about it, is not your first reaction to works of fiction your reaction to the way the authors express themselves? In other words, it is a reaction to their **style**, their choice and arrangement of words on the page. To a large extent you like or dislike certain stories not because of what their authors say, but how they say it.

Think of some of the stories you have read so far in this book. What makes "Spotted Horses" so vivid, so humorous, so moving? It is primarily the narrator's use of words, dialect, colorful metaphors and similes, precise descriptions of how the characters look and talk and act. Since "Owen Wingrave" depicts an intellectual struggling with his conscience, it uses more intricate sentences and more formal diction. In "Indian Camp" the language is simple and spare, the sentences short and uncomplicated, reflecting the characters and the primitive world they are involved in. Each story, then, has a language and an arrangement of words that suit it and that can be identified with a specific author. The styles of Faulkner, James, and Hemingway are easily recognizable because the authors use them to present their own interpretations of human experience. There is a connection between the manner in which they write and what they write about. Where James stresses the pyschological aspects of his characters, Hemingway stresses the physical world they live in, and each one's mode of expression confirms this point.

All this is, of course, general and impressionistic. Too often discussions of style become too vague to be of any real value. Faulkner's style in novels like *The Sound and the Fury* and *Absalom, Absalom!* is called rhetorical. James's style is characterized as intricate and tedious. Hemingway is said to write in a terse, hard, clean manner. Such descriptions are not very accurate or revealing. They are, for the most part, superficial. In order to find out how various writers actually express themselves you need to analyze in an objective way their diction, sentence structure, figures of speech, and dialogue. By doing this you discover what this world of words is truly like. You determine how closely related content and language are and how effective authors are in using language.

Before looking at the style of the stories in this section, it might be well to explain briefly an often confused aspect of style, **figures of speech.** Although there are hundreds, only three need be mentioned here—metaphor, simile, and allusion. A **metaphor** is an indirect comparison between two things without the use of "like" or "as"—"you are a summer day." A **simile** is a direct comparison using "like" or "as"—"you are like a summer day." An allusion is an indirect reference to an historical, biblical, literary, or mythical person, place, or thing—"my roommate is a real Hamlet." These figures not only enrich the style, but also express a point in a sharper and more suggestive way than would a mere statement of the same idea. Faulkner uses them in "Spotted Horses" for humor. A wild horse flies over the narrator's team "big as a billboard." He also uses them for pathos. Flem puts the sack of candy "into Mrs. Armstid's hand, like he would have put it into a hollow stump." Dramatic and vivid, they make memorable and significant a particular passage and enable writers to say in a few words what would otherwise take them much longer to express.

To analyze the style of a story you must first understand the author's use of style. Eudora Welty in "Death of a Travelling Salesman" (p. 224) describes a saleman's last day on the road from the standpoint of an omniscient narrator, and she gives his thoughts and feelings from his own standpoint. The standard diction, the straightforward sentences, the smooth narrative phrases, and the similes and metaphors reflect a neutral narrator depicting a character and commenting on him. In contrast, other passages contain colloquial diction, distorted sentence patterns, and fragments of interior monologue which reflect the man himself recording in his own idiom his final journey. The author integrates the two modes of expression so that you are at once outside observing R. J. Bowman suffer and inside suffering with him. By examining individual passages, you find out exactly how Welty does this. You come to appreciate her art, and you gain an insight into the meaning of the story.

John Updike in "Museums and Women" (p. 236) uses a first-person narrator. Consequently, an examination of the style will tell you a great deal about William Young, who is reminiscing about the women who have shaped his life and the museums with which he associates each one. Evidently he is a precise, formal, and analytical person preoccupied with architecture and art as well as language. You get this idea from the way he expresses himself. His diction is stiff ("the very gatekeeper of the temple"), technical ("Romanesque capitals"), and scholarly ("sixteenth-century Italian courtyard"). His sentences tend toward balance, as in the cataloguing of the contents of the museum in the second and third paragraphs. Parallelism is evident in such phrases as "to elicit with tinted reflective shadows . . . to accent with sumptuous textures. . . ." The **syntax**—the way the words are arranged to form phrases and sentences—points to an even more pedantic, word-conscious individual, as in "Homeless, we had found a home worthy of us," a repetition of words derived from the same root, a common practice throughout the story. Another prominent stylistic device is the repetition of key words such as "unsearchable," "dirty," "mystery," "timid," and "hushed," words which serve, like the museums, as "broken arcs of one curve" that connect the various people, places, and periods of William Young's life.

On the other hand, William Young is quite emotional and introspective. His words not only have a "curious formal weight," but they also "hum." They have resonance. They make music. They hint at a mystery. They pursue the ideas contained in the summary at the end of the first paragraph. William Young speaks of the "sullen, furious underworld" of the Indian statuettes, of having spent a childhood in "angry silence and timid foreboding." Even his sentences, like the last one in the story, trail off into vagueness and uncertainties while at the same time maintaining formal control. Just as the museum, like the M's in the word, forms the framework of his life, the outer structure, so women, like the M in the middle of that word, form the dark core, the inner meaning.

Most first-person narrators are not so obsessed with language as William Young. But all reveal their personalities through their forms of expression. They speak as they are. Think of Huckleberry Finn and Holden Caufield in *Catcher in the Rye*. Their language is a clue to who and what they are. And it is only by examining such language closely that you really get to know them well.

Conrad's narrator in "The Secret Sharer" (p. 245) is another person whose expression mirrors his character. His style, however, is not so constant as that of William Young. You cannot take one passage and say it is typical of the whole. In the beginning the long, ruminating sentences and the formal diction represent the mind of a brooding young man about to undertake his first command at sea. Words like "incomprehensible" and "imperceptible" create an air of mystery and foreboding. The last sentence in paragraph two conveys the heavy mood of the lonely captain setting out to test himself. The long grammatical units, the piling up of adjectives, and the picture of one waiting and wondering, poised in the stillness, are appropriate to the moment.

As the tension mounts this weightiness decreases. There are shorter sentences and paragraphs, more colloquial diction, increased dialogue, passages of uncluttered exposition and analysis. The paragraph beginning on p. 270, " 'Now,' I whispered, loudly, into the saloon . . . ," begins the shift. The brief sentences mirror the faster action yet retain some of the earlier resonance. The repetition of "dark," the account of the hands meeting in a "steady, motionless clasp," and the image of the "floppy hat," which foreshadows the saving white mark on the black water at the end, all lend gravity to the quicker pace of the prose.

Like Updike, Conrad repeats key thematic words and employs concrete language to make you see and feel what he is talking about. "Double," "strangeness," "shadowy," "secret sharer," occur over and over again. The islands on the east side of the gulf float "on silvery patches of calm water, arid and gray, or dark green and rounded like clumps of evergreen bushes." The ship sails not only into the "shadow of the land, but in the very blackness of it." You experience fully the scene. The final sentence becomes, in its structure, rhythm, diction, and imagery, a reflection of the entire story.

After moving through a series of phrases, clauses, and parenthetical expressions that seem to become entangled with one another, it suddenly leaps forward cleanly and clearly: "a free man, a proud swimmer striking out for a new destiny." Like the captain set free of the burden of the mystery, the sentence moves rapidly, resolutely forward out of the murkiness and involutions of a deeply brooding intelligence.

This approach to style, relating the expression to the content in a specific and meaningful manner, is the one you should take as you read stories. Not all of them, of course, have such distinctive styles as those by Welty, Updike, and Conrad. But you should nevertheless become sensitive to the language you are confronted with on page after page. Such awareness will enhance both your understanding and your appreciation. What is more, it will give you another way of looking at fiction and testing the effectiveness of a story.

EUDORA WELTY

Death of a Travelling Salesman

R. J. Bowman, who for fourteen years had travelled for a shoe company through Mississippi, drove his Ford along a rutted dirt path. It was a long day! The time did not seem to clear the noon hurdle and settle into soft afternoon. The sun, keeping its strength here even in winter, stayed at the top of the sky, and every time Bowman stuck his head out of the dusty car to stare up the road, it seemed to reach a long arm down and push against the top of his head, right through his hat—like the practical joke of an old drummer, long on the road. It made him feel all the more angry and helpless. He was feverish, and he was not quite sure of the way.

This was his first day back on the road after a long siege of influenza. He had had very high fever, and dreams, and had become weakened and pale, enough to tell the difference in the mirror, and he could not think clearly . . . All afternoon, in the midst of his anger, and for no reason, he had thought of his dead grandmother. She had been a comfortable soul. Once more Bowman wished he could fall into the big feather bed that had been in her room . . . Then he forgot her again.

This desolate hill country! And he seemed to be going the wrong way —it was as if he were going back, far back! There was not a house in sight. . . . There was no use wishing he were back in bed, though. By paying the hotel doctor his bill he had proved his recovery. He had not even been sorry when the pretty trained nurse said good-bye. He did not like illness, he distrusted it, as he distrusted the road without signposts. It angered him. He had given the nurse a really expensive bracelet, just because she was packing up her bag and leaving.

But now—what if in fourteen years on the road he had never been ill before and never had an accident? His record was broken, and he had even begun almost to question it . . . He had gradually put up at better hotels, in the bigger towns, but weren't they all, eternally, stuffy in summer and draughty in winter? Women? He could only remember little rooms within little rooms, like a nest of Chinese paper boxes, and if he thought of one woman he saw the worn loneliness that the furniture of that room seemed built of. And he himself—he was a man who always wore rather wide-brimmed black hats, and in the wavy hotel mirrors had looked something like a bull-fighter, as he paused for that inevitable instant on the landing, walking downstairs to supper . . . He leaned out of the car again, and once more the sun pushed at his head.

Bowman had wanted to reach Beulah by dark, to go to bed and sleep off his fatigue. As he remembered, Beulah was fifty miles away from the last town, on a gravelled road. This was only a cow trail. How had he ever come to such a place? One hand wiped the sweat from his face, and he drove on.

He had made the Beulah trip before. But he had never seen this hill or this petering-out path before—or that cloud, he thought shyly, looking up and then down quickly—any more than he had seen this day before. Why did he not admit he was simply lost and had been for miles? . . . He was not in the habit of asking the way of strangers, and these people never knew where the very roads they lived on went to; but then he had not even been close enough to anyone to call out. People standing in the fields now and then, or on top of the haystacks, had been too far away, looking like leaning sticks or weeds, turning a little at the solitary rattle of his car across their countryside, watching the pale sobered winter dust where it chunked out behind like big squashes down the road. The stares of these distant people had followed him solidly like a wall, impenetrable, behind which they turned back after he had passed.

The cloud floated there to one side like the bolster on his grandmother's bed. It went over a cabin on the edge of a hill, where two bare chinaberry trees clutched at the sky. He drove through a heap of dead oak leaves, his wheels stirring their weightless sides to make a silvery melancholy whistle as the car passed through their bed. No car had been along this way ahead of him. Then he saw that he was on the edge of a ravine that fell away, a red erosion, and that this was indeed the road's end.

He pulled the brake. But it did not hold, though he put all his strength into it. The car, tipped toward the edge, rolled a little. Without doubt, it was going over the bank.

He got out quietly, as though some mischief had been done him and he had his dignity to remember. He lifted his bag and sample case out, set them down, and stood back and watched the car roll over the edge. He heard something—not the crash he was listening for, but a slow un-uproarious crackle. Rather distastefully he went to look over, and he saw that his car had fallen into a tangle of immense grape vines as thick as his arm, which caught it and held it, rocked it like a grotesque child in a dark cradle, and then, as he watched, concerned somehow that he was not still inside it, released it gently to the ground.

He sighed.

Where am I? he wondered with a shock. Why didn't I do something? All his anger seemed to have drifted away from him. There was the house, back on the hill. He took a bag in each hand and with almost childlike willingness went toward it. But his breathing came with difficulty, and he had to stop to rest.

It was a shotgun house, two rooms and an open passage between, perched on the hill. The whole cabin slanted a little under the heavy heaped-up vine that covered the roof, light and green, as though forgotten from summer. A woman stood in the passage.

He stopped still. Then all of a sudden his heart began to behave strangely. Like a rocket set off, it began to leap and expand into uneven patterns of beats which showered into his brain, and he could not think. But in scattering and falling it made no noise. It shot up with great power, almost elation, and fell gently, like acrobats into nets. It began to pound profoundly, then waited irresponsibly, hitting in some sort of inward mockery first at his ribs, then against his eyes, then under his shoulder blades, and against the roof of his mouth when he tried to say, "Good afternoon, madam." But he could not hear his heart—it was as quiet as ashes falling. This was rather comforting; still, it was shocking to Bowman to feel his heart beating at all.

Stockstill in his confusion, he dropped his bags, which seemed to drift in slow bulks gracefully through the air and to cushion themselves on the grey prostrate grass near the doorstep.

As for the woman standing there, he saw at once that she was old. Since she could not possibly hear his heart, he ignored the pounding and now looked at her carefully, and yet in his distraction dreamily, with his mouth open.

She had been cleaning the lamp, and held it, half blackened, half clear, in front of her. He saw her with the dark passage behind her. She was a big woman with a weather-beaten but unwrinkled face; her lips were held tightly together, and her eyes looked with a curious dulled brightness into his. He looked at her shoes, which were like bundles. If it were summer she would be barefoot . . . Bowman, who automatically judged a woman's age on sight, set her age at fifty. She wore a formless garment of some grey coarse material, rough-dried from a washing, from which her arms appeared pink and unexpectedly round. When she never said a word, and sustained her quiet pose of holding the lamp, he was convinced of the strength in her body.

"Good afternoon, madam," he said.

She stared on, whether at him or at the air around him he could not tell, but after a moment she lowered her eyes to show that she would listen to whatever he had to say.

"I wonder if you would be interested—" He tried once more. "An accident—my car . . ."

Her voice emerged low and remote, like a sound across a lake. "Sonny he ain't here."

"Sonny?"

"Sonny ain't here now."

Her son—a fellow able to bring my car up, he decided in blurred relief. He pointed down the hill. "My car's in the bottom of the ditch. I'll need help."

"Sonny ain't here, but he'll be here."

She was becoming clearer to him and her voice stronger, and Bowman saw that she was stupid.

He was hardly surprised at the deepening postponement and tedium of his journey. He took a breath, and heard his voice speaking over the silent blows of his heart. "I was sick. I am not strong yet . . . May I come in?"

He stooped and laid his big black hat over the handle on his bag. It was a humble motion, almost a bow, that instantly struck him as absurd and betraying of all his weakness. He looked up at the woman, the wind blowing his hair. He might have continued for a long time in this unfamiliar attitude; he had never been a patient man, but when he was sick he had learned to sink submissively into the pillows, to wait for his medicine. He waited on the woman.

Then she, looking at him with blue eyes, turned and held open the door, and after a moment Bowman, as if convinced in his action, stood erect and followed her in.

Inside, the darkness of the house touched him like a professional hand, the doctor's. The woman set the half-cleaned lamp on a table in the centre of the room and pointed, also like a professional person, a guide, to a chair with a yellow cowhide seat. She herself crouched on the hearth, drawing her knees up under the shapeless dress.

At first he felt hopefully secure. His heart was quieter. The room was enclosed in the gloom of yellow pine boards. He could see the other room, with the foot of an iron bed showing, across the passage. The bed had been made up with a red-and-yellow pieced quilt that looked like a map or a picture, a little like his grandmother's girlhood painting of Rome burning.

He had ached for coolness, but in this room it was cold. He stared at the hearth with dead coals lying on it and iron pots in the corners. The hearth and smoked chimney were of the stone he had seen ribbing the hills, mostly slate. Why is there no fire? he wondered.

And it was so still. The silence of the fields seemed to enter and move familiarly through the house. The wind used the open hall. He felt that he was in a mysterious, quiet, cool danger. It was necessary to do what? . . . To talk.

"I have a nice line of women's low-priced shoes . . ." he said.

But the woman answered, "Sonny'll be here. He's strong. Sonny'll move your car."

"Where is he now?"

"Farms for Mr. Redmond."

Mr. Redmond. Mr. Redmond. That was someone he would never have to encounter, and he was glad. Somehow the name did not appeal to him

. . . In a flare of touchiness and anxiety, Bowman wished to avoid even mention of unknown men and their unknown farms.

"Do you two live here alone?" He was surprised to hear his old voice, chatty, confidential, inflected for selling shoes, asking a question like that—a thing he did not even want to know.

"Yes. We are alone."

He was surprised at the way she answered. She had taken a long time to say that. She had nodded her head in a deep way too. Had she wished to affect him with some sort of premonition? he wondered unhappily. Or was it only that she would not help him, after all, by talking with him? For he was not strong enough to receive the impact of unfamiliar things without a little talk to break their fall. He had lived a month in which nothing had happened except in his head and his body—an almost inaudible life of heartbeats and dreams that came back, a life of fever and privacy, a delicate life which had left him weak to the point of—what? Of begging. The pulse in his palm leapt like a trout in a brook.

He wondered over and over why the woman did not go ahead with cleaning the lamp. What prompted her to stay there across the room, silently bestowing her presence upon him? He saw that with her it was not a time for doing little tasks. Her face was grave; she was feeling how right she was. Perhaps it was only politeness. In docility he held his eyes stiffly wide; they fixed themselves on the woman's clasped hands as though she held the cord they were strung on.

Then, "Sonny's coming," she said.

He himself had not heard anything, but there came a man passing the window and then plunging in at the door, with two hounds beside him. Sonny was a big enough man, with his belt slung low about his hips. He looked at least thirty. He had a hot, red face that was yet full of silence. He wore muddy blue pants and an old military coat stained and patched. World War? Bowman wondered. Great God, it was a Confederate coat. On the back of his light hair he had a wide filthy black hat which seemed to insult Bowman's own. He pushed down the dogs from his chest. He was strong with dignity and heaviness in his way of moving . . . There was the resemblance to his mother.

They stood side by side . . . He must account again for his presence here.

"Sonny, this man, he had his car to run off over the prec'pice an' wants to know if you will git it out for him," the woman said after a few minutes.

Bowman could not even state his case.

Sonny's eyes lay upon him.

He knew he should offer explanations and show money—at least appear either penitent or authoritative. But all he could do was to shrug slightly.

Sonny brushed by him going to the window, followed by the eager dogs, and looked out. There was effort even in the way he was looking, as if he could throw his sight out like a rope. Without turning Bowman felt that his own eyes could have seen nothing: it was too far.

"Got me a mule out there an' got me a block an' tackle," said Sonny meaningfully. "I *could* catch me my mule an' git me my ropes, an' before long I'd git your car out the ravine."

He looked completely round the room, as if in meditation, his eyes roving in their own distance. Then he pressed his lips firmly and yet shyly together, and with the dogs ahead of him this time, he lowered his head and strode out. The hard earth sounded, cupping to his powerful way of walking—almost a stagger.

Mischievously, at the suggestion of those sounds, Bowman's heart leapt again. It seemed to walk about inside him.

"Sonny's goin' to do it," the woman said. She said it again, singing it almost, like a song. She was sitting in her place by the hearth.

Without looking out, he heard some shouts and the dogs barking and the pounding of hoofs in short runs on the hill. In a few minutes Sonny passed under the window with a rope, and there was a brown mule with quivering, shining, purple-looking ears. The mule actually looked in the window. Under his eyelashes it turned target-like eyes into his. Bowman averted his head and saw the woman looking serenely back at the mule, with only satisfaction in her face.

She sang a little more, under her breath. It occurred to him, and it seemed quite marvellous, that she was not really talking to him, but rather following the thing that came about with words that were unconscious and part of her looking.

So he said nothing, and this time when he did not reply he felt a curious and strong emotion, not fear, rise up in him.

This time, when his heart leapt, something—his soul—seemed to leap too, like a little colt invited out of a pen. He stared at the woman while the frantic nimbleness of his feeling made his head sway. He could not move; there was nothing he could do, unless perhaps he might embrace this woman who sat there growing old and shapeless before him.

But he wanted to leap up, to say to her, I have been sick and I found out then, only then, how lonely I am. Is it too late? My heart puts up a struggle inside me, and you may have heard it, protesting against emptiness . . . It should be full, he would rush on to tell her, thinking of his heart now as a deep lake, it should be holding love like other hearts. It should be flooded with love. There would be a warm spring day . . . Come and stand in my heart, whoever you are, and a whole river would cover your feet and rise higher and take your knees in whirlpools, and draw you down to itself, your whole body, your heart too.

But he moved a trembling hand across his eyes, and looked at the placid crouching woman across the room. She was still as a statue. He felt ashamed and exhausted by the thought that he might, in one more moment, have tried by simple words and embraces to communicate some strange thing—something which seemed always to have just escaped him . . .

Sunlight touched the farthest pot on the hearth. It was late afternoon. This time to-morrow he would be somewhere on a good gravelled road, driving his car past things that happened to people, quicker than their happening. Seeing ahead to the next day, he was glad, and knew that this was no time to embrace an old woman. He could feel in his pounding temples the readying of his blood for motion and for hurrying away.

"Sonny's hitched up your car by now," said the woman. "He'll git it out the ravine right shortly."

"Fine!" he cried with his customary enthusiasm.

Yet it seemed a long time that they waited. It began to get dark. Bowman was cramped in his chair. Any man should know enough to get up and walk around while he waited. There was something like guilt in such stillness and silence.

But instead of getting up, he listened . . . His breathing restrained, his eyes powerless in the growing dark, he listened uneasily for a warning sound, forgetting in wariness what it would be. Before long he heard something—soft, continuous, insinuating.

"What's the noise?" he asked, his voice jumping into the dark. Then wildly he was afraid it would be his heart beating so plainly in the quiet room, and she would tell him so.

"You might hear the stream," she said grudgingly.

Her voice was closer. She was standing by the table. He wondered why she did not light the lamp. She stood there in the dark and did not light it.

Bowman would never speak to her now, for the time was past. I'll sleep in the dark, he thought, in his bewilderment pitying himself.

Heavily she moved on to the window. Her arm, vaguely white, rose straight from her full side and she pointed out into the darkness.

"That white speck's Sonny," she said, talking to herself.

He turned unwillingly and peered over her shoulder; he hesitated to rise and stand beside her. His eyes searched the dusky air. The white speck floated smoothly toward her finger, like a leaf on a river, growing whiter in the dark. It was as if she had shown him something secret, part of her life, but had offered no explanation. He looked away. He was moved almost to tears, feeling for no reason that she had made a silent declaration equivalent to his own. His hand waited upon his chest.

Then a step shook the house, and Sonny was in the room. Bowman felt how the woman left him there and went to the other man's side.

"I done got your car out, mister," said Sonny's voice in the dark. "She's settin' a-waitin' in the road, turned to go back where she come from."

"Fine!" said Bowman, projecting his own voice to loudness. "I'm surely much obliged—I could never have done it myself—I was sick . . ."

"I could do it easy," said Sonny.

Bowman could feel them both waiting in the dark, and he could hear the dogs panting out in the yard, waiting to bark when he should go. He felt strangely helpless and resentful. Now that he could go, he longed to stay. From what was he being deprived? His chest was rudely shaken by the violence of his heart. These people cherished something here that he could not see, they withheld some ancient promise of food and warmth and light. Between them they had a conspiracy. He thought of the way she had moved away from him and gone to Sonny, she had flowed toward him. He was shaking with cold, he was tired, and it was not fair. Humbly and yet angrily he stuck his hand into his pocket.

"Of course I'm going to pay you for everything—"

"We don't take money for such," said Sonny's voice belligerently.

"I want to pay. But do something more . . . Let me stay—to-night . . ." He took another step toward them. If only they could see him, they would know his sincerity, his real need! His voice went on, "I'm not very strong yet, I'm not able to walk far, even back to my car, maybe, I don't know—I don't know exactly where I am—"

He stopped. He felt as if he might burst into tears. What would they think of him!

Sonny came over and put his hands on him. Bowman felt them pass (they were professional too) across his chest, over his hips. He could feel Sonny's eyes upon him in the dark.

"You ain't no revenuer come sneakin' here, mister, ain't got no gun?"

To this end of nowhere! And yet *he* had come. He made a grave answer. "No."

"You can stay."

"Sonny," said the woman, "you'll have to borry some fire."

"I'll go git it from Redmond's," said Sonny.

"What?" Bowman strained to hear their words to each other.

"Our fire, it's out, and Sonny's got to borry some, because it's dark an' cold," she said.

"But matches—I have matches—"

"We don't have no need for 'em," she said proudly. "Sonny's goin' after his own fire."

"I'm goin' to Redmond's," said Sonny with an air of importance, and he went out.

After they had waited a while, Bowman looked out the window and saw a light moving over the hill. It spread itself out like a little fan. It zig-zagged along the field, darting and swift, not like Sonny at all . . . Soon enough, Sonny staggered in, holding a burning stick behind him in tongs, fire flowing in his wake, blazing light into the corners of the room.

"We'll make a fire now," the woman said, taking the brand.

When that was done she lit the lamp. It showed its dark and light. The whole room turned golden-yellow like some sort of flower, and the walls smelled of it and seemed to tremble with the quiet rushing of the fire and the waving of the burning lampwick in its funnel of light.

The woman moved among the iron pots. With the tongs she dropped hot coals on top of the iron lids. They made a set of soft vibrations, like the sound of a bell far away.

She looked up and over at Bowman, but he could not answer. He was trembling . . .

"Have a drink, mister?" Sonny asked. He had brought in a chair from the other room and sat astride it with his folded arms across the back. Now we are all visible, to one another, Bowman thought, and cried, "Yes sir, you bet, thanks!"

"Come after me and do just what I do," said Sonny.

It was another excursion into the dark. They went through the hall, out to the back of the house, past a shed and a hooded well. They came to a wilderness of thicket.

"Down on your knees," said Sonny.

"What?" Sweat broke out on his forehead.

He understood when Sonny began to crawl through a sort of tunnel that the bushes made over the ground. He followed, startled in spite of himself when a twig or a thorn touched him gently without making a sound, clinging to him and finally letting him go.

Sonny stopped crawling and, crouched on his knees, began to dig with both his hands into the dirt. Bowman shyly struck matches and made a light. In a few minutes Sonny pulled up a jug. He poured out some of the whisky into a bottle from his coat pocket, and buried the jug again. "You never know who's liable to knock at your door," he said, and laughed. "Start back," he said, almost formally. "Ain't no need for us to drink outdoors, like hogs."

At the table by the fire, sitting opposite each other in their chairs, Sonny and Bowman took drinks out of the bottle, passing it across. The dogs slept; one of them was having a dream.

"This is good," said Bowman. "That is what I needed." It was just as though he were drinking the fire off the hearth.

"He makes it," said the woman with quiet pride.

She was pushing the coals off the pots, and the smells of corn bread and coffee circled the room. She set everything on the table before the men, with a bone-handled knife stuck into one of the potatoes, splitting out its golden fiber. Then she stood for a minute looking at them, tall and full above them where they sat. She leaned a little toward them.

"You-all can eat now," she said, and suddenly smiled.

Bowman had just happened to be looking at her. He set his cup back on the table in unbelieving protest. A pain pressed at his eyes. He saw that she was not an old woman. She was young, still young. He could think of no number of years for her. She was the same age as Sonny, and she belonged to him. She stood with the deep dark corner of the room behind her, the shifting yellow light scattering over her head and her grey formless dress, trembling over her tall body when it bent over them in its sudden communication. She was young. Her teeth were shining and her eyes glowed. She turned and walked slowly and heavily out of the room, and he heard her sit down on the cot and then lie down. The pattern on the quilt moved.

"She goin' to have a baby," said Sonny, popping a bite into his mouth.

Bowman could not speak. He was shocked with knowing what was really in this house. A marriage, a fruitful marriage. That simple thing. Anyone could have had that.

Somehow he felt unable to be indignant or protest, although some sort of joke had certainly been played upon him. There was nothing remote or mysterious here—only something private. The only secret was the ancient communication between two people. But the memory of the woman's waiting silently by the cold hearth, of the man's stubborn journey a mile away to get fire, and how they finally brought out their food and drink and filled the room proudly with all they had to show, was suddenly too clear and too enormous within him for response . . .

"You ain't as hungry as you look," said Sonny.

The woman came out of the bedroom as soon as the men had finished, and ate her supper while her husband stared peacefully into the fire.

Then they put the dogs out, with the food that was left.

"I think I'd better sleep here by the fire, on the floor," said Bowman.

He felt that he had been cheated, and that he could afford now to be generous. Ill though he was, he was not going to ask them for their bed. He was through with asking favors in this house, now that he understood what was there.

"Sure, mister."

But he had not known yet how slowly he understood. They had not meant to give him their bed. After a little interval they both rose and looking at him gravely went into the other room.

He lay stretched by the fire until it grew low and dying. He watched every tongue of blaze lick out and vanish. "There will be special reduced prices on all footwear during the month of January," he found himself repeating quietly, and then he lay with his lips tight shut.

How many noises the night had! He heard the stream running, the fire dying, and he was sure now that he heard his heart beating, too, the sound it made under his ribs. He heard breathing, round and deep, of the man and his wife in the room across the passage. And that was all. But emotion swelled patiently within him, and he wished that the child were his.

He must get back to where he had been before. He stood weakly before the red coals, and put on his overcoat. It felt too heavy on his shoulders. As he started out he looked and saw that the woman had never got through with cleaning the lamp. On some impulse he put all the money from his billfold under its fluted glass base, almost ostentatiously.

Ashamed, shrugging a little, and then shivering, he took his bags and went out. The cold of the air seemed to lift him bodily. The moon was in the sky.

On the slope he began to run, he could not help it. Just as he reached the road, where his car seemed to sit in the moonlight like a boat, his heart began to give off tremendous explosions like a rifle, bang bang bang.

He sank in fright on to the road, his bags falling about him. He felt as if all this had happened before. He covered his heart with both hands to keep anyone from hearing the noise it made.

But nobody heard it.

Writing About Style

You can write on the style of a whole story or pick out a significant passage and analyze it. For a short theme the second approach is the more practical one. It enables you to go into detail and to be objective. Furthermore, if the passage you select is truly representative, you can use your analysis to reach conclusions about the style of the whole. The danger is that you may make unwarranted assumptions about the whole based on a single passage. To avoid this pitfall read the story over several times before you begin your analysis to make certain you choose a typical passage and understand how it fits into the story.

The best way to decide on a passage is to read through the story searching for general characteristics of the style. In most instances they will fall under the headings of diction, sentence structure, and figures of speech. Next, you should reach a conclusion about how these features reflect the material. Ask yourself how they express the theme, develop the characters, suit the setting, accurately portray what happens. Why do you think the writer uses them? Finally, you should locate the section of the story where you find more of these features concentrated than anywhere else.

Once you have finished this survey, your next job is to relate the passage and its style to the whole story. For instance, how does it depict the loneliness of the protagonist, reflect the world of a child, create an aura of mystery, to name just a few common tasks style is often called upon to perform. Remember, no analysis exists for its own sake. You must show how and what the style contributes to the effectiveness of the story. Style may be the most important element of fiction since, as we have noted, all the others depend on the words authors choose and the way authors put them together to achieve their purpose.

In writing on the style of "Death of a Travelling Salesman," your first task is to select a passage to study. If you look at the story carefully, you will discover that paragraph four is more characteristic of the whole, stylistically speaking, than any other. It contains both the voice of the narrator and the voice of R. J. Bowman, the protagonist. This is exactly what you want since your principal aim is to show how Welty's style presents Bowman's character, how it shapes her concept of him. The topic sentence might read something like this: The style of "Death of a Travelling Salesman" is crucial to the development of the character of R. J. Bowman in that it reveals his loneliness, confusion, and uncertainty during his first and last day on the road after a long illness.

To develop this very comprehensive statement you have to examine all the paragraph's main stylistic features with respect to diction, sentence structure, and figurative language. In fact, such units organize the way you can approach your topic. Before beginning, you might make a list of the salient features under each of these units, keeping in mind the larger context of which the passage is a part. One danger to avoid here is cataloguing, excessive quoting, compiling lists. Details must be selective and make a significant point. They are worth bothering with only if you relate them to their function in the whole story.

Your last task is to arrive at some conclusion about the effectiveness of the style. This does not mean you will judge it on the basis of how vivid or powerful or clear it is, but rather on how well it suits the character of Bowman, how poignantly it renders his actions and thoughts on the final day of his life. With respect to this idea you should note that the point of view is basically limited omniscience, the narrator entering the mind of the character frequently to tell the story at times almost from the first-person and yet maintaining the distant omniscient pose.

Bowman's Voice

The style of "Death of a Travelling Salesman" is carefully fitted to the character of the protagonist, R. J. Bowman. Using the limited omniscient point of view, Welty adjusts the diction, sentence structure, and figures of speech to develop the portrait of a lonely and troubled shoe salesman on the last day of his life. The result is a story told with all the involvement of the first-person, yet with the sympathetic detachment of the third-person narrator. Nowhere is all of this better demonstrated than in paragraph four.

The language of the passage is a mixture of the narrator's diction with that of Bowman's to give the effect of Bowman's talking at the same time the narrator is revealing him as a character who is more than just an ordinary salesman. The first sentence contains standard expository diction and is written from the point of view of the narrator: "But now . . . what if in fourteen years on the road he had never been ill before and never had an accident?" Yet it also conveys well the flavor of Bowman's thinking, especially the abrupt break to indicate his unsteady mental condition. Later in the paragraph there are lapses into Bowman's own words and phrases: "better hotel," "in the bigger towns," "stuffy in summer and draughty in winter," "women," "the sun pushed at his head." These words and phrases evoke his past on the road as well as render faithfully his feelings and attitudes in a way that remains close to his idiom, his thought process, and his approach to experience.

The sentences even better reflect Bowman's state of mind. The deeper the narrator penetrates into Bowman's disturbed psyche, the more complex and disjointed the sentences become. When the narrator returns to the main action of the story at the end of the paragraph, they grow simpler and clearer. The majority are compound and compound-complex and feature a series of clauses loosely strung together. The first one starts out with an obvious contrast of the past with the present and then breaks to return to the past and a nostalgic recital of the salesman's life. All those that follow except the last are dislocated in some way to reflect Bowman's fuzzy thinking brought on by his illness. They are either abrupt and fragmentary or long and twisting with no close connections between the parts. Several are questions which reflect Bowman's dissatisfaction with what has happened to him and his indecisiveness about what to do now.

The rhythm of these sentences supports his jerky thoughts and mental meanderings. The first sentence indicates a lack of logical continuity and the second fades out. The fourth is one word, followed by a sentence of thirty-seven words—far in excess of the average sentence length. The next is even longer, forty-two words, and trails off like the second, again mirroring Bowman's weariness and instability. The last returns to a smooth narrative rhythm. The various changes in Bowman's train of thought are also revealed in the phrases and clauses. Sentence five has three units. The first two suggest women ("little rooms within little rooms") and furniture ("a nest of Chinese paper boxes") and are of unequal length. The final and longest concentrates on one woman and one room and acts as a fitting climax, with its stress on the loneliness of Bowman's life. The next sentence contains five uneven syntactical units, loosely linked as if part of a stream of consciousness, and concluding briefly and suddenly as if to signal the fading out of his thinking at this point. The pause near the end should be noted. It suggests Bowman's hesitation, both past and present, as he prepares to meet his fate. The last sentence brings him back to the present.

Figures of speech play a prominent part in the passage, as they do in the whole story. There are two similes which reflect the subtle and imaginative approach of the narrator to the protagonist's plight. Each one reveals something of Bowman's past and his mental condition. His mind and the hotels he stays in are compared to Chinese paper boxes. In contrast to a bullfighter, he is a weak individual, indecisive, unprofessional, lacking in confidence. At the same time he is entering into the ring a doomed man, reluctant to take that fatal step. The implications of these comparisons are clear. They reveal the type of bewildered man Bowman is and are full of foreboding.

In the end what makes the style so effective is not merely its accuracy in portraying Bowman's mind, but its suggestiveness. Bowman is more than a salesman; he is a tragic hero whose death comes with a "tremendous explosion" to evoke pity and fear. The great success of the style is that it can both remain true to local experience and at the same time suggest a universal situation. It can create a lonely salesman travelling the back roads of Mississippi and yet elevate him to the status of a genuine tragic figure who represents every man.

JOHN UPDIKE

Museums and Women

Set together, the two words are seen to be mutually transparent; the E's, the M's blend—the M's framing and squaring the structure lend resonance and a curious formal weight to the M central in the creature, which it dominates like a dark core winged with flitting syllables. Both words hum. Both suggest radiance, antiquity, mystery, and duty.

My first museum I would visit with my mother. It was a provincial museum, a stately pride to the third-class inland city it ornamented. It was approached through paradisaical grounds of raked gravel walks, humus-fed plantings of exotic flora, and trees wearing tags, as if freshly christened by Adam. The museum's contents were disturbingly various, its cases stocked with whatever scraps of foreign civilization had fallen to it from the imperious fortunes of the steel and textile barons of the province. A shredding kayak shared a room with a rack of Polynesian paddles. A mummy, its skull half masked in gold, lay in an antechamber like one more of the open-casket funerals common in my childhood. Miniature Mexican villages lit up when a switch was flicked, and a pyramid was being built by dogged brown dolls who never pulled their papier-mâché stone a fraction of an inch. An infinitely patient Chinaman, as remote from me as the resident of a star, had carved a yellow rhinoceros horn into an upright crescental city, pagoda-tipped, of balconies, vines, and thimble-sized people wearing microscopic expressions of pain.

This was downstairs. Upstairs, up a double flight of marble climaxed by a green fountain splashing greenly, the works of art were displayed. Upstairs, every fall, the county amateur artists exhibited four hundred watercolors of peonies and stone barns. The rest of the year, sombrely professional oils of rotting, tangled woodland had the walls to themselves, sharing the great cool rooms with cases of Philadelphia silver, chests decorated with hearts, tulips, and bleeding pelicans by Mennonite folk artists, thick aqua glassware left bubbled by the blowing process, quaint quilts, and strange small statues. Strange perhaps only in the impression they made on me. They were bronze statuettes, randomly burnished here and there as if by a caressing hand, of nudes or groups of nudes. The excuse for nudity varied; some of the figures were American Indians, some were mythical Greeks. One lady, wearing a refined, aloof expression, was having her clothes torn from her by a squat man with horns and hairy hooved legs hinged the wrong way. Another statue bodied forth two naked boys wrestling. Another was of an Indian, dressed in only a knife belt, sitting astride a horse bareback, his chin bowed to his chest in sorrow, his exquisitely toed feet hanging down both hard and limp, begging to be touched. I think it was the smallness of these figures that carried them so penetratingly into my mind. Each, if it could have been released into life, would have stood about twenty inches high and weighed in my arms perhaps as much as a cat. I itched to finger them, to interact with them, to insert myself into their mysterious silent world of strenuous contention—their bulged tendons burnished, their hushed violence detailed down to the fingernails. They were in their smallness like secret thoughts of mine projected into dimension and permanence, and they returned to me as a response that carried strangely into parts of my body. I felt myself a furtive animal stirring in the shadow of my mother.

My mother: like the museum, she filled her category. I knew no other, and accepted her as the index, inclusive and definitive, of women. Now I see that she too was provincial, containing much that was beautiful, but somewhat jumbled, and distorted by great gaps. She was an unsearchable mixture of knowledge and ignorance, openness and reserve; though she took me many Sundays to the museum, I do not remember our discussing anything in it except once when, noticing how the small statues fascinated me, she said, "Billy, they seem such unhappy little people." In her glancing way she had hit something true. The defeated Indian was not alone in melancholy; all the statuettes, as they engaged in the struggles or frolics that gave each group the metallic unity of a single casting, seemed caught in a tarnished fate from which I yearned to rescue them. I wanted to touch them to comfort them, yet I held my hand back, afraid of breaking the seal on their sullen, furious underworld.

My mood of dread in those high cool galleries condensed upon the small statues but did not emanate from them; it seemed to originate above and behind me, as if from another living person in the room. Often my mother, wordlessly browsing by the wall on the paintings of woods and shaggy meadows, was the only other person in the room. Who she was was a mystery so deep it never formed into a question. She had descended to me from thin clouds of preëxistent time, enveloped me, and set me moving toward an unseen goal with a vague expectation that in the beginning was more hers than mine. She was not content. I felt that the motion which brought us again and again to the museum was an agitated one, that she was pointing me through these corridors toward a radiant place she had despaired of reaching. The fountain at the head of the stairs splashed unseen; my mother's footsteps rustled and she drew me into another room, where a case of silver stood aflame with reflections like the mouth of a dragon of beauty. She let me go forward to meet it alone. I was her son and the center of her expectations. I dutifully absorbed the light-struck terror of the hushed high chambers, and went through each doorway with a kind of timid rapacity.

This museum, my first, I associate with another, less ghostly hunt; for this was one of the places—others being the telephone company, the pretzel factory, and the county fair—where schoolchildren were taken on educational expeditions. I would usually be toward the end of the line, among the unpaired stragglers, and up front, in the loud nucleus of leaders, the freckled girl I had decided I loved. The decision, perhaps, was as much my mother's as mine. The girl lived in our neighborhood, one of a pack of sisters, and from the time she could walk past our front hedge my mother had taken one of her quixotic fancies to her. She spoke admiringly of her "spirit"; this admiration surprised me, for the girl was what was known locally as "bold," and as she grew older fell in with a crowd of children whose doings would certainly have struck my mother as "unhappy." My mother always invited her to my birthday parties, where she, misplaced but rapidly forgiving the situation, animated for a few dazzling hours my circle of shadowy-faced, sheltered friends.

When I try to picture my school days, I seem to be embedded among boiling clouds straining to catch a glimpse of her, or trapped in a movie theatre behind a row of huge heads while fragmented arcs of the screen confusingly flicker. The alphabet separated us; she sat near the front of the classroom and I, William Young, toward the rear. Where the alphabet no longer obtained, other systems of distinction intervened. In the museum, a ruthless law propelled her forward to gather with the other bold spirits, tittering, around the defenseless little statues while I hung back, on the edge of the fountain, envious, angry, and brimming with things to say. I never said them. It seemed a simple matter of position; I was never in a position to declare, let alone act upon, my love. No distinction cuts as deep as the one between the worshipped and the worshipping. I am condemned by nature to be dutiful and reverent.

The girl who was to become my wife was standing at the top of some stone museum steps that I was climbing. Though it was bitterly cold, with crusts of snow packed into the stone, she wore threadbare sneakers from which her little toes stuck out, and she was smoking. Awesome sheets of smoke and frozen vapor flew from her mouth and she seemed, posed against a fluted pilaster, a white-faced priestess immolating herself in the worship of tobacco. "Aren't your feet cold?" I asked her.

"A little. I don't mind it."

"A stoic."

"Maybe I'm a masochist."

"Who isn't?"

She said nothing. Had I said something curious?

I lit a cigarette, though inhaling the raw air rasped my throat, and asked her, "Aren't you in Medieval Art? You sit near the front."

"Yes. Do you sit in the back?"

"I feel I should. I'm a history major."

"This is your first fine-arts course?"

"Yeah. It met at a good hour—late enough for a late breakfast and early enough for an early lunch. I'm trying to have a sophomore slump."

"Are you succeeding?"

"Not really. When the chips are down, I tend to grind."

"How do you like Medieval Art?"

"I love it. It's like going to a movie in the morning, which is my idea of sin."

"You have funny ideas."

"No. They're very conventional. It would never occur to me, for example, to stand outside in the snow in bare feet."

"They're not really bare."

Nevertheless, I yearned to touch them, to comfort them. There was in this girl, this pale creature of the college museum, a withdrawing that drew me forward. I felt in her an innocent sad blankness where I must stamp my name. I pursued her through the museum. It was, as museums go, rather intimate. Architecturally, it was radiantly hollow, being built around a skylight-roofed replica of a sixteenth-century Italian courtyard. At the four corners of the flagstone courtyard floor, four great gray terra-cotta statues of the seasons stood. Bigger than life, they were French, and reduced the four epic passages of the year to four charming aristocrats, two male and two female, who had chosen to attend a costume ball piquantly attired in grapes and ribbons. I remember that Spring wore a floppy hat and carried a basket of rigid flowers. The stairways and galleries that enabled the museum to communicate with itself around the courtyard were distinctly medieval in feeling, and the vagaries of benefaction had left the museum's medieval and Oriental collections disproportionately strong, though a worthy attempt had been made to piece together the history of art since the Renaissance with a painting or at least a drawing by each master. But the rooms that contained these later works—including some Cézannes and Renoirs that, because they were rarely reproduced in art books, had the secret sweetness of flowers in a forest—were off the route of the course we were both taking, so my courtship primarily led down stone corridors, past Romanesque capitals, through low gray archways giving on gilded altar panels.

I remember stalking her around a capital from Avignon; it illustrated Samson and his deeds. On one side he was bearing off the gates of Gaza, while around the corner his massive head was lying aswoon in Delilah's lap as she clumsily sawed his hair. The class had been assigned a paper on this capital, and as I rehearsed my interpretation, elaborately linear and accompanied by many agitated indications of my hands, the girl said thoughtfully, "You see awfully much in it, don't you?"

My hands froze and crept back, embarrassed; the terminology of fine-arts analysis was new to me, and in fact I did doubt that an illiterate carver of semi-barbaric Europe could have been as aesthetically ingenious as I was. "What do *you* see in it?" I asked in self-defense.

"Not very much," she said. "I wonder why they assigned it. It's not that lovely. I think the Cluny ones are much nicer."

It thrilled me to hear her speak with such careless authority. She was a fine-arts major, and there was a sense in which she contained the museum, had mastered all the priceless and timeless things that would become, in my possessing her, mine as well. She had first appeared to me as someone guarding the gates.

Once I accompanied her into Boston, to the museum there, to study, in connection with another course she was taking, an ancient Attic sphinx. This she liked, though it was just a headless winged body of white marble, very simple, sitting stiffly on its haunches, its broad breast glowing under the nicks of stylized feathers. She showed me the S-curve of its body, repeated in the tail and again, presumably, in the vanished head.

"It's a very proud little statue, isn't it?" I ventured, seeking to join her in her little careless heaven of appreciation. Again, I seemed to have said something curious.

"I love it" was all she replied, with a dent of stubborness in her mouth and an inviting blankness in her eyes.

Outside, the weather was winter, the trees medieval presences arching gray through gray. We walked and walked, and for a time the only shelter we shared was the museum. My courtship progressed; we talked solemnly; the childhood I had spent in such angry silence and timid foreboding had left me with much to say. She could listen; she was like a room of vases: you enter and find your sense of yourself abruptly sharpened by a vague, tranquil expectancy in the air. I see her sitting on the broad cold balustrade that at second-story height ran around the courtyard. Beyond her head, the flagstones shone as if wet and Printemps in her wide hat was baroquely foreshortened. An apprehension of height seized me; this girl seemed poised on the edge of a fall. I heard the volume of emptiness calling to her, calling her away from me, so full of talk. There was in her something mute and remote which spoke only once, once when, after our lying side by side an entire evening, she told me calmly, "You know I don't love you yet."

I took this as a challenge, though it may have been meant as a release. I carried the chase through exams (we both got A-minuses) and into another course, a spring-term course called, simply, Prints. My mother, surprisingly, wrote warning me that I mustn't spread myself too thin—she thought now that that had been *her* mistake at college. I was offended, for I thought that without my telling her anything she would know I was in the process of capturing the very gatekeeper of the temple of learning that must be the radiant place she had pointed me toward so long ago. The absence of her blessing seemed a tacit curse.

Here I must quickly insert, like a thin keystone, an imaginary woman I found in a faraway museum. It was another university museum, ancient and sprawling and resolutely masculine, full of battered weapons of war and unearthed agricultural tools and dull maps of diggings. All its contents seemed to need a dusting and a tasteful rearrangement by a female hand. But upstairs, in an out-of-the-way chamber, under a case of brilliantly polished glass, I one day discovered a smooth statuette of a nude asleep on a mattress. She was a dainty white dream, an eighteenth-century fancy; only that century would have thought to render a mattress in marble. Not that every stitch and seam was given the dignity of stone; but the corners were rounded, the buttoned squares of plumpness shown, and the creases of "give" lovingly sculpted. In short, it was clear that the woman was comfortable, and not posed on an arbitrary slab, or slaughtered on an altar. She was asleep, not dead; the delicate aroma of her slumber seemed to rise through the glass. She was the size of the small straining figures that had fascinated my childhood, and, as with them, smallness intensified sensual content. As I stood gazing into the eternal privacy of her sleep—her one hand resting palm up beside her averted head, one knee lifted in a light suggestion of restlessness —I was disturbed by dread and a premonition of loss. Why? Was not my wife also fair, and finely formed, and mute? Perhaps it was the mattress that brought this ideal other woman so close; it was a raft on which she had floated out of the inaccessible past and which brought her, small and intangible as a thought, ashore on the island of my bounded present. We seemed about to release each other from twin enchantments. Was not my huge face the oppressive dream that was making her stir? And was not I, out of all the thousands who had visited this museum, the first to find her here asleep? What we seek in museums is the opposite of what we seek in churches—the consoling sense of previous visitation. In museums, rather, we seek the untouched, the never-before-discovered; and it is their final unsearchability that leads us to hope, and return.

Two more, two more of each, each nameless. None have names. Museums are in the end nameless and continuous; we turn a corner in the Louvre and meet the head of a sphinx whose body is displayed in Boston. So, too, the women were broken arcs of one curve.

She was the friend of a friend, and she and I, having had lunch with the mutual friend, bade him goodbye and, both being loose in New York for the afternoon, went to a museum together. It was a new one, recently completed after the plan of a recently dead American wizard. It was shaped like a truncated top and its floor was a continuous spiral around an overweening core of empty vertical space. From the leaning, shining walls immense rectangles of torn and spattered canvas projected on thin arms of bent pipe. Menacing magnifications of textural accidents, they needed to be viewed at a distance greater than the architecture afforded. The floor width was limited by a rather slender and low concrete guard wall that more invited than discouraged a plunge into the cathedralic depths below. Too reverent to scoff and too dizzy to judge, my unexpected companion and I dutifully unwound our way down the exitless ramp, locked in a wizard's spell. Suddenly, as she lurched backward from one especially explosive painting, her high heels were tricked by the slope, and she fell against me and squeezed my arm. Ferocious gumbos splashed on one side of us; the siren chasm called on the other. She righted herself but did not let go of my arm. Pointing my eyes ahead, inhaling the presence of perfume, feeling like a cliff-climber whose companion has panicked on the sheerest part of the face, I accommodated my arm to her grip and, thus secured, we carefully descended the remainder of the museum. Not until our feet attained the safety of street level were we released. Our bodies then separated and did not touch again. Yet the spell was imperfectly broken, like the door of a chamber which, once unsealed, can never be closed quite tight.

Not far down the same avenue there is a museum which was once a mansion and still retains a homelike quality, if one can imagine people rich enough in self-esteem to inhabit walls so overripe with masterpieces, to dine from tureens by Cellini, and afterward to seat their bodies complacently on furniture invested with the blood of empires. There once were people so self-confident, and on the day of my visit I was one of them, for the woman I was with and I were perfectly in love. We had come from love-making, and were to return to it, and the museum, visited between the evaporation and the recondensation of desire, was like a bridge whose either end is dissolved in mist—its suspension miraculous, its purpose remembered only by the murmuring stream running in the invisible ravine below. Homeless, we had found a home worthy of us. We seemed hosts; surely we had walked these Persian rugs before, appraised this amphora with an eye to its purchase, debated the position of this marble-topped table whose veins foamed like gently surfing aquamarine. The woman's sensibility was more an interior decorator's than an art student's, and through her I felt furnishings unfold into a world of gilded scrolls, rubbed stuffs, cherished surfaces, painstakingly inlaid veneers, varnished cadenzas of line and curve lovingly carved by men whose hands were haunted by the memory of women. Rustling beside me, her body, which I had seen asleep on a mattress, seemed to wear clothes as a needless luxuriance, an ultra-extravagance heaped upon what was already, like the museum, both priceless and free. Room after room we entered and owned. A lingering look, a shared smile was enough to secure our claim. Once she said, of a chest whose panels were painted with pubescent cherubs after Boucher, that she didn't find it terribly "attractive." The one word, pronounced with a worried twist of her eyebrows, delighted me like the first polysyllable pronounced by an infant daughter. In this museum I was more the guide; it was I who could name the modes and deliver the appreciations. Her muteness was not a reserve but an expectancy; she and the museum were perfectly open and mutually transparent. As we passed a dark-red tapestry, her bare-shouldered summer dress, of a similar red, blended with it, isolating her head and shoulders like a bust. The stuffs of every laden room conspired to flatter her, to elicit with tinted reflective shadows the shy structure of her face, to accent with sumptuous textures her demure skin. My knowledge of how she looked asleep gave a tender nap to the alert surface of her wakefulness now. My woman, fully searched, and my museum, fully possessed; for this translucent interval—like the instant of translucence that shows in a wave between its peaking and its curling under—I had come to the limits of unsearchability. From this beautiful boundary I could imagine no retreat.

The last time I saw this woman was in another museum, where she had taken a job. I found her in a small room lined with pale books and journals, and her face as it looked up in surprise was also pale. She took me into the corridors and showed me the furniture it was her job to catalogue. When we had reached the last room of her special province, and her gay, rather matter-of-fact lecture had ended, she asked me, "Why have you come? To upset me?"

"I don't mean to upset you. I wanted to see if you're all right."

"I'm all right. Please, William. If anything's left of what you felt for me, let me alone. Don't come teasing me."

"I'm sorry. It doesn't feel like teasing to me."

Her chin reddened and the rims of her eyes went pink as tears seized her eyes. Our bodies ached to comfort each other, but at any moment someone—a professor, a nun—might wander into the room. "You know," she said, "we really had it." A sob bowed her head and rebounded from the polished surfaces around us.

"I know. I know we did."

She looked up at me, the anger of her eyes blurred. "Then why—?"

I shrugged. "Cowardice. I've always been timid. A sense of duty. I don't know. I can't do it to her. Not yet."

"Not yet," she said. "That's your little song, isn't it? That's the little song you've been singing me all along."

"Would you rather the song had been, Not ever? That would have been no song at all."

With two careful swipes of her fingers, as if she were sculpting her own face, she wiped the tears from below her eyes. "It's my fault. It's my fault for falling in love with you. In a funny way, it was unfair to you."

"Let's walk," I said.

Blind to all beauty, we walked through halls of paintings and statues and urns. A fountain splashed unseen off to our left. Through a doorway I glimpsed, still proud, its broad chest still glowing, the headless sphinx.

"No, it's my fault," I said. "I was in no position to love you. I guess I never have been." Her eyes went bold and her freckles leaped up childishly as she grinned, as if to console me.

Yet what she said was not consolatory. "Well just don't do it to anybody else."

"Lady, there is nobody else. You're all of it. You have no idea, how beautiful you are."

"You made me believe it at the time. I'm grateful for that."

"And for nothing else?"

"Oh, for lots of things, really. You got me into the museum. It's fun."

"You came here to please me?"

"Yes."

"God, it's terrible to love what you can't have. Maybe that's why you love it."

"No, I don't think so. I think that's the way you work. But not everybody works that way."

"Well, maybe one of those others will find you now."

"No. You were it. You saw something in me nobody else ever saw. I didn't know it was there myself. Now go away, unless you want to see me cry some more."

We parted and I descended marble stairs. Before pushing through the revolving doors, I looked back, and it came to me that nothing about museums is as splendid as their entrances—the sudden vault, the shapely cornices, the motionless uniformed guard like a wittily disguised archangel, the broad stairs leading upward into heaven knows what mansions of expectantly hushed treasure. And it appeared to me that now I was condemned, in my search for the radiance that had faded behind me, to enter more and more museums, and to be a little less exalted by each new entrance, and a little more quickly disenchanted by the familiar contents beyond.

Questions for Study

1. What is so significant about the word "unsearchability"? Why is it repeated so often?
2. Why do neither the museums nor the women have names?
3. Characterize the sentence structure in the paragraph on p. 240 beginning "Outside, the weather was winter . . . " and show how it reflects the narrator.
4. What is the purpose of the figures of speech in this paragraph?
5. What is the connection between the Indian figures in the first museum and the statuette of the nude in the university museum?
6. Explain the allusion to the "Attic sphinx."

Topics for Discussion and Writing

1. Compare the style William Young uses to depict the museum he visits with his mother to the style he uses to describe the other museums.
2. Compare the museum the narrator goes to with his wife-to-be and the one he visits with his mistress and explain how the style depicting each one reflects the different situations.
3. Discuss the language of the story and explain how it suits Young and his reminiscences.
4. Discuss the narrator's interest in the structure of museums and in the art found in them and show how this interest is reflected in the style.

JOSEPH CONRAD

The Secret Sharer

I

On my right hand there were lines of fishing stakes resembling a mysterious system of half-submerged bamboo fences, incomprehensible in its division of the domain of tropical fishes, and crazy of aspect as if abandoned forever by some nomad tribe of fishermen now gone to the other end of the ocean; for there was no sign of human habitation as far as the eye could reach. To the left a group of barren islets, suggesting ruins of stone walls, towers, and blockhouses, had its foundations set in a blue sea that itself looked solid, so still and stable did it lie below my feet; even the track of light from the westering sun shone smoothly, without that animated glitter which tells of an imperceptible ripple. And when I turned my head to take a parting glance at the tug which had just left us anchored outside the bar, I saw the straight line of the flat shore joined to the stable sea, edge to edge, with a perfect and unmarked closeness, in one leveled floor half brown, half blue under the enormous dome of the sky. Corresponding in their insignificance to the islets of the sea, two small clumps of trees, one on each side of the only fault in the impeccable joint, marked the mouth of the river Meinam we had just left on the first preparatory stage of our homeward journey; and, far back on the inland level, a larger and loftier mass, the grove surrounding the great Paknam pagoda, was the only thing on which the eye could rest from the vain task of exploring the monotonous sweep of the horizon. Here and there gleams as of a few scattered pieces of silver marked the windings of the great river; and on the nearest of them, just within the bar, the tug steaming right into the land became lost to my sight, hull and funnel and masts, as though the impassive earth had swallowed her up without an effort, without a tremor. My eye followed the light cloud of her smoke, now here, now there, above the plain, according to the devious curves of the stream, but always fainter and farther away, till I lost it at last behind the miter-shaped hill of the great pagoda. And then I was left alone with my ship, anchored at the head of the Gulf of Siam.

She floated at the starting point of a long journey, very still in an immense stillness, the shadows of her spars flung far to the eastward by the setting sun. At that moment I was alone on her decks. There was not a sound in her—and around us nothing moved, nothing lived, not a canoe on the water, not a bird in the air, not a cloud in the sky. In this breathless pause at the threshold of a long and arduous enterprise, the appointed task of both our existences to be carried out, far from all human eyes, with only sky and sea for spectators and for judges.

There must have been some glare in the air to interfere with one's sight, because it was only just before the sun left us that my roaming eyes made out beyond the highest ridges of the principal islet of the group something which did away with the solemnity of perfect solitude. The tide of darkness flowed on swiftly; and with tropical suddenness a swarm of stars came out above the shadowy earth, while I lingered yet, my hand resting lightly on my ship's rail as if on the shoulder of a trusted friend. But, with all that multitude of celestial bodies staring down at one, the comfort of quiet communion with her was gone for good. And there were also disturbing sounds by this time—voices, footsteps forward; the steward flitted along the main-deck, a busily ministering spirit; a hand bell tinkled urgently under the poop deck. . . .

I found my two officers waiting for me near the supper table, in the lighted cuddy. We sat down at once, and as I helped the chief mate, I said:

"Are you aware that there is a ship anchored inside the islands? I saw her mastheads above the ridge as the sun went down."

He raised sharply his simple face, overcharged by a terrible growth of whisker, and emitted his usual ejaculations: "Bless my soul, sir! You don't say so!"

My second mate was a round-cheeked, silent young man, grave beyond his years, I thought; but as our eyes happened to meet I detected a slight quiver on his lips. I looked down at once. It was not my part to encourage sneering on board my ship. It must be said, too, that I knew very little of my officers. In consequence of certain events of no particular significance, except to myself, I had been appointed to the command only a fortnight before. Neither did I know much of the hands forward. All these people had been together for eighteen months or so, and my position was that of the only stranger on board. I mention this because it has some bearing on what is to follow. But what I felt most was my being a stranger to the ship; and if all the truth must be told, I was somewhat of a stranger to myself. The youngest man on board (barring the second mate), and untried as yet by a position of the fullest responsibility, I was willing to take the adequacy of the others for granted. They had simply to be equal to their tasks; but I wondered how far I should turn out faithful to that ideal conception of one's own personality every man sets up for himself secretly.

Meantime the chief mate, with an almost visible effect of collaboration on the part of his round eyes and frightful whiskers, was trying to evolve a theory of the anchored ship. His dominant trait was to take all things into earnest consideration. He was of a painstaking turn of mind. As he used to say, he "liked to account to himself" for practically everything that came in his way, down to a miserable scorpion he had found in his cabin a week before. The why and the wherefore of that scorpion—how it got on board and came to select his room rather than the pantry (which was a dark place and more what a scorpion would be partial to), and how on earth it managed to drown itself in the inkwell of his writing desk—had exercised him infinitely. The ship within the islands was much more easily accounted for; and just as we were about to rise from table he made his pronouncement. She was, he doubted not, a ship from home lately arrived. Probably she drew too much water to cross the bar except at the top of spring tides. Therefore she went into that natural harbor to wait for a few days in preference to remaining in an open roadstead.

"That's so," confirmed the second mate, suddenly, in his slightly hoarse voice. "She draws over twenty feet. She's the Liverpool ship *Sephora* with a cargo of coal. Hundred and twenty-three days from Cardiff."

We looked at him in surprise.

"The tugboat skipper told me when he came on board for your letters, sir," explained the young man. "He expects to take her up the river the day after tomorrow."

After thus overwhelming us with the extent of his information he slipped out of the cabin. The mate observed regretfully that he "could not account for that young fellow's whims." What prevented him telling us all about it at once, he wanted to know.

I detained him as he was making a move. For the last two days the crew had had plenty of hard work, and the night before they had very little sleep. I felt painfully that I—a stranger—was doing something unusual when I directed him to let all hands turn in without setting an anchor watch. I proposed to keep on desk myself till one o'clock or thereabouts. I would get the second mate to relieve me at that hour.

"He will turn out the cook and the steward at four," I concluded, "and then give you a call. Of course at the slightest sign of any sort of wind we'll have the hands up and make a start at once."

He concealed his astonishment. "Very well, sir." Outside the cuddy he put his head in the second mate's door to inform him of my unheard-of caprice to take a five hours' anchor watch on myself. I heard the other raise his voice incredulously—"What? The Captain himself?" Then a few more murmurs, a door closed, then another. A few moments later I went on deck.

My strangeness, which had made me sleepless, had prompted that unconventional arrangement, as if I had expected in those solitary hours of the night to get on terms with the ship of which I knew nothing, manned by men of whom I knew very little more. Fast alongside a wharf, littered like any ship in port with a tangle of unrelated things, invaded by unrelated shore people, I had hardly seen her yet properly. Now, as she lay cleared for sea, the stretch of her main-deck seemed to me very fine under the stars. Very fine, very roomy for her size, and very inviting. I descended the poop and paced the waist, my mind picturing to myself the coming passage through the Malay Archipelago, down the Indian Ocean, and up the Atlantic. All its phases were familiar enough to me, every characteristic, all the alternatives which were likely to face me on the high seas—everything! . . . except the novel responsibility of command. But I took heart from the reasonable thought that the ship was like other ships, the men like other men, and that the sea was not likely to keep any special surprises expressly for my discomfiture.

Arrived at that comforting conclusion, I bethought myself of a cigar and went below to get it. All was still down there. Everybody at the after end of the ship was sleeping profoundly. I came out again on the quarterdeck, agreeably at ease in my sleeping suit on that warm breathless night, barefooted, a glowing cigar in my teeth, and, going forward, I was met by the profound silence of the fore end of the ship. Only as I passed the door of the forecastle I heard a deep, quiet, trustful sigh of some sleeper inside. And suddenly I rejoiced in the great security of the sea as compared with the unrest of the land, in my choice of that untempted life presenting no disquieting problems, invested with an elementary moral beauty by the absolute straightforwardness of its appeal and by the singleness of its purpose.

The riding light in the forerigging burned with a clear, untroubled, as if symbolic, flame, confident and bright in the mysterious shades of the night. Passing on my way aft along the other side of the ship, I observed that the rope side ladder, put over, no doubt, for the master of the tug when he came to fetch away our letters, had not been hauled in as it should have been. I became annoyed at this, for exactitude in some small matters is the very soul of discipline. Then I reflected that I had myself peremptorily dismissed my officers from duty, and by my own act had prevented the anchor watch being formally set and things properly attended to. I asked myself whether it was wise ever to interfere with the established routine of duties even from the kindest of motives. My action might have made me appear eccentric. Goodness only knew how that absurdly whiskered mate would "account" for my conduct, and what the whole ship thought of that informality of their new captain. I was vexed with myself.

Not from compunction certainly, but, as it were mechanically, I proceeded to get the ladder in myself. Now a side ladder of that sort is a light affair and comes in easily, yet my vigorous tug, which should have brought it flying on board, merely recoiled upon my body in a totally unexpected jerk. What the devil! . . . I was so astounded by the immovableness of the ladder that I remained stockstill, trying to account for it to myself like that imbecile mate of mine. In the end, of course, I put my head over the rail.

The side of the ship made an opaque belt of shadow on the darkling glassy shimmer of the sea. But I saw at once something elongated and pale floating very close to the ladder. Before I could form a guess a faint flash of phosphorescent light, which seemed to issue suddenly from the naked body of a man, flickered in the sleeping water with the elusive, silent play of summer lightning in a night sky. With a gasp I saw revealed to my stare a pair of feet, the long legs, a broad livid back immersed right up to the neck in a greenish cadaverous glow. One hand, awash, clutched the bottom rung of the ladder. He was complete but for the head. A headless corpse! The cigar dropped out of my gaping mouth with a tiny plop and a short hiss quite audible in the absolute stillness of all things under heaven. At that I suppose he raised up his face, dimly pale oval in the shadow of the ship's side. But even then I could only barely make out down there the shape of his black-haired head. However, it was enough for the horrid, frost-bound sensation which had gripped me about the chest to pass off. The moment of vain exclamations was past, too. I only climbed on the spare spar and leaned over the rail as far as I could, to bring my eyes nearer to that mystery floating alongside.

As he hung by the ladder, like a resting swimmer, the sea lightning played about his limbs at every stir; and he appeared in it ghastly, silvery, fishlike. He remained as mute as a fish, too. He made no motion to get out of the water, either. It was inconceivable that he should not attempt to come on board, and strangely troubling to suspect that perhaps he did not want to. And my first words were prompted by just that troubled incertitude.

"What's the matter?" I asked in my ordinary tone, speaking down to the face upturned exactly under mine.

"Cramp," it answered, no louder. Then slightly anxious, "I say, no need to call anyone."

"I was not going to," I said.

"Are you alone on deck?"

"Yes."

I had somehow the impression that he was on the point of letting go the ladder to swim away beyond my ken—mysterious as he came. But, for the moment, this being appearing as if he had risen from the bottom of the sea (it was certainly the nearest land to the ship) wanted only to know the time. I told him. And he, down there, tentatively:

"I suppose your captain's turned in?"

"I am sure he isn't," I said.

He seemed to struggle with himself, for I heard something like the low, bitter murmur of doubt. "What's the good?" His next words came out with a hesitating effort.

"Look here, my man. Could you call him out quietly?"

I thought the time had come to declare myself.

"*I* am the captain."

I heard a "By Jove!" whispered at the level of the water. The phosphorescence flashed in the swirl of the water all about his limbs, his other hand seized the ladder.

"My name's Leggatt."

The voice was calm and resolute. A good voice. The self-possession of that man had somehow induced a corresponding state in myself. It was very quietly that I remarked:

"You must be a good swimmer."

"Yes. I've been in the water practically since nine o'clock. The question for me now is whether I am to let go this ladder and go on swimming till I sink from exhaustion, or—to come on board here."

I felt this was no mere formula of desperate speech, but a real alternative in the view of a strong soul. I should have gathered from this that he was young; indeed, it is only the young who are ever confronted by such clear issues. But at the time it was pure intuition on my part. A mysterious communication was established already between us two—in the face of that silent, darkened tropical sea. I was young, too; young enough to make no comment. The man in the water began suddenly to climb up the ladder, and I hastened away from the rail to fetch some clothes. Before entering the cabin I stood still, listening in the lobby at the foot of the stairs. A faint snore came through the closed door of the chief mate's room. The second mate's door was on the hook, but the darkness in there was absolutely soundless. He, too, was young and could sleep like a stone. Remained the steward, but he was not likely to wake up before he was called. I got a sleeping suit out of my room and, coming back on deck, saw the naked man from the sea sitting on the main hatch, glimmering white in the darkness, his elbows on his knees and his head in his hands. In a moment he had concealed his damp body in a sleeping suit of the same gray-stripe pattern as the one I was wearing and followed me like my double on the poop. Together we moved right aft, barefooted, silent.

"What is it?" I asked in a deadened voice, taking the lighted lamp out of the binnacle, and raising it to his face.

"An ugly business."

He had rather regular features; a good mouth; light eyes under somewhat heavy, dark eyebrows; a smooth, square forehead; no growth on his cheeks; a small, brown mustache, and a well-shaped, round chin. His expression was concentrated, meditative, under the inspecting light of the lamp I held up to his face; such as a man thinking hard in solitude might wear. My sleeping suit was just right for his size. A well-knit young fellow of twenty-five at most. He caught his lower lip with the edge of white, even teeth.

"Yes," I said, replacing the lamp in the binnacle. The warm, heavy tropical night closed upon his head again.

"There's a ship over there," he murmured.

"Yes, I know. The *Sephora.* Did you know of us?"

"Hadn't the slightest idea. I am the mate of her—" He paused and corrected himself. "I should say I *was.*"

"Aha! Something wrong?"

"Yes. Very wrong indeed. I've killed a man."

"What do you mean? Just now?"

"No, on the passage. Weeks ago. Thirty-nine south. When I say a man—"

"Fit of temper," I suggested, confidently.

The shadowy, dark head, like mine, seemed to nod imperceptibly above the ghostly gray of my sleeping suit. It was, in the night, as though I had been faced by my own reflection in the depths of a somber and immense mirror.

"A pretty thing to have to own up to for a Conway boy," murmured my double, distinctly.

"You're a Conway boy?"

"I am," he said, as if startled. Then, slowly . . . "Perhaps you too—"

It was so; but being a couple of years older I had left before he joined. After a quick interchange of dates a silence fell; and I thought suddenly of my absurd mate with his terrific whiskers and the "Bless my soul—you don't say so" type of intellect. My double gave me an inkling of his thoughts by saying: "My father's a parson in Norfolk. Do you see me before a judge and jury on that charge? For myself I can't see the necessity. There are fellows that an angel from heaven—And I am not that. He was one of those creatures that are just simmering all the time with a silly sort of wickedness. Miserable devils that have no business to live at all. He wouldn't do his duty and wouldn't let anybody else do theirs. But what's the good of talking! You know well enough the sort of ill-conditioned snarling cur—"

He appealed to me as if our experiences had been as identical as our clothes. And I knew well enough the pestiferous danger of such a character where there are no means of legal repression. And I knew well enough also that my double there was no homicidal ruffian. I did not think of asking him for details, and he told me the story roughly in brusque, disconnected sentences. I needed no more. I saw it all going on as though I were myself inside that other sleeping suit.

"It happened while we were setting a reefed foresail, at dusk. Reefed foresail! You understand the sort of weather. The only sail we had left to keep the ship running; so you may guess what it had been like for days. Anxious sort of job, that. He gave me some of his cursed insolence at the sheet. I tell you I was overdone with this terrific weather that seemed to have no end to it. Terrific, I tell you—and a deep ship. I believe the fellow himself was half crazed with funk. It was no time for gentlemanly reproof, so I turned round and felled him like an ox. He up and at me. We closed just as an awful sea made for the ship. All hands saw it coming and took to the rigging, but I had him by the throat, and went on shaking him like a rat, the men above us yelling, 'Look out! look out!' Then a crash as if the sky had fallen on my head. They say that for over ten minutes hardly anything was to be seen of the ship—just the three masts and a bit of the forecastle head and of the poop all awash driving along in a smother of foam. It was a miracle that they found us, jammed together behind the forebitts. It's clear that I meant business, because I was holding him by the throat still when they picked us up. He was black in the face. It was too much for them. It seems they rushed us aft together, gripped as we were, screaming 'Murder!' like a lot of lunatics, and broke into the cuddy. And the ship running for her life, touch and go all the time, any minute her last in a sea fit to turn your hair gray only a-looking at it. I understand that the skipper, too, started raving like the rest of them. The man had been deprived of sleep for more than a week, and to have this sprung on him at the height of a furious gale nearly drove him out of his mind. I wonder they didn't fling me overboard after getting the carcass of their precious shipmate out of my fingers. They had rather a job to separate us, I've been told. A sufficiently fierce story to make an old judge and a respectable jury sit up a bit. The first thing I heard when I came to myself was the maddening howling of that endless gale, and on that the voice of the old man. He was hanging on to my bunk, staring into my face out of his sou'wester.

" 'Mr. Leggatt, you have killed a man. You can act no longer as chief mate of this ship.' "

His care to subdue his voice made it sound monotonous. He rested a hand on the end of the skylight to steady himself with, and all that time did not stir a limb, so far as I could see. "Nice little tale for a quiet tea party," he concluded in the same tone.

One of my hands, too, rested on the end of the skylight; neither did I stir a limb, so far as I knew. We stood less than a foot from each other. It occurred to me that if old "Bless my soul—you don't say so" were to put his head up the companion and catch sight of us, he would think he was seeing double, or imagine himself come upon a scene of weird witchcraft; the strange captain having a quiet confabulation by the wheel with his own gray ghost. I became very much concerned to prevent anything of the sort. I heard the other's soothing undertone.

"My father's a parson in Norfolk," it said. Evidently he had forgotten he had told me this important fact before. Truly a nice little tale.

"You had better slip down into my stateroom now," I said, moving off stealthily. My double followed my movements; our bare feet made no sound; I let him in, closed the door with care, and, after giving a call to the second mate, returned on deck for my relief.

"Not much sign of any wind yet," I remarked when he approached.

"No, sir. Not much," he assented, sleepily, in his hoarse voice, with just enough deference, no more, and barely suppressing a yawn.

"Well, that's all you have to look out for. You have got your orders."

"Yes, sir."

I paced a turn or two on the poop and saw him take up his position face forward with his elbow in the ratlines of the mizzen rigging before I went below. The mate's faint snoring was still going on peacefully. The cuddy lamp was burning over the table on which stood a vase with flowers, a polite attention from the ship's provision merchant—the last flowers we should see for the next three months at the very least. Two bunches of bananas hung from the beam symmetrically, one on each side of the rudder casing. Everything was as before in the ship—except that two of her captain's sleeping suits were simultaneously in use, one motionless in the cuddy, the other keeping very still in the captain's stateroom.

It must be explained here that my cabin had the form of the capital letter L, the door being within the angle and opening into the short part of the letter. A couch was to the left, the bed place to the right; my writing desk and the chronometers' table faced the door. But anyone opening it, unless he stepped right inside, had no view of what I call the long (or vertical) part of the letter. It contained some lockers surmounted by a bookcase; and a few clothes, a thick jacket or two, caps, oilskin coat, and such like, hung on hooks. There was at the bottom of that part a door opening into my bathroom, which could be entered also directly from the saloon. But that way was never used.

The mysterious arrival had discovered the advantage of this particular shape. Entering my room, lighted strongly by a big bulkhead lamp swung on gimbals above my writing desk, I did not see him anywhere till he stepped out quietly from behind the coats hung in the recessed part.

"I heard somebody moving about, and went in there at once," he whispered. I, too, spoke under my breath.

"Nobody is likely to come in here without knocking and getting permission."

He nodded. His face was thin and the sunburn faded, as though he had been ill. And no wonder. He had been, I heard presently, kept under arrest in his cabin for nearly seven weeks. But there was nothing sickly in his eyes or in his expression. He was not a bit like me, really; yet, as we stood leaning over my bed place, whispering side by side, with our dark heads together and our backs to the door, anybody bold enough to open it stealthily would have been treated to the uncanny sight of a double captain busy talking in whispers with his other self.

"But all this doesn't tell me how you came to hang on to our side ladder," I inquired, in the hardly audible murmurs we used, after he had told me something more of the proceedings on board the *Sephora* once the bad weather was over.

"When we sighted Java Head I had had time to think all those matters out several times over. I had six weeks of doing nothing else, and with only an hour or so every evening for a tramp on the quarter-deck."

He whispered, his arms folded on the side of my bed place, staring through the open port. And I could imagine perfectly the manner of this thinking out—a stubborn if not a steadfast operation; something of which I should have been perfectly incapable.

"I reckoned it would be dark before we closed with the land," he continued, so low that I had to strain my hearing near as we were to each other, shoulder touching shoulder almost. "So I asked to speak to the old man. He always seemed very sick when he came to see me—as if he could not look me in the face. You know, that foresail saved the ship. She was too deep to have run long under bare poles. And it was I that managed to set it for him. Anyway, he came. When I had him in my cabin—he stood by the door looking at me as if I had the halter round my neck already—I asked him right away to leave my cabin door unlocked at night while the ship was going through Sunda Straits. There would be the Java coast within two or three miles, off Angier Point. I wanted nothing more. I've had a prize for swimming my second year in the Conway."

"I can believe it," I breathed out.

"God only knows why they locked me in every night. To see some of their faces you'd have thought they were afraid I'd go about at night strangling people. Am I a murdering brute? Do I look it? By Jove! If I had been he wouldn't have trusted himself like that into my room. You'll say I might have chucked him aside and bolted out, there and then—it was dark already. Well, no. And for the same reason I wouldn't think of trying to smash the door. There would have been a rush to stop me at the noise, and I did not mean to get into a confounded scrimmage. Somebody else might have got killed—for I would not have broken out only to get chucked back, and I did not want any more of that work. He refused, looking more sick than ever. He was afraid of the men, and also of that old second mate of his who had been sailing with him for years—a gray-headed old humbug; and his steward, too, had been with him devil knows how long—seventeen years or more—a dogmatic sort of loafer who hated me like poison, just because I was the chief mate. No chief mate ever made more than one voyage in the *Sephora*, you know. Those two old chaps ran the ship. Devil only knows what the skipper wasn't afraid of (all his nerve went to pieces altogether in that hellish spell of bad weather we had)—of what the law would do to him—of his wife, perhaps. Oh, yes! she's on board. Though I don't think she would have meddled. She would have been only too glad to have me out of the ship in any way. The 'brand of Cain' business, don't you see. That's all right. I was ready enough to go off wandering on the face of the earth—and that was price enough to pay for an Abel of that sort. Anyhow, he wouldn't listen to me. 'This thing must take its course. I represent the law here.' He was shaking like a leaf. 'So you won't?' 'No!' 'Then I hope you will be able to sleep on that,' I said, and turned my back on him. 'I wonder that *you* can,' cries he, and locks the door.

"Well after that, I couldn't. Not very well. That was three weeks ago. We have had a slow passage through the Java Sea; drifted about Carimata for ten days. When we anchored here they thought, I suppose, it was all right. The nearest land (and that's five miles) is the ship's destination; the consul would soon set about catching me; and there would have been no object in bolting to these islets there. I don't suppose there's a drop of water on them. I don't know how it was, but tonight that steward, after bringing me my supper, went out to let me eat it, and left the door unlocked. And I ate it—all there was, too. After I had finished I strolled out on the quarter-deck. I don't know that I meant to do anything. A breath of fresh air was all I wanted, I believe. Then a sudden temptation came over me. I kicked off my slippers and was in the water before I had made up my mind fairly. Somebody heard the splash and they raised an awful hullabaloo. 'He's gone! Lower the boats! He's committed suicide! No, he's swimming.' Certainly I was swimming. It's not so easy for a swimmer like me to commit suicide by drowning. I landed on the nearest islet before the boat left the ship's side. I heard them pulling about in the dark, hailing, and so on, but after a bit they gave up. Everything quieted down and the anchorage became as still as death. I sat down on a stone and began to think. I felt certain they would start searching for me at daylight. There was no place to hide on those stony things—and if there had been, what would have been the good? But now I was clear of that ship, I was not going back. So after a while I took off all my clothes, tied them up in a bundle with a stone inside, and dropped them in the deep water on the outer side of that islet. That was suicide enough for me. Let them think what they liked, but I didn't mean to drown myself. I meant to swim till I sank—but that's not the same thing. I struck out for another of these little islands, and it was from that one that I first saw your riding light. Something to swim for. I went on easily, and on the way I came upon a flat rock a foot or two above water. In the daytime, I dare say, you might make it out with a glass from your poop. I scrambled up on it and rested myself for a bit. Then I made another start. That last spell must have been over a mile."

His whisper was getting fainter and fainter, and all the time he stared straight out through the porthole, in which there was not even a star to be seen. I had not interrupted him. There was something that made comment impossible in his narrative, or perhaps in himself; a sort of feeling, a quality, which I can't find a name for. And when he ceased, all I found was a futile whisper: "So you swam for our light?"

"Yes—straight for it. It was something to swim for. I couldn't see any stars low down because the coast was in the way, and I couldn't see the land, either. The water was like glass. One might have been swimming in a confounded thousand-feet deep cistern with no place for scrambling out anywhere; but what I didn't like was the notion of swimming round and round like a crazed bullock before I gave out; and as I didn't mean to go back . . . No. Do you see me being hauled back, stark naked, off one of these little islands by the scruff of the neck and fighting like a wild beast? Somebody would have got killed for certain, and I did not want any of that. So I went on. Then your ladder—"

"Why didn't you hail the ship?" I asked, a little louder.

He touched my shoulder lightly. Lazy footsteps came right over our heads and stopped. The second mate had crossed from the other side of the poop and might have been hanging over the rail for all we knew.

"He couldn't hear us talking—could he?" My double breathed into my very ear, anxiously.

His anxiety was in answer, a sufficient answer, to the question I had put to him. An answer containing all the difficulty of that situation. I closed the porthole quietly, to make sure. A louder word might have been overheard.

"Who's that?" he whispered then.

"My second mate. But I don't know much more of the fellow than you do."

And I told him a little about myself. I had been appointed to take charge while I least expected anything of the sort, now quite a fortnight ago. I didn't know either the ship or the people. Hadn't had the time in port to look about me or size anybody up. And as to the crew, all they knew was that I was appointed to take the ship home. For the rest, I was almost as much of a stranger on board as himself, I said. And at the moment I felt it most acutely. I felt that it would take very little to make me a suspect person in the eyes of the ship's company.

He had turned about meantime; and we, the two strangers in the ship, faced each other in identical attitudes.

"Your ladder—" he murmured, after a silence. "Who'd have thought of finding a ladder hanging over at night in a ship anchored out here! I felt just then a very unpleasant faintness. After the life I've been leading for nine weeks, anybody would have got out of condition. I wasn't capable of swimming round as far as your rudder chains. And, lo and behold! there was a ladder to get hold of. After I gripped it I said to myself, 'What's the good?' When I saw a man's head looking over I thought I would swim away presently and leave him shouting—in whatever language it was. I didn't mind being looked at. I—I liked it. And then you speaking to me so quietly—as if you had expected me—made me hold on a little longer. It had been a confounded lonely time—I don't mean while swimming. I was glad to talk a little to somebody that didn't belong to the *Sephora*. As to asking for the captain, that was a mere impulse. It could have been no use, with all the ship knowing about me and the other people pretty certain to be round here in the morning. I don't know—I wanted to be seen, to talk with somebody, before I went on. I don't know what I would have said. . . . 'Fine night, isn't it?' or something of the sort."

"Do you think they will be round here presently?" I asked with some incredulity.

"Quite likely," he said, faintly.

He looked extremely haggard all of a sudden. His head rolled on his shoulders.

"H'm. We shall see then. Meantime get into that bed," I whispered. "Want help? There."

It was a rather high bed place with a set of drawers underneath. This amazing swimmer really needed the lift I gave him by seizing his leg. He tumbled in, rolled over on his back, and flung one arm across his eyes. And then, with his face nearly hidden, he must have looked exactly as I used to look in that bed. I gazed upon my other self for a while before drawing across carefully the two green serge curtains which ran on a brass rod. I thought for a moment of pinning them together for greater safety, but I sat down on the couch, and once there I felt unwilling to rise and hunt for a pin. I would do it in a moment. I was extremely tired, in a peculiarly intimate way, by the strain of stealthiness, by the effort of whispering and the general secrecy of this excitement. It was three o'clock by now and I had been on my feet since nine, but I was not sleepy; I could not have gone to sleep. I sat there, fagged out, looking at the curtains, trying to clear my mind of the confused sensation of being in two places at once, and greatly bothered by an exasperating knocking in my head. It was a relief to discover suddenly that it was not in my head at all, but on the outside of the door. Before I could collect myself the words "Come in" were out of my mouth, and the steward entered with a tray, bringing in my morning coffee. I had slept, after all, and I was so frightened that I shouted, "This way! I am here, steward," as though he had been miles away. He put down the tray on the table next the couch and only then said, very quietly, "I can see you are here, sir." I felt him give me a keen look, but I dared not meet his eyes just then. He must have wondered why I had drawn the curtains of my bed before going to sleep on the couch. He went out, hooking the door open as usual.

I heard the crew washing decks above me. I knew I would have been told at once if there had been any wind. Calm, I thought, and I was doubly vexed. Indeed, I felt dual more than ever. The steward reappeared suddenly in the doorway. I jumped up from the couch so quickly that he gave a start.

"What do you want here?"

"Close your port, sir—they are washing decks."

"It is closed," I said, reddening.

"Very well, sir." But he did not move from the doorway and returned my stare in an extraordinary, equivocal manner for a time. Then his eyes wavered, all his expression changed, and in a voice unusually gentle, almost coaxingly:

"May I come in to take the empty cup away, sir?"

"Of course!" I turned my back on him while he popped in and out. Then I unhooked and closed the door and even pushed the bolt. This sort of thing could not go on very long. The cabin was as hot as an oven, too. I took a peep at my double, and discovered that he had not moved, his arm was still over his eyes; but his chest heaved; his hair was wet; his chin glistened with perspiration. I reached over him and opened the port.

"I must show myself on deck," I reflected.

Of course, theoretically, I could do what I liked, with no one to say nay to me within the whole circle of the horizon; but to lock my cabin door and take the key away I did not dare. Directly I put my head out of the companion I saw the group of my two officers, the second mate barefooted, the chief mate in long India-rubber boots, near the break of the poop, and the steward halfway down the poop ladder talking to them eagerly. He happened to catch sight of me and dived, the second ran down on the main-deck shouting some order or other, and the chief mate came to meet me, touching his cap.

There was a sort of curiosity in his eye that I did not like. I don't know whether the steward had told them that I was "queer" only, or downright drunk, but I know the man meant to have a good look at me. I watched him coming with a smile which, as he got into point-blank range, took effect and froze his very whiskers. I did not give him time to open his lips.

"Square the yards by lifts and braces before the hands go to breakfast."

It was the first particular order I had given on board that ship; and I stayed on deck to see it executed, too. I had felt the need of asserting myself without loss of time. That sneering young cub got taken down a peg or two on that occasion, and I also seized the opportunity of having a good look at the face of every foremast man as they filed past me to go to the after braces. At breakfast time, eating nothing myself, I presided with such frigid dignity that the two mates were only too glad to escape from the cabin as soon as decency permitted; and all the time the dual working of my mind distracted me almost to the point of insanity. I was constantly watching myself, my secret self, as dependent on my actions as my own personality, sleeping in that bed, behind that door which faced me as I sat at the head of the table. It was very much like being mad, only it was worse because one was aware of it.

I had to shake him for a solid minute, but when at last he opened his eyes it was in the full possession of his senses, with an inquiring look.

"All's well so far," I whispered. "Now you must vanish into the bathroom."

He did so, as noiseless as a ghost, and then I rang for the steward, and facing him boldly, directed him to tidy up my stateroom while I was having my bath—"and be quick about it." As my tone admitted of no excuses, he said, "Yes, sir," and ran off to fetch his dustpan and brushes. I took a bath and did most of my dressing, splashing, and whistling softly for the steward's edification, while the secret sharer of my life stood drawn up bolt upright in that little space, his face looking very sunken in daylight, his eyelids lowered under the stern, dark line of his eyebrows drawn together by a slight frown.

When I left him there to go back to my room the steward was finishing dusting. I sent for the mate and engaged him in some insignificant conversation. It was, as it were, trifling with the terrific character of his whiskers; but my object was to give him an opportunity for a good look at my cabin. And then I could at last shut, with a clear conscience, the door of my stateroom and get my double back into the recessed part. There was nothing else for it. He had to sit still on a small folding stool, half smothered by the heavy coats hanging there. We listened to the steward going into the bathroom out of the saloon, filling the water bottles there, scrubbing the bath, setting things to rights, whisk, bang, clatter—out again into the saloon—turn the key—click. Such was my scheme for keeping my second self invisible. Nothing better could be contrived under the circumstances. And there we sat; I at my writing desk ready to appear busy with some papers, he behind me out of sight of the door. It would not have been prudent to talk in daytime; and I could not have stood the excitement of that queer sense of whispering to myself. Now and then, glancing over my shoulder, I saw him far back there, sitting rigidly on the low stool, his bare feet close together, his arms folded, his head hanging on his breast—and perfectly still. Anybody would have taken him for me.

I was fascinated by it myself. Every moment I had to glance over my shoulder. I was looking at him when a voice outside the door said:

"Beg pardon, sir."

"Well!" . . . I kept my eyes on him, and so when the voice outside the door announced, "There's a ship's boat coming our way, sir," I saw him give a start—the first movement he had made for hours. But he did not raise his bowed head.

"All right. Get the ladder over."

I hesitated. Should I whisper something to him? But what? His immobility seemed to have been never disturbed. What could I tell him he did not know already? . . . Finally I went on deck.

II

The skipper of the *Sephora* had a thin red whisker all round his face, and the sort of complexion that goes with hair of that color; also the particular, rather smeary shade of blue in the eyes. He was not exactly a showy figure; his shoulders were high, his stature but middling—one leg slightly more bandy than the other. He shook hands, looking vaguely around. A spiritless tenacity was his main characteristic, I judged. I behaved with a politeness which seemed to disconcert him. Perhaps he was shy. He mumbled to me as if he were ashamed of what he was saying; gave his name (it was something like Archbold—but at this distance of years I hardly am sure), his ship's name, and a few other particulars of that sort, in the manner of a criminal making a reluctant and doleful confession. He had had terrible weather on the passage out—terrible—terrible—wife aboard, too.

By this time we were seated in the cabin and the steward brought in a tray with a bottle and glasses. "Thanks! No." Never took liquor. Would have some water, though. He drank two tumblerfuls. Terrible thirsty work. Ever since daylight had been exploring the islands round his ship.

"What was that for—fun?" I asked, with an appearance of polite interest.

"No!" He sighed. "Painful duty."

As he persisted in his mumbling and I wanted my double to hear every word, I hit upon the notion of informing him that I regretted to say I was hard of hearing.

"Such a young man, too!" he nodded, keeping his smeary blue, unintelligent eyes fastened upon me. "What was the cause of it—some disease?" he inquired, without the least sympathy and as if he thought that, if so, I'd got no more than I deserved.

"Yes; disease," I admitted in a cheerful tone which seemed to shock him. But my point was gained, because he had to raise his voice to give me his tale. It is not worth while to record that version. It was just over two months since all this had happened, and he had thought so much about it that he seemed completely muddled as to its bearings, but still immensely impressed.

"What would you think of such a thing happening on board your own ship? I've had the *Sephora* for these fifteen years. I am a well-known shipmaster."

He was densely distressed—and perhaps I should have sympathized with him if I had been able to detach my mental vision from the unsuspected sharer of my cabin as though he were my second self. There he was on the other side of the bulkhead, four or five feet from us, no more, as we sat in the saloon. I looked politely at Captain Archbold (if that was his name), but it was the other I saw, in a gray sleeping suit, seated on a low stool, his bare feet close together, his arms folded, and every word said between us falling into the ears of his dark head bowed on his chest.

"I have been at sea now, man and boy, for seven-and-thirty years, and I've never heard of such a thing happening in an English ship. And that it should be my ship. Wife on board, too."

I was hardly listening to him.

"Don't you think," I said, "that the heavy sea which, you told me, came aboard just then might have killed the man? I have seen the sheer weight of a sea kill a man very neatly, by simply breaking his neck."

"Good God!" he uttered, impressively, fixing his smeary blue eyes on me. "The sea! No man killed by the sea ever looked like that." He seemed positively scandalized at my suggestion. And as I gazed at him certainly not prepared for anything original on his part, he advanced his head close to mine and thrust his tongue out at me so suddenly that I couldn't help starting back.

After scoring over my calmness in this graphic way he nodded wisely. If I had seen the sight, he assured me, I would never forget it as long as I lived. The weather was too bad to give the corpse a proper sea burial. So next day at dawn they took it up on the poop, covering its face with a bit of bunting; he read a short prayer, and then, just as it was, in its oilskins and long boots, they launched it amongst those mountainous seas that seemed ready every moment to swallow up the ship herself and the terrified lives on board of her.

"That reefed foresail saved you," I threw in.

"Under God—it did," he exclaimed fervently. "It was by a special mercy, I firmly believe, that it stood some of those hurricane squalls."

"It was the setting of that sail which—" I began.

"God's own hand in it," he interrupted me. "Nothing less could have done it. I don't mind telling you that I hardly dared give the order. It seemed impossible that we could touch anything without losing it, and then our last hope would have been gone."

The terror of that gale was on him yet. I let him go on for a bit, then said, casually—as if returning to a minor subject:

"You were very anxious to give up your mate to the shore people, I believe?"

He was. To the law. His obscure tenacity on that point had in it something incomprehensible and a little awful; something, as it were, mystical, quite apart from his anxiety that he should not be suspected of "countenancing any doings of that sort." Seven-and-thirty virtuous years at sea, of which over twenty of immaculate command, and the last fifteen in the *Sephora*, seemed to have laid him under some pitiless obligation.

"And you know," he went on, groping shame-facedly amongst his feelings, "I did not engage that young fellow. His people had some interest with my owners. I was in a way forced to take him on. He looked very smart, very gentlemanly, and all that. But do you know—I never liked him, somehow. I am a plain man. You see, he wasn't exactly the sort for the chief mate of a ship like the *Sephora*."

I had become so connected in thoughts and impressions with the secret sharer of my cabin that I felt as if I, personally, were being given to understand that I, too, was not the sort that would have done for the chief mate of a ship like the *Sephora*. I had no doubt of it in my mind.

"Not at all the style of man. You understand," he insisted, superfluously, looking hard at me.

I smiled urbanely. He seemed at a loss for a while.

"I suppose I must report a suicide."

"Beg pardon?"

"Sui-cide! That's what I'll have to write to my owners directly I get in."

"Unless you manage to recover him before tomorrow," I assented, dispassionately. . . . "I mean, alive."

He mumbled something which I really did not catch, and I turned my ear to him in a puzzled manner. He fairly bawled:

"The land—I say, the mainland is at least seven miles off my anchorage."

"About that."

My lack of excitement, of curiosity, of surprise, of any sort of pronounced interest, began to arouse his distrust. But except for the felicitous pretense of deafness I had not tried to pretend anything. I had felt utterly incapable of playing the part of ignorance properly, and therefore was afraid to try. It is also certain that he had brought some ready-made suspicions with him, and that he viewed my politeness as a strange and unnatural phenomenon. And yet how else could I have received him? Not heartily! That was impossible for psychological reasons, which I need not state here. My only object was to keep off his inquiries. Surlily? Yes, but surliness might have provoked a point-blank question. From its novelty to him and from its nature, punctilious courtesy was the manner best calculated to restrain the man. But there was the danger of his breaking through my defense bluntly. I could not, I think, have met him by a direct lie, also for psychological (not moral) reasons. If he had only known how afraid I was of his putting my feeling of identity with the other to the test! But, strangely enough—(I thought of it only afterwards)—I believe that he was not a little disconcerted by the reverse side of that weird situation, by something in me that reminded him of the man he was seeking—suggested a mysterious similitude to the young fellow he had distrusted and disliked from the first.

However that might have been, the silence was not very prolonged. He took another oblique step.

"I reckon I had no more than a two-mile pull to your ship. Not a bit more."

"And quite enough, too, in this awful heat," I said.

Another pause full of mistrust followed. Necessity, they say, is mother of invention, but fear, too, is not barren of ingenious suggestions. And I was afraid he would ask me point-blank for news of my other self.

"Nice little saloon, isn't it?" I remarked, as if noticing for the first time the way his eyes roamed from one closed door to the other. "And very well fitted out, too. Here, for instance," I continued, reaching over the back of my seat negligently and flinging the door open, "is my bathroom."

He made an eager movement, but hardly gave it a glance. I got up, shut the door of the bathroom, and invited him to have a look round, as if I were very proud of my accommodation. He had to rise and be shown round, but he went through the business without any raptures whatever.

"And now we'll have a look at my stateroom," I declared, in a voice as loud as I dared to make it, crossing the cabin to the starboard side with purposely heavy steps.

He followed me in and gazed around. My intelligent double had vanished. I played my part.

"Very convenient—isn't it?"

"Very nice. Very comf . . ." He didn't finish and went out brusquely as if to escape from some unrighteous wiles of mine. But it was not to be. I had been too frightened not to feel vengeful; I felt I had him on the run, and I meant to keep him on the run. My polite insistence must have had something menacing in it, because he gave in suddenly. And I did not let him off a single item; mate's room, pantry, storerooms, the very sail locker which was also under the poop—he had to look into them all. When at last I showed him out on the quarter-deck he drew a long, spiritless sigh, and mumbled dismally that he must really be going back to his ship now. I desired my mate, who had joined us, to see to the captain's boat.

The man of whiskers gave a blast on the whistle which he used to wear hanging round his neck, and yelled, "*Sephora*'s away!" My double down there in my cabin must have heard, and certainly could not feel more relieved than I. Four fellows came running out from somewhere forward and went over the side, while my own men, appearing on deck too, lined the rail. I escorted my visitor to the gangway ceremoniously, and nearly overdid it. He was a tenacious beast. On the very ladder he lingered, and in that unique, guiltily conscientious manner of sticking to the point:

"I say . . . you . . . you don't think that—"

I covered his voice loudly:

"Certainly not. . . . I am delighted. Good-by."

I had an idea of what he meant to say, and just saved myself by the privilege of defective hearing. He was too shaken generally to insist, but my mate, close witness of that parting, looked mystified and his face took on a thoughtful cast. As I did not want to appear as if I wished to avoid all communication with my officers, he had the opportunity to address me.

"Seems a very nice man. His boat's crew told our chaps a very extraordinary story, if what I am told by the steward is true. I suppose you had it from the captain, sir?"

"Yes. I had a story from the captain."

"A very horrible affair—isn't it, sir?"

"It is."

"Beats all these tales we hear about murders in Yankee ships."

"I don't think it beats them. I don't think it resembles them in the least."

"Bless my soul—you don't say so! But of course I've no acquaintance whatever with American ships, not I, so I couldn't go against your knowledge. It's horrible enough for me. . . . But the queerest part is that those fellows seemed to have some idea the man was hidden aboard here. They had really. Did you ever hear of such a thing?"

"Preposterous—isn't it?"

We were walking to and fro athwart the quarter-deck. No one of the crew forward could be seen (the day was Sunday), and the mate pursued:

"There was some little dispute about it. Our chaps took offense. 'As if we would harbor a thing like that,' they said. 'Wouldn't you like to look for him in our coalhole?' Quite a tiff. But they made it up in the end. I suppose he did drown himself. Don't you, sir?"

"I don't suppose anything."

"You have no doubt in the matter, sir?"

"None whatever."

I left him suddenly. I felt I was producing a bad impression, but with my double down there it was most trying to be on deck. And it was almost as trying to be below. Altogether a nerve-trying situation. But on the whole I felt less torn in two when I was with him. There was no one in the whole ship whom I dared take into my confidence. Since the hands had got to know his story, it would have been impossible to pass him off for anyone else, and an accidental discovery was to be dreaded now more than ever. . . .

The steward being engaged in laying the table for dinner, we could talk only with our eyes when I first went down. Later in the afternoon we had a cautious try at whispering. The Sunday quietness of the ship was against us; the stillness of air and water around her was against us; the elements, the men were against us—everything was against us in our secret partnership; time itself—for this could not go on forever. The very trust in Providence was, I suppose, denied to his guilt. Shall I confess that this thought cast me down very much? And as to the chapter of accidents which counts for so much in the book of success, I could only hope that it was closed. For what favorable accident could be expected?

"Did you hear everything?" were my first words as soon as we took up our position side by side, leaning over my bed place.

He had. And the proof of it was his earnest whisper, "The man told you he hardly dared to give the order."

I understood the reference to be to that saving foresail.

"Yes. He was afraid of it being lost in the setting."

"I assure you he never gave the order. He may think he did, but he never gave it. He stood there with me on the break of the poop after the main topsail blew away, and whimpered about our last hope—positively whimpered about it and nothing else—and the night coming on! To hear one's skipper go on like that in such weather was enough to drive any fellow out of his mind. It worked me up into a sort of desperation. I just took it into my own hands and went away from him, boiling, and—But what's the use telling you? *You* know! . . . Do you think that if I had not been pretty fierce with them I should have got the men to do anything? Not It! The bo's'n perhaps? Perhaps! It wasn't a heavy sea—it was a sea gone mad! I suppose the end of the world will be something like that; and a man may have the heart to see it coming once and be done with it—but to have to face it day after day—I don't blame anybody. I was precious little better than the rest. Only—I was an officer of that old coal wagon, anyhow—"

"I quite understand," I conveyed that sincere assurance into his ear. He was out of breath with whispering; I could hear him pant slightly. It was all very simple. The same strung-up force which had given twenty-four men a chance, at least, for their lives, had, in a sort of recoil, crushed an unworthy mutinous existence.

But I had no leisure to weigh the merits of the matter—footsteps in the saloon, a heavy knock. "There's enough wind to get under way with, sir." Here was the call of a new claim upon my thoughts and even upon my feelings.

"Turn the hands up," I cried through the door. "I'll be on deck directly."

I was going out to make the acquaintance of my ship. Before I left the cabin our eyes met—the eyes of the only two strangers on board. I pointed to the recessed part where the little campstool awaited him and laid my finger on my lips. He made a gesture—somewhat vague—a little mysterious, accompanied by a faint smile, as if of regret.

This is not the place to enlarge upon the sensations of a man who feels for the first time a ship move under his feet to his own independent word. In my case they were not unalloyed. I was not wholly alone with my command; for there was that stranger in my cabin. Or rather, I was not completely and wholly with her. Part of me was absent. That mental feeling of being in two places at once affected me physically as if the mood of secrecy had penetrated my very soul. Before an hour had elapsed since the ship had begun to move, having occasion to ask the mate (he stood by my side) to take a compass bearing of the pagoda, I caught myself reaching up to his ear in whispers. I say I caught myself, but enough had escaped to startle the man. I can't describe it otherwise than by saying that he shied. A grave, preoccupied manner, as though he were in possession of some perplexing intelligence, did not leave him henceforth. A little later I moved away from the rail to look at the compass with such a stealthy gait that the helmsman noticed it—and I could not help noticing the unusual roundness of his eyes. These are trifling instances, though it's to no commander's advantage to be suspected of ludicrous eccentricities. But I was also more seriously affected. There are to a seaman certain words, gestures, that should in given conditions come as naturally, as instinctively as the winking of a menaced eye. A certain order should spring on to his lips without thinking; a certain sign should get itself made, so to speak, without reflection. But all unconscious alertness had abandoned me. I had to make an effort of will to recall myself back (from the cabin) to the conditions of the moment. I felt that I was appearing an irresolute commander to those people who were watching me more or less critically.

And, besides, there were the scares. On the second day out, for instance, coming off the deck in the afternoon (I had straw slippers on my bare feet) I stopped at the open pantry door and spoke to the steward. He was doing something there with his back to me. At the sound of my voice he nearly jumped out of his skin, as the saying is, and incidentally broke a cup.

"What on earth's the matter with you?" I asked, astonished.

He was extremely confused. "Beg your pardon, sir. I made sure you were in your cabin."

"You see I wasn't."

"No, sir. I could have sworn I had heard you moving in there not a moment ago. It's most extraordinary . . . very sorry, sir."

I passed on with an inward shudder. I was so identified with my secret double that I did not even mention the fact in those scanty, fearful whispers we exchanged. I suppose he had made some slight noise of some kind or other. It would have been miraculous if he hadn't at one time or another. And yet, haggard as he appeared, he looked always perfectly self-controlled, more than calm—almost invulnerable. On my suggestion he remained almost entirely in the bathroom, which, upon the whole, was the safest place. There could be really no shadow of an excuse for anyone ever wanting to go in there, once the steward had done with it. It was a very tiny place. Sometimes he reclined on the floor, his legs bent, his head sustained on one elbow. At others I would find him on the campstool, sitting in his gray sleeping suit and with his cropped dark hair like a patient, unmoved convict. At night I would smuggle him into my bed place, and we would whisper together, with the regular footfalls of the officer of the watch passing and repassing over our heads. It was an infinitely miserable time. It was lucky that some tins of fine preserves were stowed in a locker in my stateroom; hard bread I could always get hold of; and so he lived on stewed chicken, *pâté de foie gras,* asparagus, cooked oysters, sardines —on all sorts of abominable sham delicacies out of tins. My early-morning coffee he always drank; and it was all I dared do for him in that respect.

Every day there was the horrible maneuvering to go through so that my room and then the bathroom should be done in the usual way. I came to hate the sight of the steward, to abhor the voice of that harmless man. I felt that it was he who would bring on the disaster of discovery. It hung like a sword over our heads.

The fourth day out, I think (we were then working down the east side of the Gulf of Siam, tack for tack, in light winds and smooth water)—the fourth day, I say, of this miserable juggling with the unavoidable, as we sat at our evening meal, that man, whose slightest movement I dreaded, after putting down the dishes ran up on deck busily. This could not be dangerous. Presently he came down again; and then it appeared that he had remembered a coat of mine which I had thrown over a rail to dry after having been wetted in a shower which had passed over the ship in the afternoon. Sitting stolidly at the head of the table I became terrified at the sight of the garment on his arm. Of course he made for my door. There was no time to lose.

"Steward," I thundered. My nerves were so shaken that I could not govern my voice and conceal my agitation. This was the sort of thing that made my terrifically whiskered mate tap his forehead with his forefinger. I had detected him using that gesture while talking on deck with a confidential air to the carpenter. It was too far to hear a word, but I had no doubt that this pantomime could only refer to the strange new captain.

"Yes, sir," the pale-faced steward turned resignedly to me. It was this maddening course of being shouted at, checked without rhyme or reason, arbitrarily chased out of my cabin, suddenly called into it, sent flying out of his pantry on incomprehensible errands, that accounted for the growing wretchedness of his expression.

"Where are you going with that coat?"

"To your room, sir."

"Is there another shower coming?"

"I'm sure I don't know, sir. Shall I go up again and see, sir?"

"No! never mind."

My object was attained, as of course my other self in there would have heard everything that passed. During this interlude my two officers never raised their eyes off their respective plates; but the lip of that confounded cub, the second mate, quivered visibly.

I expected the steward to hook my coat on and come out at once. He was very slow about it; but I dominated my nervousness sufficiently not to shout after him. Suddenly I became aware (it could be heard plainly enough) that the fellow for some reason or other was opening the door of the bathroom. It was the end. The place was literally not big enough to swing a cat in. My voice died in my throat and I went stony all over. I expected to hear a yell of surprise and terror, and made a movement, but had not the strength to get on my legs. Everything remained still. Had my second self taken the poor wretch by the throat? I don't know what I could have done next moment if I had not seen the steward come out of my room, close the door, and then stand quietly by the sideboard.

"Saved," I thought. "But, no! Lost! Gone! He was gone!"

I laid my knife and fork down and leaned back in my chair. My head swam. After a while, when sufficiently recovered to speak in a steady voice, I instructed my mate to put the ship round at eight o'clock himself.

"I won't come on deck," I went on. "I think I'll turn in, and unless the wind shifts I don't want to be disturbed before midnight. I feel a bit seedy."

"You did look middling bad a little while ago," the chief mate remarked without showing any great concern.

They both went out, and I stared at the steward clearing the table. There was nothing to be read on that wretched man's face. But why did he avoid my eyes, I asked myself. Then I thought I should like to hear the sound of his voice.

"Steward!"

"Sir!" Startled as usual.

"Where did you hang up that coat?"

"In the bathroom, sir." The usual anxious tone. "It's not quite dry yet, sir."

For some time longer I sat in the cuddy. Had my double vanished as he had come? But of his coming there was an explanation, whereas his disappearance would be inexplicable. . . . I went slowly into my dark room, shut the door, lighted the lamp, and for a time dared not turn round. When at last I did I saw him standing bolt-upright in the narrow recessed part. It would not be true to say I had a shock, but an irresistible doubt of his bodily existence flitted through my mind. Can it be, I asked myself, that he is not visible to other eyes than mine? It was like being haunted. Motionless, with a grave face, he raised his hands slightly at me in a gesture which meant clearly, "Heavens! what a narrow escape!" Narrow indeed. I think I had come creeping quietly as near insanity as any man who has not actually gone over the border. That gesture restrained me, so to speak.

The mate with the terrific whiskers was now putting the ship on the other tack. In the moment of profound silence which follows upon the hands going to their stations I heard on the poop his raised voice: "Hard alee!" and the distant shout of the order repeated on the main-deck. The sails, in that light breeze, made but a faint fluttering noise. It ceased. The ship was coming round slowly: I held my breath in the renewed stillness of expectation; one wouldn't have thought that there was a single living soul on her decks. A sudden brisk shout, "Mainsail haul!" broke the spell, and in the noisy cries and rush overhead of the men running away with the main brace we two, down in my cabin, came together in our usual position by the bed place.

He did not wait for my question. "I heard him fumbling here and just managed to squat myself down in the bath," he whispered to me. "The fellow only opened the door and put his arm in to hang the coat up. All the same—"

"I never thought of that," I whispered back, even more appalled than before at the closeness of the shave, and marveling at that something unyielding in his character which was carrying him through so finely. There was no agitation in his whisper. Whoever was being driven distracted, it was not he. He was sane. And the proof of his sanity was continued when he took up the whispering again.

"It would never do for me to come to life again."

It was something that a ghost might have said. But what he was alluding to was his old captain's reluctant admission of the theory of suicide. It would obviously serve his turn—if I had understood at all the view which seemed to govern the unalterable purpose of his action.

"You must maroon me as soon as ever you can get amongst these islands off the Cambodge shore," he went on.

"Maroon you! We are not living in a boy's adventure tale," I protested. His scornful whispering took me up.

"We aren't indeed! There's nothing of a boy's tale in this. But there's nothing else for it. I want no more. You don't suppose I am afraid of what can be done to me? Prison or gallows or whatever they may please. But you don't see me coming back to explain such things to an old fellow in a wig and twelve respectable tradesmen, do you? What can they know whether I am guilty or not—or of *what* I am guilty, either? That's my affair. What does the Bible say? 'Driven off the face of the earth.' Very well, I am off the face of the earth now. As I came at night so I shall go."

"Impossible!" I murmured. "You can't."

"Can't? . . . Not naked like a soul on the Day of Judgment. I shall freeze on to this sleeping suit. The Last Day is not yet—and . . . you have understood thoroughly. Didn't you?"

I felt suddenly ashamed of myself. I may say truly that I understood—and my hesitation in letting that man swim away from my ship's side had been a mere sham sentiment, a sort of cowardice.

"It can't be done now till next night," I breathed out. "The ship is on the off-shore tack and the wind may fail us."

"As long as I know that you understand," he whispered. "But of course you do. It's a great satisfaction to have got somebody to understand. You seem to have been there on purpose." And in the same whisper, as if we two whenever we talked had to say things to each other which were not fit for the world to hear, he added, "It's very wonderful."

We remained side by side talking in our secret way—but sometimes silent or just exchanging a whispered word or two at long intervals. And as usual he stared through the port. A breath of wind came now and again into our faces. The ship might have been moored in dock, so gently and on an even keel she slipped through the water, that did not murmur even at our passage, shadowy and silent like a phantom sea.

At midnight I went on deck, and to my mate's great surprise put the ship round on the other tack. His terrible whiskers flitted round me in silent criticism. I certainly should not have done it if it had been only a question of getting out of that sleepy gulf as quickly as possible. I believe he told the second mate, who relieved him, that it was a great want of judgment. The other only yawned. That intolerable cub shuffled about so sleepily and lolled against the rails in such a slack, improper fashion that I came down on him sharply.

"Aren't you properly awake yet?"

"Yes, sir! I am awake."

"Well, then, be good enough to hold yourself as if you were. And keep a lookout. If there's any current we'll be closing with some islands before daylight."

The east side of the gulf is fringed with islands, some solitary, others in groups. On the blue background of the high coast they seem to float on silvery patches of calm water, arid and gray, or dark green and rounded like clumps of evergreen bushes, with the larger ones, a mile or two long, showing the outlines of ridges, ribs of gray rock under the dank mantle of matted leafage. Unknown to trade, to travel, almost to geography, the manner of life they harbor is an unsolved secret. There must be villages—settlements of fishermen at least—on the largest of them, and some communication with the world is probably kept up by native craft. But all that forenoon, as we headed for them, fanned along by the faintest of breezes, I saw no sign of man or canoe in the field of the telescope I kept on pointing at the scattered group.

At noon I gave no orders for a change of course, and the mate's whiskers became much concerned and seemed to be offering themselves unduly to my notice. At last I said:

"I am going to stand right in. Quite in—as far as I can take her."

The stare of extreme surprise imparted an air of ferocity also to his eyes, and he looked truly terrific for a moment.

"We're not doing well in the middle of the gulf," I continued, casually. "I am going to look for the land breezes tonight."

"Bless my soul! Do you mean, sir, in the dark amongst the lot of all them islands and reefs and shoals?"

"Well—if there are any regular land breezes at all on this coast one must get close inshore to find them, mustn't one?"

"Bless my soul!" he exclaimed again under his breath. All that afternoon he wore a dreamy, contemplative appearance which in him was a mark of perplexity. After dinner I went into my stateroom as if I meant to take some rest. There we two bent our dark heads over a half-unrolled chart lying on my bed.

"There," I said. "It's got to be Koh-ring. I've been looking at it ever since sunrise. It has got two hills and a low point. It must be inhabited. And on the coast opposite there is what looks like the mouth of a biggish river—with some towns, no doubt, not far up. It's the best chance for you that I can see."

"Anything. Koh-ring let it be."

He looked thoughtfully at the chart as if surveying chances and distances from a lofty height—and following with his eyes his own figure wandering on the blank land of Cochin-China, and then passing off that piece of paper clean out of sight into uncharted regions. And it was as if the ship had two captains to plan her course for her. I had been so worried and restless running up and down that I had not had the patience to dress that day. I had remained in my sleeping suit, with straw slippers and a soft floppy hat. The closeness of the heat in the gulf had been most oppressive, and the crew were used to seeing me wandering in that airy attire.

"She will clear the south point as she heads now," I whispered into his ear. "Goodness only knows when, though, but certainly after dark. I'll edge her in to half a mile, as far as I may be able to judge in the dark—"

"Be careful," he murmured, warningly—and I realized suddenly that all my future, the only future for which I was fit, would perhaps go irretrievably to pieces in any mishap to my first command.

I could not stop a moment longer in the room. I motioned him to get out of sight and made my way on the poop. That unplayful cub had the watch. I walked up and down for a while thinking things out, then beckoned him over.

"Send a couple of hands to open the two quarter-deck ports," I said, mildly.

He actually had the impudence, or else so forgot himself in his wonder at such an incomprehensible order, as to repeat:

"Open the quarter-deck ports! What for, sir?"

"The only reason you need concern yourself about is because I tell you to do so. Have them open wide and fastened properly."

He reddened and went off, but I believe made some jeering remark to the carpenter as to the sensible practice of ventilating a ship's quarter-deck. I know he popped into the mate's cabin to impart the fact to him because the whiskers came on deck, as it were by chance, and stole glances at me from below—for signs of lunacy or drunkenness, I suppose.

A little before supper, feeling more restless than ever, I rejoined, for a moment, my second self. And to find him sitting so quietly was surprising, like something against nature, inhuman.

I developed my plan in a hurried whisper.

"I shall stand in as close as I dare and then put her round. I will presently find means to smuggle you out of here into the sail locker, which communicates with the lobby. But there is an opening, a sort of square for hauling the sails out, which gives straight on the quarterdeck and which is never closed in fine weather, so as to give air to the sails. When the ship's way is deadened in stays and all the hands are aft at the main braces you will have a clear road to slip out and get overboard through the open quarter-deck port. I've had them both fastened up. Use a rope's end to lower yourself into the water so as to avoid a splash—you know. It could be heard and cause some beastly complication."

He kept silent for a while, then whispered, "I understand."

"I won't be there to see you go," I began with an effort. "The rest . . . I only hope I have understood, too."

"You have. From first to last"—and for the first time there seemed to be a faltering, something strained in his whisper. He caught hold of my arm, but the ringing of the supper bell made me start. He didn't though; he only released his grip.

After supper I didn't come below again till well past eight o'clock. The faint, steady breeze was loaded with dew; and the wet, darkened sails held all there was of propelling power in it. The night, clear and starry, sparkled darkly, and the opaque, lightless patches shifting slowly against the low stars were the drifting islets. On the port bow there was a big one more distant and shadowily imposing by the great space of sky it eclipsed.

On opening the door I had a back view of my very own self looking at a chart. He had come out of the recess and was standing near the table.

"Quite dark enough," I whispered.

He stepped back and leaned against my bed with a level, quiet glance. I sat on the couch. We had nothing to say to each other. Over our heads the officer of the watch moved here and there. Then I heard him move quickly. I knew what that meant. He was making for the companion; and presently his voice was outside my door.

"We are drawing in pretty fast, sir. Land looks rather close."

"Very well," I answered. "I am coming on deck directly."

I waited till he was gone out of the cuddy, then rose. My double moved too. The time had come to exchange our last whispers, for neither of us was ever to hear each other's natural voice.

"Look here!" I opened a drawer and took out three sovereigns. "Take this anyhow. I've got six and I'd give you the lot, only I must keep a little money to buy some fruit and vegetables for the crew from native boats as we go through Sunda Straits."

He shook his head.

"Take it," I urged him, whispering desperately. "No one can tell what—"

He smiled and slapped meaningly the only pocket of the sleeping jacket. It was not safe, certainly. But I produced a large old silk handkerchief of mine, and tying the three pieces of gold in a corner, pressed it on him. He was touched, I supposed, because he took it at last and tied it quickly round his waist under the jacket, on his bare skin.

Our eyes met; several seconds elapsed, till, our glances still mingled, I extended my hand and turned the lamp out. Then I passed through the cuddy, leaving the door of my room wide open. . . . "Steward!"

He was still lingering in the pantry in the greatness of his zeal, giving a rub-up to a plated cruet stand the last thing before going to bed. Being careful not to wake up the mate, whose room was opposite, I spoke in an undertone.

He looked round anxiously. "Sir!"

"Can you get me a little hot water from the galley?"

"I am afraid, sir, the galley fire's been out for some time now."

"Go and see."

He flew up the stairs.

"Now," I whispered, loudly, into the saloon—too loudly, perhaps, but I was afraid I couldn't make a sound. He was by my side in an instant—the double captain slipped past the stairs—through a tiny dark passage . . . a sliding door. We were in the sail locker, scrambling on our knees over the sails. A sudden thought struck me. I saw myself wandering barefooted, bareheaded, the sun beating on my dark poll. I snatched off my floppy hat and tried hurriedly in the dark to ram it on my other self. He dodged and fended off silently. I wonder what he thought had come to me before he understood and suddenly desisted. Our hands met gropingly, lingered united in a steady, motionless clasp for a second. . . . No word was breathed by either of us when they separated.

I was standing quietly by the pantry door when the steward returned.

"Sorry, sir. Kettle barely warm. Shall I light the spirit lamp?"

"Never mind."

I came out on deck slowly. It was now a matter of conscience to shave the land as close as possible—for now he must go overboard whenever the ship was put in stays. Must! There could be no going back for him. After a moment I walked over the leeward and my heart flew into my mouth at the nearness of the land on the bow. Under any other circumstances I would not have held on a minute longer. The second mate had followed me anxiously.

I looked on till I felt I could command my voice.

"She will weather," I said then in a quiet tone.

"Are you going to try that, sir?" he stammered out incredulously.

I took no notice of him and raised my tone just enough to be heard by the helmsman.

"Keep her good full."

"Good full, sir."

The wind fanned my cheek, the sails slept, the world was silent. The strain of watching the dark loom of the land grow bigger and denser was too much for me. I had shut my eyes—because the ship must go closer. She must! The stillness was intolerable. Were we standing still?

When I opened my eyes the second view started my heart with a thump. The black southern hill of Koh-ring seemed to hang right over the ship like a towering fragment of the ever-lasting night. On that enormous mass of blackness there was not a gleam to be seen, not a sound to be heard. It was gliding irresistibly towards us and yet seemed already within reach of the hand. I saw the vague figures of the watch grouped in the waist, gazing in awed silence.

"Are you going on, sir?" inquired an unsteady voice at my elbow.

I ignored it. I had to go on.

"Keep her full. Don't check her way. That won't do now," I said, warningly.

"I can't see the sails very well," the helmsman answered me, in strange, quavering tones.

Was she close enough? Already she was, I won't say in the shadow of the land, but in the very blackness of it, already swallowed up as it were, gone too close to be recalled, gone from me altogether.

"Give the mate a call," I said to the young man who stood at my elbow as still as death. "And turn all hands up."

My tone had a borrowed loudness reverberated from the height of the land. Several voices cried out together; "We are all on deck, sir."

Then stillness again, with the great shadow gliding closer, towering higher, without a light, without a sound. Such a hush had fallen on the ship that she might have been a bark of the dead floating in slowly under the very gate of Erebus.

"My God! Where are we?"

It was the mate moaning at my elbow. He was thunderstruck, and as it were deprived of the moral support of his whiskers. He clapped his hands and absolutely cried out, "Lost!"

"Be quiet," I said, sternly.

He lowered his tone, but I saw the shadowy gesture of his despair. "What are we doing here?"

"Looking for the land wind."

He made as if to tear his hair, and addressed me recklessly.

"She will never get out. You have done it, sir. I knew it'd end in something like this. She will never weather, and you are too close now to stay. She'll drift ashore before she's round. O my God!"

I caught his arm as he was raising it to batter his poor devoted head, and shook it violently.

"She's ashore already," he wailed, trying to tear himself away.

"Is she? . . . Keep good full there!"

"Good full, sir," cried the helmsman in a frightened, thin, childlike voice.

I hadn't let go the mate's arm and went on shaking it. "Ready about, do you hear? You go forward"—shake—"and stop there"—shake—"and hold your noise"—shake—"and see these head-sheets properly overhauled"—shake, shake—shake.

And all the time I dared not look towards the land lest my heart should fail me. I released my grip at last and he ran forward as if fleeing for dear life.

I wondered what my double there in the sail locker thought of this commotion. He was able to hear everything—and perhaps he was able to understand why, on my conscience, it had to be thus close—no less. My first order "Hard alee!" re-echoed ominously under the towering shadow of Koh-ring as if I had shouted in a mountain gorge. And then I watched the land intently. In that smooth water and light wind it was impossible to feel the ship coming-to. No! I could not feel her. And my second self was making now ready to ship out and lower himself overboard. Perhaps he was gone already . . . ?

The great black mass brooding over our very mastheads began to pivot away from the ship's side silently. And now I forgot the secret stranger ready to depart, and remembered only that I was a total stranger to the ship. I did not know her. Would she do it? How was she to be handled?

I swung the mainyard and waited helplessly. She was perhaps stopped, and her very fate hung in the balance, with the black mass of Koh-ring like the gate of the everlasting night towering over her taffrail. What would she do now? Had she way on her yet? I stepped to the side swiftly, and on the shadowy water I could see nothing except a faint phosphorescent flash revealing the glassy smoothness of the sleeping surface. It was impossible to tell—and I had not learned yet the feel of my ship. Was she moving? What I needed was something easily seen, a piece of paper, which I could throw overboard and watch. I had nothing on me. To run down for it I didn't dare. There was no time. All at once my strained, yearning stare distinguished a white object floating within a yard of the ship's side. White on the black water. A phosphorescent flash passed under it. What was that thing? . . . I recognized my own floppy hat. It must have fallen off his head . . . and he didn't bother. Now I had what I wanted—the saving mark for my eyes. But I hardly thought of my other self, now gone from the ship, to be hidden forever from all friendly faces, to be a fugitive and a vagabond on the earth, with no brand of the curse on his sane forehead to stay a slaying hand . . . too proud to explain.

And I watched the hat—the expression of my sudden pity for his mere flesh. It had been meant to save his homeless head from the dangers of the sun. And now—behold—it was saving the ship, by serving me for a mark to help out the ignorance of my strangeness. Ha! it was drifting forward, warning me just in time that the ship had gathered sternway.

"Shift the helm," I said in a low voice to the seaman standing still like a statue.

The man's eyes glistened wildly in the binnacle light as he jumped round to the other side and spun round the wheel.

I walked to the break of the poop. On the overshadowed deck all hands stood by the forebraces waiting for my order. The stars ahead seemed to be gliding from right to left. And all was so still in the world that I heard the quiet remark, "She's round," passed in a tone of intense relief between two seamen.

"Let go and haul."

The foreyards ran round with a great noise, amidst cheery cries. And now the frightful whiskers made themselves heard giving various orders. Already the ship was drawing ahead. And I was alone with her. Nothing! no one in the world should stand now between us, throwing a shadow on the way of silent knowledge and mute affection, the perfect communion of a seaman with his first command.

Walking to the taffrail, I was in time to make out, on the very edge of a darkness thrown by a towering black mass like the very gateway of Erebus—yes, I was in time to catch an evanescent glimpse of my white hat left behind to mark the spot where the secret sharer of my cabin and of my thoughts, as though he were my second self, had lowered himself into the water to take his punishment: a free man, a proud swimmer striking out for a new destiny.

Questions for Study

1. In what way does the narrator's speech differ from that of Captain Archbold and Leggatt?
2. Is the repetition of the word "double" and its synonyms justified? Explain your answer.
3. Analyze the paragraph on p. 268 beginning "A little before supper . . . ," indicating how the two sentences develop the mood of the captain at this point. What is the effect of the placement of key words in the sentences, especially at the end of each one?
4. What is the purpose of the images contrasting light and dark that begin in paragraph three with "a swarm of stars" and "the shadowy earth" and continue throughout the story to the picture of the "white object" on the "black water" at the end?
5. Why is Leggatt compared to "a headless corpse" while he is in the water?
6. What is the significance of the allusion to Erebus near the end of the story?

Topics for Discussion and Writing

1. Discuss the style of the paragraph on p. 271 beginning "I swung the mainyard and waited helplessly," analyzing diction, sentences, and figures of speech in order to show how the passage is integrated with the situation and the captain's mental state.
2. Discuss the diction of the narrator and explain how it reflects his position, background, and mode of thinking.
3. Discuss the images of the stranger and the secret sharer in order to show how they develop the theme of the story.
4. Analyze the style of the captain's narrative in the last two paragraphs and indicate how it reveals the changes that have taken place in him.

STORIES FOR FURTHER STUDY

JACK LONDON

To Build a Fire

Day had broken cold and gray, exceedingly cold and gray, when the man turned aside from the main Yukon trail and climbed the high earth-bank, where a dim and little-travelled trail led eastward through the fat spruce timberland. It was a steep bank, and he paused for breath at the top, excusing the act to himself by looking at his watch. It was nine o'clock. There was no sun nor hint of sun, though there was not a cloud in the sky. It was a clear day, and yet there seemed an intangible pall over the face of things, a subtle bloom that made the day dark, and that was due to the absence of sun. This fact did not worry the man. He was used to the lack of sun. It had been days since he had seen the sun, and he knew that a few more days must pass before that cheerful orb, due south, would just peep above the sky line and dip immediately from view.

The man flung a look back along the way he had come. The Yukon lay a mile wide and hidden under three feet of ice. On top of this ice were as many feet of snow. It was all pure white, rolling in gentle undulations where the ice jams of the freeze-up had formed. North and south, as far as his eye could see, it was unbroken white, save for a dark hairline that curved and twisted from around the spruce-covered island to the south, and that curved and twisted away into the north, where it disappeared behind another spruce-covered island. This dark hairline was the trail—the main trail—that led south five hundred miles to the Chilcoot Pass, Dyea, and salt water; and that led north seventy miles to Dawson, and still on to the north a thousand miles to Nulato, and finally to St. Michael, on Bering Sea, a thousand miles and half a thousand more.

But all this—the mysterious, far-reaching hairline trail, the absence of sun from the sky, the tremendous cold, and the strangeness and weirdness of it all—made no impression on the man. It was not because he was long used to it. He was a newcomer in the land, a *chechaquo*, and this was his first winter. The trouble with him was that he was without imagination. He was quick and alert in the things of life, but only in the things, and not in the significances. Fifty degrees below zero meant eighty-odd degrees of frost. Such fact impressed him as being cold and uncomfortable, and that was all. It did not lead him to meditate upon his frailty as a creature of temperature, and upon man's frailty in general, able only to live within certain narrow limits of heat and cold; and from thereon it did not lead him to the conjectural field of immortality and man's place in the universe. Fifty degrees below zero stood for a bit of frost that hurt and that must be guarded against by the use of mittens, ear flaps, warm moccasins, and thick socks. Fifty degrees below zero was to him just precisely fifty degrees below zero. That there should be anything more to it than that was a thought that never entered his head.

As he turned to go on, he spat speculatively. There was a sharp, explosive crackle that startled him. He spat again. And again, in the air, before it could fall to the snow, the spittle crackled. He knew that at fifty below spittle crackled on the snow, but this spittle had crackled in the air. Undoubtedly it was colder than fifty below—how much colder he did not know. But the temperature did not matter. He was bound for the old claim on the left fork of Henderson Creek, where the boys were already. They had come over across the divide from the Indian Creek country, while he had come the roundabout way to take a look at the possibilities of getting out logs in the spring from the islands in the Yukon. He would be in to camp by six o'clock; a bit after dark, it was true, but the boys would be there, a fire would be going, and a hot supper would be ready. As for lunch, he pressed his hand against the protruding bundle under his jacket. It was also under his shirt, wrapped up in a handkerchief and lying against the naked skin. It was the only way to keep the biscuits from freezing. He smiled agreeably to himself as he thought of those biscuits, each cut open and sopped in bacon grease, and each enclosing a generous slice of fried bacon.

He plunged in among the big spruce trees. The trail was faint. A foot of snow had fallen since the last sled had passed over, and he was glad he was without a sled, travelling light. In fact, he carried nothing but the lunch wrapped in the handkerchief. He was surprised, however, at the cold. It certainly was cold, he concluded, as he rubbed his numb nose and cheekbones with his mittened hand. He was a warm-whiskered man, but the hair on his face did not protect the high cheekbones and the eager nose that thrust itself aggressively into the frosty air.

At the man's heels trotted a dog, a big native husky, the proper wolf dog, gray-coated and without any visible or temperamental difference from its brother, the wild wolf. The animal was depressed by the tremendous cold. It knew that it was no time for travelling. Its instinct told it a truer tale than was told to the man by the man's judgment. In reality, it was not merely colder than fifty below zero; it was colder than sixty below, than seventy below. It was seventy-five below zero. Since the freezing point is thirty-two above zero, it meant that one hundred and seven degrees of frost obtained. The dog did not know anything about thermometers. Possibly in its brain there was no sharp consciousness of a condition of very cold such as was in the man's brain. But the brute had its instinct. It experienced a vague but menacing apprehension that subdued it and made it slink along at the man's heels, and that made it question eagerly every unwonted movement of the man as if expecting him to go into camp or to seek shelter somewhere and build a fire. The dog had learned fire, and it wanted fire, or else to burrow under the snow and cuddle its warmth away from the air.

The frozen moisture of its breathing had settled on its fur in a fine powder of frost, and especially were its jowls, muzzle, and eyelashes whitened by its crystalled breath. The man's red beard and mustache were likewise frosted, but more solidly, the deposit taking the form of ice and increasing with every warm, moist breath he exhaled. Also, the man was chewing tobacco, and the muzzle of ice held his lips so rigidly that he was unable to clear his chin when he expelled the juice. The result was that a crystal beard of the color and solidity of amber was increasing its length on his chin. If he fell down it would shatter itself, like glass, into brittle fragments. But he did not mind the appendage. It was the penalty all tobacco chewers paid in that country, and he had been out before in two cold snaps. They had not been so cold as this, he knew, but by the spirit thermometer at Sixty Mile he knew they had been registered at fifty below and at fifty-five.

He held on through the level stretch of woods for several miles, crossed a wide flat of nigger heads, and dropped down a bank to the frozen bed of a small stream. This was Henderson Creek, and he knew he was ten miles from the forks. He looked at his watch. It was ten o'clock. He was making four miles an hour, and he calculated that he would arrive at the forks at half-past twelve. He decided to celebrate that event by eating his lunch there.

The dog dropped in again at his heels, with a tail drooping discouragement, as the man swung along the creek bed. The furrow of the old sled trail was plainly visible, but a dozen inches of snow covered the marks of the last runners. In a month no man had come up or down that silent creek. The man held steadily on. He was not much given to thinking, and just then particularly he had nothing to think about save that he would eat lunch at the forks and that at six o'clock he would be in camp with the boys. There was nobody to talk to; and, had there been, speech would have been impossible because of the ice muzzle on his mouth. So he continued monotonously to chew tobacco and to increase the length of his amber beard.

Once in a while the thought reiterated itself that it was very cold and that he had never experienced such cold. As he walked along he rubbed his cheekbones and nose with the back of his mittened hand. He did this automatically, now and again changing hands. But, rub as he would, the instant he stopped his cheekbones went numb, and the following instant the end of his nose went numb. He was sure to frost his cheeks; he knew that, and experienced a pang of regret that he had not devised a nose strap of the sort Bud wore in cold snaps. Such a strap passed across the cheeks, as well, and saved them. But it didn't matter much, after all. What were frosted cheeks? A bit painful, that was all; they were never serious.

Empty as the man's mind was of thoughts, he was keenly observant, and he noticed the changes in the creek, the curves and bends and timber jams, and always he sharply noted where he placed his feet. Once, coming around a bend, he shied abruptly, like a startled horse, curved away from the place where he had been walking, and retreated several paces back along the trail. The creek he knew was frozen clear to the bottom—no creek could contain water in that arctic winter—but he knew also that there were springs that bubbled out from the hillsides and ran along under the snow and on top the ice of the creek. He knew that the coldest snaps never froze these springs, and he knew likewise their danger. They were traps. They hid pools of water under the snow that might be three inches deep, or three feet. Sometimes a skin of ice half an inch thick covered them, and in turn was covered by the snow. Sometimes there were alternate layers of water and ice skin, so that when one broke through he kept on breaking through for a while, sometimes wetting himself to the waist.

That was why he had shied in such panic. He had felt the give under his feet and heard the crackle of a snow-hidden ice skin. And to get his feet wet in such a temperature meant trouble and danger. At the very least it meant delay, for he would be forced to stop and build a fire, and under its protection to bare his feet while he dried his socks and moccasins. He stood and studied the creek bed and its banks, and decided that the flow of water came from the right. He reflected awhile, rubbing his nose and cheeks, then skirted to the left, stepping gingerly and testing the footing of each step. Once clear of the danger, he took a fresh chew of tobacco and swung along at his four-mile gait.

In the course of the next two hours he came upon several similar traps. Usually the snow above the hidden pools had a sunken, candied appearance that advertised the danger. Once again, however, he had a close call, and once, suspecting danger, he compelled the dog to go on in front. The dog did not want to go. It hung back until the man shoved it forward, and then it went quickly across the white, unbroken surface. Suddenly it broke through, floundered to one side, and got away to firmer footing. It had wet its forefeet and legs, and almost immediately the water that clung to it turned to ice. It made quick efforts to lick the ice off its legs, then dropped down in the snow and began to bite out the ice that had formed between the toes. This was a matter of instinct. To permit the ice to remain would mean sore feet. It did not know this. It merely obeyed the mysterious prompting that arose from the deep crypts of its being. But the man knew, having achieved a judgment on the subject, and he removed the mitten from his right hand and helped tear out the ice particles. He did not expose his fingers more than a minute, and was astonished at the swift numbness that smote them. It certainly was cold. He pulled on the mitten hastily, and beat the hand savagely across his chest.

At twelve o'clock the day was at its brightest. Yet the sun was too far south on its winter journey to clear the horizon. The bulge of the earth intervened between it and Henderson Creek, where the man walked under a clear sky at noon and cast no shadow. At half-past twelve, to the minute, he arrived at the forks of the creek. He was pleased at the speed he had made. If he kept it up, he would certainly be with the boys by six. He unbuttoned his jacket and shirt and drew forth his lunch. The action consumed no more than a quarter of a minute, yet in that brief moment the numbness laid hold of the exposed fingers. He did not put the mitten on, but, instead, struck the fingers a dozen sharp smashes against his leg. Then he sat down on a snow-covered log to eat. The sting that followed upon the striking of his fingers against his leg ceased so quickly that he was startled. He had had no chance to take a bite of biscuit. He struck the fingers repeatedly and returned them to the mitten, baring the other hand for the purpose of eating. He tried to take a mouthful, but the ice muzzle prevented. He had forgotten to build a fire and thaw out. He chuckled at his foolishness, and as he chuckled he noted the numbness creeping into the exposed fingers. Also, he noted that the stinging which had first come to his toes when he sat down was already passing away. He wondered whether the toes were warm or numb. He moved them inside the moccasins and decided that they were numb.

He pulled the mitten on hurriedly and stood up. He was a bit frightened. He stamped up and down until the stinging returned into the feet. It certainly was cold, was his thought. That man from Sulphur Creek had spoken the truth when telling how cold it sometimes got in the country. And he had laughed at him at the time! That showed one must not be too sure of things. There was no mistake about it, it *was* cold. He strode up and down, stamping his feet and threshing his arms, until reassured by the returning warmth. Then he got out matches and proceeded to make a fire. From the undergrowth, where high water of the previous spring had lodged a supply of seasoned logs, he got his firewood. Working carefully from a small beginning, he soon had a roaring fire, over which he thawed the ice from his face and in the protection of which he ate his biscuits. For the moment the cold of space was outwitted. The dog took satisfaction in the fire, stretching out close enough for warmth and far enough away to escape being singed.

When the man had finished, he filled his pipe and took his comfortable time over a smoke. Then he pulled on his mittens, settled the ear flaps of his cap firmly about his ears, and took the creek trail up the left fork. The dog was disappointed and yearned back toward the fire. This man did not know cold. Possibly all the generations of his ancestry had been ignorant of cold, of real cold, of cold one hundred and seven degrees below freezing point. But the dog knew; all its ancestry knew, and it had inherited the knowledge. And it knew that it was not good to walk abroad in such fearful cold. It was the time to lie snug in a hole in the snow and wait for a curtain of cloud to be drawn across the face of outer space whence this cold came. On the other hand, there was no keen intimacy between the dog and the man. The one was the toil slave of the other, and the only caresses it had ever received were the caresses of the whip lash and of harsh and menacing throat sounds that threatened the whip lash. So the dog made no effort to communicate its apprehension to the man. It was not concerned in the welfare of the man; it was for its own sake that it yearned back toward the fire. But the man whistled, and spoke to it with the sound of whip lashes, and the dog swung in at the man's heels and followed after.

The man took a chew of tobacco and proceeded to start a new amber beard. Also, his moist breath quickly powdered with white his mustache, eyebrows, and lashes. There did not seem to be so many springs on the left fork of the Henderson, and for half an hour the man saw no signs of any. And then it happened. At a place where there were no signs, where the soft, unbroken snow seemed to advertise solidity beneath, the man broke through. It was not deep. He wet himself halfway to the knees before he floundered out to the firm crust.

He was angry, and cursed his luck aloud. He had hoped to get into camp with the boys at six o'clock, and this would delay him an hour, for he would have to build a fire and dry out his footgear. This was imperative at that low temperature—he knew that much; and he turned aside to the bank, which he climbed. On top, tangled in the underbrush about the trunks of several small spruce trees, was a high-water deposit of dry firewood—sticks and twigs, principally, but also larger portions of seasoned branches and fine, dry, last year's grasses. He threw down several large pieces on top of the snow. This served for a foundation and prevented the young flame from drowning itself in the snow it otherwise would melt. The flame he got by touching a match to a small shred of birch bark that he took from his pocket. This burned even more readily than paper. Placing it on the foundation, he fed the young flame with wisps of dry grass and with the tiniest dry twigs.

He worked slowly and carefully, keenly aware of his danger. Gradually, as the flame grew stronger, he increased the size of the twigs with which he fed it. He squatted in the snow, pulling the twigs out from their entanglement in the brush and feeding directly to the flame. He knew there must be no failure. When it is seventy-five below zero, a man must not fail in his first attempt to build a fire—that is, if his feet are wet. If his feet are dry, and he fails, he can run along the trail for half a mile and restore his circulation. But the circulation of wet and freezing feet cannot be restored by running when it is seventy-five below. No matter how fast he runs, the wet feet will freeze the harder.

All this the man knew. The old-timer on Sulphur Creek had told him about it the previous fall, and now he was appreciating the advice. Already all sensation had gone out of his feet. To build the fire he had been forced to remove his mittens, and the fingers had quickly gone numb. His pace of four miles an hour had kept his heart pumping blood to the surface of his body and to all the extremities. But the instant he stopped, the action of the pump eased down. The cold of space smote the unprotected tip of the planet, and he, being on that unprotected tip, received the full force of the blow. The blood of his body recoiled before it. The blood was alive, like the dog, and like the dog it wanted to hide away and cover itself up from the fearful cold. So long as he walked four miles an hour, he pumped that blood, willy-nilly, to the surface; but now it ebbed away and sank down into the recesses of his body. The extremities were the first to feel its absence. His wet feet froze the faster, and his exposed fingers numbed the faster, though they had not yet begun to freeze. Nose and cheeks were already freezing, while the skin of all his body chilled as it lost its blood.

But he was safe. Toes and nose and cheeks would be only touched by the frost, for the fire was beginning to burn with strength. He was feeding it with twigs the size of his finger. In another minute he would be able to feed it with branches the size of his wrist, and then he could remove his wet footgear, and, while it dried, he could keep his naked feet warm by the fire, rubbing them at first, of course, with snow. The fire was a success. He was safe. He remembered the advice of the old-timer on Sulphur Creek, and smiled. The old-timer had been very serious in laying down the law that no man must travel alone in the Klondike after fifty below. Well, here he was; he had had the accident; he was alone; and he had saved himself. Those old-timers were rather womanish, some of them, he thought. All a man had to do was to keep his head, and he was all right. Any man who was a man could travel alone. But it was surprising, the rapidity with which his cheeks and nose were freezing. And he had not thought his fingers could go lifeless in so short a time. Lifeless they were, for he could scarcely make them move together to grip a twig, and they seemed remote from his body and from him. When he touched a twig, he had to look and see whether or not he had hold of it. The wires were pretty well down between him and his finger ends.

All of which counted for little. There was the fire, snapping and crackling and promising life with every dancing flame. He started to untie his moccasins.

They were coated with ice; the thick German socks were like sheaths of iron halfway to the knees; and the moccasin strings were rods of steel all twisted and knotted as by some conflagration. For a moment he tugged with his numb fingers, then, realizing the folly of it, he drew his sheath knife.

But before he could cut the strings, it happened. It was his own fault or, rather, his mistake. He should not have built the fire under the spruce tree. He should have built it in the open. But it had been easier to pull the twigs from the brush and drop them directly on the fire. Now the tree under which he had done this carried a weight of snow on its boughs. No wind had blown for weeks, and each bough was fully freighted. Each time he had pulled a twig he had communicated a slight agitation to the tree—an imperceptible agitation, so far as he was concerned, but an agitation sufficient to bring about the disaster. High up in the tree one bough capsized its load of snow. This fell on the boughs beneath, capsizing them. This process continued, spreading out and involving the whole tree. It grew like an avalanche, and it descended without warning upon the man and the fire, and the fire was blotted out! Where it had burned was a mantle of fresh and disordered snow.

The man was shocked. It was as though he had just heard his own sentence of death. For a moment he sat and stared at the spot where the fire had been. Then he grew very calm. Perhaps the old-timer on Sulphur Creek was right. If he had only had a trail mate he would have been in no danger now. The trail mate could have built the fire. Well, it was up to him to build the fire over again, and this second time there must be no failure. Even if he succeeded, he would most likely lose some toes. His feet must be badly frozen by now, and there would be some time before the second fire was ready.

Such were his thoughts, but he did not sit and think them. He was busy all the time they were passing through his mind. He made a new foundation for a fire, this time in the open, where no treacherous tree could blot it out. Next he gathered dry grasses and tiny twigs from the high-water flotsam. He could not bring his fingers together to pull them out, but he was able to gather them by the handful. In this way he got many rotten twigs and bits of green moss that were undesirable, but it was the best he could do. He worked methodically, even collecting an armful of the larger branches to be used later when the fire gathered strength. And all the while the dog sat and watched him, a certain yearning wistfulness in its eyes, for it looked upon him as the fire provider, and the fire was slow in coming.

When all was ready, the man reached in his pocket for a second piece of birch bark. He knew the bark was there, and, though he could not feel it with his fingers, he could hear its crisp rustling as he fumbled for it. Try as he would, he could not clutch hold of it. And all the time, in his consciousness, was the knowledge that each instant his feet were freezing. This thought tended to put him in a panic, but he fought against it and kept calm. He pulled on his mittens with his teeth, and threshed his arms back and forth, beating his hands with all his might against his sides. He did this sitting down, and he stood up to do it; and all the while the dog sat in the snow, its wolf brush of a tail curled around warmly over its forefeet, its sharp wolf ears pricked forward intently as it watched the man. And the man, as he beat and threshed with his arms and hands, felt a great surge of envy as he regarded the creature that was warm and secure in its natural covering.

After a time he was aware of the first faraway signals of sensation in his beaten fingers. The faint tingling grew stronger till it evolved into a stinging ache that was excruciating, but which the man hailed with satisfaction. He stripped the mitten from his right hand and fetched forth the birch bark. The exposed fingers were quickly going numb again. Next he brought out his bunch of sulphur matches. But the tremendous cold had already driven the life out of his fingers. In his effort to separate one match from the others, the whole bunch fell in the snow. He tried to pick it out of the snow, but failed. The dead fingers could neither touch nor clutch. He was very careful. He drove the thought of his freezing feet, and nose, and cheeks, out of his mind, devoting his whole soul to the matches. He watched, using the sense of vision in place of that of touch, and when he saw his fingers on each side of the bunch, he closed them—that is, he willed to close them, for the wires were down, and the fingers did not obey. He pulled the mitten on the right hand, and beat it fiercely against his knee. Then, with both mittened hands, he scooped the bunch of matches, along with much snow, into his lap. Yet he was no better off.

After some manipulation he managed to get the bunch between the heels of his mittened hands. In this fashion he carried it to his mouth. The ice crackled and snapped when by a violent effort he opened his mouth. He drew the lower jaw in, curled the upper lip out of the way, and scraped the bunch with his upper teeth in order to separate a match. He succeeded in getting one, which he dropped on his lap. He was no better off. He could not pick it up. Then he devised a way. He picked it up in his teeth and scratched it on his leg. Twenty times he scratched before he succeeded in lighting it. As it flamed he held it with his teeth to the birch bark. But the burning brimstone went up his nostrils and into his lungs, causing him to cough spasmodically. The match fell into the snow and went out.

The old-timer on Sulphur Creek was right, he thought in the moment of controlled despair that ensued: after fifty below, a man should travel with a partner. He beat his hands, but failed in exciting any sensation. Suddenly he bared both hands, removing the mittens with his teeth. He caught the whole bunch between the heels of his hands. His arm muscles not being frozen enabled him to press the hand heels tightly against the matches. Then he scratched the bunch along his leg. It flared into flame, seventy sulphur matches at once! There was no wind to blow them out. He kept his head to one side to escape the strangling fumes, and held the blazing bunch to the birch bark. As he so held it, he became aware of sensation in his hand. His flesh was burning. He could smell it. Deep down below the surface he could feel it. The sensation developed into pain that grew acute. And still he endured it, holding the flame of the matches clumsily to the bark that would not light readily because his own burning hands were in the way, absorbing most of the flame.

At last, when he could endure no more, he jerked his hands apart. The blazing matches fell sizzling into the snow, but the birch bark was alight. He began laying dry grasses and the tiniest twigs on the flame. He could not pick and choose, for he had to lift the fuel between the heels of his hands. Small pieces of rotten wood and green moss clung to the twigs, and he bit them off as well as he could with his teeth. He cherished the flame carefully and awkwardly. It meant life, and it must not perish. The withdrawal of blood from the surface of his body now made him begin to shiver, and he grew more awkward. A large piece of green moss fell squarely on the little fire. He tried to poke it out with his fingers, but his shivering frame made him poke too far, and he disrupted the nucleus of the little fire, the burning grasses and the tiny twigs separating and scattering. He tried to poke them together again, but in spite of the tenseness of the effort, his shivering got away with him, and the twigs were hopelessly scattered. Each twig gushed a puff of smoke and went out. The fire provider had failed. As he looked apathetically about him, his eyes chanced on the dog, sitting across the ruins of the fire from him, in the snow, making restless, hunching movements, slightly lifting one forefoot and then the other, shifting its weight back and forth on them with wistful eagerness.

The sight of the dog put a wild idea into his head. He remembered the tale of the man, caught in a blizzard, who killed a steer and crawled inside the carcass, and so was saved. He would kill the dog and bury his hands in the warm body until the numbness went out of them. Then he could build another fire. He spoke to the dog, calling it to him; but in his voice was a strange note of fear that frightened the animal, who had never known the man to speak in such a way before. Something was the matter, and its suspicious nature sensed danger—it knew not what danger, but somewhere, somehow, in its brain arose an apprehension of the man. It flattened its ears down at the sound of the man's voice, and its restless, hunching movements and the liftings and shiftings of its forefeet became more pronounced; but it would not come to the man. He got on his hands and knees and crawled toward the dog. This unusual posture again excited suspicion, and the animal sidled mincingly away.

The man sat up in the snow for a moment and struggled for calmness. Then he pulled on his mittens, by means of his teeth, and got upon his feet. He glanced down at first in order to assure himself that he was really standing up, for the absence of sensation in his feet left him unrelated to the earth. His erect position in itself started to drive the webs of suspicion from the dog's mind; and when he spoke peremptorily, with the sound of whip lashes in his voice, the dog rendered its customary allegiance and came to him. As it came within reaching distance, the man lost his control. His arms flashed out to the dog, and he experienced genuine surprise when he discovered that his hands could not clutch, that there was neither bend nor feeling in the fingers. He had forgotten for the moment that they were frozen and that they were freezing more and more. All this happened quickly, and before the animal could get away, he encircled its body with his arms. He sat down in the snow, and in this fashion held the dog, while it snarled and whined and struggled.

But it was all he could do, hold its body encircled in his arms and sit there. He realized that he could not kill the dog. There was no way to do it. With his helpless hands he could neither draw nor hold sheath knife nor throttle the animal. He realized it, and it plunged wildly away, with tail between its legs, and still snarling. It halted forty feet away and surveyed him curiously, with ears sharply pricked forward.

The man looked down at his hands in order to locate them, and found them hanging on the ends of his arms. It struck him as curious that one should have to use his eyes in order to find out where his hands were. He began threshing his arms back and forth, beating the mittened hands against his sides. He did this for five minutes, violently, and his heart pumped enough blood up to the surface to put a stop to his shivering. But no sensation was aroused in the hands. He had an impression that they hung like weights on the ends of his arms, but when he tried to run the impression down, he could not find it.

A certain fear of death, dull and oppressive, came to him. This fear quickly became poignant as he realized that it was no longer a mere matter of freezing his fingers and toes, or of losing his hands and feet, but that it was a matter of life and death with the chances against him. This threw him into a panic, and he turned and ran up the creek bed along the old, dim trail. The dog joined in behind and kept up with him. He ran blindly, without intention, in fear such as he had never known in his life. Slowly, as he plowed and floundered through the snow, he began to see things again—the banks of the creek, the old timber jams, the leafless aspens, and the sky. The running made him feel better. He did not shiver. Maybe, if he ran on, his feet would thaw out; and, anyway, if he ran far enough, he would reach camp and the boys. Without doubt he would lose some fingers and toes and some of his face; but the boys would take care of him, and save the rest of him when he got there. And at the same time there was another thought in his mind that said he would never get to the camp and the boys; that it was too many miles away, that the freezing had too great a start on him, and that he would soon be stiff and dead. This thought he kept in the background and refused to consider. Sometimes it pushed itself forward and demanded to be heard, but he thrust it back and strove to think of other things.

It struck him as curious that he could run at all on feet so frozen that he could not feel them when they struck the earth and took the weight of his body. He seemed to himself to skim along above the surface, and to have no connection with the earth. Somewhere he had once seen a winged Mercury, and he wondered if Mercury felt as he felt when skimming over the earth.

His theory of running until he reached camp and the boys had one flaw in it: he lacked the endurance. Several times he stumbled, and finally he tottered, crumpled up, and fell. When he tried to rise, he failed. He must sit and rest, he decided, and next time he would merely walk and keep on going. As he sat and regained his breath, he noted that he was feeling quite warm and comfortable. He was not shivering, and it even seemed that a warm glow had come to his chest and trunk. And yet, when he touched his nose and cheeks, there was no sensation. Running would not thaw them out. Nor would it thaw out his hands and feet. Then the thought came to him that the frozen portions of his body must be extending. He tried to keep his thought down, to forget it, to think of something else; he was aware of the panicky feeling that it caused, and he was afraid of the panic. But the thought asserted itself, and persisted, until it produced a vision of his body totally frozen. This was too much, and he made another wild run along the trail. Once he slowed down to a walk, but the thought of the freezing extending itself made him run again.

And all the time the dog ran with him, at his heels. When he fell down a second time, it curled its tail over its forefeet and sat in front of him, facing him, curiously eager and intent. The warmth and security of the animal angered him, and he cursed it till it flattened down its ears appeasingly. This time the shivering came more quickly upon the man. He was losing in his battle with the frost. It was creeping into his body from all sides. The thought of it drove him on, but he ran no more than a hundred feet, when he staggered and pitched headlong. It was his last panic. When he had recovered his breath and control, he sat up and entertained in his mind the conception of meeting death with dignity. However, the conception did not come to him in such terms. His idea of it was that he had been making a fool of himself, running around like a chicken with its head cut off—such was the simile that occurred to him. Well, he was bound to freeze anyway, and he might as well take it decently. With this new-found peace of mind came the first glimmerings of drowsiness. A good idea, he thought, to sleep off to death. It was like taking an anesthetic. Freezing was not so bad as people thought. There were lots of worse ways to die.

He pictured the boys finding his body next day. Suddenly he found himself with them, coming along the trail and looking for himself. And, still with them, he came around a turn in the trail and found himself lying in the snow. He did not belong with himself any more, for even then he was out of himself, standing with the boys and looking at himself in the snow. It certainly was cold, was his thought. When he got back to the States he could tell the folks what real cold was. He drifted on from this to a vision of the old-timer on Sulphur Creek. He could see him quite clearly, warm and comfortable, and smoking a pipe.

"You were right, old hoss; you were right," the man mumbled to the old-timer of Sulphur Creek.

Then the man drowsed off into what seemed to him the most comfortable and satisfying sleep he had ever known. The dog sat facing him and waiting. The brief day drew to a close in a long, slow twilight. There were no signs of a fire to be made, and, besides, never in a dog's experience had it known a man to sit like that in the snow and make no fire. As the twilight drew on, its eager yearning for the fire mastered it, and with a great lifting and shifting of forefeet, it whined softly, then flatted its ears down in anticipation of being chidden by the man. But the man remained silent. Later the dog whined loudly. And still later it crept close to the man and caught the scent of death. This made the animal bristle and back away. A little longer it delayed, howling under the stars that leaped and danced and shone brightly in the cold sky. Then it turned and trotted up the trail in the direction of the camp it knew, where were the other food providers and fire providers.

AMBROSE BIERCE

A Horseman in the Sky

I

One sunny afternoon in the autumn of the year 1861 a soldier lay in a clump of laurel by the side of a road in western Virginia. He lay at full length upon his stomach, his feet resting upon the toes, his head upon the left forearm. His extended right hand loosely grasped his rifle. But for the somewhat methodical disposition of his limbs and a slight rhythmic movement of the cartridge-box at the back of his belt he might have been thought to be dead. He was asleep at his post of duty. But if detected he would be dead shortly afterward, death being the just and legal penalty of his crime.

The clump of laurel in which the criminal lay was in the angle of a road which after ascending southward a steep acclivity to that point turned sharply to the west, running along the summit for perhaps one hundred yards. There it turned southward again and went zigzagging downward through the forest. At the salient of that second angle was a large flat rock, jutting out northward, overlooking the deep valley from which the road ascended. The rock capped a high cliff; a stone dropped from its outer edge would have fallen sheer downward one thousand feet to the tops of the pines. The angle where the soldier lay was on another spur of the same cliff. Had he been awake he would have commanded a view, not only of the short arm of the road and the jutting rock, but of the entire profile of the cliff below it. It might well have made him giddy to look.

The country was wooded everywhere except at the bottom of the valley to the northward, where there was a small natural meadow, through which flowed a stream scarcely visible from the valley's rim. This open ground looked hardly larger than an ordinary dooryard, but was really several acres in extent. Its green was more vivid than that of the inclosing forest. Away beyond it rose a line of giant cliffs similar to those upon which we are supposed to stand in our survey of the savage scene, and through which the road had somehow made its climb to the summit. The configuration of the valley, indeed, was such that from this point of observation it seemed entirely shut in, and one could but have wondered how the road which found a way out of it had found a way into it, and whence came and whither went the waters of the stream that parted the meadow more than a thousand feet below.

No country is so wild and difficult but men will make it a theatre of war; concealed in the forest at the bottom of that military rattrap, in which half a hundred men in possession of the exits might have starved an army to submission, lay five regiments of Federal infantry. They had marched all the previous day and night and were resting. At nightfall they would take to the road again, climb to the place where their unfaithful sentinel now slept, and descending the other slope of the ridge fall upon a camp of the enemy at about midnight. Their hope was to surprise it, for the road led to the rear of it. In case of failure, their position would be perilous in the extreme; and fail they surely would should accident or vigilance apprise the enemy of the movement.

II

The sleeping sentinel in the clump of laurel was a young Virginian named Carter Druse. He was the son of wealthy parents, an only child, and had known such ease and cultivation and high living as wealth and taste were able to command in the mountain country of western Virginia. His home was but a few miles from where he now lay. One morning he had risen from the breakfast-table and said, quietly but gravely: "Father, a Union regiment has arrived at Grafton. I am going to join it."

The father lifted his leonine head, looked at the son a moment in silence, and replied: "Well, go, sir, and whatever may occur do what you conceive to be your duty. Virginia, to which you are a traitor, must get on without you. Should we both live to the end of the war, we will speak further of the matter. Your mother, as the physician has informed you, is in a most critical condition; at the best she cannot be with us longer than a few weeks, but that time is precious. It would be better not to disturb her."

So Carter Druse, bowing reverently to his father, who returned the salute with a stately courtesy that masked a breaking heart, left the home of his childhood to go soldiering. By conscience and courage, by deeds of devotion and daring, he soon commended himself to his fellows and his officers; and it was to these qualities and to some knowledge of the country that he owed his selection for his present perilous duty at the extreme outpost. Nevertheless, fatigue had been stronger than resolution and he had fallen asleep. What good or bad angel came in a dream to rouse him from his state of crime, who shall say? Without a movement, without a sound, in the profound silence and the languor of the late afternoon, some invisible messenger of fate touched with unsealing finger the eyes of his consciousness—whispered into the ear of his spirit the mysterious awakening word which no human lips ever have spoken, no human memory ever has recalled. He quietly raised his forehead from his arm and looked between the masking stems of the laurels, instinctively closing his right hand about the stock of his rifle.

His first feeling was a keen artistic delight. On a colossal pedestal, the cliff,—motionless at the extreme edge of the capping rock and sharply outlined against the sky,—was an equestrian statue of impressive dignity. The figure of the man sat the figure of the horse, straight and soldierly, but with the repose of a Grecian god carved in the marble which limits the suggestion of activity. The gray costume harmonized with its aërial background; the metal of accoutrement and caparison was softened and subdued by the shadow; the animal's skin had no points of high light. A carbine strikingly foreshortened lay across the pommel of the saddle, kept in place by the right hand grasping it at the "grip"; the left hand, holding the bridle rein, was invisible. In silhouette against the sky the profile of the horse was cut with the sharpness of a cameo; it looked across the heights of air to the confronting cliffs beyond. The face of the rider, turned slightly away, showed only an outline of temple and beard; he was looking downward to the bottom of the valley. Magnified by its lift against the sky and by the soldier's testifying sense of the formidableness of a near enemy the group appeared of heroic, almost colossal, size.

For an instant Druse had a strange, half-defined feeling that he had slept to the end of the war and was looking upon a noble work of art reared upon that eminence to commemorate the deeds of an heroic past of which he had been an inglorious part. The feeling was dispelled by a slight movement of the group: the horse, without moving its feet, had drawn its body slightly backward from the verge; the man remained immobile as before. Broad awake and keenly alive to the significance of the situation, Druse now brought the butt of his rifle against his cheek by cautiously pushing the barrel forward through the bushes, cocked the piece, and glancing through the sights covered a vital spot of the horseman's breast. A touch upon the trigger and all would have been well with Carter Druse. At that instant the horseman turned his head and looked in the direction of his concealed foeman—seemed to look into his very face, into his eyes, into his brave, compassionate heart.

Is it then so terrible to kill an enemy in war—an enemy who has surprised a secret vital to the safety of one's self and comrades—an enemy more formidable for his knowledge than all his army for its numbers? Carter Druse grew pale; he shook in every limb, turned faint, and saw the statuesque group before him as black figures, rising, falling, moving unsteadily in arcs of circles in a fiery sky. His hand fell away from his weapon, his head slowly dropped until his face rested on the leaves in which he lay. This courageous gentleman and hardy soldier was near swooning from intensity of emotion.

It was not for long; in another moment his face was raised from earth, his hands resumed their places on the rifle, his forefinger sought the trigger; mind, heart, and eyes were clear, conscience and reason sound. He could not hope to capture that enemy; to alarm him would but send him dashing to his camp with his fatal news. The duty of the soldier was plain: the man must be shot dead from ambush—without warning, without a moment's spiritual preparation, with never so much as an unspoken prayer, he must be sent to his account. But no—there is a hope; he may have discovered nothing—perhaps he is but admiring the sublimity of the landscape. If permitted, he may turn and ride carelessly away in the direction whence he came. Surely it will be possible to judge at the instant of his withdrawing whether he knows. It may well be that his fixity of attention—Druse turned his head and looked through the deeps of air downward, as from the surface to the bottom of a translucent sea. He saw creeping across the green meadow a sinuous line of figures of men and horses—some foolish commander was permitting the soldiers of his escort to water their beasts in the open, in plain view from a dozen summits!

Druse withdrew his eyes from the valley and fixed them again upon the group of man and horse in the sky, and again it was through the sights of his rifle. But this time his aim was at the horse. In his memory, as if they were a divine mandate, rang the words of his father at their parting: "Whatever may occur, do what you conceive to be your duty." He was calm now. His teeth were firmly but not rigidly closed; his nerves were as tranquil as a sleeping babe's—not a tremor affected any muscle of his body; his breathing, until suspended in the act of taking aim, was regular and slow. Duty had conquered; the spirit had said to the body: "Peace, be still." He fired.

III

An officer of the Federal force, who in a spirit of adventure or in quest of knowledge had left the hidden *bivouac* in the valley, and with aimless feet had made his way to the lower edge of a small open space near the foot of the cliff, was considering what he had to gain by pushing his exploration further. At a distance of a quarter-mile before him, but apparently at a stone's throw, rose from its fringe of pines the gigantic face of rock, towering to so great a height above him that it made him giddy to look up to where its edge cut a sharp, rugged line against the sky. It presented a clean, vertical profile against a background of blue sky to a point half the way down, and of distant hills, hardly less blue, thence to the tops of the trees at its base. Lifting his eyes to the dizzy altitude of its summit the officer saw an astonishing sight—a man on horseback riding down into the valley through the air!

Straight upright sat the rider, in military fashion, with a firm seat in the saddle, a strong clutch upon the rein to hold his charger from too impetuous a plunge. From his bare head his long hair streamed upward, waving like a plume. His hands were concealed in the cloud of the horse's lifted mane. The animal's body was as level as if every hoof-stroke encountered the resistant earth. Its motions were those of a wild gallop, but even as the officer looked they ceased, with all the legs thrown sharply forward as in the act of alighting from a leap. But this was a flight!

Filled with amazement and terror by this apparition of a horseman in the sky—half believing himself the chosen scribe of some new Apocalypse, the officer was overcome by the intensity of his emotions; his legs failed him and he fell. Almost at the same instant he heard a crashing sound in the trees—a sound that died without an echo—and all was still.

The officer rose to his feet, trembling. The familiar sensation of an abraded shin recalled his dazed faculties. Pulling himself together he ran rapidly obliquely away from the cliff to a point distant from its foot; thereabout he expected to find his man; and thereabout he naturally failed. In the fleeting instant of his vision his imagination had been so wrought upon by the apparent grace and ease and intention of the marvelous performance that it did not occur to him that the line of march of aërial cavalry is directly downward, and that he could find the objects of his search at the very foot of the cliff. A half-hour later he returned to camp.

This officer was a wise man; he knew better than to tell an incredible truth. He said nothing of what he had seen. But when the commander asked him if in his scout he had learned anything of advantage to the expedition he answered:

"Yes, sir; there is no road leading down into this valley from the southward."

The commander, knowing better, smiled.

IV

After firing his shot, Private Carter Druse reloaded his rifle and resumed his watch. Ten minutes had hardly passed when a Federal sergeant crept cautiously to him on hands and knees. Druse neither turned his head nor looked at him, but lay without motion or sign of recognition.

"Did you fire?" the sergeant whispered.

"Yes."

"At what?"

"A horse. It was standing on yonder rock—pretty far out. You see it is no longer there. It went over the cliff."

The man's face was white, but he showed no other sign of emotion. Having answered, he turned away his eyes and said no more. The sergeant did not understand.

"See here, Druse," he said, after a moment's silence, "it's no use making a mystery. I order you to report. Was there anybody on the horse?"

"Yes."

"Well?"

"My father."

The sergeant rose to his feet and walked away. "Good God!" he said.

GRAHAM GREENE

The Blue Film

"Other people enjoy themselves," Mrs. Carter said.

"Well," her husband replied, "we've seen—"

"The reclining Buddha, the emerald Buddha, the floating markets," Mrs. Carter said. "We have dinner and go home to bed."

"Last night we went to Chez Eve. . . ."

"If you weren't with *me*," Mrs. Carter said, "you'd find . . . you know what I mean—Spots."

It was true, Carter thought, eyeing his wife over the coffee cups: her slave bangles chinked in time with her coffee spoon: she had reached an age when the satisfied woman is at her most beautiful, but the lines of discontent had formed. When he looked at her neck he was reminded of how difficult it was to unstring a turkey. Is it my fault, he wondered, or hers—or was it the fault of her birth, some glandular deficiency, some inherited characteristic? It was sad how when one was young, one so often mistook the signs of frigidity for a kind of distinction.

"You promised we'd smoke opium," Mrs. Carter said.

"Not here, darling. In Saigon. Here it's 'not done' to smoke."

"How conventional you are."

"There'd be only the dirtiest of coolie places. You'd be conspicuous. They'd stare at you." He played his winning card. "There'd be cockroaches."

"I should be taken to plenty of Spots if I wasn't with a husband."

He tried hopefully, "The Japanese strip teasers . . ." but she had heard all about them. "Ugly women in brassières," she said. His irritation rose. He thought of the money he had spent to take his wife with him and to ease his conscience—he had been away too often without her—but there is no company more cheerless than that of a woman who is not desired. He tried to drink his coffee calmly: he wanted to bite the edge of the cup.

"You've spilt your coffee," Mrs. Carter said.

"I'm sorry." He got up abruptly and said, "All right. I'll fix something. Stay here." He leant across the table. "You'd better not be shocked," he said. "You've asked for it."

"I don't think I'm usually the one who is shocked," Mrs. Carter said with a thin smile.

Carter left the hotel and walked up towards the New Road. A boy hung at his side and said, "Young girl?"

"I've got a woman of my own," Carter said gloomily.

"Boy?"

"No, thanks."

"French films?"

Carter paused. "How much?"

They stood and haggled awhile at the corner of the drab street. What with the taxi, the guide, the films, it was going to cost the best part of eight pounds, but it was worth it, Carter thought, if it closed her mouth forever from demanding "Spots." He went back to fetch Mrs. Carter.

They drove a long way and came to a halt by a bridge over a canal, a dingy lane overcast with indeterminate smells. The guide said, "Follow me."

Mrs. Carter put a hand on Carter's arm. "Is it safe?" she asked.

"How would I know?" he said, stiffening under her hand.

They walked about fifty unlighted yards and halted by a bamboo fence. The guide knocked several times. When they were admitted it was to a tiny earth-floored yard and a wooden hut. Something—presumably human—was humped in the dark under a mosquito-net. The owner showed them into a tiny stuffy room with two hard chairs and a portrait of the King. The screen was about the size of a folio volume.

The first film was peculiarly unattractive and showed the rejuvenation of an elderly man at the hands of two blonde masseuses. From the women's hairdressing the film must have been made in the late twenties. Carter and his wife sat in mutual embarrassment as the film whirled and clicked to a stop.

"Not a very good one," Carter said, as though he were a connoisseur.

"So that's what they call a blue film," Mrs. Carter said. "Ugly and not exciting."

A second film started.

There was very little story in this. A young man—one couldn't see his face because of the period soft hat—picked up a girl in the street (her cloche hat extinguished her like a meat-cover) and accompanied her to her room. The actors were young: there was some charm and excitement in the picture. Carter thought, when the girl took off her hat, I know that face, and a memory that had been buried for more than a quarter of a century moved. A doll over a telephone, a pin-up girl of the period over the double bed. The girl undressed, folding her clothes very neatly: she leant over to adjust the bed, exposing herself to the camera's eye and to the young man: he kept his head turned from the camera. Afterwards, she helped him in turn to take off his clothes. It was only then he remembered—that particular playfulness confirmed by the birthmark on the man's shoulder.

Mrs. Carter shifted on her chair. "I wonder how they find the actors," she said hoarsely.

"A prostitute," he said. "It's a bit raw, isn't it? Wouldn't you like to leave?" he urged her, waiting for the man to turn his head. The girl knelt on the bed and held the youth around the waist—she couldn't have been more than twenty. No; he made a calculation: twenty-one.

"We'll stay," Mrs. Carter said. "We've paid." She laid a dry hot hand on his knee.

"I'm sure we could find a better place than this."

"No."

The young man lay on his back and the girl for a moment left him. Briefly, as though by accident, he looked at the camera. Mrs. Carter's hand shook on his knee. "Good God," she said, "it's you."

"It *was* me," Carter said, "thirty years ago." The girl was climbing back onto the bed.

"It's revolting," Mrs. Carter said.

"I don't remember it as revolting," Carter replied.

"I suppose you went and gloated, both of you."

"No, I never saw it."

"Why did you do it? I can't look at you. It's shameful."

"I asked you to come away."

"Did they pay you?"

"They paid her. Fifty pounds. She needed the money badly."

"And you had your fun for nothing?"

"Yes."

"I'd never have married you if I'd known. Never."

"That was a long time afterwards."

"You still haven't said why. Haven't you any excuse?" She stopped. He knew she was watching, leaning forward, caught up herself in the heat of that climax more than a quarter of a century old.

Carter said, "It was the only way I could help her. She'd never acted in one before. She wanted a friend."

"A friend," Mrs. Carter said.

"I loved her."

"You couldn't love a tart."

"Oh yes, you can. Make no mistake about that."

"You queued for her, I suppose."

"You put it too crudely," Carter said.

"What happened to her?"

"She disappeared. They always disappear."

The girl leant over the young man's body and put out the light. It was the end of the film. "I have new ones coming next week," the Siamese said, bowing deeply. They followed their guide back down the dark lane to the taxi.

In the taxi Mrs. Carter said, "What was her name?"

"I don't remember." A lie was easiest.

As they turned into the New Road she broke her bitter silence again. "How could you have brought yourself . . . ? It's so degrading. Suppose someone you knew—in business—recognized you."

"People don't talk about seeing things like that. Anyway, I wasn't in business in those days."

"Did it never worry you?"

"I don't believe I have thought of it once in thirty years."

"How long did you know her?"

"Twelve months, perhaps."

"She must look pretty awful by now if she's alive. After all, she was common even then."

"I thought she looked lovely," Carter said.

They went upstairs in silence. He went straight to the bathroom and locked the door. The mosquitoes gathered around the lamp and the great jar of water. As he undressed he caught glimpses of himself in the small mirror; thirty years had not been kind: he felt his thickness and his middle-age. He thought, I hope to God she's dead. Please, God, he said, let her be dead. When I go back in there, the insults will start again.

But when he returned Mrs. Carter was standing by the mirror. She had partly undressed. Her thin bare legs reminded him of a heron waiting for fish. She came and put her arms round him: a slave bangle joggled against his shoulder. She said, "I'd forgotten how nice you looked."

"I'm sorry. One changes."

"I didn't mean that. I like you as you are."

She was dry and hot and implacable in her desire. "Go on," she said, "go on," and then she screamed like an angry and hurt bird. Afterwards she said, "It's years since that happened," and continued to talk for what seemed a long half hour excitedly at his side. Carter lay in the dark silent, with a feeling of loneliness and guilt. It seemed to him that he had betrayed that night the only woman he loved.

FLANNERY O'CONNOR

Enoch and the Gorilla

Enoch Emery had borrowed his landlady's umbrella and he discovered as he stood in the entrance of the drugstore, trying to open it, that it was at least as old as she was. When he finally got it hoisted, he pushed his dark glasses back on his eyes and re-entered the downpour.

The umbrella was one his landlady had stopped using fifteen years before (which was the only reason she had lent it to him) and as soon as the rain touched the top of it, it came down with a shriek and stabbed him in the back of the neck. He ran a few feet with it over his head and then backed into another store entrance and removed it. Then to get it up again, he had to place the tip of it on the ground and ram it open with his foot. He ran out again, holding his hand up near the spokes to keep them open and this allowed the handle, which was carved to represent the head of a fox terrier, to jab him every few seconds in the stomach. He proceeded for another quarter of a block this way before the back half of the silk stood up off the spokes and allowed the storm to sweep down his collar. Then he ducked under the marquee of a movie house. It was Saturday and there were a lot of children standing more or less in a line in front of the ticket box.

Enoch was not very fond of children, but children always seemed to like to look at him. The line turned and twenty or thirty eyes began to observe him with a steady interest. The umbrella had assumed an ugly position, half up and half down, and the half that was up was about to come down and spill more water under his collar. When this happened the children laughed and jumped up and down. Enoch glared at them and turned his back and lowered his dark glasses. He found himself facing a life-size four-color picture of a gorilla. Over the gorilla's head, written in red letters was "GONGA! Giant Jungle Monarch and a Great Star! HERE IN PERSON! ! !" At the level of the gorilla's knee, there was more that said, "Gonga will appear in person in front of this theater at 12 A.M. *TODAY!* A free pass to the first ten brave enough to step up and shake his hand!"

Enoch was usually thinking of something else at the moment that Fate began drawing back her leg to kick him. When he was four years old, his father had brought him home a tin box from the penitentiary. It was orange and had a picture of some peanut brittle on the outside of it and green letters that said, "A NUTTY SURPRISE!" When Enoch had opened it, a coiled piece of steel had sprung out at him and broken off the ends of his two front teeth. His life was full of so many happenings like that that it would seem he should have been more sensitive to his times of danger. He stood there and read the poster twice through carefully. To his mind, an opportunity to insult a successful ape came from the hand of Providence.

He turned around and asked the nearest child what time it was. The child said it was twelve-ten and that Gonga was already ten minutes late. Another child said that maybe the rain had delayed him. Another said, no not the rain, his director was taking a plane from Hollywood. Enoch gritted his teeth. The first child said that if he wanted to shake the star's hand, he would have to get in line like the rest of them and wait his turn. Enoch got in line. A child asked him how old he was. Another observed that he had funny-looking teeth. He ignored all this as best he could and began to straighten out the umbrella.

In a few minutes a black truck turned around the corner and came slowly up the street in the heavy rain. Enoch pushed the umbrella under his arm and began to squint through his dark glasses. As the truck approached, a phonograph inside it began to play "Tarara Boom Di Aye," but the music was almost drowned out by the rain. There was a large illustration of a blonde on the outside of the truck, advertising some picture other than the gorilla's.

The children held their line carefully as the truck stopped in front of the movie house. The back door of it was constructed like a paddy wagon, with a grate, but the ape was not at it. Two men in raincoats got out of the cab part, cursing, and ran around to the back and opened the door. One of them stuck his head in and said, "Okay, make it snappy, willya?" The other jerked his thumb at the children and said, "Get back willya, willya get back?"

A voice on the record inside the truck said, "Here's Gonga, folks, Roaring Gonga and a Great Star! Give Gonga a big hand, folks!" The voice was barely a mumble in the rain.

The man who was waiting by the door of the truck stuck his head in again. "Okay willya get out?" he said.

There was a faint thump somewhere inside the van. After a second a dark furry arm emerged just enough for the rain to touch it and then drew back inside.

"Goddamn," the man who was under the marquee said; he took off his raincoat and threw it to the man by the door, who threw it into the wagon. After two or three minutes more, the gorilla appeared at the door, with the raincoat buttoned up to his chin and the collar turned up. There was an iron chain hanging from around his neck; the man grabbed it and pulled him down and the two of them bounded under the marquee together. A motherly-looking woman was in the glass ticket box, getting the passes ready for the first ten children brave enough to step up and shake hands.

The gorilla ignored the children entirely and followed the man over to the other side of the entrance where there was a small platform raised about a foot off the ground. He stepped up on it and turned facing the children and began to growl. His growls were not so much loud as poisonous; they appeared to issue from a black heart. Enoch was terrified and if he had not been surrounded by the children, he would have run away.

"Who'll step up first?" the man said. "Come on come on, who'll step up first? A free pass to the first kid stepping up."

There was no movement from the group of children. The man glared at them. "What's the matter with you kids?" he barked. "You yellow? He won't hurt you as long as I got him by this chain." He tightened his grip on the chain and jangled it at them to show he was holding it securely.

After a minute a little girl separated herself from the group. She had long wood-shaving curls and a fierce triangular face. She moved up to within four feet of the star.

"Okay okay," the man said, rattling the chain, "make it snappy."

The ape reached out and gave her hand a quick shake. By this time there was another little girl ready and then two boys. The line re-formed and began to move up.

The gorilla kept his hand extended and turned his head away with a bored look at the rain. Enoch had got over his fear and was trying frantically to think of an obscene remark that would be suitable to insult him with. Usually he didn't have any trouble with this kind of composition but nothing came to him now. His brain, both parts, was completely empty. He couldn't think even of the insulting phrases he used every day.

There were only two children in front of him by now. The first one shook hands and stepped aside. Enoch's heart was beating violently. The child in front of him finished and stepped aside and left him facing the ape, who took his hand with an automatic motion.

It was the first hand that had been extended to Enoch since he had come to the city. It was warm and soft.

For a second he only stood there, clasping it. Then he began to stammer. "My name is Enoch Emery," he mumbled. "I attended the Rodemill Boys' Bible Academy. I work at the city zoo. I seen two of your pictures. I'm only eighteen years old but I already work for the city. My daddy made me come . . ." and his voice cracked.

The star leaned slightly forward and a change came in his eyes: an ugly pair of human ones moved closer and squinted at Enoch from behind the celluloid pair. "You go to hell," a surly voice inside the ape-suit said, low but distinctly, and the hand was jerked away.

Enoch's humiliation was so sharp and painful that he turned around three times before he realized which direction he wanted to go in. Then he ran off into the rain as fast as he could.

In spite of himself, Enoch couldn't get over the expectation that something was going to happen to him. The virtue of hope, in Enoch, was made up of two parts suspicion and one part lust. It operated on him all the rest of the day. He had only a vague idea what he wanted, but he was not a boy without ambition: he wanted to become something. He wanted to better his condition. He wanted, some day, to see a line of people waiting to shake his hand.

All afternoon he fidgeted and fooled in his room, biting his nails and shredding what was left of the silk off the landlady's umbrella. Finally he denuded it entirely and broke off the spokes. What was left was a black stick with a sharp steel point at one end and a dog's head at the other. It might have been an instrument for some specialized kind of torture that had gone out of fashion. Enoch walked up and down his room with it under his arm and realized that it would distinguish him on the sidewalk.

About seven o'clock in the evening he put on his coat and took the stick and headed for a little restaurant two blocks away. He had the sense that he was setting off to get some honor, but he was very nervous, as if he were afraid he might have to snatch it instead of receive it.

He never set out for anything without eating first. The restaurant was called the Paris Diner; it was a tunnel about six feet wide, located between a shoeshine parlor and a dry-cleaning establishment. Enoch slid in and climbed up on the far stool at the counter and said he would have a bowl of split-pea soup and a chocolate malted milk shake.

The waitress was a tall woman with a big yellow dental plate and the same color hair done up in a black hairnet. One hand never left her hip; she filled orders with the other one. Although Enoch came in every night, she had never learned to like him.

Instead of filling his order, she began to fry bacon; there was only one other customer in the place and he had finished his meal and was reading a newspaper; there was no one to eat the bacon but her. Enoch reached over the counter and prodded her hip with the stick. "Listen here," he said, "I got to go. I'm in a hurry."

"Go then," she said. Her jaw began to work and she stared into the skillet with a fixed attention.

"Lemme just have a piece of theter cake yonder," he said, pointing to a half of pink and yellow cake on a round glass stand. "I think I got something to do. I got to be going. Set it up there next to him," he said, indicating the customer reading the newspaper. He slid over the stools and began reading the outside sheet of the man's paper.

The man lowered the paper and looked at him. Enoch smiled. The man raised the paper again. "Could I borrow some part of your paper that you ain't studying?" Enoch asked. The man lowered it again and stared at him; he had muddy unflinching eyes. He leafed deliberately through the paper and shook out the sheet with the comic strips and handed it to Enoch. It was Enoch's favorite part. He read it every evening like an office. While he ate the cake that the waitress had torpedoed down the counter at him, he read and felt himself surge with kindness and courage and strength.

When he finished one side, he turned the sheet over and began to scan the advertisements for movies that filled the other side. His eye went over three columns without stopping; then it came to a box that advertised Gonga, Giant Jungle Monarch, and listed the theaters he would visit on his tour and the hours he would be at each one. In thirty minutes he would arrive at the Victory on 57th Street and that would be his last appearance in the city.

If anyone had watched Enoch read this, he would have seen a certain transformation in his countenance. It still shone with the inspiration he had absorbed from the comic strips, but something else had come over it: a look of awakening.

The waitress happened to turn around to see if he hadn't gone. "What's the matter with you?" she said. "Did you swallow a seed?"

"I know what I want," Enoch murmured.

"I know what I want too," she said with a dark look.

Enoch felt for his stick and laid his change on the counter. "I got to be going."

"Don't let me keep you," she said.

"You may not see me again," he said, "—the way I am."

"Any way I don't see you will be all right with me," she said.

Enoch left. It was a pleasant damp evening. The puddles on the sidewalk shone and the store windows were steamy and bright with junk. He disappeared down a side street and made his way rapidly along the darker passages of the city, pausing only once or twice at the end of an alley to dart a glance in each direction before he ran on. The Victory was a small theater, suited to the needs of the family, in one of the closer subdivisions; he passed through a succession of lighted areas and then on through more alleys and back streets until he came to the business section that surrounded it. Then he slowed up. He saw it about a block away, glittering in its darker setting. He didn't cross the street to the side it was on but kept on the far side, moving forward with his squint fixed on the glary spot. He stopped when he was directly across from it and hid himself in a narrow stair cavity that divided a building.

The truck that carried Gonga was parked across the street and the star was standing under the marquee, shaking hands with an elderly woman. She moved aside and a gentleman in a polo shirt stepped up and shook hands vigorously, like a sportsman. He was followed by a boy of about three who wore a tall Western hat that nearly covered his face; he had to be pushed ahead by the line. Enoch watched for some time, his face working with envy. The small boy was followed by a lady in shorts, she by an old man who tried to draw extra attention to himself by dancing up instead of walking in a dignified way. Enoch suddenly darted across the street and slipped noiselessly into the open back door of the truck.

The handshaking went on until the feature picture was ready to begin. Then the star got back in the van and the people filed into the theater. The driver and the man who was master of ceremonies climbed in the cab part and the truck rumbled off. It crossed the city rapidly and continued on the highway, going very fast.

There came from the van certain thumping noises, not those of the normal gorilla, but they were drowned out by the drone of the motor and the steady sound of wheels against the road. The night was pale and quiet, with nothing to stir it but an occasional complaint from a hoot owl and the distant muted jarring of a freight train. The truck sped on until it slowed for a crossing, and as the van rattled over the tracks, a figure slipped from the door and almost fell, and then limped hurriedly off toward the woods.

Once in the darkness of a pine thicket, he laid down a pointed stick he had been clutching and something bulky and loose that he had been carrying under his arm, and began to undress. He folded each garment neatly after he had taken it off and then stacked it on top of the last thing he had removed. When all his clothes were in the pile, he took up the stick and began making a hole in the ground with it.

The darkness of the pine grove was broken by paler moonlit spots that moved over him now and again and showed him to be Enoch. His natural appearance was marred by a gash that ran from the corner of his lip to his collarbone and by a lump under his eye that gave him a dulled insensitive look. Nothing could have been more deceptive for he was burning with the intensest kind of happiness.

He dug rapidly until he had made a trench about a foot long and a foot deep. Then he placed the stack of clothes in it and stood aside to rest a second. Burying his clothes was not a symbol to him of burying his former self; he only knew he wouldn't need them any more. As soon as he got his breath, he pushed the displaced dirt over the hole and stamped it down with his foot. He discovered while he did this that he still had his shoes on, and when he finished, he removed them and threw them from him. Then he picked up the loose bulky object and shook it vigorously.

In the uncertain light, one of his lean white legs could be seen to disappear and then the other, one arm and then the other: a black heavier shaggier figure replaced his. For an instant, it had two heads, one light and one dark, but after a second, it pulled the dark back head over and the other and corrected this. It busied itself with certain hidden fastenings and what appeared to be minor adjustments of its hide.

For a time after this, it stood very still and didn't do anything. Then it began to growl and beat its chest; it jumped up and down and flung its arms and thrust its head forward. The growls were thin and uncertain at first but they grew louder after a second. They became low and poisonous, louder again, low and poisonous again; they stopped altogether. The figure extended its hand, clutched nothing, and shook its arm vigorously; it withdrew the arm, extended it again, clutched nothing, and shook. It repeated this four or five times. Then it picked up the pointed stick and placed it at a cocky angle under its arm and left the woods for the highway. No gorilla anywhere, Africa or California or New York, was happier than he.

A man and woman sitting close together on a rock just off the highway were looking across an open stretch of valley at a view of the city in the distance and they didn't see the shaggy figure approaching. The smokestacks and square tops of buildings made a black uneven wall against the lighter sky and here and there a steeple cut a sharp wedge out of a cloud. The young man turned his neck just in time to see the gorilla standing a few feet away, hideous and black, with its hand extended. He eased his arm from around the woman and disappeared silently into the woods. She, as soon as she turned her eyes, fled screaming down the highway. The gorilla stood as though surprised and presently its arm fell to its side. It sat down on the rock where they had been sitting and stared over the valley at the uneven skyline of the city.

JAMES ALAN McPHERSON

Gold Coast

I

That spring, when I had a great deal of potential and no money at all, I took a job as a janitor. That was when I was still very young and spent money very freely, and when, almost every night, I drifted off to sleep lulled by sweet anticipation of that time when my potential would suddenly be realized and there would be capsule biographies of my life on dust jackets of many books, all proclaiming: ". . . He knew life on many levels. From shoeshine boy, free-lance waiter, 3rd cook, janitor, he rose to . . ." I had never been a janitor before, and I did not really have to be one, and that is why I did it. But now, much later, I think it might have been because it is possible to be a janitor without becoming one, and at parties or at mixers, when asked what it was I did for a living, it was pretty good to hook my thumbs in my vest pockets and say comfortably: "Why, I am an apprentice janitor." The hippies would think it degenerate and really dig me and it made me feel good that people in Philosophy and Law and Business would feel uncomfortable trying to make me feel better about my station while wondering how the hell I managed to crash the party.

"What's an apprentice janitor?" they would ask.

"I haven't got my card yet," I would reply. "Right now I'm just taking lessons. There's lots of complicated stuff you have to learn before you get your card and your own building."

"What kind of stuff?"

"Human nature, for one thing. *Race* nature, for another."

"Why race?"

"Because," I would say in a low voice, looking around lest someone else should overhear, "you have to be able to spot Jews and Negroes who are passing."

"That's terrible," would surely be said then with a hint of indignation.

"It's an art," I would add masterfully.

After a good pause I would invariably be asked: "But you're a Negro yourself, how can you keep your own people out?"

At which point I would look terribly disappointed and say: "*I* don't keep them out. But if they get in it's my job to make their stay just as miserable as possible. Things are changing."

Now the speaker would just look at me in disbelief.

"It's Janitorial Objectivity," I would say to finish the thing as the speaker began to edge away. "Don't hate me," I would call after him to his considerable embarrassment. "Somebody has to do it."

It was an old building near Harvard Square. Conrad Aiken had once lived there, and in the days of the Gold Coast, before Harvard built its great houses, it had been a very fine haven for the rich; but that was a world ago, and this building was one of the few monuments of that era which had survived. The lobby had a high ceiling with thick redwood beams, and it was replete with marble floor, fancy ironwork, and an old-fashioned house telephone that no longer worked. Each apartment had a small fireplace, and even the large bathtubs and chain toilets, when I was having my touch of nature, made me wonder what prominent personage of the past had worn away all the newness. And, being there, I felt a certain affinity toward the rich.

It was a funny building, because the people who lived there made it old. Conveniently placed as it was between the Houses and Harvard Yard, I expected to find it occupied by a company of hippies, hopeful working girls, and assorted graduate students. Instead, there were a majority of old maids, dowagers, asexual middle-aged men, homosexual young men, a few married couples, and a teacher. No one was shacking up there, and walking through the quiet halls in the early evening, I sometimes had the urge to knock on a door and expose myself just to hear someone breathe hard for once.

It was a Cambridge spring: down by the Charles happy students were making love while sad-eyed middle-aged men watched them from the bridge. It was a time of activity: Law students were busy sublimating, Business School people were making records of the money they would make, the Harvard Houses were clearing out, and in the Square bearded pot-pushers were setting up their restaurant tables in anticipation of the Summer School faithfuls. There was a change of season in the air, and to comply with its urgings, James Sullivan, the old superintendent, passed his three beaten garbage cans on to me with the charge that I should take up his daily rounds of the six floors, and with unflinching humility, gather whatever scraps the old-maid tenants had refused to husband.

I then became very rich, with my own apartment, a sensitive girl, a stereo, two speakers, one tattered chair, one fork, a job, and the urge to acquire. Having all this and youth besides made me pity Sullivan: he had been in that building thirty years and had its whole history recorded in the little folds of his mind, as his own life was recorded in the wrinkles of his face. All he had to show for his time there was a berserk dog, a wife almost as mad as the dog, three cats, bursitis, acute myopia, and a drinking problem. He was well over seventy and could hardly walk, and his weekly check of twenty-two dollars from the company that managed the building would not support anything. So, out of compromise, he was retired to superintendent of my labor.

My first day as a janitor, while I skillfully lugged my three overflowing cans of garbage out of the building, he sat on his bench in the lobby, faded and old and smoking, in patched, loose blue pants. He watched me. He was a chain smoker, and I noticed right away that he very carefully dropped all of the ashes and butts on the floor and crushed them under his feet until there was a yellow and gray smear. Then he laboriously pushed the mess under the bench with his shoe, all the while eyeing me like a cat in silence as I hauled the many cans of muck out to the big disposal unit next to the building. When I had finished, he gave me two old plates to help stock my kitchen and his first piece of advice.

"Sit down, for Chrissake, and take a load off your feet," he told me.

I sat on the red bench next to him and accepted the wilted cigarette he offered me from the crushed package he kept in his sweater pocket.

"Now, I'll tell you something to help you get along in the building," he said.

I listened attentively.

"If any of these sons of bitches ever ask you to do something extra, be sure to charge them for it."

I assured him that I absolutely would.

"If they can afford to live here, they can afford to pay. The bastards."

"Undoubtedly," I assured him again.

"And another thing," he added. "Don't let any of these girls shove any cat shit under your nose. That ain't your job. You tell them to put it in a bag and take it out themselves."

I reminded him that I knew very well my station in life, and that I was not about to haul cat shit or anything of that nature. He looked at me through his thick-lensed glasses. He looked like a cat himself. "That's right," he said at last. "And if they still try to sneak it in the trash be sure to make the bastards pay. They can afford it." He crushed his seventh butt on the floor and scattered the mess some more while he lit up another. "I never hauled out no cat shit in the thirty years I been here, and you don't do it either."

"I'm going up to wash my hands," I said.

"Remember," he called after me, "don't take no shit from any of them."

I protested once more that, upon my life, I would never, never do it, not even for the prettiest girl in the building. Going up in the elevator, I felt comfortably resolved that I would never do it. There were no pretty girls in the building.

I never found out what he had done before he came there, but I do know that being a janitor in that building was as high as he ever got in life. He had watched two generations of the rich pass the building on their way to the Yard, and he had seen many governors ride white horses thirty times into that same Yard to send sons and daughters of the rich out into life to produce, to acquire, to procreate, and to send back sons and daughters so that the cycle would continue. He had watched the cycle from when he had been able to haul the cans out for himself, and now he could not, and he was bitter.

He was Irish, of course, and he took pride in Irish accomplishments when he could have none of his own. He had known Frank O'Connor when that writer had been at Harvard. He told me on many occasions how O'Connor had stopped to talk every day on his way to the Yard. He had also known James Michael Curley, and his most colorful memory of the man was a long-ago day when he and James Curley sat in a Boston bar and one of Curley's runners had come in and said: "Hey, Jim, Sol Bernstein the Jew wants to see you." And Curley, in his deep, memorial voice, had said to James Sullivan: "Let us go forth and meet this Israelite Prince." These were his memories, and I would obediently put aside my garbage cans and laugh with him over the hundred or so colorful, insignificant little details which made up a whole lifetime of living in the basement of Harvard. And although they were of little value to me then, I knew that they were the reflections of a lifetime and the happiest moments he would ever have, being sold to me cheap, as youthful time is cheap, for as little time and interest as I wanted to spend. It was a buyer's market.

II

In those days I believed myself gifted with a boundless perception and attacked my daily garbage route with a gusto superenforced by the happy knowledge that behind each of the fifty or so doors in our building lived a story which would, if I chose to grace it with the magic of my pen, become immortal. I watched my tenants fanatically, noting their perversions, their visitors, and their eating habits. So intense was my search for material that I had to restrain myself from going through their refuse scrap by scrap; but at the topmost layers of muck, without too much hand soiling in the process, I set my perception to work. By late June, however, I had discovered only enough to put together a skimpy, rather naive Henry Miller novel, the most colorful discoveries being:

1. The lady in #24 was an alumna of Paducah College
2. The couple in #55 made love at least 500 times a week, and the wife had not yet discovered the pill
3. The old lady in #36 was still having monthly inconvenience
4. The two fatsos in #56 consumed nightly an extraordinary amount of chili
5. The fat man in #54 had two dogs that were married to each other, but he was not married to anyone at all
6. The middle-aged single man in #63 threw out an awful lot of flowers.

Disturbed by the snail's progress I was making, I confessed my futility to James one day as he sat on his bench chain-smoking and smearing butts on my newly waxed lobby floor. "So you want to know about the tenants?" he said, his cat's eyes flickering over me.

I nodded.

"Well, the first thing to notice is how many Jews there are."

"I haven't noticed many Jews," I said.

He eyed me in amazement.

"Well, a few," I said quickly to prevent my treasured perception from being dulled any further.

"A few, hell," he said. "There's more Jews here than anybody."

"How can you tell?"

He gave me that undecided look again. "Where do you think all that garbage comes from?" He nodded feebly toward my bulging cans. I looked just in time to prevent a stray noodle from slipping over the brim. "That's right," he continued. "Jews are the biggest eaters in the world. They eat the best too."

I confessed then that I was of the chicken-soup generation and believed that Jews ate only enough to muster strength for their daily trips to the bank.

"Not so!" he replied emphatically. "You never heard the expression: 'Let's get to the restaurant before the Jews get there'?"

I shook my head sadly.

"You don't know that in certain restaurants they take the free onions and pickles off the tables when they see Jews coming?"

I held my head down in shame over the bounteous heap.

He trudged over to my can and began to turn back the leaves of noodles and crumpled tissues from #47 with his hand. After a few seconds of digging, he unmucked an empty pâté can. "Look at that," he said triumphantly. "Gourmet stuff, no less."

"That's from #44," I said.

"What else?" he said, all-knowingly. "In 1946 a Swedish girl moved in up there and took a Jewish girl for her roommate. Then the Swedish girl moved out and there's been a Jewish Dynasty up there ever since."

I recalled that #44 was occupied by a couple that threw out a good number of S. S. Pierce cans, Chivas Regal bottles, assorted broken records, and back issues of *Evergreen* and the *Realist.*

"You're right," I said.

"Of course," he replied, as if there were never any doubt. "I can spot them anywhere, even when they think they're passing." He leaned closer and said in a you-and-me voice: "But don't ever say anything bad about them in public, the Anti-Defamation League will get you."

Just then his wife screamed for him from the second floor, and the dog joined her and beat against the door. He got into the elevator painfully and said: "Don't ever talk about them in public. You don't know who they are, and that Defamation League will take everything you got."

Sullivan did not really hate Jews. He was just bitter toward anyone better off than himself. He liked me because I seemed to like hauling garbage and because I listened to him and seemed to respect what he said and seemed to imply, by lingering even when he repeated himself, that I was eager to take what wisdom he had for no other reason than that I needed it in order to get along.

He lived with his wife on the second floor, and his apartment was very dirty because both of them were sick and old, and neither could move very well. His wife swept dirt out into the hall, and two hours after I had mopped and waxed their section of the floor, there was sure to be a layer of dirt, grease, and crushed-scattered tobacco from their door to the end of the hall. There was a smell of dogs and cats and age and death about their door, and I did not ever want to have to go in there for any reason because I feared something about it I cannot name.

Mrs. Sullivan, I found out, was from South Africa. She loved animals much more than people, and there was a great deal of pain in her face. She kept little cans of meat posted at strategic points about the building, and I often came across her in the early morning or late at night throwing scraps out of the second-floor window to stray cats. Once, when James was about to throttle a stray mouse in their apartment, she had screamed at him to give the mouse a sporting chance. Whenever she attempted to walk she had to balance herself against a wall or a rail, and she hated the building because it confined her. She also hated James and most of the tenants. On the other hand, she loved the *Johnny Carson Show,* she loved to sit outside on the front steps (because she could get no further unassisted), and she loved to talk to anyone who would stop to listen. She never spoke coherently except when she was cursing James, and then she had a vocabulary like a sailor. She had great, shrill lungs, and her screams, accompanied by the rabid barks of the dog, could be heard all over the building. She was never really clean, her teeth were bad, and the first most pathetic thing in the world was to see her sitting on the steps in the morning watching the world pass, in a stained smock and a fresh summer blue hat she kept just to wear downstairs, with no place in the world to go. James told me, on the many occasions of her screaming, that she was mentally disturbed and could not control herself. The admirable thing about him was that he never lost his temper with her, no matter how rough her curses became and no matter who heard them. And the second most pathetic thing in the world was to see them slowly making their way in Harvard Square, he supporting her, through the hurrying crowds of miniskirted summer girls, J-Pressed Ivy Leaguers, beatniks, and bused Japanese tourists, decked in cameras, who would take pictures of every inch of Harvard Square except them. Once he told me a hippie had brushed past them and called back over his shoulder: "Don't break any track records, Mr. and Mrs. Speedy Molasses."

Also on the second floor lived Miss O'Hara, a spinster who hated Sullivan as only an old maid can hate an old man. Across from her lived a very nice, gentle celibate named Murphy, who had once served with Montgomery in North Africa and who was now spending the rest of his life cleaning his little apartment and gossiping with Miss O'Hara. It was an Irish floor.

I never found out just why Miss O'Hara hated the Sullivans with such a passion. Perhaps it was because they were so unkempt and she was so superciliously clean. Perhaps it was because Miss O'Hara had a great deal of Irish pride, and they were stereotyped Irish. Perhaps it was because she merely had no reason to like them. She was a fanatic about cleaniness and put out her little bit of garbage wrapped very neatly in yesterday's *Christian Science Monitor* and tied in a bow with a fresh piece of string. Collecting all those little neat packages, I would wonder where she got the string and imagined her at night breaking meat market locks with a hairpin and hobbling off with yards and yards of white cord concealed under the gray sweater she always wore. I could even imagine her back in her little apartment chuckling and rolling the cord into a great white ball by candlelight. Then she would stash it away in her bread box. Miss O'Hara kept her door slightly open until late at night, and I suspected that she heard everything that went on in the building. I had the feeling that I should never dare to make love with gusto for fear that she would overhear and write down all my happy-time phrases, to be maliciously recounted to me if she were ever provoked.

She had been in the building longer than Sullivan, and I suppose that her greatest ambition in life was to outlive him and then attend his wake with a knitting ball and needles. She had been trying to get him fired for twenty-five years or so, and did not know when to quit. On summer nights when I painfully mopped the second floor, she would offer me root beer, apples, or cupcakes while trying to pump me for evidence against him.

"He's just a filthy old man, Robert," she would declare in a little-old-lady whisper. "And don't think you have to clean up those dirty old butts of his. Just report him to the Company."

"Oh, I don't mind," I would tell her, gulping the root beer as fast as possible.

"Well, they're both a couple of lushes, if you ask me. They haven't been sober a day in twenty-five years."

"Well, she's sick too, you know."

"Ha!" She would throw up her hands in disgust. "She's only sick when he doesn't give her the booze."

I fought to keep down a burp. "How long have *you* been here?"

She motioned for me to step out of the hall and into her dark apartment. "Don't tell him"—she nodded toward Sullivan's door—"but I've been here for thirty-four years." She waited for me to be taken aback. Then she added:

"And it was a better building before those two lushes came."

She then offered me an apple, asked five times if the dog's barking bothered me, forced me to take a fudge brownie, said that the cats had wet the floor again last night, got me to dust the top of a large chest too high for her to reach, had me pick up the minute specks of dust which fell from my dustcloth, pressed another root beer on me, and then showed me her family album. As an afterthought, she had me take down a big old picture of her great-grandfather, also too high for her to reach, so that I could dust that too. Then together we picked up the dust from it which might have fallen to the floor. "He's really a filthy old man, Robert," she said in closing, "and don't be afraid to report him to the Property Manager anytime you want."

I assured her that I would do it at the slightest provocation from Sullivan, finally accepted an apple but refused the money she offered, and escaped back to my mopping. Even then she watched me, smiling, from her half-opened door.

"Why does Miss O'Hara hate you?" I asked James once.

He lifted his cigarette hand and let the long ash fall elegantly to the floor. "That old bitch has been an albatross around my neck ever since I got here," he said. "Don't trust her, Robert. It was her kind that sat around singing hymns and watching them burn saints in this state."

There was never an adequate answer to my question. And even though the dog was noisy and would surely kill someone if it ever got loose, no one could really dislike the old man because of it. The dog was all they had. In his garbage each night, for every wine bottle, there would be an equally empty can of dog food. Some nights he took the brute out for a long walk, when he could barely walk himself, and both of them had to be led back to the building.

III

In those days I had forgotten that I was first of all a black and I had a very lovely girl who was not first of all a black. We were both very young and optimistic then, and she believed with me in my potential and liked me partly because of it; and I was happy because she belonged to me and not to the race, which made her special. It made me special too because I did not have to wear a beard or hate or be especially hip or ultra-Ivy Leagueish. I did not have to smoke pot or supply her with it, or be for any other cause at all except myself. I only had to be myself, which pleased me; and I only had to produce, which pleased both of us. Like many of the artistically inclined rich, she wanted to own in someone else what she could not own in herself. But this I did not mind, and I forgave her for it because she forgave me moods and the constant smell of garbage and a great deal of latent hostility. She only minded James Sullivan, and all the valuable time I was wasting listening to him rattle on and on. His conversations, she thought, were useless, repetitious, and promised nothing of value to me. She was accustomed to the old-rich, whose conversations meandered around a leitmotiv of how well off they were and how much they would leave behind very soon. She was not at all cold, but she had been taught how to tolerate the old-poor and perhaps toss them a greeting in passing. But nothing more.

Sullivan did not like her when I first introduced them because he saw that she was not a hippie and could not be dismissed. It is in the nature of things that liberal people will tolerate two interracial hippies more than they will an intelligent, serious-minded mixed couple. The formal liaison is easy to dismiss as the dregs of both races, deserving of each other and the contempt of both races; but the latter poses a threat because there is no immediacy or overpowering sensuality or "you-pick-my-fleas-I'll-pick-yours" apparent on the surface of things, and people, even the most publicly liberal, cannot dismiss it so easily.

"That girl is Irish, isn't she?" he had asked one day in my apartment soon after I had introduced them.

"No," I said definitely.

"What's her name again?"

"Judy Smith," I said, which was not her name at all.

"Well, I can spot it," he said. "She's got Irish blood all right."

"Everybody's got a little Irish blood," I told him.

He looked at me cattily and craftily from behind his thick lenses. "Well, she's from a good family, I suppose."

"I suppose," I said.

He paused to let some ashes fall to the rug. "They say the Colonel's Lady and Nelly O'Grady are sisters under the skin." Then he added: "Rudyard Kipling."

"That's true," I said with equal innuendo, "that's why you have to maintain a distinction by marrying the Colonel's Lady."

An understanding passed between us then, and we never spoke more on the subject.

Almost every night the cats wet the second floor while Meg Sullivan watched the *Johnny Carson Show* and the dog howled and clawed the door. During the commercials Meg would curse James to get out and stop dropping ashes on the floor or to take the dog out or something else, totally unintelligible to those of us on the fourth, fifth, and sixth floors. Even after the *Carson Show* she would still curse him to get out, until finally he would go down to the basement and put away a bottle or two of wine. There was a steady stench of cat functions in the basement, and with all the grease and dirt, discarded trunks, beer bottles, chairs, old tools, and the filthy sofa on which he sometimes slept, seeing him there made me want to cry. He drank the cheapest sherry, the wino kind, straight from the bottle; and on many nights that summer at 2:00 A.M. my phone would ring me out of bed.

"Rob? Jimmy Sullivan here. What are you doing?"

There was nothing suitable to say.

"Come on down to the basement for a drink."

"I have to be at work at 8:30," I would protest.

"Can't you have just one drink?" he would say pathetically.

I would carry down my own glass so that I would not have to drink out of the bottle. Looking at him on the sofa, I could not be mad because now I had many records for my stereo, a story that was going well, a girl who believed in me and belonged to me and not to the race, a new set of dishes, and a tomorrow morning with younger people.

"I don't want to burden you unduly," he would always preface.

I would force myself not to look at my watch and say: "Of course not."

"My Meg is not in the best health, you know," he would say, handing the bottle to me.

"She's just old."

"The doctors say she should be in an institution."

"That's no place to be."

"I'm a sick man myself, Rob. I can't take much more. She's crazy."

"Anybody who loves animals can't be crazy."

He took another long draw from the bottle. "I won't live another year, I'll be dead in a year."

"You don't know that."

He looked at me closely, without his glasses, so that I could see the desperation in his eyes. "I just hope Meg goes before I do. I don't want them to put her in an institution after I'm gone."

At 2:00 A.M., with the cat stench in my nose and a glass of bad sherry standing still in my hand because I refuse in my mind to touch it, and all when my dreams of greatness were above him and the basement and the building itself, I did not know what to say. The only way I could keep from hating myself was to talk about the AMA or the Medicare program or hippies. He was pure hell on all three. To him, the medical profession was "morally bankrupt," Medicare was a great farce which deprived oldsters like himself of their "rainy-day dollars," and hippies were "dropouts from the human race." He could rage on and on in perfect phrases about all three of his major dislikes, and I had the feeling that because the sentences were so well constructed and well turned, he might have memorized them from something he had read. But then he was extremely well read, and it did not matter if he had borrowed a phrase or two from someone else. The ideas were still his own.

It would be 3:00 A.M. before I knew it, and then 3:30, and still he would go on. He hated politicians in general and liked to recount, at these times, his private catalogue of political observations. By the time he got around to Civil Rights it would be 4:00 A.M., and I could not feel sorry or responsible for him at that hour. I would begin to yawn, and at first he would just ignore it. Then I would start to edge toward the door, and he would see that he could hold me no longer, not even by declaring that he wanted to be an honorary Negro because he loved the race so much.

"I hope I haven't burdened you unduly," he would say again.

"Of course not," I would say, because it was over then, and I could leave him and the smell of the cats there, and sometimes I would go out in the cool night and walk around the Yard and be thankful that I was only an assistant janitor, and a transient one at that. Walking in the early dawn and seeing the Summer School fellows sneak out of the girls' dormitories in the Yard gave me a good feeling, and I thought that tomorrow night it would be good to make love myself so that I could be busy when he called.

IV

"Why don't you tell that old man your job doesn't include babysitting with him," Jean told me many times when she came over to visit during the day and found me sleeping.

I would look at her and think to myself about social forces and the pressures massing and poised, waiting to attack us. It was still July then. It was hot, and I was working good.

"He's just an old man," I said. "Who else would listen to him?"

"You're too soft. As long as you do your work you don't have to be bothered with him."

"He could be a story if I listened long enough."

"There are too many stories about old people."

"No," I said, thinking about us again, "there are just too many people who have no stories."

Sometimes he would come up and she would be there, but I would let him come in anyway, and he would stand in the room looking dirty and uncomfortable, offering some invented reason for having intruded. At these times something silent would pass between them, something I cannot name, which would reduce him to exactly what he was: an old man, come out of his basement to intrude where he was not wanted. But all the time this was being communicated, there would be a surface, friendly conversation between them. And after five minutes or so of being unwelcome, he would apologize for having come, drop a few ashes on the rug, and back out the door. Downstairs we could hear his wife screaming.

We endured and aged and August was almost over. Inside the building the cats were still wetting, Meg was still screaming, the dog was getting madder, and Sullivan began to drink during the day. Outside it was hot and lush and green, and the Summer girls were wearing shorter miniskirts and no panties and the middle-aged men down by the Charles were going wild on their bridge. Everyone was restless for change, for August is the month when undone summer things must be finished or regretted all through the winter.

V

Being imaginative people, Jean and I played a number of original games. One of them we called "Social Forces," the object of which was to see which side could break us first. We played it with the unknown night riders who screamed obscenities from passing cars. And because that was her side I would look at her expectantly, but she would laugh and say: "No." We played it at parties with unaware blacks who attempted to enchant her with skillful dances and hip vocabulary, believing her to be community property. She would be polite and aloof, and much later, it then being my turn, she would look at me expectantly. And I would force a smile and say: "No." The last round was played while taking her home in a subway car, on a hot August night, when one side of the car was black and tense and hating and the other side was white and of the same mind. There was not enough room on either side for the two of us to sit and we would not separate; and so we stood, holding on to a steel post through all the stops, feeling all the eyes, between the two sides of the car and the two sides of the world. We aged. And getting off finally at the stop which was no longer ours, we looked at each other, again expectantly, and there was nothing left to say.

I began to avoid the old man, would not answer the door when I knew it was he who was knocking, and waited until very late at night, when he could not possibly be awake, to haul the trash down. I hated the building then; and I was really a janitor for the first time. I slept a lot and wrote very little. And I did not give a damn about Medicare, the AMA, the building, Meg, or the crazy dog. I began to consider moving out.

In that same month, Miss O'Hara finally succeeded in badgering Murphy, the celibate Irishman, and a few other tenants into signing a complaint about the dog. No doubt Murphy signed because he was a nice fellow and women like Miss O'Hara had always dominated him. He did not really mind the dog: he did not really mind anything. She called him "Frank Dear," and I had the feeling that when he came to that place, fresh from Montgomery's Campaign, he must have had a will of his own; but she had drained it all away, year by year, so that now he would do anything just to be agreeable.

One day soon after the complaint, the Property Manager came around to tell Sullivan that the dog had to be taken away. Miss O'Hara told me the good news later, when she finally got around to my door.

"Well, that crazy dog is gone now, Robert. Those two are enough."

"Where is the dog?" I asked.

"I don't know, but Albert Rustin made them get him out. You should have seen the old drunk's face," she said. "That dirty useless old man."

"You should be at peace now," I said.

"Almost," was her reply. "The best thing would be to get rid of those two old boozers along with the dog."

I congratulated Miss O'Hara again and then went out. I knew that the old man would be drinking and would want to talk. I did not want to talk. But very late that evening he called on the telephone and caught me in.

"Rob?" he said. "James Sullivan here. Would you come down to my apartment like a good fellow? I want to ask you something important."

I had never been in his apartment before and did not want to go then. But I went down anyway.

They had three rooms, all grimy from corner to corner. There was a peculiar odor in that place I did not want to ever smell again, and his wife was dragging herself around the room talking in mumbles. When she saw me come in the door, she said: "I can't clean it up. I just can't. Look at that window. I can't reach it. I can't keep it clean." She threw up both her hands and held her head down and to the side. "The whole place is dirty, and I can't clean it up."

"What do you want?" I said to Sullivan.

"Sit down." He motioned me to a kitchen chair. "Have you changed that bulb on the fifth floor?"

"It's done."

He was silent for a while, drinking from a bottle of sherry, and he offered me some and a dirty glass. "You're the first person who's been in here in years," he said. "We couldn't have company because of the dog."

Somewhere in my mind was a note that I should never go into his apartment. But the dog had not been the reason. "Well, he's gone now," I said, fingering the dirty glass of sherry.

He began to cry. "They took my dog away," he said. "It was all I had. How can they take a man's dog away from him?"

There was nothing I could say.

"I couldn't do nothing," he continued. After a while he added: "But I know who it was. It was that old bitch O'Hara. Don't ever trust her, Rob. She smiles in your face, but it was her kind that laughed when they burned Joan of Arc in this state."

Seeing him there, crying and making me feel unmanly because I wanted to touch him or say something warm, also made me eager to be far away and running hard.

"Everybody's got problems," I said. "I don't have a girl now."

He brightened immediately, and for a while he looked almost happy in his old cat's eyes. Then he staggered over to my chair and held out his hand. I did not touch it, and he finally pulled it back. "I know how you feel," he said. "I know just how you feel."

"Sure," I said.

"But you're a young man, you have a future. But not me. I'll be dead inside of a year."

Just then his wife dragged in to offer me a cigar. They were being hospitable, and I forced myself to drink a little of the sherry.

"They took my dog away today," she mumbled. "That's all I had in the world, my dog."

I looked at the old man. He was drinking from the bottle.

VI

During the first week of September one of the middle-aged men down by the Charles got tired of looking and tried to take a necking girl away from her boyfriend. The police hauled him off to jail, and the girl pulled down her dress tearfully. A few days later another man exposed himself near the same spot. And that same week a dead body was found on the banks of the Charles.

The miniskirted brigade had moved out of the Yard, and it was quiet and green and peaceful there. In our building another Jewish couple moved into #44. They did not eat gourmet stuff, and on occasion, threw out pork-and-beans cans. But I had lost interest in perception. I now had many records for my stereo, loads of S. S. Pierce stuff, and a small bottle of Chivas Regal which I never opened. I was working good again, and did not miss other things as much; or at least I told myself that.

The old man was coming up steadily now, at least three times a day, and I had resigned myself to it. If I refused to let him in, he would always come back later with a missing bulb on the fifth floor. We had taken to buying cases of beer together, and when he had finished his half, which was very frequently, he would come up to polish off mine. I began to enjoy talking about politics, the AMA, Medicare, hippies, and listening to him recite from books he had read. I discovered that he was very well read in history, philosophy, literature, and law. He was extraordinarily fond of saying: "I am really a cut above being a building superintendent. Circumstances made me what I am." And even though he was drunk and dirty and it was very late at night, I believed him and liked him anyway because having him there was much better than being alone. After he had gone I could sleep, and I was not lonely in sleep; and it did not really matter how late I was at work the next morning because when I really thought about it all, I discovered that nothing really matters except not being old and being alive and having potential to dream about, and not being alone.

Whenever I passed his wife on the steps she would say: "That no-good bastard let them take my dog away." And whenever her husband complained that he was sick she said: "That's good for him. He took my dog away."

Sullivan slept in the basement on the sofa almost every night because his wife would think about the dog after the *Carson Show* and blame him for letting it be taken away. He told her, and then me, that the dog was on a farm in New Hampshire; but that was unlikely because the dog had been near mad, and it did not appease her. It was nearing autumn and she was getting violent. Her screams could be heard for hours through the halls and I knew that beyond her quiet door Miss O'Hara was plotting again. Sullivan now had little cuts and bruises on his face and hands, and one day he said: "Meg is like an albatross around my neck. I wish she was dead. I'm sick myself and I can't take much more. She blames me for the dog and I couldn't help it."

"Why don't you take her out to see the dog?" I said.

"I couldn't help it Rob," he went on. "I'm old and I couldn't help it."

"You ought to just get her out of here for a while."

He looked at me, drunk as usual. "Where would we go? We can't even get past the Square."

There was nothing left to say.

"Honest to God, I couldn't help it," he said. He was not saying it to me.

That night I wrote a letter from a mythical New Hampshire farmer telling them that the dog was very fine and missed them a great deal because he kept trying to run off. I said that the children and all the other dogs liked him and that he was not vicious any more. I wrote that the open air was doing him a lot of good and added that they should feel absolutely free to come up to visit the dog any time. That same night I gave him the letter.

One evening, some days later, I asked him about it.

"I tried to mail it, I really tried," he said.

"What happened?"

I went down to the Square and looked for cars with New Hampshire license plates. But I never found anybody."

"That wasn't even necessary, was it?"

"It had to have a New Hampshire postmark. You don't know my Meg."

"Listen," I said. "I have a friend who goes up there. Give me the letter and I'll have him mail it."

He held his head down. "I'll tell you the truth. I carried that letter in my pocket so much it got ragged and dirty and I got tired of carrying it. I finally just tore it up."

Neither one of us said anything for a while.

"If I could have sent it off it would have helped some," he said at last. "I know it would have helped."

"Sure," I said.

"I wouldn't have to ask anybody it I had my strength."

"I know."

"If I had my strength I would have mailed it myself."

"I know," I said.

That night we both drank from his bottle of sherry and it did not matter at all that I did not provide my own glass.

VII

In late September the Cambridge police finally picked up the bearded pot-pusher in the Square. He had been in a restaurant all summer, at the same table, with the same customers flocking around him; but now that summer was over, they picked him up. The leaves were changing. In the early evening students passed the building and Meg, blue-hatted and waiting on the steps, carrying sofas and chairs and coffee tables to their suites in the Houses. Down by the Charles the middle-aged men were catching the last phases of summer sensuality before the grass grew cold and damp, and before the young would be forced indoors to play. I wondered what those hungry, spying men did in the winter or at night when it was too dark to see. Perhaps, I thought, they just stood there and listened.

In our building Miss O'Hara was still listening. She had never stopped. When Meg was outside on the steps it was very quiet and I felt good that Miss O'Hara had to wait a long, long time before she heard anything. The company gave the halls and ceilings a new coat of paint, but it was still old in the building. James Sullivan got his yearly two-week vacation and they went to the Boston Common for six hours: two hours going, two hours sitting on the benches, and two hours coming back. Then they both sat on the steps, watching, and waiting.

At first I wanted to be kind because he was old and dying in a special way and I was young and ambitious. But at night, in my apartment, when I heard his dragging feet in the hall outside and knew that he would be drunk and repetitious and imposing on my privacy, I did not want to be kind any more. There were girls outside and I knew that I could have one now because that desperate look had finally gone somewhere deep inside. I was young and now I did not want to be bothered.

"Did you read about the lousy twelve per cent Social Security increase those bastards in Washington gave us?"

"No."

He would force himself past me, trying to block the door with my body, and into the room. "When those old pricks tell me to count my blessings, I tell them, 'You're not one of them.' " He would seat himself at the table without meeting my eyes. "The cost of living's gone up more than twelve per cent in the last six months."

"I know."

"What unmitigated bastards."

I would try to be busy with something on my desk.

"But the Texas Oil Barons got another depletion allowance."

"They can afford to bribe politicians," I would mumble.

"They tax away our rainy-day dollars and give us a lousy twelve per cent."

"It's tough."

He would know that I did not want to hear any more and he would know that he was making a burden of himself. It made me feel bad that it was so obvious to him, but I could not help myself. It made me feel bad that I disliked him more every time I heard a girl laugh on the street far below my window. So I would nod occasionally and say half-phrases and smile slightly at something witty he was saying for the third time. If I did not offer him a drink he would go sooner and so I gave him Coke when he hinted at how dry he was. Then, when he had finally gone, saying, "I hope I haven't burdened you unduly," I went to bed and hated myself.

VIII

If I am a janitor it is either because I have to be a janitor or because I want to be a janitor. And if I do not have to do it, and if I no longer want to do it, the easiest thing in the world, for a young man, is to step up to something else. Any move away from it is a step up because there is no job more demeaning than that of a janitor. One day I made myself suddenly realize that the three dirty cans would never contain anything of value to me, unless, of course, I decided to gather material for Harold Robbins or freelance for the *Realist*. Neither alternative appealed to me.

Toward dawn one day, during the first part of October, I rented a U-Haul truck and took away two loads of things I had accumulated. The records I packed very carefully, and the stereo I placed on the front seat of the truck beside me. I slipped the Chivas Regal and a picture of Jean under some clothes in a trunk I will not open for a long time. And I left the rug on the floor because it was dirty and too large for my new apartment. I also left the two plates given to me by James Sullivan, for no reason at all. Sometimes I want to go back to get them, but I do not know how to ask for them or explain why I left them in the first place. But sometimes at night, when there is a sleeping girl beside me, I think that I cannot have them again because I am still young and do not want to go back into that building.

I saw him once in the Square walking along very slowly with two shopping bags, and they seemed very heavy. As I came up behind him I saw him put them down and exercise his arms while the crowd moved in two streams around him. I had an instant impulse to offer help and I was close enough to touch him before I stopped. I will never know why I stopped. And after a few seconds of standing behind him and knowing that he was not aware of anything at all except the two heavy bags waiting to be lifted after his arms were sufficiently rested, I moved back into the stream of people which passed on the left of him. I never looked back.

JAMES JOYCE

An Encounter

It was Joe Dillon who introduced the Wild West to us. He had a little library made up of old numbers of *The Union Jack, Pluck* and *The Halfpenny Marvel.* Every evening after school we met in his back garden and arranged Indian battles. He and his fat young brother Leo, the idler, held the loft of the stable while we tried to carry it by storm; or we fought a pitched battle on the grass. But, however well we fought, we never won siege or battle and all our bouts ended with Joe Dillon's war dance of victory. His parents went to eight-o'clock mass every morning in Gardiner Street and the peaceful odour of Mrs. Dillon was prevalent in the hall of the house. But he played too fiercely for us who were younger and more timid. He looked like some kind of an Indian when he capered round the garden, an old tea-cosy on his head, beating a tin with his fist and yelling:

"Ya! yaka, yaka, yaka!"

Everyone was incredulous when it was reported that he had a vocation for the priesthood. Nevertheless it was true.

A spirit of unruliness diffused itself among us and, under its influence, differences of culture and constitution were waived. We banded ourselves together, some boldly, some in jest and some almost in fear: and of the number of these latter, the reluctant Indians who were afraid to seem studious or lacking in robustness, I was one. The adventures related in the literature of the Wild West were remote from my nature but, at least, they opened doors of escape. I liked better some American detective stories which were traversed from time to time by unkempt fierce and beautiful girls. Though there was nothing wrong in these stories and though their intention was sometimes literary they circulated secretly at school. One day when Father Butler was hearing the four pages of Roman History clumsy Leo Dillon was discovered with a copy of *The Halfpenny Marvel.*

"This page or this page? This page? Now, Dillon, up! *'Hardly had the day'* . . . Go on! What day? *'Hardly had the day dawned'* . . . Have you studied it? What have you there in your pocket?"

Everyone's heart palpitated as Leo Dillon handed up the paper and everyone assumed an innocent face. Father Butler turned over the pages, frowning.

"What is this rubbish?" he said. "*The Apache Chief!* Is this what you read instead of studying your Roman History? Let me not find any more of this wretched stuff in this college. The man who wrote it, I suppose, was some wretched fellow who writes these things for a drink. I'm surprised at boys like you, educated, reading such stuff. I could understand it if you were . . . National School boys. Now, Dillon, I advise you strongly, get at your work or . . ."

This rebuke during the sober hours of school paled much of the glory of the Wild West for me and the confused puffy face of Leo Dillon awakened one of my consciences. But when the restraining influence of the school was at a distance I began to hunger again for wild sensations, for the escape which those chronicles of disorder alone seemed to offer me. The mimic warfare of the evening became at last as wearisome to me as the routine of school in the morning because I wanted real adventures to happen to myself. But real adventures, I reflected, do not happen to people who remain at home: they must be sought abroad.

The summer holidays were near at hand when I made up my mind to break out of the weariness of schoollife for one day at least. With Leo Dillon and a boy named Mahony I planned a day's miching. Each of us saved up sixpence. We were to meet at ten in the morning on the Canal Bridge. Mahony's big sister was to write an excuse for him and Leo Dillon was to tell his brother to say he was sick. We arranged to go along the Wharf Road until we came to the ships, then to cross in the ferryboat and walk out to see the Pigeon House. Leo Dillon was afraid we might meet Father Butler or someone out of the college; but Mahony asked, very sensibly, what would Father Butler be doing out at the Pigeon House. We were reassured: and I brought the first stage of the plot to an end by collecting sixpence from the other two, at the same time showing them my own sixpence. When we were making the last arrangements on the eve we were all vaguely excited. We shook hands, laughing, and Mahony said:

"Till to-morrow, mates!"

That night I slept badly. In the morning I was firstcomer to the bridge as I lived nearest. I hid my books in the long grass near the ashpit at the end of the garden where nobody ever came and hurried along the canal bank. It was a mild sunny morning in the first week of June. I sat up on the coping of the bridge admiring my frail canvas shoes which I had diligently pipe-clayed overnight and watching the docile horses pulling a tramload of business people up the hill. All the branches of the tall trees which lined the mall were gay with little light green leaves and the sunlight slanted through them on to the water. The granite stone of the bridge was beginning to be warm and I began to pat it with my hands in time to an air in my head. I was very happy.

When I had been sitting there for five or ten minutes I saw Mahony's grey suit approaching. He came up the hill, smiling, and clambered up beside me on the bridge. While we were waiting he brought out the catapult which bulged from his inner pocket and explained some improvements which he had made in it. I asked him why he had brought it and he told me he had brought it to have some gas with the birds. Mahoney used slang freely, and spoke of Father Butler as Old Bunser. We waited on for a quarter of an hour more but there was still no sign of Leo Dillon. Mahony, at last, jumped down and said:

"Come along. I knew Fatty'd funk it."

"And his sixpence . . . ?" I said.

"That's forfeit," said Mahony. "And so much the better for us—a bob and a tanner instead of a bob."

We walked along the North Strand Road till we came to the Vitriol Works and then turned to the right along the Wharf Road. Mahony began to play the Indian as soon as we were out of public sight. He chased a crowd of ragged girls, brandishing his unloaded catapult and, when two ragged boys began, out of chivalry, to fling stones at us, he proposed that we should charge them. I objected that the boys were too small, and so we walked on, the ragged troop screaming after us: "*Swaddlers! Swaddlers!*" thinking that we were Protestants because Mahony, who was dark-complexioned, wore the silver badge of a cricket club in his cap. When we came to the Smoothing Iron we arranged a siege; but it was a failure because you must have at least three. We revenged ourselves on Leo Dillon by saying what a funk he was and guessing how many he would get at three o'clock from Mr. Ryan.

We came then near the river. We spent a long time walking about the noisy streets flanked by high stone walls, watching the working of cranes and engines and often being shouted at for our immobility by the drivers of groaning carts. It was noon when we reached the quays and, as all the labourers seemed to be eating their lunches, we bought two big currant buns and sat down to eat them on some metal piping beside the river. We pleased ourselves with the spectacle of Dublin's commerce—the barges signalled from far away by their curls of woolly smoke, the brown fishing fleet beyond Ringsend, the big white sailingvessel which was being discharged on the opposite quay. Mahony said it would be right skit to run away to sea on one of those big ships and even I, looking at the high masts, saw, or imagined, the geography which had been scantily dosed to me at school gradually taking substance under my eyes. School and home seemed to recede from us and their influences upon us seemed to wane.

We crossed the Liffey in the ferryboat, paying our toll to be transported in the company of two labourers and a little Jew with a bag. We were serious to the point of solemnity, but once during the short voyage our eyes met and we laughed. When we landed we watched the discharging of the graceful three-master which we had observed from the other quay. Some bystander said that she was a Norwegian vessel. I went to the stern and tried to decipher the legend upon it but, failing to do so, I came back and examined the foreign sailors to see had any of them green eyes for I had some confused notion. . . . The sailors' eyes were blue and grey and even black. The only sailor whose eyes could have been called green was a tall man who amused the crowd on the quay by calling out cheerfully every time the planks fell:

"All right! All right!"

When we were tired of this sight we wandered slowly into Ringsend. The day had grown sultry, and in the windows of the grocers' shops musty biscuits lay bleaching. We bought some biscuits and chocolate which we ate sedulously as we wandered through the squalid streets where the families of the fishermen live. We could find no dairy and so we went to the huckster's shop and bought a bottle of raspberry lemonade each. Refreshed by this, Mahony chased a cat down a lane, but the cat escaped into a wide field. We both felt rather tired and when we reached the field we made at once for a sloping bank over the ridge of which we could see the Dodder.

It was too late and we were too tired to carry out our project of visiting the Pigeon House. We had to be home before four o'clock lest our adventure should be discovered. Mahony looked regretfully at his catapult and I had to suggest going home by train before he regained any cheerfulness. The sun went in behind some clouds and left us to our jaded thoughts and the crumbs of our provisions.

There was nobody but ourselves in the field. When we had lain on the bank for some time without speaking I saw a man approaching from the far end of the field. I watched him lazily as I chewed one of those green stems on which girls tell fortunes. He came along by the bank slowly. He walked with one hand upon his hip and in the other hand he held a stick with which he tapped the turf lightly. He was shabbily dressed in a suit of greenish-black and wore what we used to call a jerry hat with a high crown. He seemed to be fairly old for his moustache was ashen-grey. When he passed at our feet he glanced up at us quickly and then continued his way. We followed him with our eyes and saw that when he had gone on for perhaps fifty paces he turned about and began to retrace his steps. He walked towards us very slowly, always tapping the ground with his stick, so slowly that I thought he was looking for something in the grass.

He stopped when he came level with us and bade us good-day. We answered him and he sat down beside us on the slope slowly and with great care. He began to talk of the weather, saying that it would be a very hot summer and adding that the seasons had changed greatly since he was a boy—a long time ago. He said that the happiest time of one's life was undoubtedly one's schoolboy days and that he would give anything to be young again. While he expressed these sentiments which bored us a little we kept silent. Then he began to talk of school and of books. He asked us whether we had read the poetry of Thomas Moore or the works of Sir Walter Scott and Lord Lytton. I pretended that I had read every book he mentioned so that in the end he said:

"Ah, I can see you are a bookworm like myself. Now," he added, pointing to Mahony who was regarding us with open eyes, "he is different; he goes in for games."

He said he had all Sir Walter Scott's works and all Lord Lytton's works at home and never tired of reading them. "Of course," he said, "there were some of Lord Lytton's works which boys couldn't read." Mahony asked why couldn't boys read them—a question which agitated and pained me because I was afraid the man would think I was as stupid as Mahony. The man, however, only smiled. I saw that he had great gaps in his mouth between his yellow teeth. Then he asked us which of us had the most sweethearts. Mahony mentioned lightly that he had three totties. The man asked me how many I had. I answered that I had none. He did not believe me and said he was sure I must have one. I was silent.

"Tell us," said Mahony pertly to the man, "how many have you yourself?"

The man smiled as before and said that when he was our age he had lots of sweethearts.

"Every boy," he said, "has a little sweetheart."

His attitude on this point struck me as strangely liberal in a man of his age. In my heart I thought that what he said about boys and sweethearts was reasonable. But I disliked the words in his mouth and I wondered why he shivered once or twice as if he feared something or felt a sudden chill. As he proceeded I noticed that his accent was good. He began to speak to us about girls, saying what nice soft hair they had and how soft their hands were and how all girls were not so good as they seemed to be if one only knew. There was nothing he liked, he said, so much as looking at a nice young girl, at her nice white hands and her beautiful soft hair. He gave me the impression that he was repeating something which he had learned by heart or that, magnetised by some words of his own speech, his mind was slowly circling round and round in the same orbit. At times he spoke as if he were simply alluding to some fact that everybody knew, and at times he lowered his voice and spoke mysteriously as if he were telling us something secret which he did not wish others to overhear. He repeated his phrases over and over again, varying them and surrounding them with his monotonous voice. I continued to gaze towards the foot of the slope, listening to him.

After a long while his monologue paused. He stood up slowly, saying that he had to leave us for a minute or so, a few minutes, and, without changing the direction of my gaze, I saw him walking slowly away from us towards the near end of the field. We remained silent when he had gone. After a silence of a few minutes I heard Mahony exclaim:

"I say! Look what he's doing!"

As I neither answered nor raised my eyes Mahony exclaimed again:

"I say . . . He's a queer old josser!"

"In case he asks us for our names," I said, "let you be Murphy and I'll be Smith."

We said nothing further to each other. I was still considering whether I would go away or not when the man came back and sat down beside us again. Hardly had he sat down when Mahony, catching sight of the cat which had escaped him, sprang up and pursued her across the field. The man and I watched the chase. The cat escaped once more and Mahony began to throw stones at the wall she had escaladed. Desisting from this, he began to wander about the far end of the field, aimlessly.

After an interval the man spoke to me. He said that my friend was a very rough boy and asked did he get whipped often at school. I was going to reply indignantly that we were not National School boys to be whipped, as he called it; but I remained silent. He began to speak on the subject of chastising boys. His mind, as if magnetised again by his speech, seemed to circle slowly round and round its new centre. He said that when boys were that kind they ought to be whipped and well whipped. When a boy was rough and unruly there was nothing would do him any good but a good sound whipping. A slap on the hand or a box on the ear was no good: what he wanted was to get a nice warm whipping. I was surprised at this sentiment and involuntarily glanced up at his face. As I did so I met the gaze of a pair of bottle-green eyes peering at me from under a twitching forehead. I turned my eyes away again.

The man continued his monologue. He seemed to have forgotten his recent liberalism. He said that if ever he found a boy talking to girls or having a girl for a sweetheart he would whip him and whip him; and that would teach him not to be talking to girls. And if a boy had a girl for a sweetheart and told lies about it then he would give him such a whipping as no boy ever got in this world. He said that there was nothing in this world he would like so well as that. He described to me how he would whip such a boy as if he were unfolding some elaborate mystery. He would love that, he said, better than anything in this world; and his voice, as he led me monotonously through the mystery, grew almost affectionate and seemed to plead with me that I should understand him.

I waited till his monologue paused again. Then I stood up abruptly. Lest I should betray my agitation I delayed a few moments pretending to fix my shoe properly and then, saying that I was obliged to go, I bade him good-day. I went up the slope calmly but my heart was beating quickly with fear that he would seize me by the ankles. When I reached the top of the slope I turned round and, without looking at him, called loudly across the field:

"Murphy!"

My voice had an accent of forced bravery in it and I was ashamed of my paltry stratagem. I had to call the name again before Mahony saw me and hallooed in answer. How my heart beat as he came running across the field to me! He ran as if to bring me aid. And I was penitent; for in my heart I had always despised him a little.

ISAAC BASHEVIS SINGER

Powers

I

As a rule, those who come for advice to the newspaper where I work do not ask for anyone in particular. We have a reporter who turns out a regular column of advice to readers, and anyone dropping around is usually referred to him. But this man asked especially for me. He was shown my room: a tall man—he had to bend his head to come through the door—without a hat, with a shock of black hair mixed with gray. His black eyes, under shaggy brows, had a wild look that rather frightened me. He had on a light raincoat, although it was snowing outside. His square face was red from the cold. He wore no tie, and his shirt was open, showing a chest covered with hair as thick as fur. He had a broad nose and thick lips. When he talked, he revealed large, separated teeth that appeared unusually strong.

He said, "Are you the writer?"

"I am."

He seemed surprised. "This little man who sits at this table?" he said. "I imagined you somewhat different. Well, things don't have to be exactly as we imagine them. I read every word you write—Yiddish and English both. When I hear that you've published something in a magazine, I run right out to buy it."

"Thank you very much. Please sit down."

"I'd rather stand—but—well—I will sit down. May I smoke?"

"Certainly."

"I should tell you I am not an American. I came here after the Second World War. I've been through Hitler's hell, Stalin's hell, and a couple of other hells besides. But that's not why I came to you. Do you have time to listen to me?"

"Yes, I have."

"Well, everybody in America is busy. How do you have time to write all those things and to see people too?"

"There is time for everything."

"Perhaps. Here in America time disappears—a week is nothing and a month is nothing, and a year passes by between yes and no. In those hells on the other side, a day seemed longer than a year does here. I've been in this country since 1950, and the years have gone like a dream. Now it's summer, now it's winter, the years just roll away. How old do you think I am?"

"In the forties—maybe fifty."

"Add thirteen years more. In April I will be sixty-three."

"You look young—knock on wood."

"That's what everybody says. In our family we don't turn gray. My grandfather died at ninety-three and he had hardly any gray hair. He was a blacksmith. On my mother's side, they were scholars. I studied at a yeshiva—I was a student at the yeshiva of Gur, and for a while in Lithuania. Only until I was seventeen, it's true, but I have a good memory. When I learn something, it stays stuck in my brain. I forget nothing, in a sense, and this is my tragedy. Once I was convinced that poring over the Talmud would be useless, I took to studying worldly books. The Russians had left by that time and the Germans had taken over. Then Poland became independent and I was drafted into the army. I helped to drive the Bolsheviks to Kiev. Then they drove us back to the Vistula. The Poles are not too fond of Jews, but I advanced. They made me a top sergeant—*chorázy*—the highest rank you can reach without military school, and after the war they offered to send me to a military academy. I might have become a colonel or something, but the barracks was not my ambition. I read a lot, painted, and tried to become a sculptor. I began to carve all sorts of figures out of wood. I ended up making furniture. Cabinet work—I specialized in repairing furniture, mostly antiques. You know how it is—inlays fall out, bits break off. It takes skill to make the patch invisible. I still don't know why I threw myself into it with such enthusiasm. To find the right grain of wood, the right color, and to fit it in so that the owner himself couldn't spot the place—for this, one needs iron patience, and instinct too.

"Now I'll tell you why I came to you. It's because you write about the mysterious powers: telepathy, spirits, hypnotism, fatalism, and so on—I read it all. I read it because I possess the powers you describe. I didn't come to boast, and don't get the idea I want to become a newspaperman. Here in America I work at my trade and I earn enough. I'm single—no wife, no children. They killed off my family. I take a drink of whisky, but I'm not a drunkard. I have an apartment here in New York, and a cottage in Woodstock. I don't need help from anybody.

"But to get back to the powers. You're right when you say a person is born with them. We're born with everything. I was a child of six when I first began to carve. Later I neglected it, but the gift stayed with me. And that's how it is with the powers. I had them but I didn't know what they were. I got up one morning and it came into my mind that someone in our building was going to fall out the window that day. We lived in Warsaw on Twarda Street. I didn't like the thought—it frightened me. I left for cheder, and when I came home the courtyard was black with people. The ambulance was just arriving. A glazier had been replacing a pane in a window on the second floor, and had fallen out. If such things had happened once, twice—even five times—I might have called it coincidence, but they happened so frequently there could be no question of coincidence. Strange, I began to understand that I should conceal this—as if it were an ugly birthmark. And I was right, because powers like this are a misfortune. It's better to be born deaf or lame than to possess them.

"But, no matter how careful you are, you can't hide everything. Once, I was sitting in the kitchen. My mother—peace be with her—was knitting a stocking. My father earned good money, even though he was a laborer. Our apartment was comfortable, and as clean as a rich man's house. We had a lot of copper dishes, which my mother used to scour each week until they shone. I was sitting on a low bench. I wasn't more than seven years old at the time. All of a sudden I said, 'Mama, there's money under the floor! There is money!' My mother stopped knitting and looked at me in amazement. 'What sort of money? What are you babbling about?' 'Money,' I said. 'Gold pieces.' My mother said, 'Are you crazy? How do you know what's under the floor?' 'I know,' I said. Already I realized that I shouldn't have said it, but it was too late.

"When my father came home for dinner, my mother told him what I had said. I wasn't there, but my father was so astonished he confessed that he had hidden a number of golden coins under the floor. I had an older sister and my father was saving a dowry for her—putting money into a bank was not the custom for simple people. When I returned from cheder, my father began to question me. 'Are you spying on me?' Actually, my father had hidden the money when I was in cheder and my mother was out marketing. My sister had gone to visit a friend. He had locked and bolted the door, and we lived on the third floor. He had even been careful enough to stuff the keyhole with cotton. I got a beating, but no matter how I tried I could not explain to him how I knew about those coins. 'This boy is a devil!' my father said, and he gave me an extra box on the ear. It was a good lesson to me to keep my mouth shut.

"I could tell you a hundred things like that about my childhood, but I'll add just one. Across the street from our home there was a store that sold dairy products. In those years, you went to the store to buy boiled milk. They boiled it on a gas range. One morning my mother gave me a pan and told me, 'Go to Zelda across the street and buy a quart of boiled milk.' I went over to the store and there was only one customer—a girl who was buying a few ounces of butter. In Warsaw they used to slice the butter from a big chunk with a bow, like the ones children carried at the Feast of Omer when they went picnicking in the Praga forest. I looked up and saw a strange thing: a light was burning over Zelda's head, as if there were a Hanukkah lamp in her wig. I stood and gaped—how was it possible? Nearby, at the counter, the girl spoke to Zelda as though there was nothing out of the way. After Zelda weighed the butter on the scale and the girl left, Zelda said, 'Come in, come in. Why are you standing there on the threshold?' I wanted to ask her, 'Why does a light burn over your head?' But I already had a hunch that I was the only one who saw it.

"The next day, when I came home from cheder, my mother said to me, 'Did you hear what happened? Zelda from the dairy store dropped dead.' You can imagine my fright. I was only about eight. Since then I've seen the same kind of light many times over the heads of those who were about to die. Thank God, I haven't seen it for the last twenty years. At my age, and among those I spend my days with, I could see those lights all the time."

II

"A while ago, you wrote that in every great love there is an element of telepathy. I was struck by this and decided that I had to see you. In my own life this happened not once, not ten times, but over and over again. In my young years I was romantic. I would see a woman and fall in love with her at first sight. In those days you couldn't just approach a woman and tell her you were in love with her. Girls were delicate creatures. A mere word was considered an insult. Also, in my own way, I was shy. Proud, too. It's not in my nature to run after women. To make it short, instead of talking to a girl, I would think about her—day and night. I fancied all kinds of impossible encounters and adventures. Then I began to notice that my thoughts took effect. The girl I had been thinking about so hard would actually come to me. Once, I deliberately waited for a woman on a crowded street in Warsaw until she appeared. I'm no mathematician, but I know the odds that this woman might cross that street at that very time were about one in twenty million. But she came, as though attracted by an invisible magnet.

"I'm not too credulous; even today I have my doubts. We want to believe that everything happens in a rational way and according to order. We're afraid of mysteries—if there are good powers, it's likely there are also evil ones, and who knows what they might do! But so many irrational things happened to me I would have to be an idiot to ignore them.

"Perhaps because I have this kind of magnetism, I never married. Anyway, I'm not the kind of man who is satisfied with one woman. I had other powers, too, but those I'm not going to boast about. I lived, as they say, in a Turkish paradise—often with as many as five or six lovers at the same time. In the drawing rooms where I used to fix furniture, I often made the acquaintance of beautiful women—mostly Gentiles. And I always heard the same song from them—I was different from other Jews, and all that kind of chatter. I had a room with a separate entrance, and that's all a bachelor needs. I kept brandy and liquors and a good supply of delicacies in my cupboard. If I were to tell you what took place in this room on my sofa, you could make a book out of it—but who cares? The older I grew, the clearer it became to me that for modern man marriage is sheer insanity. Without religion, the whole institution is absurd. Naturally, your mother and my mother were faithful women. For them there was one God and one husband.

"Now I come to the main point. In spite of all the women I had in those years, there was one I stayed with for almost thirty years—actually, until the day the Nazis bombed Warsaw. That day thousands of men crossed the bridge to Praga. I wanted to take Manya with me—Manya was her name—but she had the grippe, and I couldn't wait for her. I had plenty of connections in Poland, but in such a catastrophe they are not worth a sniff of tobacco. Later I was told that the house where I lived was hit by a bomb and reduced to a pile of lime and bricks. I never heard from Manya again.

"This Manya might have been considered an ordinary girl. She came from some little village in Greater Poland. When we met, we were both virgins. But no power and no treachery on my part could destroy the love between us. Somehow she knew of all my abominations and kept warning me that she would leave me, get married, and whatnot. But she came to me regularly every week—often more. The other women never spent the night in my room, but when Manya came she stayed. She was not particularly beautiful—dark, not tall, with black eyes. She had curly hair. In her village they called her Manya the Gypsy. She had all the antics of a gypsy. She told fortunes from cards and read palms. She believed in all kinds of witchcraft and superstitions. She even dressed like a gypsy in flowered skirts and shawls, wore large hoop earrings, and red beads around her neck. There was always a cigarette between her lips. She made a living as a salesgirl in a lingerie shop. The owners were an elderly couple without children, and Manya became almost a daughter to them. She was an excellent saleswoman. She could sew, embroider, and even learned how to make corsets. She managed the whole business. If she had been willing to steal, she could have had a fortune, but she was one hundred per cent honest. Anyhow, the old people were going to leave her the store in their will. In later years, the old man had a liver ailment, so they traveled to Carlsbad, Marienbad, and to Piszczany. And they left everything with Manya. Why did she need to get married? What she needed was a man, and I was that man. This girl, who could barely read and write, was, in her way, very refined—especially in sex. In my life I had God knows how many women, but there was never one like Manya. She had her own caprices and peculiarities, and when I think about them I don't know whether to laugh or cry. Sadism is sadism and masochism is masochism—are there names for all this nonsense? Each time we quarreled we were both terribly unhappy, and making peace was a great ceremony. She could cook fit for a king. When her bosses went to the spas, she cooked meals for me in their apartment. I used to say that her food had sex appeal, and there was some truth in it. This was her good side. The bad side was that Manya could never make peace with the idea that I had other women. She did everything she could to spoil my pleasure. By nature I am not a liar, but because of her I became one. Automatically. I didn't have to invent lies—my tongue did it by itself, and I was often astonished at how clever and farsighted a tongue can be. It foresaw events and situations—a matter I realized only later. However, you cannot fool anybody for thirty years. Manya knew my habits and she never stopped spying on me; my telephone used to ring in the middle of the night. At the same time, my business with other women gave her a perverse enjoyment. Now and again I confessed to her and she would ask for details, call me the worst names, cry, laugh, and become wild. I often felt like an animal trainer—like one who puts his head in the mouth of a lion. I always knew that my successes with other women made sense only as long as Manya was in the background. If I had Manya, the Countess Potocka was a bargain. Without Manya, no conquest was worth a groschen.

"It sometimes happened that I returned from one of my adventures, perhaps at an inn or at a nobleman's estate, and I would be with Manya that same night. She refreshed me and I would begin all over again as if nothing had happened. But as I grew older I began to worry that too much love might do me some damage. I am something of a hypochondriac. I read medical books and articles in the newspapers. I worried that I might be ruining my health. Once, when I returned completely exhausted and was to meet Manya, the thought ran through my mind: how good it would be if Manya would get her period and I would not have to spend the night with her. I called her and she said, 'A funny thing happened, I got my holiday'—this is what she called it—'in the middle of the month.' 'So you've turned into a miracle worker,' I said to myself. But I remained skeptical about its really having anything to do with my wish. Only after such things repeated themselves many times did I realize that I had the power to give orders to Manya's body. Every word I'm telling you is pure truth. A few times I willed her to become sick—of course, just for a while, because I loved her very much—and she immediately got a high fever. It became clear that I ruled over her body completely. If I had wanted her to die, she would have died. I had read books and pamphlets about mesmerism, animal magnetism, and such topics, but it never occurred to me that I possessed this power myself, and in such measure.

"Besides being able to do anything I wanted with her, I also knew her thoughts. I could literally read her mind. Once, after a bitter fight, Manya left, slamming the door so hard that the windowpanes trembled. The moment she left, it occurred to me that she was going to the Vistula to drown herself. I grabbed my overcoat and started after her silently. She went from one street to another and I trailed her like a detective. She never looked back. Finally she reached the Vistula and began to move straight toward the water. I ran after her and grabbed her shoulder. She screamed and struggled. I had saved her from death. After that, I ordered her in my mind never to think of suicide again. Later she told me, 'How strange, I often used to think of making an end to myself. Lately these thoughts have stopped completely. Can you explain this?'

"I could have explained everything. Once when she came to me, I told her, 'You have lost money today.' She became pale. It was the truth. She had returned from a savings bank and had lost six hundred zlotys."

III

"I will tell you the story about the dog and one story more and that will be enough. One summer—it must have been 1928 or 1929—I was overcome by a terrible fatigue. Hypochondria, too. I was entangled in so many affairs and complications that I almost fell apart. My telephone rang constantly. There were bitter quarrels between Manya and me that began to take on an uncanny character. At the place where she worked, the old man's wife had died, and

Manya kept threatening to marry him. She had a cousin in South Africa who wrote her love letters and offered to send her an affidavit. Her great love suddenly turned to terrible hatred. She talked about poisoning herself and me. She proposed a double suicide. A fire kindled in her black eyes, which made her look like a Tartar. We are all the descendants of God knows what murderers. Did you or someone else write in your newspaper that every man is potentially a Nazi? At night I usually slept like the dead, but now I suffered from insomnia. When I finally fell asleep, I had nightmares. One morning I felt that my end had come. My legs were shaky, everything whirled before my eyes, there was a ringing in my ears. I saw that if I did not make some change, I would be finished. I decided to leave everything and go away. I packed a bag. As I packed, the telephone rang madly, but I did not answer it. I went down the street and took a droshky to the Vienna depot. A train was about to leave for Krakow, and I bought a ticket. I sat down on the second-class bench and I was so tired that I slept through the whole trip. The conductor woke me at Krakow. In Krakow I again took a droshky and told the driver to take me to a hotel. The moment I entered the hotel room, I fell down on the bed in my clothes and dozed until dawn. I say dozed, because my sleep was fitful—I slept and I did not sleep. I went to the toilet and voices screamed in my ears and bells rang. I literally heard Manya crying and calling me back. I was on the verge of a breakdown. But with my last strength I curbed myself. I had fasted for a day and a night, and when I woke at about eleven o'clock in the morning I was more dead than alive. There are no baths in the Krakow hotel rooms—if you wanted a bath, you had to order it from the maid. There was a washstand and a pitcher of water in the room. Somehow I managed to shave, eat breakfast, and get myself to a railroad station. I rode a few stops, and there the rails ended. Of course I wanted to go to the mountains, but it was not the line to Zakopane but a spur. I arrived at a village near Babia Góra. This is a mountain apart from the other mountains—a mountain individualist—and few tourists go there. There was no hotel or rooming house and I got a room with an old peasant couple—*gazdas*. I guess you know the region and I don't have to tell you how beautiful it is. But this particular village was especially beautiful and wild, perhaps because it was so isolated. The old pair had a dog—a huge specimen—I don't know what breed. They warned me that he would bite and one should be careful. I patted him on the head, I tickled his neck, and he immediately became my pal. That's an understatement—the dog fell madly in love with me—and it happened almost at once. He did not leave me for a minute. The old couple rented the room every summer, but the dog had never become attached to any lodger. To make it short, I ran away from human love and fell into canine love. Burek had all the ways of a woman, even though he was a male. He made scenes of jealousy that were worse than Manya's. I took long walks and he ran after me everywhere. There were whole packs of dogs in the village and if I only looked at another dog Burek became wild. He bit them, and me too. At night he insisted upon sleeping on my bed. In those places, dogs have fleas. I tried not to let him into my room, but he howled and wailed so, he woke half the village. I had to let him in and he immediately jumped on the bed. He cried with a human voice. They began to say in the village that I was a sorcerer. I didn't stay long, because you could die there from boredom. I had taken a few books with me, but I soon read them all. I had rested and was ready for new entanglements. But parting from Burek was not an easy business. He had sensed, with God knows what instinct, that I was about to leave. I had telephoned Manya from the post office and had received telegrams and registered letters in that Godforsaken village. The dog kept on barking and howling. The last day, he went into some kind of spasm; he foamed at the mouth. The peasants were afraid he was mad. Until then, he hadn't even been tied up, but his owner got a chain and tied him to a stake. His clamor and his tearing at the chain shattered my nerves.

"I returned to Warsaw, sunburned but not really rested. What the dog did to me in that village, Manya and a few other females did in Warsaw. They all clung to me and bit me. I had orders to mend furniture, and the owners kept phoning me. A few days passed—or perhaps a few weeks; I don't remember exactly. After a difficult day, I went to bed early. I put out the lamp. I was so exhausted that I fell asleep immediately. Suddenly I woke up. Waking up in the middle of the night was not unusual for me, but this time I woke with the feeling that someone was in my room. I used to waken with a heaviness in my chest, but this time I felt an actual weight on my feet. I looked up and there was a dog lying on my blanket. The lamp was out, but it wasn't completely dark because a street lamp shone in. I recognized Burek.

"At first I had the idea that the dog had run after the train to Warsaw. But this was sheer nonsense. In the first place, he was tied up; then, no dog could run for so long after an express train. Even if the dog could have found his way to Warsaw by himself—and found my house—he could not have climbed up three flights of stairs. Besides, my door was always locked. I grasped that this was not a real dog, flesh and blood—it was a phantom. I saw his eyes, I felt the heaviness on my feet, but I didn't dare to touch him. I sat there terrified, and he looked me in the eyes with an expression utterly sad—and something else for which I have no name. I wanted to push him off and free my feet, but felt restrained. This was not a dog but a ghost. I lay down again and tried to fall asleep. After a while I succeeded. A nightmare? Call it a nightmare. But it was Burek just the same. I recognized his eyes, ears, his expression, his fur. The next day I wanted to write to the peasant to ask about the dog. But I knew that he couldn't read, and then I was too busy to write letters. I wouldn't have got an answer anyhow. I am absolutely convinced that the dog had died—what had visited me was not of this world.

"That wasn't the only time he came—over a number of years he kept returning, so that I had ample time to observe him even though he never appeared in the light. The dog was old when I left the village, and the way he looked that last day, I knew that he couldn't have lasted long. Astral body, spirit, soul—call it what you like—it is a fact so far as I'm concerned that a ghost of a dog came to me and lay on my legs, not once but dozens of times. Almost every night at first, then rarely. A dream? No, I wasn't dreaming—unless the whole of life is one dream."

IV

"I will tell you one last incident. I have already told you that a number of the women with whom I had affairs I met in the drawing rooms where I went to repair furniture. This plain man who sits here has made love to Polish countesses. What is a countess? We are all made of the same stuff. But once I met a young woman who really made me jump out of my skin. I was hired to go to a noblewoman's house in Vilanov, to mend an old pianoforte decorated with gilded garlands. While I was working, a young woman glided through the drawing room. She stopped for no more than a second, saw what I was doing, and our eyes met. How can I describe to you how she looked? Both Polish aristocrat and strangely Jewish—as if, by some magic, a gentle yeshiva student had turned into a Polish *panienka*. She had a narrow face and black eyes, such deep ones that I became confused. They actually burned me. Everything about this woman was full of spirituality. Never before have I seen such beauty. She disappeared in an instant, and I remained shattered. Later I asked the owner who that beauty was, and she said it was a niece who was visiting. She mentioned the name of some estate or town from which she came. But in my confusion I wasn't able to pay attention. I could easily have learned her name and address if I hadn't been so dazed. I finished my work; she did not show up again. But her image always stood before my eyes. I began to think about her day and night without stopping. My thoughts wore me out, and I decided to make an end of them, no matter what the cost. Manya realized that I wasn't myself and this was the cause of new scenes. I was so mixed up that, even though I knew Warsaw like my ten fingers, I got lost in the streets and made silly mistakes. It went on like this for months. Slowly my obsession weakened—or perhaps it just sank deeper inside me; I could think about someone else and at the same time brood about her. So the summer passed and it was winter, then it was spring again. One late afternoon—almost dusk—I don't remember if it was April or May—my telephone rang. I said hello, and no one answered. However, somebody was holding the receiver at the end of the line. I called again, 'Hello, hello, hello!' and I heard a crackle and a stammering voice. I said, 'Whoever you are, be so good as to speak up.'

"After a while I heard a voice that was a woman's voice but also the voice of a boy. She said to me, 'You once worked in Vilanov, in such and such a house. Do you happen to remember someone passing through the drawing room?' My throat became tight, and I almost lost the ability to move my tongue. 'Yes, I remember you,' I said. 'Could anyone forget your face?' She was so quiet I thought she had hung up. But she began to speak again—murmur is more like it. She said, 'I have to talk to you. Where can we meet?' 'Wherever you wish,' I said. 'Would you want to come to me?' 'No, out of the question,' she said. 'Perhaps in a café—' 'No, not in a café,' I said, 'Tell me where you could meet me and I will be there.' She became silent; then she mentioned a little street near the city library, way uptown, near Mokotow. 'When do you want it to be?' I asked. And she said, 'As soon as possible.' 'Perhaps now?' 'Yes, if you can make it.' I knew that there was no café, no restaurant, not even a bench to sit on in that little street, but I told her that I was leaving at once. There had been a time when I thought that if this miracle should happen I would jump for joy. But somehow everything was silent in me. I was neither happy nor unhappy—only amazed.

"When I arrived at our meeting place, it was already night. The street had trees on both sides and few lamps. I could see her in the half darkness. She seemed leaner, and her hair was combed up in a bun. She stood near a tree, wrapped in shadow. Except for her, the street was deserted. She started when I approached her. The trees were blooming and the gutter was full of blossoms. I said to her, 'Here I am. Where can we go?' 'What I want to tell you can be said right here,' she replied. 'What do you want to tell me?' I asked. She hesitated. 'I want to ask you to leave me in peace.'

"I was startled, and said, 'I don't know what you mean.' 'You know very well,' she said. 'You don't leave me in peace. I have a husband and I am happy with him. I want to be a faithful wife.' It wasn't talking but stammering. She paused after each word. She said, 'It wasn't easy to learn who you were and your telephone number. I had to invent a story about a broken chest to get the information from my aunt. I am not a liar; my aunt did not believe me. Still, she gave me your name and address.' Then she became silent.

"I asked, 'Why can't we go somewhere to talk it over?' 'I can't go anywhere. I could have told you this on the telephone—it is all so strange, absolutely insane—but now you know the truth.' 'I really don't know what's on your mind,' I said, just to prolong the conversation. She said, 'I beseech you, by whatever is holy to you, to stop tormenting me. What you want I cannot do—I'd rather die.' And her face became as pale as chalk.

"I still played the fool and said, 'I want nothing from you. It is true that when I saw you in your aunt's drawing room you made a strong impression on me—but I haven't done anything that should upset you.' 'Yes, you have. If you weren't living in the twentieth century, I would think you were a sorcerer. Believe me,' she went on, 'I didn't come easily to the decision to call you. I was even afraid that you might not know who I was—but you knew immediately.'

" 'We cannot stand here on the street and talk,' I said. 'We have to go somewhere.' 'Where? If someone who knows me should see me, I am lost.' I said, 'Come with me.' She hesitated for a while, and then she followed me. She seemed to have difficulty walking on her high heels and she took my arm. I noticed, even though she was wearing gloves, that she had most beautiful hands. Her hand fluttered on my arm, and each time a shudder ran through my body. After a while the young woman became more relaxed with me, and she said, 'What kind of powers do you possess? I have heard your voice several times. I have seen you, too. I woke up in the middle of the night and you were standing at the foot of my bed. Instead of eyes, two green beams shone from your sockets. I woke my husband, but in a second you vanished.'

" 'It's a hallucination,' I said. 'No, you wander in the night.' 'If I do, it's without knowing it.'

"We approached the shore of the Vistula and sat down on a log. It's quiet there. It's not completely safe because it's full of drunks and bums. But she sat with me. She said, 'My aunt will not know what has become of me. I told her that I was going for a walk. She even offered to accompany me. Give me a holy promise that you will let me go. Perhaps you have a wife and you wouldn't want anybody to molest her.'

" 'I have no wife," I said, 'but I promise you that, as far as it depends on me, I will not molest you. That's all I can promise.'

" 'I will be grateful to you until my last breath.'

"That is the story. I never saw the woman again. I don't even know her name. I don't know why, but of all the strange things that have happened to me this made the strongest impression. Well, that's all. I won't disturb you any more."

"You don't disturb me," I said. "It's good to meet a person with such powers. It strengthens my own faith. But how did it happen that Manya had the grippe when you left Warsaw? Why didn't you order her to get well?"

"What? I ask myself this question constantly. It seems that my power is only negative. To heal the sick, one must be a saint and, as you see, I am far from being a saint. Or it may be—who knows—that to have a woman along in those days was dangerous."

The stranger hung his head. He began to drum on the table with his fingers and to hum to himself. Then he got up. It seemed to me that his face had changed; it had become gray and wrinkled. Suddenly he looked his age. He even appeared less tall than before. I noticed that his raincoat was full of spots. He gave me his hand to say goodbye, and I accompanied him to the elevator.

"Do you still think about women?" I asked.

He thought it over as though he hadn't grasped my words. He looked at me sadly, with suspicion. "Only about dead women."

BERNARD MALAMUD

The Silver Crown

Gans, the father, lay dying in a hospital bed. Different doctors said different things, held different theories. There was talk of an exploratory operation but they thought it might kill him. One doctor said cancer.

"Of the heart," the old man said bitterly.

"It wouldn't be impossible."

The young Gans, Albert, a high school biology teacher, in the afternoons walked the streets in sorrow. What can anybody do about cancer? His soles wore thin with walking. He was easily irritated; angered by the war, atom bomb, pollution, death, obviously the strain of worrying about his father's illness. To be able to do nothing for him made him frantic. He had done nothing for him all his life.

A female colleague, an English teacher he had slept with once, a girl who was visibly aging, advised, "If the doctors don't know, Albert, try a faith healer. Different people know different things; nobody knows everything. You can't tell about the human body."

Albert laughed mirthlessly but listened. If specialists disagree who do you agree with? If you've tried everything what else can you try?

One afternoon after a long walk alone, as he was about to descend the subway stairs somewhere in the Bronx, still burdened by his worries, uneasy that nothing had changed, he was accosted by a fat girl with bare meaty arms who thrust a soiled card at him that he tried to avoid. She was a stupefying sight, retarded at the very least. Fifteen, he'd say, though she looks thirty and probably has the mentality of age ten. Her skin glowed, face wet, fleshy, the small mouth open and would be forever; eyes set wide apart on the broad unfocused face, either washed-out green or brown, or one of each—he wasn't sure. She seemed not to mind his appraisal, gurgled faintly. Her thick hair was braided in two ropelike strands; she wore bulging cloth slippers, bursting at seams and soles; a faded red skirt down to massive ankles; and a heavy brown sweater vest, buttoned over blown breasts, though the weather was still hot September.

The teacher's impulse was to pass by her outthrust plump baby hand. Instead he took the card from her. Simple curiosity—once you had learned to read you read anything? Charitable impulse?

Albert recognized Yiddish and Hebrew but read in English: "Heal The Sick. Save The Dying. Make A Silver Crown."

"What kind of silver crown would that be?"

She uttered impossible noises. Depressed, he looked away. When his eyes turned to hers she ran off.

He studied the card. "Make A Silver Crown." It gave a rabbi's name and address no less: Jonas Lifschitz, close by in the neighborhood. The silver crown mystified him. He had no idea what it had to do with saving the dying but felt he ought to know. Although at first repelled by the thought, he made up his mind to visit the rabbi and felt, in a way, relieved.

The teacher hastened along the street a few blocks until he came to the address on the card, a battered synagogue in a store, Congregation Theodor Herzl, painted in large uneven white letters on the plate-glass window. The rabbi's name, in smaller, gold letters, was A. Marcus. In the doorway to the left of the store the number of the house was repeated in tin numerals, and on a card under the vacant name plate under the mezuzah, appeared in pencil, "Rabbi J. Lifschitz. Retired. Consultations. Ring The Bell." The bell, when he decided to chance it, did not work—seemed dead to the touch—so Albert, his heartbeat erratic, turned the knob. The door gave easily enough and he hesitantly walked up a dark flight of narrow wooden stairs. Ascending, assailed by doubts, peering up through the gloom, he thought of turning back but at the first-floor landing compelled himself to knock loudly on the door.

"Anybody home here?"

He rapped harder, annoyed with himself for being there, engaging in the act of entrance—who would have predicted it an hour ago? The door opened a crack and that broad, badly formed face appeared. The retarded girl, squinting one bulbous eye, made noises like two eggs frying, and ducked back, slamming the door. The teacher, after momentary reflection, thrust it open in time to see her, bulky as she was, running swiftly along the long tight corridor, her body bumping the walls before she disappeared into a room at the rear.

Albert entered cautiously, with a sense of embarrassment, if not danger, warning himself to depart at once; yet stayed to peek curiously into a front room off the hallway, darkened by lowered green shades through which thread-like rivulets of light streamed. The shades resembled faded maps of ancient lands. An old gray-bearded man with thickened left eyelid, wearing a yarmulke, sat heavily asleep, a book in his lap, on a sagging armchair. Someone in the room gave off a stale odor, unless it was the armchair. As Albert stared, the old man awoke in a hurry. The small thick book on his lap fell with a thump to the floor, but instead of picking it up, he shoved it with a kick of his heel under the chair.

"So where were we?" he inquired pleasantly, a bit breathless.

The teacher removed his hat, remembered whose house he was in, and put it back on his head.

He introduced himself. "I was looking for Rabbi J. Lifschitz. Your—ah —girl let me in."

"Rabbi Lifschitz; this was my daughter Rifkele. She's not perfect, though God who made her in His image is Himself perfection. What this means I don't have to tell you."

His heavy eyelid went down in a wink, apparently involuntarily.

"What does it mean?" Albert asked.

"In her way she is also perfect."

"Anyway she let me in and here I am."

"So what did you decide?"

"Concerning what if I may ask?"

"What did you decide about what we were talking about—the silver crown?"

His eyes roved as he spoke; he rubbed a nervous thumb and forefinger. Crafty type, the teacher decided. Him I have to watch myself with.

"I came here to find out about this crown you advertised," he said, "but actually we haven't talked about it or anything else. When I entered here you were sound asleep."

"At my age—" the rabbi explained with a little laugh.

"I don't mean any criticism. All I'm saying is I am a stranger to you."

"How can we be strangers if we both believe in God?"

Albert made no argument of it.

The rabbi raised the two shades and the last of daylight fell into the spacious high-ceilinged room, crowded with at least a dozen stiff-back and folding chairs, plus a broken sofa. What kind of operation is he running here? Group consultations? He dispensed rabbinic therapy? The teacher felt renewed distaste for himself for having come. On the wall hung a single oval mirror, framed in gold-plated groupings of joined metal circles, large and small; but no pictures. Despite the empty chairs, or perhaps because of them, the room seemed barren.

The teacher observed that the rabbi's trousers were a week from ragged. He was wearing an unpressed worn black suit-coat and a yellowed white shirt without a tie. His wet grayish-blue eyes were restless. Rabbi Lifschitz was a dark-faced man with brown eye pouches and smelled of old age. This was the odor. It was hard to say whether he resembled his daughter; Rifkele resembled her species.

"So sit," said the old rabbi with a light sigh. "Not on the couch, sit on a chair."

"Which in particular?"

"You have a first-class humor." Smiling absently he pointed to two kitchen chairs and seated himself in one.

He offered a thin cigarette.

"I'm off them," the teacher explained.

"I also." The old man put the pack away. "So who is sick?" he inquired.

Albert tightened at the question as he recalled the card he had taken from the girl: "Heal The Sick, Save The Dying."

"To come to the point, my father's in the hospital with a serious ailment. In fact, he's dying."

The rabbi, nodding gravely, dug into his pants pocket for a pair of glasses, wiped them with a large soiled handkerchief and put them on, lifting the wire earpieces over each fleshy ear.

"So we will make then a crown for him?"

"That depends. The crown is what I came here to find out about."

"What do you wish to find out?"

"I'll be frank with you." The teacher blew his nose and slowly wiped it. "My cast of mind is naturally empiric and objective—you might say non-mystical. I'm suspicious of faith healing but I've come here, frankly, because I want to do anything possible to help my father recover his former health. To put it otherwise, I don't want anything to go untried."

"You love your father?" the rabbi clucked, a glaze of sentiment veiling his eyes.

"What I feel is obvious. My real concern right now mainly is how does the crown work. Could you be explicit about the mechanism of it all? Who wears it, for instance? Does he? Do you? Or do I have to? In other words, how does it function? And if you wouldn't mind saying, what's the principle, or rationale, behind it? This is terra incognita for me, but I think I might be willing to take a chance if I could justify it to myself. Could I see a sample of the crown, for instance, if you have one on hand?"

The rabbi, with an absent-minded start, seemed to interrupt himself about to pick his nose.

"What is the crown?" he asked, at first haughtily, then again, gently. "It's a crown, nothing else. There are crowns in Mishna, Proverbs, Kabbalah; the holy scrolls of the Torah are often protected by crowns. But this one is different, this you will understand when it does the work. It's a miracle. A sample doesn't exist. The crown has to be made individual for your father. Then his health will be restored. There are two prices—"

"Kindly explain what's supposed to cure the sickness," Albert said. "Does it work like sympathetic magic? I'm not nay-saying, you understand. I just happen to be interested in all kinds of phenomena. Is the crown supposed to draw off the illness like some kind of poultice, or what?"

"The crown is not a medicine, it is the health of your father. We offer the crown to God and God returns to your father his health. But first we got to make it the way it must be made—this I will do with my assistant, a retired jeweler. He has helped me to make a thousand crowns. Believe me, he knows silver—the right amount to the ounce according to the size you wish. Then I will say the blessings. Without the right blessings, exact to each word, the crown don't work. I don't have to tell you why. When the crown is finished your father will get better. This I will guarantee you. Let me read you some words from the mystic book."

"The Kabbalah?" the teacher asked respectfully.

"Like the Kabbalah."

The rabbi rose, went to his armchair, got slowly down on his hands and knees and withdrew the book he had shoved under the misshapen chair, a thick small volume with faded purple covers, not a word imprinted on it. The rabbi kissed the book and murmured a prayer.

"I hid it for a minute," he explained, "when you came in the room. It's a terrible thing nowadays, goyim come in your house in the middle of the day and take away that which belongs to you, if not your life itself."

"I told you right away that your daughter had let me in," Albert said in embarrassment.

"Once you mentioned I knew."

The teacher then asked, "Suppose I am a non-believer? Will the crown work if it's ordered by a person who has his doubts?"

"Doubts we all got. We doubt God and God doubts us. This is natural on account of the nature of existence. Of this kind doubts I am not afraid so long as you love your father."

"You're putting it as sort of a paradox."

"So what's so bad about a paradox?"

"My father wasn't the easiest man in the world to get along with, and neither am I for that matter, but he has been generous to me and I'd like to repay him in some way."

"God respects a grateful son. If you love your father this will go in the crown and help him to recover his health. Do you understand Hebrew?"

"Unfortunately not."

The rabbi flipped a few pages of his thick tome, peered at one closely and read aloud in Hebrew which he then translated into English. " 'The crown is the fruit of God's grace. His grace is love of creation.' These words I will read seven times over the silver crown. This is the most important blessing."

"Fine. But what about those two prices you mentioned a minute ago?"

"This depends how quick you wish the cure."

"I want the cure to be immediate, otherwise there's no sense to the whole deal," Albert said, controlling anger. "If you're questioning my sincerity, I've already told you I'm considering this recourse even though it goes against the grain of some of my strongest convictions. I've gone out of my way to make my pros and cons absolutely clear."

"Who says no?"

The teacher became aware of Rifkele standing at the door, eating a slice of bread with lumps of butter on it. She beheld him in mild stupefaction, as though seeing him for the first time.

"Shpeter, Rifkele," the rabbi said patiently.

The girl shoved the bread into her mouth and ran ponderously down the passageway.

"Anyway, what about those two prices?" Albert asked, annoyed by the interruption. Every time Rifkele appeared his doubts of the enterprise rose before him like warriors with spears.

"We got two kinds crowns," said the rabbi. "One is for 401 and the other is 986."

"Dollars, you mean, for God's sake?—that's fantastic."

"The crown is pure silver. The client pays in silver dollars. So the silver dollars we melt—more for the large-size crown, less for the medium."

"What about the small?"

"There is no small. What good is a small crown?"

"I wouldn't know, but the assumption seems to be the bigger the better. Tell me, please, what can a 986 crown do that a 401 can't? Does the patient get better faster with the larger one? It hastens the reaction?"

The rabbi, five fingers hidden in his limp beard, assented.

"Are there any other costs?"

"Costs?"

"Over and above the quoted prices?"

"The price is the price, there is no extra. The price is for the silver and for the work and for the blessings."

"Now would you kindly tell me, assuming I decide to get involved in this, where am I supposed to lay my hands on 401 silver dollars? Or if I should opt for the 986 job, where can I get a pile of cartwheels of that amount? I don't suppose that any bank in the whole Bronx would keep that many silver dollars on hand nowadays. The Bronx is no longer the Wild West, Rabbi Lifschitz. But what's more to the point, isn't it true the mint isn't making silver dollars all silver any more?"

"So if they are not making we will get wholesale. If you will leave with me the cash I will order the silver from a wholesaler, and we will save you the trouble to go to the bank. It will be the same amount of silver, only in small bars, I will weigh them on a scale in front of your eyes."

"One other question. Would you take my personal check in payment? I could give it to you right away once I've made my final decision."

"I wish I could, Mr. Gans," said the rabbi, his veined hand still nervously exploring his beard, "but it's better cash when the patient is so sick, so I can start to work right away. A check sometimes comes back, or gets lost in the bank, and this interferes with the crown."

Albert did not ask how, suspecting that a bounced check, or a lost one, wasn't the problem. No doubt some customers for crowns had stopped their checks on afterthought.

As the teacher reflected concerning his next move—should he, shouldn't he?—weighing a rational thought against a sentimental, the old rabbi sat in his chair, reading quickly in his small mystic book, his lips hastening along silently.

Albert at last got up.

"I'll decide the question once and for all tonight. If I go ahead and commit myself on the crown I'll bring you the cash after work tomorrow."

"Go in good health," said the rabbi. Removing his glasses he wiped both eyes with his handkerchief.

Wet or dry? thought the teacher.

As he let himself out of the downstairs door, more inclined than not toward trying the crown, he felt relieved, almost euphoric.

But by the next morning, after a difficult night, Albert's mood had about-faced. He fought gloom, irritation, felt flashes of hot and cold anger. It's throwing money away, pure and simple. I'm dealing with a clever confidence man, that's plain to me, but for some reason I am not resisting strongly. Maybe my subconscious is telling me to go along with a blowing wind and have the crown made. After that we'll see what happens—whether it rains, snows, or spring comes. Not much will happen, I suppose, but whatever does, my conscience will be in the clear.

But when he visited Rabbi Lifschitz that afternoon in the same roomful of empty chairs, though the teacher carried the required cash in his wallet, he was still uncomfortable about parting with it.

"Where do the crowns go after they are used and the patient recovers his health?" he cleverly asked the rabbi.

"I'm glad you asked me this question," said the rabbi alertly, his thick lid drooping. "They are melted and the silver we give to the poor. A mitzvah for one makes a mitzvah for another."

"To the poor you say?"

"There are plenty poor people, Mr. Gans. Sometimes they need a crown for a sick wife or a sick child. Where will they get the silver?"

"I see what you mean—recycled, sort of, but can't a crown be re-used as it is? I mean do you permit a period of time to go by before you melt them down? Suppose a dying man who recovers gets seriously ill again at a future date?"

"For a new sickness you will need a new crown. Tomorrow the world is not the same as today, though God listens with the same ear."

"Look, Rabbi Lifschitz," Albert said impatiently, "I'll tell you frankly that I am inching toward ordering the crown, but it would make my decision a whole lot easier all around if you would let me have a quick look at one of them—it wouldn't have to be for more than five seconds—at a crown-in-progress for some other client."

"What will you see in five seconds?"

"Enough—whether the object is believable, worth the fuss and not inconsequential investment."

"Mr. Gans," replied the rabbi, "this is not a showcase business. You are not buying from me a new Chevrolet automobile. Your father lays now dying in the hospital. Do you love him? Do you wish me to make a crown that will cure him?"

The teacher's anger flared. "Don't be stupid, rabbi, I've answered that. Please don't sidetrack the real issue. You're working on my guilt so I'll suspend my perfectly reasonable doubts of the whole freaking business. I won't fall for that."

They glared at each other. The rabbi's beard quivered. Albert ground his teeth.

Rifkele, in a nearby room, moaned.

The rabbi, breathing emotionally, after a moment relented.

"I will show you the crown," he sighed.

"Accept my apologies for losing my temper."

The rabbi accepted. "Now tell me please what kind of sickness your father has got."

"Ah," said Albert, "nobody is certain for sure. One day he got into bed, turned to the wall and said, 'I'm sick.' They suspected leukemia at first but the lab tests didn't confirm it."

"You talked to the doctors?"

"In droves. Till I was blue in the face. A bunch of ignoramuses," said the teacher hoarsely. "Anyway, nobody knows exactly what he has wrong with him. The theories include rare blood diseases, also a possible carcinoma of certain endocrine glands. You name it, I've heard it, with complications suggested, like Parkinson's or Addison's disease, multiple sclerosis, or something similar, alone or in combination with other sicknesses. It's a mysterious case, all in all."

"This means you will need a special crown," said the rabbi.

The teacher bridled. "What do you mean special? What will it cost?"

"The cost will be the same," the rabbi answered dryly, "but the design and the kind of blessings will be different. When you are dealing with such a mystery you got to make another one but it must be bigger."

"How would that work?"

"Like two winds that they meet in the sky. A white and a blue. The blue says, 'Not only I am blue but inside I am also purple and orange.' So the white goes away."

"If you can work it up for the same price, that's up to you."

Rabbi Lifschitz then drew down the two green window shades and shut the door, darkening the room.

"Sit," he said in the heavy dark, "I will show you the crown."

"I'm sitting."

"So sit where you are, but turn your head to the wall where is the mirror."

"But why so dark?"

"You will see light."

He heard the rabbi strike a match and it flared momentarily, casting shadows of candles and chairs amid the empty chairs in the room.

"Look now in the mirror."

"I'm looking."

"What do you see?"

"Nothing."

"Look with your eyes."

A silver candelabrum, first with three, then five, then seven burning bony candlesticks appeared like ghostly hands with flaming fingertips in the oval mirror. The heat of it hit Albert in the face and for a moment he was stunned.

But recalling the games of his childhood, he thought, who's kidding who? It's one of those illusion things I remember from when I was a kid. In that case I'm getting the hell out of here. I can stand maybe mystery but not magic tricks or dealing with a rabbinical magician.

The candelabrum had vanished, although not its light, and he now saw the rabbi's somber face in the glass, his gaze addressing him. Albert glanced quickly around to see if anyone was standing at his shoulder, but nobody was. Where the rabbi was hiding at the moment the teacher did not know; but in the lit glass appeared his old man's lined and shrunken face, his sad eyes, compelling, inquisitive, weary, perhaps even frightened, as though they had seen more than they had cared to but were still looking.

What's this, slides or home movies? Albert sought some source of projection but saw no ray of light from wall or ceiling, nor object or image that might be reflected by the mirror.

The rabbi's eyes glowed like sun-filled clouds. A moon rose in the blue sky. The teacher dared not move, afraid to discover he was unable to. He then beheld a shining crown on the rabbi's head.

It had appeared at first like a braided mother-of-pearl turban, then had luminously become—like an intricate star in the night sky—a silver crown, constructed of bars, triangles, half-moons and crescents, spires, turrets, trees, points of spears; as though a wild storm had swept them up from the earth and flung them together in its vortex, twisted into a single glowing interlocked sculpture, a forest of disparate objects.

The sight in the ghostly mirror, a crown of rare beauty—very impressive, Albert thought—lasted no longer than five short seconds, then the reflecting glass by degrees turned dark and empty.

The shades were up. The single bulb in a frosted lily fixture on the ceiling shone harshly in the room. It was night.

The old rabbi sat, exhausted, on the broken sofa.

"So you saw it?"

"I saw something."

"You believe what you saw—the crown?"

"I believe I saw. Anyway, I'll take it."

The rabbi gazed at him blankly.

"I mean I agree to have the crown made," Albert said, having to clear his throat.

"Which size?"

"Which size was the one I saw?"

"Both sizes. This is the same design for both sizes, but there is more silver and also more blessings for the $986 size."

"But didn't you say that the design for my father's crown, because of the special nature of his illness, would have a different style, plus some special blessings?"

The rabbi nodded. "This comes also in two sizes—the $401 and $986."

The teacher hesitated a split second. "Make it the big one," he said decisively.

He had his wallet in his hand and counted out fifteen new bills—nine one hundreds, four twenties, a five and a single—adding to $986.

Putting on his glasses, the rabbi hastily counted the money, snapping with thumb and forefinger each crisp bill as though to be sure none had stuck together. He folded the stiff paper and thrust the wad into his pants pocket.

"Could I have a receipt?"

"I would like to give you a receipt," said Rabbi Lifschitz earnestly, "but for the crowns there are no receipts. Some things are not a business."

"If money is exchanged, why not?"

"God will not allow. My father did not give receipts and also my grandfather."

"How can I prove I paid you if something goes wrong?"

"You have my word, nothing will go wrong."

"Yes, but suppose something unforeseen did," Albert insisted, "would you return the cash?"

"Here is your cash," said the rabbi, handing the teacher the packet of folded bills.

"Never mind," said Albert hastily. "Could you tell me when the crown will be ready?"

"Tomorrow night before Shabbos, the latest."

"So soon?"

"Your father is dying."

"That's right, but the crown looks like a pretty intricate piece of work to put together out of all those odd pieces."

"We will hurry."

"I wouldn't want you to rush the job in any way that would—let's say—prejudice the potency of the crown, or for that matter, in any way impair the quality of it as I saw it in the mirror—or however I saw it."

Down came the rabbi's eyelid, quickly raised without a sign of self-consciousness.

"Mr. Gans, all my crowns are first-class jobs. About this you got nothing to worry about."

They then shook hands. Albert, still assailed by doubts, stepped into the corridor. He felt he did not, in essence, trust the rabbi; and suspected that Rabbi Lifschitz knew it and did not, in essence, trust him.

Rifkele, panting like a cow for a bull, let him out the front door, perfectly.

In the subway, Albert figured he would call it an investment in experience and see what came of it. Education costs money, but how else can you get it? He pictured the crown as he had seen it established on the rabbi's head, and then seemed to remember that as he had stared at the man's shifty face in the mirror the thickened lid of his right eye had slowly dropped into a full wink. Did he recall this in truth, or was he seeing in his mind's eye and transposing into the past something that had happened just before he left the house? What does he mean by his wink?—not only is he a fake but he kids you? Uneasy once more, the teacher clearly remembered, when he was staring into the rabbi's fish eyes in the glass, after which they had lit in visionary light, that he had fought a hunger to sleep; and the next thing there's the sight of the old boy, as though on the television screen, wearing this high-hat magic crown.

Albert, rising, cried, "Hypnosis! The bastard magician hypnotized me! He never did produce a silver crown, it's out of my imagination—I've been suckered!"

He was outraged by the knavery, hypocrisy, fat nerve of Rabbi Jonas Lifschitz. The concept of a curative crown, if he had ever for a moment believed in it, crumbled in his brain and all he could think of were 986 blackbirds flying in the sky. As three curious passengers watched, Albert bolted out of the car at the next stop, rushed up the stairs, hurried across the street, then cooled his impatient heels for twenty-two minutes till the next train clattered into the station, and he rode back to the stop near the rabbi's house. Though he banged with both fists on the door, kicked at it, "rang" the useless bell until his thumb was blistered, the boxlike wooden house, including dilapidated synagogue store, was dark, monumentally starkly still, like a gigantic, slightly tilted tombstone in a vast graveyard; and in the end unable to arouse a soul, the teacher, long past midnight, had to head home.

He awoke next morning cursing the rabbi and his own stupidity for having got involved with a faith healer. This is what happens when a man—even for a minute—surrenders his true beliefs. There are less punishing ways to help the dying. Albert considered calling the cops but had no receipt and did not want to appear that much a fool. He was tempted, for the first time in six years of teaching, to phone in sick; then take a cab to the rabbi's house and demand the return of his cash. The thought agitated him. On the other hand, suppose Rabbi Lifschitz was seriously at work assembling the crown with his helper; on which, let's say, after he had bought the silver and paid the retired jeweler for his work, he made, let's say, a hundred bucks clear profit—not so very much; and there really *was* a silver crown, and the rabbi sincerely and religiously believed it would reverse the course of his father's illness? Although nervously disturbed by his suspicions, Albert felt he had better not get the police into the act too soon because the crown wasn't promised—didn't the old gent say—until before the Sabbath, which gave him till sunset tonight.

If he produces the thing by then, I have no case against him even if it's a piece of junk. So I better wait. But what a dope I was to order the $986 job instead of the $401. On that decision alone I lost $585.

After a distracted day's work Albert taxied to the rabbi's house and tried to rouse him, even hallooing at the blank windows facing the street; but either nobody was home or they were both hiding, the rabbi under the broken sofa, Rifkele trying to shove her bulk under a bathtub. Albert decided to wait them out. Soon the old boy would have to leave the house to step into the shul on Friday night. He would speak to him, warn him to come clean. But the sun set; dusk settled on the earth; and though the autumn stars and a sliver of moon gleamed in the sky, the house was dark, shades drawn; and no Rabbi Lifschitz emerged. Lights had gone on in the little shul, candles were lit. It occurred to Albert, with chagrin, that the rabbi might be already worshipping; he might all this time have been in the synagogue.

The teacher entered the long, brightly lit store. On yellow folding chairs scattered around the room sat a dozen men holding worn prayer books, praying. The Rabbi A. Marcus, a middle-aged man with a high voice and a short reddish beard, was dovening at the Ark, his back to the congregation.

As Albert entered and embarrassedly searched from face to face, the congregants stared at him. The old rabbi was not among them. Disappointed, the teacher withdrew.

A man sitting by the door touched his sleeve.

"Stay awhile and read with us."

"Excuse me, I'd like to but I'm looking for a friend."

"Look," said the man, "maybe you'll find him."

Albert waited across the street under a chestnut tree losing its leaves. He waited patiently—till tomorrow if he had to.

Shortly after nine the lights went out in the synagogue and the last of the worshippers left for home. The red-bearded rabbi then emerged with his key in his hand to lock the store door.

"Excuse me, rabbi," said Albert, approaching. "Are you acquainted with Rabbi Jonas Lifschitz, who lives upstairs with his daughter Rifkele—if she is his daughter?"

"He used to come here," said the rabbi with a small smile, "but since he retired he prefers a big synagogue on Mosholu Parkway, a palace."

"Will he be home soon, do you think?"

"Maybe in an hour. It's Shabbat, he must walk."

"Do you—ah—happen to know anything about his work on silver crowns?"

"What kind of silver crowns?"

"To assist the sick, the dying?"

"No," said the rabbi, locking the shul door, pocketing the key, and hurrying away.

The teacher, eating his heart, waited under the chestnut tree till past midnight, all the while urging himself to give up and go home but unable to unstick the glue of his frustration and rage. Then shortly before 1 A.M. he saw some shadows moving and two people drifting up the shadow-encrusted street. One was the old rabbi, in a new caftan and snappy black Homburg, walking tiredly. Rifkele, in sexy yellow mini, exposing to above the big-bone knees her legs like poles, walked lightly behind him, stopping to strike her ears with her hands. A long white shawl, pulled short on the right shoulder, hung down to her left shoe.

"On my income their glad rags."

Rifkele chanted a long "boooo" and slapped both ears with her pudgy hands to keep from hearing it.

They toiled up the ill-lit narrow staircase, the teacher trailing them.

"I came to see my crown," he told the pale, astonished rabbi, in the front room.

"The crown," the rabbi said haughtily, "is already finished. Go home and wait, your father will soon get better."

"I called the hospital before leaving my apartment, there's been no improvement."

"How can you expect so soon improvement if the doctors themselves don't know what is the sickness? You must give the crown a little more time. God Himself has trouble to understand human sickness."

"I came to see the thing I paid for."

"I showed you already, you saw before you ordered."

"That was an image of a facsimile, maybe, or something of the sort. I insist on seeing the real thing, for which I paid close to one thousand smackers."

"Listen, Mr. Gans," said the rabbi patiently, "there are some things we are allowed to see which He lets us see them. Sometimes I wish He didn't let us. There are other things we are not allowed to see—Moses knew this—and one is God's face, and another is the real crown that He makes and blesses it. A miracle is a miracle, this is God's business."

"Don't you see it?"

"Not with my eyes."

"I don't believe a word of it, you faker, two-bit magician."

"The crown is a real crown. If you think there is magic, it is on account those people that they insist to see it—we try to give them an idea. For those who believe, there is no magic."

"Rifkele," the rabbi said hurriedly, "bring to Papa my book of letters."

She left the room, after a while, a little in fright, her eyes evasive; and returned in ten minutes, after flushing the toilet, in a shapeless long flannel nightgrown, carrying a large yellowed notebook whose loose pages were thickly interleaved with old correspondence.

"Testimonials," said the rabbi.

Turning several loose pages, with trembling hand he extracted a letter and read it aloud, his voice husky with emotion.

" 'Dear Rabbi Lifschitz: Since the miraculous recovery of my mother, Mrs. Max Cohen, from her recent illness, my impulse is to cover your bare feet with kisses. Your crown worked wonders and I am recommending it to all my friends. Yours truly and sincerely, (Mrs.) Esther Polatnik.' "

"This is a college teacher."

He read another. " 'Dear Rabbi Lifschitz, Your $986 crown totally and completely cured my father of cancer of the pancreas, with serious complications of the lungs, after nothing else had worked. Never before have I believed in miraculous occurrences, but from now on I will have less doubts. My thanks to you and God. Most sincerely, Daniel Schwartz.' "

"A lawyer," said the rabbi.

He offered the book to Albert. "Look yourself, Mr. Gans, hundreds of letters."

Albert wouldn't touch it.

"There's only one thing I want to look at, Rabbi Lifschitz, and it's not a book of useless testimonials. I want to see my father's silver crown."

"This is impossible. I already explained to you why I can't do this. God's word is God's law."

"So if it's the law you're citing, either I see the crown in the next five minutes, or the first thing tomorrow morning I'm reporting you and your activities to the Bronx County District Attorney."

"Booo-ooo," sang Rifkele, banging her ears.

"Shut up!" Albert said.

"Have respect," cried the rabbi. "Grubber yung!"

"I will swear out a complaint and the D.A. will shut you down, the whole freaking plant, if you don't at once return the $986 you swindled me out of."

The rabbi wavered in his tracks. "Is this the way to talk to a rabbi of God?"

"A thief is a thief."

Rifkele blubbered, squealed.

"Sha," the rabbi thickly whispered to Albert, clasping and unclasping his gray hands. "You'll frighten the neighbors. Listen to me, Mr. Gans, you saw with your eyes what it looks like the real crown. I give you my word that nobody of my whole clientele ever saw this before. I showed you for your father's sake so you would tell me to make the crown which will save him. Don't spoil now the miracle."

"Miracle," Albert bellowed, "it's a freaking fake magic, with an idiot girl for a come-on and hypnotic mirrors. I was mesmerized, suckered by you."

"Be kind," begged the rabbi, tottering as he wandered amid empty chairs. "Be merciful to an old man. Think of my poor child. Think of your father who loves you."

"He hates me, the son-of-a-bitch, I hope he croaks."

In an explosion of silence the girl slobbered in fright.

"Aha," cried the wild-eyed rabbi, pointing a finger at God in heaven.

"Murderer," he cried, aghast.

Moaning, father and daughter rushed into each other's arms, as Albert, wearing a massive, spike-laden headache, rushed down the booming stairs.

An hour later the elder Gans shut his eyes and expired.

RALPH ELLISON

Battle Royal

It goes a long way back, some twenty years. All my life I had been looking for something, and everywhere I turned someone tried to tell me what it was. I accepted their answers too, though they were often in contradiction and even self-contradictory. I was naïve. I was looking for myself and asking everyone except myself questions which I, and only I, could answer. It took me a long time and much painful boomeranging of my expectations to achieve a realization everyone else appears to have been born with: That I am nobody but myself. But first I had to discover that I am an invisible man!

And yet I am no freak of nature, nor of history. I was in the cards, other things having been equal (or unequal) eighty-five years ago. I am not ashamed of my grandparents for having been slaves. I am only ashamed of myself for having at one time been ashamed. About eighty-five years ago they were told that they were free, united with others of our country in everything pertaining to the common good, and, in everything social, separate like the fingers of the hand. And they believed it. They exulted in it. They stayed in their place, worked hard, and brought up my father to do the same. But my grandfather is the one. He was an odd old guy, my grandfather, and I am told I take after him. It was he who caused the trouble. On his deathbed he called my father to him and said, "Son, after I'm gone I want you to keep up the good fight. I never told you, but our life is a war and I have been a traitor all my born days, a spy in the enemy's country ever since I give up my gun back in the Reconstruction. Live with your head in the lion's mouth. I want you to overcome 'em with yeses, undermine 'em with grins, agree 'em to death and destruction, let 'em swoller you till they vomit or bust wide open." They thought the old man had gone out of his mind. He had been the meekest of men. The younger children were rushed from the room, the shades drawn and the flame of the lamp turned so low that it sputtered on the wick like the old man's breathing. "Learn it to the younguns," he whispered fiercely; then he died.

But my folks were more alarmed over his last words than over his dying. It was as though he had not died at all, his words caused so much anxiety. I was warned emphatically to forget what he had said and, indeed, this is the first time it has been mentioned outside the family circle. It had a tremendous effect upon me, however. I could never be sure of what he meant. Grandfather had been a quiet old man who never made any trouble, yet on his deathbed he had called himself a traitor and a spy, and he had spoken of his meekness as a dangerous activity. It became a constant puzzle which lay unanswered in the back of my mind. And whenever things went well for me I remembered my grandfather and felt guilty and uncomfortable. It was as though I was carrying out his advice in spite of myself. And to make it worse, everyone loved me for it. I was praised by the most lily-white men of the town. I was considered an example of desirable conduct—just as my grandfather had been. And what puzzled me was that the old man had defined it as *treachery*. When I was praised for my conduct I felt a guilt that in some way I was doing something that was really against the wishes of the white folks, that if they understood they would have desired me to act just the opposite, that I should have been sulky and mean, and that that really would have been what they wanted, even though they were fooled and thought they wanted me to act as I did. It made me afraid that some day they would look upon me as a traitor and I would be lost. Still I was more afraid to act any other way because they didn't like that at all. The old man's words were like a curse. On my graduation day I delivered an oration in which I showed that humility was the secret, indeed, the very essence of progress. (Not that I believed this—how could I, remembering my grandfather?—I only believed that it worked.) It was a great success. Everyone praised me and I was invited to give the speech at a gathering of the town's leading white citizens. It was a triumph for our whole community.

It was in the main ballroom of the leading hotel. When I got there I discovered that it was on the occasion of a smoker, and I was told that since I was to be there anyway I might as well take part in the battle royal to be fought by some of my classmates as part of the entertainment. The battle royal came first.

All of the town's big shots were there in their tuxedoes, wolfing down the buffet foods, drinking beer and whiskey and smoking black cigars. It was a large room with a high ceiling. Chairs were arranged in neat rows around three sides of a portable boxing ring. The fourth side was clear, revealing a gleaming space of polished floor. I had some misgivings over the battle royal, by the way. Not from a distaste for fighting, but because I didn't care too much for the other fellows who were to take part. They were tough guys who seemed to have no grandfather's curse worrying their minds. No one could mistaken their toughness. And besides, I suspected that fighting a battle royal might detract from the dignity of my speech. In those pre-invisible days I visualized myself as a potential Booker T. Washington. But the other fellows didn't care too much for me either, and there were nine of them. I felt superior to them in my way, and I didn't like the manner in which we were all crowded together into the servants' elevator. Nor did they like my being there. In fact, as the warmly lighted floors flashed past the elevator we had words over the fact that I, by taking part in the fight, had knocked one of their friends out of a night's work.

We were led out of the elevator through a rococo hall into an anteroom and told to get into our fighting togs. Each of us was issued a pair of boxing gloves and ushered into the big mirrored hall, which we entered looking cautiously about us and whispering, lest we might accidentally be heard above the noise of the room. It was foggy with cigar smoke. And already the whiskey was taking effect. I was shocked to see some of the most important men of the town quite tipsy. They were all there—bankers, lawyers, judges, doctors, fire chiefs, teachers, merchants. Even one of the more fashionable pastors. Something we could not see was going on up front. A clarinet was vibrating sensuously and the men were standing up and moving eagerly forward. We were a small tight group, clustered together, our bare upper bodies touching and shining with anticipatory sweat; while up front the big shots were becoming increasingly excited over something we still could not see. Suddenly I heard the school superintendent, who had told me to come, yell, "Bring up the shines, gentlemen! Bring up the little shines!"

We were rushed up to the front of the ballroom, where it smelled even more strongly of tobacco and whiskey. Then we were pushed into place. I almost wet my pants. A sea of faces, some hostile, some amused, ringed around us, and in the center, facing us, stood a magnificent blonde—stark naked. There was a dead silence. I felt a blast of cold air chill me. I tried to back away, but they were behind me and around me. Some of the boys stood with lowered heads, trembling. I felt a wave of irrational guilt and fear. My teeth chattered, my skin turned to goose flesh, my knees knocked. Yet I was strongly attracted and looked in spite of myself. Had the price of looking been blindness, I would have looked. The hair was yellow like that of a circus kewpie doll, the face heavily powdered and rouged, as though to form an abstract mask, the eyes hollow and smeared a cool blue, the color of a baboon's butt. I felt a desire to spit upon her as my eyes brushed slowly over her body. Her breasts were firm and round as the domes of East Indian temples, and I stood so close as to see the fine skin texture and beads of pearly perspiration glistening like dew around the pink and erected buds of her nipples. I wanted at one and the same time to run from the room, to sink through the floor, or go to her and cover her from my eyes and the eyes of the others with my body; to feel the soft thighs, to caress her and destroy her, to love her and murder her, to hide from her, and yet to stroke where below the small American flag was tattooed upon her belly her thighs formed a capital V. I had a notion that of all in the room she saw only me with her impersonal eyes.

And then she began to dance, a slow sensuous movement; the smoke of a hundred cigars clinging to her like the thinnest of veils. She seemed like a fair bird-girl girdled in veils calling to me from the angry surface of some gray and threatening sea. I was transported. Then I became aware of the clarinet playing and the big shots yelling at us. Some threatened us if we looked and others if we did not. On my right I saw one boy faint. And now a man grabbed a silver pitcher from a table and stepped close as he dashed ice water upon him and stood him up and forced two of us to support him as his head hung and moans issued from his thick bluish lips. Another boy began to plead to go home. He was the largest of the group, wearing dark red fighting trunks much too small to conceal the erection which projected from him as though in answer to the insinuating low-registered moaning of the clarinet. He tried to hide himself with his boxing gloves.

And all the while the blonde continued dancing, smiling faintly at the big shots who watched her with fascination, and faintly smiling at our fear. I noticed a certain merchant who followed her hungrily, his lips loose and drooling. He was a large man who wore diamond studs in a shirtfront which swelled with the ample paunch underneath, and each time the blonde swayed her undulating hips he ran his hand through the thin hair of his bald head and, with his arms upheld, his posture clumsy like that of an intoxicated panda, wound his belly in a slow and obscene grind. This creature was completely hypnotized. The music had quickened. As the dancer flung herself about with a detached expression on her face, the men began reaching out to touch her. I could see their beefy fingers sink into the soft flesh. Some of the others tried to stop them and she began to move around the floor in graceful circles, as they gave chase, slipping and sliding over the polished floor. It was mad. Chairs went crashing, drinks were spilt, as they ran laughing and howling after her. They caught her just as she reached the door, raised her from the floor, and tossed her as college boys are tossed at a hazing, and above her red, fixed-smiling lips I saw the terror and disgust in her eyes, almost like my own terror and that which I saw in some of the other boys. As I watched, they tossed her twice and her soft breasts seemed to flatten against the air and her legs flung wildly as she spun. Some of the more sober ones helped her to escape. And I started off the floor, heading for the anteroom with the rest of the boys.

Some were still crying and in hysteria. But as we tried to leave we were stopped and ordered to get into the ring. There was nothing to do but what we were told. All ten of us climbed under the ropes and allowed ourselves to be blindfolded with broad bands of white cloth. One of the men seemed to feel a bit sympathetic and tried to cheer us up as we stood with our backs against the ropes. Some of us tried to grin. "See that boy over there?" one of the men said. "I want you to run across at the bell and give it to him right in the belly. If you don't get him, I'm going to get you. I don't like his looks." Each of us was told the same. The blindfolds were put on. Yet even then I had been going over my speech. In my mind each word was as bright as flame. I felt the cloth pressed into place, and frowned so that it would be loosened when I relaxed.

But now I felt a sudden fit of blind terror. I was unused to darkness. It was as though I had suddenly found myself in a dark room filled with poisonous cottonmouths. I could hear the bleary voices yelling insistently for the battle royal to begin.

"Get going in there!"

"Let me at the big nigger!"

I strained to pick up the school superintendent's voice, as though to squeeze some security out of that slightly more familiar sound.

"Let me at those black sonsabitches!" someone yelled.

"No, Jackson, no!" another voice yelled. "Here, somebody, help me hold Jack."

"I want to get at that ginger-colored nigger. Tear him limb from limb," the first voice yelled.

I stood against the ropes trembling. For in those days I was what they called ginger-colored, and he sounded as though he might crunch me between his teeth like a crisp ginger cookie.

Quite a struggle was going on. Chairs were being kicked about and I could hear voices grunting as with a terrific effort. I wanted to see, to see more desperately than ever before. But the blindfold was as tight as a thick skin-puckering scab and when I raised my gloved hands to push the layers of white aside a voice yelled, "Oh, no you don't, black bastard! Leave that alone!"

"Ring the bell before Jackson kills him a coon!" someone boomed in the sudden silence. And I heard the bell clang and the sound of feet scuffling forward.

A glove smacked against my head. I pivoted, striking out stiffly as someone went past, and felt the jar ripple along the length of my arm to my shoulder. Then it seemed as though all nine of the boys had turned upon me at once. Blows pounded me from all sides while I struck out as best I could. So many blows landed upon me that I wondered if I were not the only blindfolded fighter in the ring, or if the man called Jackson hadn't succeeded in getting me after all.

Blindfolded, I could no longer control my motions. I had no dignity. I stumbled about like a baby or a drunken man. The smoke had become thicker and with each new blow it seemed to sear and further restrict my lungs. My saliva became like hot bitter glue. A glove connected with my head, filling my mouth with warm blood. It was everywhere. I could not tell if the moisture I felt upon my body was sweat or blood. A blow landed hard against the nape of my neck. I felt myself going over, my head hitting the floor. Streaks of blue light filled the black world behind the blindfold. I lay prone, pretending that I was knocked out, but felt myself seized by hands and yanked to my feet. "Get going, black boy! Mix it up!" My arms were like lead, my head smarting from blows. I managed to feel my way to the ropes and held on, trying to catch my breath. A glove landed in my midsection and I went over again, feeling as though the smoke had become a knife jabbed into my guts. Pushed this way and that by the legs milling around me, I finally pulled erect and discovered that I could see the black, sweat-washed forms weaving in the smoky-blue atmosphere like drunken dancers weaving to the rapid drum-like thuds of blows.

Everyone fought hysterically. It was complete anarchy. Everybody fought everybody else. No group fought together for long. Two, three, four, fought one, then turned to fight each other, were themselves attacked. Blows landed below the belt and in the kidney, with the gloves open as well as closed, and with my eye partly opened now there was not so much terror. I moved carefully, avoiding blows, although not too many to attract attention, fighting from group to group. The boys groped about like blind, cautious crabs crouching to protect their mid-sections, their heads pulled in short against their shoulders, their arms stretched nervously before them, with their fists testing the smoke-filled air like the knobbed feelers of hypersensitive snails. In one corner I glimpsed a boy violently punching the air and heard him scream in pain as he smashed his hand against a ring post. For a second I saw him bent over holding his hand, then going down as a blow caught his unprotected head. I played one group against the other, slipping in and throwing a punch then stepping out of range while pushing the others into the melee to take the blows blindly aimed at me. The smoke was agonizing and there were no rounds, no bells at three minute intervals to relieve our exhaustion. The room spun round me, a swirl of lights, smoke, sweating bodies surrounded by tense white faces. I bled from both nose and mouth, the blood spattering upon my chest.

The men kept yelling, "Slug him, black boy! Knock his guts out!"

"Uppercut him! Kill him! Kill that big boy!"

Taking a fake fall, I saw a boy going down heavily beside me as though we were felled by a single blow, saw a sneaker-clad foot shoot into his groin as the two who had knocked him down stumbled upon him. I rolled out of range, feeling a twinge of nausea.

The harder we fought the more threatening the men became. And yet, I had begun to worry about my speech again. How would it go? Would they recognize my ability? What would they give me?

I was fighting automatically when suddenly I noticed that one after another of the boys was leaving the ring. I was surprised, filled with panic, as though I had been left alone with an unknown danger. Then I understood. The boys had arranged it among themselves. It was the custom for the two men left in the ring to slug it out for the winner's prize. I discovered this too late. When the bell sounded two men in tuxedoes leaped into the ring and removed the blindfold. I found myself facing Tatlock, the biggest of the gang. I felt sick at my stomach. Hardly had the bell stopped ringing in my ears than it clanged again and I saw him moving swiftly toward me. Thinking of nothing else to do I hit him smash on the nose. He kept coming, bringing the rank sharp violence of stale sweat. His face was a black blank of a face, only his eyes alive—with hate of me and aglow with a feverish terror from what had happened to us all. I became anxious. I wanted to deliver my speech and he came at me as though he meant to beat it out of me. I smashed him again and again, taking his blows as they came. Then on a sudden impulse I struck him lightly and as we clinched, I whispered, "Fake like I knocked you out, you can have the prize."

"I'll break your behind," he whispered hoarsely.

"For *them?*"

"For *me,* sonofabitch."

They were yelling at us to break it up and Tatlock spun me half around with a blow, and as a joggled camera sweeps in a reeling scene, I saw the howling red faces crouching tense beneath the cloud of blue-gray smoke. For a moment the world wavered, unraveled, flowed, then my head cleared and Tatlock bounced before me. That fluttering shadow before my eyes was his jabbing left hand. Then falling forward, my head against his damp shoulder, I whispered,

"I'll make it five dollars more."

"Go to hell!"

But his muscles relaxed a trifle beneath my pressure and I breathed, "Seven?"

"Give it to your ma," he said, ripping me beneath the heart.

And while I still held him I butted him and moved away. I felt myself bombarded with punches. I fought back with hopeless desperation. I wanted to deliver my speech more than anything else in the world, because I felt only these men could judge truly my ability, and now this stupid clown was ruining my chances. I began fighting carefully now, moving in to punch him and out again with my greater speed. A lucky blow to his chin and I had him going too—until I heard a loud voice yell, "I got my money on the big boy."

Hearing this, I almost dropped my guard. I was confused: Should I try to win against the voice out there? Would not this go against my speech, and was not this a moment for humility, for nonresistance? A blow to my head as I danced about sent my right eye popping like a jack-in-the-box and settled my dilemma. The room went red as I fell. It was a dream fall, my body languid and fastidious as to where to land, until the floor became impatient and smashed up to meet me. A moment later I came to. An hypnotic voice said FIVE emphatically. And I lay there, hazily watching a dark red spot of my own blood shaping itself into a butterfly, glistening and soaking into the soiled gray world of the canvas.

When the voice drawled TEN I was lifted up and dragged to a chair. I sat dazed. My eye pained and swelled with each throb of my pounding heart and I wondered if now I would be allowed to speak. I was wringing wet, my mouth still bleeding. We were grouped along the wall now. The other boys ignored me as they congratulated Tatlock and speculated as to how much they would be paid. One boy whimpered over his smashed hand. Looking up front, I saw attendants in white jackets rolling the portable ring away and placing a small square rug in the vacant space surrounded by chairs. Perhaps, I thought, I will stand on the rug to deliver my speech.

Then the M.C. called to us, "Come on up here boys and get your money."

We ran forward to where the men laughed and talked in their chairs, waiting. Everyone seemed friendly now.

"There it is on the rug," the man said. I saw the rug covered with coins of all dimensions and a few crumpled bills. But what excited me, scattered here and there, were the gold pieces.

"Boys, it's all yours," the man said. "You get all you grab."

"That's right, Sambo," a blond man said, winking at me confidentially.

I trembled with excitement, forgetting my pain. I would get the gold and the bills, I thought. I would use both hands. I would throw my body against the boys nearest me to block them from the gold.

"Get down around the rug now," the man commanded, "and don't anyone touch it until I give the signal."

"This ought to be good," I heard.

As told, we got around the square rug on our knees. Slowly the man raised his freckled hand as we followed it upward with our eyes.

I heard, "These niggers look like they're about to pray!"

Then, "Ready," the man said. "Go!"

I lunged for a yellow coin lying on the blue design of the carpet, touching it and sending a surprised shriek to join those rising around me. I tried frantically to remove my hand but could not let go. A hot, violent force tore through my body, shaking me like a wet rat. The rug was electrified. The hair bristled up on my head as I shook myself free. My muscles jumped, my nerves jangled, writhed. But I saw that this was not stopping the other boys. Laughing in fear and embarrassment, some were holding back and scooping up the coins knocked off by the painful contortions of the others. The men roared above us as we struggled.

"Pick it up, goddamnit, pick it up!" someone called like a bass-voiced parrot. "Go on, get it!"

I crawled rapidly around the floor, picking up the coins, trying to avoid the coppers and to get greenbacks and the gold. Ignoring the shock by laughing, as I brushed the coins off quickly, I discovered that I could contain the electricity—a contradiction, but it works. Then the men began to push us onto the rug. Laughing embarrassedly, we struggled out of their hands and kept after the coins. We were all wet and slippery and hard to hold. Suddenly I saw a boy lifted into the air, glistening with sweat like a circus seal, and dropped, his wet back landing flush upon the charged rug, heard him yell and saw him literally dance upon his back, his elbows beating a frenzied tattoo upon the floor, his muscles twitching like the flesh of a horse stung by many flies. When he finally rolled off, his face was gray and no one stopped him when he ran from the floor amid booming laughter.

"Get the money," the M.C. called. "That's good hard American cash!"

And we snatched and grabbed, snatched and grabbed. I was careful not to come too close to the rug now, and when I felt the hot whisky breath descend upon me like a cloud of foul air I reached out and grabbed the leg of a chair. It was occupied and I held on desperately.

"Leggo nigger! Leggo!"

The huge face wavered down to mine as he tried to push me free. But my body was slippery and he was too drunk. It was Mr. Colcord, who owned a chain of movie houses and "entertainment palaces." Each time he grabbed me I slipped out of his hands. It became a real struggle. I feared the rug more than I did the drunk, so I held on, surprising myself for a moment by trying to topple *him* upon the rug. It was such an enormous idea that I found myself actually carrying it out. I tried not to be obvious, yet when I grabbed his leg, trying to tumble him out of the chair, he raised up roaring with laughter, and, looking at me with soberness dead in the eye, kicked me viciously in the chest. The chair leg flew out of my hand and I felt myself going and rolled. It was as though I had rolled through a bed of hot coals. It seemed a whole century would pass before I would roll free, a century in which I seared through the deepest levels of my body to the fearful breath within me and the breath seared and heated to the point of explosion. It'll all be over in a flash, I thought as I rolled clear. It'll all be over in a flash.

But not yet, the men on the other side were waiting, red faces swollen as though from apoplexy as they bent forward in their chairs. Seeing their fingers coming toward me I rolled away as a fumbled football rolls off the receiver's fingertips, back into the coals. That time I luckily sent the rug sliding out of place and heard the coins ringing against the floor and the boys scuffling to pick them up and the M.C. calling, "All right, boys, that's all. Go get dressed and get your money."

I was limp as a dish rag. My back felt as though it had been beaten with wires.

When we had dressed the M.C. came in and gave us each five dollars, except Tatlock, who got ten for being last in the ring. Then he told us to leave. I was not to get a chance to deliver my speech, I thought. I was going out into the dim alley in despair when I was stopped and told to go back. I returned to the ballroom, where the men were pushing back their chairs and gathering in groups to talk.

The M.C. knocked on a table for quiet. "Gentlemen," he said, "we almost forgot an important part of the program. A most serious part, gentlemen. This boy was brought here to deliver a speech which he made at his graduation yesterday . . ."

"Bravo!"

"I'm told that he is the smartest boy we've got out there in Greenwood. I'm told that he knows more big words than a pocket-sized dictionary."

Much applause and laughter.

"So now, gentlemen, I want you to give him your attention."

There was still laughter as I faced them, my mouth dry, my eye throbbing. I began slowly, but evidently my throat was tense, because they began shouting, "Louder! Louder!"

"We of the younger generation extol the wisdom of that great leader and educator," I shouted, "who first spoke these flaming words of wisdom: 'A ship lost at sea for many days suddenly sighted a friendly vessel. From the mast of the unfortunate vessel was seen a signal: "Water, water; we die of thirst!" The answer from the friendly vessel came back: "Cast down your bucket where you are." The captain of the distressed vessel, at last heeding the injunction, cast down his bucket, and it came up full of fresh sparkling water from the mouth of the Amazon River.' And like him I say, and in his words, 'To those of my race who depend upon bettering their condition in a foreign land, or who underestimate the importance of cultivating friendly relations with the Southern white man, who is his next-door neighbor, I would say: "Cast down your bucket where you are"—cast it down in making friends in every manly way of the people of all races by whom we are surrounded. . . .' "

I spoke automatically and with such fervor that I did not realize that the men were still talking and laughing until my dry mouth, filling up with blood from the cut, almost strangled me. I coughed, wanting to stop and go to one of the tall brass, sand-filled spittoons to relieve myself, but a few of the men, especially the superintendent, were listening and I was afraid. So I gulped it down, blood, saliva and all, and continued. (What powers of endurance I had during those days! What enthusiasm! What a belief in the rightness of things!) I spoke even louder in spite of the pain. But still they talked and still they laughed, as though deaf with cotton in dirty ears. So I spoke with greater emotional emphasis. I closed my ears and swallowed blood until I was nauseated. The speech seemed a hundred times as long as before, but I could not leave out a single word. All had to be said, each memorized nuance considered, rendered. Nor was that all. Whenever I uttered a word of three or more syllables a group of voices would yell for me to repeat it. I used the phrase "social responsibility" and they yelled:

"What's that word you say, boy?"

"Social responsibility," I said.

"What?"

"Social . . ."

"Louder."

". . . responsibility."

"More!"

"Respon—"

"Repeat!"

"—sibility."

The room filled with the uproar of laughter until, no doubt, distracted by having to gulp down my blood, I made a mistake and yelled a phrase I had often seen denounced in newspaper editorials, heard debated in private.

"Social . . ."

"What?" they yelled.

". . . equality—"

The laughter hung smokelike in the sudden stillness. I opened my eyes, puzzled. Sounds of displeasure filled the room. The M.C. rushed forward. They shouted hostile phrases at me. But I did not understand.

A small dry mustached man in the front row blared out, "Say that slowly, son!"

"What sir?"

"What you just said!"

"Social responsibility, sir," I said.

"You weren't being smart, were you, boy?" he said, not unkindly.

"No, sir!"

"You sure that about 'equality' was a mistake?"

"Oh, yes, sir," I said. "I was swallowing blood."

"Well, you had better speak more slowly so we can understand. We mean to do right by you, but you've got to know your place at all times. All right, now, go on with your speech."

I was afraid. I wanted to leave but I wanted also to speak and I was afraid they'd snatch me down.

"Thank you, sir," I said, beginning where I had left off, and having them ignore me as before.

Yet when I finished there was a thunderous applause. I was surprised to see the superintendent come forth with a package wrapped in white tissue paper, and, gesturing for quiet, address the men.

"Gentlemen, you see that I did not overpraise this boy. He makes a good speech and some day he'll lead his people in the proper paths. And I don't have to tell you that that is important in these days and times. This is a good, smart boy, and so to encourage him in the right direction, in the name of the Board of Education I wish to present him a prize in the form of this . . ."

He paused, removing the tissue paper and revealing a gleaming calfskin brief case.

". . . in the form of this first-class article from Shad Whitmore's shop."

"Boy," he said, addressing me, "take this prize and keep it well. Consider it a badge of office. Prize it. Keep developing as you are and some day it will be filled with important papers that will help shape the destiny of your people."

I was so moved that I could hardly express my thanks. A rope of bloody saliva forming a shape like an undiscovered continent drooled upon the leather and I wiped it quickly away. I felt an importance that I had never dreamed.

"Open it and see what's inside," was told.

My fingers a-tremble, I complied, smelling the fresh leather and finding an official-looking document inside. It was a scholarship to the state college for Negroes. My eyes filled with tears and I ran awkwardly off the floor.

I was overjoyed; I did not even mind when I discovered that the gold pieces I had scrambled for were brass pocket tokens advertising a certain make of automobile.

When I reached home everyone was excited. Next day the neighbors came to congratulate me. I even felt safe from grandfather, whose death-bed curse usually spoiled my triumphs. I stood beneath his photograph with my brief case in hand and smiled triumphantly into his stolid black peasant's face. It was a face that fascinated me. The eyes seemed to follow everywhere I went.

That night I dreamed I was at a circus with him and that he refused to laugh at the clowns no matter what they did. Then later he told me to open my brief case and read what was inside and I did, finding an official envelope stamped with the state seal; and inside the envelope I found another and another, endlessly, and I thought I would fall of weariness. "Them's years," he said. "Now open that one." And I did and in it I found an engraved document containing a short message in letters of gold. "Read it," my grandfather said. "Out loud."

"To Whom It May Concern," I intoned. "Keep This Nigger-Boy Running."

I awoke with the old man's laughter ringing in my ears.

(It was a dream I was to remember and dream again for many years after. But at that time I had no insight into its meaning. First I had to attend college.)

JAMES BALDWIN

This Morning, This Evening, So Soon

"You are full of nightmares," Harriet tells me. She is in her dressing gown and has cream all over her face. She and my older siser, Louisa, are going out to be girls together. I suppose they have many things to talk about—they have *me* to talk about, certainly—and they do not want my presence. I have been given a bachelor's evening. The director of the film which has brought us such incredible and troubling riches will be along later to take me out to dinner.

I watch her face. I know that it is quite impossible for her to be as untroubled as she seems. Her self-control is mainly for my benefit—my benefit, and Paul's. Harriet comes from orderly and progressive Sweden and has reacted against all the advanced doctrines to which she has been exposed by becoming steadily and beautifully old-fashioned. We never fought in front of Paul, not even when he was a baby. Harriet does not so much believe in protecting children as she does in helping them to build a foundation on which they can build and build again, each time life's high-flying steel ball knocks down everything they have built.

Whenever I become upset, Harriet becomes very cheerful and composed. I think she began to learn how to do this over eight years ago, when I returned from my only visit to America. Now, perhaps, it has become something she could not control if she wished to. This morning, at breakfast, when I yelled at Paul, she averted Paul's tears and my own guilt by looking up and saying, "My God, your father is cranky this morning, isn't he?"

Paul's attention was immediately distracted from his wounds, and the unjust inflicter of those wounds, to his mother's laughter. He watched her.

"It is because he is afraid they will not like his songs in New York. Your father is an *artiste, mon chou*, and they are very mysterious people, *les artistes*. Millions of people are waiting for him in New York, they are begging him to come, and they will give him a *lot* of money, but he is afraid they will not like him. Tell him he is wrong."

She succeeded in rekindling Paul's excitement about places he has never seen. I was also, at once, reinvested with all my glamour. I think it is sometimes extremely difficult for Paul to realize that the face he sees on record sleeves and in the newspapers and on the screen is nothing more or less than the face of his father—who sometimes yells at him. Of course, since he is only seven—going on eight, he will be eight years old this winter—he cannot know that I am baffled, too.

"Of course, you are wrong, you are silly," he said with passion—and caused me to smile. His English is strongly accented and is not, in fact, as good as his French, for he speaks French all day at school. French is really his first language, the first he ever heard. "You are the greatest singer in France"—sounding exactly as he must sound when he makes this pronouncement to his schoolmates—"the greatest *American* singer"—this concession was so gracefully made that it was not a concession at all, it added inches to my stature, America being only a glamorous word for Paul. It is the place from which his father came, and to which he now is going, a place which very few people have ever seen. But his aunt is one of them and he looked over at her. "Mme. Dumont says so, and she says he is a *great actor, too.*" Louisa nodded, smiling. "And she has seen *Les Fauves Nous Attendent*—five times!" This clinched it, of course. Mme. Dumont is our concierge and she has know Paul all his life. I suppose he will not begin to doubt anything she says until he begins to doubt everything.

He looked over at me again. "So you are wrong to be afraid."

"I was wrong to yell at you, too. I won't yell at you any more today."

"All right." He was very grave.

Louisa poured more coffee. "He's going to knock them dead in New York. You'll see."

"*Mais bien sur,*" said Paul, doubtfully. He does not quite know what "knock them dead" means, though he was sure, from her tone, that she must have been agreeing with him. He does not quite understand this aunt, whom he met for the first time two months ago, when she arrived to spend the summer with us. Her accent is entirely different from anything he has ever heard. He does not really understand why, since she is my sister and his aunt, she should be unable to speak French.

Harriet, Louisa, and I looked at each other and smiled. "Knock them dead," said Harriet, "means *d'avoir un succès fou.* But you will soon pick up all the American expressions." She looked at me and laughed. "So will I."

"That's what he's afraid of." Louisa grinned. "We have *got* some expressions, believe me. Don't let anybody ever tell you America hasn't got a culture. Our culture is as thick as clabber milk."

"Ah," Harriet answered, "I know. I know."

"I'm going to be practicing later, I told Paul.

His face lit up. "*Bon.*" This meant that, later, he would come into my study and lie on the floor with his papers and crayons while I worked out with the piano and the tape recorder. He knew that I was offering this as an olive branch. All things considered, we get on pretty well, my son and I.

He looked over at Louisa again. She held a coffee cup in one hand and a cigarette in the other; and something about her baffled him. It was early, so she had not yet put on her face. Her short, thick, graying hair was rougher than usual, almost as rough as my own—later, she would be going to the hairdresser's; she is fairer than I, and better-looking; Louisa, in fact, caught all the looks in the family. Paul knows that she is my older sister and that she helped to raise me, though he does not, of course, know what this means. He knows that she is a schoolteacher in the *American* South, which is not, for some reason, the same place as South America. I could see him trying to fit all those exotic details together into a pattern which would explain her strangeness—strangeness of accent, strangeness of manner. In comparison with the people he has always known, Louisa must seem, for all her generosity and laughter and affection, peculiarly uncertain of herself, peculiarly hostile and embattled.

I wondered what he would think of his Uncle Norman, older and much blacker than I, who lives near the Alabama town in which we were born. Norman will meet us at the boat.

Now Harriet repeats, "Nightmares, nightmares. Nothing ever turns out as badly as you think it will—in fact," she adds laughing, "I am happy to say that that would scarcely be possible."

Her eyes seek mine in the mirror—dark-blue eyes, pale skin, black hair. I had always thought of Sweden as being populated entirely by blondes, and I thought that Harriet was abnormally dark for a Swedish girl. But when we visited Sweden, I found out differently. "It is all a great racial salad, Europe, that is why I am sure that I will never understand your country," Harriet said. That was in the days when we never imagined that we would be going to it.

I wonder what she is really thinking. Still, she is right, in two days we will be on a boat, and there is simply no point in carrying around my load of apprehension. I sit down on the bed, watching her fix her face. I realize that I am going to miss this old-fashioned bedroom. For years, we've talked about throwing out the old junk which came with the apartment and replacing it with less massive, modern furniture. But we never have.

"Oh, everything will probably work out," I say. "I've been in a bad mood all day long. I just can't sing any more." We both laugh. She reaches for a wad of tissues and begins wiping off the cream. "I wonder how Paul will like it, if he'll make friends—that's all."

"Paul will like any place where you are, where we are. Don't you worry about Paul."

Paul has never been called any names, so far. Only, once he asked us what the word *métis* meant and Harriet explained to him that it meant mixed blood, adding that the blood of just about everybody in the world was mixed by now. Mme. Dumont contributed bawdy and detailed corroboration from her own family tree, the roots of which were somewhere in Corsica; the moral of the story, as she told it, was that women were weak, men incorrigible, and *le bon Dieu* appallingly clever. Mme. Dumont's version is the version I prefer, but it may not be, for Paul, the most utilitarian.

Harriet rises from the dressing table and comes over to sit in my lap. I fall back with her on the bed, and she smiles down into my face.

"Now, don't worry," she tells me, "please try not to worry. Whatever is coming, we will manage it all very well, you will see. We have each other and we have our son and we know what we want. So, we are luckier than most people."

I kiss her on the chin. "I'm luckier than most men."

"I'm a very lucky woman, too."

And for a moment we are silent, alone in our room, which we have shared so long. The slight rise and fall of Harriet's breathing creates an intermittent pressure against my chest, and I think how, if I had never left America, I would never have met her and would never have established a life of my own, would never have entered my own life. For everyone's life begins on a level where races, armies, and churches stop. And yet everyone's life is always shaped by races, churches, and armies; races, churches, armies menace, and have taken, many lives. If Harriet had been born in America, it would have taken her a long time, perhaps forever, to look on me as a man like other men; if I had met her in America, I would never have been able to look on her as a woman like all other women. The habits of public rage and power would also have been our private compulsions, and would have blinded our eyes. We would never have been able to love each other. And Paul would never have been born.

Perhaps, if I had stayed in America, I would have found another woman and had another son. But that other woman, that other son are in the limbo of vanished possibilities. I might also have become something else, instead of an actor-singer, perhaps a lawyer, like my brother, or a teacher, like my sister. But no, I am what I have become and this woman beside me is my wife, and I love her. All the sons I might have had mean nothing, since I *have* a son, I named him, Paul, for my father, and I love him.

I think of all the things I have seen destroyed in America, all the things that I have lost there, all the threats it holds for me and mine.

I grin up at Harriet. "Do you love me?"

"Of course not. I simply have been madly plotting to get to America all these years."

"What a patient wench you are."

"The Swedes are very patient."

She kisses me again and stands up. Louisa comes in, also in a dressing gown.

"I hope you two aren't sitting in here yakking about the *subject*." She looks at me. "My, you are the sorriest-looking celebrity I've ever seen. I've always wondered why people like you hired press agents. Now I know." She goes to Harriet's dressing table. "Honey, do you mind if I borrow some of that *mad* nail polish?"

Harriet goes over to the dressing table. "I'm not sure I know *which* mad nail polish you mean."

Harriet and Louisa, somewhat to my surprise, get on very well. Each seems to find the other full of the weirdest and most delightful surprises. Harriet has been teaching Louisa French and Swedish expressions, and Louisa has been teaching Harriet some of the saltier expressions of the black South. Whenever one of them is not playing straight man to the other's accent, they become involved in long speculations as to how a language reveals the history and the attitudes of a people. They discovered that all the European languages contain a phrase equivalent to "to work like a nigger." ("Of course," says Louisa, "they've had black men working for them for a long time.") "Language is experience and language is power," says Louisa, after regretting that she does not know any of the African dialects. "That's what I kept trying to tell those dirty bastards down South. They get their own experience into the language, we'll have a great language. But, no, they all want to talk like white folks." Then she leans forward, grasping Harriet by the knee. "I tell them, honey, white folks ain't saying *nothing*. Not a thing are they saying—and *some* of them know it, they *need* what you got, the whole world needs it." Then she leans back, in disgust. "You think they listen to me? Indeed they do not. They just go right on, trying to talk like white folks." She leans forward again, in tremendous indignation. "You know some of them folks are *ashamed* of Mahalia Jackson? *Ashamed* of her, one of the greatest singers alive! They think she's common." Then she looks about the room as though she held a bottle in her hand and were looking for a skull to crack.

I think it is because Louisa has never been able to talk like this to any white person before. All the white people she has ever met needed, in one way or another, to be reassured, consoled, to have their consciences pricked but not blasted; could not, could not afford to hear a truth which would shatter, irrevocably, their image of themselves. It is astonishing the lengths to which a person, or a people, will go in order to avoid a truthful mirror. But Harriet's necessity is precisely the opposite: it is of the utmost importance that she learn everything that Louisa can tell her, and then learn more, much more. Harriet is really trying to learn from Louisa how best to protect her husband and her son. This is why they are going out alone tonight. They will have, tonight, as it were, a final council of war. I may be moody, but they, thank God, are practical.

Now Louisa turns to me while Harriet rummages about on the dressing table. "What time is Vidal coming for you?"

"Oh, around seven-thirty, eight o'clock. He says he's reserved tables for us in some very chic place, but he won't say where." Louisa wriggles her shoulders, raises her eyebrows, and does a tiny bump and grind. I laugh. "That's right. And then I guess we'll go out and get drunk."

"I hope to God you do. You've been about as cheerful as a cemetery these last few days. And, that way, your hangover will keep you from bugging us tomorrow."

"What about *your* hangovers? I know the way you girls drink."

"Well, we'll be paying for our own drinks," says Harriet, "so I don't think we'll have that problem. But *you're* going to be feted, like an international movie star."

"You sure you don't want to change your mind and come out with Vidal and me?"

"We're sure," Louisa says. She looks down at me and gives a small, amused grunt. "An international movie star. And I used to change your diapers. I'll be damned." She is grave for a moment. "Mama'd be proud of you, you know that?" We look at each other and the air between us is charged with secrets which not even Harriet will ever know. "Now, get the hell out of here, so we can get dressed."

"I'll take Paul on down to Mme. Dumont's."

Paul is to have supper with her children and spend the night there.

"For the last time," says Mme. Dumont and she rubs her hand over Paul's violently curly black hair. "*Tu vas nous manquer, tu sais?*" Then she looks up at me and laughs. "He doesn't care. He is only interested in seeing the big ship and all the wonders of New York. Children are never sad to make journeys."

"I would be very sad to go," says Paul, "but my father must go to New York to work and he wants me to come with him."

Over his head, Mme. Dumont and I smile at each other. "*Il est malin, ton gosse!*" She looks down at him again. "And do you think, my little diplomat, that you will like New York?"

"We aren't only going to New York," Paul answers, "we are going to California, too."

"Well, do you think you will like California?"

Paul looks at me. "I don't know. If we don't like it, we'll come back."

"So simple. Just like that," says Mme. Dumont. She looks at me. "It is the best way to look at life. Do come back. You know, we feel that you belong to us, too, here in France."

"I hope you do," I say. "I hope you do. I have always felt—always felt at home here." I bend down and Paul and I kiss each other on the cheek. We have always done so—but will we be able to do so in America? American fathers never kiss American sons. I straighten, my hand on Paul's shoulder. "You be good. I'll pick you up for breakfast, or, if you get up first you come and pick me up and we can hang out together tomorrow, while your *Maman* and your Aunt Louisa finish packing. They won't want two men hanging around the house."

"*D'accord.* Where shall we hang out?" On the last two words he stumbles a little and imitates me.

"Maybe we can go to the zoo, I don't know. And I'll take you to lunch at the Eiffel Tower, would you like that?"

"Oh, yes," he says, "I'd love that." When he is pleased, he seems to glow. All the energy of his small, tough, concentrated being charges an unseen battery and adds an incredible luster to his eyes, which are large and dark brown—like mine—and to his skin, which always reminds me of the colors of honey and the fires of the sun.

"OK, then." I shake hands with Mme. Dumont. "*Bonsoir, Madame,*" I ring for the elevator, staring at Paul. "*Ciao, Pauli.*"

"*Bonsoir, Papa.*"

And Mme. Dumont takes him inside.

Upstairs, Harriet and Louisa are finally powdered, perfumed, and jeweled, and ready to go: dry martinis at the Ritz, supper, "in some *very* expensive little place," says Harriet, and perhaps the Folies Bergère afterwards. "A real cornball, tourist evening," says Louisa. "I'm working on the theory that if I can get Harriet to act like an American now, she won't have so much trouble later."

"I very much doubt," Harriet says, "that I will be able to endure the

Folies Bergère for three solid hours."

"Oh, then we'll duck across town to Harry's New York bar and drink mint juleps," says Louisa.

I realize that, quite apart from everything else, Louisa is having as much fun as she has ever had in her life. Perhaps she, too, will be sad to leave Paris, even though she has only known it for such a short time.

"Do people drink those in New York?" Harriet asks. I think she is making a list of the things people do or do not do in New York.

"*Some* people do." Louisa winks at me. "Do you realize that this Swedish chick's picked up an Alabama drawl?"

We laugh together. The elevator chugs to a landing.

"We'll stop and say goodnight to Paul," Harriet says. She kisses me. "Give our best to Vidal."

"Right. Have a good time. Don't let any Frenchmen run off with Louisa."

"I did not come to Paris to be protected, and if I had, this wild chick *you* married couldn't do it. I just *might* upset everybody and come home with a French count." She presses the elevator button and the cage goes down.

I walk back into our dismantled apartment. It stinks of departure. There are bags and crates in the hall which will be taken away tomorrow, there are no books in the bookcases, the kitchen looks as though we never cooked a meal there, never dawdled there, in the early morning or late at night, over coffee. Presently, I must shower and shave but now I pour myself a drink and light a cigarette and step out on our balcony. It is dusk, the brilliant light of Paris is beginning to fade, and the green of the trees is darkening.

I have lived in this city for twelve years. This apartment is on the top floor of a corner building. We look out over the trees and the roof tops to the Champ de Mars, where the Eiffel Tower stands. Beyond this field is the river, which I have crossed so often, in so many states of mind. I have crossed every bridge in Paris, I have walked along every *quai*. I know the river as one finally knows a friend, know it when it is black, guarding all the lights of Paris in its depths, and seeming, in its vast silence, to be communing with the dead who lie beneath it; when it is yellow, evil, and roaring, giving a rough time to tugboats and barges, and causing people to remember that it has been known to rise, it has been known to kill; when it is peaceful, a slick dark, dirty green, playing host to rowboats and *les bateaux mouches* and throwing up from time to time an extremely unhealthy fish. The men who stand along the *quais* all summer with their fishing lines gratefully accept the slimy object and throw it in a rusty can. I have always wondered who eats those fish.

And I walk up and down, up and down, glad to be alone.

It is August, the month when all Parisians desert Paris and one has to walk miles to find a barbershop or a laundry open in some tree-shadowed, silent side street. There is a single person on the avenue, a paratrooper walking toward École Militaire. He is also walking, almost certainly, and rather sooner than later, toward Algeria. I have a friend, a good-natured boy who was always hanging around the clubs in which I worked in the old days, who has just returned from Algeria, with a recurring, debilitating fever, and minus one eye. The government has set his pension at the sum, arbitrary if not occult, of fifty-three thousand francs every three months. Of course, it is quite impossible to live on this amount of money without working—but who will hire a half-blind invalid? This boy has been spoiled forever, long before his thirtieth birthday, and there are thousands like him all over France.

And there are fewer Algerians to be found on the streets of Paris now. The rug sellers, the peanut vendors, the postcard peddlers and moneychangers have vanished. The boys I used to know during my first years in Paris are scattered—or corralled—the Lord knows where.

Most of them had no money. They lived three and four together in rooms with a single skylight, a single hard cot, or in buildings that seemed abandoned, with cardboard in the windows, with erratic plumbing in a wet, cobblestoned yard, in dark, dead-end alleys, or on the outer, chilling heights of Paris.

The Arab cafés are closed—those dark, acrid cafés in which I used to meet with them to drink tea, to get high on hashish, to listen to the obsessive, stringed music which has no relation to any beat, any time, that I have ever known. I once thought of the North Africans as my brothers and that is why I went to their cafés. They were very friendly to me, perhaps one or two of them remained really fond of me even after I could no longer afford to smoke Lucky Strikes and after my collection of American sport shirts had vanished—mostly into their wardrobes. They seemed to feel that they had every right to them, since I could only have wrested these things from the world by cunning—it meant nothing to say that I had had no choice in the matter; perhaps I had wrested these things from the world by treason, by refusing to be identified with the misery of my people. Perhaps, indeed, I identified myself with those who were responsible for this misery.

And this was true. Their rage, the only note in all their music which I could not fail to recognize, to which I responded, yet had the effect of setting us more than ever at a division. They were perfectly prepared to drive all Frenchmen into the sea, and to level the city of Paris. But I could not hate the French, because they left me alone. And I love Paris, I will always love it, it is the city which saved my life. It saved my life by allowing me to find out who I am.

It was on a bridge, one tremendous, April morning, that I knew I had fallen in love. Harriet and I were walking hand in hand. The bridge was the Pont Royal, just before us was the great *horloge*, high and lifted up, saying ten to ten; beyond this, the golden statue of Joan of Arc, with her sword uplifted. Harriet and I were silent, for we had been quarreling about something. Now, when I look back, I think we had reached that state when an affair must either end or become something more than an affair.

I looked sideways at Harriet's face, which was still. Her dark-blue eyes were narrowed against the sun, and her full, pink lips were still slightly sulky, like a child's. In those days, she hardly ever wore make-up. I was in my shirt sleeves. Her face made me want to laugh and run my hand over her short dark hair. I wanted to pull her to me and say, *Baby, don't be mad at me*, and at that moment something tugged at my heart and made me catch my breath. There were millions of people all around us, but I was alone with Harriet. She was alone with me. Never, in all my life, until that moment, had I been alone with anyone. The world had always been with us, between us, defeating the quarrel we could not achieve, and making love impossible. During all the years of my life, until that moment, I had carried the menacing, the hostile, killing world with me everywhere. No matter what I was doing or saying or feeling, one eye had always been on the world—that world which I had learned to distrust almost as soon as I learned my name, that world on which I knew one could never turn one's back, the white man's world. And for the first time in my life I was free of it; it had not existed for me; I had been quarreling with my girl. It was our quarrel, it was entirely between us, it had nothing to do with anyone else in the world. For the first time in my life I had not been afraid of the patriotism of the mindless, in uniform or out, who would beat me up and treat the woman who was with me as though she were the lowest of untouchables. For the first time in my life I felt that no force jeopardized my right, my power, to possess and to protect a woman; for the first time, the first time, felt that the woman was not, in her own eyes or in the eyes of the world, degraded by my presence.

The sun fell over everything, like a blessing, people were moving all about us, I will never forget the feeling of Harriet's small hand in mine, dry and trusting, and I turned to her, slowing our pace. She looked up at me with her enormous, blue eyes, and she seemed to wait. I said, "*Harriet. Harriet. Tu sais, il y a quelque chose de très grave qui m'est arrivé. Je t'aime. Je t'aime. Tu me comprends*, or shall I say it in English?"

This was eight years ago, shortly before my first and only visit home.

That was when my mother died. I stayed in America for three months. When I came back, Harriet thought that the change in me was due to my grief—I was very silent, very thin. But it had not been my mother's death which accounted for the change. I had known that my mother was going to die. I had not known what America would be like for me after nearly four years away.

I remember standing at the rail and watching the distance between myself and Le Havre increase. Hands fell, ceasing to wave, handkerchiefs ceased to flutter, people turned away, they mounted their bicycles or got into their cars and rode off. Soon, Le Havre was nothing but a blur. I thought of Harriet, already miles from me in Paris, and I pressed my lips tightly together in order not to cry.

Then, as Europe dropped below the water, as the days passed and passed, as we left behind us the skies of Europe and the eyes of everyone on the ship began, so to speak, to refocus, waiting for the first glimpse of America, my apprehension began to give way to a secret joy, a checked anticipation. I thought of such details as showers, which are rare in Paris, and I thought of such things as rich, cold, American milk and heavy, chocolate cake. I wondered about my friends, wondered if I had any left, and wondered if they would be glad to see me.

The Americans on the boat did not seem to be so bad, but I was fascinated, after such a long absence from it, by the nature of their friendliness. It was a friendliness which did not suggest, and was not intended to suggest, any possibility of friendship. Unlike Europeans, they dropped titles and used first names almost at once, leaving themselves, unlike the Europeans, with nowhere thereafter to go. Once one had become "Pete" or "Jane" or "Bill" all that could decently be known was known and any suggestion that there might be further depths, a person, so to speak, behind the name, was taken as a violation of that privacy which did not, paradoxically, since they trusted it so little, seem to exist among Americans. They apparently equated privacy with the unspeakable things they did in the bathroom or the bedroom, which they related only to the analyst, and then read about in the pages of best sellers. There was an eerie and unnerving irreality about everything they said and did, as though they were all members of the same team and were acting on orders from some invincibly cheerful and tirelessly inventive coach. I was fascinated by it. I found it oddly moving, but I cannot say that I was displeased. It had not occurred to me before that Americans, who had never treated me with any respect, had no respect for each other.

On the last night but one, there was a gala in the big ballroom and I sang. It had been a long time since I had sung before so many Americans. My audience had mainly been penniless French students, in the weird, Left Bank bistros I worked in those days. Still, I was a great hit with them and by this time I had become enough of a drawing card, in the Latin quarter and in St. Germain des Prés, to have attracted a couple of critics, to have had my picture in *France-soir,* and to have acquired a legal work permit which allowed me to make a little more money. Just the same, no matter how industrious and brilliant some of the musicians had been, or how devoted my audience, they did not know, they could not know, what my songs came out of. They did not know what was funny about it. It was impossible to translate: It damn well better be funny, or Laughing to keep from crying, or What did *I* do to be so black and blue?

The moment I stepped out on the floor, they began to smile, something opened in them, they were ready to be pleased. I found in their faces, as they watched me, smiling, waiting, an artless relief, a profound reassurance. Nothing was more familiar to them than the sight of a dark boy, singing, and there were few things on earth more necessary. It was under cover of darkness, my own darkness, that I could sing for them of the joys, passions, and terrors they smuggled about with them like steadily depreciating contraband. Under cover of the midnight fiction that I was unlike them because I was black, they could stealthily gaze at those treasures which they had been mysteriously forbidden to possess and were never permitted to declare.

I sang *I'm Coming, Virginia,* and *Take This Hammer,* and *Precious Lord.* They wouldn't let me go and I came back and sang a couple of the oldest blues I knew. Then someone asked me to sing *Swanee River,* and I did, astonished that I could, astonished that this song, which I had put down long ago, should have the power to move me. Then, if only, perhaps, to make the record complete, I wanted to sing *Strange Fruit,* but, on this number, no one can surpass the great, tormented Billie Holiday. So I finished with *Great*

Getting-Up Morning and I guess I can say that if I didn't stop the show I certainly ended it. I got a big hand and I drank at a few tables and I danced with a few girls.

After one more day and one more night, the boat landed in New York. I woke up, I was bright awake at once, and I thought, *We're here.* I turned on all the lights in my small cabin and I stared into the mirror as though I were committing my face to memory. I took a shower and I took a long time shaving and I dressed myself very carefully. I walked the long ship corridors to the dining room, looking at the luggage piled high before the elevators and beside the steps. The dining room was nearly half empty and full of a quick and joyous excitement which depressed me even more. People ate quickly, chattering to each other, anxious to get upstairs and go on deck. Was it my imagination or was it true that they seemed to avoid my eyes? A few people waved and smiled, but let me pass; perhaps it would have made them uncomfortable, this morning, to try to share their excitement with me; perhaps they did not want to know whether or not it was possible for me to share it. I walked to my table and sat down. I munched toast as dry as paper and drank a pot of coffee. Then I tipped my waiter, who bowed and smiled and called me "sir" and said that he hoped to see me on the boat again. "I hope so, too," I said.

And was it true, or was it my imagination, that a flash of wondering comprehension, a flicker of wry sympathy, then appeared in the waiter's eyes? I walked upstairs to the deck.

There was a breeze from the water but the sun was hot and made me remember how ugly New York summers could be. All of the deck chairs had been taken away and people milled about in the space where the deck chairs had been, moved from one side of the ship to the other, clambered up and down the steps, crowded the rails, and they were busy taking photographs—of the harbor, of each other, of the sea, of the gulls. I walked slowly along the deck, and an impulse stronger than myself drove me to the rail. There it was, the great, unfinished city, with all its towers blazing in the sun. It came toward us slowly and patiently, like some enormous, cunning, and murderous beast, ready to devour, impossible to escape. I watched it come closer and I listened to the people around me, to their excitement and their pleasure. There was no doubt that it was real. I watched their shining faces and wondered if I were mad. For a moment I longed, with all my heart, to be able to feel whatever they were feeling, if only to know what such a feeling was like. As the boat moved slowly into the harbor, they were being moved into safety. It was only I who was being floated into danger. I turned my head, looking for Europe, but all that stretched behind me was the sky, thick with gulls. I moved away from the rail. A big, sandy-haired man held his daughter on his shoulders, showing her the Statue of Liberty. I would never know what this statue meant to others, she had always been an ugly joke for me. And the American flag was flying from the top of the ship, above my head. I had seen the French flag drive the French into the most unspeakable frenzies, I had seen the flag which was nominally mine used to dignify the vilest purposes: now I would never, as long as I lived, know what others saw when they saw a flag.

"There's no place like home," said a voice close by, and I thought, *There damn sure isn't.* I decided to go back to my cabin and have a drink.

There was a cablegram from Harriet in my cabin. It said: Be good. Be quick. I'm waiting. I folded it carefully and put it in my breast pocket. Then I wondered if I would ever get back to her. How long would it take me to earn the money to get out of this land? Sweat broke out on my forehead and I poured myself some whiskey from my nearly empty bottle. I paced the tiny cabin. It was silent. There was no one down in the cabins now.

I was not sober when I faced the uniforms in the first-class lounge. There were two of them; they were not unfriendly. They looked at my passport, they looked at me. "You've been away a long time," said one of them.

"Yes," I said, "it's been a while."

"What did you do over there all that time?"—with a grin meant to hide more than it revealed, which hideously revealed more than it could hide.

I said, "I'm a singer," and the room seemed to rock around me. I held on to what I hoped was a calm, open smile. I had not had to deal with these faces in so long that I had forgotten how to do it. I had once known how to pitch my voice precisely between curtness and servility, and known what razor's edge of a pickaninny's smile would turn away wrath. But I had forgotten all the tricks on which my life had once depended. Once I had been an expert at baffling these people, at setting their teeth on edge, and dancing just outside the trap laid for me. But I was not an expert now. These faces were no longer merely the faces of two white men, who were my enemies. They were the faces of two white people whom I did not understand, and I could no longer plan my moves in accordance with what I knew of their cowardice and their needs and their strategy. That moment on the bridge had undone me forever.

"That's right," said one of them, "that's what it says, right here on the passport. Never heard of you, though." They looked up at me. "Did you do a lot of singing over there?"

"Some."

"What kind—concerts?"

"No." I wondered what I looked like, sounded like. I could tell nothing from their eyes. "I worked a few nightclubs."

"Nightclubs, eh? I guess they liked you over there."

"Yes," I said, "they seemed to like me all right."

"Well"—and my passport was stamped and handed back to me—"let's hope they like you over here."

"Thanks." They laughed—was it at me, or was it my imagination? and I picked up the one bag I was carrying and threw my trench coat over one shoulder and walked out of the first-class lounge. I stood in the slow-moving, murmuring line which led to the gangplank. I looked straight ahead and watched heads, smiling faces, step up to the shadow of the gangplank awning and then swiftly descend out of sight. I put my passport back in my breast pocket—*Be quick. I'm waiting*—and I held my landing card in my hand. Then, suddenly, there I was, standing on the edge of the boat, staring down the long ramp to the ground. At the end of the plank, on the ground, stood a heavy man in a uniform. His cap was pushed back from his gray hair and his face was red and wet. He looked up at me. This was the face I remembered, the face of my nightmares; perhaps hatred had caused me to know this face better than I would ever know the face of any lover. "Come on, boy," he cried, "come on, come on!"

And I almost smiled. I was home. I touched my breast pocket. I thought of a song I sometimes sang, *When will I ever get to be a man?* I came down the gangplank, stumbling a little, and gave the man my landing card.

Much later in the day, a customs inspector checked my baggage and waved me away. I picked up my bags and started walking down the long stretch which led to the gate, to the city.

And I heard someone call my name.

I looked up and saw Louisa running toward me. I dropped my bags and grabbed her in my arms and tears came to my eyes and rolled down my face. I did not know whether the tears were for joy at seeing her, or from rage, or both.

"How are you? How are you? You look wonderful, but, oh, haven't you lost weight? It's wonderful to see you again."

I wiped my eyes. "It's wonderful to see you, too, I bet you thought I was never coming back."

Louisa laughed. "I wouldn't have blamed you if you hadn't. These people are just as corny as ever, I swear I don't believe there's any hope for them. How's your French? Lord, when I think that it was I who studied French and now I can't speak a word. And you never went near it and you probably speak it like a native."

I grinned. "*Pas mal. Te me défends pas mal.*" We started down the wide steps into the street. "My God," I said. "New York." I was not aware of its towers now. We were in the shadow of the elevated highway but the thing which most struck me was neither light nor shade, but noise. It came from a million things at once, from trucks and tires and clutches and brakes and doors; from machines shuttling and stamping and rolling and cutting and pressing; from the building of tunnels, the checking of gas mains, the laying of wires, the digging of foundations; from the chattering of rivets, the scream of the pile driver, the clanging of great shovels; from the battering down and the raising up of walls; from millions of radios and television sets and juke boxes. The human voices distinguished themselves from the roar only by their note of strain and hostility. Another fleshy man, uniformed and red faced, hailed a cab for us and touched his cap politely but could only manage a peremptory growl: "Right this way, miss. Step up, sir." He slammed the cab door behind us. Louisa directed the driver to the New Yorker Hotel.

"Do they take us there?"

She looked at me. "They got laws in New York, honey, it'd be the easiest thing in the world to spend all your time in court. But over at the New Yorker, I believe they've already got the message." She took my arm. "You see? In spite of all this chopping and booming, this place hasn't really changed very much. You still can't hear yourself talk."

And I thought to myself, Maybe that's the point.

Early the next morning we checked out of the hotel and took the plane for Alabama.

I am just stepping out of the shower when I hear the bell ring. I dry myself hurriedly and put on a bathrobe. It is Vidal, of course, and very elegant he is, too, with his bushy gray hair quite lustrous, his swarthy, cynical, gypsy-like face shaved and lotioned. Usually he looks just any old way. But tonight his brief bulk is contained in a dark-blue suit and he has an ironical pearl stickpin in his blue tie.

"Come in, make yourself a drink. I'll be with you in a second."

"I am, *hélas!*, on time. I trust you will forgive me for my thoughtlessness."

But I am already back in the bathroom. Vidal puts on a record: Mahalia Jackson, singing *I'm Going to Live the Life I Sing About in My Song.*

When I am dressed, I find him sitting in a chair before the open window. The daylight is gone, but it is not exactly dark. The trees are black now against the darkening sky. The lights in windows and the lights of motorcars are yellow and ringed. The street lights have not yet been turned on. It is as though, out of deference to the departed day, Paris waited a decent interval before assigning her role to a more theatrical but inferior performer.

Vidal is drinking a whiskey and soda. I pour myself a drink. He watches me.

"Well. How are you, my friend? You are nearly gone. Are you happy to be leaving us?"

"No." I say this with more force than I had intended. Vidal raises his eyebrows, looking amused and distant. "I never really intended to go back there. I certainly never intended to raise my kid there—"

"*Mais, mon cher,*" Vidal says, calmly, "you are an intelligent man, you must have known that you would probably be returning one day." He pauses. "And, as for Paul—did it never occur to you that he might wish one day to see the country in which his father and his father's fathers were born?"

"To do that, really, he'd have to go to Africa."

"America will always mean more to him than Africa, you know that."

"I don't know." I throw my drink down and pour myself another. "Why should he want to cross all that water just to be called a nigger? America never gave him anything."

"It gave him his father."

I look at him. "You mean, his father escaped."

Vidal throws back his head and laughs. If Vidal likes you, he is certain to laugh at you and his laughter can be very unnerving. But the look, the silence which follows this laughter can be very unnerving, too. And, now, in the silence, he asks me, "Do you really think that you have escaped anything? Come. I know you for a better man than that." He walks to the table which holds the liquor. "In that movie of ours which has made you so famous, and, as I now see, so troubled, what are you playing, after all? What is the tragedy of this half-breed troubadour if not, precisely, that he has taken all the possible roads to escape and that all these roads have failed him?" He pauses, with the bottle in one hand, and looks at me. "Do you remember the trouble I had to get a performance out of you? How you hated me, you sometimes looked as though you wanted to shoot me! And do you remember when the role of Chico began to come alive?" He pours his drink. "Think back, remember. I am a very great director, *mais pardon!* I could not have got such a performance out of anyone but you. And what were you thinking of, what was in your mind, what nightmare were you living with when you began, at last, to play the role—truthfully?" He walks back to his seat.

Chico, in the film, is the son of a Martinique woman and a French *colon* who hates both his mother and his father. He flees from the island to the capital, carrying his hatred with him. This hatred has now grown, naturally, to include all dark women and all white men, in a word, everyone. He descends into the underworld of Paris, where he dies. *Les fauves*—the wild beasts—refers to the life he has fled and to the life which engulfs him. When I agreed to do the role, I felt that I could probably achieve it by bearing in mind the North Africans I had watched in Paris for so long. But this did not please Vidal. The blowup came while we were rehearsing a fairly simple, straightforward scene. Chico goes into a sleazy Pigalle dance hall to beg the French owner for a particularly humiliating job. And this Frenchman reminds him of his father.

"You are playing this boy as though you thought of him as the noble savage," Vidal said, icily. "*Ça vient d'où*—all these ghastly mannerisms you are using all the time?"

Everyone fell silent, for Vidal rarely spoke this way. This silence told me that everyone, the actor with whom I was playing the scene and all the people in the "dance hall," shared Vidal's opinion of my performance and were relieved that he was going to do something about it. I was humiliated and too angry to speak; but perhaps I also felt, at the very bottom of my heart, a certain relief, an unwilling respect.

"You are doing it all wrong," he said, more gently. Then, "Come, let us have a drink together."

We walked into his office. He took a bottle and two glasses out of his desk. "Forgive me, but you put me in mind of some of those English *lady* actresses who love to play *putain* as long as it is always absolutely clear to the audience that they are really ladies. So perhaps they read a book, not usually, *hélas!*, *Fanny Hill*, and they have their chauffeurs drive them through Soho once or twice—and they come to the stage with a performance so absolutely loaded with detail, every bit of it meaningless, that there can be no doubt that they are acting. It is what the British call a triumph." He poured two cognacs. "That is what you are doing. Why? Who do you think this boy is, what do you think he is feeling, when he asks for this job?" He watched me carefully and I bitterly resented his look. "You come from America. The situation is not so pretty there for boys like you. I know you may not have been as poor as—as some—but is it really impossible for you to understand what a boy like Chico feels? Have you never, yourself, been in a similar position?"

I hated him for asking the question because I knew he knew the answer to it. "I would have had to be a very lucky black man not to have been in such a position."

"You would have had to be a very lucky *man*."

"Oh, God," I said, "please don't give me any of this equality-in-anguish business."

"It is perfectly possible," he said, sharply, "that there is not another kind."

Then he was silent. He sat down behind his desk. He cut a cigar and lit it, puffing up clouds of smoke, as though to prevent us from seeing each other too clearly. "Consider this,' he said. "I am a French director who has never seen your country. I have never done you any harm, except, perhaps, historically—I mean, because I am white—but I cannot be blamed for that—"

"But *I* can be," I said, "and I am! I've never understood why, if *I* have to pay for the history written in the color of my skin, *you* should get off scot-free!" But I was surprised at my vehemence, I had not known I was going to say these things, and by the fact that I was trembling and from the way he looked at me I knew that, from a professional point of view anyway, I was playing into his hands.

"What makes you think I *do?*" His face looked weary and stern. "I am a Frenchman. Look at France. You think that I—we—are not paying for our history?" He walked to the window, staring out at the rather grim little town in which the studio was located. "If it is revenge that you want, well, then, let me tell you, you will have it. You will probably have it, whether you want it or not, our stupidity will make it inevitable." He turned back into the room. "But I beg you not to confuse me with the happy people of your country, who scarcely know that there is such a thing as history and so, naturally, imagine that they can escape, as you put it, scot-free. That is what you are doing, that is what I was about to say. I was about to say that I am a French director and I have never been in your country and I have never done you any harm—but you are not talking to that man, in this room, now. You are not talking to Jean Luc Vidal, but to some other white man, whom you remember, who has nothing to do with me." He paused and went back to his desk. "Oh, most of the time you are not like this, I know. But it is there all the time, it must be, because when you are upset, this is what comes out. So you are not playing Chico truthfully, you are lying about him, and I will not let you do it. When you go back, now, and play this scene again, I want you to remember what has just happened in this room. You brought your past into this room. That is what Chico does when he walks into the dance hall. The Frenchman whom he begs for a job is not merely a Frenchman—he is the father who disowned and betrayed him and all the Frenchmen whom he hates." He smiled and poured me another cognac. "Ah! If it were not for *my* history, I would not have so much trouble to get the truth out of you." He looked into my face, half smiling. "And you, you are angry—are you not?—that I *ask* you for the truth. You think I have no right to ask." Then he said something which he knew would enrage me. "Who are you then, and what good has it done you to come to France, and how will you raise your son? Will you teach him never to tell the truth to anyone?" And he moved behind his desk and looked at me, as though from behind a barricade.

"You have no right to talk to me this way."

"Oh, yes, I do," he said. "I have a film to make and a reputation to maintain and I am going to get a performance out of you." He looked at his watch. "Let us go back to work."

I watch him now, sitting quietly in my living room, tough, cynical, crafty old Frenchman, and I wonder if he knows that the nightmare at the bottom of my mind, as I played the role of Chico, was all the possible fates of Paul. This is but another way of saying that I relived the disasters which had nearly undone me; but, because I was thinking of Paul, I discovered that I did not want my son ever to feel toward me as I had felt toward my own father. He had died when I was eleven, but I had watched the humiliations he had to bear, and I had pitied him. But was there not, in that pity, however painfully and unwillingly, also some contempt? For how could I *know* what he had borne? I knew only that I was his son. However he had loved me, whatever he had borne, I, his son, was despised. Even had he lived, he could have done nothing to prevent it, nothing to protect me. The best that he could hope to do was to prepare me for it; and even at that he had failed. How can one be prepared for the spittle in the face, all the tireless ingenuity which goes into the spite and fear of small, unutterably miserable people, whose greatest terror is the singular identity, whose joy, whose safety, is entirely dependent on the humiliation and anguish of others?

But for Paul, I swore it, such a day would never come. I would throw my life and my work between Paul and the nightmare of the world. I would make it impossible for the world to treat Paul as it had treated my father and me.

Mahalia's record ends. Vidal rises to turn it over. "Well?" He looks at me very affectionately. "Your nightmares, please!"

"Oh, I was thinking of that summer I spent in Alabama, when my mother died." I stop. "You know, but when we finally filmed that bar scene, I was thinking of New York. I was scared in Alabama, but I almost went crazy in New York. I was sure I'd never make it back here—back here to Harriet. And I knew if I didn't, it was going to be the end of me." Now Mahalia is singing *When the Saints Go Marching In*. "I got a job in the town as an elevator boy, in the town's big department store. It was a special favor, one of my father's white friends got it for me. For a long time, in the South, we all—depended—on the—*kindness*—of white friends." I take out a handkerchief and wipe my face. "But this man didn't like me. I guess I didn't seem grateful enough, wasn't enough like my father, what he thought my father was. And I couldn't get used to the town again, I'd been away too long, I hated it. It's a terrible town, anyway, the whole thing looks as though it's been built around a jailhouse. There's a room in the courthouse, a room where they beat you up. Maybe you're walking along the street one night, it's usually at night, but it happens in the daytime, too. And the police car comes up behind you and the cop says, 'Hey, boy. Come on over here.' So you go on over. He says, 'Boy, I believe you're drunk.' And, you see, if you say, 'No, no sir,' he'll beat you because you're calling him a liar. And if you say anything else, unless it's something to make him laugh, he'll take you in and beat you, just for fun. The trick is to think of some way for them to have their fun without beating you up."

The street lights of Paris click on and turn all the green leaves silver. "Or to go along with the ways *they* dream up. And they'll do anything, anything at all, to prove that you're no better than a dog and to make you feel like one. And they hated me because I'd been North and I'd been to Europe. People kept saying, I hope you didn't bring no foreign notions back here with you, boy. And I'd say, 'No sir,' or 'No ma'am,' but I never said it right. And there was a time, all of them remembered it, when I *had* said it right. But now they could tell that I despised them—I guess, no matter what, I wanted them to know that I despised them. But I didn't despise them any more than everyone else did, only the others never let it show. They knew how to keep the white folks happy, and it was easy—you just had to keep them feeling like they were God's favor to the universe. They'd walk around with great, big, foolish grins on their faces and the colored folks loved to see this, because they hated them so much. "Just look at So-and-So," somebody'd say. "His white is *on* him today." And when we didn't hate them, we pitied them. In America, that's usually what it means to have a white friend. You pity the poor bastard because he was born believing the world's a great place to be, and you know it's not, and you can see that he's going to have a terrible time getting used to this idea, if he ever gets used to it."

Then I think of Paul again, those eyes which still imagine that I can do anything, that skin, the color of honey and fire, his jet-black, curly hair. I look out at Paris again, and I listen to Mahalia. "Maybe it's better to have the terrible times first. I don't know. Maybe, then, you can have, *if* you live, a better life, a real life, because you had to fight so hard to get it away—you know?—from the mad dog who held it in his teeth. But then your life has all those tooth marks, too, all those tatters, and all that blood." I walk to the bottle and raise it. "One for the road?"

"Thank you," says Vidal.

I pour us a drink, and he watches me. I have never talked so much before, not about those things anyway. I know that Vidal has nightmares, because he knows so much about them, but he has never told me what his are. I think that he probably does not talk about his nightmares any more. I know that the war cost him his wife and his son, and that he was in prison in Germany. He very rarely refers to it. He has a married daughter who lives in England, and he rarely speaks of her. He is like a man who has learned to live on what is left of an enormous fortune.

We are silent for a moment.

"Please go on," he says, with a smile. "I am curious about the reality behind the reality of your performance."

"My sister, Louisa, never married," I say, abruptly, "because, once, years ago, she and the boy she was going with and two friends of theirs were out driving in a car and the police stopped them. The girl who was with them was very fair and the police pretended not to believe her when she said she was colored. They made her get out and stand in front of the headlights of the car and pull down her pants and raise her dress—they said that was the only way they could be sure. And you can imagine what they said, and what they did—and they were lucky, at that, that it didn't go any further. But none of the men could do anything about it. Louisa couldn't face the boy again, and I guess he couldn't face her." Now it is really growing dark in the room and I cross to the light switch. "You know, I know what that boy felt, I've felt it. They want you to feel that you're not a man, maybe that's the only way they can feel like men, I don't know. I walked around New York with Harriet's cablegram in my pocket as though it were some atomic secret, in *code,* and they'd kill me if they ever found out what it meant. You know, there's something wrong with people like that. And thank God Harriet was here, she *proved* that the world was bigger than the world they wanted me to live in, I *had* to get back here, get to a place where people were too busy with their own lives, *their private lives,* to make fantasies about mine, to set up walls around mine." I look at him. The light in the room has made the night outside blue-black and golden and the great searchlight of the Eiffel Tower is turning in the sky. "That's what it's like in America, for me, anyway. I always feel that I don't exist there, except in someone else's—usually dirty—mind. I don't know if you know what that means, but I do, and I don't want to put Harriet through that and I don't want to raise Paul there."

"Well," he says at last, "you are not required to remain in America forever, are you? You will sing in that elegant club which apparently feels that it cannot, much longer, so much as open its doors without you, and you will probably accept the movie offer, you would be very foolish not to. You will make a lot of money. Then, one day, you will remember that airlines and steamship companies are still in business and that France still exists. *That* will certainly be cause for astonishment."

Vidal was a Gaullist before de Gaulle came to power. But he regrets the manner of de Gaulle's rise and he is worried about de Gaulle's regime. "It is not the fault of *mon général,*" he sometimes says, sadly. "Perhaps it is history's fault. I *suppose* it must be history which always arranges to bill a civilization at the very instant it is least prepared to pay."

Now he rises and walks out on the balcony, as though to reassure himself of the reality of Paris. Mahalia is singing *Didn't It Rain?* I walk out and stand beside him.

"You are a good boy—Chico," he says. I laugh. "You believe in love. You do not know all the things love cannot do, but"—he smiles—"love will teach you that."

We go, after dinner, to a Left Bank discothèque which can charge outrageous prices because Marlon Brando wandered in there one night. By accident, according to Vidal. "Do you know how many people in Paris are becoming rich—to say nothing of those, *hélas!,* who are going broke—on the off chance that Marlon Brando will lose his way again?"

He has not, presumably, lost his way tonight, but the discothèque is crowded with those strangely faceless people who are part of the night life of all great cities, and who always arrive, moments, hours, or decades late, on the spot made notorious by an event or a movement or a handful of personalities. So here are American boys, anything but beardless, scratching around for Hemingway; American girls, titillating themselves with Frenchmen and existentialism, while waiting for the American boys to shave off their beards; French painters, busily pursuing the revolution which ended thirty years ago; and the young, bored, perverted, American *arrivistes* who are buying their way into the art world via flattery and liquor, and the production of canvases as arid as their greedy little faces. Here are boys, of all nations, one step above the pimp, who are occasionally walked across a stage or trotted before a camera. And the girls, their enemies, whose faces are sometimes seen in ads, one of whom will surely have a tantrum before the evening is out.

In a corner, as usual, surrounded, as usual, by smiling young men, sits the drunken blonde woman who was once the mistress of a famous, dead painter. She is a figure of some importance in the art world, and so rarely has to pay for either her drinks or her lovers. An older Frenchman, who was once a famous director, is playing *quatre cent vingt-et-un* with the woman behind the cash register. He nods pleasantly to Vidal and me as we enter, but makes no move to join us, and I respect him for this. Vidal and I are obviously cast tonight in the role vacated by Brando: our entrance justifies the prices and sends a kind of shiver through the room. It is marvelous to watch the face of the waiter as he approaches, all smiles and deference and grace, not so much honored by our presence as achieving his reality from it; excellence, he seems to be saying, gravitates naturally toward excellence. We order two whiskey and sodas. I know why Vidal sometimes comes here. He is lonely. I do not think that he expects ever to love one woman again, and so he distracts himself with many.

Since this is a discothèque, jazz is blaring from the walls and record sleeves are scattered about with a devastating carelessness. Two of them are mine and no doubt, presently, someone will play the recording of the songs I sang in the film.

"I thought," says Vidal, with a malicious little smile, "that your farewell to Paris would not be complete without a brief exposure to the perils of fame. Perhaps it will help prepare you for America, where, I am told, the populace is yet more carnivorous than it is here."

I can see that one of the vacant models is preparing herself to come to our table and ask for an autograph, hoping, since she is pretty—she has, that is, the usual female equipment, dramatized in the usual, modern way—to be invited for a drink. Should the maneuver succeed, one of her boy friends or girl friends will contrive to come by the table, asking for a light or a pencil or a lipstick, and it will be extremely difficult not to invite this person to join us, too. Before the evening ends, we will be surrounded. I don't, now, know what I expected of fame, but I suppose it never occurred to me that the light could be just as dangerous, just as killing, as the dark.

"Well, let's make it brief," I tell him. "Sometimes I wish that you weren't quite so fond of me."

He laughs. "There are some very interesting people here tonight. Look."

Across the room from us, and now staring at our table, are a group of American Negro students, who are probably visiting Paris for the first time. There are four of them, two boys and two girls, and I suppose that they must be in their late teens or early twenties. One of the boys, a gleaming, curly-haired, golden-brown type—the color of his mother's fried chicken—is carrying a guitar. When they realize we have noticed them, they smile and wave—wave as though I were one of their possessions, as, indeed, I am. Golden-brown is a mime. He raises his guitar, drops his shoulders, and his face falls into the lugubrious lines of Chico's face as he approaches death. He strums a little of the film's theme music, and I laugh and the table laughs. It is as though we were all back home and had met for a moment, on a Sunday morning, say, before a church or a poolroom or a barbershop.

And they have created a sensation in the discothèque, naturally, having managed, with no effort whatever, to outwit all the gleaming boys and girls. Their table, which had been of no interest only a moment before, has now become the focus of a rather pathetic attention; their smiles have made it possible for the others to smile, and to nod in our direction.

"Oh," says Vidal, "he does that far better than you ever did, perhaps I will make him a star."

"Feel free, *m'sieu, le bon Dieu,* I got mine." But I can see that his attention has really been caught by one of the girls, slim, tense, and dark, who seems, though it is hard to know how one senses such things, to be treated by the others with a special respect. And, in fact, the table now seems to be having a council of war, to be demanding her opinion or her cooperation. She listens, frowning, laughing; the quality, the force of her intelligence causes her face to keep changing all the time, as though a light played on it. And, presently, with a gesture she might once have used to scatter feed to chickens, she scoops up from the floor one of those dangling rag bags women love to carry. She holds it loosely by the drawstrings, so that it is banging somewhere around her ankle, and walks over to our table. She has an honest, forthright walk, entirely unlike the calculated, pelvic workout by means of which most women get about. She is small, but sturdily, economically, put together.

As she reaches our table, Vidal and I rise, and this throws her for a second. (It has been a long time since I have seen such an attractive girl.)

Also, everyone, of course, is watching us. It is really a quite curious moment. They have put on the record of Chico singing a sad, angry Martinique ballad; my own voice is coming at us from the walls as the girl looks from Vidal to me, and smiles.

"I guess you know," she says, "we weren't *about* to let you get out of here without bugging you just a little bit. We've only been in Paris just a couple of days and we thought for sure that we wouldn't have a chance of running into you anywhere, because it's in all the papers that you're coming home."

"Yes," I say, "yes. I'm leaving the day after tomorrow."

"Oh!" She grins. "Then we really *are* lucky." I find that I have almost forgotten the urchin-like grin of a colored girl. "I guess, before I keep babbling on, I'd better introduce myself. My name is Ada Holmes."

We shake hands. "This is Monsieur Vidal, the director of the film."

"I'm very honored to meet you, sir."

"Will you join us for a moment? Won't you sit down?" And Vidal pulls a chair out for her.

But she frowns contritely. "I really ought to get back to my friends." She looks at me. "I really just came over to say, for myself and all the kids, that we've got your records and we've seen your movie, and it means so much to us"—and she laughs, breathlessly, nervously, it is somehow more moving than tears—"more than I can say. Much more. And we wanted to know if you and your friend"—she looks at Vidal—"your *director,* Monsieur Vidal, would allow us to buy you a drink? We'd be very honored if you would."

"It is we who are honored," says Vidal, promptly, "*and* grateful. We were getting terribly bored with one another, thank God you came along."

The three of us laugh, and we cross the room.

The three at the table rise, and Ada makes the introductions. The other girl, taller and paler than Ada, is named Ruth. One of the boys is named Talley—"short for Talliafero"—and Golden-brown's name is Pete. "Man," he tells me, "I dig you the most. You tore me up, baby, tore me *up*."

"You tore up a lot of people," Talley says, cryptically, and he and Ruth laugh. Vidal does not know, but I do, that Talley is probably referring to white people.

They are from New Orleans and Tallahassee and North Carolina; are college students, and met on the boat. They have been in Europe all summer, in Italy and Spain, but are only just getting to Paris.

"We meant to come sooner," says Ada, "but we could never make up our minds to leave a place. I thought we'd never pry Ruth loose from Venice."

"I resigned myself," says Pete, "and just sat in the Piazza San Marco, drinking gin fizz and being photographed with the pigeons, while Ruth had herself driven *all* up and down the Grand Canal." He looks at Ruth. "Finally, thank heaven, it rained."

"She was working off her hostilities," says Ada, with a grin. "We thought we might as well let her do it in Venice, the opportunities in North Carolina are really terribly limited."

"There are some very upset people walking around down there," Ruth says, "and a couple of tours around the Grand Canal might do them a world of good."

Pete laughs. "Can't you just see Ruth escorting them to the edge of the water?"

"I haven't lifted my hand in anger yet," Ruth says, "but, oh Lord," and she laughs, clenching and unclenching her fists.

"You haven't been back for a long time, have you?" Talley asks me.

"Eight years. I haven't really lived there for twelve years."

Pete whistles. "I fear you are in for some surprises, my friend. There have been some changes made." Then, "Are you afraid?"

"A little."

"We all are," says Ada, "that's why I was so glad to get away for a little while."

"Then you haven't been back since Black Monday," Talley says. He laughs. "That's how it's gone down in Confederate history." He turns to Vidal. "What do people think about it here?"

Vidal smiles, delighted. "It seems extraordinarily infantile behavior, even for Americans, from whom, I must say, I have never expected very much in the way of maturity." Everyone at the table laughs. Vidal goes on. "But I cannot really talk about it, I do not understand it. I have never really understood Americans; I am an old man now, and I suppose I never will. There is something very nice about them, something very winning, but they seem so ignorant—so ignorant of life. Perhaps it is strange, but the only people from your country with whom I have ever made contact are black people—like my good friend, my discovery, here," and he slaps me on the shoulder. "Perhaps it is because we, in Europe, whatever else we do not know, or have forgotten, know about suffering. We have suffered here. You have suffered, too. But most Americans do not yet know what anguish is. It is too bad, because the life of the West is in their hands." He turns to Ada. "I cannot help saying that I think it is a scandal—and we may all pay very dearly for it—that a civilized nation should elect to represent it a man who is so simple that he thinks the world is simple." And silence falls at the table and the four young faces stare at him.

"Well," says Pete, at last, turning to me, "you won't be bored, man, when you get back there."

"It's much too nice a night," I say, "to stay cooped up in this place, where all I can hear is my own records." We laugh. "Why don't we get out of here and find a sidewalk café?" I tap Pete's guitar. "Maybe we can find out if you've got any talent."

"Oh, talent I've got," says Pete, "but character, man, I'm lacking."

So, after some confusion about the bill, for which Vidal has already made himself responsible, we walk out into the Paris night. It is very strange to feel that, very soon now, these boulevards will not exist for me. People will be walking up and down, as they are tonight, and lovers will be murmuring in the black shadows of the plane trees, and there will be these same still figures on the benches or in the parks—but they will not exist for me, I will not be here. For a long while Paris will no longer exist for me, except in my mind; and only in the minds of some people will I exist any longer for Paris. After departure, only invisible things are left, perhaps the life of the world is held together by invisible chains of memory and loss and love. So many things, so many people, depart! And we can only repossess them in our minds. Perhaps this is what the old folks meant, what my mother and my father meant, when they counseled us to keep the faith.

We have taken a table at the Deux Magots and Pete strums on his guitar and begins to play this song:

Preach the word, preach the word, preach the word!
If I never, never see you any more.
Preach the word, preach the word.
And I'll meet you on Canaan's shore.

He has a strong, clear, boyish voice, like a young preacher's, and he is smiling as he sings his song. Ada and I look at each other and grin, and Vidal is smiling. The waiter looks a little worried, for we are already beginning to attract a crowd, but it is a summer night, the gendarmes on the corner do not seem to mind, and there will be time, anyway, to stop us.

Pete was not there, none of us were, the first time this song was needed; and no one now alive can imagine what that time was like. But the song has come down the bloodstained ages. I suppose this to mean that the song is still needed, still has its work to do.

The others are all, visibly, very proud of Pete; and we all join him, and people stop to listen:

Testify! Testify!
If I never, never see you any more!
Testify! Testify!
I'll meet you on Canaan's shore!

In the crowd that has gathered to listen to us, I see a face I know, the face of a North African prize fighter, who is no longer in the ring. I used to know him well in the old days, but have not seen him for a long time. He looks quite well, his face is shining, he is quite decently dressed. And something about the way he holds himself, not quite looking at our table, tells me that he has seen me, but does not want to risk a rebuff. So I call him. "Boona!"

And he turns, smiling, and comes loping over to our table, his hands in his pockets. Pete is still singing and Ada and Vidal have taken off on a conversation of their own. Ruth and Talley look curiously, expectantly, at Boona. Now that I have called him over, I feel somewhat uneasy. I realize that I do not know what he is doing now, or how he will get along with any of these people, and I can see in his eyes that he is delighted to be in the presence of two young girls. There are virtually no North African women in Paris, and not even the dirty, rat-faced girls who live, apparently, in cafés are willing to go with an Arab. So Boona is always looking for a girl, and because he is so deprived and because he is not Western, his techniques can be very unsettling. I know he is relieved that the girls are not French and not white. He looks briefly at Vidal and Ada. Vidal, also, though for different reasons, is always looking for a girl.

But Boona has always been very nice to me. Perhaps I am sorry that I called him over, but I did not want to snub him.

He claps one hand to the side of my head, as is his habit. "*Comment vas-tu, mon frère?* I have not seen you, oh, for long time." And he asks me, as in the old days, "You all right? Nobody bother you?" And he laughs. "Ah! *Tu as fait le chemin, toi!* Now you are *vedette,* big star—wonderful!" He looks around the table, made a little uncomfortable by the silence that has fallen, now that Pete has stopped singing. "I have seen you in the movies—you know?—and I tell everybody, I know *him!*" He points to me, and laughs, and Ruth and Talley laugh with him. "That's right, man, you make me real proud, you make me cry!"

"Boona, I want you to meet some friends of mine." And I go round the table: "Ruth, Talley, Ada, Pete"—and he bows and shakes hands, his dark eyes gleaming with pleasure—"*et Monsieur Vidal, le metteur en scène du film qui t'a arraché des larmes.*"

"*Enchanté.*" But his attitude toward Vidal is colder, more distrustful. "Of course I have heard of Monsieur Vidal. He is the director of many films, many of them made me cry." This last statement is utterly, even insolently, insincere.

But Vidal, I think, is relieved that I will now be forced to speak to Boona and will leave him alone with Ada.

"Sit down," I say, "have a drink with us, let me have your news. What's been happening with you, what are you doing with yourself these days?"

"Ah," he sits down, "nothing very brilliant, my brother." He looks at me quickly, with a little smile. "You know, we have been having hard times here."

"Where are you from?" Ada asks him.

His brilliant eyes take her in entirely, but she does not flinch. "I am from Tunis." He says it proudly, with a little smile.

"From Tunis. I have never been to Africa, I would love to go one day."

He laughs. "Africa is a big place. Very big. There are many countries in Africa, many"—he looks briefly at Vidal—"different kinds of people, many colonies."

"But Tunis," she continues, in her innocence, "is free? Freedom is happening all over Africa. That's why I would like to go there."

"I have not been back for a long time," says Boona, "but all the news I get from Tunis, from my people, is not good."

"Wouldn't you like to go back?" Ruth asks.

Again he looks at Vidal. "That is not so easy."

Vidal smiles. "You know what I would like to do? There's a wonderful Spanish place not far from here, where we can listen to live music and dance a little." He turns to Ada. "Would you like that?"

He is leaving it up to me to get rid of Boona, and it is, of course, precisely for this reason that I cannot do it. Besides, it is no longer so simple.

"Oh, I'd love that," says Ada, and she turns to Boona. "Won't you come, too?"

"Thank you, mam'selle," he says, softly, and his tongue flicks briefly over his lower lip, and he smiles. He is very moved, people are not often nice to him.

In the Spanish place there are indeed a couple of Spanish guitars, drums, castanets, and a piano, but the uses to which these are being put carry one back, as Pete puts it, to the levee. "These are the wailingest Spanish cats I ever heard," says Ruth. "They didn't learn how to do this in Spain, no, they didn't, they been rambling. You ever hear anything like this going on in Spain?" Talley takes her out on the dance floor, which is already crowded. A very handsome Frenchwoman is dancing with an enormous, handsome black man, who seems to be her lover, who seems to have taught her how to dance. Apparently, they are known to the musicians, who egg them on with small cries of "*Olé!*" It is a very good-natured crowd, mostly foreigners, Spaniards, Swedes, Greeks. Boona takes Ada out on the dance floor while Vidal is answering some questions put to him by Pete on the entertainment situation in France. Vidal looks a little put out, and I am amused.

We are there for perhaps an hour, dancing, talking, and I am, at last, a little drunk. In spite of Boona, who is a very good and tireless dancer, Vidal continues his pursuit of Ada, and I begin to wonder if he will make it and I begin to wonder if I want him to.

I am still puzzling out my reaction when Pete, who has disappeared, comes in through the front door, catches my eye, and signals to me. I leave the table and follow him into the streets.

He looks very upset. "I don't want to bug you, man," he says, "but I fear your boy has goofed."

I know he is not joking. I think he is probably angry at Vidal because of Ada, and I wonder what I can do about it and why he should be telling me.

I stare at him, gravely, and he says, "It looks like he stole some money."

"Stole *money?* Who, Vidal?"

And then, of course, I get it, in the split second before he says, impatiently, "No, are you kidding? Your friend, the Tunisian."

I do not know what to say or what to do, and so I temporize with questions. All the time I am wondering if this can be true and what I can do about it if it is. The trouble is, I know that Boona steals, he would probably not be alive if he didn't, but I cannot say so to these children, who probably still imagine that everyone who steals is a thief. But he has never, to my knowledge, stolen from a friend. It seems unlike him. I have always thought of him as being better than that, and smarter than that. And so I cannot believe it, but neither can I doubt it. I do not know anything about Boona's life, these days. This causes me to realize that I do not really know much about Boona.

"Who did he steal it from?"

"From Ada. Out of her bag."

"How much?"

"Ten dollars. It's not an awful lot of money, but"—he grimaces—"none of us *have* an awful lot of money."

"I know." The dark side street on which we stand is nearly empty. The only sound on the street is the muffled music of the Spanish club. "How do you know it was Boona?"

He anticipates my own unspoken rejoinder. "Who else could it be? Besides—somebody *saw* him do it."

"Somebody saw him?"

"Yes."

I do not ask him who this person is, for fear that he will say it is Vidal.

"Well," I say, "I'll try to get it back." I think that I will take Boona aside and then replace the money myself. "Was it in dollars or in francs?"

"In francs."

I have no dollars and this makes it easier. I do not know how I can possibly face Boona and accuse him of stealing money from my friends. I would rather give him the benefit of even the faintest doubt. But, "Who saw him?" I ask.

"Talley. But we didn't want to make a thing about it—"

"Does Ada know it's gone?"

"Yes." He looks at me helplessly. "I know this makes you feel pretty bad, but we thought we'd better tell you, rather than"—lamely—"anybody else."

Now, Ada comes out of the club, carrying her ridiculous handbag, and with her face all knotted and sad. "Oh," she says, "I hate to cause all this trouble, it's not worth it, not for ten lousy dollars." I am astonished to see that she has been weeping, and tears come to her eyes now.

I put my arm around her shoulder. "Come on, now. You're not causing anybody any trouble and, anyway, it's nothing to cry about."

"It isn't your fault, Ada," Pete says, miserably.

"Oh, I ought to get a sensible handbag," she says, "like you're always telling me to do," and she laughs a little, then looks at me. "Please don't try to do anything about it. Let's just forget it."

"What's happening inside?" I ask her.

"Nothing. They're just talking. I think Mr. Vidal is dancing with Ruth. He's a great dancer, that little Frenchman."

"He's a great talker, too," Pete says.

"Oh, he doesn't mean anything," says Ada, "he's just having fun. He probably doesn't get a chance to talk to many American girls."

"He certainly made up for lost time tonight."

"Look," I say, "if Talley and Boona are alone, maybe you better go back in. We'll be in in a minute. Let's try to keep this as quiet as we can."

"Yeah," he says, "okay. We're going soon anyway, okay?"

"Yes," she tells him, "right away."

But as he turns away, Boona and Talley step out into the street, and it is clear that Talley feels that he has Boona under arrest. I almost laugh, the whole thing is beginning to resemble one of those mad French farces with people flying in and out of doors; but Boona comes straight to me.

"They say I stole money, my friend. You know me, you are the only one here who knows me, you know I would not do such a thing."

I look at him and I do not know what to say. Ada looks at him with her eyes full of tears and looks away. I take Boona's arm.

"We'll be back in a minute," I say. We walk a few paces up the dark, silent street.

"She say I take her money," he says. He, too, looks as though he is about to weep—but I do not know for which reason. "You know me, you know me almost twelve years, you think I do such a thing?"

Talley saw you, I want to say, but I cannot say it. Perhaps Talley only thought he saw him. Perhaps it is easy to see a boy who looks like Boona with his hand in an American girl's purse.

"If you do not believe me," he says, "search me. Search me!" And he opens his arms wide, theatrically, and now there are tears standing in his eyes.

I do not know what his tears mean, but I certainly cannot search him. I want to say, I know you steal, I know you have to steal. Perhaps you took the money out of this girl's purse in order to eat tomorrow, in order not to be thrown into the streets tonight, in order to stay out of jail. This girl means nothing to you, after all, she is only an American, an American like me. Perhaps, I suddenly think, no girl means anything to you, or ever will again, they have beaten you too hard and kept you out in the gutter too long. And I also think, if you would steal from her, then of course you would lie to me, neither of us means anything to you; perhaps, in your eyes, we are simply luckier gangsters in a world which is run by gangsters. But I cannot say any of these things to Boona. I cannot say, Tell me the truth, nobody cares about the money any more.

So I say, "Of course I will not search you." And I realize that he knew I would not.

"I think it is that Frenchman who say I am a thief. They think we all are thieves." His eyes are bright and bitter. He looks over my shoulder. "They have all come out of the club now."

I look around and they are all there, in a little dark knot on the sidewalk.

"Don't worry," I say. "It doesn't matter."

"You believe me? My brother?" And his eyes look into mine with a terrible intensity.

"Yes," I force myself to say, "yes, of course, I believe you. Someone made a mistake, that's all."

"You know, the way American girls run around, they have their sack open all the time, she could have lost the money anywhere. Why she blame me? Because I come from Africa?" Tears are glittering on his face. "Here she come now."

And Ada comes up the street with her straight, determined walk. She walks straight to Boona and takes his hand. "I am sorry," she says, "for everything that happened. Please believe me. It isn't worth all this fuss. I'm sure you're a very nice person, and"—she falters—"I must have lost the money, I'm sure I lost it." She looks at him. "It isn't worth hurting your feelings, and I'm terribly sorry about it."

"I no take your money," he says. "Really, truly, I no take it. Ask him"—pointing to me, grabbing me by the arm, shaking me—"he know me for years, he will tell you that I never, never steal!"

"I'm sure," she says. "I'm sure."

I take Boona by the arm again. "Let's forget it. Let's forget it all. We're all going home now, and one of these days we'll have a drink again and we'll forget all about it, all right?"

"Yes," says Ada, "let us forget it." And she holds out her hand.

Boona takes it, wonderingly. His eyes take her in again. "You are a very nice girl. Really. A very nice girl."

"I'm sure you're a nice person, too." She pauses. "Goodnight."

"Goodnight," he says, after a long silence.

Then he kisses me on both cheeks. "*Au revoir, mon frère.*"

"*Au revoir, Boona.*"

After a moment we turn and walk away, leaving him standing there.

"Did he take it?" asks Vidal.

"I tell you, I *saw* him," says Talley.

"Well," I say, "it doesn't matter now." I look back and see Boona's stocky figure disappearing down the street.

"No," says Ada, "it doesn't matter." She looks up. "It's almost morning."

"I would gladly," says Vidal, stammering, "gladly—"

But she is herself again. "I wouldn't think of it. We had a wonderful time tonight, a wonderful time, and I wouldn't think of it." She turns to me with that urchin-like grin. "It was wonderful meeting you. I hope you won't have too much trouble getting used to the States again."

"Oh, I don't think I will," I say. And then, "I hope you won't."

"No," she says, "I don't think anything they can do will surprise me any more."

"Which way are we all going?" asks Vidal. "I hope someone will share my taxi with me."

But he lives in the sixteenth arrondissement, which is not in anyone's direction. We walk him to the line of cabs standing under the clock at Odéon.

And we look each other in the face, in the growing morning light. His face looks weary and lined and lonely. He puts both hands on my shoulders and then puts one hand on the nape of my neck. "Do not forget me, Chico," he says. "You must come back and see us, one of these days. Many of us depend on you for many things."

"I'll be back," I say. "I'll never forget you."

He raises his eyebrows and smiles. "*Alors, Adieu.*"

"*Adieu, Vidal.*"

"I was happy to meet all of you," he says. He looks at Ada. "Perhaps we will meet again before you leave."

"Perhaps," she says. "Goodby, Monsieur Vidal."

"Goodby."

Vidal's cab drives away. "I also leave you now," I say. "I must go home and wake up my son and prepare for our journey."

I leave them standing on the corner, under the clock, which points to six. They look very strange and lost and determined, the four of them. Just before my cab turns off the boulevard, I wave to them and they wave back.

Mme. Dumont is in the hall, mopping the floor.

"Did all my family get home?" I ask. I feel very cheerful, I do not know why.

"Yes," she says, "they are all here. Paul is still sleeping."

"May I go in and get him?"

She looks at me in surprise. "Of course."

So I walk into her apartment and walk into the room where Paul lies sleeping. I stand over his bed for a long time.

Perhaps my thoughts traveled—travel through to him. He opens his eyes and smiles up at me. He puts a fist to his eyes and raises his arms. "*Bonjour, Papa.*"

I lift him up. "*Bonjour.* How do you feel today?"

"Oh, I don't know yet," he says.

I laugh. I put him on my shoulder and walk out into the hall. Mme. Dumont looks up at him with her radiant, aging face.

"Ah," she says, "you are going on a journey! How does it feel?"

"He doesn't know yet," I tell her. I walk to the elevator door and open it, dropping Paul down to the crook of my arm.

She laughs again. "He will know later. What a journey! *Jusqu'au nouveau monde!*"

I open the cage and we step inside. "Yes," I say, "all the way to the new world." I press the button and the cage, holding my son and me, goes up.

NATHANIEL HAWTHORNE

Wakefield

In some old magazine or newspaper I recollect a story, told as truth of a man—let us call him Wakefield—who absented himself for a long time from his wife. The fact, thus abstractedly stated, is not very uncommon, nor —without a proper distinction of circumstances—to be condemned either as naughty or nonsensical. Howbeit, this, though far from the most aggravated, is perhaps the strangest, instance on record, of marital delinquency; and, moreover, as remarkable a freak as may be found in the whole list of human oddities. The wedded couple lived in London. The man, under pretence of going a journey, took lodgings in the next street to his own house, and there, unheard of by his wife or friends, and without the shadow of a reason for such self-banishment, dwelt upwards of twenty years. During that period, he beheld his home every day, and frequently the forlorn Mrs. Wakefield. And after so great a gap in his matrimonial felicity—when his death was reckoned certain, his estate settled, his name dismissed from memory, and his wife, long, long ago, resigned to her autumnal widowhood—he entered the door one evening, quietly, as from a day's absence, and became a loving spouse till death.

This outline is all that I remember. But the incident, though of the purest originality, unexampled, and probably never to be repeated, is one, I think, which appeals to the generous sympathies of mankind. We know, each for himself, that none of us would perpetrate such a folly, yet feel as if some other might. To my own contemplations, at least, it has often recurred, always exciting wonder, but with a sense that the story must be true, and a conception of its hero's character. Whenever any subject so forcibly affects the mind, time is well spent in thinking of it. If the reader choose, let him do his own meditation; or if he prefer to ramble with me through the twenty years of Wakefield's vagary, I bid him welcome; trusting that there will be a pervading spirit and a moral, even should we fail to find them, done up neatly, and condensed into the final sentence. Thought has always its efficacy, and every striking incident its moral.

What sort of a man was Wakefield? We are free to shape out our own idea, and call it by his name. He was now in the meridian of life; his matrimonial affections, never violent, were sobered into a calm, habitual sentiment; of all husbands, he was likely to be the most constant, because a certain sluggishness would keep his heart at rest, wherever it might be placed. He was intellectual, but not actively so; his mind occupied itself in long and lazy musings, that ended to no purpose, or had not vigor to attain it; his thoughts were seldom so energetic as to seize hold of words. Imagination, in the proper meaning of the term, made no part of Wakefield's gifts. With a cold but not depraved nor wandering heart, and a mind never feverish with riotous thoughts, nor perplexed with orginality, who could have anticipated that our friend would entitle himself to a foremost place among the doers of eccentric deeds? Had his acquaintances been asked, who was the man in London the surest to perform nothing today which should be remembered on the morrow, they would have thought of Wakefield. Only the wife of his bosom might have hesitated. She, without having analyzed his character, was partly aware of a quiet selfishness, that had rusted into his inactive mind; of a peculiar sort of vanity, the most uneasy attribute about him; of a disposition to craft which had seldom produced more positive effects than the keeping of petty secrets, hardly worth revealing; and, lastly, of what she called a little strangeness, sometimes, in the good man. This latter quality is indefinable, and perhaps non-existent.

Let us now imagine Wakefield bidding adieu to his wife. It is the dusk of an October evening. His equipment is a drab great-coat, a hat covered with an oilcloth, top-boots, an umbrella in one hand and a small portmanteau in the other. He has informed Mrs. Wakefield that he is to take the night coach into the country. She would fain inquire the length of his journey, its object, and the probable time of his return; but, indulgent to his harmless love of mystery, interrogates him only by a look. He tells her not to expect him positively by the return coach, nor to be alarmed should he tarry three or four days; but, at all events, to look for him at supper on Friday evening. Wakefield himself, be it considered, has no suspicion of what is before him. He holds out his hand, she gives her own, and meets his parting kiss in the matter-of-course way of a ten years' matrimony; and forth goes the middle-aged Mr. Wakefield, almost resolved to perplex his good lady by a whole week's absence. After the door has closed behind him, she perceives it thrust partly open, and a vision of her husband's face through the aperture, smiling on her, and gone in a moment. For the time, this little incident is dismissed without a thought. But, long afterwards, when she has been more years a widow than a wife, that smile recurs, and flickers across all her reminiscences of Wakefield's visage. In her many musings, she surrounds the original smile with a multitude of fantasies, which make it strange and awful: as, for instance, if she imagines him in a coffin that parting look is frozen on his pale features; or, if she dreams of him in heaven, still his blessed spirit wears a quiet and crafty smile. Yet, for its sake, when all others have given him up for dead, she sometimes doubts whether she is a widow.

But our business is with the husband. We must hurry after him along the street, ere he lose his individuality, and melt into the great mass of London life. It would be vain searching for him there. Let us follow close at his heels, therefore, until, after several superfluous turns and doublings, we find him comfortably established by the fireside of a small apartment, previously bespoken. He is in the next street to his own, and at his journey's end. He can scarcely trust his good fortune, in having got thither unperceived—recollecting that, at one time, he was delayed by the throng, in the very focus of a lighted lantern; and, again, there were footsteps that seemed to tread behind his own, distinct from the multitudinous tramp around him; and, anon, he heard a voice shouting afar, and fancied that it called his name. Doubtless, a dozen busybodies had been watching him, and told his wife the whole affair. Poor Wakefield! Little knowest thou thine own insignificance in this great world! No mortal eye but mine has traced thee. Go quietly to thy bed, foolish man; and, on the morrow, if thou wilt be wise, get thee home to good Mrs. Wakefield, and tell her the truth. Remove not thyself, even for a little week, from thy place in her chaste bosom. Were she, for a single moment, to deem thee dead, or lost, or lastingly divided from her, thou wouldst be wofully conscious of a change in thy true wife forever after. It is perilous to make a chasm in human affections; not that they gape so long and wide—but so quickly close again!

Almost repenting of his frolic, or whatever it may be termed, Wakefield lies down betimes, and starting from his first nap, spreads forth his arms into the wide and solitary waste of the unaccustomed bed. "No,"—thinks he, gathering the bedclothes about him,—"I will not sleep alone another night."

In the morning he rises earlier than usual, and sets himself to consider what he really means to do. Such are his loose and rambling modes of thought that he has taken this very singular step with the consciousness of a purpose, indeed, but without being able to define it sufficiently for his own contemplation. The vagueness of the project, and the convulsive effort with which he plunges into the execution of it, are equally characteristic of a feeble-minded man. Wakefield sifts his ideas, however, as minutely as he may, and finds himself curious to know the progress of matters at home—how his exemplary wife will endure her widowhood of a week; and, briefly, how the little sphere of creatures and circumstances, in which he was a central object, will be affected by his removal. A morbid vanity, therefore, lies nearest the bottom of the affair. But, how is he to attain his ends? Not, certainly, by keeping close in this comfortable lodging, where, though he slept and awoke in the next street to his home, he is as effectually abroad as if the stage-coach had been whirling him away all night. Yet, should he reappear, the whole project is knocked in the head. His poor brains being hopelessly puzzled with this dilemma, he at length ventures out, partly resolving to cross the head of the street, and send one hasty glance towards his forsaken domicile. Habit—for he is a man of habits—takes him by the hand, and guides him, wholly unaware, to his own door, where, just at the critical moment, he is aroused by the scraping of his foot upon the step. Wakefield! whither are you going?

At that instant his fate was turning on the pivot. Little dreaming of the doom to which his first backward step devotes him, he hurries away, breathless with agitation hitherto unfelt, and hardly dares turn his head at the distant corner. Can it be that nobody caught sight of him? Will not the whole household—the decent Mrs. Wakefield, the smart maid servant, and the dirty little footboy—raise a hue and cry, through London streets, in pursuit of their fugitive lord and master? Wonderful escape! He gathers courage to pause and look homeward, but is perplexed with a sense of change about the familiar edifice, such as affects us all, when, after a separation of months or years, we again see some hill or lake, or work of art, with which we were friends of old. In ordinary cases, this indescribable impression is caused by the comparison and contrast between our imperfect reminiscences and the reality. In Wakefield, the magic of a single night has wrought a similar transformation, because, in that brief period, a great moral change has been effected. But this is a secret from himself. Before leaving the spot, he catches a far and momentary glimpse of his wife, passing athwart the front window, with her face turned towards the head of the street. The crafty nincompoop takes to his heels, scared with the idea that, among a thousand such atoms of mortality, her eye must have detected him. Right glad is his heart, though his brain be somewhat dizzy, when he finds himself by the coal fire of his lodgings.

So much for the commencement of this long whimwham. After the initial conception, and the stirring up of the man's sluggish temperament to put it in practice, the whole matter evolves itself in a natural train. We may suppose him, as the result of deep deliberation, buying a new wig, of reddish hair, and selecting sundry garments, in a fashion unlike his customary suit of brown, from a Jew's old-clothes bag. It is accomplished. Wakefield is another man. The new system being now established, a retrograde movement to the old would be almost as difficult as the step that placed him in his unparalleled position. Furthermore, he is rendered obstinate by a sulkiness occasionally incident to his temper, and brought on at present by the inadequate sensation which he conceives to have been produced in the bosom of Mrs. Wakefield. He will not go back until she be frightened half to death. Well; twice or thrice has she passed before his sight, each time with a heavier step, a paler cheek, and more anxious brow; and in the third week of his non-appearance he detects a portent of evil entering the house, in the guise of an apothecary. Next day the knocker is muffled. Towards nightfall comes the chariot of a physician, and deposits its big-wigged and solemn burden at Wakefield's door, whence, after a quarter of an hour's visit, he emerges, perchance the herald of a funeral. Dear woman! Will she die? By this time, Wakefield is excited to something like energy of feeling, but still lingers away from his wife's bedside, pleading with his conscience that she must not be disturbed at such a juncture. If aught else restrains him, he does not know it. In the course of a few weeks she gradually recovers; the crisis is over; her heart is sad, perhaps, but quiet; and, let him return soon or late, it will never be feverish for him again. Such ideas glimmer through the midst of Wakefield's mind, and render him indistinctly conscious that an almost impassable gulf divides his hired apartment from his former home. "It is but in the next street!" he sometimes says. Fool! It is in another world. Hitherto, he has put off his return from one particular day to another; henceforward, he leaves the precise time undetermined. Not tomorrow—probably next week—pretty soon. Poor man! The dead have nearly as much chance of revisiting their earthly homes as the self-banished Wakefield.

Would that I had a folio to write, instead of an article of a dozen pages! Then might I exemplify how an influence beyond our control lays its strong hand on every deed which we do, and weaves its consequences into an iron tissue of necessity. Wakefield is spell-bound. We must leave him, for ten years or so, to haunt around his house, without once crossing the threshold, and to be faithful to his wife, with all the affection of which his heart is capable, while he is slowly fading out of hers. Long since, it must be remarked, he had lost the perception of singularity in his conduct.

Now for a scene! Amid the throng of a London street we distinguish a man, now waxing elderly, with few characteristics to attract careless observers, yet bearing, in his whole aspect, the handwriting of no common fate, for such as have the skill to read it. He is meagre; his low and narrow forehead is deeply wrinkled; his eyes, small and lustreless, sometimes wander apprehensively about him, but oftener seem to look inward. He bends his head, and moves with an indescribable obliquity of gait, as if unwilling to display his full front to the world. Watch him long enough to see what we have described, and you will allow that circumstances—which often produce remarkable men from nature's ordinary handiwork—have produced one such here. Next, leaving him to sidle along the footwalk, cast your eyes in the opposite direction, where a portly female, considerably in the wane of life, with a prayer-book in her hand, is proceeding to yonder church. She has the placid mien of settled widowhood. Her regrets have either died away, or have become so essential to her heart, that they would be poorly exchanged for joy. Just as the lean man and well-conditioned woman are passing, a slight obstruction occurs, and brings these two figures directly in contact. Their hands touch; the pressure of the crowd forces her bosom against his shoulder; they stand, face to face, staring into each other's eyes. After a ten years' separation, thus Wakefield meets his wife!

The throng eddies away, and carries them asunder. The sober widow, resuming her former pace, proceeds to church, but pauses in the portal, and throws a perplexed glance along the street. She passes in, however, opening her prayer-book as she goes. And the man! with so wild a face that busy and selfish London stands to gaze after him, he hurries to his lodgings, bolts the door, and throws himself upon the bed. The latent feelings of years break out; his feeble mind acquires a brief energy from their strength; all the miserable strangeness of his life is revealed to him at a glance: and he cries out, passionately, "Wakefield! Wakefield! You are mad!"

Perhaps he was so. The singularity of his situation must have so moulded him to himself, that, considered in regard to his fellow-creatures and the business of life, he could not be said to possess his right mind. He had contrived, or rather he had happened, to dissever himself from the world —to vanish—to give up his place and privileges with living men, without being admitted among the dead. The life of a hermit is nowise parallel to his. He was in the bustle of the city, as of old; but the crowd swept by and saw him not; he was, we may figuratively say, always beside his wife and at his hearth, yet must never feel the warmth of the one nor the affection of the other. It was Wakefield's unprecedented fate to retain his original share of human sympathies, and to be still involved in human interests, while he had lost his reciprocal influence on them. It would be a most curious speculation to trace out the effect of such circumstances on his heart and intellect, separately, and in unison. Yet, changed as he was, he would seldom be conscious of it, but deem himself the same man as ever; glimpses of the truth, indeed, would come, but only for the moment; and still he would keep saying, "I shall soon go back!"—nor reflect that he had been saying so for twenty years.

I conceive, also, that these twenty years would appear, in the retrospect, scarcely longer than the week to which Wakefield had at first limited his absence. He would look on the affair as no more than an interlude in the main business of his life. When, after a little while more, he should deem it time to reënter his parlor, his wife would clap her hands for joy, on beholding the middle-aged Mr. Wakefield. Alas, what a mistake! Would Time but await the close of our favorite follies, we should be young men, all of us, and till Doomsday.

One evening, in the twentieth year since he vanished, Wakefield is taking his customary walk towards the dwelling which he still calls his own. It is a gusty night of autumn, with frequent showers that patter down upon the pavement, and are gone before a man can put up his umbrella. Pausing near the house, Wakefield discerns, through the parlor windows of the second floor, the red glow and the glimmer and fitful flash of a comfortable fire. On the ceiling appears a grotesque shadow of good Mrs. Wakefield. The cap, the nose and chin, and the broad waist, form an admirable caricature, which dances, moreover, with the up-flickering and down-sinking blaze, almost too merrily for the shade of an elderly widow. At this instant a shower chances to fall, and is driven, by the unmannerly gust, full into Wakefield's face and bosom. He is quite penetrated with its autumnal chill. Shall he stand, wet and shivering here, when his own hearth has a good fire to warm him, and his own wife will run to fetch the gray coat and small-clothes, which, doubtless, she has kept carefully in the closet of their bed chamber? No! Wakefield is no such fool. He ascends the steps—heavily—for twenty years have stiffened his legs since he came down—but he knows it not. Stay, Wakefield! Would you go to the sole home that is left you? Then step into your grave! The door opens. As he passes in, we have a parting glimpse of his visage, and recognize the crafty smile, which was the precursor of the little joke that he has ever since been playing off at his wife's expense. How unmercifully has he quizzed the poor woman! Well, a good night's rest to Wakefield!

This happy event—supposing it to be such—could only have occurred at an unpremeditated moment. We will not follow our friend across the threshold. He has left us much food for thought, a portion of which shall lend its wisdom to a moral, and be shaped into a figure. Amid the seeming confusion of our mysterious world, individuals are so nicely adjusted to a system, and systems to one another and to a whole, that, by stepping aside for a moment, a man exposes himself to a fearful risk of losing his place forever. Like Wakefield, he may become, as it were, the Outcast of the Universe.

HEINRICH BÖLL

Murke's Collected Silences

Every morning, after entering Broadcasting House, Murke performed an existential exercise. Here in this building the elevator was the kind known as a paternoster—open cages carried on a conveyor belt, like beads on a rosary, moving slowly and continuously from bottom to top, across the top of the elevator shaft, down to the bottom again, so that passengers could step on and off at any floor. Murke would jump onto the paternoster but, instead of getting off at the second floor, where his office was, he would let himself be carried on up, past the third, fourth, fifth floors, and he was seized with panic every time the cage rose above the level of the fifth floor and ground its way up into the empty space where oily chains, greasy rods and groaning machinery pulled and pushed the elevator from an upward into a downward direction, and Murke would stare in terror at the bare brick walls, and sigh with relief as the elevator passed through the lock, dropped into place, and began its slow descent, past the fifth, fourth, third floors. Murke knew his fears were unfounded: obviously nothing would ever happen, nothing could ever happen, and even if it did it could be nothing worse than finding himself up there at the top when the elevator stopped moving and being shut in for an hour or two at the most. He was never without a book in his pocket, and cigarettes; yet as long as the building had been standing, for three years, the elevator had never once failed. On certain days it was inspected, days when Murke had to forego those four and a half seconds of panic, and on these days he was irritable and restless, like people who had gone without breakfast. He needed this panic, the way other people need their coffee, their oatmeal or their fruit juice.

So when he stepped off the elevator at the second floor, the home of the Cultural Department, he felt light-hearted and relaxed, as light-hearted and relaxed as anyone who loves and understands his work. He would unlock the door to his office, walk slowly over to his armchair, sit down and light a cigarette. He was always first on the job. He was young, intelligent, and had a pleasant manner, and even his arrogance, which occasionally flashed out for a moment—even that was forgiven him since it was known he had majored in psychology and graduated *cum laude*.

For two days now, Murke had been obliged to go without his panic-breakfast: unusual circumstances had required him to get to Broadcasting House at eight A.M., dash off to a studio and begin work right away, for he had been told by the Director of Broadcasting to go over the two talks on The Nature of Art which the great Bur-Malottke had taped and to cut them according to Bur-Malottke's instructions. Bur-Malottke, who had converted to Catholicism during the religious fervor of 1945, had suddenly, "overnight," as he put it, "felt religious qualms," he had "suddenly felt he might be blamed for contributing to the religious overtones in radio," and he had decided to omit God, Who occurred frequently in both his half-hour talks on The Nature of Art, and replaced Him with a formula more in keeping with the mental outlook which he had professed before 1945. Bur-Malottke had suggested to the producer that the word God be replaced by the formula "that higher Being Whom we revere," but he had refused to retape the talks, requesting instead that God be cut out of the tapes and replaced by "that higher Being Whom we revere." Bur-Malottke was a friend of the Director, but this friendship was not the reason for the Director's willingness to oblige him: Bur-Malottke was a man one simply did not contradict. He was the author of numerous books of a belletristic-philosophical-religious and art-historical nature, he was on the editorial staff of three periodicals and two newspapers, and closely connected with the largest publishing house. He had agreed to come to Broadcasting House for fifteen minutes on Wednesday and tape the words "that higher Being Whom we revere" as often as God was mentioned in his talks: the rest was up to the technical experts.

It had not been easy for the Director to find someone whom he could ask to do the job; he thought of Murke, but the suddenness with which he thought of Murke made him suspicious—he was a dynamic, robust individual—so he spent five minutes going over the problem in his mind, considered Schwendling, Humkoke, Miss Broldin, but he ended up with Murke. The Director did not like Murke; he had, of course, taken him on as soon as his name had been put forward, the way a zoo director, whose real love is the rabbits and the deer, naturally accepts wild animals too for the simple reason that a zoo must contain wild animals—but what the Director really loved was rabbits and deer, and for him Murke was an intellectual wild animal. In the end his dynamic personality triumphed, and he instructed Murke to cut Bur-Malottke's talks. The talks were to be given on Thursday and Friday, and Bur-Malottke's misgivings had come to him on Sunday night—one might just as well commit suicide as contradict Bur-Malottke, and the Director was much too dynamic to think of suicide.

So Murke spent Monday afternoon and Tuesday morning listening three times to the two half-hour talks on The Nature of Art; he had cut out God, and in the short breaks which he took, during which he silently smoked a cigarette with the technician, reflected on the dynamic personality of the Director and the inferior Being Whom Bur-Malottke revered. He had never read a line of Bur-Malottke, never heard one of his talks before. Monday night he had dreamed of a staircase as tall and steep as the Eiffel Tower, and he had climbed it but soon noticed that the stairs were slippery with soap, and the Director stood down below and called out: "Go on, Murke, go on . . . show us what you can do—go on!" Tuesday night the dream had been similar: he had been at a fairground, strolled casually over to the roller coaster, paid his thirty pfennigs to a man whose face seemed familiar, and as he got on the roller coaster he saw that it was at least ten miles long, he knew there was no going back, and realized that the man who had taken his thirty pfennigs had been the Director. Both mornings after these dreams he had not needed the harmless panic-breakfast up there in the empty space above the paternoster.

Now it was Wednesday. He was smiling as he entered the building, got into the paternoster, let himself be carried up as far as the sixth floor—four and a half seconds of panic, the grinding of the chains, the bare brick walls—he rode down as far as the fourth floor, got out and walked toward the studio where he had an appointment with Bur-Malotke. It was two minutes to ten as he sat down in his green chair, waved to the technician and lit his cigarette. His breathing was quiet, he took a piece of paper out of his breast pocket and glanced at the clock: Bur-Malottke was always on time, at least he had a reputation for being punctual; and as the second hand completed the sixtieth minute of the tenth hour, the minute hand slipped onto the twelve, the hour hand onto the ten, the door opened, and in walked Bur-Malottke. Murke got up, and with a pleasant smile walked over to Bur-Malottke and introduced himself. Bur-Malottke shook hands, smiled and said: "Well, let's get started!" Murke picked up the sheet of paper from the table, put his cigarette between his lips, and, reading from the list, said to Bur-Malottke:

"In the two talks, God occurs precisely twenty-seven times—so I must ask you to repeat twenty-seven times the words we are to splice. We would appreciate it if we might ask you to repeat them thirty-five times, so as to have a certain reserve when it comes to splicing."

"Granted," said Bur-Malottke with a smile, and sat down.

"There is one difficulty, however," said Murke: "where God occurs in the genitive, such as 'God's will,' 'God's love,' 'God's purpose,' He must be replaced by the noun in question followed by the words 'of that higher Being Whom we revere.' I must ask you, therefore, to repeat the words 'the will' twice, 'the love' twice, and 'the purpose' three times, followed each time by 'of that higher Being Whom we revere,' giving us a total of seven genitives. Then there is one spot where you use the vocative and say 'O God'—here I suggest you substitute 'O Thou higher Being Whom we revere.' Everywhere else only the nominative case applies."

It was clear that Bur-Malottke had not thought of these complications; he began to sweat, the grammatical transposition bothered him. Murke went on: "In all," he said, in his pleasant, friendly manner, "the twenty-seven sentences will require one minute and twenty seconds radio time, whereas the twenty-seven times 'God' occurs require only twenty seconds. In other words, in order to take care of your alterations we shall have to cut half a minute from each talk."

Bur-Malottke sweated more heavily than ever; inwardly he cursed his sudden misgivings and asked: "I suppose you've already done the cutting, have you?"

"Yes, I have," said Murke, pulling a flat metal box out of his pocket; he opened it and held it out to Bur-Malottke: it contained some darkish sound-tape scraps, and Murke said softly: "God twenty-seven times, spoken by you. Would you care to have them?"

"No I would not," said Bur-Malottke, furious. "I'll speak to the Director about the two half-minutes. What comes after my talks in the program?"

"Tomorrow," said Murke, "your talk is followed by the regular program Neighborly News, edited by Grehm."

"Damn," said Bur-Malottke, "it's no use asking Grehm for a favor."

"And the day after tomorrow," said Murke, "your talk is followed by Let's Go Dancing."

"Oh God that's Huglieme," groaned Bur-Malottke, "never yet has Light Entertainment given way to Culture by as much as a fifth of a minute."

"No," said Murke, "it never has, at least—" and his youthful face took on an expression of irreproachable modesty—"at least not since I've been working here."

"Very well," said Bur-Malottke and glanced at the clock, "we'll be through here in ten minutes, I take it, and then I'll have a word with the Director about that minute. Let's go. Can you leave me your list?"

"Of course," said Murke, "I know the figures by heart."

The technician put down his newspaper as Murke entered the little glass booth. The technician was smiling. On Monday and Tuesday, during the six hours they listened to Bur-Malottke's talks and did their cutting, Murke and the technician had not exchanged a single personal word; now and again they exchanged glances, and when they stopped for a breather the technician had passed his cigarettes to Murke and the next day Murke passed his to the technician, and now when Murke saw the technician smiling he thought: If there is such a thing as friendship in this world, then this man is my friend. He laid the metal box with the snippets from Bur-Malottke's talk on the table and said quietly: "Here we go." He plugged into the studio and said into the microphone: "I'm sure we can dispense with the run-through, Professor. We might as well start right away—would you please begin with the nominatives?"

Bur-Malottke nodded, Murke switched off his own microphone, pressed the button which turned on the green light in the studio and heard Bur-Malottke's solemn, carefully articulated voice intoning: "That higher Being Whom we revere—that higher Being . . ."

Bur-Malottke pursed his lips toward the muzzle of the mike as if he wanted to kiss it, sweat ran down his face, and through the glass Murke observed with cold detachment the agony that Bur-Malottke was going through; then he suddenly switched Bur-Malottke off, stopped the moving tape that was recording Bur-Malottke's words, and feasted his eyes on the spectacle of Bur-Malottke behind the glass, soundless, like a fat, handsome fish. He switched on his microphone and his voice came quietly into the studio: "I'm sorry, but our tape was defective, and I must ask you to begin again at the beginning with the nominatives." Bur-Malottke swore, but his curses were silent ones which only he could hear, for Murke had disconnected him and did not switch him on again until he had begun to say "that higher Being . . ." Murke was too young, considered himself too civilized, to approve of the word hate. But here, behind the glass pane, while Bur-Malottke repeated his genitives, he suddenly knew the meaning of hatred: he hated this great fat, handsome creature, whose books—two million three hundred and fifty thousand copies of them—lay around in libraries, bookstores, bookshelves and bookcases, and not for one second did he dream of suppressing this hatred. When Bur-Malottke had repeated two genitives, Murke switched on his own mike and said quietly: "Excuse me for interrupting you: the nominatives were excellent, so was the first genitive, but would you mind doing the second genitive again? Rather gentler in tone, rather more relaxed—I'll play it back to you." And although Bur-Malottke shook his head violently he signaled to the technician to play back the tape in the studio. They saw Bur-Malottke give a start, sweat more profusely than ever, then hold his hands over his ears until the tape came to an end. He said something, swore, but Murke and the technician could not hear him; they had disconnected him. Coldly Murke waited until he could read from Bur-Malottke's lips that he had begun again with the higher Being, he turned on the mike and the tape, and Bur-Malottke continued with the genitives.

When he was through, he screwed up Murke's list into a ball, rose from his chair, drenched in sweat and fuming, and made for the door; but Murke's quiet, pleasant young voice called him back. Murke said: "But Professor, you've forgotten the vocative." Bur-Malottke looked at him, his eyes blazing with hate, and said into the mike: "O Thou higher Being Whom we revere!"

As he turned to leave, Murke's voice called him back once more. Murke said: "I'm sorry, Professor, but, spoken like that, the words are useless."

"For God's sake," whispered the technician, "watch it!" Bur-Malottke was standing stock-still by the door, his back to the glass booth, as if transfixed by Murke's voice.

Something had happened to him which had never happened to him before: he was helpless, and this young voice, so pleasant, so remarkably intelligent, tortured him as nothing had ever tortured him before. Murke went on:

"I can, of course, paste it into the talk the way it is, but I must point out to you, Professor, that it will have the wrong effect."

Bur-Malottke turned, walked back to the microphone, and said in low and solemn tones:

"O Thou higher Being Whom we revere."

Without turning to look at Murke, he left the studio. It was exactly quarter past ten, and in the doorway he collided with a young, pretty woman carrying some sheet music. The girl, a vivacious redhead, walked briskly to the microphone, adjusted it, and moved the table to one side so she could stand directly in front of the mike.

In the booth Murke chatted for half a minute with Huglieme, who was in charge of Light Entertainment. Pointing to the metal container, Huglieme said: "Do you still need that?" And Murke said, "Yes, I do." In the studio the redhead was singing, "Take my lips, just as they are, they're so lovely." Huglieme switched on his microphone and said quietly: "D'you mind keeping your trap shut for another twenty seconds, I'm not quite ready." The girl laughed, made a face, and said: "O.K., pansy dear." Murke said to the technician: "I'll be back at eleven; we can cut it up then and splice it all together."

"Will we have to hear it through again after that?" asked the technician. "No," said Murke, "I wouldn't listen to it again for a million marks."

The technician nodded, inserted the tape for the red-haired singer, and Murke left.

He put a cigarette between his lips, did not light it, and walked along the rear corridor toward the second paternoster, the one on the south side leading down to the coffee shop. The rugs, the corridors, the furniture and the pictures, everything irritated him. The rugs were impressive, the corridors were impressive, the furniture was impressive, and the pictures were in excellent taste, but he suddenly felt a desire to take the sentimental picture of the Sacred Heart which his mother had sent him and see it somewhere here on the wall. He stopped, looked round, listened, took the picture from his pocket and stuck it between the wallpaper and the frame of the door to the Assistant Drama Producer's office. The tawdry little print was highly colored, and beneath the picture of the Sacred Heart were the words: *I prayed for you at St. James' Church.*

Murke continued along the corridor, got into the paternoster, and was carried down. On this side of the building the Schrumsnot ashtrays, which had won a Good Design Award, had already been installed. They hung next to the illuminated red figures indicating the floor: a red four, a Schrumsnot ashtray, a red three, a Schrumsnot ashtray, a red two, a Schrumsnot ashtray. They were handsome ashtrays, scallop-shaped, made of beaten copper, the beaten copper base an exotic marine plant, nodular seaweed—and each ashtray had cost two hundred and fifty-eight marks and seventy-seven pfennigs. They were so handsome that Murke could never bring himself to soil them with cigarette ash, let alone anything as sordid as a butt. Other smokers all seemed to have had the same feeling—empty packs, butts and ash littered the floor under the handsome ashtrays: apparently no one had the courage to use them as ashtrays; they were copper, burnished, forever empty.

Murke saw the fifth ashtray next to the illuminated red zero rising toward him, the air was getting warmer, there was a smell of food. Murke jumped off and stumbled into the coffee shop. Three free-lance colleagues were sitting at a table in the corner. The table was covered with used plates, cups, and saucers.

The three men were the joint authors of a radio series, *The Lung, A Human Organ;* they had collected their fee together, breakfasted together, were having a drink together, and were now throwing dice for the expense voucher. One of them, Wendrich, Murke knew well, but just then Wendrich shouted: "Art!"—"art," he shouted again, "art, art!" and Murke felt a spasm, like the frog when Galvani discovered electricity. The last two days Murke had heard the word *art* too often, from Bur-Malottke's lips; it occurred exactly one hundred and thirty-four times in the two talks; and he had heard the talks three times, which meant he had heard the word *art* four hundred and two times, too often to feel any desire to discuss it. He squeezed past the counter toward a booth in the far corner and was relieved to find it empty. He sat down, lit his cigarette, and when Wulla, the waitress, came, he said: "Apple juice, please," and was glad when Wulla went off again at once. He closed his eyes tight, but found himself listening willy-nilly to the conversation of the free-lance writers over in the corner, who seemed to be having a heated argument about art; each time one of them shouted "art" Murke winced. It's like being whipped, he thought.

As she brought him the apple juice Wulla looked at him in concern. She was tall and strongly built, but not fat, she had a healthy, cheerful facc, and as she poured the apple juice from the jug into the glass she said: "You ought to take a vacation, sir, and quit smoking."

She used to call herself Wilfriede-Ulla, but later, for the sake of simplicity, she combined the names into Wulla. She especially admired the people from the Cultural Department.

"Lay off, will you?" said Murke, "please!"

"And you ought to take some nice ordinary girl to the movies one night," said Wulla.

"I'll do that this evening," said Murke, "I promise you."

"It doesn't have to be one of those dolls," said Wulla, "just some nice, quiet, ordinary girl, with a kind heart. There are still some of those around."

"Yes," said Murke, "I know they're still around, as a matter of fact I know one." Well, that's fine then, thought Wulla, and went over to the free lances, one of whom had ordered three drinks and three coffees. Poor fellows, thought Wulla, art will be the death of them yet. She had a soft spot for the free lances and was always trying to persuade them to economize. The minute they have any money, she thought, they blow it; she went up to the counter and, shaking her head, passed on the order for the three drinks and the three coffees.

Murke drank some of the apple juice, stubbed out his cigarette in the ashtray, and thought with apprehension of the hours from eleven to one when he had to cut up Bur-Malottke's sentences and paste them into the right places in the talks. At two o'clock the Director wanted both talks played back to him in his studio. Murke thought about soap, about staircases, steep stairs and roller coasters, he thought about the dynamic personality of the Director, he thought about Bur-Malottke, and was startled by the sight of Schwendling coming into the coffee shop.

Schwendling had on a shirt of large red and black checks and made a beeline for the booth where Murke was hiding. Schwendling was humming the tune which was very popular just then: "Take my lips, just as they are, they're so lovely. . . ." He stopped short when he saw Murke, and said: "Hullo, you here? I thought you were busy carving up that crap of Bur-Malottke's."

"I'm going back at eleven," said Murke.

"Wulla, let's have some beer," shouted Schwendling over to the counter, "a pint. Well," he said to Murke, "you deserve extra time off for that, it must be a filthy job. The old man told me all about it."

Murke said nothing, and Schwendling went on:

"Have you heard the latest about Muckwitz?"

Murke, not interested, first shook his head, then for politeness' sake asked: "What's he been up to?"

Wulla brought the beer, Schwendling swallowed some, paused for effect, and announced: "Muckwitz is doing a feature about the Steppes."

Murke laughed and said: "What's Fenn doing?"

"Fenn," said Schwendling, "Fenn's doing a feature about the Tundra."

"And Wegucht?"

"Wegucht is doing a feature about me, and after that I'm going to do a feature about him, you know the old saying: You feature me, I'll feature you. . . ."

Just then one of the free lances jumped up and shouted across the room: "Art—art—that's the only thing that matters!"

Murke ducked, like a soldier when he hears the mortars being fired from the enemy trenches. He swallowed another mouthful of apple juice and winced again when a voice over the loudspeaker said: "Mr. Murke is wanted in Studio Thirteen—Mr. Murke is wanted in Studio Thirteen." He looked at his watch, it was only half-past ten, but the voice went on relentlessly: "Mr. Murke is wanted in Studio Thirteen—Mr. Murke is wanted in Studio Thirteen." The loudspeaker hung above the counter, immediately below the motto the Director had had painted on the wall: *Discipline Above All.*

"Well," said Schwendling, "that's it, you'd better go."

"Yes," said Murke, "that's it."

He got up, put money for the apple juice on the table, pressed past the free lances' table, got into the paternoster outside and was carried up once more past the five Schrumsnot ashtrays. He saw his Sacred Heart picture still sticking in the Assistant Producer's doorframe and thought:

"Thank God, now there's at least one corny picture in this place."

He opened the door of the studio booth, saw the technician sitting alone and relaxed in front of three cardboard boxes, and asked wearily: "What's up?"

"They were ready sooner than expected, and we've got an extra half hour in hand," said the technician. "I thought you'd be glad of the extra time."

"I certainly am," said Murke, "I've got an appointment at one. Let's get on with it then. What's the idea of the boxes?"

"Well," said the technician, "for each grammatical case I've got one box —the nominatives in the first, the genitives in the second, and in that one—" he pointed to the little box on the right with the words "Pure Chocolate" on it, and said: "in that one I have the two vocatives, the good one in the right-hand corner, the bad one in the left."

"That's terrific," said Murke, "so you've already cut up the crap."

"That's right," said the technician, "and if you've made a note of the order in which the cases have to be spliced it won't take us more than an hour. Did you write it down?"

"Yes, I did," said Murke. He pulled a piece of paper from his pocket with the numbers 1 to 27; each number was followed by a grammatical case.

Murke sat down, held out his cigarette pack to the technician; they both smoked while the technician laid the cut tapes with Bur-Malottke's talks on the roll.

"In the first cut," said Murke, "we have to stick in a nominative."

The technician put his hand into the first box, picked up one of the snippets and stuck it into the space.

"Next comes a genitive," said Murke.

They worked swiftly, and Murke was relieved that it all went so fast.

"Now," he said, "comes the vocative; we'll take the bad one, of course."

The technician laughed and stuck Bur-Malottke's bad vocative into the tape.

"Next," he said, "next!" "Genitive," said Murke.

The Director conscientiously read every listener's letter. The one he was reading at this particular moment went as follows:

Dear Radio,

I am sure you can have no more faithful listener than myself. I am an old woman, a little old lady of seventy-seven, and I have been listening to you every day for thirty years. I have never been sparing with my praise. Perhaps you remember my letter about the program: "The Seven Souls of Kaweida the Cow." It was a lovely program—but now I have to be angry with you! The way the canine soul is being neglected in radio is gradually becoming a disgrace. And you call that humanism. I am sure Hitler had his bad points: if one is to believe all one hears, he was a dreadful man, but one thing he did have: a real affection for dogs, and he did a lot for them. When are dogs going to come into their own again in German radio? The way you tried to do it in the program "Like Cat and Dog" is certainly not the right one: it was an insult to every canine soul. If my little Lohengrin could only talk, he'd tell you! And the way he barked, poor darling, all through your terrible program, it almost made me die of shame. I pay my two marks a month like any other listener and stand on my rights and demand to know: When are dogs going to come into their own again in German radio?

With kind regards—in spite of my being so cross with you,

Sincerely yours,

Jadwiga Herchen (retired)

P.S. In case none of those cynics of yours who run your programs should be capable of doing justice to the canine soul, I suggest you make use of my modest attempts, which are enclosed herewith. I do not wish to accept any fee. You may send it direct to the S.P.C.A. Enclosed: 35 manuscripts.

Yours,

J.H.

The Director sighed. He looked for the scripts, but his secretary had evidently filed them away. The Director filled his pipe, lit it, ran his tongue over his dynamic lips, lifted the receiver and asked to be put through to Krochy. Krochy had a tiny office with a tiny desk, although in the best of taste, upstairs in Culture and was in charge of a section as narrow as his desk: Animals in the World of Culture.

"Krochy speaking," he said diffidently into the telephone.

"Say, Krochy," said the Director, "when was the last time we had a program about dogs?"

"Dogs, sir?" said Krochy. "I don't believe we ever have, at least not since I've been here."

"And how long have you been here, Krochy?" And upstairs in his office Krochy trembled, because the Director's voice was so gentle; he knew it boded no good when that voice became gentle.

"I've been here ten years now, sir," said Krochy.

"It's a disgrace," said the Director, "that you've never had a program about dogs; after all, that's your department. What was the title of your last program?"

"The title of my last program was—" stammered Krochy.

"You don't have to repeat every sentence," said the Director, "we're not in the army."

"Owls in the Ruins," said Krochy timidly.

"Within the next three weeks," said the Director, gentle again now, "I would like to hear a program about the canine soul."

"Certainly, sir," said Krochy; he heard the click as the Director put down the receiver, sighed deeply and said: "Oh God!"

The Director picked up the next listener's letter.

At this moment Bur-Malottke entered the room. He was always at liberty to enter unannounced, and he made frequent use of this liberty. He was still sweating as he sank wearily into a chair opposite the Director and said:

"Well, good morning."

"Good morning," said the Director, pushing the listener's letter aside. "What can I do for you?"

"Could you give me one minute?"

"Bur-Malottke," said the Director, with a generous, dynamic gesture, "does not have to ask me for one minute; hours, days, are at your disposal."

"No," said Bur-Malottke, "I don't mean an ordinary minute, I mean one minute of radio time. Due to the changes my talk has become one minute longer."

The Director grew serious, like a satrap distributing provinces. "I hope," he said, sourly, "it's not a political minute."

"No," said Bur-Malottke, "it's half a minute of Neighborly News and half a minute of Light Entertainment."

"Thank God for that," said the Director. "I've got a credit of seventy-nine seconds with Light Entertainment and eighty-three seconds with Neighborly News. I'll be glad to let someone like Bur-Malottke have one minute."

"I am overcome," said Bur-Malottke.

"Is there anything else I can do for you?" asked the Director.

"I would appreciate it," said Bur-Malottke, "if we could gradually start correcting all the tapes I have made since 1945. One day," he said—he passed his hand over his forehead and gazed wistfully at the genuine Kokoschkla above the Director's desk—"one day I shall—" he faltered, for the news he was about to break to the Director was too painful for posterity "—one day I shall—die," and he paused again, giving the Director a chance to look gravely shocked and raise his hand in protest, "and I cannot bear the thought that after my death tapes may be run off on which I say things I no longer believe in. Particularly in some of my political utterances, during the fervor of 1945, I let myself be persuaded to make statements which today fill me with serious misgivings and which I can only account for on the basis of that spirit of youthfulness which has always distinguished my work. My written works are already in process of being corrected, and I would like to ask you to give me the opportunity of correcting my spoken works as well."

The Director was silent, he cleared his throat slightly, and little shining beads of sweat appeared on his forehead: it occurred to him that Bur-Malottke had spoken for at least an hour every month since 1945, and he made a swift calculation while Bur-Malottke went on talking: twelve times ten hours meant one hundred and twenty hours of spoken Bur-Malottke.

"Pedantry," Bur-Malottke was saying, "is something that only impure spirits regard as unworthy of genius; we know, of course"—and the Director felt flattered to be ranked by the We among the pure spirits—"that the true geniuses, the great geniuses, were pedants. Himmelsheim once had a whole printed edition of his *Seelon* rebound at his own expense because he felt that three or four sentences in the central portion of the work were no longer appropriate. The idea that some of my talks might be broadcast which no longer correspond to my convictions when I depart this earthly life—I find such an idea intolerable. How do you propose we go about it?"

The beads of sweat on the Director's forehead had become larger. "First of all," he said in a subdued voice, "an exact list would have to be made of all your broadcast talks, and then we would have to check in the archives to see if all the tapes were still there."

"I should hope," said Bur-Malottke, "that none of the tapes has been erased without notifying me. I have not been notified, therefore no tapes have been erased."

"I will see to everything," said the Director.

"Please do," said Bur-Malottke curtly, and rose from his chair. "Good-by."

"Good-by," said the Director, as he accompanied Bur-Malottke to the door.

The free lances in the coffee shop had decided to order lunch. They had had some more drinks, they were still talking about art, their conversation was quieter now but no less intense. They all jumped to their feet when Wanderburn suddenly came in. Wanderburn was a tall, despondent-looking writer with dark hair, an attractive face somewhat etched by the stigma of fame. On this particular morning he had not shaved, which made him look even more attractive. He walked over to the table where the three free lances were sitting, sank exhausted into a chair and said: "For God's sake, give me a drink. I always have the feeling in this building that I'm dying of thirst."

They passed him a drink, a glass that was still standing on the table, and the remains of a bottle of soda water. Wanderburn swallowed the drink, put down his glass, looked at each of the three men in turn, and said: "I must warn you about the radio business, about this pile of junk—this immaculate, shiny, slippery pile of junk. I'm warning you. It'll destroy us all." His warning was sincere and impressed the three young men very much; but the three young men did not know that Wanderburn had just come from the accounting department where he had picked up a nice fat fee for a quick job of editing the Book of Job.

"They cut us," said Wanderburn, "they consume our substance, splice us together again, and it'll be more than any of us can stand."

He finished the soda water, put the glass down on the table and, his coat flapping despondently about him, strode to the door.

On the dot of noon Murke finished the splicing. They had just stuck in the last snippet, a genitive, when Murke got up. He already had his hand on the doorknob when the technician said: "I wish I could afford a sensitive and expensive conscience like that. What'll we do with the box?" He pointed to the flat tin lying on the shelf next to the cardboard boxes containing the new tapes.

"Just leave it there," said Murke.

"What for?"

"We might need it again."

"D'you think he might get pangs of conscience all over again?"

"He might," said Murke, "we'd better wait and see. So long." He walked to the front paternoster, rode down to the second floor, and for the first time that day entered his office. His secretary had gone to lunch; Murke's boss, Humkoke, was sitting by the phone reading a book. He smiled at Murke, got up and said: "Well, I see you survived. Is this your book? Did you put it on the desk?" He held it out for Murke to read the title, and Murke said: "Yes, that's mine." The book had a jacket of green, gray and orange and was called "Batley's Lyrics of the Gutter"; it was about a young English writer a hundred years ago who had drawn up a catalogue of London slang.

"It's a marvelous book," said Murke.

"Yes," said Humkoke, "it is marvelous, but you never learn."

Murke eyed him questioningly.

"You never learn that one doesn't leave marvelous books lying around when Wanderburn is liable to turn up, and Wanderburn is always liable to turn up. He saw it at once, of course, opened it, read it for five minutes, and what's the result?"

Murke said nothing.

"The result," said Humkoke, "is two hour-long broadcasts by Wanderburn on 'Lyrics of the Gutter.' One day this fellow will do a feature about his own grandmother, and the worst of it is that one of his grandmothers was one of mine too. Please, Murke, try and remember: never leave marvelous books around when Wanderburn is liable to turn up, and, I repeat, he's always liable to turn up. That's all, you can go now, you've got the afternoon off, and I'm sure you've earned it. Is the stuff ready? Did you hear it through again?"

"It's all done," said Murke, "but I can't hear the talks through again, I simply can't."

" 'I simply can't' is a very childish thing to say," said Humkoke.

"If I have to hear the word Art one more time today I shall become hysterical," said Murke.

"You already are," said Humkoke, "and I must say you've every reason to be. Three hours of Bur-Malottke, that's too much for anybody, even the toughest of us, and you're not even tough." He threw the book on the table, took a step toward Murke and said: "When I was your age I once had to cut three minutes out of a four-hour speech of Hitler's, and I had to listen to the speech three times before I was considered worthy of suggesting which three minutes should be cut. When I began listening to the tape for the first time I was still a Nazi, but by the time I had heard the speech for the third time I wasn't a Nazi any more; it was a drastic cure, a terrible one, but very effective."

"You forget," said Murke quietly, "that I had already been cured of Bur-Malottke before I had to listen to his tapes."

"You really are a vicious beast!" said Humkoke with a laugh. "That'll do for now, the Director is going to hear it through again at two. Just see that you're available in case anything goes wrong."

"I'll be at home from two to three," said Murke.

"One more thing," said Humkoke, pulling out a yellow biscuit tin from a shelf next to Murke's desk, "what's this scrap you've got here?"

Murke colored. "It's—" he stammered, "I collect a certain kind of left-overs."

"What kind of left-overs?" asked Humkoke.

"Silences," said Murke, "I collect silences."

Humkoke raised his eyebrows, and Murke went on: "When I have to cut tapes, in the places where the speakers sometimes pause for a moment—or sigh, or take a breath, or there is absolute silence—I don't throw that away, I collect it. Incidentally, there wasn't a single second of silence in Bur-Malottke's tapes."

Humkoke laughed: "Of course not, he would never be silent. And what do you do with the scrap?"

"I splice it together and play back the tape when I'm at home in the evening. There's not much yet, I only have three minutes so far—but then people aren't silent very often."

"You know, don't you, that it's against regulations to take home sections of tape?"

"Even silences?" asked Murke.

Humkoke laughed and said: "For God's sake, get out!" And Murke left.

When the Director entered his studio a few minutes after two, the Bur-Malottke tape had just been turned on:

> . . . and wherever, however, why ever, and whenever we begin to discuss the Nature of Art, we must first look to that higher Being Whom we revere, we must bow in awe before that higher Being Whom we revere, and we must accept Art as a gift from that higher Being Whom we revere. Art . . . .

No, thought the Director, I really can't ask anyone to listen to Bur-Malottke for a hundred and twenty hours. No, he thought, there are some things one simply cannot do, things I wouldn't want to wish even on Murke. He returned to his office and switched on the loudspeaker just in time to hear Bur-Malottke say: "O Thou higher Being Whom we revere. . . ." No, thought the Director, no, no.

Murke lay on his chesterfield at home smoking. Next to him on a chair was a cup of tea, and Murke was gazing at the white ceiling of the room. Sitting at his desk was a very pretty blonde who was staring out of the window at the street. Between Murke and the girl, on a low coffee table, stood a tape recorder, recording. Not a word was spoken, not a sound was made. The girl was pretty and silent enough for a photographer's model.

"I can't stand it," said the girl suddenly, "I can't stand it, it's inhuman, what you want me to do. There are some men who expect a girl to do immoral things, but it seems to me that what you are asking me to do is even more immoral than the things other men expect a girl to do."

Murke sighed. "Oh hell," he said, "Rina dear, now I've got to cut all that out; do be sensible, be a good girl and put just five more minutes' silence on the tape."

"Put silence," said the girl, with what thirty years ago would have been called a pout. "Put silence, that's another of your inventions. I wouldn't mind putting words onto a tape—but putting silence. . . ."

Murke had got up and switched off the tape recorder. "Oh Rina," he said, "if you only knew how precious your silence is to me. In the evening, when I'm tired, when I'm sitting here alone, I play back your silence. Do be a dear and put just three more minutes' silence on the tape for me and save me the cutting; you know how I feel about cutting." "Oh all right," said the girl, "but give me a cigarette at least."

Murke smiled, gave her a cigarette and said: "This way I have your silence in the original and on tape, that's terrific." He switched the tape on again, and they sat facing one another in silence till the telephone rang. Murke got up, shrugged helplessly, and lifted the receiver.

"Well," said Humkoke, "the tapes ran off smoothly, the boss couldn't find a thing wrong with them. . . . You can go to the movies now. And think about snow."

"What snow?" asked Murke, looking out onto the street, which lay basking in brilliant summer sunshine.

"Come on now," said Humkoke, "you know we have to start thinking about the winter programs. I need songs about snow, stories about snow—we can't fool around for the rest of our lives with Schubert and Stifter. No one seems to have any idea how badly we need snow songs and snow stories. Just imagine if we have a long hard winter with lots of snow and freezing temperatures: where are we going to get our snow programs from? Try and think of something snowy."

"All right," said Murke, "I'll try and think of something." Humkoke had hung up.

"Come along," he said to the girl, "we can go to the movies."

"May I speak again now?" said the girl.

"Yes," said Murke, "speak!"

It was just at this time that the Assistant Drama Producer had finished listening again to the one-act play scheduled for that evening. He liked it, only the ending did not satisfy him. He was sitting in the glass booth in Studio Thirteen next to the technician, chewing a match and studying the script.

(*Sound-effects of a large empty church*)

ATHEIST: (*in a loud clear voice*) Who will remember me when I have become the prey of worms?

(*Silence*)

ATHEIST: (*his voice a shade louder*) Who will wait for me when I have turned into dust?

(*Silence*)

ATHEIST: (*louder still*) And who will remember me when I have turned into leaves?

(*Silence*)

There were twelve such questions called out by the atheist into the church, and each question was followed by—? Silence.

The Assistant Producer removed the chewed match from his lips, replaced it with a fresh one and looked at the technician, a question in his eyes.

"Yes," said the technician, "if you ask me: I think there's a bit too much silence in it."

"That's what I thought," said the Assistant Producer; "the author thinks so too and he's given me leave to change it. There should just be a voice saying: "God"—but it ought to be a voice without church sound-effects, it would have to be spoken somehow in a different acoustical environment. Have you any idea where I can get hold of a voice like that at this hour?"

The technician smiled, picked up the metal container which was still lying on the shelf. "Here you are," he said, "here's a voice saying 'God' without any sound-effects."

The Assistant Producer was so surprised he almost swallowed the match, choked a little and got it up into the front of his mouth again. "It's quite all right," the technician said with a smile, "we had to cut it out of a talk, twenty-seven times."

"I don't need it that often, just twelve times," said the Assistant Producer.

"It's a simple matter, of course," said the technician, "to cut out the silence and stick in God twelve times—if you'll take the responsibility."

"You're a godsend," said the Assistant Producer, "and I'll be responsible. Come on, let's get started." He gazed happily at the tiny, lusterless tape snippets in Murke's tin box. "You really are a godsend," he said, "come on, let's go!"

The technician smiled, for he was looking forward to being able to present Murke with the snippets of silence: it was a lot of silence, altogether nearly a minute; it was more silence than he had ever been able to give Murke, and he liked the young man.

"O.K.," he said with a smile, "here we go."

The Assistant Producer put his hand in his jacket pocket, took out a pack of cigarettes; in doing so he touched a crumpled piece of paper, he smoothed it out and passed it to the technician: "Funny, isn't it, the corny stuff you can come across in this place? I found this stuck in my door."

The technician took the picture, looked at it, and said: "Yes, it's funny," and he read out the words under the picture:

I prayed for you at St. James' Church.

VLADIMIR NABOKOV

The Potato Elf

I

Actually his name was Frederic Dobson. To his friend the conjuror, he talked about himself thus:

"There was no one in Bristol who didn't know Dobson the tailor for children's clothes. I am his son—and am proud of it out of sheer stubbornness. You should know that he drank like an old whale. Some time around 1900, a few months before I was born, my gin-soaked dad rigged up one of those wax-work cherubs, you know—sailor suit, with a lad's first long trousers—and put it in my mother's bed. It's a wonder the poor thing did not have a miscarriage. As you can well understand, I know all this only by hearsay—yet, if my kind informers were not liars, this is, apparently, the secret reason I am—"

And Fred Dobson, in a sad and good-natured gesture, would spread out his little hands. The conjuror, with his usual dreamy smile, would bend down, pick up Fred like a baby, and, sighing, place him on the top of a wardrobe, where the Potato Elf would meekly roll up and start to sneeze softly and whimper.

He was twenty, and weighed less than fifty pounds, being only a couple of inches taller than the famous Swiss dwarf, Zimmermann (dubbed "Prince Balthazar"). Like friend Zimmermann, Fred was extremely well built, and had there not been those wrinkles on his round forehead and at the corners of his narrowed eyes, as well as a rather eerie air of tension (as if he were resisting growth), our dwarf would have easily passed for a gentle eight-year-old boy. His hair, the hue of damp straw, was sleeked down and evenly parted by a line which ran up the exact middle of his head to conclude a cunning agreement with its crown. Fred walked lightly, had an easy demeanor, and danced rather well, but his very first manager deemed it wise to weight the notion of "elf" with a comic epithet upon noticing the fat nose inherited by the dwarf from his plethoric and naughty father.

The Potato Elf, by his sole aspect, aroused a storm of applause and laughter throughout England, and then in the main cities of the Continent. He differed from most dwarfs in being of a mild and friendly nature. He became greatly attached to the miniature pony Snowdrop on which he trotted diligently around the arena of a Dutch circus; and, in Vienna, he conquered the heart of a stupid and glum giant hailing from Omsk by stretching up to him the first time he saw him and pleading like an infant to be taken up in Nurse's arms.

He usually performed not alone. In Vienna, for example, he appeared with the Russian giant and minced around him, neatly attired in striped trousers and a smart jacket, with a voluminous roll of music under his arm. He brought the giant's guitar. The giant stood like a tremendous statue and took the instrument with the motions of an automaton. A long frock coat that looked carved out of ebony, elevated heels, and a top hat with a sheen of columnar reflections increased the height of the stately three-hundred-and-fifty-pound Siberian. Thrusting out his powerful jaw, he beat the strings with one finger. Backstage, in womanish tones, he complained of giddiness. Fred grew very fond of him and even shed a few tears at the moment of separation, for he rapidly became accustomed to people. His life, like a circus horse's, went round and round with smooth monotony. One day in the dark of the wings he tripped over a bucket of house paint and mellowly plopped into it—an occurrence he kept recalling for quite a long while as something out of the ordinary.

In this way the dwarf traveled around most of Europe, and saved money, and sang with a *castrato*-like silvery voice, and in German variety theaters the audience ate thick sandwiches and candied nuts on sticks, and in Spanish ones, sugared violets and also nuts on sticks. The world was invisible to him. There remained in his memory the same faceless abyss laughing at him, and afterwards, when the performance was over, the soft, dreamy echo of a cool night that seems of such a deep blue when you leave the theater.

Upon returning to London he found a new partner in the person of Shock, the conjuror. Shock had a tuneful delivery, slender, pale, virtually ethereal hands, and a lick of chestnut brown hair that came down on one eyebrow. He resembled a poet more than a stage magician, and demonstrated his skill with a sort of tender and graceful melancholy, without the fussy patter characteristic of his profession. The Potato Elf assisted him amusingly, and, at the end of the act, would turn up in the gallery with a cooing exclamation of joy, although a minute before everyone had seen Shock lock him up in a black box right in the middle of the stage.

All this happened in one of those London theaters where there are acrobats soaring in the tinkle and shiver of the trapezes, and a foreign tenor (a failure in his own country) singing barcaroles, and a ventriloquist in naval uniform, and bicyclists, and the inevitable clown-eccentric shuffling about in a minuscule hat and a waistcoat coming down to his knees.

II

Latterly Fred had been growing gloomy, and sneezing a lot, soundlessly and sadly, like a little Japanese spaniel. While not experiencing for months any hankering after a woman, the virginal dwarf would be beset now and then by sharp pangs of lone amorous anguish which went as suddenly as they came, and again, for a while, he would ignore the bare shoulders showing white beyond the velvet boundary of loges, as well as the little girl acrobats, or the Spanish dancer whose sleek thighs were revealed for a moment when the orange-red curly fluff of her nether flounces would whip up in the course of a rapid swirl.

"What you need is a female dwarf," said pensively Shock, producing with a familiar flick of finger and thumb a silver coin from the ear of the dwarf whose little arm went up in a brushing-away curve as if chasing a fly.

That same night, as Fred, after his number, snuffling and grumbling, in bowler and tiny topcoat, was toddling along a dim backstage passage, a door came ajar with a sudden splash of gay light and two voices called him in. It was Zita and Arabella, sister acrobats, both half-undressed, sun-tanned, black-haired, with elongated blue eyes. A shimmer of theatrical disorder and the fragrance of lotions filled the room. The dressing table was littered with powder puffs, combs, cut-glass atomizers, hairpins in an ex-chocolate box, and rouge sticks.

The two girls instantly deafened Fred with their chatter. They tickled and squeezed the dwarf, who, glowering, and empurpled with lust, rolled like a ball in the embrace of the bare-armed teases. Finally, when frolicsome Arabella drew him to her and fell backward upon the couch, Fred lost his head and began to wriggle against her, snorting and clasping her neck. In attempting to push him away, she raised her arm and, slipping under it, he lunged and glued his lips to the hot pricklish hollow of her shaven axilla. The other girl, weak with laughter, tried in vain to drag him off by his legs. At that moment the door banged open, and the French partner of the two aerialists came into the room wearing marble-white tights. Silently, without any resentment, he grabbed the dwarf by the scruff of the neck (all you heard was the snap of Fred's wing collar as one side broke loose from the stud), lifted him in the air and threw him out like a monkey. The door slammed. Shock, who happened to be wandering past, managed to catch a glimpse of the marble-bright arm and of a black little figure with feet retracted in flight.

Fred hurt himself in falling and now lay motionless in the corridor. He was not really stunned, but had gone all limp with eyes fixed on one point, and fast chattering teeth.

"Bad luck, old boy," sighed the conjurer, picking him up from the floor. He palpated with translucent fingers the dwarf's round forehead and added, "I told you not to butt in. Now you got it. A dwarf woman is what you need."

Fred, his eyes bulging, said nothing.

"You'll sleep at my place to-night," decided Shock and carried the Potato Elf toward the exit.

III

There existed also a Mrs. Shock.

She was a lady of uncertain age, with dark eyes which had a yellowish tinge around the iris. Her skinny frame, parchment complexion, lifeless black hair, a habit of strongly exhaling tobacco smoke through her nostrils, the studied untidiness of her attire and hairdo—all this could hardly attract many men, but, no doubt, was to Mr. Shock's liking, though actually he never seemed to notice his wife, as he was always engaged in imagining secret devices for his show, always appeared unreal and shifty, thinking of something else when talking about trivialities, but keenly observing everything around him when immersed in astral fancies. Nora had to be constantly on the lookout since he never missed the occasion to contrive some small, inutile, yet subtly artful deception. There had been, for instance, that time when he amazed her by his unusual gluttony: he smacked his lips juicily, sucked chicken bones clean, again and again heaped up food on his plate; then he departed after giving his wife a sorrowful glance; and a little later the maid, giggling into her apron, informed Nora that Mr. Shock had not touched one scrap of his dinner, and had left all of it in three brand-new pans under the table.

She was the daughter of a respectable artist who painted only horses, spotty hounds, and huntsmen in pink coats. She had lived in Chelsea before her marriage, had admired the hazy Thames sunsets, taken drawing lessons, gone to ridiculous meetings attended by the local Bohemian crowd—and it was there that the ghost-gray eyes of a quiet slim man had singled her out. He talked little about himself, and was still unknown. Some people believed him to be a composer of lyrical poems. She fell headlong in love with him. The poet absentmindedly became engaged to her, and on the very first day of matrimony explained, with a sad smile, that he did not know how to write poetry, and there and then, in the middle of the conversation, he transformed an old alarm-clock into a nickel-plated chronometer, and the chronometer into a miniature gold watch, which Nora had worn ever since on her wrist. She understood that nevertheless conjuror Shock was, in his own way, a poet; only she could not get used to his demonstrating his art every minute, in all circumstances. It is hard to be happy when one's husband is a mirage, a peripatetic legerdemain of a man, a deception of all five senses.

IV

She was idly tapping a fingernail against the glass of a bowl in which several goldfish that looked cut out of orange peel breathed and fin-flashed when the door opened noiselessly, and Shock appeared (silk hat askew, strand of brown hair on his brow) with a little creature all screwed up in his arms.

"Brought him," said the conjuror with a sigh.

Nora thought fleetingly: child. Lost. Found. Her dark eyes grew moist.

"Must be adopted," softly added Shock, lingering in the doorway.

The small thing suddenly came alive, mumbled something and started to scrabble shyly against the conjuror's starched shirtfront. Nora glanced at the tiny boots in chamois spats, at the little bowler.

"I'm not so easy to fool," she sneered.

The conjuror looked at her reproachfully. Then he laid Fred on a plush couch and covered him with a lap-robe.

"Blondinet roughed him up," explained Shock, and could not help adding, "Bashed him with a dumbbell. Right in the tummy."

And Nora, kind-hearted as childless women frequently are, felt such an especial pity that she almost broke into tears. She proceeded to mother the dwarf, she fed him, gave him a glass of port, rubbed his forehead with eau-de-cologne, moistened with it his temples and the infantine hollows behind his ears.

Next morning Fred woke up early, inspected the unfamiliar room, talked to the goldfish, and after a quiet sneeze or two, settled on the ledge of the bay-window like a little boy.

A melting, enchanting mist washed London's gray roofs. Somewhere in the distance an attic window was thrown open, and its pane caught a glint of sunshine. The horn of an automobile sang out in the freshness and tenderness of dawn.

Fred's thoughts dwelt on the previous day. The laughing accents of the girl tumblers got oddly mixed up with the touch of Mrs. Shock's cold fragrant hands. At first he had been ill-treated, then he had been caressed; and, mind you, he was a very affectionate, very ardent dwarf. He dwelt in fancy on the possibility of his rescuing Nora some day from a strong, brutal man resembling that Frenchman in white tights. Incongruously, there floated up the memory of a fifteen-year-old female dwarf with whom he appeared together at one time. She was a bad-tempered, sick, sharp-nosed little thing. The two were presented to the spectators as an engaged couple, and, shivering with disgust, he had to dance an intimate tango with her.

Again a lone klaxon sang out and swept by. Sunlight was beginning to infuse the mist over London's soft wilderness.

Around half-past seven the flat came to life. With an abstract smile Mr. Shock left for an unknown destination. From the dining room came the delicious smell of bacon and eggs. With her hair done anyhow, wearing a kimono embroidered with sunflowers, appeared Mrs. Shock.

After breakfast she offered Fred a perfumed cigarette with a red-petaled tip and half-closing her eyes had him tell her about his existence. At such narrative moments Fred's little voice deepened slightly: he spoke slowly, choosing his words, and, strange to say, that unforeseen dignity of diction became him. Bent-headed, solemn, and elastically tense, he sat sideways at Nora's feet. She reclined on the plush divan, her arms thrown back, revealing her sharp bare elbows. The dwarf, having finished his tale, lapsed into silence but still kept turning this way and that the palm of his tiny hand, as if softly continuing to speak. His black jacket, inclined face, fleshy little nose, tawny hair, and that middle parting reaching the back of his head vaguely moved Nora's heart. As she looked at him through her lashes she tried to imagine that it was not an adult dwarf sitting there, but her non-existing little son in the act of telling her how his schoolmates bullied him. Nora stretched her hand and stroked his head lightly—and, at that moment, by an enigmatic association of thought, she called forth something else, a curious vindictive vision.

Upon feeling those light fingers in his hair, Fred at first sat motionless, then began to lick his lips in feverish silence. His eyes, turned askance, could not detach their gaze from the green pompon on Mrs. Shock's slipper. And all at once, in some absurd and intoxicating way, everything came into motion.

V

On that smoke-blue day, in the August sun, London was particularly lovely. The tender and festive sky was reflected in the smooth spread of the asphalt, the glossy pillar boxes glowed crimson at the street corners, through the Gobelin green of the Park cars flashed and rolled with a low hum—the entire city shimmered and breathed in the mellow warmth, and only underground, on the platforms of the Tube, could one find a region of coolness.

Every separate day in the year is a gift presented to only one man—the happiest one; all other people use his day, to enjoy the sunshine or berate the rain, never knowing, however, to whom that day really belongs; and its fortunate owner is pleased and amused by their ignorance. A person cannot foreknow which day exactly will fall to his lot, what trifle he will remember forever: the ripple of reflected sunlight on a wall bordering water or the revolving fall of a maple leaf; and it often happens that he recognizes *his* day only in retrospection, long after he has plucked, and crumpled, and chucked under his desk the calendar leaf with the forgotten figure.

Providence granted Fred Dobson, a dwarf in mouse-gray spats, the merry August day in 1920 which began with the melodious hoot of a motor horn and the flash of a casement swung open in the distance. Children coming back from a walk told their parents, with gasps of wonder, that they had met a dwarf in a bowler hat and striped trousers, with a cane in one hand and a pair of tan gloves in the other.

After ardently kissing Nora good-bye (she was expecting visitors), the Potato Elf came out on the broad smooth street, flooded with sunlight, and instantly knew that the whole city had been created for him and only for him. A cheerful taxi driver turned down with a resounding blow the iron flag of his meter; the street started to flow past, and Fred kept slipping off the leathern seat, while chuckling and cooing under his breath.

He got out at the Hyde Park entrance, and without noticing the looks of curiosity, minced along, by the green folding chairs, by the pond, by the great rhododendron bushes, darkling under the shelter of elms and lindens, above a turf as bright and bland as billiard cloth. Riders sped past, lightly going up and down on their saddles, the yellow leather of their leggings creaking, the slender faces of their steeds springing up, their bits clinking; and expensive black motor cars, with a dazzling glitter of wheel spokes, progressed sedately over the ample lacework of violet shade.

The dwarf walked, inhaling the warm whiffs of benzine, the smell of foliage that seemed to rot with the over-abundance of green sap, and twirled his cane, and pursed his lips as if about to whistle, so great was the sense of liberation and lightness overwhelming him. His mistress had seen him off with such hurried tenderness, had laughed so nervously, that he realized how much she feared that her old father, who always came to lunch, would begin to suspect something if he found a strange gentleman in the house.

That day he was seen everywhere: in the park where a rosy nurse in a starched bonnet offered him for some reason a ride in the pram she was pushing; and in the halls of a great museum; and on the escalator that slowly crept out of rumbling depths where electric winds blew among brilliant posters; and in an elegant shop where only men's handkerchiefs were sold; and on the crest of a bus where he was hoisted by someone's kind hands.

And after a while he became tired—all that motion and glitter dazed him, the laughing eyes staring at him got on his nerves, and he felt he must ponder carefully the ample sensation of freedom, pride, and happiness which kept accompanying him.

When finally a hungry Fred entered the familiar restaurant where all kinds of performers gathered and where his presence could not surprise anyone, and when he looked around at those people, at the old dull clown who was already drunk, at the Frenchman, a former enemy, who now gave him a friendly nod, Mr. Dobson realized with perfect clarity that never again would he appear on the stage.

The place was darkish, with not enough lamps lit inside and not enough outside day filtering in. The dull clown resembling a ruined banker, and the acrobat who looked oddly uncouth in mufti, were playing a silent game of dominoes. The Spanish dancing girl, wearing a cartwheel hat that cast a blue shadow on her eyes, sat with crossed legs all alone at a corner table. There were half-a-dozen people whom Fred did not know; he examined their features which years of make-up had bleached; meanwhile the waiter brought a cushion to prop him up, changed the tablecloth, nimbly laid the cover.

All at once, in the dim depths of the restaurant, Fred distinguished the delicate profile of the conjuror, who was talking in undertone to an obese old man of an American type. Fred had not expected to run here into Shock—who never frequented taverns—and in point of fact had totally forgotten about his existence. He now felt so sorry for the poor magician that, at first, he decided to conceal everything; but then it occurred to him that Nora could not cheat anyway and would probably tell her husband that very evening ("I've fallen in love with Mr. Dobson. . . . I'm leaving you")—and that she should be spared a difficult, disagreeable confession, for was he not her knight, did he not feel proud of her love, should he not, therefore, be justified in causing her husband pain, no matter the pity?

The waiter brought him a piece of kidney pie and a bottle of ginger beer. He also switched on more light. Here and there, above the dusty plush, crystal flowers glowed forth, and the dwarf saw from afar a golden gleam bring out the conjuror's chestnut forelock and the light and shade shuttle over his tender transparent fingers. His interlocutor rose, clawing at the belt of his pants and obsequiously grinning, and Shock accompanied him to the cloakroom. The fat American donned a wide-brimmed hat, shook Shock's ethereal hand, and, still hitching up his pants, made for the exit. Momentarily one discerned a chink of lingering daylight, while the restaurant lamps glowed yellower. The door closed with a thud.

"Shock!" called the Potato Elf, wiggling his short feet under the table.

Shock came over. On his way, he pensively took a lighted cigar out of his breast pocket, inhaled, let out a puff of smoke, and put the cigar back. Nobody knew how he did it.

"Shock," said the dwarf, whose nose had reddened from the ginger beer, "I must speak to you. It is most important."

The conjuror sat down at Fred's table and leaned his elbow upon it.

"How's your head—doesn't hurt?" he inquired indifferently.

Fred wiped his lips with the napkin; he did not know how to start, still fearing to cause his friend too much anguish.

"By the way," said Shock, "tonight I appear together with you for the last time. That chap is taking me to America. Things look pretty good."

"I say, Shock—" and the dwarf, crumbling bread, groped for adequate words. "The fact is. . . . Be brave, Shock. I love your wife. This morning, after you left, she and I, we two, I mean, she—"

"Only I'm a bad sailor," mused the conjuror, "and it's a week to Boston. I once sailed to India. Afterwards I felt as a leg does when it goes to sleep."

Fred, flushing purple, rubbed the tablecloth with his tiny fist. The conjuror chuckled softly at his own thoughts, and then asked, "You were about to tell me something, my little friend?"

The dwarf looked into his ghostly eyes and shook his head in confusion.

"No, no, nothing. . . . One can't talk to you."

Shock's hand stretched out—no doubt he intended to snip out a coin from Fred's ear—but for the first time in years of masterly magic, the coin, not grasped by the palm muscles firmly enough, fell out the wrong way. He caught it up and rose.

"I'm not going to eat here," said he, examining curiously the crown of the dwarf's head. "I don't care for this place."

Sulky and silent, Fred was eating a baked apple.

The conjuror quietly left. The restaurant emptied. The languorous Spanish dancer in the large hat was led off by a shy, exquisitely dressed young man with blue eyes.

"Well, if he doesn't want to listen, that settles it," reflected the dwarf; he sighed with relief and decided that after all Nora would explain things better. Then he asked for notepaper and proceeded to write her a letter. It closed as follows:

Now you understand why I cannot continue to live as before. What feelings would you experience knowing that every evening the common herd rocks with laughter at the sight of your chosen one? I am breaking my contract, and tomorrow I shall be leaving. You will receive another letter from me as soon as I find a peaceful nook where after your divorce we shall be able to love one another, my Nora.

Thus ended the swift day given to a dwarf in mouse-colored spats.

VI

London was cautiously darkening. Street sounds blended in a soft hollow note, as if someone had stopped playing but still kept his foot on the piano pedal. The black leaves of the limes in the park were patterned against the transparent sky like aces of spades. At this or that turning, or between the funereal silhouettes of twin towers, a burning sunset was revealed like a vision.

It was Shock's custom to go home for dinner and change into professional tails so as to drive afterwards straight to the theater. That evening Nora awaited him most impatiently, quivering with evil glee. How glad she was to have now her own private secret! The image of the dwarf himself she dismissed. The dwarf was a nasty little worm.

She heard the lock of the entrance door emit its delicate click. As so often happens when one has betrayed a person, Shock's face struck her as new, as almost that of a stranger. He gave her a nod, and shamefully, sadly lowered his long-lashed eyes. He took his place opposite her at the table without a word. Nora considered his light gray suit that made him seem still more slender, still more elusive. Her eyes lit up with warm triumph; one corner of her mouth twitched malevolently.

"How's your dwarf?" she inquired, relishing the casualness of her question. "I thought you'd bring him along."

"Haven't seen him today," answered Shock, beginning to eat. All at once he thought better of it—took out a vial, uncorked it with a careful squeak, and tipped it over a glassful of wine.

Nora expected with irritation that the wine would turn a bright blue, or become as translucent as water, but the claret did not change its hue. Shock caught his wife's glance and smiled dimly.

"For the digestion—just drops," he murmered. A shadow rippled across his face.

"Lying as usual," said Nora. "You've got an excellent stomach."

The conjuror laughed softly. Then he cleared his throat in a businesslike way, and drained his glass in one gulp.

"Get on with your food," said Nora. "It will be cold."

With grim pleasure she thought, "Ah, if you only knew. You'll never find out. That's my power!"

The conjuror ate in silence. Suddenly he made a grimace, pushed his plate away, and started to speak. As usual, he kept looking not directly at her, but a little above her, and his voice was melodious and soft. He described his day, telling her he had visited the King at Windsor where he had been invited to amuse the little dukes who wore velvet jackets and lace collars. He related all this with light vivid touches, mimicking the people he had seen, twinkling, cocking his head slightly.

"I produced a whole flock of white doves from my gibus," said Shock.

"And the dwarf's little palms were clammy, and you're making it all up," reflected Nora in brackets.

"Those pigeons, you know, went flying around the Queen. She shoo-flied them but kept smiling out of politeness."

Shock got up, swayed, lightly leaned on the table edge with two fingers, and said, as if completing his story:

"I'm not feeling well, Nora. That was poison I drank. You shouldn't have been unfaithful to me."

His throat swelled convulsively, and, pressing a handkerchief to his lips, he left the dining room. Nora sprang up; the amber beads of her long necklace caught at the fruit knife upon her plate and brushed it off.

"It's all an act," she thought bitterly. "Wants to scare me, to torment me. No, my good man, it's no use. You shall see!"

How vexing that Shock had somehow discovered her secret! But at least she would now have the opportunity to reveal all her feelings to him, to shout that she hated him, that she despised him furiously, that he was not a person, but a phantom of rubber, that she could not bear to live with him any longer, that—

The conjuror sat on the bed, all huddled up and gritting his teeth in anguish, but he managed a faint smile when Nora stormed into the bedroom.

"So you thought I'd believe you," she said, gasping. "Oh no, that's the end! I, too, know how to cheat. You repel me, oh, you're a laughingstock with your unsuccessful tricks—"

Shock, still smiling helplessly, attempted to get off the bed. His foot scraped against the carpet. Nora paused in an effort to think what else she could yell in the way of insult.

"Don't," uttered Shock with difficulty. "If there was something that I . . . please, forgive. . . ."

The vein in his forehead was tensed. He hunched up still more, his throat rattled, the moist lock on his brow shook, and the handkerchief at his mouth got all soaked with bile and blood.

"Stop playing the fool!" cried Nora and stamped her foot.

He managed to straighten up. His face was wax pale. He threw the balled rag into a corner.

"Wait, Nora. . . . You don't understand. . . . This is my very last trick. . . . I won't do any other. . . ."

Again a spasm distorted his terrible, shiny face. He staggered, fell on the bed, threw back his head on the pillow.

She came near, she looked, knitting her brows. Shock lay with closed eyes and his clenched teeth creaked. When she bent over him, his eyelids quivered; he glanced at her vaguely, not recognizing his wife, but suddenly he did recognize her and his eyes flickered with a humid light of tenderness and pain.

At that instant Nora knew that she loved him more than anything in the world. Horror and pity overwhelmed her. She whirled about the room, poured out some water, left the glass on the washstand, dashed back to her husband, who had raised his head and was pressing the edge of the sheet to his lips, his whole body shuddering as he retched heavily, staring with unseeing eyes which Death had already veiled. Then Nora with a wild gesture dashed into the next room, where there was a telephone, and there, for a long time, she joggled the holder, repeated the wrong number, rang again, sobbing for breath and hammering the telephone table with her fist; and finally when the doctor's voice responded, Nora cried that her husband had poisoned himself, that he was dying; upon which she flooded the receiver with a storm of tears, and cradling it crookedly, ran back into the bedroom.

The conjuror, bright-faced and sleek, in white waistcoat and impeccably pressed black trousers, stood before the pier glass and, elbows parted, was meticulously working upon his tie. He saw Nora in the mirror, and without turning gave her an absentminded twinkle while whistling softly and continuing to knead with transparent fingertips the black ends of his silk bow.

VII

Drowse, a tiny town in the north of England, looked, indeed, so somnolent that one suspected it might have been somehow mislaid among those misty, gentle-sloped fields where it had fallen asleep forever. It had a post office, a bicycle shop, two or three tobacconists with red and blue signs, an ancient gray church surrounded by tombstones over which stretched sleepily the shade of an enormous chestnut tree. The main street was lined with hedges, small gardens, and brick cottages diagonally girt with ivy. One of these had been rented to a certain F. R. Dobson whom nobody knew except his housekeeper and the local doctor, and he was no gossiper. Mr. Dobson, apparently, never went out. The housekeeper, a large stern woman, who had formerly been employed in an insane asylum, would answer the casual questions of neighbors by explaining that Mr. Dobson was an aged paralytic, doomed to vegetate in curtained silence. No wonder the inhabitants forgot him the same year that he arrived in Drowse: he became an unnoticeable presence whom people took for granted as they did the unknown bishop whose stone effigy had been standing so long in its niche above the church portal. The mysterious old man was thought to have a grandchild—a quiet fair-haired little boy who sometimes, at dusk, used to come out of the Dobson cottage with small, timid steps. This happened, however, so seldom that nobody could say for sure that it was always the same child, and, of course, twilight at Drowse was particularly blurry and blue, softening every outline. Thus the uncurious and sluggish Drowsians missed the fact that the supposed grandson of the supposed paralytic did not grow as the years went by and that his flaxen hair was nothing but an admirably made wig; for the Potato Elf started to go bald at the very beginning of his new existence, and his head was soon so smooth and glossy that Ann, his housekeeper, thought at times what fun it would be to fit one's palm over that globe. Otherwise, he had not much changed: his tummy, perhaps, had grown plumper, and purple veins showed through on his dingier, fleshier nose which he powdered when dressed up as a little boy. Furthermore, Ann and his doctor knew that the heart attacks besetting the dwarf would come to no good.

He lived peacefully and inconspicuously in his three rooms, subscribed to a circulating library at the rate of three or four books (mostly novels) per week, acquired a black yellow-eyed cat because he mortally feared mice (which bumped about somewhere behind the wardrobe as if rolling minute balls of wood), ate a lot, especially sweetmeats (sometimes jumping up in the middle of the night and pattering along the chilly floor, eerily small and shivery in his long nightshirt, to get, like a little boy, at the chocolate-coated biscuits in the pantry), and recalled less and less frequently his love affair and the first dreadful days he had spent in Drowse.

Nevertheless, in his desk, among wispy, neatly folded playbills, he still preserved a sheet of peach-colored notepaper with a dragon-shaped watermark, scribbled over in an angular, barely legible hand. Here is what it said:

> Dear Mr. Dobson
>
> I received your first letter, as well as your second one, in which you ask me to come to D. All this, I am afraid, is an awful misunderstanding. Please try to forget and forgive me. Tomorrow my husband and I are leaving for the States and shall probably not be back for quite some time. I simply do not know what more I can write you, my poor Fred.

It was then that the first attack of angina pectoris occurred. A meek look of astonishment remained since then in his eyes. And during a number of days afterwards he would walk from room to room, swallowing his tears and gesturing in front of his face with one trembling tiny hand.

Presently, though, Fred began to forget. He grew fond of the coziness he had never known before—of the blue film of flame over the coals in the fireplace, of the dusty small vases on their own rounded small shelves, of the print between two casements: a St. Bernard dog, complete with barrelet, reviving a mountaineer on his bleak rock. Rarely did he recollect his past life. Only in dream did he sometimes see a starry sky come alive with the tremor of many trapezes while he was being clapped into a black trunk: through its walls he distinguished Shock's bland singsong voice but could not find the trap in the floor of the stage and suffocated in sticky darkness, while the conjuror's voice grew sadder and more remote and melted away, and Fred would wake up with a groan on his spacious bed, in his snug, dark room, with its faint fragrance of lavender, and would stare for a long time, gasping for breath and pressing his child's fist to his stumbling heart, at the pale blur of the window blind.

As the years passed, the yearning for a woman's love sighed in him fainter and fainter, as if Nora had drained him of all the ardor that had tormented him once. True, there were certain times, certain vague spring evenings, when the dwarf, having shyly put on short pants and the blond wig, left the house to plunge into crepuscular dimness, and there, stealing along some path in the fields, would suddenly stop as he looked with anguish at a dim pair of lovers locked in each other's arms near a hedge, under the protection of brambles in blossom. Presently that too passed, and he ceased seeing the world altogether. Only once in a while the doctor, a white-haired man with piercing black eyes, would come for a game of chess and, across the board, would consider with scientific delight those tiny soft hands, that little bulldoggish face, whose prominent brow would wrinkle as the dwarf pondered a move.

VIII

Eight years elapsed. It was Sunday morning. A jug of cocoa under a cozy in the guise of a parrot's head was awaiting Fred on the breakfast table. The sunny greenery of apple trees streamed through the window. Stout Ann was in the act of dusting the little pianola on which the dwarf occasionally played wobbly waltzes. Flies settled on the jar of orange marmalade and rubbed their front feet.

Fred came in, slightly sleep-rumpled, wearing carpet slippers and a little black dressing gown with yellow frogs. He sat down slitting his eyes and stroking his bald head. Ann left for church. Fred pulled open the illustrated section of a Sunday paper and, alternately drawing in and pouting his lips, examined at length prize pups, a Russian ballerina folding up in a swan's languishing agony, the top hat and mug of a financier who had bamboozled everyone. . . . Under the table the cat, curving her back, rubbed herself against his bare ankle. He finished his breakfast; rose, yawning: he had had a very bad night, never yet had his heart caused him such pain, and now he felt too lazy to dress, although his feet were freezing. He transferred himself to the window-nook armchair and curled up in it. He sat there without a thought in his head, and near him the black cat stretched, opening tiny pink jaws.

The doorbell tinkled.

"Doctor Knight," reflected Fred indifferently, and remembering that Ann was out, went to open the door himself.

Sunlight poured in. A tall lady all in black stood on the threshold. Fred recoiled, muttering and fumbling at his dressing gown. He dashed back into the inner rooms, losing one slipper on the way but ignoring it, his only concern being that whoever had come must not notice he was a dwarf. He stopped, panting, in the middle of the parlor. Oh, why hadn't he simply slammed shut the entrance door! And who on earth could be calling on him? A mistake, no doubt.

And then he heard distinctly the sound of approaching steps. He retreated to the bedroom; wanted to lock himself up, but there was no key. The second slipper remained on the rug in the parlor.

"This is dreadful," said Fred under his breath and listened.

The steps had entered the parlor. The dwarf emitted a little moan and made for the wardrobe, looking for a hiding place.

A voice that he certainly knew pronounced his name, and the door of the room opened:

"Fred, why are you afraid of me?"

The dwarf, bare-footed, black-robed, his pate beaded with sweat, stood by the wardrobe, still holding on to the ring of its lock. He recalled with the utmost clarity the orange-gold fish in their glass bowl.

She had aged unhealthily. There were olive-brown shadows under her eyes. The little dark hairs above her upper lip had become more distinct than before; and from her black hat, from the severe folds of her black dress, there wafted something dusty and woeful.

"I never expected—" Fred slowly began, looking up at her warily.

Nora took him by the shoulders, turned him to the light, and with eager, sad eyes examined his features. The embarrassed dwarf blinked, deploring his wiglessness and marveling at Nora's excitement. He had ceased thinking of her so long ago that now he felt nothing except sadness and surprise. Nora, still holding him, shut her eyes, and then, lightly pushing the dwarf away, turned toward the window.

Fred cleared his throat and said:

"I lost sight of you entirely. Tell me, how's Shock?"

"Still performing his tricks," replied Nora absently. "We returned to England only a short while ago."

Without removing her hat she sat down near the window and kept staring at him with odd intensity.

"It means that Shock—" hastily resumed the dwarf, feeling uneasy under her gaze.

"—Is the same as ever," said Nora, and, still not taking her glistening eyes from the dwarf, quickly peeled off and crumpled her glossy black gloves which were white inside.

"Can it be that she again—?" abruptly wondered the dwarf. There rushed through his mind the fish bowl, the smell of eau de cologne, the green pompoms on her slippers.

Nora got up. The black balls of her gloves rolled on the floor.

"It's not a big garden but it has apple trees," said Fred, and continued to wonder inwardly: had there really been a moment when I—? Her skin is quite sallow. She has a mustache. And why is she so silent?

"I seldom go out, though," said he, rocking slightly back and forth in his seat and massaging his knees.

"Fred, do you know why I'm here?" asked Nora.

She rose and came up to him quite close. Fred with an apologetic grin tried to escape by slipping off his chair.

It was then that she told him in a very soft voice:

"The fact is I had a son from you."

The dwarf froze, his gaze fixing a minuscule casement burning on the side of a dark blue cup. A timid smile of amazement flashed at the corners of his lips, then it spread, and lit up his cheeks with a purplish flush.

"My . . . son. . . ."

And all at once he understood everything, all the meaning of life, of his long anguish, of the little bright window upon the cup.

He slowly raised his eyes. Nora sat sideways on a chair and was shaking with violent sobs. The glass head of her hat-pin glittered like a teardrop. The cat, purring tenderly, rubbed itself against her legs.

He dashed up to her, he remembered a novel read a short while ago: "You have no cause," said Mr. Dobson, "no cause whatever for fearing that I may take him away from you. I am so happy!"

She glanced at him through a mist of tears. She was about to explain something, but gulped—saw the tender and joyful radiance with which the dwarf's countenance breathed—and explained nothing.

She hastened to pick up her crumpled gloves.

"Well, now you know. Nothing more is necessary. I must be going."

A sudden thought stabbed Fred. Acute shame joined the quivering joy. He inquired, fingering the tassel of his dressing gown.

"And . . . and what is he like? He is not—"

"Oh, on the contrary," replied Nora rapidly. "A big boy, like all boys." And again she burst into tears.

Fred lowered his eyes.

"I would like to see him."

Joyously he corrected himself:

"Oh, I understand! He must not know that I am like this. But perhaps you might arrange—"

"Yes, by all means," said Nora, hurriedly, and almost sharply, as she stepped through the hall. "Yes, we'll arrange something. I must be on my way. It's a twenty-minute walk to the railway station."

She turned her head in the doorway and for the last time, avidly and mournfully, she examined Fred's features. Sunlight trembled on his bald head, his ears were of a translucent pink. He understood nothing in his amazement and bliss. And after she had gone, Fred remained standing for a long time in the hallway, as if afraid to spill his full heart with an imprudent movement. He kept trying to imagine his son, and all he could do was to imagine his own self dressed as a schoolboy and wearing a little blond wig. And by the act of transferring his own aspect onto his boy, he ceased to feel that he was a dwarf.

He saw himself entering a house, a hotel, a restaurant, to meet his son. In fancy, he stroked the boy's fair hair with poignant parental pride. . . . And then, with his son and Nora (silly goose—to fear he would snatch him away!), he saw himself walking down a street, and there—

Fred clapped his thighs. He had forgotten to ask Nora where and how he could reach her!

Here commenced a crazy, absurd sort of phase. He rushed to his bedroom, began to dress in a wild hurry. He put on the best things he had, an expensive starched shirt, practically new, striped trousers, a jacket made by Resartre of Paris years ago—and as he dressed, he kept chuckling and breaking his fingernails in the chinks of tight commode drawers, and had to sit down once or twice to let his swelling and knocking heart rest; and again he went skipping about the room looking for the bowler he had not worn for years, and at last, on consulting a mirror in passing, he glimpsed the image of a stately elderly gentleman, in smart formal dress, and ran down the steps of the porch, dazzled by a new idea: to travel back with Nora—whom he would certainly manage to overtake—and to see his son that very evening!

A broad dusty road led straight to the station. It was more or less deserted on Sundays—but unexpectedly a boy with a cricket bat appeared at a corner. He was the first to notice the dwarf. In gleeful surprise he slapped himself on the top of his bright-colored cap as he watched Fred's receding back and the flicking of his mouse-gray spats.

And instantly, from God knows where, more boys appeared, and with gaping stealthiness started to follow the dwarf. He walked faster and faster, now and then looking at his watch, and chuckling excitedly. The sun made him feel a little queasy. Meanwhile, the number of boys increased, and chance passers-by stopped to look in wonder. Somewhere afar church chimes rang forth: the drowsy town was coming to life—and all of a sudden it burst into uncontrollable, long-restrained laughter.

The Potato Elf, unable to master his eagerness, switched to a jog. One of the lads darted in front of him to have a look at his face; another yelled something in a rude hoarse voice. Fred, grimacing because of the dust, ran on, and abruptly it seemed to him that all those boys crowding in his wake were his sons, merry, rosy, well-built sons—and he smiled a bewildered smile as he trotted along, puffing and trying to forget the heart breaking his chest with a burning ram.

A cyclist, riding beside the dwarf on glittering wheels, pressed his fist to his mouth like a megaphone and urged the sprinter along as they do at a race. Women came out on their porches and, shading their eyes and laughing loudly, pointed out the running dwarf to one another. All the dogs of the town woke up. The parishioners in the stuffy church could not help listening to the barking, to the inciting halloos. And the crowd that kept up with the dwarf continued to grow around him. People thought it was all a capital stunt, circus publicity, or the shooting of a picture.

Fred was beginning to stumble, there was a singing in his ears, the front stud of his collar dug into his throat, he could not breathe. Moans of mirth, shouts, the tramping of feet deafened him. Then through the fog of sweat he saw at last her black dress. She was slowly walking along a brick wall in a torrent of sun. She looked back, she stopped. The dwarf reached her and clutched at the folds of her skirt.

With a smile of happiness he glanced up at her, attempted to speak, but instead raised his eyebrows in surprise and collapsed in slow motion on the sidewalk. All around people noisily swarmed. Someone, realizing that this was no joke, bent over the dwarf, then whistled softly and bared his head. Nora looked listlessly at Fred's tiny body resembling a crumpled black glove. She was jostled. A hand grasped her elbow.

"Leave me alone," said Nora in a toneless voice. "I don't know anything. My son died a few days ago."

FRANZ KAFKA

The Metamorphosis

I

As Gregor Samsa awoke one morning from uneasy dreams he found himself transformed in his bed into a gigantic insect. He was lying on his hard, as it were armor-plated, back and when he lifted his head a little he could see his dome-like brown belly divided into stiff arched segments on top of which the bed quilt could hardly keep in position and was about to slide off completely. His numerous legs, which were pitifully thin compared to the rest of his bulk, waved helplessly before his eyes.

What has happened to me? he thought. It was no dream. His room, a regular human bedroom, only rather too small, lay quiet between the four familiar walls. Above the table on which a collection of cloth samples was unpacked and spread out—Samsa was a commercial traveler—hung the picture which he had recently cut out of an illustrated magazine and put into a pretty gilt frame. It showed a lady, with a fur cap on and a fur stole, sitting upright and holding out to the spectator a huge fur muff into which the whole of her forearm had vanished!

Gregor's eyes turned next to the window, and the overcast sky—one could hear rain drops beating on the window gutter—made him quite melancholy. What about sleeping a little longer and forgetting all this nonsense, he thought, but it could not be done, for he was accustomed to sleep on his right side and in his present condition he could not turn himself over. However violently he forced himself towards his right side he always rolled on to his back again. He tried it at least a hundred times, shutting his eyes to keep from seeing his struggling legs, and only desisted when he began to feel in his side a faint dull ache he had never experienced before.

Oh God, he thought, what an exhausting job I've picked on! Traveling about day in, day out. It's much more irritating work than doing the actual business in the office, and on top of that there's the trouble of constant traveling, of worrying about train connections, the bed and irregular meals, casual acquaintances that are always new and never become intimate friends. The devil take it all! He felt a slight itching up on his belly; slowly pushed himself on his back nearer to the top of the bed so that he could lift his head more easily; identified the itching place which was surrounded by many small white spots the nature of which he could not understand and made to touch it with a leg, but drew the leg back immediately, for the contact made a cold shiver run through him.

He slid down again into his former position. This getting up early, he thought, makes one quite stupid. A man needs his sleep. Other commercials live like harem women. For instance, when I come back to the hotel of a morning to write up the orders I've got, these others are only sitting down to breakfast. Let me just try that with my chief; I'd be sacked on the spot.

Anyhow, that might be quite a good thing for me, who can tell? If I didn't have to hold my hand because of my parents I'd have given notice long ago, I'd have gone to the chief and told him exactly what I think of him. That would knock him endways from his desk! It's a queer way of doing, too, this sitting on high at a desk and talking down to employees, especially when they have to come quite near because the chief is hard of hearing. Well, there's still hope; once I've saved enough money to pay back my parents' debts to him—that should take another five or six years—I'll do it without fail. I'll cut myself completely loose then. For the moment, though, I'd better get up, since my train goes at five.

He looked at the alarm clock ticking on the chest. Heavenly Father! he thought. It was half-past six o'clock and the hands were quietly moving on, it was even past the half-hour, it was getting on toward a quarter to seven. Had the alarm clock not gone off? From the bed one could see that it had been properly set for four o'clock; of course it must have gone off. Yes, but was it possible to sleep quietly through that ear-splitting noise? Well, he had not slept quietly, yet apparently all the more soundly for that. But what was he to do now? The next train went at seven o'clock; to catch that he would need to hurry like mad and his samples weren't even packed up, and he himself wasn't feeling particularly fresh and active. And even if he did catch the train he wouldn't avoid a row with the chief, since the firm's porter would have been waiting for the five o'clock train and would have long since reported his failure to turn up. The porter was a creature of the chief's, spineless and stupid. Well, supposing he were to say he was sick? But that would be most unpleasant and would look suspicious, since during his five years' employment he had not been ill once. The chief himself would be sure to come with the sick-insurance doctor, would reproach his parents with their son's laziness and would cut all excuses short by referring to the insurance doctor, who of course regarded all mankind as perfectly healthy malingerers. And would he be so far wrong on this occasion? Gregor really felt quite well, apart from a drowsiness that was utterly superfluous after such a long sleep, and he was even unusually hungry.

As all this was running through his mind at top speed without his being able to decide to leave his bed—the alarm clock had just struck a quarter to seven—there came a cautious tap at the door behind the head of his bed. "Gregor," said a voice—it was his mother's—"it's a quarter to seven. Hadn't you a train to catch?" That gentle voice! Gregor had a shock as he heard his own voice answering hers, unmistakably his own voice, it was true, but with a persistent horrible twittering squeak behind it like an undertone, that left the words in their clear shape only for the first moment and then rose up reverberating round them to destroy their sense, so that one could not be sure one had heard them rightly. Gregor wanted to answer at length and explain everything, but in the circumstances he confined himself to saying: "Yes, yes, thank you, Mother, I'm getting up now." The wooden door between them must have kept the change in his voice from being noticeable outside, for his mother contented herself with this statement and shuffled away. Yet this brief exchange of words had made the other members of the family aware that Gregor was still in the house, as they had not expected, and at one of the side doors his father was already knocking, gently, yet with his fist. "Gregor, Gregor," he called, "what's the matter with you?" And after a little while he called again in a deeper voice: "Gregor! Gregor!" At the other side door his sister was saying in a low, plaintive tone: "Gregor? Aren't you well? Are you needing anything?" He answered them both at once: "I'm just ready," and did his best to make his voice sound as normal as possible by enunciating the words very clearly and leaving long pauses between them. So his father went back to his breakfast, but his sister whispered: "Gregor, open the door, do." However, he was not thinking of opening the door, and felt thankful for the prudent habit he had acquired in traveling of locking all doors during the night, even at home.

His immediate intention was to get up quietly without being disturbed, to put on his clothes and above all eat his breakfast, and only then to consider what else was to be done, since in bed, he was well aware, his meditations would come to no sensible conclusion. He remembered that often enough in bed he had felt small aches and pains, probably caused by awkward postures, which had proved purely imaginary once he got up, and he looked forward eagerly to seeing this morning's delusions gradually fall away. That the change in his voice was nothing but the precursor of a severe chill, a standing ailment of commercial travelers, he had not the least possible doubt.

To get rid of the quilt was quite easy; he had only to inflate himself a little and it fell off by itself. But the next move was difficult, especially because he was so uncommonly broad. He would have needed arms and hands to hoist himself up; instead he had only the numerous little legs which never stopped waving in all directions and which he could not control in the least. When he tried to bend one of them it was the first to stretch itself straight; and did he succeed at last in making it do what he wanted, all the other legs meanwhile waved the more wildly in a high degree of unpleasant agitation. "But what's the use of lying idle in bed," said Gregor to himself.

He thought that he might get out of bed with the lower part of his body first, but this lower part, which he had not yet seen and of which he could form no clear conception, proved too difficult to move; it shifted so slowly; and when finally, almost wild with annoyance, he gathered his forces together and thrust out recklessly, he had miscalculated the direction and bumped heavily against the lower end of the bed, and the stinging pain he felt informed him that precisely this lower part of his body was at the moment probably the most sensitive.

So he tried to get the top part of himself out first, and cautiously moved his head towards the edge of the bed. That proved easy enough, and despite its breadth and mass bulk his body at last slowly followed the movement of his head. Still, when he finally got his head free over the edge of the bed he felt too scared to go on advancing, for after all if he let himself fall in this way it would take a miracle to keep his head from being injured. And at all costs he must not lose consciousness now, precisely now; he would rather stay in bed.

But when after a repetition of the same efforts he lay in his former position again, sighing, and watched his little legs struggling against each other more wildly than ever, if that were possible, and saw no way of bringing any order into this arbitrary confusion, he told himself again that it was impossible to stay in bed and that the most sensible course was to risk everything for the smallest hope of getting away from it. At the same time he did not forget meanwhile to remind himself that cool reflection, the coolest possible, was much better than desperate resolves. In such moments he focused his eyes as sharply as possible on the window, but, unfortunately, the prospect of the morning fog, which muffled even the other side of the narrow street, brought him little encouragement and comfort. "Seven o'clock already," he said to himself when the alarm clock chimed again, "seven o'clock already and still such a thick fog." And for a little while he lay quiet, breathing lightly, as if perhaps expecting such complete repose to restore all things to their real and normal condition.

But then he said to himself: "Before it strikes a quarter past seven I must be quite out of this bed, without fail. Anyhow, by that time someone will have come from the office to ask for me, since it opens before seven." And he set himself to rocking his whole body at once in a regular rhythm, with the idea of swinging it out of the bed. If he tipped himself out in that way he could keep his head from injury by lifting it at an acute angle when he fell. His back seemed to be hard and was not likely to suffer from a fall on the carpet. His biggest worry was the loud crash he would not be able to help making, which would probably cause anxiety, if not terror, behind all the doors. Still, he must take the risk.

When he was already half out of the bed—the new method was more a game than an effort, for he needed only to hitch himself across by rocking to and fro—it struck him how simple it would be if he could get help. Two strong people—he thought of his father and the servant girl—would be amply sufficient; they would only have to thrust their arms under his convex back, lever him out of bed, bend down with their burden and then be patient enough to let him turn himself right over on to the floor, where it was to be hoped his legs would then find their proper function. Well, ignoring the fact that the doors were all locked, ought he really to call for help? In spite of his misery he could not suppress a smile at the very idea of it.

He had got so far that he could barely keep his equilibrium when he rocked himself strongly, and he would have to nerve himself very soon for the final decision since in five minutes' time it would be a quarter past seven—when the front door bell rang. "That's someone from the office," he said to himself, and grew almost rigid, while his little legs only jigged about all the faster. For a moment everything stayed quiet. "They're not going to open the door," said Gregor to himself, catching at some kind of irrational hope. But then of course the servant girl went as usual to the door with her heavy tread and opened it. Gregor needed only to hear the first good morning of the visitor to know immediately who it was—the chief clerk himself. What a fate, to be condemned to work for a firm where the smallest omission at once gave rise to the gravest suspicion! Were all employees in a body nothing but scoundrels, was there not among them one single loyal devoted man who, had he wasted only an hour or so of the firm's time in a morning, was so tormented by conscience as to be driven out of his mind and actually incapable of leaving his bed? Wouldn't it really have been sufficient to send an apprentice to inquire—if any inquiry were necessary at all—did the chief clerk himself have to come and thus indicate to the entire family, an innocent family, that this suspicious circumstance could be investigated by no one less versed in affairs than himself? And more through the agitation caused by these reflections than through any act of will Gregor swung himself out of bed with all his strength. There was a loud thump, but it was not really a crash. His fall was broken to some extent by the carpet, his back, too, was less stiff than he thought, and so there was merely a dull thud, not so very startling. Only he had not lifted his head carefully enough and had hit it; he turned it and rubbed it on the carpet in pain and irritation.

"That was something falling down in there," said the chief clerk in the next room to the left. Gregor tried to suppose to himself that something like what had happened to him today might some day happen to the chief clerk; one really could not deny that it was possible. But as if in brusque reply to this supposition the chief clerk took a couple of firm steps in the next-door room and his patent leather boots creaked. From the right-hand room his sister was whispering to inform him of the situation: "Gregor, the chief clerk's here." "I know," muttered Gregor to himself; but he didn't dare to make his voice loud enough for his sister to hear it.

"Gregor," said his father now from the left-hand room, "the chief clerk has come and wants to know why you didn't catch the early train. We don't know what to say to him. Besides, he wants to talk to you in person. So open the door, please. He will be good enough to excuse the untidiness of your room." "Good morning, Mr. Samsa," the chief clerk was calling amiably meanwhile. "He's not well," said his mother to the visitor, while his father was still speaking through the door, "he's not well, sir, believe me. What else would make him miss a train! The boy thinks about nothing but his work. It makes me almost cross the way he never goes out in the evenings; he's been here the last eight days and has stayed at home every single evening. He just sits there quietly at the table reading a newspaper or looking through railway timetables. The only amusement he gets is doing fretwork. For instance, he spent two or three evenings cutting out a little picture frame; you would be surprised to see how pretty it is; it's hanging in his room; you'll see it in a minute when Gregor opens the door. I must say I'm glad you've come, sir; we should never have got him to unlock the door by ourselves; he's so obstinate; and I'm sure he's unwell, though he wouldn't have it to be so this morning." "I'm just coming," said Gregor slowly and carefully, not moving an inch for fear of losing one word of the conversation. "I can't think of any other explanation, madam," said the chief clerk, "I hope it's nothing serious. Although on the other hand I must say that we men of business—fortunately or unfortunately—very often simply have to ignore any slight indisposition, since business must be attended to." "Well, can the chief clerk come in now?" asked Gregor's father impatiently, again knocking on the door. "No," said Gregor. In the left-hand room a painful silence followed this refusal, in the right-hand room his sister began to sob.

Why didn't his sister join the others? She was probably newly out of bed and hadn't even begun to put on her clothes yet. Well, why was she crying? Because he wouldn't get up and let the chief clerk in, because he was in danger of losing his job, and because the chief would begin dunning his parents again for the old debts? Surely these were things one didn't need to worry about for the present. Gregor was still at home and not in the least thinking of deserting the family. At the moment, true, he was lying on the carpet and no one who knew the condition he was in could seriously expect him to admit the chief clerk. But for such a small discourtesy, which could plausibly be explained away somehow later on, Gregor could hardly be dismissed on the spot. And it seemed to Gregor that it would be much more sensible to leave him in peace for the present than to trouble him with tears and entreaties. Still, of course, their uncertainty bewildered them all and excused their behavior.

"Mr. Samsa," the chief clerk called now in a louder voice, "what's the matter with you? Here you are, barricading yourself in your room, giving only 'yes' and 'no' for answers, causing your parents a lot of unnecessary trouble and neglecting—I mention this only in passing—neglecting your business duties in an incredible fashion. I am speaking here in the name of your parents and of your chief, and I beg you quite seriously to give me an immediate and precise explanation. You amaze me, you amaze me. I thought you were a quiet, dependable person, and now all at once you seem bent on making a disgraceful exhibition of yourself. The chief did hint to me early this morning a possible explanation for your disappearance—with reference to the cash payments that were entrusted to you recently—but I almost pledged my solemn word of honor that this could not be so. But now that I see how incredibly obstinate you are, I no longer have the slightest desire to take your part at all. And your position in the firm is not so unassailable. I came with the intention of telling you all this in private, but since you are wasting my time so needlessly I don't see why your parents shouldn't hear it too. For some time past your work has been most unsatisfactory; this is not the season of the year for a business boom, of course, we admit that, but a season of the year for doing no business at all, that does not exist, Mr. Samsa, must not exist."

"But, sir," cried Gregor, beside himself and in his agitation forgetting everything else, "I'm just going to open the door this very minute. A slight illness, an attack of giddiness, has kept me from getting up. I'm still lying in bed. But I feel all right again. I'm getting out of bed now. Just give me a moment or two longer! I'm not quite so well as I thought. But I'm all right, really. How a thing like that can suddenly strike one down! Only last night I was quite well, my parents can tell you, or rather I did have a slight presentiment. I must have showed some sign of it. Why didn't I report it at the office! But one always thinks that an indisposition can be got over without staying in the house. Oh sir, do spare my parents! All that you're reproaching me with now has no foundation; no one has ever said a word to me about it. Perhaps you haven't looked at the last orders I sent in. Anyhow, I can still catch the eight o'clock train, I'm much the better for my few hours' rest. Don't let me detain you here, sir; I'll be attending to business very soon, and do be good enough to tell the chief so and to make my excuses to him!"

And while all this was tumbling out pell-mell and Gregor hardly knew what he was saying, he had reached the chest quite easily, perhaps because of the practice he had had in bed, and was now trying to lever himself upright by means of it. He meant actually to open the door, actually to show himself and speak to the chief clerk; he was eager to find out what the others, after all their insistence, would say at the sight of him. If they were horrified then the responsibility was no longer his and he could stay quiet. But if they took it calmly, then he had no reason either to be upset, and could really get to the station for the eight o'clock train if he hurried. At first he slipped down a few times from the polished surface of the chest, but at length with a last heave he stood upright; he paid no more attention to the pains in the lower part of his body, however they smarted. Then he let himself fall against the back of a near-by chair, and clung with his little legs to the edges of it. That brought him into control of himself again and he stopped speaking, for now he could listen to what the chief clerk was saying.

"Did you understand a word of it?" the chief clerk was asking; "surely he can't be trying to make fools of us?" "Oh dear," cried his mother, in tears, "perhaps he's terribly ill and we're tormenting him. Grete! Grete!" she called out then. "Yes Mother?" called his sister from the other side. They were calling to each other across Gregor's room. "You must go this minute for the doctor. Gregor is ill. Go for the doctor, quick. Did you hear how he was speaking?" "That was no human voice," said the chief clerk in a voice noticeably low beside the shrillness of the mother's. "Anna! Anna!" his father was calling through the hall to the kitchen, clapping his hands, "get a locksmith at once!" And the two girls were already running through the hall with a swish of skirts—how could his sister have got dressed so quickly?—and were tearing the front door open. There was no sound of its closing again; they had evidently left it open, as one does in houses where some great misfortune has happened.

But Gregor was now much calmer. The words he uttered were no longer understandable, apparently, although they seemed clear enough to him, even clearer than before, perhaps because his ear had grown accustomed to the sound of them. Yet at any rate people now believed that something was wrong with him, and were ready to help him. The positive certainty with which these first measures had been taken comforted him. He felt himself drawn once more into the human circle and hoped for great and remarkable results from both the doctor and the locksmith, without really distinguishing precisely between them. To make his voice as clear as possible for the decisive conversation that was now imminent he coughed a little, as quietly as he could, of course, since this noise too might not sound like a human cough for all he was able to judge. In the next room meanwhile there was complete silence. Perhaps his parents were sitting at the table with the chief clerk, whispering, perhaps they were all leaning against the door and listening.

Slowly Gregor pushed the chair towards the door, then let go of it, caught hold of the door for support—the soles at the end of his little legs were somewhat sticky—and rested against it for a moment after his efforts. Then he set himself to turning the key in the lock with his mouth. It seemed, unhappily, that he hadn't really any teeth—what could he grip the key with?—but on the other hand his jaws were certainly very strong; with their help he did manage to set the key in motion, heedless of the fact that he was undoubtedly damaging them somewhere, since a brown fluid issued from his mouth, flowed over the key and dripped on the floor. "Just listen to that," said the chief clerk next door; "he's turning the key." That was a great encouragement to Gregor; but they should all have shouted encouragement to him, his father and mother too: "Go on, Gregor," they should have called out, "keep going, hold on to that key!" And in the belief that they were all following his efforts intently, he clenched his jaws recklessly on the key with all the force at his command. As the turning of the key progressed he circled round the lock, holding on now only with his mouth, pushing on the key, as required, or pulling it down again with all the weight of his body. The louder click of the finally yielding lock literally quickened Gregor. With a deep breath of relief he said to himself: "So I didn't need the locksmith," and laid his head on the handle to open the door wide.

Since he had to pull the door towards him, he was still invisible when it was really wide open. He had to edge himself slowly round the near half of the double door, and to do it very carefully if he was not to fall plump upon his back just on the threshold. He was still carrying out this difficult manoeuvre, with no time to observe anything else, when he heard the chief clerk utter a loud "Oh!"—it sounded like a gust of wind—and now he could see the man, standing as he was nearest to the door, clapping one hand before his open mouth and slowly backing away as if driven by some invisible steady pressure. His mother—in spite of the chief clerk's being there her hair was still undone and sticking up in all directions—first clasped her hands and looked at his father, then took two steps towards Gregor and fell on the floor among her outspread skirts, her face quite hidden on her breast. His father knotted his fist with a fierce expression on his face as if he meant to knock Gregor back into his room, then looked uncertainly round the living room, covered his eyes with his hands and wept till his great chest heaved.

Gregor did not go now into the living room, but leaned against the inside ot the firmly shut wing of the door, so that only half his body was visible and his head above it bending sideways to look at the others. The light had meanwhile strengthened; on the other side of the street one could see clearly a section of the endlessly long, dark gray building opposite—it was a hospital—abruptly punctuated by its row of regular windows; the rain was still falling, but only in large singly discernible and literally singly splashing drops. The breakfast dishes were set out on the table lavishly, for breakfast was the most important meal of the day to Gregor's father, who lingered it out for hours over various newspapers. Right opposite Gregor on the wall hung a photograph of himself on military service, as a lieutenant, hand on sword, a carefree smile on his face, inviting one to respect his uniform and military bearing. The door leading to the hall was open, and one could see that the front door stood open too, showing the landing beyond and the beginning of the stairs going down.

"Well," said Gregor, knowing perfectly that he was the only one who had retained any composure, "I'll put my clothes on at once, pack up my samples and start off. Will you only let me go? You see, sir, I'm not obstinate, and I'm willing to work; traveling is a hard life, but I couldn't live without it. Where are you going, sir? To the office? Yes? Will you give a true account of all this? One can be temporarily incapacitated, but that's just the moment for remembering former services and bearing in mind that later on, when the incapacity has been got over, one will certainly work with all the more industry and concentration. I'm loyally bound to serve the chief, you know that very well. Besides, I have to provide for my parents and my sister. I'm in great difficulties, but I'll get out of them again. Don't make things any worse for me than they are. Stand up for me in the firm. Travelers are not popular there, I know. People think they earn sacks of money and just have a good time. A prejudice there's no particular reason for revising. But you, sir, have a more comprehensive view of affairs than the rest of the staff, yes, let me tell you in confidence, a more comprehensive view than the chief himself, who, being the owner, lets his judgment easily be swayed against one of his employees. And you know very well that the traveler, who is never seen in the office almost the whole year round, can so easily fall a victim to gossip and ill luck and unfounded complaints, which he mostly knows nothing about, except when he comes back exhausted from his rounds, and only then suffers in person from their evil consequences, which he can no longer trace back to the original causes. Sir, sir, don't go away without a word to me to show that you think me in the right at least to some extent!"

But at Gregor's very first words the chief clerk had already backed away and only stared at him with parted lips over one twitching shoulder. And while Gregor was speaking he did not stand still one moment but stole away towards the door, without taking his eyes off Gregor, yet only an inch at a time, as if obeying some secret injunction to leave the room. He was already at the hall, and the suddenness with which he took his last step out of the living room would have made one believe he had burned the sole of his foot. Once in the hall he stretched his right arm before him towards the staircase, as if some supernatural power were waiting there to deliver him.

Gregor perceived that the chief clerk must on no account be allowed to go away in this frame of mind if his position in the firm were not to be endanged to the utmost. His parents did not understand this so well; they had convinced themselves in the course of years that Gregor was settled for life in this firm, and besides they were so occupied with their immediate troubles that all foresight had forsaken them. Yet Gregor had this foresight. The chief clerk must be detained, soothed, persuaded and finally won over; the whole future of Gregor and his family depended on it! If only his sister had been there! She was intelligent; she had begun to cry while Gregor was still lying quietly on his back. And no doubt the chief clerk, so partial to ladies, would have been guided by her; she would have shut the door of the flat and in the hall talked him out of his horror. But she was not there, and Gregor would have to handle the situation himself. And without remembering that he was still unaware what powers of movement he possessed, without even remembering that his words in all possibility, indeed in all likelihood, would again be unintelligible, he let go the wing of the door, pushed himself through the opening, started to walk towards the chief clerk, who was already ridiculously clinging with both hands to the railing on the landing; but immediately, as he was feeling for a support, he fell down with a little cry upon all his numerous legs. Hardly was he down when he experienced for the first time this morning a sense of physical comfort; his legs had firm ground under them; they were completely obedient, as he noted with joy; they even strove to carry him forward in whatever direction he chose; and he was inclined to believe that a final relief from all his sufferings was at hand. But in the same moment as he found himself on the floor, rocking with suppressed eagerness to move, not far from his mother, indeed just in front of her, she, who had seemed so completely crushed, sprang all at once to her feet, her arms and fingers outspread, cried: "Help, for God's sake, help!" bent her head down as if to see Gregor better, yet on the contrary kept backing senselessly away; had quite forgotten that the laden table stood behind her; sat upon it hastily, as if in absence of mind, when she bumped into it; and seemed altogether unaware that the big coffee pot beside her was upset and pouring coffee in a flood over the carpet.

"Mother, Mother," said Gregor in a low voice, and looked up at her. The chief clerk, for the moment, had quite slipped from his mind; instead, he could not resist snapping his jaws together at the sight of the streaming coffee. That made his mother scream again, she fled from the table and fell into the arms of his father, who hastened to catch her. But Gregor had now no time to spare for his parents; the chief clerk was already on the stairs; with his chin on the banisters he was taking one last backward look. Gregor made a spring, to be as sure as possible of overtaking him; the chief clerk must have divined his intention, for he leaped down several steps and vanished; he was still yelling "Ugh!" and it echoed through the whole staircase.

Unfortunately, the flight of the chief clerk seemed completely to upset Gregor's father, who had remained relatively calm until now, for instead of running after the man himself, or at least not hindering Gregor in his pursuit, he seized in his right hand the walking stick which the chief clerk had left behind on a chair, together with a hat and greatcoat, snatched in his left hand a large newspaper from the table and began stamping his feet and flourishing the stick and the newspaper to drive Gregor back into his room. No entreaty of Gregor's availed, indeed no entreaty was even understood, however humbly he bent his head his father only stamped on the floor the more loudly. Behind his father his mother had torn open a window, despite the cold weather, and was leaning far out of it with her face in her hands. A strong draught set in from the street to the staircase, the window curtains blew in, the newspapers on the table fluttered, stray pages whisked over the floor. Pitilessly Gregor's father drove him back, hissing and crying "Shoo!" like a savage. But Gregor was quite unpracticed in walking backwards, it really was a slow business. If he only had a chance to turn round he could get back to his room at once, but he was afraid of exasperating his father by the slowness of such a rotation and at any moment the stick in his father's hand might hit him a fatal blow on the back or on the head. In the end, however, nothing else was left for him to do since to his horror he observed that in moving backwards he could not even control the direction he took; and so, keeping an anxious eye on his father all the time over his shoulder, he began to turn round as quickly as he could, which was in reality very slowly. Perhaps his father noted his good intentions, for he did not interfere except every now and then to help him in the manoeuvre from a distance with the point of the stick. If only he would have stopped making that unbearable hissing noise! It made Gregor quite lose his head. He had turned almost completely round when the hissing noise so distracted him that he even turned a little the wrong way again. But when at last his head was fortunately right in front of the doorway, it appeared that his body was too broad simply to get through the opening. His father, of course, in his present mood was far from thinking of such a thing as opening the other half of the door, to let Gregor have enough space. He had merely the fixed idea of driving Gregor back into his room as quickly as possible. He would never have suffered Gregor to make the circumstantial preparations for standing up on end and perhaps slipping his way through the door. Maybe he was now making more noise than ever to urge Gregor forward, as if no obstacle impeded him; to Gregor, anyhow, the noise in his rear sounded no longer like the voice of one single father; this was really no joke, and Gregor thrust himself—come what might—into the doorway. One side of his body rose up, he was tilted at an angle in the doorway, his flank was quite bruised, horrid blotches stained the white door, soon he was stuck fast and, left to himself, could not have moved at all, his legs on one side fluttered trembling in the air, those on the other were crushed painfully to the floor—when from behind his father gave him a strong push which was literally a deliverance and he flew far into the room, bleeding freely. The door was slammed behind him with the stick, and then at last there was silence.

II

Not until it was twilight did Gregor awake out of a deep sleep, more like a swoon than a sleep. He would certainly have waked up of his own accord not much later, for he felt himself sufficiently rested and well-slept, but it seemed to him as if a fleeting step and a cautious shutting of the door leading into the hall had aroused him. The electric lights in the street cast a pale sheen here and there on the ceiling and the upper surfaces of the furniture, but down below, where he lay, it was dark. Slowly, awkwardly trying out his feelers, which he now first learned to appreciate, he pushed his way to the door to see what had been happening there. His left side felt like one single long, unpleasantly tense scar, and he had actually to limp on his two rows of legs. One little leg, moreover, had been severely damaged in the course of that morning's events—it was almost a miracle that only one had been damaged—and trailed uselessly behind him.

He had reached the door before he discovered what had really drawn him to it: the smell of food. For there stood a basin filled with fresh milk in which floated little sops of white bread. He could almost have laughed with joy, since he was now still hungrier than in the morning, and he dipped his head almost over the eyes straight into the milk. But soon in disappointment he withdrew it again; not only did he find it difficult to feed because of his tender left side—and he could only feed with the palpitating collaboration of his whole body—he did not like the milk either, although milk had been his favorite drink and that was certainly why his sister had set it there for him, indeed it was almost with repulsion that he turned away from the basin and crawled back to the middle of the room.

He could see through the crack of the door that the gas was turned on in the living room, but while usually at this time his father made a habit of reading the afternoon newspaper in a loud voice to his mother and occasionally to his sister as well, not a sound was now to be heard. Well, perhaps his father had recently given up this habit of reading aloud, which his sister had mentioned so often in conversation and in her letters. But there was the same silence all around, although the flat was certainly not empty of occupants. "What a quiet life our family has been leading," said Gregor to himself, and as he sat there motionless staring into the darkness he felt great pride in the fact that he had been able to provide such a life for his parents and sister in such a fine flat. But what if all the quiet, the comfort, the contentment were now to end in horror? To keep himself from being lost in such thoughts Gregor took refuge in movement and crawled up and down the room.

Once during the long evening one of the side doors was opened a little and quickly shut again, later the other side door too; someone had apparently wanted to come in and then thought better of it. Gregor now stationed himself immediately before the living-room door, determined to persuade any hesitating visitor to come in or at least to discover who it might be; but the door was not opened again and he waited in vain. In the early morning, when the doors were locked, they had all wanted to come in, now that he had opened one door and the other had apparently been opened during the day, no one came in and even the keys were on the other side of the doors.

It was late at night before the gas went out in the living room, and Gregor could easily tell that his parents and his sister had all stayed awake until then, for he could clearly hear the three of them stealing away on tiptoe. No one was likely to visit him, not until the morning, that was certain; so he had plenty of time to meditate at his leisure on how he was to arrange his life afresh. But the lofty, empty room in which he had to lie flat on the floor filled him with an apprehension he could not account for, since it had been his very own room for the past five years—and with a half-unconscious action, not without a slight feeling of shame, he scuttled under the sofa, where he felt comfortable at once, although his back was a little cramped and he could not lift his head up, and his only regret was that his body was too broad to get the whole of it under the sofa.

He stayed there all night, spending the time partly in a light slumber, from which his hunger kept waking him up with a start, and partly in worrying and sketching vague hopes, which all led to the same conclusion, that he must lie low for the present and, by exercising patience and the utmost consideration, help the family to bear the inconvenience he was bound to cause them in his present condition.

Very early in the morning, it was still almost night, Gregor had the chance to test the strength of his new resolutions, for his sister, nearly fully dressed, opened the door from the hall and peered in. She did not see him at once, yet when she caught sight of him under the sofa—well, he had to be somewhere, he couldn't have flown away, could he?—she was so startled that without being able to help it she slammed the door shut again. But as if regretting her behavior she opened the door again immediately and came in on tiptoe, as if she were visiting an invalid or even a stranger. Gregor had pushed his head forward to the very edge of the sofa and watched her. Would she notice that he had left the milk standing, and not for lack of hunger, and would she bring in some other kind of food more to his taste? If she did not do it of her own accord, he would rather starve than draw her attention to the fact, although he felt a wild impulse to dart out from under the sofa, throw himself at her feet and beg her for something to eat. But his sister at once noticed, with surprise, that the basin was still full, except for a little milk that had been spilt all around it, she lifted it immediately, not with her bare hands, true, but with a cloth and carried it away. Gregor was wildly curious to know what she would bring instead, and made various speculations about it. Yet what she actually did next, in the goodness of her heart, he could never have guessed at. To find out what he liked she brought him a whole selection of food, all set out on an old newspaper. There were old, half-decayed vegetables, bones from last night's supper covered with a white sauce that had thickened; some raisins and almonds; a piece of cheese that Gregor would have called uneatable two days ago; a dry roll of bread, a buttered roll, and a roll both buttered and salted. Besides all that, she set down again the same basin, into which she had poured some water, and which was apparently to be reserved for his exclusive use. And with fine tact, knowing that Gregor would not eat in her presence, she withdrew quickly and even turned the key, to let him understand that he could take his ease as much as he liked. Gregor's legs all whizzed towards the food. His wounds must have healed completely, moreover, for he felt no disability, which amazed him and made him reflect how more than a month ago he had cut one finger a little with a knife and had still suffered pain from the wound only the day before yesterday. Am I less sensitive now? he thought, and sucked greedily at the cheese, which above all the other edibles attracted him at once and strongly. One after another and with tears of satisfaction in his eyes he quickly devoured the cheese, the vegetables and the sauce; the fresh food, on the other hand, had no charms for him, he could not even stand the smell of it and actually dragged away to some little distance the things he could eat. He had long finished his meal and was only lying lazily on the same spot when his sister turned the key slowly as a sign for him to retreat. That roused him at once, although he was nearly asleep, and he hurried under the sofa again. But it took considerable self-control for him to stay under the sofa, even for the short time his sister was in the room, since the large meal had swollen his body somewhat and he was so cramped he could hardly breathe. Slight attacks of breathlessness afflicted him and his eyes were starting a little out of his head as he watched his unsuspecting sister sweeping together with a broom not only the remains of what he had eaten but even the things he had not touched, as if these were now of no use to anyone, and hastily shoveling it all into a bucket, which she covered with a wooden lid and carried away. Hardly had she turned her back when Gregor came from under the sofa and stretched and puffed himself out.

In this manner Gregor was fed, once in the early morning while his parents and the servant girl were still asleep, and a second time after they had all had their midday dinner, for then his parents took a short nap and the servant girl could be sent out on some errand or other by his sister. Not that they would have wanted him to starve, of course, but perhaps they could not have borne to know more about his feeding than from hearsay, perhaps too his sister wanted to spare them such little anxieties wherever possible, since they had quite enough to bear as it was.

Under what pretext the doctor and the locksmith had been got rid of on that first morning Gregor could not discover, for since what he said was not understood by the others it never struck any of them, not even his sister, that he could understand what they said, and so whenever his sister came into his room he had to content himself with hearing her utter only a sigh now and then and an occasional appeal to the saints. Later on, when she had got a little used to the situation—of course she could never get completely used to it—she sometimes threw out a remark which was kindly meant or could be so interpreted. "Well, he liked his dinner today," she would say when Gregor had made a good clearance of his food; and when he had not eaten, which gradually happened more and more often, she would say almost sadly: "Everything's been left standing again."

But although Gregor could get no news directly, he overheard a lot from the neighboring rooms, and as soon as voices were audible, he would run to the door of the room concerned and press his whole body against it. In the first few days especially there was no conversation that did not refer to him somehow, even if only indirectly. For two whole days there were family consultations at every mealtime about what should be done; but also between meals the same subject was discussed, for there were always at least two members of the family at home, since no one wanted to be alone in the flat and to leave it quite empty was unthinkable. And on the very first of these days the household cook—it was not quite clear what and how much she knew of the situation—went down on her knees to his mother and begged leave to go, and when she departed, a quarter of an hour later, gave thanks for her dismissal with tears in her eyes as if for the greatest benefit that could have been conferred on her, and without any prompting swore a solemn oath that she would never say a single word to anyone about what had happened.

Now Gregor's sister had to cook too, helping her mother; true, the cooking did not amount to much, for they ate scarcely anything. Gregor was always hearing one of the family vainly urging another to eat and getting no answer but: "Thanks, I've had all I want," or something similar. Perhaps they drank nothing either. Time and again his sister kept asking his father if he wouldn't like some beer and offered kindly to go and fetch it herself, and when he made no answer suggested that she could ask the concierge to fetch it, so that he need feel no sense of obligation, but then a round "No" came from his father and no more was said about it.

In the course of that very first day Gregor's father explained the family's financial position and prospects to both his mother and his sister. Now and then he rose from the table to get some voucher or memorandum out of the small safe he had rescued from the collapse of his business five years earlier. One could hear him opening the complicated lock and rustling papers out and shutting it again. This statement made by his father was the first cheerful information Gregor had heard since his imprisonment. He had been of the opinion that nothing at all was left over from his father's business, at least his father had never said anything to the contrary, and of course he had not asked him directly. At that time Gregor's sole desire was to do his utmost to help the family to forget as soon as possible the catastrophe which had overwhelmed the business and thrown them all into a state of complete despair. And so he had set to work with unusual ardor and almost overnight had become a commercial traveler instead of a little clerk, with of course much greater chances of earning money, and his success was immediately translated into good round coin which he could lay on the table for his amazed and happy family. These had been fine times, and they had never recurred, at least not with the same sense of glory, although later on Gregor had earned so much money that he was able to meet the expenses of the whole household and did so. They had simply got used to it, both the family and Gregor; the money was gratefully accepted and gladly given, but there was no special uprush of warm feeling. With his sister alone had he remained intimate, and it was a secret plan of his that she, who loved music, unlike himself, and could play movingly on the violin, should be sent next year to study at the Conservatorium, despite the great expense that would entail, which must be made up in some other way. During his brief visits home the Conservatorium was often mentioned in the talks he had with his sister, but always merely as a beautiful dream which could never come true, and his parents discouraged even these innocent references to it; yet Gregor had made up his mind firmly about it and meant to announce the fact with due solemnity on Christmas Day.

Such were the thoughts, completely futile in his present condition, that went through his head as he stood clinging upright to the door and listening. Sometimes out of sheer weariness he had to give up listening and let his head fall negligently against the door, but he always had to pull himself together again at once, for even the slight sound his head made was audible next door and brought all conversation to a stop. "What can he be doing now?" his father would say after a while, obviously turning towards the door, and only then would the interrupted conversation gradually be set going again.

Gregor was now informed as amply as he could wish—for his father tended to repeat himself in his explanations, partly because it was a long time since he had handled such matters and partly because his mother could not always grasp things at once—that a certain amount of investments, a very small amount it was true, had survived the wreck of their fortunes and had even increased a little because the dividends had not been touched meanwhile. And besides that, the money Gregor brought home every month—he had kept only a few dollars for himself—had never been quite used up and now amounted to a small capital sum. Behind the door Gregor nodded his head eagerly, rejoiced at this evidence of unexpected thrift and foresight. True, he could really have paid off some more of his father's debts to the chief with his extra money, and so brought much nearer the day on which he could quit his job, but doubtless it was better the way his father had arranged it.

Yet this capital was by no means sufficient to let the family live on the interest of it; for one year, perhaps, or at the most two, they could live on the principal, that was all. It was simply a sum that ought not to be touched and should be kept for a rainy day; money for living expenses would have to be earned. Now his father was still hale enough but an old man, and he had done no work for the past five years and could not be expected to do much; during these five years, the first years of leisure in his laborious though unsuccessful life, he had grown rather fat and become sluggish. And Gregor's old mother, how was she to earn a living with her asthma, which troubled her even when she walked through the flat and kept her lying on a sofa every other day panting for breath beside an open window? And was his sister to earn her bread, she who was still a child of seventeen and whose life hitherto had been so pleasant, consisting as it did in dressing herself nicely, sleeping long, helping in the housekeeping, going out to a few modest entertainments and above all playing the violin? At first whenever the need for earning money was mentioned Gregor let go his hold on the door and threw himself down on the cool leather sofa beside it, he felt so hot with shame and grief.

Often he just lay there the long nights through without sleeping at all, scrabbling for hours on the leather. Or he nerved himself to the great effort of pushing an armchair to the window, then crawled up over the window sill and, braced against the chair, leaned against the window panes, obviously in some recollection of the sense of freedom that looking out of a window always used to give him. For in reality day by day things that were even a little way off were growing dimmer to his sight; the hospital across the street, which he used to execrate for being all too often before his eyes, was now quite beyond his range of vision, and if he had not known that he lived in Charlotte Street, a quiet street but still a city street, he might have believed that his window gave on a desert waste where gray sky and gray land blended indistinguishably into each other. His quick-witted sister only needed to observe twice that the armchair stood by the window; after that whenever she had tidied the room she always pushed the chair back to the same place at the window and even left the inner casements open.

If he could have spoken to her and thanked her for all she had to do for him, he could have borne her ministrations better; as it was, they oppressed him. She certainly tried to make as light as possible of whatever was disagreeable in her task, and as time went on she succeeded, of course, more and more, but time brought more enlightenment to Gregor too. The very way she came in distressed him. Hardly was she in the room when she rushed to the window, without even taking time to shut the door, careful as she was usually to shield the sight of Gregor's room from the others, and as if she were almost suffocating tore the casements open with hasty fingers, standing then in the open draught for a while even in the bitterest cold and drawing deep breaths. This noisy scurry of hers upset Gregor twice a day; he would crouch trembling under the sofa all the time, knowing quite well that she would certainly have spared him such a disturbance had she found it at all possible to stay in his presence without opening the window.

On one occasion, about a month after Gregor's metamorphosis, when there was surely no reason for her to be still startled at his appearance, she came a little earlier than usual and found him gazing out of the window, quite motionless, and thus well placed to look like a bogey. Gregor would not have been surprised had she not come in at all, for she could not immediately open the window while he was there, but not only did she retreat, she jumped back as if in alarm and banged the door shut; a stranger might well have thought that he had been lying in wait for her there meaning to bite her. Of course he hid himself under the sofa at once, but he had to wait until midday before she came again, and she seemed more ill at ease than usual. This made him realize how repulsive the sight of him still was to her, and that it was bound to go on being repulsive, and what an effort it must cost her not to run away even from the sight of the small portion of his body that stuck out from under the sofa. In order to spare her that, therefore, one day he carried a sheet on his back to the sofa—it cost him four hours' labor—and arranged it there in such a way as to hide him completely, so that even if she were to bend down she could not see him. Had she considered the sheet unnecessary, she would certainly have stripped it off the sofa again, for it was clear enough that this curtaining and confining of himself was not likely to conduce Gregor's comfort, but she left it where it was, and Gregor even fancied that he caught a thankful glance from her eye when he lifted the sheet carefully a very little with his head to see how she was taking the new arrangement.

For the first fortnight his parents could not bring themselves to the point of entering his room, and he often heard them expressing their appreciation of his sister's activities, whereas formerly they had frequently scolded her for being as they thought a somewhat useless daughter. But now, both of them often waited outside the door, his father and his mother, while his sister tidied his room, and as soon as she came out she had to tell them exactly how things were in the room, what Gregor had eaten, how he had conducted himself this time and whether there was not perhaps some slight improvement in his condition. His mother, moreover, began relatively soon to want to visit him, but his father and sister dissuaded her at first with arguments which Gregor listened to very attentively and altogether approved. Later, however, she had to be held back by main force, and when she cried out: "Do let me in to Gregor, he is my unfortunate son! Can't you understand that I must go to him?" Gregor thought that it might be well to have her come in, not every day, of course, but perhaps once a week; she understood things, after all, much better than his sister, who was only a child despite the efforts she was making and had perhaps taken on so difficult a task merely out of childish thoughtlessness.

Gregor's desire to see his mother was soon fulfilled. During the daytime he did not want to show himself at the window, out of consideration for his parents, but he could not crawl very far around the few square yards of floor space he had, nor could he bear lying quietly at rest all during the night, while he was fast losing any interest he had ever taken in food, so that for mere recreation he had formed the habit of crawling crisscross over the walls and ceiling. He especially enjoyed hanging suspended from the ceiling; it was much better than lying on the floor; one could breathe more freely; one's body swung and rocked lightly; and in the almost blissful absorption induced by this suspension it could happen to his own surprise that he let go and fell plump on the floor. Yet he now had his body much better under control than formerly, and even such a big fall did him no harm. His sister at once remarked the new distraction Gregor had found for himself—he left traces behind him of the sticky stuff on his soles wherever he crawled—and she got the idea in her head of giving him as wide a field as possible to crawl in and of removing the pieces of furniture that hindered him, above all the chest of drawers and the writing desk. But that was more than she could manage all by herself; she did not dare ask her father to help her; and as for the servant girl, a young creature of sixteen who had had the courage to stay on after the cook's departure, she could not be asked to help, for she had begged as an especial favor that she might keep the kitchen door locked and open it only on a definite summons; so there was nothing left but to apply to her mother at an hour when her father was out. And the old lady did come, with exclamations of joyful eagerness, which, however, died away at the door of Gregor's room. Gregor's sister, of course, went in first, to see that everything was in order before letting his mother enter. In great haste Gregor pulled the sheet lower and tucked it more in folds so that it really looked as if it had been thrown accidentally over the sofa. And this time he did not peer out from under it; he renounced the pleasure of seeing his mother on this occasion and was only glad that she had come at all. "Come in, he's out of sight," said his sister, obviously leading her mother in by the hand. Gregor could now hear the two women struggling to shift the heavy old chest from its place, and his sister claiming the greater part of the labor for herself, without listening to the admonitions of her mother who feared she might overstrain herself. It took a long time. After at least a quarter of an hour's tugging his mother objected that the chest had better be left where it was, for in the first place it was too heavy and could never be got out before his father came home, and standing in the middle of the room like that it would only hamper Gregor's movements, while in the second place it was not at all certain that removing the furniture would be doing a service to Gregor. She was inclined to think to the contrary; the sight of the naked walls made her own heart heavy, and why shouldn't Gregor have the same feeling, considering that he had been used to his furniture for so long and might feel forlorn without it. "And doesn't it look," she concluded in low voice—in fact she had been almost whispering all the time as if to avoid letting Gregor, whose exact whereabouts she did not know, hear even the tones of her voice, for she was convinced that he could not understand her words—"doesn't it look as if we were showing him, by taking away his furniture, that we have given up hope of his ever getting better and are just leaving him coldly to himself? I think it would be best to keep his room exactly as it has always been, so that when he comes back to us he will find everything unchanged and be able all the more easily to forget what has happened in between."

On hearing these words from his mother Gregor realized that the lack of all direct human speech for the past two months together with the monotony of family life must have confused his mind, otherwise he could not account for the fact that he had quite earnestly looked forward to having his room emptied of furnishing. Did he really want his warm room, so comfortably fitted with old family furniture, to be turned into a naked den in which he would certainly be able to crawl unhampered in all directions but at the price of shedding simultaneously all recollection of his human background? He had indeed been so near the brink of forgetfulness that only the voice of his mother, which he had not heard for so long, had drawn him back from it. Nothing should be taken out of his room; everything must stay as it was; he could not dispense with the good influence of the furniture on his state of mind; and even if the furniture did hamper him in his senseless crawling round and round, that was no drawback but a great advantage.

Unfortunately his sister was of the contrary opinion; she had grown accustomed, and not without reason, to consider herself an expert in Gregor's affairs as against her parents, and so her mother's advice was now enough to make her determined on the removal not only of the chest and the writing desk, which had been her first intention, but of all the furniture except the indispensable sofa. This determination was not, of course, merely the outcome of childish recalcitrance and of the self-confidence she had recently developed so unexpectedly and at such cost; she had in fact perceived that Gregor needed a lot of space to crawl about in, while on the other hand he never used the furniture at all, so far as could be seen. Another factor might have been also the enthusiastic temperament of an adolescent girl, which seeks to indulge itself on every opportunity and which now tempted Grete to exaggerate the horror of her brother's circumstances in order that she might do all the more for him. In a room where Gregor lorded it all alone over empty walls no one save herself was likely ever to set foot.

And so she was not to be moved from her resolve by her mother who seemed moreover to be ill at ease in Gregor's room and therefore unsure of herself, was soon reduced to silence and helped her daughter as best she could to push the chest outside. Now, Gregor could do without the chest, if need be, but the writing desk he must retain. As soon as the two women had got the chest out of his room, groaning as they pushed it, Gregor stuck his head out from under the sofa to see how he might intervene as kindly and cautiously as possible. But as bad luck would have it, his mother was the first to return, leaving Grete clasping the chest in the room next door where she was trying to shift it all by herself, without of course moving it from the spot. His mother however was not accustomed to the sight of him, it might sicken her and so in alarm Gregor backed quickly to the other end of the sofa, yet could not prevent the sheet from swaying a little in front. That was enough to put her on the alert. She paused, stood still for a moment and then went back to Grete.

Although Gregor kept reassuring himself that nothing out of the way was happening, but only a few bits of furniture were being changed round, he soon had to admit that all this trotting to and fro of the two women, their little ejaculations and the scraping of furniture along the floor affected him like a vast disturbance coming from all sides at once, and however much he tucked in his head and legs and cowered to the very floor he was bound to confess that he would not be able to stand it for long. They were clearing his room out; taking away everything he loved; the chest in which he kept his fret saw and other tools was already dragged off; they were now loosening the writing desk which had almost sunk into the floor, the desk at which he had done all his homework when he was at the commercial academy, at the grammar school before that, and, yes, even at the primary school—he had no more time to waste in weighing the good intentions of the two women, whose existence he had by now almost forgotten, for they were so exhausted that they were laboring in silence and nothing could be heard but the heavy scuffling of their feet.

And so he rushed out—the women were just leaning against the writing desk in the next room to give themselves a breather—and four times changed his direction, since he really did not know what to rescue first, then on the wall opposite, which was already otherwise cleared, he was struck by the picture of the lady muffled in so much fur and quickly crawled up to it and pressed himself to the glass, which was a good surface to hold on to and comforted his hot belly. This picture at least, which was entirely hidden beneath him, was going to be removed by nobody. He turned his head towards the door of the living room so as to observe the women when they came back.

They had not allowed themselves much of a rest and were already coming; Grete had twined her arm round her mother and was almost supporting her. "Well, what shall we take now?" said Grete, looking round. Her eyes met Gregor's from the wall. She kept her composure, presumably because of her mother, bent her head down to her mother, to keep her from looking up, and said, although in a fluttering, unpremeditated voice: "Come, hadn't we better go back to the living room for a moment?" Her intentions were clear enough to Gregor, she wanted to bestow her mother in safety and then chase him down from the wall. Well, just let her try it! He clung to his picture and would not give it up. He would rather fly in Grete's face.

But Grete's words had succeeded in disquieting her mother, who took a step to one side, caught sight of the huge brown mass on the flowered wall-paper, and before she was really conscious that what she saw was Gregor screamed in a loud, hoarse voice: "Oh God, oh God!" fell with outspread arms over the sofa as if giving up and did not move. "Gregor!" cried his sister, shaking her fist and glaring at him. This was the first time she had directly addressed him since his metamorphosis. She ran into the next room for some aromatic essence with which to rouse her mother from her fainting fit. Gregor wanted to help too—there was still time to rescue the picture—but he was stuck fast to the glass and had to tear himself loose; he then ran after his sister into the next room as if he could advise her, as he used to do; but then had to stand helplessly behind her; she meanwhile searched among various small bottles and when she turned round started in alarm at the sight of him; one bottle fell on the floor and broke; a splinter of glass cut Gregor's face and some kind of corrosive medicine splashed him; without pausing a moment longer Grete gathered up all the bottles she could carry and ran to her mother with them; she banged the door shut with her foot. Gregor was now cut off from his mother, who was perhaps nearly dying because of him; he dared not open the door for fear of frightening away his sister, who had to stay with her mother; there was nothing he could do but wait; and harassed by self-reproach and worry he began now to crawl to and fro, over everything, walls, furniture and ceiling, and finally in his despair, when the whole room seemed to be reeling round him, fell down on to the middle of the big table.

A little while elapsed, Gregor was still lying there feebly and all around was quiet, perhaps that was a good omen. Then the doorbell rang. The servant girl was of course locked in her kitchen, and Grete would have to open the door. It was her father. "What's been happening?" were his first words; Grete's face must have told him everything. Grete answered in a muffled voice, apparently hiding her head on his breast: "Mother has been fainting, but she's better now. Gregor's broken loose." "Just what I expected," said her father, "just what I've been telling you, but you women would never listen." It was clear to Gregor that his father had taken the worst interpretation of Grete's all too brief statement and was assuming that Gregor had been guilty of some violent act. Therefore Gregor must now try to propitiate his father, since he had neither time nor means for an explanation. And so he fled to the door of his own room and crouched against it, to let his father see as soon as he came in from the hall that his son had the good intention of getting back into his room immediately and that it was not necessary to drive him there, but that if only the door were opened he would disappear at once.

Yet his father was not in the mood to perceive such fine distinctions. "Ah!" he cried as soon as he appeared, in a tone which sounded at once angry and exultant. Gregor drew his head back from the door and lifted it to look at his father. Truly, this was not the father he had imagined to himself; admittedly he had been too absorbed of late in his new recreation of crawling over the ceiling to take the same interest as before in what was happening elsewhere in the flat, and he ought really to be prepared for some changes. And yet, and yet, could that be his father? The man who used to lie wearily sunk in bed whenever Gregor set out on a business journey; who welcomed him back of an evening lying in a long chair in a dressing gown; who could not really rise to his feet but only lifted his arms in greeting, and on the rare occasions when he did go out with his family, on one or two Sundays a year and on high holidays, walked between Gregor and his mother, who were slow walkers anyhow, even more slowly than they did, muffled in his old greatcoat, shuffling laboriously forward with the help of his crook-handled stick which he set down most cautiously at every step and, whenever he wanted to say anything, nearly always came to a full stop and gathered his escort around him? Now he was standing there in fine shape; dressed in a smart blue uniform with gold buttons, such as bank messengers wear; his strong double chin bulged over the stiff high collar of his jacket; from under his bushy eyebrows his black eyes darted fresh and penetrating glances; his onetime tangled white hair had been combed flat on either side of a shining and carefully exact parting. He pitched his cap, which bore a gold monogram, probably the badge of some bank, in a wide sweep across the whole room on to a sofa and with the tail-ends of his jacket thrown back, his hands in his trouser pockets, advanced with a grim visage towards Gregor. Likely enough he did not himself know what he meant to do; at any rate he lifted his feet uncommonly high, and Gregor was dumbfounded at the enormous size of his shoe soles. But Gregor could not risk standing up to him, aware as he had been from the very first day of his new life that his father believed only the severest measures suitable for dealing with him. And so he ran before his father, stopping when he stopped and scuttling forward again when his father made any kind of move. In this way they circled the room several times without anything decisive happening, indeed the whole operation did not even look like a pursuit because it was carried out so slowly. And so Gregor did not leave the floor, for he feared that his father might take as a piece of peculiar wickedness any excursion of his over the walls or the ceiling. All the same, he could not stay this course much longer, for while his father took one step he had to carry out a whole series of movements. He was already beginning to feel breathless, just as in his former life his lungs had not been very dependable. As he was staggering along, trying to concentrate his energy on running, hardly keeping his eyes open; in his dazed state never even thinking of any other escape than simply going forward; and having almost forgotten that the walls were free to him, which in this room were well provided with finely carved pieces of furniture full of knobs and crevices—suddenly something lightly flung landed close behind him and rolled before him. It was an apple; a second apple followed immediately; Gregor came to a stop in alarm; there was no point in running on, for his father was determined to bombard him. He had filled his pockets with fruit from the dish on the sideboard and was now shying apple after apple, without taking particularly good aim for the moment. The small red apples rolled about the floor as if magnetized and cannoned into each other. An apple thrown without much force grazed Gregor's back and glanced off harmlessly. But another following immediately landed right on his back and sank in; Gregor wanted to drag himself forward, as if this startling, incredible pain could be left behind him; but he felt as if nailed to the spot and flattened himself out in a complete derangement of all his senses. With his last conscious look he saw the door of his room being torn open and his mother rushing out ahead of his screaming sister, in her underbodice, for her daughter had loosened her clothing to let her breathe more freely and recover from her swoon, he saw his mother rushing towards his father, leaving one after another behind her on the floor her loosened petticoats, stumbling over her petticoats straight to his father and embracing him, in complete union with him—but here Gregor's sight began to fail—with her hands clasped round his father's neck as she begged for her son's life.

III

The serious injury done to Gregor, which disabled him for more than a month—the apple went on sticking in his body as a visible reminder, since no one ventured to remove it—seemed to have made even his father recollect that Gregor was a member of the family, despite his present unfortunate and repulsive shape, and ought not to be treated as an enemy, that, on the contrary, family duty required the suppression of disgust and the exercise of patience, nothing but patience.

And although his injury had impaired, probably for ever, his power of movement, and for the time being it took him long, long minutes to creep across his room like an old invalid—there was no question now of crawling up the wall—yet in his own opinion he was sufficiently compensated for this worsening of his condition by the fact that towards evening the living-room door, which he used to watch intently for an hour or two beforehand, was always thrown open, so that lying in the darkness of his room, invisible to the family, he could see them all at the lamp-lit table and listen to their talk, by general consent as it were, very different from his earlier eavesdropping.

True, their intercourse lacked the lively character of former times, which he had always called to mind with a certain wistfulness in the small hotel bedrooms where he had been wont to throw himself down, tired out, on damp bedding. They were now mostly very silent. Soon after supper his father would fall asleep in his armchair; his mother and sister would admonish each other to be silent; his mother, bending low over the lamp, stitched at fine sewing for an underwear firm; his sister, who had taken a job as a salesgirl, was learning shorthand and French in the evenings on the chance of bettering herself. Sometimes his father woke up, and as if quite unaware that he had been sleeping said to his mother: "What a lot of sewing you're doing today!" and at once fell asleep again, while the two women exchanged a tired smile.

With a kind of mulishness his father persisted in keeping his uniform on even in the house; his dressing gown hung uselessly on its peg and he slept fully dressed where he sat, as if he were ready for service at any moment and even here only at the beck and call of his superior. As a result, his uniform, which was not brand-new to start with, began to look dirty, despite all the loving care of the mother and sister to keep it clean, and Gregor often spent whole evenings gazing at the many greasy spots on the garment, gleaming with gold buttons always in a high state of polish, in which the old man sat sleeping in extreme discomfort and yet quite peacefully.

As soon as the clock struck ten his mother tried to rouse his father with gentle words and to persuade him after that to get into bed, for sitting there he could not have a proper sleep and that was what he needed most, since he had to go to duty at six. But with the mulishness that had obsessed him since he became a bank messenger he always insisted on staying longer at the table, although he regularly fell asleep again and in the end only with the greatest trouble could be got out of his armchair and into his bed. However insistently Gregor's mother and sister kept urging him with gentle reminders, he would go on slowly shaking his head for a quarter of an hour, keeping his eyes shut, and refuse to get to his feet. The mother plucked at his sleeve, whispering endearments in his ear, the sister left her lessons to come to her mother's help, but Gregor's father was not to be caught. He would only sink down deeper in his chair. Not until the two women hoisted him up by the armpits did he open his eyes and look at them both, one after the other, usually with the remark: "This is a life. This is the peace and quiet of my old age." And leaning on the two of them he would heave himself up, with difficulty, as if he were a great burden to himself, suffer them to lead him as far as the door and then wave them off and go on alone, while the mother abandoned her needlework and the sister her pen in order to run after him and help him farther.

Who could find time, in this overworked and tired-out family, to bother about Gregor more than was absolutely needful? The household was reduced more and more; the servant girl was turned off; a gigantic bony charwoman with white hair flying round her head came in morning and evening to do the rough work; everything else was done by Gregor's mother, as well as great piles of sewing. Even various family ornaments, which his mother and sister used to wear with pride at parties and celebrations, had to be sold, as Gregor discovered of an evening from hearing them all discuss the prices obtained. But what they lamented most was the fact that they could not leave the flat which was much too big for their present circumstances, because they could not think of any way to shift Gregor. Yet Gregor saw well enough that consideration for him was not the main difficulty preventing the removal, for they could have easily shifted him in some suitable box with a few air holes in it; what really kept them from moving into another flat was rather their own complete hopelessness and the belief that they had been singled out for a misfortune such as had never happened to any of their relations or acquaintances. They fulfilled to the uttermost all that the world demands of poor people, the father fetched breakfast for the small clerks in the bank, the mother devoted her energy to making underwear for strangers, the sister trotted to and fro behind the counter at the behest of customers, but more than this they had not the strength to do. And the wound in Gregor's back began to nag at him afresh when his mother and sister, after getting his father into bed, came back again, left their work lying, drew close to each other and sat cheek by cheek; when his mother, pointing towards his room, said: "Shut that door now, Grete," and he was left again in darkness, while next door the women mingled their tears or perhaps sat dry-eyed staring at the table.

Gregor hardly slept at all by night or by day. He was often haunted by the idea that next time the door opened he would take the family's affairs in hand again just as he used to do; once more, after this long interval, there appeared in his thoughts the figures of the chief and the chief clerk, the commercial travelers and the apprentices, the porter who was so dull-witted, two or three friends in other firms, a chambermaid in one of the rural hotels, a sweet and fleeting memory, a cashier in a milliner's shop, whom he had wooed earnestly but too slowly—they all appeared, together with strangers or people he had quite forgotten, but instead of helping him and his family they were one and all unapproachable and he was glad when they vanished. At other times he would not be in the mood to bother about his family, he was only filled with rage at the way they were neglecting him, and although he had no clear idea of what he might care to eat he would make plans for getting into the larder to take the food that was after all his due, even if he were not hungry. His sister no longer took thought to bring him what might especially please him, but in the morning and at noon before she went to business hurriedly pushed into his room with her foot any food that was available, and in the evening cleared it out again with one sweep of the broom, heedless of whether it had been merely tasted, or—as most frequently happened—left untouched. The cleaning of his room, which she now did always in the evenings, could not have been more hastily done. Streaks of dirt stretched along the walls, here and there lay balls of dust and filth. At first Gregor used to station himself in some particularly filthy corner when his sister arrived, in order to reproach her with it, so to speak. But he could have sat there for weeks without getting her to make any improvements; she could see the dirt as well as he did, but she had simply made up her mind to leave it alone. And yet, with a touchiness that was new to her, which seemed anyhow to have infected the whole family, she jealously guarded her claim to be the sole caretaker of Gregor's room. His mother once subjected his room to a thorough cleaning, which was achieved only by means of several buckets of water—all this dampness of course upset Gregor too and he lay widespread, sulky and motionless on the sofa—but she was well punished for it. Hardly had his sister noticed the changed aspect of his room that evening than she rushed in high dudgeon into the living room and despite the imploringly raised hands of her mother, burst into a storm of weeping, while her parents—her father had of course been startled out of his chair—looked on at first in helpless amazement; then they too began to go into action; the father reproached the mother on his right for not having left the cleaning of Gregor's room to his sister; shrieked at the sister on his left that never again was she to be allowed to clean Gregor's room; while the mother tried to pull the father into his bedroom, since he was beyond himself with agitation; the sister, shaken with sobs, then beat upon the table with her small fists; and Gregor hissed loudly with rage because not one of them thought of shutting the door to spare him such a spectacle and so much noise.

Still, even if the sister, exhausted by her daily work, had grown tired of looking after Gregor as she did formerly, there was no need for his mother's intervention or for Gregor's being neglected at all. The charwoman was there. This old widow, whose strong bony frame had enabled her to survive the worst a long life could offer, by no means recoiled from Gregor. Without being in the least curious she had once by chance opened the door of his room and at the sight of Gregor, who, taken by surprise, began to rush to and fro although no one was chasing him, merely stood there with her arms folded. From that time she never failed to open his door a little for a moment, morning and evening, to have a look at him. At first she even used to call him to her, with words which apparently she took to be friendly, such as: "Come along, then, you old dung beetle!" or "Look at the old dung beetle, then!" To such allocutions Gregor made no answer, but stayed motionless where he was, as if the door had never been opened. Instead of being allowed to disturb him so senselessly whenever the whim took her, she should rather have been ordered to clean out his room daily, that charwoman! Once, early in the morning—heavy rain was lashing on the windowpanes, perhaps a sign that spring was on the way—Gregor was so exasperated when she began addressing him again that he ran at her, as if to attack her, although slowly and feebly enough. But the charwoman instead of showing fright merely lifted high a chair that happened to be beside the door, and as she stood there with her mouth wide open it was clear that she meant to shut it only when she brought the chair down on Gregor's back. "So you're not coming any nearer?" she asked, as Gregor turned away again, and quietly put the chair back into the corner.

Gregor was now eating hardly anything. Only when he happened to pass the food laid out for him did he take a bit of something in his mouth as a pastime, kept it there for an hour at a time and usually spat it out again. At first he thought it was chagrin over the state of his room that prevented him from eating, yet he soon got used to the various changes in his room. It had become a habit in the family to push into his room things there was no room for elsewhere, and there were plenty of these now, since one of the rooms had been let to three lodgers. These serious gentlemen—all three of them with full beards, as Gregor once observed through a crack in the door—had a passion for order, not only in their own room but, since they were now members of the household, in all its arrangements, especially in the kitchen. Superfluous, not to say dirty, objects they could not bear. Besides, they had brought with them most of the furnishings they needed. For this reason many things could be dispensed with that it was no use trying to sell but that should not be thrown away either. All of them found their way into Gregor's room. The ash can likewise and the kitchen garbage can. Anything that was not needed for the moment was simply flung into Gregor's room by the charwoman, who did everything in a hurry; fortunately Gregor usually saw only the object, whatever it was, and the hand that held it. Perhaps she intended to take the things away again as time and opportunity offered, or to collect them until she could throw them all out in a heap, but in fact they just lay wherever she happened to throw them, except when Gregor pushed his way through the junk heap and shifted it somewhat, at first out of necessity, because he had not room enough to crawl, but later with increasing enjoyment, although after such excursions, being sad and weary to death, he would lie motionless for hours. And since the lodgers often ate their supper at home in the common living room, the living-room door stayed shut many an evening, yet Gregor reconciled himself quite easily to the shutting of the door, for often enough on evenings when it was opened he had disregarded it entirely and lain in the darkest corner of his room, quite unnoticed by the family. But on one occasion the charwoman left the door open a little and it stayed ajar even when the lodgers came in for supper and the lamp was lit. They set themselves at the top end of the table where formerly Gregor and his father and mother had eaten their meals, unfolded their napkins and took knife and fork in hand. At once his mother appeared in the other doorway with a dish of meat and close behind her his sister with a dish of potatoes piled high. The food steamed with a thick vapor. The lodgers bent over the food set before them as if to scrutinize it before eating, in fact the man in the middle, who seemed to pass for an authority with the other two, cut a piece of meat as it lay on the dish, obviously to discover if it were tender or should be sent back to the kitchen. He showed satisfaction, and Gregor's mother and sister, who had been watching anxiously, breathed freely and began to smile.

The family itself took its meals in the kitchen. None the less, Gregor's father came into the living room before going into the kitchen and with one prolonged bow, cap in hand, made a round of the table. The lodgers all stood up and murmured something in their beards. When they were alone again they ate their food in almost complete silence. It seemed remarkable to Gregor that among the various noises coming from the table he could always distinguish the sound of their masticating teeth, as if this were a sign to Gregor that one needed teeth in order to eat, and that with toothless jaws even of the finest make one could do nothing. "I'm hungry enough," said Gregor sadly to himself, "but not for that kind of food. How these lodgers are stuffing themselves, and here am I dying of starvation!"

On that very evening—during the whole of his time there Gregor could not remember ever having heard the violin—the sound of violin-playing came from the kitchen. The lodgers had already finished their supper, the one in the middle had brought out a newspaper and given the other two a page apiece, and now they were leaning back at ease reading and smoking. When the violin began to play they pricked up their ears, got to their feet, and went on tiptoe to the hall door where they stood huddled together. Their movements must have been heard in the kitchen, for Gregor's father called out: "Is the violin-playing disturbing you, gentlemen? It can be stopped at once." "On the contrary," said the middle lodger, "could not Fräulein Samsa come and play in this room, beside us, where it is much more convenient and comfortable?" "Oh certainly," cried Gregor's father, as if he were the violin-player. The lodgers came back into the living room and waited. Presently Gregor's father arrived with the music stand, his mother carrying the music and his sister with the violin. His sister quietly made everything ready to start playing; his parents, who had never let rooms before and so had an exaggerated idea of the courtesy due to lodgers, did not venture to sit down on their own chairs; his father leaned against the door, the right hand thrust between two buttons of his livery coat, which was formally buttoned up; but his mother was offered a chair by one of the lodgers and, since she left the chair just where he had happened to put it, sat down in a corner to one side.

Gregor's sister began to play; the father and mother, from either side, intently watched the movements of her hands. Gregor, attracted by the playing, ventured to move forward a little until his head was actually inside the living room. He felt hardly any surprise at his growing lack of consideration for the others; there had been a time when he prided himself on being considerate. And yet just on this occasion he had more reason than ever to hide himself, since owing to the amount of dust which lay thick in his room and rose into the air at the slightest movement, he too was covered with dust; fluff and hair and remnants of food trailed with him, caught on his back and along his sides; his indifference to everything was much too great for him to turn on his back and scrape himself clean on the carpet, as once he had done several times a day. And in spite of his condition, no shame deterred him from advancing a little over the spotless floor of the living room.

To be sure, no one was aware of him. The family was entirely absorbed in the violin-playing; the lodgers, however, who first of all had stationed themselves, hands in pockets, much too close behind the music stand so that they could all have read the music, which must have bothered his sister, had soon retreated to the window, half-whispering with downbent heads, and stayed there while his father turned an anxious eye on them. Indeed, they were making it more than obvious that they had been disappointed in their expectation of hearing good or enjoyable violin-playing, that they had had more than enough of the performance and only out of courtesy suffered a continued disturbance of their peace. From the way they all kept blowing the smoke of their cigars high in the air through nose and mouth one could divine their irritation. And yet Gregor's sister was playing so beautifully. Her face leaned sideways, intently and sadly her eyes followed the notes of music. Gregor crawled a little farther forward and lowered his head to the ground so that it might be possible for his eyes to meet hers. Was he an animal, that music had such an effect upon him? He felt as if the way were opening before him to the unknown nourishment he craved. He was determined to push forward till he reached his sister, to pull at her skirt and so let her know that she was to come into his room with her violin, for no one here appreciated her playing as he would appreciate it. He would never let her out of his room, at least, not so long as he lived; his frightful appearance would become, for the first time, useful to him; he would watch all the doors of his room at once and spit at intruders; but his sister should need no constraint, she should stay with him of her own free will; she should sit beside him on the sofa, bend down her ear to him and hear him confide that he had had the firm intention of sending her to the Conservatorium, and that, but for his mishap, last Christmas—surely Christmas was long past?—he would have announced it to everybody without allowing a single objection. After this confession his sister would be so touched that she would burst into tears, and Gregor would then raise himself to her shoulder and kiss her on the neck, which, now that she went to business, she kept free of any ribbon or collar.

"Mr. Samsa!" cried the middle lodger, to Gregor's father, and pointed, without wasting any more words, at Gregor, now working himself slowly forwards. The violin fell silent, the middle lodger first smiled to his friends with a shake of the head and then looked at Gregor again. Instead of driving Gregor out, his father seemed to think it more needful to begin by soothing down the lodgers, although they were not at all agitated and apparently found Gregor more entertaining than the violin-playing. He hurried towards them and, spreading out his arms, tried to urge them back into their own room and at the same time to block their view of Gregor. They now began to be really a little angry, one could not tell whether because of the old man's behavior or because it had just dawned on them that all unwittingly they had such a neighbor as Gregor next door. They demanded explanations of his father, they waved their arms like him, tugged uneasily at their beards, and only with reluctance backed towards their room. Meanwhile Gregor's sister, who stood there as if lost when her playing was so abruptly broken off, came to life again, pulled herself together all at once after standing for a while holding violin and bow in nervelessly hanging hands and staring at her music, pushed her violin into the lap of her mother, who was still sitting in her chair fighting asthmatically for breath, and ran into the lodgers' room to which they were now being shepherded by her father rather more quickly than before. One could see the pillows and blankets on the beds flying under her accustomed fingers and being laid in order. Before the lodgers had actually reached their room she had finished making the beds and slipped out.

The old man seemed once more to be so possessed by his mulish self-assertiveness that he was forgetting all the respect he should show to his lodgers. He kept driving them on and driving them on until in the very door of the bedroom the middle lodger stamped his foot loudly on the floor and so brought him to a halt. "I beg to announce," said the lodger, lifting one hand and looking also at Gregor's mother and sister, "that because of the disgusting conditions prevailing in this household and family"—here he spat on the floor with emphatic brevity—"I give you notice on the spot. Naturally I won't pay you a penny for the days I have lived here, on the contrary I shall consider bringing an action for damages against you, based on claims—believe me—that will be easily susceptible of proof." He ceased and stared straight in front of him, as if he expected something. In fact his two friends at once rushed into the breach with these words: "And we too give notice on the spot." On that he seized the door-handle and shut the door with a slam.

Gregor's father, groping with his hands, staggered forward and fell into his chair; it looked as if he were stretching himself there for his ordinary evening nap, but the marked jerkings of his head, which was as if uncontrollable, showed that he was far from asleep. Gregor had simply stayed quietly all the time on the spot where the lodgers had espied him. Disappointment at the failure of his plan, perhaps also the weakness arising from extreme hunger, made it impossible for him to move. He feared, with a fair degree of certainty, that at any moment the general tension would discharge itself in a combined attack upon him, and he lay waiting. He did not react even to the noise made by the violin as it fell off his mother's lap from under her trembling fingers and gave out a resonant note.

"My dear parents," said his sister, slapping her hand on the table by way of introduction, "things can't go on like this. Perhaps you don't realize that, but I do. I won't utter my brother's name in the presence of this creature, and so all I say is: we must try to get rid of it. We've tried to look after it and to put up with it as far as is humanly possible, and I don't think anyone could reproach us in the slightest."

"She is more than right," said Gregor's father to himself. His mother, who was still choking for lack of breath, began to cough hollowly into her hand with a wild look in her eyes.

His sister rushed over to her and held her forehead. His father's thoughts seemed to have lost their vagueness at Grete's words, he sat more upright, fingering his service cap that lay among the plates still lying on the table from the lodgers' supper, and from time to time looked at the still form of Gregor.

"We must try to get rid of it," his sister now said explicitly to her father, since her mother was coughing too much to hear a word, "it will be the death of both of you, I can see that coming. When one has to work as hard as we do, all of us, one can't stand this continual torment at home on top of it. At least I can't stand it any longer." And she burst into such a passion of sobbing that her tears dropped on her mother's face, where she wiped them off mechanically.

"My dear," said the old man sympathetically, and with evident understanding, "but what can we do?"

Gregor's sister merely shrugged her shoulders to indicate the feeling of helplessness that had now overmastered her during her weeping fit, in contrast to her former confidence.

"If he could understand us," said her father, half questioningly; Grete, still sobbing, vehemently waved a hand to show how unthinkable that was.

"If he could understand us," repeated the old man, shutting his eyes to consider his daughter's conviction that understanding was impossible, "then perhaps we might come to some agreement with him. But as it is—"

"He must go," cried Gregor's sister, "that's the only solution, Father. You must just try to get rid of the idea that this is Gregor. The fact that we've believed it for so long is the root of all our trouble. But how can it be Gregor? If this were Gregor, he would have realized long ago that human beings can't live with such a creature, and he'd have gone away on his own accord. Then we wouldn't have any brother, but we'd be able to go on living and keep his memory in honor. As it is, this creature persecutes us, drives away our lodgers, obviously wants the whole apartment to himself and would have us all sleep in the gutter. Just look, Father," she shrieked all at once, "he's at it again!" And in an access of panic that was quite incomprehensible to Gregor she even quitted her mother, literally thrusting the chair from her as if she would rather sacrifice her mother than stay so near to Gregor, and rushed behind her father, who also rose up, being simply upset by her agitation, and half-spread his arms out as if to protect her.

Yet Gregor had not the slightest intention of frightening anyone, far less his sister. He had only begun to turn round in order to crawl back to his room, but it was certainly a startling operation to watch, since because of his disabled condition he could not execute the difficult turning movements except by lifting his head and then bracing it against the floor over and over again. He paused and looked round. His good intentions seemed to have been recognized; the alarm had only been momentary. Now they were all watching him in melancholy silence. His mother lay in her chair, her legs stiffly outstretched and pressed together, her eyes almost closing for sheer weariness; his father and his sister were sitting beside each other, his sister's arm around the old man's neck.

Perhaps I can go on turning round now, thought Gregor, and began his labors again. He could not stop himself from panting with the effort, and had to pause now and then to take breath. Nor did anyone harass him, he was left entirely to himself. When he had completed the turn-round he began at once to crawl straight back. He was amazed at the distance separating him from his room and could not understand how in his weak state he had managed to accomplish the same journey so recently, almost without remarking it. Intent on crawling as fast as possible, he barely noticed that not a single word, not an ejaculation from his family, interfered with his progress. Only when he was already in the doorway did he turn his head round, not completely, for his neck muscles were getting stiff, but enough to see that nothing had changed behind him except that his sister had risen to her feet. His last glance fell on his mother, who was not quite overcome by sleep.

Hardly was he well inside his room when the door was hastily pushed shut, bolted and locked. The sudden noise in his rear startled him so much that his little legs gave beneath him. It was his sister who had shown such haste. She had been standing ready waiting and had made a light spring forward, Gregor had not even heard her coming, and she cried "At last!" to her parents as she turned the key in the lock.

"And what now?" said Gregor to himself, looking round in the darkness. Soon he made the discovery that he was now unable to stir a limb. This did not surprise him, rather it seemed unnatural that he should ever actually have been able to move on these feeble little legs. Otherwise he felt relatively comfortable. True, his whole body was aching, but it seemed that the pain was gradually growing less and would finally pass away. The rotting apple in his back and the inflamed area around it, all covered with soft dust, already hardly troubled him. He thought of his family with tenderness and love. The decision that he must disappear was one that he held to even more strongly than his sister, if that were possible. In this state of vacant and peaceful meditation he remained until the tower clock struck three in the morning. The first broadening of light in the world outside the window entered his consciousness once more. Then his head sank to the floor of its own accord and from his nostrils came the last faint flicker of his breath.

When the charwoman arrived early in the morning—what between her strength and her impatience she slammed all the doors so loudly, never mind how often she had been begged not to do so, that no one in the whole apartment could enjoy any quiet sleep after her arrival—she noticed nothing unusual as she took her customary peep into Gregor's room. She thought he was lying motionless on purpose, pretending to be in the sulks; she credited him with every kind of intelligence. Since she happened to have the long-handled broom in her hand she tried to tickle him up with it from the doorway. When that too produced no reaction she felt provoked and poked at him a little harder, and only when she had pushed him along the floor without meeting any resistance was her attention aroused. It did not take her long to establish the truth of the matter, and her eyes widened, she let out a whistle, yet did not waste much time over it but tore open the door of the Samsas' bedroom and yelled into the darkness at the top of her voice: "Just look at this, it's dead, it's lying here dead and done for!"

Mr. and Mrs. Samsa started up in their double bed and before they realized the nature of the charwoman's announcement had some difficulty in overcoming the shock of it. But then they got out of bed quickly, one on either side, Mr. Samsa throwing a blanket over his shoulders, Mrs. Samsa in nothing but her nightgown; in this array they entered Gregor's room. Meanwhile the door of the living room opened, too, where Grete had been sleeping since the advent of the lodgers; she was completely dressed as if she had not been to bed, which seemed to be confirmed also by the paleness of her face. "Dead?" said Mrs. Samsa, looking questioningly at the charwoman, although she could have investigated for herself, and the fact was obvious enough without investigation. "I should say so," said the charwoman, proving her words by pushing Gregor's corpse a long way to one side with her broomstick. Mrs. Samsa made a movement as if to stop her, but checked it. "Well," said Mr. Samsa, "now thanks be to God." He crossed himself, and the three women followed his example. Grete, whose eyes never left the corpse, said: "Just see how thin he was. It's such a long time since he's eaten anything. The food came out again just as it went in." Indeed, Gregor's body was completely flat and dry, as could only now be seen when it was no longer supported by the legs and nothing prevented one from looking closely at it.

"Come in beside us, Grete, for a little while," said Mrs. Samsa with a tremulous smile, and Grete, not without looking back at the corpse, followed her parents into their bedroom. The charwoman shut the door and opened the window wide. Although it was so early in the morning a certain softness was perceptible in the fresh air. After all, it was already the end of March.

The three lodgers emerged from their room and were surprised to see no breakfast; they had been forgotten. "Where's our breakfast?" said the middle lodger peevishly to the charwoman. But she put her finger to her lips and hastily, without a word, indicated by gestures that they should go into Gregor's room. They did so and stood, their hands in the pockets of their somewhat shabby coats, around Gregor's corpse in the room where it was now fully light.

At that the door of the Samsas's bedroom opened and Mr. Samsa appeared in his uniform, his wife on one arm, his daughter on the other. They all looked a little as if they had been crying; from time to time Grete hid her face on her father's arm.

"Leave my house at once!" said Mr. Samsa, and pointed to the door without disengaging himself from the women. "What do you mean by that?" said the middle lodger, taken somewhat aback, with a feeble smile. The two others put their hands behind them and kept rubbing them together, as if in gleeful expectation of a fine set-to in which they were bound to come off the winners. "I mean just what I say," answered Mr. Samsa, and advanced in a straight line with his two companions toward the lodger. He stood his ground at first quietly, looking at the floor as if his thoughts were taking a new pattern in his head. "Then let us go by all means," he said, and looked up at Mr. Samsa as if in a sudden access of humility he were expecting some renewed sanction for this decision. Mr. Samsa merely nodded once or twice with meaning eyes. Upon that the lodger really did go with long strides into the hall, his two friends had been listening and had quite stopped rubbing their hands for some moments and now went scuttling after him as if afraid that Mr. Samsa might get into the hall before them and cut them off from their leader. In the hall they all three took their hats from the rack, their sticks from the umbrella stand, bowed in silence and quitted the apartment. With a suspiciousness which proved quite unfounded Mr. Samsa and the two women followed them out to the landing; leaning over the banister they watched the three figures slowly but surely going down the long stairs, vanishing from sight at a certain turn of the staircase on every floor and coming into view again after a moment or so; the more they dwindled, the more the Samsa family's interest in them dwindled, and when a butcher's boy met them and passed them on the stairs coming up proudly with a tray on his head, Mr. Samsa and the two women soon left the landing and as if a burden had been lifted from them went back into their apartment.

They decided to spend this day in resting and going for a stroll; they had not only deserved such a respite from work, but absolutely needed it. And so they sat down at the table and wrote three notes of excuse, Mr. Samsa to his board of management, Mrs. Samsa to her employer and Grete to the head of her firm. While they were writing, the charwoman came in to say that she was going now, since her morning's work was finished. At first they only nodded without looking up, but as she kept hovering there they eyed her irritably. "Well?" said Mr. Samsa. The charwoman stood grinning in the doorway as if she had good news to impart to the family but meant not to say a word unless properly questioned. The small ostrich feather standing upright on her hat, which had annoyed Mr. Samsa ever since she was engaged, was waving gaily in all directions. "Well, what is it then?" asked Mr. Samsa, who obtained more respect from the charwoman than the others. "Oh," said the charwoman, giggling so amiably that she could not at once continue, "just this, you don't need to bother about how to get rid of the thing next door. It's been seen to already." Mrs. Samsa and Grete bent over their letters again, as if preoccupied; Mr. Samsa, who perceived that she was eager to begin describing it all in detail, stopped her with a decisive hand. But since she was not allowed to tell her story, she remembered the great hurry she was in, being obviously deeply huffed: "Bye, everybody," she said, whirling off violently, and departed with a frightful slamming of doors.

"She'll be given notice tonight," said Mr. Samsa, but neither from his wife nor his daughter did he get any answer, for the charwoman seemed to have shattered again the composure they had barely achieved. They rose, went to the window and stayed there, clasping each other tight. Mrs. Samsa turned in his chair to look at them and quietly observed them for a little. Then he called out: "Come along, now, do. Let bygones be bygones. And you might have some consideration for me." The two of them complied at once, hastened to him, caressed him and quickly finished their letters.

Then they all three left the apartment together, which was more than they had done for months, and went by tram into the open country outside the town. The tram, in which they were the only passengers, was filled with warm sunshine. Leaning comfortably back in their seats they canvassed their prospects for the future, and it appeared on closer inspection that these were not at all bad, for the jobs they had got, which so far they had never really discussed with each other, were all three admirable and likely to lead to better things later on. The greatest immediate improvement in their condition would of course arise from moving to another house; they wanted to take a smaller and cheaper but also better situated and more easily run apartment than the one they had, which Gregor had selected. While they were thus conversing, it struck both Mr. and Mrs. Samsa, almost at the same moment, as they became aware of their daughter's increasing vivacity, that in spite of all the sorrow of recent times, which had made her cheeks pale, she had bloomed into a pretty girl with a good figure. They grew quieter and half unconsciously exchanged glances of complete agreement, having come to the conclusion that it would soon be time to find a good husband for her. And it was like a confirmation of their new dreams and excellent intentions that at the end of their journey their daughter sprang to her feet first and stretched her young body.

JOYCE CAROL OATES

The Metamorphosis

Matthew woke suddenly from a daydream that was not his.

He shook himself awake, startled. He dislodged the dream from himself, out of his head. No one had noticed; the place was gleaming and empty, only the three new automobiles out on the floor, brilliant and massive and unseeing, all curves and sleek precise lines; no one else was around. Peter, one of the younger salesmen, was just coming through the door at the far end of the showroom, looking nervous, perplexed. . . .

Matthew hoped that Peter would not stop at his cubicle to talk with him.

He had stirred himself from a dream that was not his. It could not have belonged to him. He had never had such a dream before, he would not acknowledge it. Not his. He never daydreamed, he never let his thoughts wander. The dream had been someone else's, not his own. The tag end of a stranger's dream. . . . It was possible; you could be infected by the fears of strangers.

He looked through the calendar on his desk; he must make himself concentrate on something real. What was the date? His birthday was approaching —he would be forty-six in two weeks. He felt much younger. He looked much younger, a man of broad, vigorous shoulders, thighs thick and still muscular, like the trunks of small trees. That hard grainy muscularity. He was proud of his body and of his face—he had an intelligent, kindly face, marred only by the deep lines made by smiles. Years of smiling. His hair was brown, streaked with red; there was something exclamatory in the way he frequently raised his eyebrows.

He had been selling cars for twenty years here at Overmeyer Ford.

. . . On the gleaming fake-brick floor, a man of obvious energy. Excellent clothes, shoes, his hair kept carefully trimmed. He knew everything. He could answer any question about any car manufactured by Ford. He could answer the questions of the most methodical, suspicious customer. Everyone knew him, Matthew Brown; he had sold thousands of cars, old customers kept coming back to him, making appointments specifically with him . . . he knew everyone's name, he shook hands easily and yet without presumption; there was a sacred space around all men, a few feet of air, and he knew enough not to blunder into it. Though he was almost forty-six he could judge by the look in women's eyes his own youthful appearance, that blond, broad, generous Irish face, the good looks he had had for decades without especially prizing them. He was proud of his work, not of himself. Proud of his family. Not himself; his family. He was devoted to his wife and five children.

He did not think about the strange dream he had had, sitting here awake. He was a man who did not believe in dreams.

Yes, it said here on his calendar that someone was supposed to have come to see him at three o'clock. He would wait. No reason for uneasiness.

Customers were often late. This month had been a slow month . . . interest rates had risen again . . . there were rumors of another dealer going bankrupt . . . but it did no good to think of any of these things. He would sit in his cubicle and wait quietly. He wondered if Peter had lost his customer—that woman with the bone-white hair, bleached and sullen, who had talked so loudly. It might be a good idea to stop by Peter's cubicle on the way out, say something kind to him, it was the least he could do. He felt sorry for Peter, who had not made any sales yet this month. . . . Waiting, he looked idly at the tiny crack on his desk top. It seemed that his daydream had sprung somehow out of that crack. It was an irritant, the crack. Faint and thin and curving as a hair. He often tried to brush it away while talking with customers. His voice could move on, rapidly, knowing the answers to all questions, heading off questions before they were asked, gauging by the customers' faces how well he was doing. He usually did well. Very well. He could work swiftly with numbers, adding up long columns, subtracting, figuring out discounts, a routine performance of his that impressed customers. If the trade-in is $1200, then. . . . Minus this. Minus. Plus.

Months in a long wavering column, adding up to decades.

Father came home early, about four-thirty, on that day. . . .

"Do you want some coffee, Matt? I'm going over now," Gardie said. She wore a navy blue dress, trim as a uniform. Gardie. Hildegarde. He must have said yes because in a few minutes she appeared again with coffee for him. He accepted the paper cup, touched. Women had always liked him, had always been concerned about him. She leaned against the partition, her dress stark and neutral against the frosted glass. Five or six years now of Gardie's cheerful sagging face. Cheerful conversation, the words slightly sagging as the years passed. A troubled marriage—Matthew knew only a little, didn't want to know more. In spite of his tall, broad, leggy personality he didn't want to know much about people, resisted their hints of private, personal, grieved lives, didn't want to get snagged by them. He carried himself cautiously through crowds.

He had five children of his own and thought about them constantly.

One of us saw his car coming up the boulevard, the big black Lincoln he drove in 1970. That was Ronnie, delivering papers. Then Len saw the car parked in front of the garage. Why wasn't it inside the garage the way Father always wanted it? He didn't want oil stains on the concrete . . . he had poured the concrete himself for the new driveway. But now the car was parked outside and might drip oil onto the concrete.

He drank the coffee slowly, grateful for its warmth. A bad habit, all this coffee. It was almost four o'clock. Someone named Mr. Yates had called Gardie yesterday to make this appointment with Matthew, but he had never heard of the man before; no Mr. Yates in his file of old customers. Should he have known him?

He would not think of Yates. Customers often came late, or showed up the next day. He would not think of the daydream that had disturbed him. Instead, he concentrated on the crack in his desk. The top was plastic, an unclean light yellow. Almost white. The crack was a stream, a river . . . a faint lifeline he must follow . . . a stubborn little artery. The daydream had come from this line, somehow. It had not been about automobiles. The automobiles, those magnificent new models, were right out there on the floor, a few yards away from him, and he had only to glance up to see how massive and patient they were. He did not dream about them. Never about them. He did not dream about selling cars, about breaking his own record, made three years ago. Not about his wife Florence. Not about his sons, his daughters. . . . This strange dream had been about sleep. A dream about sleep. There had been a body, a kind of mummy, lying very still beneath heavy covers. Sheets pulled up to the chin. A faceless face. Formless bulges, ridges. A mystery. The figure had appeared in his mind's eye and had held itself there for some minutes, frightening him.

But it was not his dream. It must have belonged to someone else.

One of us, Vicky, heard Mother's voice upstairs. "Matt? What do you mean? Why is the door locked?" Vicky backed away from that sound in her mother's voice. She felt a sharp terrified thrill in the pit of her stomach; why was Father home, up in the bedroom, at four-thirty on a Tuesday afternoon?

She noticed a crack on the living-room ceiling. Had she ever seen that crack before?

Someone was infecting him with bad dreams, Matthew thought. He could hear Peter talking on the telephone—making a show of sounding efficient, talking too fast. Peter should know that customers did not trust salesmen who talked too fast. Peter was several years younger than Matthew, but he had stomach troubles, he probably had bad dreams. His commissions dissolved; too anxious to knock down prices. But Matthew had never talked with Peter about these tactics. Better not to talk. In the long run. . . . In the long run, he thought vaguely, the best salesman does best.

A rattle of voices. Mother washing dishes as if nothing was wrong, Vicky drying. Tommy fooling around. "Is Daddy sick? Why is the door locked?" Mother using the pink sponge, which was worn out. It looked eroded. Tommy pulled his lips away from his gums, making a face. He was five years old. Vicky stood with her back to him, her shoulders thin and tense. She kept listening for Father's footsteps upstairs. First the creaking of the bedsprings, then the heavy footsteps. Mother set dishes in the drying rack, her fingers slippery with soap. "Why didn't Daddy have supper with us? Is he sick?" Tommy whined.

He followed the crack with his eyes, then with his forefinger. Strange. It was a small river leading him up, back . . . up into what, back into what? The dream had come out of that small river. But he did not want to remember it. He did not want to see that figure in bed, hardly a human figure, lying so stiffly in bed, aged and silent. Where the hell was this Mr. Yates?

The telephone rang.

Gardie answered it and he knew before she buzzed him that it would be for him. He picked up the receiver: "This is Matthew Brown." He began talking at once. No trouble. Quoting prices: the advertisement in the Sunday paper. Yes. Subtract two hundred dollars. Three years to pay. His words rattled on with a false, bright energy of their own, while he stared at the little crack on his desk top. He had a sensation of falling and only the telephone conversation kept him upright.

He hung up. Gardie hurried over.

"That guy who just called," she said in a whisper, "he was Peter's customer a few years ago . . . oh, when was it? . . . caused all that trouble, do you remember? Something about the turn lights not working right. . . ."

He remembered exactly, every detail. No, he did not remember.

In the middle of their conversation—such a normal, conspiratorial conversation, of the kind they had every day!—he got to his feet. Not well. Sick. Must go home. Gardie's face immediately crinkling and maternal. "I have to go home. I'm not well," he said suddenly.

"Not well?" she said, shocked.

"Not well? You're not well?" Mother was saying outside the bedroom door. "Why can't you answer me?" Vicky next to her. Another one of us—Sally—was by the bathroom door, pretending to be swinging on it. Wanting attention. She had hold of the doorknob and stood with her knees on either side of the door, trying clumsily to swing on it. If Mother noticed, she would be scolded. Why were Mother and Vicky standing there like that, so strange, by the bedroom door? Mother and Vicky: the same height. Vicky was thirteen then. Her hair was cut very short, almost as short as a boy's. A deeper brown than Father's. She had Father's nose, wide at the bridge, making her eyes look clear and wise because they were spaced far apart. Vicky's wise monkeyish look. Mother, with her hair in a tangle, rapped on the door to her own bedroom. A strange, formal gesture. "Why is the door locked? Why is the door locked?" she cried.

He left the agency and drove home. His car responded at once—the powerful motor made hardly any sound. So much strength, yet nearly silent. These machines were miraculous. No one could invent them if their secret were lost. The car leaped forward, hurtled itself forward. . . . Carrying him home. Safe. Back up that winding little river, safely back to something, into something, into darkness. His heart beat calmly in his chest. When he got home he would go upstairs at once and into the bedroom and lock the door. Better to lie down and rest. A short nap before dinner. He hoped that his wife would not be in the house.

Turning onto Claremont Boulevard he felt that he was losing strength, that it was somehow flowing out of his legs and into the engine of his car. Must get home, to bed. A sense of despair in his stomach—the very pit of his stomach—everything was settling down darkly, heavily. He must get home. Get to bed. He was dangerous, out here on the street, driving this large vehicle. Its mass hurtled itself across the pavement without much warning sound, a terrible danger to other people in spite of its beauty. What if he crashed into someone?—he did not even own this car—his legs had grown very weak—what if he crashed this car into one driven by an old customer of his, a car he himself had sold?

Other cars on the boulevard appeared to be winking and grimacing at him. Happy grillwork in front of the cars. The slope of the bumper: a happy look. Chrome, tinted windshield, whitewall tires that seemed to be winking, gesturing. . . .

His house was at the far end of the block. Two colonials had been built at the same time, identical except that one had dark orange brick and the other had pale buff brick. The dark orange brick home was his. His lawn had a clump of three birch trees, not doing well, and his neighbor's lawn had a single red-leafed tree, not doing well. Though he was nearly home, he felt very weak. Maybe he should park in front of the house, not risk turning up the drive. His wrists and knees were especially weak. But he turned up the driveway and parked just in front of the garage, not daring to drive in because he feared brushing the side of the doorway. He turned off the ignition. Left the keys inside. Went into the house, through the back hall, upstairs, before anyone saw him. Florence called out, "Matt? . . ."

He closed the bedroom door behind him and locked it.

"What is happening to me?" he thought.

We sat around the kitchen table while Mother and Vicky were upstairs. The air was all jumbled. What was happening? Tommy was sniveling. Ronnie sat with his elbows on the table and his hands pressed against his forehead, imitating Father: the way Father someimes sat at the table, by himself, in the evening. "What are they talking about up there? Where is Daddy?" Sally kept saying.

His hands were shaking. He tore off his suitcoat and threw it onto a chair. Must get these hot, heavy clothes off. They were suffocating him. Unbottoned his shirt, took off his necktie. Everything was damp. Smelled. There was a sour, panicked smell about him. Must get his clothes off. Must get naked. Already Florence was hurrying up the stairs. "Matt? Is that you? Is something wrong?"

Already it was beginning.

He slid in bed, trembling. Pulled the covers up to his chin. Every part of his body trembled. Lying flat, he could feel the panic spread everywhere inside him, like a pool of mercury. That sharp acrid taste. But he would force himself to think calmly, logically. He would relax, take a nap. A nap would restore his strength. Yes, a nap before supper, and then he would be feeling as good as ever . . . if only Florence would let him alone. . . . But she was right outside the door now, calling out in that surprised, slightly annoyed voice she used on the children: "Are you in there? Is the door locked? What on earth is wrong?"

He got a grip on his teeth, his jaws locked firmly together. Good. He would relax every part of his body and sleep. It would do no good to reply to his wife because he would only be lying down here for a few minutes. The sensation of panic would pass. It was a foreign sensation, not his own. He did not recognize it. . . . What was that noise? A telephone ringing. Someone was running—one of the children—there was always someone running in this house. The boys wrestled one another, elbowed one another on the stairs and at meals. He closed his eyes and saw his oldest son's face. He loved Len more than any of the other children because he was the first child. Never another child, another miraculous birth, like that. But Vicky, sweet and waifish, he loved Vicky very much, he must explain to her that he loved her. . . .

Florence was saying: "Matt, it's Gardie. She wants to know if you're all right. Matt? Matt? Did you get sick at work?"

He must have slept. He saw now that the room was darker. It was not a very large room, but he had always liked it. Florence complained that the walls and ceiling should be painted. Everything was very still. The curtains caught his eye, pale green fishnet curtains. Dime-store curtains. His wife had always been clever at sewing, fixing up cheap things, searching for bargains. The curtains and the bureau and the rocking chair were very familiar, in the proper scale. He thought that perhaps he himself was out of proportion. He felt smaller. His legs seemed shorter. The covers on his chest formed a shallow ridge and he could not look past it. His mouth tasted sour from the spread of panic. What was that smell in the air? He had carried it up here with him, to bed—the odor of gasoline, exhaust fumes, the close smooth stench of oil. The rainbow stench of oil. He peered along his chest but could not see to the foot of the bed. His gaze skimmed the bottom of his eyebrows and came away tangled and befuddled. The fishnet material of the curtains was confused with the tangle of his eyebrows and the bumpy ridge of his chest.

Len with the screwdriver. Mother's angry tears. "Why doesn't he answer us?" Something harsh and soiled about her face. When we used to see her out on the street, shopping, the oldest of us would flinch a little from the sight of our mother—her breeziness, the rapid skittish walk of hers—as if she were free, a woman and not a mother, just a person out on her own—and we would call out to her, to bring her to a halt. The oldest of us—Len and Vicky and Ronnie—were embarrassed because she was so pretty. But that day she wasn't a pretty woman, not a woman at all but something frightened, smelling of fear. "He won't answer me! He must be sick!" Mother kept saying.

Len stood with his cheek pressed against the locked door. Silence inside. "Father, this is Len. Father? I'm going to take the lock off the door. . . . Father? Can you hear me?"

In bed he was thinking seriously about getting up. Like commandments, certain phrases were going through his head: *front wheel drive, liquid suspension but no springs or shock absorbers, a fully synchronized transmission, a luxurious all-vinyl interior, nylon carpeting wall-to-wall, eight cylinders. . . .* These words were like summonses from another world. They were like shouts from a cliff down to him as he lay here so peacefully in bed, preparing his strength. . . . What was that about a lock on a door? What did that mean?

Someone was rapping on wood and he thought of Mr. Yates, the customer who had never shown up. Maybe he was knocking now on a door, trying to get to see Matthew. Well, let him knock. Matthew had survived many disappointments and now he felt himself stronger, almost independent of his customers; he would not even glance up to see who was knocking. So many disappointments! But they belonged to the past, to another Matthew, and he felt that he had grown beyond them.

"No, don't open it! He doesn't want us to open it!" Vicky cried suddenly. The screwdriver fell to the floor—she knocked it out of Len's hand.

The problem: he had to think through his plans for the evening. He had to think through all the moves he would make. "Getting up"—a generalized expression that took in a complex, an almost hopelessly complex, sequence of particularized movements, some of them muscular and some of them entirely cerebral. Just thinking about this made him exhausted. It was nearly more than the human brain could assimilate. And, behind all this, behind the demand placed upon him by the command "Get up," was the mysterious rapping, the jumble of voices, which seemed to be shouting individual and uncoordinated commandments to him. The need for "getting up" was one he could recognize clearly, privately, as originating inside himself, but these other voices with their curious demands—they were obviously the voices of other people, actual existing human beings who could not even agree with one another.

. . . The world was busy and it wanted nothing so much as to drag him out into it, sweep him along the river where he would be lost, in all that shouting, that busyness. . . . What a kindness, if someone should think of bringing him a cup of coffee! But no one thought of it and he was too tired to get it himself.

Instead, the voices of arguing people.

Mother hurrying downstairs. She embraced Tommy and Sally, who were crying. "Daddy is sick, just a bad cold. Yes. He said so. I'm going to call the doctor." Ronnie backed away from her, bumped into a table. His face stern, rigid, small droplets of perspiration on his forehead. He wore a T-shirt and soiled khaki pants and sneakers. Looking down at himself, he saw that he was dressed like a kid and he was ashamed.

Mother was wearing old slacks and a white blouse we thought was too sheer—you could see straps at her shoulders—we hated that.

She called the doctor and Ronnie ran out to the back fence, where everything was weedy. He pressed against the fence.

In the corner of the room, his wife's sewing machine. Photographs on the wall—the children when they were very young—Florence and himself—posed for Christmas cards a few years ago. How fast the children grew! A miracle. He loved them tenderly, fiercely . . . he could feel a warm, blinding haze of love for them in his own body, located in his chest . . . or in the base of his skull? . . . He thought of Len. A healthy, husky boy. Vicky: that cap of dark close-cropped hair, her thin arms and legs, her thin face. Len was handsomer. Golden-tanned, curly hair lighter than his father's, energetic arms and legs, a sudden smile that could break his father's heart. When he confessed to stealing a bicycle from school, years before, Matthew had been the one to break down. Unashamed to cry before his oldest son. The two of them in the basement of the house, talking quietly, a father and his son. Matthew was unashamed to cry. Unashamed.

If he cried now the tears would run down sideways, comically, on his cheeks. No need to cry. Florence did not cry. . . . One day he stood in the doorway of the bedroom, watching her at the sewing machine, the rapid tonguelike flicking of the needle, her skillful hands guiding the cloth, the rattling noise, the vibrations he could feel beneath his feet, the look of danger, of relentlessness about her bent head and narrowed, skillful eyes. . . . She had been unaware of him.

Dr. Crane was talking to him suddenly. The door stood open. Florence in the doorway, a blur. Where were the children? Dr. Crane was talking to him, asking him something, and he felt his parched lips cracking into a smile. Must smile. Must communicate. Dr. Crane was wrapping something about his upper arm,. tighter and tighter. The pressure was enormous. Matthew tried not to notice it. He must not seem too sensitive. What should he say to Dr. Crane? It was important to communicate. Communication was the first step in sales, in civilization itself. Nothing happened between people unless there was communication first. You could have a miraculous product but it would not sell itself. It would sit there, inert. The three enormous cars in the showroom—the sedan, the convertible, the station wagon—would remain there forever, unsold, unacknowledged, until they were explained to the customer. All their energy, their godliness inert for centuries! Unless they were explained, translated, sold. The product and the customer had to be brought together by a handshake and certain words, which were magical and very powerful. Each word was extremely important. . . . Last winter, when things had gone so slowly, the salemen were advised to telephone old customers: "Hello. This is ——— ——— of Overmeyer Ford. I was wondering how you are. . . ." No: "I was wondering if you might happen to be in the market for a new car this winter." No, too direct. "Hello, this is ——— ——— of Overmeyer Ford. I hope I'm not disturbing you? I was wondering. . . ." But no, it was a poor idea to apologize and to suggest that the telephone call might be a disturbance. Poor psychology. Begin again: "Hello. This is ——— ——— of Overmeyer Ford. Maybe you remember, in 19— you bought a car from me, and I was just wondering if. . . ."

Something was decided at the bedside, Dr. Crane and his wife conferring, and he felt suddenly very relieved. He would not have to explain himself tonight, then. Evidently they had decided to let him alone. He would rest. Sleep. In the morning everything would be back to normal and perhaps when he got to the agency he would come across Mr. Yates himself, that mischievous mysterious Mr. Yates!

Eleven o'clock already. One of us turned on the news. We had forgotten about the whole evening, suddenly it was eleven o'clock. Mother heated up some chicken gumbo soup from cans. Tommy looked feverish but wouldn't go to bed. Mother's face pale and lined. We will all go to bed at once, we said. All fall asleep at once. Make a vow: we will all fall asleep at the same minute.

In the morning, a peculiar stillness to the house. A foreign stillness. He woke from troubled dreams, dreams that did not belong to him. They must have been someone else's dreams, infecting him. Diseases were spread by germs, and bad dreams could be spread by germs. Why did he dream about flesh that was rosy turning to lard? About handshakes falling away to nothing, a hand coming loose in his own grip? He refused to think about these dreams. Maybe they belonged to Peter. Or Gardie. Maybe they belonged to Florence herself. They lay together at night, every night, side by side in the same bed, and between them there was an enormous distance of inches. . . . They never spoke of this distance. They would have had to shout across it. He would have had to telephone her from the agency, an impersonal voice: "Hello. Mrs. Brown? This is ——— ——— of Overmeyer Ford. I came across your name in my files and I was wondering if. . . ."

Maybe he was dreaming his wife's dreams?

But they were such ugly dreams! Himself in bed. Matthew Brown himself, still and cold in bed, wrapped up in blankets like a mummy. Ugh! How could she dream such dreams about her husband? His face flabby and old, the color drained out of it, wormy, grainy, pale, aged, no longer a handsome man, his hair plastered close to his skull. . . .

Len said to Vicky and Ronnie: "One of us better stay home today, it better be me." Ronnie agreed at once. He wanted to get out of the house. All A's at school. Father was very proud of him, but we all knew that he loved Len best. Vicky said, "I feel sick but I want to go to school. . . . I'm afraid to stay home here. . . ." "You're crazy!" Len said, reddening.

. . . Or maybe the dreams were Mr. Overmeyer's? He was a plump, big-voiced man of about five feet eight, fat grown on the outside of his body from too much drinking, alcoholic flab, soft wrinkles in the face and neck that seemed to gesticulate like Mr. Overmeyer's hands. Matthew was his best salesman. Mr. Overmeyer liked him best because Matthew did not ask for any favors. And he sold the most cars: a fact. Statistical fact. But sales were down, the economy was crazily inflated, who could pay such interest rates? . . . In the past no one noticed the interest rates, but now they did. The younger customers, college educated, scanning the figures Matthew gave them, their young foreheads wrinkling as they saw what the car would really cost. . . . "Jesus Christ," one of them whispered the other day. . . . Mr. Overmeyer lived out in Hanley Park, along the river. He had three daughters, all taller than himself.

Mr. Overmeyer came out on Saturday, four days after Father had gotten sick. Stood eye to eye with Len and shook hands gravely. "You've got to be the man of the house, until your father gets well."

"Exhaustion," someone was saying to him. "Sick leave." "Busy period." "Too much strain." It sounded like Mr. Overmeyer. But why would he be here, at Matthew's bedside? Was Florence pushing the two of them together, urging Mr. Overmeyer to get closer, to get in bed with Matthew? A crowded bed! Matthew had a sudden idea: he would telephone customers from his bed. Very simple. Gardie could bring his files over, he could prop himself up with pillows, and use the telephone. An excellent idea. He would suggest it to Mr. Overmeyer, as soon as Mr. Overmeyer stopped talking and stopped moving his hands. Why did that man always move his hands!—it marked him as common. Matthew's mother had always noted gestures that marked people as *common,* even if they had money. As soon as Mr. Overmeyer stopped talking Matthew would tell him about his plan: telephoning from bed. That way he would still be at work. It would be quite an experiment, to see how many cars he could sell like that, over the telephone. Maybe it would be written up in the *Ford Times.*

The mess in the bed. The smell. Vicky imagining she carried it with her to school. Mother had to go to a medical supply store and buy a bedpan. The youngest of us were kept out of the sickroom. We hung around downstairs and watched cartoons on television all day long. Loud enough to hear all over the house. At school, Vicky thought of that pasty face, the strange dark sockets of his eyes, the flabby lips, the raspy breathing, the bedpan emptied in the bathroom, the whispering, Mother's vague hands and eyes, the television set and the endless cartoons, the smell that was in her own clothes and wouldn't come out . . . she had to excuse herself and run to the rest room, where she was sick to her stomach for the second time that day.

Ronnie hated collection day. By now many people knew about Father: stray sly little questions, holding the money in their hands so that Ronnie couldn't escape, always asking if "things were any better at his house? . . ."

The hell with them all, Ronnie thought.

The hell with his sister Vicky puking in the bathroom.

The hell with the little kids, always giggling or bursting into tears.

The hell with Len, bossing everyone around.

The hell with Mother.

The hell with Father: let him stink.

His mother came to see him, that noble ravaged face, that harsh gray hair. She must have had some news to tell him. But he could not make sense of her words. Why didn't Florence come closer, why didn't Florence make his mother speak up? He could not make sense of her words, no. All his life he had been hearing them: *Matthew! I own you! My son!* But now they eluded him. She was only inches away. She might have come here to remind him that he was not just a father but also a son, he had been a son for forty-six years and could not escape that fact, hiding in his smelly cocoon. No. But he could not hear her. He wanted to weep: why was she leaning so close?

Mother, Len, and Vicky fed him. The doctor showed them how. The rest of us were kept downstairs. Bickering. Tommy throwing himself around. Ronnie yelled: "Goddamn you little bastards! I could kill you!" Father upstairs, drooling. The best thing to feed him, Dr. Crane said, is baby food. Why not? He did not spit the food out, but sometimes it came back out by itself.

Ronnie said: "I'm going to set that bed on fire. Get that big worm up and moving fast!" Len punched him in the chest. They wrestled together, falling back against the wall, Ronnie giggled and sucked blood from his bleeding nose and began to choke.

Sounds of battle in the distance. Beyond the range of his bed the world was in perpetual twilight and turmoil. Struggle—arguing—vibrations from angry footsteps—weeping—the ringing of the telephone. Two figures standing at the foot of his bed, speaking gravely. Was that his wife? Was that the doctor? The world was filling up with strangers, people whose names he did not know. Hands he could not shake. His customers were being taken away from him . . . perhaps his files had already been divided up among the salesmen at the agency. . . . What were these two saying, were they talking about him? He strained to hear, he tried to lift himself up on one elbow. . . .

One of us was waiting out on the verandah. Dr. Crane said: "There's nothing else to do. You'd better take this opening while you can. Yes, he did move, he seemed about to get up, but then he fell back again. . . . But it isn't enough. He's very sick." Mother stumbled over something of Tommy's on the porch. She was crying again.

Mother, why did you cry so much!—small pale rivulets worn in your cheeks—it took months of sunlight to erase them—

The doorway had widened. The whole world was trooping through it, into his room, trying to get into bed with him. Over the years the children had run in here, jumping in bed with him and Florence, what a noisy giggling bunch!—but now there were strangers coming in. They gripped him hard, skillfully. Eased him up. His body ached, his spine flashed pain. Someone was saying, "Come on. That's it. Okay. Fine. Get his feet. Hold steady."

He wondered if they would let him drive his own car. Why was he being put in the back of someone else's car? A small truck? The car he drove was not really his own, but it was given to him for his use; he always had a new car. But now his legs were strangely shortened, very limp. What had happened? Maybe if he were placed in his car, behind the wheel, he would be able to reach the accelerator and the brake. His heartbeat quickened at the thought of driving his car himself. Even if it was the last time he was allowed to drive. He was proud of that car. His sons had always been proud of the new cars he drove, because their friends' fathers did not have such expensive cars. Would they think of letting him drive, would they be that kind? Or would he have to request this favor himself?

We all watched. The stretcher, the blankets still wrapped around him, that face. Tommy, who hadn't seen him for a while, screamed: "That's not Daddy!" Len helped the attendants with the stretcher. Mother had to get out of the way, she looked vague and confused, as if she were having difficulty making sense of the scene before her.

The ambulance was driven away like an ordinary car. No siren, no red light. Down to the end of our street and onto Claremont Boulevard and out of sight. It did not seem right that Father should be taken away so quietly.

We kept waking up at night. Was somebody in the room? In bed with us? We kept running in to Mother, Tommy and Sally especially. Tommy screamed until his eyes filled up with blood. Wanted to kick at the rest of us. He pounded at his own face with his fists. Mother took him in with her every night, in the new bed. Everything new about it: a shiny smooth headboard, a new mattress, new pillows, new box springs, new sheets. Even there Tommy would wake up, frightened. "Was somebody here in bed?" Mother said, "No." "Wasn't there somebody?" Tommy cried. Mother said, "No."

One day one of us came home from school and couldn't find Mother. He walked through the house calling, "Mother? . . ." and then saw her out the back window. He ran out, back to the fence. Mother was digging in the weeds. A hot weedy garden, the smell of earth and sunlight and plants and Mother's warm dress, all yellow and purple streaks. . . .

"Mother? Mother?" She let the hoe fall back against the fence and opened her arms for an embrace.

DONALD BARTHELME

City Life

I

Elsa and Ramona entered the complicated city. They found an apartment without much trouble, several rooms on Porter Street. Curtains were hung. Bright paper things from a Japanese store were placed here and there.

—You'd better tell Charles that he can't come see us until everything is ready.

Ramona thought: I don't want him to come at all. He will go into a room with Elsa and close the door. I will be sitting outside reading the business news. Britain Weighs Economic Curbs. Bond Rate Surge Looms. Time will pass. Then, they will emerge. Acting as if nothing had happened. Elsa will make coffee. Charles will put brandy from his flat silver flask into the coffee. We will all drink the coffee with the brandy in it. Ugh!

—Where shall we put the telephone books?

—Put them over there, by the telephone.

Elsa and Ramona went to the $2 plant store. A man stood outside selling individual peacock feathers. Elsa and Ramona bought several hanging plants in white plastic pots. The proprietor put the plants in brown paper bags.

—Water them every day, girls. Keep them wet.

—We will.

Elsa uttered a melancholy reflection on life: It goes faster and faster! Ramona said: It's so difficult!

Charles accepted a position with greater responsibilities in another city.

—I'll be able to get in on weekends sometimes.

—Is this a real job?

—Of course, Elsa. You don't think I'd fool you, do you?

Clad in an extremely dark gray, if not completely black, suit, he had shaved his mustache.

—This outfit doesn't let you wear them.

Ramona heard Elsa sobbing in the back bedroom. I suppose I should sympathize with her. But I don't.

II

Ramona received the following letter from Charles:

Dear Ramona—

Thank you, Ramona, for your interesting and curious letter. It is true that I have noticed you sitting there, in the living room, when I visit Elsa. I have many times made mental notes about your appearance, which I consider in no way inferior to that of Elsa herself. I get a pretty electric reaction to your taste in clothes, too. Those upper legs have not been lost on me. But the trouble is, when two girls are living together, one must make a choice. One can't have them both, in our society. This prohibition is enforced by you girls, chiefly, together with older ladies, who if the truth were known probably don't care, but nevertheless feel that standards must be upheld, somewhere. I have Elsa, therefore I can't have you. (I know that there is a philosophical problem about "being" and "having" but I can't discuss that now because I'm a little rushed due to the pressures of my new assignment.) So that's what obtains at the moment, most excellent Ramona. That's where we stand. Of course the future may be different. It not infrequently is.

Hastily,
Charles.

—What are you reading?
—Oh, it's just a letter.
—Who is it from?
—Oh, just somebody I know.
—Who?
—Oh, nobody.
—Oh.

Ramona's mother and father came to town from Montana. Ramona's thin father stood on the Porter Street sidewalk wearing a business suit and a white cowboy hat. He was watching his car. He watched from the steps of the house for a while, and then watched from the sidewalk a little, and then watched from the steps again. Ramona's mother looked in the suitcases for the present she had brought.

—Mother! You shouldn't have bought me such an expensive present!

—Oh, it wasn't all that expensive. We wanted you to have something for the new apartment.

—An original gravure by René Magritte!

—Well, it isn't very big. It's just a small one.

Whenever Ramona received a letter forwarded to her from her Montana home, the letter had been opened and the words "Oops! Opened by mistake!" written on the envelope. But she forgot that in gazing at the handsome new Magritte print, a picture of a tree with a crescent moon cut out of it.

—It's fantastically beautiful! Where shall we hang it?

—How about on the wall?

III

At the University the two girls enrolled in the Law School.

—I hear the Law School's tough, Elsa stated, but that's what we want, a tough challenge.

—You are the only two girls ever to be admitted to our Law School, the Dean observed. Mostly, we have men. A few foreigners. Now I am going to tell you three things to keep an eye on: 1) Don't try to go too far too fast. 2) Wear plain clothes. And 3) Keep your notes clean. And if I hear the words "Yoo hoo" echoing across the quadrangle, you will be sent down instantly. We don't use those words in this school.

—I like what I already know, Ramona said under her breath.

Savoring their matriculation, the two girls wandered out to sample the joys of Pascin Street. They were closer together at this time than they had ever been. Of course, they didn't want to get too close together. They were afraid to get too close together.

Elsa met Jacques. He was deeply involved in the struggle.

—What is this struggle about, exactly, Jacques?

—My God, Elsa, your eyes! I have never seen that shade of umber in anyone's eyes before. Ever.

Jacques took Elsa to a Mexican restaurant. Elsa cut into her *cabrito con queso.*

—To think that this food was once a baby goat!

Elsa, Ramona, and Jacques looked at the dawn coming up over the hanging plants. Patterns of silver light and so forth.

—You're not afraid that Charles will bust in here unexpectedly and find us?

—Charles is in Cleveland. Besides, I'd say you were with Ramona. Elsa giggled.

Ramona burst into tears.

Elsa and Jacques tried to comfort Ramona.

—Why don't you take a 21-day excursion-fare trip to "preserves of nature"?

—If I went to a "preserve of nature," it would turn out to be nothing but a terrible fen!

Ramona thought: He will go into a room with Elsa and close the door. Time will pass. Then they will emerge, acting as if nothing had happened. Then the coffee. Ugh!

IV

Charles in Cleveland.

"Whiteness"

"Vital skepticism"

Charles advanced very rapidly in the Cleveland hierarchy. That sort of situation that develops sometimes wherein managers feel threatened by gifted subordinates and do not assign them really meaningful duties but instead shunt them aside into dead areas where their human potential is wasted did not develop in Charles' case. His devoted heart lifted him to the highest levels. It was Charles who pointed out that certain operations had been carried out more efficiently "when the cathedrals were white," and in time the entire Cleveland structure was organized around his notions: "whiteness," "vital skepticism."

Two men held Charles down on the floor and a third slipped a needle into his hip.

He awakened in a vaguely familiar room.

—Where am I? he asked the nurselike person who appeared to answer his ring.

—Porter Street, this creature said. Mlle. Ramona will see you shortly. In the meantime, drink some of this orange juice.

Well, Charles thought to himself, I cannot but admire the guts and address of this brave girl, who wanted me so much that she engineered this whole affair—my abduction from Cleveland and removal to these beloved rooms, where once I was entertained by the beautiful Elsa. And now I must see whether my key concepts can get me out of this "fix," for "fix" it is. I shouldn't have written that letter. Perhaps if I wrote another letter? A followup?

Charles formed the letter to Ramona in his mind.

Dear Ramona—

Now that I am back in your house, tied down to this bed with these steel bands around my ankles, I understand that perhaps my earlier letter to you was subject to misinterpretation etc. etc.

Elsa entered the room and saw Charles tied down on the bed.

—That's against the law!

—Sit down, Elsa. Just because you are a law student you want to proclaim the rule of law everywhere. But some things don't have to do with the law. Some things have to do with the heart. The heart, which was our great emblem and cockade, when the cathedrals were white.

—I'm worried about Ramona, Elsa said. She has been missing lectures. And she has been engaging in hilarity at the expense of the law.

—Jokes?

—Gibes. And now this extra-legality. Your sequestration.

Charles and Elsa looked out of the window at the good day.

—See that blue in the sky. How wonderful. After all the gray we've had.

V

Elsa and Ramona watched the Motorola television set in their pajamas.

—What else is on? Elsa asked.

Ramona looked in the newspaper.

—On 7 there's "Johnny Allegro" with George Raft and Nina Foch. On 9 "Johnny Angel" with George Raft and Claire Trevor. On 11 there's "Johnny Apollo" with Tyrone Power and Dorothy Lamour. On 13 is "Johnny Concho" with Frank Sinatra and Phyllis Kirk. On 2 is "Johnny Dark" with Tony Curtis and Piper Laurie. On 4 is "Johnny Eager" with Robert Taylor and Lana Turner. On 5 is "Johnny O'Clock" with Dick Powell and Evelyn Keyes. On 31 is "Johnny Trouble" with Stuart Whitman and Ethel Barrymore.

—What's this one we're watching?

—What time is it?

—Eleven-thirty-five.

—"Johnny Guitar" with Joan Crawford and Sterling Hayden.

VI

Jacques, Elsa, Charles and Ramona sat in a row at the sun dance. Jacques was sitting next to Elsa and Charles was sitting next to Ramona. Of course Charles was also sitting next to Elsa but he was leaning toward Ramona mostly. It was hard to tell what his intentions were. He kept his hands in his pockets.

—How is the struggle coming, Jacques?

—Quite well, actually. Since the Declaration of Rye we have accumulated many hundreds of new members.

Elsa leaned across Charles to say something to Ramona.

—Did you water the plants?

The sun dancers were beating the ground with sheaves of wheat.

—Is that supposed to make the sun shine, or what? Ramona asked.

—Oh, I think it's just sort of to . . . honor the sun. I don't think it's supposed to make it do anything.

Elsa stood up.

—That's against the law!

—Sit down, Elsa.

Elsa became pregnant.

VII

"This young man, a man though only eighteen . . ."

A large wedding scene

Charles measures the church

Elsa and Jacques bombarded with flowers

Fathers and mothers riding on the city railway

The minister raises his hands

Evacuation of the sacristy: bomb threat

Black limousines with ribbons tied to their aerials

Several men on balconies who appear to be signalling, or applauding

Traffic lights

Pieces of blue cake

Champagne

VIII

—Well, Ramona, I am glad we came to the city. In spite of everything.

—Yes, Elsa, it has turned out well for you. You are Mrs. Jacques Tope now. And soon there will be a little one.

—Not so soon. Not for eight months. I am sorry, though, about one thing. I hate to give up Law School.

—Don't be sorry. The Law needs knowledgeable civilians as well as practitioners. Your training will not be wasted.

—That's dear of you. Well, goodbye.

Elsa and Jacques and Charles went into the back bedroom. Ramona remained outside with the newspaper.

—Well, I suppose I might as well put the coffee on, she said to herself. Rats!

IX

Laughing aristocrats moved up and down the corridors of the city.

Elsa, Jacques, Ramona and Charles drove out to the combined race track and art gallery. Ramona had a Heineken and everyone else had one too. The tables were crowded with laughing aristocrats. More laughing aristocrats arrived in their carriages drawn by dancing matched pairs. Some drifted in from Flushing and São Paulo. Management of the funded indebtedness was discussed;

the Queen's behavior was discussed. All of the horses ran very well, and the pictures ran well too. The laughing aristocrats sucked on the heads of their gold-headed canes some more.

Jacques held up his degrees from the New Yorker Theatre, where he had been buried in the classics, when he was twelve.

—I remember the glorious debris underneath the seats, he said, and I remember that I hated then, as I do now, laughing aristocrats.

The aristocrats heard Jacques talking. They all raised their canes in the air, in rage. A hundred canes shattered in the sun, like a load of antihistamines falling out of an airplane. More laughing aristocrats arrived in phaetons and tumbrels.

As a result of absenting himself from Cleveland for eight months, Charles had lost his position there.

—It is true that I am part of the laughing-aristocrat structure, Charles said. I don't mean I am one of them. I mean I am their creature. They hold me in thrall.

Laughing aristocrats who invented the cost-plus contract . . .

Laughing aristocrats who invented the real estate broker . . .

Laughing aristocrats who invented Formica . . .

Laughing aristocrats wiping their surfaces clean with a damp cloth . . .

Charles poured himself another brilliant green Heineken.

—To the struggle!

x

The Puerto Rican painters have come, as they do every three years, to paint the apartment!

The painters, Emmanuel and Curtis, heaved their buckets, rollers, ladders and drop cloths up the stairs into the apartment.

—What shade of white do you want this apartment painted?

A consultation.

—How about plain white?

—Fine, Emmanuel said. That's a mighty good-looking Motorola television set you have there. Would you turn it to Channel 47, *por favor?* There's a film we'd like to see. We can paint and watch at the same time.

—What's the film?

—"Victimas de Pecado," with Pedro Vargas and Ninon Sevilla.

Elsa spoke to her husband, Jacques.

—Ramona has frightened me.

—How?

—She said one couldn't sleep with someone more than four hundred times without being bored.

—How does she know?

—She saw it in a book.

—Well, Jacques said, we only do what we really want to do about 11 per cent of the time. In our lives.

—11 per cent!

At the Ingres Gardens, the great singer Moonbelly sang a song of rage.

XI

Vercingetorix, leader of the firemen, reached for his red telephone.

—Hello, is this Ramona?

—No, this is Elsa. Ramona's not home.

—Will you tell her that the leader of all the firemen called?

Ramona went out of town for a weekend with Vercingetorix. They went to his farm, about eighty miles away. In the kitchen of the farm, bats attacked them. Vercingetorix could not find his broom.

—Put a paper bag over them. Where is a paper bag?

—The groceries, Vercingetorix said.

Ramona dumped the groceries on the floor. The bats were zooming around the room uttering audible squeaks. With the large paper bag in his hands Vercingetorix made weak capturing gestures toward the bats.

—God, if one gets in my hair, Ramona said.

—They don't want to fly into the bag, Vercingetorix said.

—Give me the bag, if one gets in my hair I'll croak right here in front of you.

Ramona put the paper bag over her head just as a bat banged into her.

—What was that?

—A bat, Vercingetorix said, but it didn't get into your hair.

—Damn you, Ramona said, inside the bag, why can't you stay in the city like other men?

Moonbelly emerged from the bushes and covered her arms with kisses.

XII

Jacques persuaded Moonbelly to appear at a benefit for the signers of the Declaration of Rye, who were having a little legal trouble. Three hundred younger people sat in the church. Paper plates were passed up and down the rows. A number of quarters were collected.

Moonbelly sang a new song called "The System Cannot Withstand Close Scrutiny."

The system cannot withstand close scrutiny
The system cannot withstand close scrutiny
The system cannot withstand close scrutiny
The system cannot withstand close scrutiny
Etc.

Jacques spoke briefly and well. A few more quarters showered down on the stage.

At the party after the benefit Ramona spoke to Jacques, because he was handsome and flushed with triumph.

—Tell me something.

—All right Ramona what do you want to know?

—Do you promise to tell me the truth?

—Of course. Sure.

—Can one be impregnated by a song?

—I think not. I would say no.

—While one is asleep, possibly?

—It's not very likely.

—What sort of people have hysterical pregnancies?

—Well, you know. Sort of nervous girls.

—If a hysterical pregnancy results in a birth, is it still considered hysterical?

—No.

—Rats!

XIII

Charles and Jacques were trying to move a parked Volkswagen. When a Volkswagen is parked with its parking brake set you need three people to move it, usually.

A third person was sighted moving down the street.

—Say, buddy, could you give us a hand for a minute?

—Sure, the third person said.

Charles, Jacques, and the third person grasped the VW firmly in their hands and heaved. It moved forward opening up a new parking space where only half a space had been before.

—Thanks, Jacques said. Now would you mind helping us unload this panel truck here? It contains printed materials pertaining to the worldwide struggle for liberation from outmoded ways of thought that hold us in thrall.

—I don't mind.

Charles, Jacques, and Hector carried the bundles of printed material up the stairs into the Porter Street apartment.

—What does this printed material say, Jacques?

—It says that the government has promised to give us some of our money back if it loses the war.

—Is that true?

—No. And now, how about a drink?

Drinking their drinks they regarded the black trombone case which rested under Hector's coat.

—Is that a trombone case?

Hector's eyes glazed.

Moonbelly sat on the couch, his great belly covered with plants and animals.

—It's good to be what one is, he said.

XIV

Ramona's child was born on Wednesday. It was a boy.

—But Ramona! Who is responsible? Charles? Jacques? Moonbelly? Vercingetorix?

—It was a virgin birth, unfortunately, Ramona said.

—But what does this imply about the child?

—Nothing, Ramona said. It was just an ordinary virgin birth. Don't bother your pretty head about it, Elsa dear.

However much Ramona tried to soft-pedal the virgin birth, people persisted in getting excited about it. A few cardinals from the Sacred Rota dropped by.

—What is this you're claiming here, foolish girl?

—I claim nothing, Your Eminence. I merely report.

—Give us the name of the man who has compromised you!

—It was a virgin birth, sir.

Cardinal Maranto frowned in several directions.

—There can't be another Virgin Birth!

Ramona modestly lowered her eyes. The child, Sam, was wrapped in a blanket with his feet sticking out.

—Better cover those feet.

—Thank you, Cardinal. I will.

XV

Ramona went to class at the Law School carrying Sam on her hip in a sling.

—What's that?

—My child.

—I didn't know you were married.

—I'm not.

—That's against the law! I think.

—What law is it against?

The entire class regarded the teacher.

—Well there is a law against fornication on the books, but of course it's not enforced very often ha ha. It's sort of difficult to enforce ha ha.

—I have to tell you, Ramona said, that this child is not of human man conceived. It was a virgin birth. Unfortunately.

A few waves of smickers washed across the classroom.

A law student named Harold leaped to his feet.

—Stop this smickering! What are we thinking of? To make mock of this fine girl! Rot me if I will permit it! Are we gentlemen? Is this lady our colleague? Or are we rather beasts of the field? This Ramona, this trull . . . No, that's not what I mean. I mean that we should think not upon her peculations but on our own peculations. For, as Augustine tells us, if for some error or sin of our own, sadness seizes us, let us not only bear in mind that an afflicted spirit is a sacrifice to God but also the words: for as water quencheth a flaming fire, so almsgiving quencheth sin; and for I desire, He says, mercy rather than sacrifice. As, therefore, if we were in danger from fire, we should, of course, run for water with which to extinguish it, and should be thankful if someone showed us water nearby, so if some flame of sin has arisen from the hay of our passions, we should take delight in this, that the ground for a work of great mercy is given to us. Therefore—

Harold collapsed, from the heat of his imagination.

A student in a neighboring seat looked deeply into Sam's eyes.

—They're brown.

XVI

Moonbelly was fingering his axe.

—A birth hymn? Do I really want to write a birth hymn?

—What do I really think about this damn birth?

—Of course it's within the tradition.

—Is this the real purpose of cities? Is this why all these units have been brought together, under the red, white and blue?

—Cities are erotic, in a depressing way. Should that be my line?

—Of course I usually do best with something in the rage line. However—

—C . . . F . . . C . . . F . . . C . . . F . . . G7 . . .

Moonbelly wrote "Cities Are Centers of Copulation."

The recording company official handed Moonbelly a gold record marking the sale of a million copies of "Cities Are Centers of Copulation."

XVII

Charles and Jacques were still talking to Hector Guimard, the former trombone player.

—Yours is not a modern problem, Jacques said. The problem today is not angst but lack of angst.

—Wait a minute, Jacques. Although I myself believe that there is nothing wrong with being a trombone player, I can understand Hector's feeling. I know a painter who feels the same way about being a painter. Every morning he gets up, brushes his teeth, and stands before the empty canvas. A terrible feeling of being *de trop* comes over him. So he goes to the corner and buys the Times, at the corner newsstand. He comes back home and reads the Times. During the period in which he's coupled with the Times he is all right. But soon the Times is exhausted. The empty canvas remains. So (usually) he makes a mark on it, some kind of mark that is not what he means. That is, any old mark, just to have something on the canvas. Then he is profoundly depressed because what is there is not what he meant. And it's time for lunch. He goes out and buys a pastrami sandwich at the deli. He comes back and eats the sandwich meanwhile regarding the canvas with the wrong mark on it out of the corner of his eye. During the afternoon, he paints out the mark of the morning. This affords him a measure of satisfaction. The balance of the afternoon is spent in deciding whether or not to venture another mark. The new mark, if one is ventured, will also, inevitably, be misconceived. He ventures it. It is misconceived. It is, in fact, the worst kind of vulgarity. He paints out the second mark. Anxiety accumulates. However, the canvas is now, in and of itself, because of the wrong moves and the painting out, becoming rather interesting-looking. He goes to the A. & P. and buys a TV Mexican dinner and many bottles of Carta Blanca. He comes back to his loft and eats the Mexican dinner and drinks a couple of Carta Blancas, sitting in front of his canvas. The canvas is, for one thing, no longer empty. Friends drop in and congratulate him on having a not-empty canvas. He begins feeling better. A something has been wrested from the nothing. The quality of the something is still at issue —he is by no means home free. And of course all of painting—the whole art —has moved on somewhere else, it's not where his head is, and he knows that, but nevertheless he—

—How does this apply to trombone playing? Hector asked.

—I had the connection in my mind when I began, Charles said.

—As Goethe said, theory is gray, but the golden tree of life is green.

XVIII

Everybody in the city was watching a movie about an Indian village menaced by a tiger. Only Wendell Corey stood between the village and the tiger. Furthermore Wendell Corey had dropped his rifle—or rather the tiger had knocked it out of his hands—and was left with only his knife. In addition, the tiger had Wendell Corey's left arm in his mouth up to the shoulder.

Ramona thought about the city.

—I have to admit we are locked in the most exquisite mysterious muck. This muck heaves and palpitates. It is multi-directional and has a mayor. To describe it takes many hundreds of thousands of words. Our muck is only a part of a much greater muck—the nation-state—which is itself the creation of that muck of mucks, human consciousness. Of course all these things also have a touch of sublimity—as when Moonbelly sings, for example, or all the lights go out. What a happy time that was, when all the electricity went away! If only we could re-create that paradise! By, for instance, all forgetting to pay our electric bills at the same time. All nine million of us. Then we'd all get those little notices that say unless we remit within five days the lights will go out. We all stand up from our chairs with the notice in our hands. The same thought drifts across the furrowed surface of nine million minds. We wink at each other, through the walls.

At the Electric Company, a nervousness appeared as Ramona's thought launched itself into parapsychological space.

Ramona arranged names in various patterns.

Vercingetorix
Moonbelly
Charles

Moonbelly
Charles
Vercingetorix

Charles
Vercingetorix
Moonbelly

—Upon me, their glance has fallen. The engendering force was, perhaps, the fused glance of all of them. From the millions of units crawling about on the surface of the city, their wavering desirous eyes selected me. The pupil enlarged to admit more light: more me. They began dancing little dances of suggestion and fear. These dances constitute an invitation of unmistakable import—an invitation which, if accepted, leads one down many muddy roads. I accepted. What was the alternative?

JOHN BARTH

Lost in the Funhouse

For whom is the funhouse fun? Perhaps for lovers. For Ambrose it is *a place of fear and confusion.* He has come to the seashore with his family for the holiday, *the occasion of their visit is Independence Day, the most important secular holiday of the United States of America.* A single straight underline is the manuscript mark for italic type, *which in turn* is the printed equivalent to oral emphasis of words and phrases as well as the customary type for titles of complete works, not to mention. Italics are also employed, in fiction-stories especially, for "outside," intrusive, or artificial voices, such as radio announcements, the texts of telegrams and newspaper articles, *et cetera.* They should be used *sparingly.* If passages originally in roman type are italicized by someone repeating them, it's customary to acknowledge the fact. *Italics mine.*

Ambrose was "at that awkward age." His voice came out high-pitched as a child's if he let himself get carried away; to be on the safe side, therefore, he moved and spoke with *deliberate calm* and *adult gravity.* Talking soberly of unimportant or irrelevant matters and listening consciously to the sound of your own voice are useful habits for maintaining control in this difficult interval. *En route* to Ocean City he sat in the back seat of the family car with his brother, Peter, age fifteen, and Magda G——, age fourteen, a pretty girl an exquisite young lady, who lived not far from them on B—— Street in the town of D——, Maryland. Initials, blanks, or both were often substituted for proper names in nineteenth-century fiction to enhance the illusion of reality. It is as if the author felt it necessary to delete the names for reasons of tact or legal liability. Interestingly, as with other aspects of realism, it is an *illusion* that is being enhanced, by purely artificial means. Is it likely, does it violate the principle of verisimilitude, that a thirteen-year-old boy could make such a sophisticated observation? A girl of fourteen is *the psychological coeval* of a boy of fifteen or sixteen; a thirteen-year-old boy, therefore, even one precocious in some other respects, might be three years *her emotional junior.*

Thrice a year—on Memorial, Independence, and Labor Days—the family visits Ocean City for the afternoon and evening. When Ambrose and Peter's father was their age the excursion was made by train, as mentioned in the novel *The 42nd Parallel* by John Dos Passos. Many families from the same neighborhood used to travel together, with dependent relatives and often with Negro servants; schoolfuls of children swarmed through the railway cars; everyone shared everyone else's Maryland fried chicken, Virginia ham, deviled eggs, potato salad, beaten biscuits, iced tea. Nowadays (that is, in 19——, the year of our story) the journey is made by automobile—more comfortably and quickly though without the extra fun though without the *camaraderie* of a general excursion. It's all part of the deterioration of American life, their father declares; Uncle Karl supposes that when the boys take *their* families to Ocean City for the holidays, they'll fly in Autogiros. Their mother, sitting in the middle of the front seat like Magda in the second, only with her arms on the seat-back behind the men's shoulders, wouldn't want the good old days back again, the steaming trains and stuffy long dresses; on the other hand, she can do without Autogiros, too, if she has to become a grandmother to fly in them.

Description of physical appearance and mannerisms is one of several standard methods of characterization used by writers of fiction. It is also important to "keep the senses operating"; when a detail from one of the five senses, say visual, is "crossed" with a detail from another, say auditory, the reader's imagination is oriented to the scene, perhaps unconsciously. This procedure may be compared to the way surveyors and navigators determine their positions by two or more compass-bearings, a process known as triangulation. The brown hair on Ambrose's mother's forearms gleamed in the sunlight. Though right-handed, she took her left arm from the seat-back to press the dashboard cigar-lighter for Uncle Karl. When the glass bead in its handle glowed red, the lighter was ready for use. The smell of Uncle Karl's cigar-smoke reminded one of. The fragance of the ocean came strong to the picnic-ground where they always stopped for lunch, two miles inland from Ocean City. Having to pause for a full hour almost within sound of the breakers was difficult for Peter and Ambrose when they were younger; even at their present age it was not easy to keep their anticipation, *stimulated by the briny spume*, from turning into short temper. The Irish author James Joyce, in his unusual novel entitled *Ulysses*, now available in this country, uses the adjectives *snot-green* and *scrotum-tightening* to describe the sea. Visual, auditory, tactile, olfactory, gustatory. Peter and Ambrose's father, while steering their black 1936 LaSalle sedan with one hand, could with the other remove the first cigarette from a white pack of Lucky Strikes and, more remarkably, light it with a match forefingered from its book and thumbed against the flint-paper without being detached. The matchbook cover merely advertised U.S. War Bonds and Stamps. A fine metaphor, simile, or other figure of speech, in addition to its obvious "first-order" relevance to the thing it describes, will be seen upon reflection to have a second order of significance: it may be drawn from the *milieu* of the action, for example, or be particularly appropriate to the sensibility of the narrator, even hinting to the reader things of which the narrator is unaware; or it may cast further and subtler lights upon the thing it describes, sometimes ironically qualifying the more evident sense of the comparison.

To say that Ambrose and Peter's mother was *pretty* is to accomplish nothing; the reader may acknowledge the proposition, but his imagination is not engaged. Besides, Magda was pretty, yet in an altogether different way. Although she lived on B—— Street, she had very good manners and did better than average in school. Her figure was very well developed for her age. Her right hand lay casually on the plush upholstery of the seat, very near Ambrose's left leg, on which his own hand rested. The space between their legs, between her right and his left leg, was out of the line of sight of anyone sitting on the other side of Magda, as well as anyone glancing into the rearview mirror. Uncle Karl's face resembled Peter's—rather, vice versa. Both had dark hair and eyes, short husky statures, deep voices. Magda's left hand was probably in a similar position on her left side. The boy's father is difficult to describe; no particular feature of his appearance or manner stood out. He wore glasses and taught English in the T—— County High School. Uncle Karl was a masonry contractor.

Although Peter must have known as well as Ambrose that the latter, because of his position in the car, would be the first to see the electrical towers of the power plant at V——, the halfway point of their trip, he leaned forward and slightly toward the center of the car and pretended to be looking for them through the flat pinewoods and tuckahoe creeks along the highways. For as long as the boys could remember, "looking for the Towers" had been a feature of the first half of their excursions to Ocean City, "looking for the standpipe" of the second. Though the game was childish, their mother preserved the tradition of rewarding the first to see the Towers with a candybar or piece of fruit. She insisted now that Magda play the game; the prize, she said, was "something hard to get nowadays." Ambrose decided not to join in; he sat back in his seat. Magda, like Peter, leaned forward. Two sets of straps were discernible through the shoulders of her sun-dress; the inside right one, a brassiere-strap, was fastened or shortened with a small safety-pin. The right armpit of her dress, presumably the left as well, was damp with perspiration. The simple strategy for being first to espy the Towers, which Ambrose had understood by the age of four, was to sit on the right-hand side of the car. Whoever sat there, however, had also to put up with the worst of the sun, and so Ambrose, without mentioning the matter, chose sometimes the one and sometimes the other. Not impossibly, Peter had never caught on to the trick, or thought that his brother hadn't, simply because Ambrose on occasion preferred shade to a Baby Ruth or tangerine.

The shade-sun situation didn't apply to the front seat, owing to the windshield; if anything the driver got more sun, since the person on the passenger side not only was shaded below by the door and dashboard but might swing down his sun visor all the way too.

"Is that them?" Magda asked. Ambrose's mother teased the boys for letting Magda win, insinuating that "somebody [had] a girlfriend." Peter and Ambrose's father reached a long thin arm across their mother to butt his cigarette in the dashboard ashtray, under the lighter. The prize this time for seeing the Towers first was a banana. Their mother bestowed it after chiding their father for wasting a half-smoked cigarette when everything was so scarce. Magda, to take the prize, moved her hand from so near Ambrose's that he could have touched it as though accidentally. She offered to share the prize, things like that were so hard to find; but everyone insisted it was hers alone. Ambrose's mother sang an iambic trimeter couplet from a popular song, femininely rhymed:

What's good is in the Army;
What's left will never harm me.

Uncle Karl tapped his cigar-ash out the ventilator window; some particles were sucked by the slip-stream back into the car through the rear window on the passenger side. Magda demonstrated her ability to hold a banana in one hand and peel it with her teeth. She still sat forward; Ambrose pushed his glasses back onto the bridge of his nose with his left hand, which he then negligently let fall to the seat-cushion immediately behind her. He even permitted the single hair, gold, on the second joint of his thumb to brush the fabric of her skirt. Should she have sat back at that instant, his hand would have been caught under her.

Plush upholstery prickles uncomfortably through gabardine slacks in the July sun. The function of the *beginning* of the story is to introduce the principal characters, establish their initial relationships, set the scene for the main action, expose the background of the situation if necessary, plant motifs and foreshadowings where appropriate, and initiate the first complication or whatever of the "rising action." Actually, if one imagines a story called "The Funhouse," or "Lost in the Funhouse," the details of the drive to Ocean City don't seem especially relevant. The *beginning* should recount the events between Ambrose's first sight of the funhouse early in the afternoon and his entering it with Magda and Peter in the evening. The *middle* would narrate all relevant events from the time he goes in to the time he loses his way; middles have the double and contradictory function of delaying the climax while at the same time preparing the reader for it and fetching him to it. Then the *ending* would tell what Ambrose does while he's lost, how he finally finds his way out, and what everybody makes of the experience. So far there's been no real dialogue, very little sensory detail, and nothing in the way of a *theme*. And a long time has gone by already without anything happening; it makes a person wonder. We haven't even reached Ocean City yet: we will never get out of the funhoue.

The more closely an author identifies with the narrator, literally or metaphorically, the less advisable it is as a rule to use the first-person narrative viewpoint. Once five years previously the three young people *aforementioned* played Niggers and Masters in the backyard; when it was Ambrose's turn to be Master and theirs to be Niggers, Peter had to go serve his evening papers; Ambrose was afraid to punish Magda alone, but she led him to the whitewashed Torture Chamber between the woodshed and the privy in the Slaves Quarters; there she knelt sweating among bamboo rakes and dusty mason jars, pleadingly embraced his knees, and while bumblebees droned in the lattice as if on an ordinary summer afternoon, purchased clemency at a surprising price set by herself. Doubtless she remembered nothing of this event; Ambrose on the other hand seemed unable to forget the least detail of his life. He even recalled how, standing beside himself with awed impersonality in the reeky heat, he'd stared the while at an empty cigar-box in which Uncle Karl kept stonecutting chisels: beneath the words *El Producto,* a laureled, loose-toga'd lady regarded the sea from a marble bench; beside her, forgotten or not yet turned to, was a five-stringed lute. Her chin reposed on the back of her right hand; her left depended negligently from the bench-arm. The lower half of scene and lady was peeled away; the words EXAMINED BY —— were inked there into the wood. Nowadays cigar-boxes are made of pasteboard. Ambrose wondered what Magda would have done, Ambrose wondered what Magda would do when she sat back on his hand as he resolved she should. Be angry. Make a teasing joke of it. Give no sign at all. For a long time she leaned forward, playing cow-poker with Peter against Uncle Karl and Mother and watching for the first sign of Ocean City. At nearly the same instant picnic-ground and Ocean-City standpipe hove into view; an Amoco filling station on their side of the road cost Mother and Uncle Karl fifty cows and the game; Magda bounced back, clapping her right hand on Mother's right arm; Ambrose moved clear "in the nick of time."

At this rate our hero, at this rate our protagonist will remain in the funhouse forever. Narrative ordinarily consists of alternating dramatization and summarization. One symptom of nervous tension, paradoxically, is repeated and violent yawning; neither Peter nor Magda nor Uncle Karl nor Mother reacted in this manner. Although they were no longer small children, Peter and Ambrose were each given a dollar to spend on boardwalk amusements in addition to what money of their own they'd brought along. Magda too, though she protested she had ample spending money. The boys' mother made a little scene out of distributing the bills; she pretended that her sons and Magda were small children and cautioned them not to spend the sum too quickly or in one place. Magda promised with a merry laugh, and having both hands free, took the bill with her left. Peter laughed also and pledged in a falsetto to be a good boy. His imitation of a child was not clever. The boys' father was tall and thin, balding, fair-complexioned. Assertions of that sort are not effective; the reader may acknowledge the proposition, but. We should be much farther along than we are; something has gone wrong; not much of this preliminary rambling seems relevant. Yet everyone begins in the same place; how is it that most go along without difficulty but a few lose their way?

"Stay out from under the boardwalk," Uncle Karl growled from the side of his mouth. The boys' mother pushed his shoulder *in mock annoyance*. They were all standing before Fat May the Laughing Lady, who advertised the funhouse. Larger than life, Fat May mechanically shook, rocked on her heels, slapped her thighs while recorded laughter—uproarious, female—came amplified from a hidden loudspeaker. It chuckled, wheezed, wept; tried in vain to catch its breath; tittered, groaned, exploded raucous and anew. You couldn't hear it without laughing yourself, no matter how you felt. Father came back from talking to a Coast-Guardsman on duty and reported that the surf was spoiled with crude oil from tankers recently torpedoed offshore. Lumps of it, difficult to remove, made tarry tidelines on the beach and stuck on swimmers. Many bathed in the surf nevertheless and came out speckled; others paid to use a municipal pool and only sunbathed on the beach. We would do the latter. We would do the latter. We would do the latter.

Under the boardwalk, cold sand littered with cigar-butts, treasured with cigarette-stubs, Coco-Cola caps, cardboard lollipop-sticks, matchbook-covers warning that A Slip of the Lip Can Sink a Ship, grainy other things. What is the story's point? Ambrose is ill. He perspires in the dark passages; candied apples-on-a-stick, delicious-looking, disappointing to eat. Funhouses need men's and ladies' rooms at intervals.

Magda's teeth. She *was* left-handed. Perspiration. They've gone all the way, through, Magda and Peter, they've been waiting for hours with Mother and Uncle Karl while Father searches for his lost son; they draw french-fried potatoes from a paper cup and shake their heads. They've named the children they'll one day have and bring to Ocean City on holidays. Can spermatozoa properly be thought of as male animalcules when there are no female spermatozoa? They grope through hot dark windings, past Love's Tunnel's fearsome obstacles. Some perhaps lose their way.

Peter suggested then and there that they do the funhouse; he had been through it before, so had Magda, Ambrose hadn't and suggested, his voice cracking on account of Fat May's laughter, that they swim first. All were chuckling, couldn't help it; Ambrose's father, Ambrose and Peter's father came up grinning like a lunatic with two boxes of syrup-coated popcorn, one for Mother, one for Magda; the men were to help themselves. Ambrose walked on Magda's right; being by nature left-handed, she carried the box in her left hand. Up front the situation was reversed.

"What are you limping for?" Magda inquired of Ambrose. He supposed in a husky tone that his foot had gone to sleep in the car. Her teeth flashed. "Pins and needles?" It was the honeysuckle on the lattice of the former privy that drew the bees. Imagine being stung there. How long is this going to take?

The adults decided to forgo the pool, but Uncle Karl insisted they change into swimsuits and do the beach. "He wants to watch the pretty girls," Peter teased, and ducked behind Magda from Uncle Karl's pretended wrath. "You've got all the pretty girls you need right here," Magda declared, and Mother said: "Now that's the gospel truth." Magda scolded Peter, who reached over her shoulder to sneak some popcorn. "Your brother and father aren't getting any." Uncle Karl wondered if they were going to have fireworks that night, what with the shortages. It wasn't the shortages, Mr. M—— replied; Ocean City had fireworks from pre-war. But it was too risky on account of the enemy submarines, some people thought.

"Don't seem like Fourth of July without fireworks," said Uncle Karl. The inverted tag in dialogue-writing is still considered permissible with proper names or epithets, but sounds old-fashioned with personal pronouns. "We'll have 'em again soon enough," predicted the boys' father. Their mother declared she could do without fireworks: they reminded her too much of the real thing. Their father said all the more reason to shoot off a few now and again. Uncle Karl asked *rhetorically* who needed reminding, just look at people's hair and skin.

"The oil, yes," said Mrs. M——.

Ambrose had a pain in his stomach and so didn't swim but enjoyed watching the others. He and his father burned red easily. Magda's figure was exceedingly well developed for her age. She too declined to swim, and got mad, and became angry when Peter attempted to drag her into the pool. She always swam, he insisted; what did she mean not swim? Why did a person come to Ocean City?

"Maybe I want to lay here with Ambrose," Magda teased.

Nobody likes a pedant.

"Aha," said Mother. Peter grabbed Magda by one ankle and ordered Ambrose to grab the other. She squealed and rolled over on the beach blanket. Ambrose pretended to help hold her back. Her tan was darker than even Mother's and Peter's. "Help out, Uncle Karl!" Peter cried. Uncle Karl went to seize the other ankle. Inside the top of her swimsuit, however, you could see the line where the sunburn ended and, when she hunched her shoulders and squealed again, one nipple's auburn edge. Mother made them behave themselves. "*You* should certainly know," she said to Uncle Karl. Archly. "that when a lady says she doesn't feel like swimming, a gentleman doesn't ask questions." Uncle Karl said excuse *him;* Mother winked at Magda; Ambrose blushed; stupid Peter kept saying "Phooey on *feel like!*" and tugging at Magda's ankle; then even he got the point, and cannon-balled with a holler into the pool.

"I swear," Magda said, in mock *in feigned* exasperation.

The diving would make a suitable literary symbol. To go off the high board you had to wait in a line along the poolside and up the ladder. Fellows tickled girls and goosed one another and shouted to the ones at the top to hurry up, or razzed them for bellyfloppers. Once on the springboard some took a great while posing or clowning or deciding on a dive or getting up their nerve; others ran right off. Especially among the younger fellows the idea was to strike the funniest pose or do the craziest stunt as you fell, a thing that got harder to do as you kept on and kept on. But whether you hollered *Geronimo!* or *Sig heil!*, held your nose or "rode a bicycle," pretended to be shot or did a perfect jackknife or changed your mind halfway down and ended up with nothing, it was over in two seconds, after all that wait. Spring, pose, splash. Spring, neat-o, splash. Spring, aw shit, splash.

The grown-ups had gone on; Ambrose wanted to converse with Magda; she was remarkably well developed for her age; it was said that that came from rubbing with a Turkish towel, and there were other theories. Ambrose could think of nothing to say except how good a diver Peter was, who was showing off for her benefit. You could pretty well tell by looking at their bathing suits and arm-muscles how far along the different fellows were. Ambrose was glad he hadn't gone in swimming, the cold water shrank you up so. Magda pretended not to be interested in the diving; she probably weighed as much as he did. If you knew your way around in the funhouse like your own bedroom you could wait until a girl came along and then slip away without ever getting caught, even if her boyfriend was right with her. She'd think *he* did it! It would be better to be the boyfriend, and act outraged, and tear the funhouse apart. Not act; *be.*

"He's a master diver," Ambrose said. In feigned admiration. "You really have to slave away at it to get that good." What would it matter anyway if he asked her right out whether she remembered, even teased her with it as Peter would have?

There's no point in going farther; this isn't getting anybody anywhere; they haven't even come to the funhouse yet. Ambrose is off the track, in some new or old part of the place that's not supposed to be used; he strayed into it by some one-in-a-million chance, like the time the roller-coaster-car left the tracks in the nineteen-teens against all the laws of physics and sailed over the boardwalk in the dark. And they can't locate him because they don't know where to look. Even the designer and operator has forgotten this other part, that winds around on itself like a whelk-shell. That winds around the right part like the snakes on Mercury's caduceus. Some people, perhaps, don't "hit their stride" until their twenties, when the growing-up business is over and women appreciate other things besides wisecracks and teasing and strutting. Peter didn't have one-tenth the imagination *he* had, not one-tenth. Peter did this naming-their-children thing as a joke, making up names like Aloysius and Murgatroyd, but Ambrose knew *exactly* how it would feel to be married and have children of your own, and be a loving husband and father, and go comfortably to work in the mornings and to bed with your wife at night, and wake up with her there. With a breeze coming through the sash and birds and mockingbirds singing in the chinese-cigar trees. His eyes watered, there aren't enough ways to say that. He would be quite famous in his line of work. Whether Magda was his wife or not, one evening when he was wise-lined and gray at the temples, he'd smile gravely, at a fashionable dinner-party, and remind her of his youthful passion. The time they went with his family to Ocean City; the *erotic fantasies* he used to have about her. How long ago it seemed, and childish! Yet tender, too, *n'est-ce pas?* Would she have imagined that the world-renowned whatever remembered how many strings were on the lute on the bench beside the girl on the label of the cigar-box he'd stared at in the toolshed at age eight while she, age nine. Even then he had felt *wise beyond his years*: he'd stroked her hair and said in his deepest voice and correctest English, as to a dear child: "I shall never forget this moment."

But though he had breathed heavily, groaned as if ecstatic, what he'd really felt throughout was an odd detachment, as though someone else were Master. Strive as he might to be transported, he heard his mind take notes upon the scene: *This is what they call* passion. *I am experiencing it*. Many of the digger-machines were out of order in the penny arcades and could not be repaired or replaced for the duration. Moreover, the prizes, made now in USA, were less interesting than formerly, pasteboard items for the most part, and some of the machines wouldn't work on white pennies. The gypsy-fortuneteller machine might have provided a foreshadowing of the climax of this story if Ambrose had operated it. It was even dilapidateder than most: the silver coating was worn off the brown metal handles, the glass windows around the dummy were cracked and taped, her kerchiefs and silks long faded. If a man lived by himself he could take a department-store mannequin with flexible joints and modify her in certain ways. *However*: by the time he was that old he'd have a real woman. There was a machine that stamped your name around a white-metal coin with a star in the middle: A—. His son would be the Third, and when the lad reached thirteen or so he would put a strong arm around his shoulder and tell him calmly: "It is perfectly normal. We have all been through it. It will not last forever." Nobody knew how to be what they were right. He'd smoke a pipe, teach his son how to fish and softcrab, assure him he needn't worry about himself. Magda would certainly give, Magda would certainly yield a great deal of milk, although guilty of occasional solecisms. It don't taste so bad. Suppose the lights came on now!

The day wore on. You think you're yourself, but there are other persons in you. Ambrose gets an erection when Ambrose doesn't want one, *and obversely.* Ambrose watches them disagreeing; Ambrose watches him watch. In the funhouse mirror-room you can't see yourself go on forever, because no matter how you stand your head gets in the way. Even if you had a glass periscope, the image of your eye would cover up the thing you really wanted to see. The police will come; there'll be a story in the papers. That must be where it happened. Unless he can find a surprise exit, an unofficial backdoor or escape-hatch opening on an alley, say, and then stroll up to the family in front of the funhouse and ask where everybody's been; *he's* been out of the place for ages. That's just where it happened, in that last lighted room: Peter and Magda found the right exit; he found one that you weren't supposed to find and strayed off into the works somewhere. In a perfect funhouse you'd be able to go only one way, like the divers off the high board; getting lost would be impossible; the doors and halls would work like minnow-traps or the valves in veins.

On account of German U-boats Ocean City was "browned out": streetlights were shaded on the seaward side; shopwindows and boardwalk amusement-places were kept dim, not to silhouette tankers and Liberty-ships for torpedoing. In a short-story about Ocean City, Maryland, during World War II the author could make use of the image of sailors on leave in the penny arcades and shooting-galleries, sighting through the cross hairs to toy machine-guns as swastika'd subs, while out in the black Atlantic a U-boat skipper squints through his periscope at real ships outlined by the glow of penny arcades. After dinner the family strolled back to the amusement end of the boardwalk. The boys' father had burnt red as always and was masked with Noxzema, a minstrel in reverse. The grown-ups stood at the end of the boardwalk where the Hurricane of '33 had cut an inlet from the ocean to Assawoman Bay.

"Pronounced with a long *o*," Uncle Karl reminded Magda with a wink. His shirt-sleeves were rolled up; Mother punched his brown biceps with the arrowed heart on it and said his mind was naughty. Fat May's laugh came suddenly from the funhouse, as if she'd just got the joke; the family laughed too at the coincidence. Ambrose went under the boardwalk to search for out-of-town matchbook-covers with the aid of his pocket flashlight; he looked out from the edge of the North American continent and wondered how far their laughter carried over the water. Spies in rubber rafts; survivors in lifeboats. If the joke had been beyond his understanding, he could have said: "*The laughter was over his head.*" And let the reader see the serious wordplay on second reading.

He turned the flashlight on and then off at once even before the woman whooped. He sprang away, heart athud, dropping the light. The man had snarled "Cut da friggin' light!" Perspiration drenched and chilled him by the time he scrambled up to the family. "See anything?" his father asked. His voice wouldn't come; he shrugged and violently brushed sand from his pantslegs.

"Let's ride the old flying-horses!" Magda cried. I'll never be an author. It's been forever already, everybody's gone home. Ocean City's deserted, the ghost-crabs are tickling across the beach and down the littered cold streets. And the empty halls of clapboard hotels and abandoned funhouses. A tidal wave; an enemy air raid; a monster-crab swelling like an island from the sea. *The Inhabitants fled in terror.* Magda clung to his trouserleg; he alone knew the maze's secret. "He gave his life that we might live," said Uncle Karl with a scowl of pain, as he. The woman's legs had been twined behind the man's neck; he'd spread her fat cheeks with tatooed hands and pumped like a whippet. *An astonishing coincidence.* He yearned to tell Peter. He wanted to throw up for excitement. They hadn't even chased him. He wished he were dead.

One possible ending would be to have Ambrose come across another lost person in the dark. They'd match their wits together against the funhouse, struggle like Ulysses past obstacle after obstacle, help and encourage each other. Or a girl. By the time they found the exit they'd be closest friends, sweethearts if it were a girl; they'd know each other's inmost souls, be bound together *by the cement of shared adventure;* then they'd emerge into the light, and it would turn out that his friend was a Negro. A blind girl. President Roosevelt's son. Ambrose's former arch-enemy.

Shortly after the mirror-room he'd groped along a musty corridor, his heart already misgiving him at the absence of phosphorescent arrows and other signs. He'd found a crack of light—not a door, it turned out, but a seam between the plyboard wall-panels—and squinting up to it, espied a small old man nodding upon a stool beneath a bare speckled bulb. A crude panel of toggle- and knife-switches hung besides the open fuse-box near his head; elsewhere in the little room were wooden levers and ropes belayed to boat-cleats. At the time, Ambrose wasn't lost enough to rap or call; later he couldn't find that crack. Now it seemed to him that he'd possibly dozed off for a few minutes somewhere along the way; certainly he was exhausted from the afternoon's sunshine and the evening's problems; he couldn't be sure he hadn't dreamed part or all of the sight. Had an old black wall fan droned like bumble-bees and shimmied two flypaper streamers? Had the funhouse operator—gentle, somewhat sad and tired-appearing—murmured in his sleep? Is there really such a person as Ambrose, or is he a figment of the author's imagination? Was it Assawoman Bay or Sinepuxent? Are there other errors of fact in this fiction? Was there another sound besides the little slap slap of thigh on ham, like water sucking at the chineboards of a skiff?

When you're lost, the smartest thing to do is stay put till you're found, hollering if necessary. But to holler guarantees humiliation as well as rescue; keeping silent permits some saving of face—you can act surprised at the fuss when your rescuers find you and swear you weren't lost, if they do. What's more you might find your own way yet, *however belatedly.*

"Don't tell me your foot's still asleep!" Magda exclaimed as the three young people walked from the inlet to the area set aside for ferris-wheels, carrousels, and other carnival rides, they having decided in favor of the vast and ancient merry-go-round instead of the funhouse. What a sentence, everything was wrong from the outset. People don't know what to make of him, he doesn't know what to make of himself, he's only thirteen, *athletically and socially inept,* not astonishingly bright, but there are antennae; he has . . . some sort of receivers in his head; things speak to him, he understands more than he should, the world winks at him through its objects, grabs grinning at his coat. Everybody else is in on some secret he doesn't know; they've forgotten to tell him. Through simple *procrastination* his mother put off his baptism until this year. Everyone else had it done as a baby; he'd assumed the same of himself, as had his mother so she claimed, until it was time for him to join Grace Methodist-Protestant and the oversight came out. He was mortified, but pitched sleepless through his private catechizing, intimidated by the ancient mysteries, a thirteen-year-old would never say that, resolved to experience conversion like St. Augustine. When the water touched his brow and Adam's sin left him, he contrived by a strain like defecation to bring tears into his eyes—but felt nothing. There was some simple, radical difference about him; he hoped it was genius, feared it was madness, devoted himself to amiability and inconspicuousness. Alone on the seawall near his house he was seized by the terrifying transports he'd thought to find in summershed, in Communion-cup. The grass was alive! The town, the river, himself, were not imaginary; time roared in his ears like wind; the world was *going on!* This part ought to be dramatized. The Irish author James Joyce once wrote. Ambrose M—— is going to scream.

There is no *texture of rendered sensory detail,* for one thing. The faded distorting mirrors beside Fat May; the impossibility of choosing a mount when one had but a single ride on the great carrousel; the *vertigo attendant on his recognition* that Ocean City was worn out, the place of fathers and grandfathers, straw-boatered men and parasoled ladies survived by their amusements. Money spent, the three paused at Peter's insistence beside Fat May to watch the girls get their skirts blown up. The object was to tease Magda, who said, "I swear, Peter M——, you've got a one-track mind! Amby and me aren't *interested* in such things." In the tumbling-barrel, too, just inside the Devil's-mouth entrance to the funhouse, the girls were upended, and their boyfriends and others could see up their dresses if they cared to. Which was the whole point, Ambrose realized. Of the entire funhouse! If you looked around, you noticed that almost all the people on the boardwalk were paired off into couples except the small children; in a way, that was the whole point of Ocean City! If you had X-ray eyes and could see everything going on at that instant under the boardwalk and in all the hotel-rooms and cars and alleyways, you'd realize that all that normally *showed,* like restaurants and dance-halls and clothing and test-your-strength machines, was merely preparation and intermission. Fat May screamed.

Because he watched the goings-on from the corner of his eye, it was Ambrose who spied the half-dollar on the boardwalk near the tumbling-barrel. Losers weepers. The first time he'd heard some people moving through a corridor not far away, just after he'd lost sight of the crack of light, he'd decided not to call to them, for fear they'd guess he was scared and poke fun; it sounded like roughnecks; he'd hoped they'd come by and he could follow in the dark without their knowing. Another time he'd heard just one person, unless he imagined it, bumping along as if on the other side of the plywood; perhaps Peter coming back for him, or Father, or Magda lost too. Or the owner and operator of the funhouse. He'd called out once, as though merrily: "Anybody know where the heck we are?" But the query was too stiff, his voice cracked when the sounds stopped he was terrified: maybe it was a queer who waited for fellows to get lost, or a longhaired filthy monster that lived in some cranny of the funhouse. He stood rigid for hours it seemed like, scarcely respiring. His future was shockingly clear, in outline. He tried holding his breath to the point of unconsciousness. There ought to be a button you could push to end your life absolutely without pain; disappear in a flick, like turning out a light. He would push it instantly! He despised Uncle Karl. But he despised his father too, for not being what he was supposed to be. Perhaps his father hated *his* father, and so on, and his son would hate him, and so on. Instantly!

Naturally he didn't have nerve enough to ask Magda to go through the funhouse with him. With incredible nerve and to everyone's surprise he invited Magda, quietly and politely, to go through the funhouse with him. "I warn you, I've never been through it before," he added, *laughing easily;* "but I reckon we can manage somehow. The important thing to remember, after all, is that it's meant to be a *fun*house; that is, a place of amusement. If people really got lost or injured or too badly frightened in it, the owner'd go out of business. There'd even be lawsuits. No character in a work of fiction can make a speech this long without interruption or acknowledgment from the other characters."

Mother teased Uncle Karl: "Three's a crowd, I always heard." But actually Ambrose was relieved that Peter now had a quarter too. Nothing was what it looked like. Every instant, under the surface of the Atlantic Ocean, millions of living animals devoured one another. Pilots were falling in flames over Europe; women were being forcibly raped in the South Pacific. His father should have taken him aside and said: "There is a simple secret to getting through the funhouse, as simple as being first to see the Towers. Here it is. Peter does not know it; neither does your Uncle Karl. You and I are different. Not surprisingly, you've often wished you weren't. Don't think I haven't noticed how unhappy your childhood has been! But you'll understand, when I tell you, why it had to be kept secret until now. And you won't regret not being like your brother and your uncle. *On the contrary.*" If you knew all the stories behind all the people on the boardwalk you'd see that *nothing* was what it looked like. Husbands and wives often hated each other; parents didn't necessarily love their children; et cetera. A child took things for granted because he had nothing to compare his life to, and everybody acted as if things were as they should be. Therefore each saw himself as the hero of the story, when the truth might turn out to be that he's the villain, or the coward. And there wasn't one thing you could do about it!

Hunchbacks, fat ladies, fools—that no one chose what they were was unbearable. In the movies he'd meet a beautiful young girl in the funhouse; they'd have hairsbreadth escapes from real dangers; he'd do and say the right things; she also; in the end they'd be lovers; their dialogue-lines would match up; he'd be perfectly at ease; she'd not only like him well enough, she'd think he was *marvelous*; she'd lie awake thinking about *him*, instead of vice versa—the way *his* face looked in different lights and how he stood and exactly what he'd said—and yet that would be only one small episode in his wonderful life, among many many others. Not a *turning-point* at all. What had happened in the toolshed was nothing. He hated, he loathed his parents! One reason for not writing a lost-in-the-funhouse story is that either everybody's felt what Ambrose feels, in which case it goes without saying, or else no normal person feels such things, in which case Ambrose is a freak. "Is anything more tiresome, in fiction, than the problems of sensitive adolescents?" And it's all too long and rambling, as if the author. For all a person knows the first time through, the end could be just around any corner; perhaps, *not impossibly* it's been within reach any number of times. On the other hand he may be scarcely past the start, with everything yet to get through, an intolerable idea.

Fill in: His father's raised eyebrows when he announced his decision to do the funhouse with Magda. Ambrose understands now, but didn't then, that his father was wondering whether he knew what the funhouse was *for*—especially since he didn't object, as he should have, when Peter decided to come along too. The ticket-woman, witchlike, mortifying him when inadvertently he gave her his name-coin instead of the half-dollar, then unkindly calling Magda's attention to the birthmark on his temple: "Watch out for him, girlie, he's a marked man!" She wasn't even cruel, he understood, only vulgar and insensitive. Somewhere in the world there was a young woman with such splendid understanding that she'd see him entire, like a poem or story, and find his words so valuable after all that when he confessed his apprehensions she would explain why they were in fact the very things that made him precious to her . . . and to Western Civilization! There was no such girl, the simple truth being. Violent yawns as they approached the mouth. Whispered advice from an old-timer on a bench near the barrel: "Go crabwise and ye'll get an eyeful without upsetting!" Composure vanished at the first pitch: Peter hollered joyously, Magda tumbled, shrieked, clutched her skirt, Ambrose scrambled crabwise, tightlipped with terror, was soon out, watched his dropped name-coin slide among the couples. Shamefaced he saw that to get through expeditiously was not the point; Peter feigned assistance in order to trip Magda up, shouted "I see Christmas!" when her legs went flying. The old man, his latest betrayer, cackled approval. A dim hall then of blackthread cobwebs and recorded gibber: he took Magda's elbow to steady her against revolving discs set in the slanted floor to throw your feet out from under, and explained to her in a calm deep voice his theory that each phase of the funhouse was triggered either automatically, by a series of photoelectric devices, or else manually by operators stationed at peepholes. But he lost his voice thrice as the discs unbalanced him; Magda was anyhow squealing; but at one point she clutched him about the waist to keep from falling, and her right cheek pressed for a moment against his belt-buckle. Heroically he drew her up, it was his chance to clutch her close as if for support and say: "I love you." He even put an arm lightly about the small of her back before a sailor-and-girl pitched into them from behind, sorely treading his left big toe and knocking Magda asprawl with them. The sailor's girl was a string-haired hussy with a loud laugh and light-blue drawers; Ambrose realized that he wouldn't have said "I love you" anyhow, and was smitten with self-contempt. How much better it would be to be that common sailor! A wiry little Seaman 3rd, the fellow squeezed a girl to each side and stumbled hilarious into the mirror-room, closer to Magda in thirty seconds than Ambrose had got in thirteen years. She giggled at something the fellow said to Peter; she drew her hair from her eyes with a movement so womanly it struck Ambrose's heart; Peter's smacking her backside then seemed particularly coarse. But Magda made a pleased indignant face and cried, "All right for *you*, mister!" and pursued Peter into the maze without a backward glance. The sailor followed after, leisurely drawing his girl against his hip; Ambrose understood not only that they were all so relieved to be rid of his burdensome company that they didn't even notice his absence, but that he himself shared their relief. Stepping from the treacherous passage at last into the mirror-maze, he saw once again, more clearly than ever, how readily he deceived himself into supposing he was a person. He even foresaw, wincing at his dreadful self-knowledge, that he would repeat the deception, at ever-rarer intervals, all his wretched life, so fearful were the alternatives. Fame, madness, suicide; perhaps all three. It's not believable that so young a boy could articulate that reflection, and in fiction the merely true must always yield to the plausible. Yet Ambrose M—— understood, as few adults do, that the famous loneliness of the great was no popular myth but a general truth—and moreover, that it was as much cause as effect.

All the preceding except the last few sentences is exposition that should've been done earlier or interspersed with the present action instead of lumped together. No reader would put up with so much with such *prolixity*. It's interesting that Ambrose's father, though presumably an intelligent man (as indicated by his role as high-school teacher), neither encouraged nor discouraged his children at all in any way—as if he either didn't care about them or cared all right but didn't know how to act. If this fact should contribute to one of his children's becoming a celebrated but wretchedly unhappy scientist, was it a good thing or not? He too might someday face that question; it would be useful to know whether it had tortured his father for years, for example, or never once crossed his mind.

In the mirror-maze two important things happened. First, our hero found a name-coin someone else had lost or discarded: *AMBROSE*, suggestive of the famous lightship and of his father's favorite dessert, which his mother prepared on special occasions out of coconut, oranges, grapes, and what else. Second, as he wondered at the endless replication of his image in the mirrors—second, as he *lost himself in the reflection* that the necessity for an observer makes perfect observation impossible, better make him eighteen at least, yet that would render other things unlikely, he heard Peter and Magda chuckling somewhere in the maze. "Here!" "No, here!" they shouted to each other; Peter said, "Where's Amby?" Magda murmured. "Amb?" Peter called. In a pleased, friendly voice. He didn't reply. The truth was, his brother was a *happy-go-lucky youngster* who'd've been better off with a regular brother of his own, but who seldom complained of his lot and was generally cordial. Ambrose's throat ached; there aren't enough different ways to say that. He stood quietly while the two young people giggled and thumped through the glittering maze, hurrah'd their discovery of its exit, cried out in joyful alarm at what next beset them. Then he set his mouth and followed after, as he supposed, took a wrong turn, strayed into the pass *wherein he lingers yet.*

The action of conventional dramatic narrative may be represented by a diagram called Freitag's Triangle

or more accurately by a variant of that diagram

in which *AB* represents the exposition, *B* the introduction of conflict, *BC* the "rising action," complication, or development of the conflict, *C* the climax or turn of the action, *CD* the *dénouement* or resolution of the conflict.

While there is no reason to regard this pattern as an absolute necessity, like many other conventions it became conventional because great numbers of people over great numbers of years learned by trial and error that it was effective; one ought not to forsake it, therefore, unless one wishes to forsake as the effect of drama or has clear cause to feel that deliberate violation of the "normal" pattern can better can better effect that effect. This can't go on much longer; it can go on forever. He died telling stories to himself in the dark; years later, when that vast unsuspected area of the funhouse came to light, the first expedition found his skeleton in one of its labyrinthine corridors and mistook it for part of the entertainment. He died of starvation telling himself stories in the dark; but unbeknownst unbeknownst to him, an assistant operator of the funhouse, happening to overhear him, crouched just behind the plyboard partition and wrote down his every word. The operator's daughter, an exquisite young woman with a figure unusually well developed for her age, crouched just behind the partition and transcribed his every word. Though she had never laid eyes on him, she recognized that here was one of Western Culture's truly great imaginations, the eloquence of whose suffering would be an inspiration to unnumbered. And her heart was torn between her love for the misfortunate young man (yes, she loved him, though she had never laid though she knew him only—but how well!—through his words, and the deep, calm voice in which he spoke them) between her love et cetera and her woman's intuition that only in suffering and isolation could he give voice et cetera. Lone dark dying. Quietly she kissed the rough plyboard, and a tear fell upon the page. Where she had written in shorthand *Where she had written in shorthand* Where she had written in shorthand *Where she* et cetera. A long time ago we should have passed the apex of Freitag's Triangle and made brief work of the *dénouement;* the plot doesn't rise by meaningful steps but winds upon itself, digresses, retreats, hesitates, sighs, collapses, expires. The climax of the story must be its protagonist's discovery of a way to get through the funhouse. But he has found none, may have ceased to search.

What relevance does the war have to the story? Should there be fireworks outside or not?

Ambrose wandered, languished, dozed. Now and then he fell into his habit of rehearsing to himself the unadventurous story of his life, narrated from the third-person point of view, from his earliest memory parenthesis of maple-leaves stirring in the summer breath of tidewater Maryland end of parenthesis to the present moment. Its principal events, on this telling, would appear to have been *A*, *B*, *C*, and *D*.

He imagined himself years hence, successful, married, at ease in the world, the trials of his adolescence far behind him. He has come to the seashore with his family for the holiday: how Ocean City has changed! But at one seldom at one ill-frequented end of the boardwalk a few derelict amusements survive from times gone by: the great carrousel from the turn of the century, with its monstrous griffins and mechanical concert-band; the roller-coaster rumored since 1916 to have been condemned; the mechanical shooting-gallery in which only the image of our enemies changed. His own son laughs with Fat May and wants to know what a funhouse is; Ambrose hugs the sturdy lad close and smiles around his pipestem at his wife.

The family's going home. Mother sits between Father and Uncle Karl, who teases him good-naturedly who chuckles over the fact that the comrade with whom he'd fought his way shoulder to shoulder through the funhouse had turned out to be a colored boy—to their mutual discomfort, as they'd opened their souls. But such are the walls of custom, which even. Whose arm is where? How must it feel. He dreams of a funhouse vaster by far than any yet constructed; but by then they may be out of fashion, like steamboats and excursion-trains. Already quaint and seedy: the draperied ladies on the frieze of the carrousel are his father's father's mooncheeked dreams; if he thinks of it more he will vomit his apple-on-a-stick.

He wonders: will he become a regular person? Something has gone wrong; his vaccination didn't take; at the Boy-Scout initiation campfire he only pretended to be deeply moved, as he pretends to this hour that it is not so bad after all in the funhouse, and that he has a little limp. How long will it last? He envisions a truly astonishing funhouse, incredibly complex yet utterly controlled from a great central switchboard like the console of a pipeorgan. Nobody had enough imagination. He could design such a place himself, wiring and all, and he's only thirteen years old. He would be its operator: panel-lights would show what was up in every cranny of its cunning of its multifarious vastness; a switchflick would ease this fellow's way, complicate that's, to balance things out; if anyone seemed lost or frightened, all the operator had to do was.

He wishes he had never entered the funhouse. No: he wishes he had never been born. But he was. Then he wishes he were dead. But he's not. Therefore he will construct funhouses for others and be their secret operator—though he would rather be among the lovers for whom funhouses are designed.

Biographical Sketches

ISAAC BABEL

One of the finest short story writers in Russian literature, Isaac Babel was born in Odessa in 1894 and lived there in the Jewish community until 1915. He then settled in St. Petersburg, now Leningrad, and came under the influence of Maxim Gorky, an important literary figure in Russia at that time. Babel served with the Red army on several fronts during the civil war that followed the revolution, and in 1926 he published a collection of stories, *The Red Cavalry,* based on his military experiences. Another volume of stories, *Odessa Tales,* appeared in 1924. Unable to accept the demands that he make his writing conform to Soviet dogma, Babel opposed the government and was finally arrested in 1939 during the Stalinist purges. He was executed in a slave labor camp in 1941. An edition of his work was published in Russia in 1957. Two volumes of uncollected stories have been published in recent years in this country: *Isaac Babel: The Lonely Years, 1925–1939* (1964) and *You Must Know Everything: Stories 1915–1937* (1969).

JAMES BALDWIN

No other living black writer has written so provocatively and so intensely about the plight of blacks in a white society as James Baldwin. Born in Harlem in 1924, the stepson of a storefront preacher, he drifted from one menial job to another after high school. Discouraged about his writing career, despite the help given him by Richard Wright, Baldwin went to Paris in 1948 and remained for eight years. The expatriate experience is the subject of the story in this book, as well as the subject of his second novel, *Giovanni's Room* (1955), which contains a strong homosexual theme. His first and still his best novel, *Go Tell It on the Mountain* (1953), is a semi-autobiographical story of the Grimes family in Harlem, their conflicts, their religious fervor, and their struggle to survive in the ghetto. Baldwin's next two novels, *Another Country* (1962) and *Tell Me How Long the Train's Been Gone* (1968), continue his preoccupation with the racial and homosexual themes of his earlier works, though in a more violent and diffuse manner. His fifth novel, *If Beale Street Could Talk,* was published in 1974. Baldwin has written one book of stories, *Going to Meet the Man* (1965), two plays, and several collections of essays that are in many ways his most brilliant work. The most important of these are *Notes of a Native Son* (1955), *Nobody Knows My Name* (1961), and *The Fire Next Time* (1963).

JOHN BARTH

John Barth is the supreme parodist. He parodies the real world around him with wild fantasies. He parodies the art of fiction by constantly mocking its basic elements, such as plot, setting, and point of view. He parodies style, playing games with language. At the same time he is a serious writer intent on confronting the "intellectual dead end" of traditional fiction writing and employing it "against itself to accomplish new human work." As one critic remarks, "He pits the imagination against the void as no other American writer can, making art of heroic absurdity." The title "Lost in the Funhouse" is a precise description of Barth's fictional world and his attitude toward it. Born in Cambridge, Maryland, in 1930, he went to the Juilliard School of Music and Johns Hopkins, where he now teaches. His early novels, *The Floating Opera* (1956) and *The End of the Road* (1958), are fairly traditional, but with *The Sot-Weed Factor*

(1960), a brilliant parody of the historical novel, he breaks new ground. *Giles Goat-Boy* (1967) and his collections of short fiction, *Lost in the Funhouse* (1968) and *Chimera* (1972), with their original use of myth and their technical innovations, present striking new approaches to fiction. Barth won the National Book Award in 1973.

DONALD BARTHELME

Like John Barth and other experimental writers who deal in the absurd and the surrealistic, Donald Barthelme is a satirist of American life, especially city life, and a defier of conventional fictional techniques. Where he differs is in the brevity of his pieces, his dependence on clichés and advertising jargon, and his use of grotesque drawings to enhance his text. His meaning is also more elusive. Born in Philadelphia in 1931, Barthelme served in the army and was once a museum director in Houston and a managing editor of the magazine *Location*. He lives in New York and writes for *The New Yorker*. His only novel is *Snow White* (1967). Barthelme's principal volumes of stories are *Come Back, Dr. Caligari* (1964), *Unspeakable Practices, Unnatural Acts* (1968), *City Life* (1971), *Sadness* (1972), and *Guilty Pleasures* (1974).

AMBROSE BIERCE

The master of the bizarre psychological tale and the surprise ending, Ambrose Bierce was born in Ohio in 1842, the son of an indigent farmer whom he loathed. He rose from a drummer boy to a brevet major in the Union army and was wounded several times. After the Civil War he journeyed to San Francisco and became a reporter. There Bierce joined the literary circle of Bret Harte and Mark Twain and began a writing career. For a time he was a Hearst correspondent in Washington, D.C. His marriage to the daughter of a wealthy silver miner ended in divorce in 1904. Unhappy about his personal life, he vanished into Mexico in 1913. Bierce is thought to have died the next year. His reputation rests on three volumes: *In the Midst of Life* (1898), *Can Such Things Be?* (1893), and *The Devil's Dictionary* (1911).

HEINRICH BÖLL

Heinrich Böll was born in Cologne, Germany, in 1917, the son of a cabinetmaker and woodcarver. After serving in the army from 1939 to 1945, he became a full-time writer in 1951. His first books, such as the collection of stories *The Train Was on Time* (1956), are about the senselessness of war and are written in a simple, spare style reminiscent of Hemingway. *Tomorrow and Yesterday* (1957) depicts the postwar alienation in Germany and reveals a nostalgia for the prewar days. Other novels are *Billiards at Half-Past Nine* (1961), *The Clown* (1965), and his most accomplished work, *Group Portrait with Lady* (1973). Böll won the Nobel Prize in 1972. Though a satirist, especially in his short fiction, and a surrealist who elaborates logically on "an absurd situation," as in "Murke's Collected Silences," he uses conventional fictional techniques and espouses a Christian humanism. His characters have been described as "depressed innocents trying hard to live decently in an indecent world." Böll has published not only fiction, but also plays, essays, and translations, and is considered one of Germany's most important living authors.

JORGE LUIS BORGES

Jorge Luis Borges is one of the most scholarly and enigmatic writers living today, rendering reality in an elusive and haunting manner. Like Kafka, he is obsessed with "the fabulous complexity of the universe confronting man's ridiculously inadequate attempts at unraveling it." Born in Buenos Aires, Argentina, in 1899, the son of a poet, novelist, and translator, Borges traveled widely in Europe as a young man, acquiring a vast knowledge of the literature of many countries. He turned from poetry to fiction in the 1930s, though he never wrote a novel. His opposition to Nazism and Peron during World War II cost him his position as a librarian and reduced him to the post of a chicken inspector. Borges regained favor after Peron's ouster in 1955. In the 1950s his sight failed and he had to confine himself to writing short pieces. He came to the attention of the literary world outside of Argentina when he shared the International Publishers' Prize with Samuel Beckett in 1961. Among his best collections of translated stories are *Ficciones* (1962), *Labyrinths* (1962), *A Personal Anthology* (1967), and *Dr. Brodie's Report* (1972). Most of Borges's stories are a combination of myth, parable, essay, and poetry. As one critic put it, to Borges "life is a literary dream."

ANTON CHEKHOV

The father of the modern short story, Anton Chekhov began his literary career in a most unliterary way. Born in 1860, the grandson of a serf and the son of a bankrupt grocer in Taganrog in southern Russia, he went to Moscow as a young man to study medicine. While in school Chekhov supported himself and his struggling family by writing humorous pieces for Moscow newspapers and St. Petersburg periodicals. From these sketches developed his ironic, plotless stories, which have so influenced twentieth-century authors. Among his more famous stories are "The Lady with a Dog," "Ward No. 6," and "Peasants." Toward the end of his life Chekhov gave up the medical profession completely and devoted himself to fiction and playwriting. *Uncle Vanya* (1899) and *The Cherry Orchard* (1904) are two of his most successful plays. He died at the age of forty-four of tuberculosis.

JOHN CHEEVER

Chronicler of the American middle class, John Cheever is one of the subtlest and shrewdest observers of suburban manners and morals writing today. His ironic stories of people caught up in the tensions and failures that lie beneath the smug, smiling surfaces of the commuting status seeker present a depressing yet faithful picture of life in a large segment of our society. Born in Quincy, Massachusetts, in 1912, Cheever was educated at Thayer Academy and served in the army during World War II. He has received many honors, most notably the National Book Award in 1958. He lives with his family in Ossining, New York. Cheever's work includes three novels and seven collections of stories. Of the novels, *The Wapshot Chronicle* (1957) is the best. *The Enormous Radio* (1953) and *World of Apples* (1973) are among his liveliest and most incisive volumes of stories.

JOSEPH CONRAD

Joseph Conrad spoke Polish as a child, learned French as a young man, and wrote in English in his maturity. Born Josef Teodor Konrad Nalecz Korzeniowski in Poland in 1857, the son of a translator and outspoken patriot, he and his family were sent into exile near Moscow because of his father's championing of Polish freedom during the partition of that country. At the age of seventeen Conrad left home for Marseilles, France, where he became a seaman on a French ship. Transferring to the British merchant marine, he attained his first command in 1888. He began writing stories in English, encouraged by John Galsworthy, a passenger on his ship *The Torrens* in 1893. Conrad left the sea in 1894 and settled down in England, intent on becoming a writer. Although he did not attain popular success until *Chance* (1913) was published, his works, such as *The Nigger of the Narcissus* (1897), *The Heart of Darkness* (1899), *Lord Jim* (1900), and *Nostromo* (1904), earned him a secure reputation among critics and fellow novelists. He died in 1924. Conrad's attitude toward his craft can best be summed up in his own words: "My task which I am trying to achieve is, by the power of the written word, to make you hear, to make you feel—it is, before all, to make you *see*."

STEPHEN CRANE

Stephen Crane died before he fulfilled his promise. Born in Newark, New Jersey, in 1871, the son of a Methodist minister, he studied briefly at Lafayette College and Syracuse University. As a reporter for the New York *Journal* he covered the Spanish-American and the Greco-Turkish wars. Crane published his first book, *Maggie: A Girl of the Streets* (1893), at his own expense. His next novel, *The Red Badge of Courage* (1895), brought him fame and remains today the classic treatment of the Civil War. His most famous story, "The Open Boat" (1898), is one of the finest examples of the naturalistic school of writing in American literature. Crane also wrote poetry. He died of tuberculosis at Badenweiler, Germany, in 1900 after a sojourn in England, where he was a friend of Joseph Conrad and Henry James.

RALPH ELLISON

Few authors have been honored so greatly for one novel as Ralph Ellison for *Invisible Man* (1952). He has won literary prizes, served as visiting professor at numerous colleges and universities, been elected to various academies and organizations, and received honorary degrees. Born in Oklahoma City, Oklahoma, in 1914, Ellison attended Tuskegee Institute, went to New York in 1936, where he met Richard Wright and worked at a variety of odd jobs, and served in the merchant marine during World War II. His other published work consists of uncollected short stories, excerpts from a novel-in-progress, and a volume of essays, *Shadow and Act* (1964). On the occasion of winning the National Book Award in 1953 he said, "If I were asked . . . what I considered to be the chief significance of *Invisible Man* I would reply . . . its attempt to return to the mood of personal moral responsibility for democracy which typified the best of our nineteenth-century fiction." His novel, of which "Battle Royal" is the first chapter, is not only about the black experience in America, but also about the experience of all persons coming to grips with their freedom and their responsibility. Both in theme and in form, the book is a major work of fiction.

WILLIAM FAULKNER

Hailed today as America's greatest twentieth-century novelist, William Faulkner had to wait a long time for recognition. It was not until after World War II that he finally received the praise and critical attention he deserved for such original novels as *The Sound and the Fury* (1929), *As I Lay Dying* (1930), *Light in August* (1932), *Absalom, Absalom!* (1936), and *The Hamlet* (1940). Although he served in the Canadian and British air forces during World War I and lived abroad as well as in New York, New Orleans, and Hollywood, all his best work is set in the South and particularly Mississippi, where he was born in New Albany in 1897. The town in which Faulkner spent most of his life, Oxford, Mississippi, closely resembles the Jefferson of his fiction, and the surrounding country, the legendary Yoknapatawpha County that serves as a microcosm of the South and ultimately of the world. He won the Nobel Prize in 1950. On that occasion he made a statement about his beliefs which shocked readers accustomed to thinking of his fiction as portraying violence and degeneracy: "I believe that man will not merely endure: he will prevail. He is immortal, not because he alone among creatures has an inexhaustible voice, but because he has a soul, a spirit capable of compassion and sacrifice and endurance. The poet's, the writer's, duty is to write about these things." Faulkner spent his last years as writer-in-residence at the University of Virginia and died in 1962 in Oxford, Mississippi.

CAROLINE GORDON

Not so well known as other Southern writers, Caroline Gordon deserves recognition for her careful rendering of the history and character of the South. Conservative, Catholic, and agrarian in outlook, she has portrayed her region in a series of novels and stories with perception and sympathy. A precise stylist in the manner of Flaubert, she writes clearly and vividly of the aristocratic society of the old South, its heroics, its failures, its enduring values. Born in Trenton, Kentucky, in 1895, and educated at Bethany College, West Virginia, Gordon married Allen Tate, the poet and critic, in 1924 and was divorced from him in 1959. She has taught at many colleges and universities and is currently at the University of Dallas. Her work consists of nine novels, two collections of stories, and several volumes of criticism. Her most important books are *Aleck Maury, Sportsman* (1934), *The Malefactors* (1956), and *Old Red and Other Stories* (1963).

GRAHAM GREENE

A Catholic novelist with a powerful sense of human sinfulness and alienation in a violent world, Graham Greene was born in 1904 in Hertfordshire, England, the son of a headmaster. He went to Oxford and then became a journalist in London. His first books, featuring murder and suspense, he called "entertainments." Two successful ones are *This Gun for Hire* (1936) and *The Ministry of Fear* (1943). With *Brighton Rock* (1938) Greene began to write serious novels while retaining his man-on-the-run plots and his "thriller" atmosphere. His novels take place in various parts of the globe: *The Power and the Glory* (1940) in Mexico, *The Heart of the Matter* (1948) in West Africa, *The Quiet American* (1955) in Vietnam, and *The Honorary Consul* (1974) in South America. Greene has also written plays, several volumes of stories, a collection of literary essays entitled *The Lost Childhood* (1951), and an autobiography, *A Sort of Life* (1971). He now lives in France.

ERNEST HEMINGWAY

Ernest Hemingway was born in Oak Park, Illinois, in 1899, the son of a doctor. He had no formal education beyond high school. Following a brief career as a reporter on the Kansas City *Star*, he went to Italy during World War I to drive an ambulance and was severely wounded. *A Farewell to Arms* (1929) is based on his experiences there. After the war he lived in Paris and wrote a volume of stories, *In Our Time* (1925), in which "Indian Camp" appeared, and a novel, *The Sun Also Rises* (1926), about the postwar "lost generation" of Americans abroad. Hemingway went to Spain in the 1930s to report on the civil war and gather material for his novel *For Whom the Bell Tolls* (1940). *Across the River and into the Trees* (1950) draws on his participation as a correspondent in World War II. *The Old Man and the Sea* (1952) is set in Cuba, where he lived during his last years. Hemingway won the Nobel Prize in 1954. His work includes not only novels and volumes of stories, but also a book about bullfighting in Spain, *Death in the Afternoon* (1932), and a "true autobiography" about a safari in Africa, *The Green Hills of Africa* (1935). Ill and despondent, Hemingway committed suicide in Ketchum, Idaho, in 1961. A memoir of Paris in the 1920s, *A Moveable Feast* (1964), a novel, *Islands in the Stream* (1970), and *The Nick Adams Stories* (1972) were published posthumously.

NATHANIEL HAWTHORNE

A descendant of the Puritans of Salem, Massachusetts, where he was born on Independence Day, 1804, Nathaniel Hawthorne carried within him both the Puritan sense of sin and guilt and a strong sense of his country's past. He was a brooding, retiring man whose life alternated between periods of withdrawal and sociability. After graduating from Bowdoin in 1825, he retreated to the family home for twelve years, where he wrote the stories that make up his first volume, *Twice-Told Tales* (1837). Prior to the publication of his first important novel, *The Scarlet Letter* (1850), Hawthorne worked in the custom house in Salem. His next novel was *The House of the Seven Gables* (1851). In 1852 he published *The Blithedale Romance,* a satire of the utopian community of Brook Farm, where he had lived for a short period in 1841. Despite his shy nature, Hawthorne was a friend of Emerson, Thoreau, and particularly Melville, who admired him above all other American writers. He traveled extensively in England and was for a time United States consul at Liverpool. Out of his Italian experiences he wrote *The Marble Faun* (1860), his last novel. A master of the psychological-moral tale, Hawthorne set his stories in a kind of twilight zone between dreams and reality. They deal with the violation of the human heart as well as the effects of sin, guilt, and isolation on introspective individuals.

HENRY JAMES

Henry James was born in New York in 1843. His father was a prominent theologian and his older brother William became a renowned psychologist and philosopher. Educated at Harvard and in England, France, and Switzerland, James spent most of his life after 1875 in Europe, writing about innocent, wealthy Americans abroad and the contrasts and conflicts between the Old World and the New. These are his concerns in his best early novel, *The Portrait of a Lady* (1881), as well as in his best late one, *The Ambassadors* (1903). During his middle period he wrote about the decadence of English society in such books as *The Princess Casamassima* (1886) and *The Awkward Age* (1899). A bachelor, James made his living through his writing. He published not only two dozen novels and as many novellas, but also stories, plays, travel essays, biographies, and critical pieces on art, drama, and literature. His fiction is known for its psychological realism, its intricate style, and its concern for social relationships. James's great theme, apart from the international one, is the unlived life. Just before his death in 1916 he became a British subject. He was buried in Cambridge, Massachusetts, with his family.

JAMES JOYCE

James Joyce was born in Dublin in 1882, the son of a talented but irresponsible father. Educated by the Jesuits at University College, he turned against them, the Church, his family, and his country in 1904 when he left Ireland to live on the continent with Nora Barnacle, whom he married years later. Yet all his work is about them. His first book of fiction, *Dubliners* (1914), contains realistic stories of Dublin life, and his first novel, *A Portrait of the Artist as a Young Man* (1916), is largely autobiographical. *Ulysses* (1922) is concerned with one day, June 16, 1904, in the life of his native city. Its "stream of consciousness" technique, mingling of myth and reality, and highly original style changed the approach many took to the novel and influenced such writers as Faulkner and Barth. Joyce's last book, *Finnegan's Wake* (1939), is even more innovative in its form and language. He also wrote a book of verse, *Chamber Music* (1907), and a play, *Exiles* (1918). In his last years he suffered from failing eyesight, and died in Zurich, Switzerland, in 1941.

FRANZ KAFKA

More poignantly than any other twentieth-century writer, Franz Kafka expressed the loneliness, the insignificance, and the trapped feeling of modern men and women obsessed with nameless guilt and victimized by forces beyond their control. He was born in Prague in 1883, the son of a successful Jewish merchant whose expectations for him he could never fulfill and who haunts his work as a stern father figure. He received a doctorate of jurisprudence in 1906 at a German university and in 1908 worked as a civil servant in an insurance office. By 1917 Kafka discovered he had tuberculosis. He never married, although he was engaged three times and suffered an unhappy love affair with a German woman. Several of his major books were published posthumously despite instructions to a friend that all his work should be destroyed upon his death. His two most important novels are *The Trial* (1925) and *The Castle* (1926). His volumes of stories include *Metamorphosis* (1915) and *The Penal Colony* (1919). Kafka died in 1924 at the Kierling Sanitarium near Vienna.

D. H. LAWRENCE

D. H. Lawrence was born in Eastwood, Nottinghamshire, England, in 1885, the son of a coal miner. His first novel, *Sons and Lovers* (1913), is about his family and an early love affair. He taught school briefly and married Frieda von Richthofen, cousin of a famous German pilot of World War II. Under constant attack by the government and the public for his views on the war, morality, and art, and unhappy with the reception of his work, Lawrence left England in 1919 and traveled to Italy, Australia, Mexico, the American Southwest, and France searching for a place to live. He died in the south of France in 1930 of tuberculosis. His best novels are *The Rainbow* (1915) and *Women in Love* (1920), but he is better known to the reading public for *Lady Chatterly's Lover* (1928), which contains explicit sexual scenes and frank language. In addition to stories and novels, Lawrence wrote poems, plays, travel essays, and literary and social criticism. He remains today one of the major forces in modern British literature.

DORIS LESSING

Doris Lessing is one of England's leading novelists. She was born in Persia in 1919, the daughter of a banker, and grew up in southern Rhodesia, where she attended a convent school. She came to London in 1949 after a divorce and, because of her interest in Communism, was not allowed to return to Rhodesia. Lessing remained in England, determined to make a living as a writer. The book that brought her into prominence was *The Golden Notebook* (1962). Her other outstanding novels are the five-volume *Children of Violence* (1952–1969) and *Briefing for a Descent into Hell* (1971). Among her several collections of short stories are *The Habit of Loving* (1957), *African Stories* (1964), and *The Temptation of Jack Orkney* (1972). She has also written verse, plays, and essays. Lessing's work, among other things, deals with the position of women in society and the relationship between the sexes, racial tension in Africa, madness and extrasensory perception, and what she calls "the individual conscience in its relations with the collective."

JACK LONDON

Jack London led a rough but spectacular life. Born in San Francisco in 1876, the illegitimate son of a vagabond Irish astrologer, he spent his youth as a wanderer, sailor, and gold prospector in the Klondike. It was his Alaskan adventures that furnished him with material for his most famous novels, such as *The Call of the Wild* (1903) and *White Fang* (1906). Influenced by Nietzsche and his concept of the superman in *The Sea Wolf* (1904) and by Marx in *The Iron Heel* (1908), London stressed in his work the primitive and the realistic in a highly charged adventure atmosphere. He committed suicide in 1916, like the hero of his autobiographical novel *Martin Eden* (1909). Among the best of his short story collections are *Tales of the Far North* (1900) and *Love of Life* (1907). Few writers of his day enjoyed his fame or commanded such high fees for their work.

JAMES ALAN McPHERSON

Representing a new generation of black writers intent on presenting racial situations in a subtler and less violent manner than their literary fathers such as Richard Wright, James Alan McPherson has shown in his only book of stories, *Hue and Cry* (1969), how effectively he can depict individuals, white and black, interacting in society without making a special point of their race. McPherson was born in Savannah, Georgia, in 1943, attended Morgan State and Morris Brown, and then went to Harvard Law School while working as a janitor. His story "Gold Coast" comes out of his Cambridge experience. He has also worked in a supermarket and in a dining car and as a research assistant at Harvard Business School and as a recruiter for Harvard Law School. Upon completion of his work at Harvard, McPherson took a M.F.A. at the University of Iowa and taught English and Afro-American literature. He is presently an editor of *The Atlantic Monthly.*

BERNARD MALAMUD

Bernard Malamud is the American Jewish writer of the big city, with its ethnic neighborhoods and small stores, its synagogues and rabbis, its tenements and racial conflicts. His work is filled with Yiddish lore and the cadences of Jewish speech. Born in Brooklyn in 1914, he grew up during the Depression and records in his stories people enduring suffering with dignity, humor, and love. Malamud graduated from City College in 1936 and received an M.A. from Columbia University in 1942. He now teaches at Bennington College in Vermont. His first novel, *The Natural* (1952), was about baseball; his next, *The Assistant* (1957), about becoming a Jew. The latter immediately established him as an important writer. Out of his teaching experience at Oregon State College from 1949 to 1961 Malamud wrote *A New Life* (1961), one of the funniest academic novels ever written by an American. *The Fixer* (1966), set in Russia and dealing with the persecution of the Jews, received the Pulitzer Prize. His other novels are *Pictures of Fidelman: An Exhibition* (1969) and *The Tenants* (1971). A collection of stories, *The Magic Barrel* (1958), won the National Book Award. A more recent volume of stories is *Rembrandt's Hat* (1974).

VLADIMIR NABOKOV

Like the conjuror Shock in "The Potato Elf," Vladimir Nabokov is a combination magician and poet. He dazzles the reader with his verbal magic and startling images, ingenious situations and comically sad characters. One never quite knows what everything means, but one is fascinated by the prestidigitator's art. Few authors are as learned or as quick-witted. Born in St. Petersburg in 1899 to a prominent family, Nabokov was educated there and at Cambridge University. After living in France and Germany for twenty years and writing novels in Russian, he came to the United States in 1940 to teach Russian and creative writing at Stanford, Wellesley, and Cornell. His first novel in English was *The Real Life of Sebastian Knight* (1941). With *Lolita* (1955) he gained worldwide acclaim. Among his other novels in English, the most important are *Pnin* (1957), *Pale Fire* (1962), and *Ada* (1969). Nabokov has published plays, verse, numerous volumes of short stories, an autobiography, *Speak, Memory* (1952), and a four-volume edition of Pushkin's narrative poem *Eugene Onegin* (1964). It is said that his works would run to thirty or forty volumes if collected. Now an American citizen, Nabokov lives in Switzerland.

JOYCE CAROL OATES

Rarely has a writer produced so much so early in her career as Joyce Carol Oates. Still in her thirties, she has published to date six novels, five short story collections, several volumes of poetry, two plays, and two books of criticism. What is more, all her fiction is charged with a controlled intensity unusual in a writer so young. Oates deals with violent, depressing subjects in a melodramatic way, carrying the reader along at a breathless pace through sordid scenes that remind one of Dreiser and Faulkner as well as Flaubert and Kafka. At the same time she is constantly experimenting with fictional techniques that stamp her work as her own. Her world is primarily that of the middle class and her main concerns are love and marriage and the explosive situations they can create. Born in Lockport, New York, in 1938, educated at Syracuse University and the University of Wisconsin, Oates taught at the University of Detroit and now is Professor of English at the University of Windsor in Canada. Her best novel, *them* (1969), won the National Book Award. Her most successful collections of stories are *The Wheel of Love* (1970) and *Marriages and Infidelities* (1972). An insight into her work can be gleaned by reading her critical examination of other writers in *New Heaven, New Earth: The Visionary Experience in Literature* (1974).

FLANNERY O'CONNOR

Few writers can portray grotesque characters and weird situations with such power and grim humor as Flannery O'Connor. Possibly some of her power and vision stem from the fact that she was a Catholic in a Protestant region. Born in Savannah, Georgia, in 1925, she lived most her life in Milledgeville, Georgia, and graduated from the Georgia State College for Women. While at the Writers' Workshop at the University of Iowa, she published her first story. Despite a crippling disease which struck her in 1950 and which finally killed her in 1964, O'Connor continued to write a series of strange, disturbing tales about the South, most of them colored with religious significance and her own sense of distorted reality. They are collected in two volumes, *A Good Man Is Hard to Find* (1955) and *Everything That Rises Must Converge* (1965). She also wrote two novels, *Wise Blood* (1952) and *The Violent Bear It Away* (1960), and a book of essays and notes on fiction, *Mystery and Manners* (1969). A collection of all O'Connor's stories was published in 1972.

KATHERINE ANNE PORTER

Although she has written only one novel, *Ship of Fools* (1962), a book which took her twenty years to complete, and a handful of short stories and novellas, Katherine Anne Porter has established herself as one of the most poised American writers with her precise characterizations, her clear prose style, and her vivid evocation of place, especially of Mexico and the South. Porter was born in Indian Creek, Texas, in 1890, a descendant of Daniel Boone, and educated in Texas and Louisiana. But she did not remain in her native region. She traveled extensively throughout North America and Europe. Her stay in Mexico in 1920 led to her first published story in 1922, "María Concepción." It became part of her first book, *Flowering Judas* (1930), which immediately brought her favorable critical recognition. Other volumes of short fiction followed: *Noon Wine* (1937), *Pale Horse, Pale Rider* (1938), *The Leaning Tower* (1944), and *Collected Stories* (1965). Porter has also published a volume of essays, reviews, and occasional pieces, *The Days Before* (1952). She won the National Book Award and the Pulitzer Prize for Fiction in 1966. She presently lives in College Park, Maryland.

PHILIP ROTH

One of the most talented writers to appear on the literary scene after World War II, Philip Roth gained almost instant fame with his first book of stories, *Goodbye, Columbus* (1959.). The short novel from which the title is taken is set in the Jewish community of Newark where Roth was born in 1933. His first novel, *Letting Go* (1962), reflects his life as a graduate student at the University of Chicago, his teaching at the University of Iowa, and his interest in becoming a writer. *When She Was Good* (1967), of which "In Trouble" is a part, differs from his other works in that it deals not with Jewish life or graduate students, but with a midwestern family. Few authors have Roth's ear for dialogue, his outrageous humor, and his sharp sense of mimicry, all demonstrated so remarkably in his best book, *Portnoy's Complaint* (1969). His other novels are

Our Gang (1971), *The Breast* (1972), *The Great American Novel* (1973), and *My Life as a Man* (1974).

ISAAC BASHEVIS SINGER

Of all the contemporary writers in this book, Isaac Bashevis Singer seems the most old-fashioned. One of the reasons is that he belongs to the tradition of Yiddish literature so remote from the modernist literary movement, with its technical experiments and themes of alienation and revolt. In fact, all his work is written in Yiddish. Another reason he seems so old-fashioned is that, in his own words, he believes "in storytelling" and dislikes "commentary by the author. The events must speak for themselves. A fiction writer who tries to explain his story from a psychological or sociological point of view destroys his chance to endure." Singer's story "Powers" illustrates this point. It also illustrates the subject matter of much of his work—"senility and the diseases, loneliness and hopelessness of the discarded old." Born in Poland in 1904, Singer emigrated to the United States in 1935 and became a naturalized citizen in 1943. Among his many novels are *Satan in Goray* (1955) and *Enemies: A Love Story* (1972). His best story collections are *Gimpel the Fool* (1957), *The Spinoza of Market Street* (1961), and *A Crown of Feathers* (1973), which won the National Book Award. Singer lives in New York.

ALEXANDER SOLZHENITSYN

Following the tradition of Russian writers from Pushkin to Pasternak who have opposed the government, Alexander Solzhenitsyn is, in addition to being an artist, a vigorous critic of a tyrannical society. Born in the Caucasus in 1918, he studied mathematics and physics at Rostov University and became a teacher before joining the Soviet army in 1941. Although decorated for bravery several times, he was imprisoned in 1945 for criticizing Stalin in a letter. Solzhenitsyn's experiences during eleven years in slave labor camps form the basis of his early novels—*One Day in the Life of Ivan Denisovich* (1963), *The First Circle* (1968), and *Cancer Ward* (1968). Khrushchev permitted the publication of the first in order to discredit the Stalin regime, but when he fell from power Solzhenitsyn's writings were banned and the rest of his work has been published only in the West. He was not allowed to leave Russia in 1970 to accept his Nobel Prize. *August 1914* appeared in 1972, the first in a series of novels Solzhenitsyn planned to write on World War I. His next book was *The Gulag Archipelago* (1974), a massive indictment of the Soviet system of slave labor. With its publication he was denounced in his country and threatened with arrest. Because of worldwide pressure, however, he was exiled rather than imprisoned. He now lives in the West, where he carries on his struggle against Communism and tyranny and for a Christian society.

JOHN UPDIKE

An elaborate stylist with a painter's eye and a love of language, John Updike was born in Shillington, Pennsylvania, in 1932, the son of a high-school teacher. That area is the setting of much of his early fiction. After graduating from Harvard, Updike attended the Ruskin School of Drawing and Fine Art, Oxford, and then became a staff member of *The New Yorker*, where many of his poems, stories, and reviews have appeared. He now lives with his family in Ipswich, Massachusetts. Updike has published seven novels, most notably *Rabbit Run* (1960) and *The Centaur* (1963), six volumes of short stories, several books of poetry, one play, and a collection of essays. Strong biblical and mythical currents run through all his work, including the very erotic *Couples* (1968). Much of his fiction concerns the sexual and moral tensions that arise in marriage and family life as men and women in a chaotic and often empty world seek some meaningful pattern for their lives.

KURT VONNEGUT, JR.

Kurt Vonnegut, Jr., is one of the most popular writers on the American campus today. His opposition to the establishment, his satire of contemporary life, and his startling juxtaposition of the realistic and the fantastic make him an appealing figure for a generation disillusioned with the technological society they live in and appalled at the horrors of war. He was born in Indianapolis, Indiana, in 1922, the son of an architect, and was educated at Cornell and the University of Chicago. After serving in the army in World War II, Vonnegut worked in public relations for General Electric before becoming a free-lance writer in 1950. He has written seven novels, two collections of stories, and three plays. His first important book, *Cat's Cradle* (1963), was a work of science fiction. *Slaughterhouse Five* (1969), based on his experiences as a prisoner of the Germans in Dresden during the bombing of that city, brought him worldwide recognition. Vonnegut now lives with his family on Cape Cod.

EUDORA WELTY

Eudora Welty belongs to that distinguished group of Southern women writers that includes Katherine Anne Porter, Caroline Gordon, Flannery O'Connor, and Carson McCullers. In fact, it was Porter who wrote an introduction to her first book of stories, *A Curtain of Green* (1941). Welty was born in Jackson, Mississippi, in 1909, the daughter of the president of an insurance company, and has remained there most of her life. She attended Mississippi State College for Women, the University of Wisconsin, and Columbia University. Among her volumes of stories are *The Wide Net* (1943) and *The Bride of Innisfallen* (1955). Her novels include *The Robber Bridegroom* (1942), *Delta Wedding* (1946), *The Ponder Heart* (1954), *Losing Battles* (1970), and *The Optimist's Daughter* (1972). A collection of essays, *Place in Fiction* (1957), presents her views on the writing of fiction. Most of Welty's stories are located in the South and especially in her native state, but they are not local in significance. She has a "multiple" vision of the world that transcends her region. Her work is filled with the ironies, the ambiguities, and the mythical patterns so characteristic of modern literature.

INDEX OF LITERARY TERMS

Allegory, 185
Allusion, 222
Antagonist, 37–38

Believability, 1

Characterization, 37–39
Character analysis, 39, 53
Character sketch, 53
Climax, 2
Conflict, 39
Contrast
  in plot, 4
  of characters, 53–54
Conventional symbol, 184
Created symbol, 184–185

Denouement, 2
Dialogue, 110
Dramatic irony, 2
Dramatic method
  in characterization, 38
Dramatic point of view, 109
Dynamic character, 37

Epiphany, 2
Exposition, 2

Falling action, 2
Figures of speech, 222
First-person point of view, 107–108
Flashback, 4
Flat character, 38
Foil, 38
Foreshadowing, 4
Framing device, 147–148, 158

Inevitability, 1

Interior monologue, 38
Irony, 2
Irony of situation, 2

Limited omniscience, 109

Metaphor, 222
Motif, 11

Pictorial method
  in characterization, 38
Plot, 1–4
Point of view, 107–110
Protagonist, 37

Reportorial method
  in characterization, 38
Rising action, 2
Round character, 37

Scenic method
  in characterization, 38
Setting, 147–149
Simile, 222
Stock figures, 38
Stream of consciousness, 38–39
Style, 221–224
Symbol, 184–185
Syntax, 222–223

Theme, 182–185
Third-person omniscient point
  of view, 108–109
Tone, 109–110

Verbal irony, 2

INDEX OF AUTHORS AND TITLES

Babel, Isaac, 116
Baldwin, James, 355
Barth, John, 475
Barthelme, Donald, 464
Battle Royal, 344
Bierce, Ambrose, 287
Blue Film, The, 291
Blue Hotel, The, 200
Böll, Heinrich, 390
Borges, Jorge Luis, 196

Captive, The, 120
Cheever, John, 149
City Life, 464
Conrad, Joseph, 245
Chekhov, Anton, 14
Crane, Stephen, 200

Death of a Travelling Salesman, 224

Ellison, Ralph, 344
Encounter, An, 316
Enemies, 14
Enoch and the Gorilla, 294

Faulkner, William, 23

Gold Coast, 300
Gordon, Caroline, 120
Gospel According to Mark, The, 196
Greene, Graham, 291

Hawthorne, Nathaniel, 384
Hemingway, Ernest, 110
Horseman in the Sky, A, 287

Indian Camp, 110
In Trouble, 40

James, Henry, 56
Joyce, James, 316

Kafka, Franz, 420

Lawrence, D. H., 186
Lessing, Doris, 161
London, Jack, 276
Lost in the Funhouse, 475

Malamud, Bernard, 331
María Concepcíon, 167
Matryona's House, 80
McPherson, James Alan, 300
Metamorphosis, The, (Kafka) 204
Metamorphosis, The, (Oates) 453
Murke's Collected Silences, 390
Museums and Women, 236

Nabokov, Vladimir, 405
Next Door, 5

Oates, Joyce Carol, 453
O'Connor, Flannery, 294
Owen Wingrave, 56

Porter, Katherine Anne, 167
Potato Elf, The, 405
Powers, 321

Roth, Philip, 40

Secret Sharer, The, 245
Silver Crown, The, 331
Sin of Jesus, The, 116
Singer, Isaac Bashevis, 321
Solzhenitsyn, Alexander, 80

Spotted Horses, 23
Sunrise on the Veld, A, 161
Swimmer, The, 149

Things, 186
This Morning, This Evening, So Soon, 355
To Build A Fire, 276

Updike, John, 236

Vonnegut, Kurt, Jr., 5

Wakefield, 384
Welty, Eudora, 224